ALSO BY STEPHEN FOX

The Guardian of Boston: William Monroe Trotter

JOHN MUIR
AND HIS LEGACY

John Muir at twenty-eight (Meserve Collection, as published in American Heritage, *February 1965)*

❧ JOHN MUIR
AND HIS
LEGACY ❧

The American Conservation Movement

STEPHEN FOX

Little, Brown and Company—Boston—Toronto

FIRST EDITION

LIBRARY OF CONGRESS CATALOGING IN PUBLICATION DATA
Fox, Stephen R.
  John Muir and his legacy.

  Includes bibliographical references and index.
  1. Nature conservation—United States—History.
2. Muir, John, 1838-1914.   3. Conservationists—United
States—Biography.   4. Naturalists—United States—
Biography.   I. Title.
QH76.F69   333.95′0973   81-1852
ISBN 0-316-29110-2   AACR2

VB
Designed by Susan Windheim
*Published simultaneously in Canada
by Little, Brown & Company (Canada) Limited*

PRINTED IN THE UNITED STATES OF AMERICA

For Chloe and Theo Goodfellow

Preface

To make my bias clear at the outset: I consider myself a conservationist, at least by sympathy if not by affiliation or activity. I know hardly anything about birds or trees or wild animals. My idea of a wilderness trip is a long walk through the woods followed by a return to four walls before nightfall. Camping out or testing myself against a serious mountain appeals to me not in the least. But the ideas behind conservation do appeal to me. When the people in this book discuss the meaning of technology, modern progress, and the dubious sweep of Western history, they are speaking for me too.

Three years ago I set out to write a general history of the American conservation movement. At an initial point in my research I noticed that of the early pioneers in conservation, only one — John Muir of the Sierra Club — still seemed an active force in the movement today, with his books in print and his name familiar to contemporary activists. When I looked at Muir more closely, I found that his religious ideology and the part he took in the movement set patterns for his successors in conservation. Gradually I realized that I should organize this book around him.

Next occurred one of those strokes of plain, dumb luck that so gladden the hearts of historians: I learned that, although Muir had died in 1914, his personal papers and manuscripts had just recently been opened for scholarly research. All the proliferating picture books on Muir and juvenile biographies of him had essentially been drawn from two authorized, uncritical studies published in 1924 and 1945. These two books were about as good as their genre can be. It seemed likely that Muir's papers, examined anew with no restrictions on interpretation, might yield a fresh picture of the man.

The first section of this book, then, presents a new biography of Muir. The second section offers a chronological history of the conservation movement from 1890 to 1975, stressing the role of the amateur radical that Muir so epitomized. The third section, topical rather than chronological in organization, generalizes about what conservation means in historical terms. The book thus moves from the specific to the general, from biography through history to analysis. But it ends where it starts, with Muir in Yosemite Valley; and my basic argument also circles back to where it begins. This book, and the view of history behind it, imply not a line but a cycle.

— STEPHEN RUSSELL FOX

Somerville, Massachusetts
October 16, 1980

Contents

��

I. A CONSERVATIONIST PROTOTYPE

�✺

II. THE AMERICAN CONSERVATION MOVEMENT, 1890–1975

✺✺

III. CONSERVATION IN AMERICAN HISTORY

❧ I ❧

A CONSERVATIONIST
PROTOTYPE

1

The Yosemite Prophet

HALFWAY down the western slope of the Sierra Nevada mountains in California, the valley was gouged out of obdurate granite a million years ago. The chiseling glaciers left a broad, flat floor, seven miles long and up to a mile wide. A meandering little river of variable temperament bisects the floor. On its flanks lie meadows of wildflowers: blue and white violet, geranium, columbine, larkspur, goldenrod, daisy, honeysuckle, orchid, and lily. Their aromas mingle with those of bay laurel and incense cedar. At four thousand feet the air is dry, the sunlight vivid. Sounds of wildlife and the colors of plants and flowers mingle crisply, with an effect oddly combining discreteness and aggregate power. Fringing the grassy meadows are stands of oversized forests — oak and maple dominated by Douglas spruce, sugar pine, silver fir, and ponderosa reaching two hundred feet and more. Over them, ornamented by ferns and lichens, loom the iron-gray walls of the valley, averaging some thirty-five hundred feet in height. Parts of the rock structure reach even higher. A massive dome, sliced in half as though by a giant cleaver, rises almost a mile above the floor.

These sheer granite cliffs dominate the valley, surrounding it both physically and emotionally. Everything else, even the tall pines, seems small by comparison. Five waterfalls cascade down the cliffs. The largest, ten times higher than Niagara, rumbles forth a steady bass roar. Under a full moon the spray sometimes arranges itself into a lunar rainbow with a five-hundred-foot arc. The depth and steepness of the walls cause abrupt contrasts in climate and vegetation. Most of the south wall remains in constant shadow through the winter; meanwhile, the granite of the north wall absorbs sunlight, which raises its temperature above that of the air, so that flowers bloom and butterflies hatch even as a blizzard descends on the south wall, less than a mile away.

For centuries the valley served as refuge and ancestral home for the Ahwahneechee Indians. The tribe's leaders were so fierce in battle they claimed kinship with the grizzly bear, the Uzumaiti. In the early 1850s they made quixotic war against the white gold miners encroaching on their game fields and acorn orchards. A white battalion of troops pursued the Ahwahneechee to their hideaway and thus "discovered" (once again) the valley. The Indians were removed but the grizzly-bear name, written as Yo Semite and finally Yosemite, stuck to the area.

Barren of gold, too remote for much agriculture, Yosemite Valley quickly became celebrated for its scenery. People made the trek from San Francisco and Sacramento — by railroad, stagecoach, and finally mule-back — to have their senses assaulted by the grand unexpectedness of the place. In 1864 it was ceded by the federal government to the state of California for purposes of "public use, resort, and recreation." Californians claimed it with pride as the first wilderness park in the United States. "You have to go," a British visitor to San Francisco was told in 1870. "It is *the* big thing of the world right now. You ain't got no rocks in Europe near so tall nor so straight. You are bound to go, I *tell* you."

In the spring of 1871 a party of Boston literati arrived in Yosemite for a holiday. They were grouped around their benign leader, Ralph Waldo Emerson, at sixty-eight the most revered man in American letters. The local accommodations, generously called hotels, did not please the Bostonians. (One morning a member of the party was awakened by a chicken traversing his bed.) But the scenery, at least, did not disappoint them. "This valley," Emerson declared, "is the only place that comes up to the brag about it, and exceeds it." The resident population was equally impressed by the famous visitor. Every evening a small crowd gathered at his hotel to stand back and look at the great man. On the fringe of the crowd lingered a young sawyer, John Muir. A mutual friend had told him of Emerson's coming, had extolled each man to the other. Now Muir held back, yearning to introduce himself but too bashful to come forward.

After two years in the valley Muir was regarded as a local curiosity, eccentric but harmless. At times of high water he made a spare living by running a sawmill. Otherwise he seemed a tramp, vague about his background, with no firm plans or even much interest in the future. On his days off he would set out alone into the hills and return by moonlight, laden not with gold or anything valuable, but with sketches and botanical specimens. Given any encouragement at all, he would spout an implausible mixture of religious rhapsodies and scientific theories about the geology of the mountains.

As he stood outside Emerson's hotel, he heard with alarm that the Bostonians planned to leave in a day or two. With that nudge he bravely took himself in hand and — left a note. "Do not thus drift away with the mob," he wrote, "while the spirits of these rocks and waters hail you after long waiting as their kinsman and persuade you to closer communion. . . . I invite you to join me in a month's worship with Nature in the high temples of the great Sierra Crown beyond our holy Yosemite. It will cost you nothing save the time and very little of that for you will be mostly in eternity. . . . In the name of a hundred cascades that barbarous visitors never see . . . in the name of all the spirit creatures of these rocks and of this whole spiritual atmosphere Do not leave us *now*. With most cordial regards I am yours in Nature, John Muir."

The note struck venerable chords in the old transcendentalist. In the morning he and a companion rode over to the sawmill to meet this John Muir. The old man climbed a precarious plank to a tiny boxlike room Muir had attached to the outside of the mill, just below the gable. Perched in his "hang-nest," with the stream gurgling below and a view of the valley stretching to the west (and South Dome visible through a hole in the roof), young Muir puttered away amid a litter of rocks and dried plants. Muir brought forth his treasures. Emerson's questions provoked a deluge of arcane information. Muir repeated his offer of a camping trip to the high mountains. Emerson seemed willing but deferred to his companions, who would not hear of it. "His party, full of indoor philosophy, failed to see the natural beauty and fullness of promise of my wild plan," Muir later recalled, "and laughed at it in good-natured ignorance, as if it were necessarily amusing to imagine that Boston people might be led to accept Sierra manifestations of God at the price of rough camping."

On the last day of Emerson's visit, the party rode out to the Mariposa sequoia grove south of the valley. The Bostonians were amused by the young man's uncertain literary tastes; but he in turn taught them the name of every tree they passed. Again he urged Emerson to camp out, if only for one night, among the giant sequoias. ("I wanted to steal him," Muir explained.) But his solicitous companions intervened once more, fearing the old man might catch cold. So they took him away, leaving Muir alone in the forest. At the top of a distant ridge Emerson stopped, turned his horse, and taking off his hat waved a final goodbye. Though accustomed to his own company, Muir suddenly felt lonesome for the first time in the Sierra. After lingering for a moment he went back to the grove and made a bed of ferns and sequoia plumes. At sundown he built a great fire and started to feel better.

Still tingling from his meeting with Emerson, Muir sent fan letters and plant specimens to Concord. "Would you were here to sing our Yosemite snowbound," he wrote in the following winter. "What prayers push my pen for your coming, but I must hush them all back for our roads are deep blocked with snowbloom." The botanical sawyer was nothing if not persistent. Besieged by his letters and packages, Emerson finally responded in kind: "I have everywhere testified to my friends, who should also be yours, my happiness in finding you — the right man in the right place — in your mountain tabernacle." He repeated the advice he had given his earlier protégé Thoreau years ago. Eventually, when Muir wearied of his solitude ("a sublime mistress, but an intolerable wife"), he should pack up his drawings and herbaria, and come meet society in Concord. Emerson would introduce him to the larger world he deserved. In the meantime Emerson sent two volumes of his collected essays.

The protégé had his own ideas. Yet again he asked Emerson to come back to Yosemite, this time for an entire summer. Concord could learn as much from the mountains, he was sure, as the mountains from Concord. In reading Emerson's essays for the first time, he found the author surprisingly ignorant of the natural world. Scribbling rejoinders in the margins, he carried on a running debate with one of the most formidable intellects of the time.

Emerson: "The squirrel hoards nuts, and the bee gathers honey, without knowing what they do." Muir: *How do we know this.*

Nature "takes no thought for the morrow." *Are not buds and seeds thought for the morrow.*

"It never troubles the sun that some of his rays fall wide and vain into ungrateful space, and only a small part on the reflecting planet." *How do we know that space is ungrateful.*

"The soul that ascends to worship the great God is plain and true; has no rose-color." *Why not? God's sky has rose color and so has his flower.*

"The beauty of nature must always seem unreal and mocking, until the landscape has human figures." *God is in it.*

"The trees are imperfect men, and seem to bemoan their imprisonment, rooted in the ground." *No.*

"There is in woods and waters a certain enticement and flattery, together with a failure to yield a present satisfaction. This disappointment is felt in every landscape." *No — always we find more than we expect.*

The Concord philosopher, it seemed, could only accept nature in human terms, measured by human scales. Muir reasoned in the opposite direction, bringing humans to the test of nature and usually finding them deficient. In reading his Sierra landscapes Muir was overwhelmed by a sense of human insignificance. For all his puffing and striving, man was dwarfed by the mountains and valleys around Yosemite. His power seemed puny compared with a glacier's. His entire history on earth was a blink of the eye in geological time. Yet he arrogated all the Creator's intentions to himself. As Emerson had said, a landscape required human figures, and trees were only imperfect men. When Muir finally sat down to read his hero, he found him all too literally human.

Emerson was an old man, an institution beyond cavil. Muir never told him of his disappointment. Occasionally he used Emersonian terms — such as the "transparent eyeball" — in his own writing. Whatever Emerson's philosophical shortcomings, Muir always loved him for his personal qualities. "The most serene, majestic, sequoia-like soul I ever met," said Muir. "His smile was as sweet and calm as morning light on mountains. There was a wonderful charm in his presence . . . sensed at once by everybody." As for Emerson, at some point in his last years he took another look at an unpublished list among his papers. Entitled *My Men,* it included Carlyle, Agassiz, Thoreau, Lowell, Holmes, and a dozen others. The old man scratched in a final name: John Muir.

❧❧

The nature-struck tramp leaps out from Emerson's list of Brahmins and scholars — the odd man in the group, as he was in any group. He belonged to nobody and followed no plans. He was pulled and pushed by some internal mechanism, but he claimed no control over the device.

In such manner he had arrived in California, on a steamer from New York by way of Panama, three years before his encounter with Emerson. "I am lost — absorbed — captivated with the divine and unfathomable loveliness and grandeur of Nature," he said then. "Somehow I feel separated from the mass of mankind, and I do not know whether I can return to the ordinary modes of feeling and thinking or not." He decided to stay in California for a few months before setting out on a botanizing trip to South America.

He drifted into the great central valley nestled between the coastal mountain range and the distant Sierra Nevada. He spent the summer stalking plants and working odd jobs: hiring himself out at harvesttime, breaking horses, and shearing sheep. In the fall he took charge of eighteen hundred sheep for the winter. Settled in a squalid little hut, two miles from the nearest town, he lived for five months with the company of his two sheep dogs. "I never was so thoroughly hermitized as at present," he noted. "Not a sheep in my flock or bird on the plains lives a more simple uncompounded life than I." His charges, bred for their fleece to the exclusion of any other attributes, were helplessly stupid, quick to panic, and unable to fend for themselves. The shepherd regarded them as typical examples of civilization and progress. Whenever possible he turned his back on them and amused himself with his plants and sketches. He felt happier, he decided, than ever before in his life. Looming to the east, the Sierra exerted a mysteriously perceptible force, like an implausible sun clothed in snow. "If I want the Sierra Mountain feeling on my back, I stand with my back to them just as I would to a fire."

When spring came, the despised sheep took him toward the Sierra. With the valley vegetation quickly burned off, the flock started up toward the high green summer pastures. In typically planless fashion he was drawn to Yosemite. Passing over the foothills, into the mountains, he experienced his first prolonged immersion in the high country. It seemed eerily familiar — like returning to a home he had never known, or recognizing a friend he had never met. As he climbed higher he felt at ease, then exalted, then transformed. "Now we are fairly into the mountains, and they are into us," he wrote in his journal at twenty-five hundred feet. "What bright seething white fire enthusiasm is bred in us — without our help or knowledge a perfect influx into every pore and cell of us fusing, vaporizing, by its heat until the boundary walls of our heavy flesh tabernacle seem taken down and we flow out diffuse into the very air. . . . How glorious a conversion, so complete and wholesome is it. . . . Now I am no longer a shepherd with a few bruised beans and crackers in my stomach and wrapped in a woolen blanket but a free bit of everything."

Yet even in his ecstasies he could not escape reminders of civilized hubris. Finding a growth of poison oak, he reflected that most humans would dismiss it as worthless — as though it had not been created for itself first of all. He measured such manipulative attitudes against those of the region's Indians, who had lived there for centuries without damaging the land. But the whites bustled around building mills, damming streams, cutting roads into granite, working like slaves in the played-out gold mines. "Perhaps no such excess of industry was ever before seen in the history of the world," Muir supposed.

The wretched sheep ("hoofed locusts," he called them) kept chewing their way through the mountain meadows, transforming the carpets of grasses and flowers into dusty wastelands, and therefore always climbing to higher pastures, up to six thousand feet. On a day in mid-July of 1869, feeling guilty about the sheep but exhilarated by the atmosphere, Muir was rambling around the Tuolumne Divide when he suddenly happened on his first comprehensive view of Yosemite Valley. Almost the whole gorge opened itself at his feet: the domes and battlements of the walls, the booming waterfalls, the floor blooming like a garden, the meandering Merced River flashing glints of sunlight. He had stopped in the valley briefly the year before. But now, after weeks in the mountains, he was primed to take it all in. He skirted the rim to the westward, looking for a vantage point from which to peer straight down the face of the wall to the bottom. "When such places were found, and I had cautiously set my feet and drawn my body erect, I could not help fearing a little that the rock might split off and let me down, and what a down! — more than three thousand feet."

He had never taken such chances in the mountains before, but the valley led him on. His body took on an independent will. The internal mechanism seized control. At the top of Upper Yosemite Fall, the largest in the valley, he took off his shoes and crept toward the edge with his hands and feet pressed against the granite. Just below him, another small brow obscured the view into the heart of the torrent. At the very brink he saw a shelf, three inches wide. To reach it he would have to descend a steep slope with nothing to hold onto. "I therefore concluded not to venture farther, but did nevertheless." Somehow he crept down to the shelf, scuttled another thirty feet horizontally, and gazed down into the roaring, streaming current. Settling into his precarious perch, he no longer felt any danger. Nor did he sense any passage of time, lost as he was in the reveries of an incipient mountaineer. Finally he pulled himself back and returned to camp at sundown. That night he tossed in his blankets, awakened repeatedly by a dream that the rim had collapsed and he was falling to a mountaineer's death at the bottom of Yosemite Valley.

Wild, mysterious forces were loose in those mountains. A few days later he received a letter from a former teacher, James Davie Butler, announcing his arrival in California but indicating no intention to visit Yosemite. Muir put the letter aside and made camp in a grove of silver firs, a mile from the North Dome. At about four o'clock on the afternoon of August 1, he sat on the rim sketching, engrossed in his work. "I suddenly stopped, as if something had held my hand," he recalled, "and I jumped up, gazed down into the valley towards the base of the great El Capitan rock; and in a bewildered way, said aloud: 'Can it be possible that Professor Butler is down there.' " Muir started to run down into the valley, but it was late and he did not know the way. The next morning he donned his best clothes and was pulled down a path he could not see. At Vernal Fall he found his man; at four o'clock the previous afternoon Butler had passed the base of El Capitan. "This is the most wonderful example of pure telepathy that I have ever heard of," the professor exclaimed. Muir, amazed and shaken, shrugged it off with a jest: "Hawthorne, I fancy, could weave one of his weird romances out of this little telepathic episode . . . probably replacing my good old Professor by an attractive woman." (But the experience perplexed him for the rest of his life. He never found an explanation.)

With fall approaching, Muir took his hoofed locusts back down to the lowlands. Again he thought about heading for South America. The mountains pulled him back. In mid-November he set out for Yosemite. "I am told that the winter storms there will not be easily borne," he conceded, "but I am bewitched, enchanted." Presenting himself to James Hutchings, one of the valley's original white settlers, he asked for a job and was engaged to build and operate a sawmill. At a site near the base of Lower Yosemite Fall he constructed a simple cabin. It boasted running water: a little brook running through a corner, complete with frogs and ferns in season. His hammock bed offered a view of the fall at night. In December Yosemite was transformed by the first deep snowfall. He rode to the end of the valley, gazing from side to side, gorging on the spectacle yet unable to get his fill. On New Year's Day he marked the occasion by running up a mountain. When the spring thaw swelled the falls he started his mill, quivering at the sacrilege of drowning out the torrents with the screech of his saw. "I have run wild," he declared.

The sawmill at least held him more lightly than the sheep did, and was never threatened by coyotes or snowstorms. Since he cut only fallen timber, yellow pine mostly, the mill did no violence to Sierra vegetation. He enjoyed tinkering with the machinery and showing off his own modifications. He loved the fragrance as the blade sliced into the soft pine. It was idyllic: agreeable employment in the most beautiful spot he had ever seen. South America receded from his plans, replaced by a different kind of wanderlust. As he worked and botanized in the valley, he would look up at the walls, and then to the beckoning peaks beyond. By summertime the spring cascades were only trickling down. Freed of the mill, he could take blocks of time — up to three weeks — and disappear into the Sierra.

Mountaineering in 1870 was barely recognized as a sport. Its few adherents, mainly on the East Coast and in Europe, had developed only the rudiments of technique. In any case Muir knew nothing about them. Over the course of several years, by trial and error he devised his own notions of how to go about it. Normally he wore loose-fitting trousers of duck or blue denim, a woolen shirt, a vest, and a light broad-brimmed hat. The vest pockets were filled with small instruments, such as a watch, barometer, thermometer, and a hand lens. He never wore a coat because it impeded his arms, flapped in the wind, and was liable to catch on bushes or rock outcroppings. On the hardest climbs he stripped down to his drawers to free his limbs completely. He wore low, well-fitted shoes, with thick soles and roundheaded hobnails, tied over both ankle and instep with well-stretched buckskin strings. (Boots, he explained, were liable to shrink or expand when wet, with no means of adjustment — but shoes could simply be retied.) A perfect fit was crucial, not only to avoid blisters but to enable the climber to cross glacial moraines or earthquake taluses: "the sole forms as it were a portion of the foot and we can tell exactly in making a leap where the foot will strike." On level ground he walked with a peculiar shuffling gait, barely lifting his feet, apparently to save energy. In more difficult terrain he shifted into a "dancing rhythm," as he called it, "so that in leaping from boulder to boulder one's feet keep time to music." The rocks were arranged in a definite order, he explained, best approached by a particular cadence.

Heading into a timbered region, he usually packed blankets and provisions on a small mustang that learned to jump rocks like a goat. The pony carried a pair of thick blankets, eight or ten pounds of bread or crackers, a few pounds of oatmeal, a package of tea, and two tin cans fitted with wire handles for cooking. These were packed in strong canvas bags that could withstand stiff underbrush and even those occasions when the pony stumbled and rolled down a canyon side. "The crackers were of course pounded into meal," Muir noted, "and the bread into mere crumbs which made some difficulty in fitting into one's mouth, but its nourishment was not impaired thereby which was the main thing." If the cans were jammed or broken, the oatmeal could be parched on hot stones, or wetted and kneaded on a smooth rock and then baked on the coals. The tea could be dispensed with or chewed in small quantities like tobacco. "A very strong mouthful of tea is thus made," he said with some understatement, "which may be diluted to any required strength after it is swallowed by drinking cold water."

On climbs above timberline he had to leave the pony behind and scale down his needs accordingly. He carried the same quantities of bread, crackers, oatmeal, and tea, along with two cans fitted into each other. Each article was tied in a separate cloth sack, "then all tied in one sack so that in descending dangerous gorges or snow-slopes it could be tumbled down ahead and bear the battering without getting mixed." Blankets were too heavy to carry. At night he would come back down to his camp at timberline and gather enough pitchy pine roots to last the night. Constructing a bed of boughs on the leeward side of some dwarf pines, he would sleep for twenty or thirty minutes and then be awakened by the cold. "I would start up the fire and get a little warmed, and then try it again, and so wear the night out. When I was asleep one side of me roasted, while the other froze. In the morning I was naturally stiff and cold, but soon from the effect of tea and sunshine I felt 'lifted up.' " Before leaving camp he hung his food bag on a high limb to keep it from wood rats and coyotes. A piece of bread or a little bag of crumbs attached to his belt sustained him through the day and even through the next night if he didn't return to camp. With his pocket instruments and ice ax he would stride into the day's exploration. "The higher the peak to be climbed and the greater the difficulty anticipated, the earlier the start, thus shortening the cold night at both ends." Carried away by the adventure, he might go three hard days without food, or stretch one week's provisions over three.

Why did he do it? What made him endure the hunger and cold and the endless nights without blankets? Before his first summer in the Sierra, Muir had scarcely set foot on a mountain. Then overnight he was displaying all the zealous symptoms of the new convert. "Who wouldn't be a mountaineer!" he exclaimed. Again: "I feel like preaching these mountains like an apostle." Emerson caught the full brunt of the young man's missionary intensity. But what did Muir find on those peaks? He pursued his botanical and geological studies, but initially with no intention of publishing the results. He made many first ascents of mountains considered unclimbable, but never left his name on a summit. The people in the valley scratched their heads and considered him more than a little daft.

What he found was a degree of psychic integration previously unknown to him. After years of wandering he felt as though he belonged up there. This sense overwhelmed him especially at moments of danger, when a wrong decision or a clumsy step would have killed him. At such times his conscious mind yielded to what he called his "other self," a mysterious force, neither outside nor inside his body but surrounding it, that calmed him and gave directions. The other self never appeared among civilized surroundings, was never needed there. Only in the wilderness, when he was poised against some natural obstacle, could he sense its unbidden presence: an apparent proof that he was at home in the mountains. Sometimes he would approach a climbing maneuver of no obvious risk, only to be driven back by the other self. More typically it helped him over emergencies. In the fall of 1872, in making the first ascent of Mount Ritter he found himself stuck halfway up a sheer face, clinging to the rock with no further handholds in sight, frozen by indecision. Enter the other self. "Then my trembling muscles became firm again," he recalled, "every rift and flaw in the rock was seen as through a microscope, and my limbs were moved with a positiveness and precision with which I seemed to have nothing at all to do." His own will suspended, buoyed up by the other self, he fused with the mountain.

The union verified his intuitive notion of the indivisible harmony of the natural world. Nature included no accidents, no dissonance, no absolute separations. Everything, from the man on the mountain down to the smallest speck, was arranged and loved *in equal measure* by the Creator. "There is no mystery but the mystery of harmony," Muir wrote in his journal, "no inexplicable caprice, no anomalous or equivocal expression on all the grandly inscribed mountains." The common distinction between animate and inanimate matter meant nothing to Muir. The ranking of "higher" and "lower" creatures was only another human conceit. All had their own purposes, regardless of the Draconian judgments passed by man.

Muir reserved a special sympathy for those species most lacking in human friends. During his first year in the Sierra he killed two rattlesnakes — but regretted the executions and did not repeat them. He regarded the coyote as "a beautiful animal, graceful in motion," skilled at picking off an occasional dinner of mutton. Even bears aroused only admiration, never fear, when he encountered them on the trail. He did not carry a gun and was never harmed. Only one creature made him wonder about the universality of divine love and natural harmony: a vicious species of small black ant, found in the Sierra foothills, that would attack any bystander without provocation. "I can't understand the need of their ferocious courage," he said, perplexed. "Their bodies are mostly jaws curved like ice-hooks, and to get work for these weapons seems to be their chief aim and pleasure." But otherwise the wilderness offered a friendly refuge to even the most assertive of bipeds.

Shuttling between the mountains and Yosemite Valley, he felt these ideas resonate through every cell of his body. He picked them up from direct experience in nature, not from books, so contrary arguments evolved from books carried no weight with him. Even Emerson seemed misguided, sitting in his Concord study. The error was only compounded by larger urban settlements. The bigger the city, the further from divine harmony. "The gross heathenism of civilization has generally destroyed nature, and poetry, and all that is spiritual," said Muir. The senses so alive on a mountain would quickly atrophy in a city. Far from the wonders of nature, humans might entertain an excessive opinion of their importance and cleverness.

Shortly after his ascent of Mount Ritter, two friends dragged Muir off to San Francisco for his first visit to a city in three years. In short order he fled back to Yosemite and embarked on "a good hard trip" to purge the city from his body. Climbing a shoulder of Mount Watkins, at the edge of a thousand-foot gorge, he fell and hit his head. He had never so much as stumbled before. Unconscious, rolling toward the brink, he was stopped by some bushes at the edge. When he came around he was furious with himself. The corrupting city had nearly killed him, Muir decided. "I ran back to the spot from whence I had fallen, every nerve and muscle aroused and firm, rounded the shoulder and pushed on up the canyon rejoicing that a single tap on the head had proved sufficient to shake out and clear away every trace of lowland confusion, degeneration and dust."

❧❧

Preaching the mountains, he hoped the multitude would come and be baptized. About two thousand tourists passed through Yosemite each summer in the 1870s. Muir watched them and occasionally helped guide them around the valley. They came "more to show than to see," he thought. Immured in their city ways, they saw only the obvious; too much lowland confusion. "All sorts of human stuff is being poured into our valley this year," he noted in the spring of 1870, "and the blank, fleshly apathy with which most of it comes in contact with the rock and water spirits of the place is most amazing. . . . They climb sprawlingly to their saddles like overgrown frogs pulling themselves up a stream-bank through the bent sedges, ride up the valley with about as much emotion as the horses they ride upon . . . and long for the safety and flatness of their proper homes." When Muir looked at the rocks he saw religion, science, philosophy — and more. Others saw only rocks.

The irony of his caustic response to the tourists was that he seemed just as peculiar to them as they to him. A grown man, he would take a swim and then thrash around in the snow; or roll boulders down the slope of a mile-long canyon; or climb to the top of a tree to celebrate a howling storm; or soak a sequoia cone in water and drink the resulting purple liquid, "hoping thereby to improve my color and render myself more tree-wise and sequoical." He worked barely hard enough to buy his meager diet. In encountering a stranger in the high Sierra, Muir said he came from Yosemite and was looking at trees. "Oh, then," said the stranger, "you must be John Muir." For no one else would have been so engaged. "Idle sentimental transcendental dreaming is the only sensible and substantial business that one can engage in," he wrote in his journal.

A British writer named Thérèse Yelverton spent the summer of 1870 in the valley. She found Muir so striking that she included him, down to the last detail and with speeches borrowed from his journals, in her novel *Zanita,* published two years later. "Kenmuir" was modeled so closely on the original article — with an occasional exaggeration such as his pet rattlesnake — that the book provides the fullest portrait of the valley's most striking human phenomenon.

The novel opens as the narrator is making her way down into Yosemite. "What on earth is that?" she exclaims, pointing to a man standing at the edge of a cliff, stretching himself as though about to take wing. "It's that darned idiot Kenmuir," her guide replies, "and the sooner he dashes out that rum mixture of his he calls brains the sooner his troubles'll be over, that's my idee." Approaching this curiosity, the intrepid narrator sees him "swaying to and fro with extended arms as if moved by the wind, the head thrown back as in swimming, and the long brown hair falling wildly about his face and neck." Snapped out of his reverie, the apparition springs lithely toward his observers, "skipping over the rough boulders, poising with the balance of an athlete, or skirting a shelf of rock with the cautious activity of a goat, never losing for a moment the rhythmic motion of his flexile form." Seen at close range he seems quite normal. "His bright intelligent eyes revealed no trace of insanity, and his open blue eyes of honest questioning, and glorious auburn hair might have stood as a portrait of the angel Raphael. His figure was about five feet nine, well knit, and bespoke that active grace which only trained muscles can assume."

Then he opens his mouth and once again seems — unusual. "Can I do anything for you?" he asks. "She wants to know what you were doing out on that bloody knob overhanging eternity," says the guide. "Praising God," Kenmuir declares solemnly. ("Thought that would start him," the guide interjects.) "Praising God, madam, for his mighty works, his glorious earth, and the sublimity of these fleecy clouds, the majesty of that great roaring torrent" (pointing to the Nevada) "that leaps from rock to rock in exultant joy, and laves them, and kisses them with caresses of downiest foam. O, no mother ever pressed her child in tenderer embrace. . . ."

Proceeding down into the valley with Kenmuir, the narrator takes her measure of this creature. "Truly his garments had the tatterdemalion style of a Mad Tom. The waist of his trousers was eked out with a grass band; a long flowing sedge rush stuck in the solitary button-hole of his shirt, the sleeves of which were ragged and forlorn, and his shoes appeared to have known hard and troublous times." Yet his speech, the rhetorical flourishes aside, suggests a man of culture and breeding. "I soon divined that his refinement was innate, his education collegiate, not only from his scientific treatment of his subject, but his correct English. Kenmuir, I decided in my mind, was a gentleman." Of obvious eccentricity, but a gentleman — a breed familiar enough to the British writer. "Man is the only mistake, it seems to me, in the works of the Creator," Kenmuir announces, "and there does appear to be something radically wrong about him."

Evidently Muir liked mankind in general no better than the lowland tourists in particular. Yet his strictures by their shrill, overstated insistence betrayed an implicit defensiveness — as though, unable to connect with human society, he protected himself by throwing up a screen of misanthropic growls and then running away to the wilderness. Did he love the mountains more, or humans less? By his own admission he was "desperately bashful and shy." His wild appearance and manner of living, not to mention his peculiar ideas, further cut him off from people. Usually forced by circumstances to climb mountains by himself, since nobody would go with him, he bore his loneliness by telling himself he would see more and work harder without distractions.

In his years of rambling through nature Muir had never been reconciled to the essential solitariness of it. "I am always a little lonesome," he had said shortly after arriving in California. "I cannot accustom myself to the coldness of strangers, nor to the shiftings and wanderings of this Arab life." Six months later: "I have not made a single friend in California." His associates among ranchers and sheepherders shared none of his intellectual interests. Timidly, haltingly, he sought the human affection he craved. But he was so *different.* Even in Yosemite, the resonating sympathies of the natural setting did not quite compensate for his impregnable isolation. "I am lonely among my enjoyments," he noted dolefully; "the valley is full of visitors, but I have no one to talk to."

He seemed most at ease around small children. They could respond directly to nature with the same awed delight he did; they liked to laugh and play games; they took no special notice of ragged clothes or irregular employment. When he started working for James Hutchings in the fall of 1869 he made immediate friends of the boss's two little girls, five-year-old Floy and two-year-old Cosie. Muir held them on his knee, pointing out the parts of flowers. They trotted after him as he botanized through the meadows of the valley floor. Their mother, Elvira Sproat Hutchings, also liked to collect plant specimens, sometimes reproducing them in paintings. With botany as the common ground, Muir began to know the mother better. Thérèse Yelverton put her in *Zanita* too: "a slight semi-girlish semi-matronly figure, with a Madonna cast of countenance, deep, pensive hazel eyes, a blush-rose complexion, and brown hair. She moved dreamily, as if under a spell." Normally calm and reposed, with a soft musical voice, she seemed to float rather than walk, with an ethereal quality not entirely of this world.

As a valley resident later recalled it, James and Elvira Hutchings were "ill mated." More than twenty years her senior, he looked even older, with his snowy beard and sparse white hair. After three babies in five years, the last a crippled boy only a few months old, she felt exhausted by her marriage and resentful of her husband's expectations. Further, their stake in the valley had been jeopardized by the federal cession to the state, which had invalidated their previously filed claim. Within a few days of hiring Muir, James Hutchings left to spend the winter in Washington seeking compensation for his loss. Muir was charged with taking care of the family during his absence. Given the circumstances — Elvira's restiveness, Muir's loneliness, the absence of James, and the isolation of being snowed into the valley during a long winter — it would have been remarkable if something had *not* happened.

Something did happen, though precisely what can only be conjectured. Apparently Muir lived in the Hutchings home briefly, then moved to his nearby cabin and continued to eat with the family. (Years later, in dictating his autobiography Muir recalled: "I boarded with Mr. Hutchings' family while I built a cabin myself." Then he revised the sentence to read: "I boarded with Mr. Hutchings' family but occupied a cabin that I built for myself.") Even allowing for Yelverton's literary exaggerations, Muir was a sharply handsome young man; Elvira in her frailness called on his protective instincts. Both delighted in the children. Both loved to launch into intricate botanical discussions, Muir "all vigor, and arguing in little puffs and dashes," according to *Zanita,* while Elvira "glided out her sentences like soft falling snow." So the winter passed, Muir's first in Yosemite. "I have a great deal to say to you," he wrote a confidante in early April, "which I will not try to write."

After being held up in Washington, James Hutchings finally returned in May. However odd Muir might have seemed, with his irrepressible good cheer he was universally liked in the valley; but for some reason Hutchings conceived an implacable animosity toward him. "My father had a violent, unreasoning dislike for him — unwarranted and most regrettable," Cosie Hutchings said later. Perhaps he resented the mountaineering time Muir took from the sawmill. Perhaps he felt displaced by Muir's budding fame as a celebrant of the valley. (Hutchings guarded the "apparently accepted mission" of his life, as he wrote in his Sierra guidebook, "the dissemination of knowledge on the charming realities of Yo Semite." With this proprietary interest, he may have felt threatened by the newly arrived upstart.) And finally, perhaps he sensed some involvement between Muir and his wife.

(In *Zanita* the Elvira character dies an early, sentimental death. "Hers is the only death I cannot bring myself to look upon with philosophy," says Kenmuir. "She is the only person I ever knew who seemed to be ever with God and to lean upon Him." At the funeral, "Kenmuir wept softly like a woman, every now and then approaching the lounge to look at the dead." Years later he falls in love — with her daughter.)

For whatever reason the disaffection between the two men was deeply felt on both sides. "J. M. Hutchings wasn't much of a man," a mutual friend conceded to Muir much later. "I can see it now but ... I did not follow you as much as I had ought to." In the summer of 1870 Muir and Hutchings competed in subtle ways for the attention of visiting celebrities. While they feuded, Muir continued to visit Elvira and the children. Late that fall Hutchings abruptly announced that Muir could not stay in the cabin near the family home, explaining that it was needed by his sister. He had expressly promised it to Muir for the winter. "Were it not that Mr. Hutchings owes me money," said Muir, "and that I have a lot of loose notes and outline sketches to work up I should set out for South America at once." The ploy, if ploy it was, did not work. Muir built his hang-nest and stayed in the valley through the winter, partaking occasionally of Elvira's company.

When summer came the Hutchingses moved down the valley to the hotel they operated, and Muir saw less of Elvira. Despite this separation his dealings with James grew steadily more disagreeable. Muir suspected him of trying to cheat him out of his proper wages. In August Muir left his employ and moved out of the hang-nest. The following winter James again departed for Washington, but this time he took Elvira along. "I am more lonely this winter than ever," said Muir. Without Elvira, "there is not left one soul with whom I can exchange a thought."

He spent the winter of 1871–1872 in gloomy isolation at the other hotel in the valley. The Yosemite snows could still revive him. In such surroundings he was constitutionally incapable of a prolonged depression. He was starting to think about a writing career, and receiving his first wisps of encouragement. The season passed. When Elvira came back to the valley they resumed their conversations. "Mrs. Hutchings is always kind to me, and the clearness of her views on all spiritual things is very extraordinary," said Muir. "Her little Cosie is as pure a piece of sunbeam as ever was condensed to human form."

᙭᙭

Acquaintances kept telling Muir to write. The torrents of nature-struck verbiage that cascaded from his mouth at the slightest provocation should, they said, be preserved on paper. For a long time he would not consider it. The act of writing would hold him indoors, away from his real work in the mountains. Even guiding the froglike tourists through the valley at least kept him outside, his senses alert and his legs tuned. Though he obviously loved the play and music of spoken English, he distrusted the written word. "I have a low opinion of books; they are but piles of stones set up to show travelers where other minds have been, or at best signal smokes to call attention," he noted in his journal. "No amount of word-making will ever make a single soul to *know* these mountains. . . . One day's exposure to mountains is better than cartloads of books." The mountains spoke directly, immediately, to the whole body. Books were artificial, vicarious, dead, the all-too-predictable fabrication of lowland society.

In 1871 someone sent him a book about Alpine explorations by John Tyndall, the English physicist and mountaineer. It confirmed Muir's suspicion of literary exploration. Tyndall seemed preoccupied with the physical aspects of mountain climbing and thus missed the larger purposes. "There is no such thing," Muir scribbled into the book, "as mere scrambling on the mountains though some seem to think so, as if a man could be found who was legs only." Tyndall compounded his error by making dubious statements about the geological structure of mountains — a predictable misstep by someone who only climbed from the waist down. All such celebrated experts, Muir decided, needed to raise their heads and open their eyes. Unless they did he expected to learn nothing from them. "It is astonishing to see how little the greatest know in this field," he told Emerson. "If Tyndall would leave his lectures and books and dwell with the Alps he would finally make a speech or book of everlasting worth, but he does not allow himself time to fill."

Despite his untamed postures and contempt for book learning, Muir usually bowled over any scientist who came his way. He caught visitors off guard because his appearance was so at odds with his talk. And how he talked! A geology professor from Berkeley, Joseph Le Conte, encountered an unprepossessing man in the rough clothing of the sawmill. But he had

an "intelligent face and earnest, clear blue eye," and a considerable knowledge of botany. "A man of so much intelligence tending a sawmill!" Le
Conte exclaimed. They set forth into the high country around the valley.
The professor was amazed by Muir's unquenchable passion for everything
in sight. "Mr. Muir gazes and gazes, and cannot get his fill," Le Conte
noted. "He seems to revel in the freedom of this life. I think he would pine
away in a city or in conventional life of any kind." Muir was a powerful,
serious personality, the professor concluded, with an original and meticulously observing mind.

Muir liked Le Conte well enough and invited him to go on further rambles. But they disagreed about the geological history of the Sierra. Muir
badgered and taunted Le Conte into coming back for another look; Le
Conte pleaded his responsibilities in Berkeley. "If you could be made to
feel the truth chapters which are here," Muir shot back, "you would come
at once without looking at times and duties like an attracted atom going to
a magnet. Strange that manufactured proprieties and duties should so
shackle and cobweb God's human flies, but next year you will have what
you call vacation and then mankind and your wife will let you come."
Having no wife and few duties, and being on a more or less permanent vacation, Muir was perplexed by the normal constraints of civilization. Perhaps offended by his tone, Le Conte ignored the challenge. Muir tried
again, more conciliatorily: "you know how gladly I will see you this summer when we will burn our thoughts together instead of struggling with
distance and the penghosts of language." Always he favored direct immersion over the written word. The professor wasn't sure.

They were arguing about the geological origins of the valley and the
surrounding region. Muir was hooked on the problem. It dominated his
trips to the mountains and even intruded into his dreams at night. Waking
or sleeping, he puzzled over it, ran it through his mind one more time,
flicked through his notes yet again, looking for the evidence to nail down
his intuitions. Following the work of Charles Lyell, the founder of modern
geology, he believed in the "uniformitarian" theory of gradual, steady
geological forces working relentlessly over the millennia, continuing on to
the present day. Specifically, under the influence of Louis Agassiz, Muir
stressed the role of glaciers. He accepted (initially) Agassiz's exaggerated
notion that a single polar ice cap had spread down from the North Pole
and carved out the major features of the Northern Hemisphere. During his
first summer in the Sierra, Muir had noticed many examples of glacial
striations and polishing on the rocks. "This entire region must have been
overswept by ice," he wrote in his journal. But the dominant theory of Yo-

semite's origins, as propounded by the state geologist of California, Josiah Dwight Whitney, dismissed glaciers in favor of random "cataclysmic" shiftings and heavings of the earth's crust. Thus Yosemite was an accident: the earth quaked and the valley floor collapsed some thirty-five hundred feet.

Yosemite an *accident?* It was inconceivable to Muir. From his years in the wilderness he knew, with a certainty beyond the reach of books or professors, that a single, orderly harmony embraced all nature. The Creator made no mistakes, no offhand gestures. Surely Yosemite had been scooped out by slow, intentional glaciers. If it was only the result of a random catastrophe, then what of other gorges like it, such as the Hetch Hetchy Valley a few miles to the north? All such glacial phenomena, with their visible scorings, were "landscapes fresh from God's hand," Muir declared. "As if this were the very dawn of creation and we had been blessed in being made spectators of it all." The cataclysmic theory made God a prankster. The glacial theory suggested a cosmic plan. It harmonized science and religion by adducing empirical evidence of the divine scheme. When Muir rejected the Whitney theory "most devoutly," he used the word with precision. Proving the glacial origin of Yosemite became an act of devotion for him.

Whitney's assistant on the state geological survey, Clarence King, had found traces of large glaciers that had entered the valley at three separate points. But King did not recognize that they had scooped out the valley, and Whitney would not even acknowledge the visible evidence of the glaciers. Muir had to establish their credibility and — by correlating the effects of gravity, sun and shadow, and the peculiar structure of the granite peaks and valleys — trace their probable course through the valley and across the entire nearby range. He had no scientific credentials, severely limited resources, and no one to help him.

At least he had the advantage of knowing his conclusions a priori. For over a year he was mystified by a deep canyon southwest of Lower Yosemite Fall. It looked glacial in origin, but could not have been dug by any of the valley glaciers identified by King. Finally, on one of his Sundays away from the mill, he climbed to the valley rim and set out for the upper end of the basin above the fall, looking for traces of his missing glacier in the higher, deeper portions of its channel, where it would have lingered longest. After about four miles he found glacial scoring in a small hollow. "You might have heard a shout in Concord," he wrote Emerson. By following such inferential hunches, imagining where glaciers must have been, he could make the smallest of clues stand forth in bold relief. It appeared that glaciers had entered Yosemite by all its canyons, slicing off Half Dome and the other upper battlements in the process, and carved the sheer stone walls dominating the valley.

The Lyell thesis extended ancient processes into the present. One day in the upper Merced basin Muir ran across a stream bottomed by fine gray silt. Supposing it might be glacial mud, he followed the stream up its course and found a small residual glacier, a living remnant of the massive mountain carvers. In the next few years he found scores of other living glaciers, but the news was skeptically received. "My friends regarded my deductions and statements with distrust," he recalled; "therefore, I determined to collect proofs of the common, measured, arithmetical kind." He planted stakes on several of the snowfields. The stakes measured steady movement in a glacial pattern, about an inch a day. With that Muir had his proof.

The amateur geologist thus found himself with a major discovery on his hands. After a final show of diffidence he was at last prevailed on to try writing for publication, to risk the penghosts of language. Clinton L. Merriam, a New York congressman with an interest in natural history, visited Yosemite in the summer of 1871. "I have no objection to your publishing what I have told you," said Muir, ". . . trusting as I do in your judgement, and kindness of heart." Merriam instead insisted that Muir write up his own discoveries, which Merriam then submitted to Horace Greeley's New York *Tribune*. (Greeley had visited Yosemite in 1859, declaring it "the grandest marvel of the continent.") The article, "Yosemite Glaciers," was published by the *Tribune* on December 5, 1871, a remarkable debut: Muir's first formally published writing appeared in the most influential American newspaper of the day. "I have been drifting about among the rocks of this region for several years," Muir explained, "anxious to spell out some of the mountain truths which are written here." Then followed an account of his work, punctuated with an occasional sally of the kind known to his friends: "There is sublimity in the life of a glacier . . . working on unwearied through unmeasured times, unhalting as the stars."

In starting to write he was only meeting the professors halfway. Along with the necessary obeisance to sober scientific discourse, he would include an ecstatic tribute to the natural wonder of it all to make his philosophical point: man the scientist was only the reporter; the credit belonged to the infinite mystery of nature's design. People from the lowland, he would suggest, were liable to entertain an exaggerated notion of human significance in the grand scheme. Despite the flattering attention of noted professors, he continued to denigrate books in favor of reading the landscape directly. He took John Daniel Runkle of the Massachusetts Institute of

Technology on a tour of Yosemite glaciers, pointing out the rock forms and canyons and preaching his theories. "He soon said 'It is true,' " Muir reported to Emerson, "receiving knowledge by absorption past all his flinty mathematics quite forgetful of his ghaunt rawboned Euclidal 'Wherefors.' He thinks that if the damp mosses and lichens were scraped off I might make a teacher — a professor faggot to burn beneath their Technological furnaces. All in kindness but I'd rather grow green in the sky."

He might shrug off such offers, but he could not miss their implication. He was on to something. Formerly complacent about having his discoveries published by others, he now felt more protective when he was plagiarized without credit, more intent on writing up his ideas himself. Freed of the sawmill, he had ample time. "My life work is now before me plain enough," he declared. He wrote a series of glacial articles for *Overland Monthly,* the California version of an eastern literary magazine. The pieces were illustrated with his own primitive sketches, of which he was inordinately proud. Parts of these articles were also published in such recognized scientific periodicals as the *American Journal of Science* and the *Proceedings* of the American Association for the Advancement of Science, thus bringing Muir's work to the national scientific community. "It appears that all the mountains of the range between lat. 36°, 30' and 39°," he concluded in the AAAS *Proceedings,* ". . . owe their development to the ice-sheet of the great winter, which brooded them all, and flowed grandly above them like a wind."

A characteristic flourish, even before the prestigious AAAS. Though his ambitions and intellectual horizons were expanding, he remained the mountaineer. The scientists held serious discussions about methods of study and cool objectivity, with a manipulative attitude of picking things apart and dominating them. For man was the lord of creation. Muir followed his instincts and let Nature talk to him on her own terms. "This was my 'method of study,' " he explained with a nod to the professors: "I drifted about from rock to rock, from stream to stream, from grove to grove. Where night found me, there I camped. When I discovered a new plant, I sat down beside it for a minute or a day, to make its acquaintance and hear what it had to tell. . . . I asked the boulders I met, whence they came and whither they were going." His unstructured, even whimsical approach — that yielded such substantial results — no doubt offended the sensibilities of his professional audience.

Josiah Whitney and Clarence King, at least, were evidently wounded by both the method and the findings. Muir dismissed the state survey's efforts to discover living glaciers ("a slight reconnaissance"), and he casually recounted climbs that had forced King to turn back. Thus provoked, Whitney spurned the theories of "that shepherd." King quite agreed, and heaped particular scorn on the claim of living glaciers in the Sierra. "It is to be hoped that Mr. Muir's vagaries will not deceive geologists who are personally unacquainted with California," said King, "and that the ambitious amateur himself may divert his evident enthusiastic love of nature into a channel, if there is one, in which his attainments would save him from hopeless floundering." (Later work would support the amateur, except on two points. It was not a single glacial age, as envisioned by Agassiz, but a series of smaller epochs; and Muir missed the substantial role of water erosion in scooping out the Yosemite. Still, he was more nearly right than Whitney or King, or any other geologist of his time.)

Glaciers were his passion, the focus of his life in these years. But a nineteenth-century naturalist was expected to have at least some acquaintance with all the natural world; the blinders of specialization had not yet locked into place. When he stalked his glaciers he still took due notice of the plant and animal life of the Sierra. Occasionally he sent specimens and vivid accounts of his rambles to the Harvard botanist Asa Gray. "What a splendid *plant-finder* you are," Gray wrote back, "and I envy, while I shudder over your walk. It seems to me here and now just astonishing." In the summer of 1872 Gray brought his own mentor John Torrey to Yosemite, and the three men went up into the high country together. At night, by the campfire, Muir sat enthralled by the amiable company of the two most distinguished American botanists of the day. "They told the stories of their lives," Muir recalled, "Torrey fondly telling all about Gray, Gray about Torrey." Gray later sent Muir four of his books "so you can set to studying Botany again" and, like Emerson and Runkle, urged him to come to Boston for more education. Muir inevitably told Gray to come back to Yosemite; after which, he allowed, Gray might return to his Cambridge classes "and to all of the just and proper ding dong of civilization."

To the civilized unfortunates he served as press agent for the mountains. The New York *Tribune* published more articles about the Yosemite region, as did the Boston *Evening Transcript,* the favored newspaper of his Brahmin friends. He celebrated the flooding of the Merced River and the major Yosemite earthquakes in the spring of 1872: they implied no danger, he assured his readers, because destruction always brought creation. Tourists were guaranteed the full panoply of natural attractions, food and lodging for three dollars a day, and smiles for free. Muir included loving evocations of all the sights, sounds, and smells. In the end he generally reverted to his favorite theme. "The last days of this glacial winter are not yet past, so young is our world," he exulted. "The morning stars still sing together, and the world, not yet half made, becomes more beautiful every day."

※※

And yet: despite his glacial work, the beginnings of a writing career, and his insatiable joy when absorbed by the wilderness, something was missing. He still felt lonesome, unable to connect in a fundamental way with other human beings. "In all God's mountain mansions," he wrote in his journal in the fall of 1872, "I find no human sympathy, and I hunger." Five months later, at the end of another isolated Yosemite winter: "To live without human love is impossible. Quench love, and what is left of a man's life but the folding of a few jointed bones and square inches of flesh. Who would call that life?" The question dangles, teasingly ambiguous. Had he spent the winter in his normal, garrisoned solitude? Or had he experienced love that was then forcibly quenched?

The marriage of James and Elvira Hutchings was disintegrating. She was devoutly religious, the daughter of Christian missionaries, and she did not contemplate lightly the possibility of a formal separation. She sent Muir a note. In reply, he urged her not to think so deeply about it. She went to him, confused and desperate; his response is not known. Finally she decided to leave her husband, apparently in September 1873. She sent Muir a second note, loving and elliptical, to tell him she was all right and confidently looked forward to making a new life.

"Dear friend," she wrote. "I feel that I must talk to you a little while, and perhaps can say more fully what I wish in this way than in another. You know me, now, more fully than any other living soul upon earth, for you have known me when most weak in body and mind, when deeply hurt and most anxious, and doubtful about myself. I feel stronger now, and wish you to know me at all times. I believe I went to you, in my loneliness, as a bird would fly to a grand old cedar in a storm — as I would have gone to Christ had He been here in human shape, and I believe that He sent me, for I prayed to Him to help me. . . . There are plenty of dear old trees to rest under, and I should not starve. So you see I have no fear for the future, and though I have seen many living lives that seem to run through peaceful sunny days without storm, or shadow, I would not exchange my life for theirs; No — not even when walking, barefoot, over the rough stones in the canyon's shadow. Where will the deeply learned and keen-eyed scholar go for comfort and strength in bereavement, when the veil seems partly to withdraw and material things lie far below?"

Muir saved the letter but neither then nor later left any overt record of his feelings in the matter. Elvira Hutchings was his dearest friend in the valley. Wounded and vulnerable, she approached him for help and found, evidently, little consolation of the kind she needed. In fact, Muir fled the valley. Just back from his longest and hardest trip into the high country, he took off again, traversing some thousand miles in the next two months. Then he went down to Oakland, ostensibly to spend the winter writing. But he stayed away from the valley for ten months, his longest absence since 1869. For that entire period, his collected papers contain no outgoing correspondence. Apparently he spent the time writing up his discoveries. As to his emotional state during those ten months, the record is mute.

Finally he could stand the absence of wilderness no longer. "Tell me what you will of the benefactions of city civilization," he wrote in his journal, "of the sweet security of streets — all as part of the natural upgrowth of man towards the high destiny we hear so much of. . . . All are more or less sick; there is not a perfectly sane man in San Francisco." In September 1874 he went back to the valley, but only for a visit. He felt like a stranger there. The rocks and mountains, once so eloquent, were silent. He avoided Elvira Hutchings. "I have not seen Mrs. H. and hope I shall not." Their friendship, indeed the whole four-year Yosemite period of his life, seemed irrevocably finished. "Surely this Merced and Tuolumne chapter of my life is done," he decided. His Yosemite years — his glacier work — his friendship with Elvira Hutchings: bound together by circumstances, they all ended at the same time. For the rest of his life he came to the valley on occasional visits, but never stayed for long.

2

Before Yosemite:
Nature and the Biped Lord

 MUIR was thirty years old when he first set foot in Yosemite. The hegira that brought him there had stretched from a town in Scotland to a farm in Wisconsin, then to college in Madison and a forced flight to the Canadian woods, then to a factory in Indianapolis, where he had a traumatic accident, and a thousand-mile hike to Florida. This wandering course, Muir claimed, had simply unrolled before him, without direction or comprehension on his part. "We never know where we must go nor what guides we are to get," he said during his first summer in the Sierra. "All the wilderness seems to be full of tricks and plans to drive and draw us up into God's Light." According to Muir, he simply followed the wilderness. By a mysterious process it brought him home to Yosemite.

Muir did not care to inquire into the matter more deeply. Ascribing everything to the lure of the wilderness left unexplained the major tensions in his personality — between people and nature, civilized constraints and wild freedom, love and loneliness. He spent his whole life moving back and forth between these sets of polar opposites. The pattern had been set during the thirty years before Yosemite, a motif repeated four times: a period of bondage followed by a release and leave-taking to an unknown destination. In this rhythm of bondage and release lies the key to understanding what made John Muir so different from most Americans of his time. The recurrent alternation of freedom and restraint made each seem all the more vivid by contrast and set up the unresolved polarities in his character. Projected onto the unequal battle that the American wilderness was losing to nineteenth-century technology, these internal tensions found external expression in a life poised between the mountains and the city. Through working out his private quarrels, Muir was to become the central figure in the history of American conservation.

❧❧

He was born on April 21, 1838, in the town of Dunbar, which faced the North Sea near the mouth of the Firth of Forth thirty miles east of Edinburgh. Both parents were descended from Highlanders. Daniel Muir — "a comet whose course Heaven only knows," according to his son — was a Christian zealot who spent his life looking for a church that met his exacting standards. When not reading his Bible, the only book he approved, he ran a prosperous grocery business with the thrift and integrity expected of a Scotsman. Ann Gilrye Muir, softer and less dour, balanced her husband's austerity. "A representative Scotch woman," as John Muir described her, "quiet, conservative, of pious, affectionate character, fond of painting and poetry." She delighted in the wild, swirling Highland ballads that he later recalled as his first conscious memories. But in time Daniel Muir banned the ancient songs from the house as pagan blasphemies.

As the third child but first son among eight offspring, John held a favored position in the family. His older sisters spoiled their little brother, mothering him without stint, though on occasion they scolded him for talking too much (a lifelong habit). With servants in the home and doting grandparents across the street, his preschool years passed by in a single unbroken idyll. His grandfather took him for walks by the ocean and out into the country around Dunbar. From the age of three the boy was drawn to the natural world. (Merely present a boy to nature, he said years later, "and nature does the rest. It is like simply pressing a button!") For the rest of his life, many chance encounters in the wilderness might trigger sharp memories of his earliest years in Scotland: the lapping of a lake on the shore, ferns by Yosemite Fall that recalled the purple dulses in Scottish tidal pools, a snowfall, the fragrance of spring flowers, the birdsong of a lark or a mavis.

The gently enveloping idyll ended when John started grammar school. In a schoolboy reader he found his first snatches of natural history, descriptions of American fauna by Wilson and Audubon. According to his later testimony, these sketches left an indelible impression on the future naturalist. At the time, though, he showed little promise as a latent conservationist. He and his schoolmates roamed the town and countryside in a bristling, caterwauling little gang, stealing apples and turnips and abusing any helpless creatures they could find. They threw stones at cats, delighted in provoking dogfights, shot fecklessly at seagulls with homemade guns and fanned out into the country to rob birds' nests of their eggs. ("Damn it!" he said remorsefully sixty years later. "We would be doing things to drive them out of their nests!")

In visiting cruelty on others, he felt it rebound on himself. At night he and his cohorts would creep out of their houses and run to the country and back, overtly for eggs or apples but probably more for the forbidden thrill of it. Then he would return to a meticulous thrashing by his father, applied with Scotch thoroughness. As a matter of pride the boy would not be deterred — the first gesture of a prolonged rebellion against his father. The round of nocturnal runs and methodical beatings went on. "But, mark you! it never was the means of preventing us from going out one single time," John recalled. "As a preventive it was of no use at all; simply taught us to lie, without being of any use or benefit." He always disapproved of such punishment and did not spank his own children.

But in Dunbar in the 1840s both pedagogy and child rearing relied heavily on corporal punishment. When Muir and his little band of hooligans attacked wildlife and domestic animals, and started fights with other schoolboy gangs, they were only expressing in their own way the prevailing belief in salutary violence. At best the school curriculum offered a grim diet of religious and classical fare, taught by rote and recited by the squirming scholars before a cane-wielding martinet. Even worse than the dull lessons was the invariable penalty for failure. "The Scotch simply made the discovery that there was a connection between the skin and the memory," Muir said later. "The whole educational system was founded on leather." The school also forcibly imposed English cultural standards. It was only a century since the Battle of Culloden Moor had settled, apparently, the question of Scottish nationalism. Inside the school only strict English was spoken. Lapses into Scottish vernacular were punished in the usual way. Yet on the playground or in the home a single sentence of proper English would invite the same retaliation. In school and out, conduct was regulated by a constant threat of being struck and striking back. Always, at the risk of greater humiliation, the victim was expected to bear his pain with stoic indifference. "Public opinion on a Scotch playground was a very powerful agent in controlling our behavior," Muir recalled; "so we managed to keep our features in a state of repose while enduring pain that would try an American Indian."

Late in life, when he mulled over his schoolboy days in Scotland, Muir was amazed and revolted by the unending cycles of violence-pain-retaliation, carried on for the most trivial causes, often for no reason at all. A bloody fight on the playground might be sparked by a raised eyebrow or a suspect look in the eye. Home offered no escape. Every day he was expected to memorize a few verses of the Bible. Any dereliction brought the usual corrective measures. By the age of eleven he had learned to recite "by heart and by sore flesh" all the New Testament, from Matthew through Revelation, and most of the Old. The extent to which Muir objected to his lot *at the time* cannot be known. His later recollections were filtered through the nonviolent attitudes of his maturity. As a boy he probably accepted the world as he found it, knowing no other possibilities. A boy must expect to be beaten at regular intervals by father, teacher, and schoolmates: at least in Dunbar in the middle of the nineteenth century.

Although his father's religious zeal pounded the Bible into him, it ultimately provided the way out of Dunbar. Daniel Muir broke from the established Presbyterian Church, rejecting both its institutional structure and the Calvinist notion of a predestined elect. He joined many sects, one after the other, before settling on the Campbellite Disciples of Christ. The Disciples attracted him by their ecumenical spirit of returning to the primitive Christianity of the Apostles. The Campbells had pursued their mission to the wilderness of North America; Daniel Muir determined to do the same. He would set out, with three of the older children, and establish a home. Then the rest of the family would follow. John, not yet eleven years old, was giddy with the chance for adventure and — in particular — for release from the dreary Scotch school regimen. "With all that wilderness before us," he recalled, "especially a schoolless, bookless wilderness (By Jove! we didn't want any books) . . . we couldn't even get up a decent regret in having to leave for a time mother and part of the children." Their destination was vague — perhaps a Campbellite settlement in Ontario. When they embarked in February 1849, the boy experienced his first release.

❧❧

On the boat they heard of Scotch settlements in the rich farmland of southeastern Wisconsin. Seeking fertile ground for both agriculture and the gospel, Daniel Muir bought a tract of eighty virgin acres in Marquette County, four miles from the nearest neighbor. Covered with dense stands of oak and hickory, the property edged up to a small glacial lake bordered by rushes and white pond lilies. North of the lake a brook flowed through a meadow of wildflowers, its banks overgrown with willows, mosses, and ferns. On this site the Muirs put up a fine eight-room house, the best in the township, and started cutting trees and grubbing out the roots. In the fall the rest of the family arrived and settled into life at Fountain Lake Farm.

At first it seemed a paradise to the boy. "I was set down in the midst of pure wildness where every object excited endless admiration and wonder," he said later. The whole panoply of an untouched wilderness in a strange new land stretched before him, arousing his first direct interest in nature by its sheer profusion and variety. In the spring and fall the sky would darken with millions of passenger pigeons in migration, extending from horizon to horizon all day long. During the winter he would hunt hares for sport; at other times he stalked muskrats, gophers, ducks, and prairie chickens. His great ambition was to kill a loon. ("We cannot but pity the boy who has never fired a gun," he reflected in old age, although "no humane being past the thoughtless age of childhood will wantonly murder any creature.") Even at this early stage he began to have misgivings about hunting. When he finally shot a loon he only wounded it and brought it home as a pet.

While opening his senses to the natural world, the wilderness also exacted its inevitable price in isolation. The surrounding countryside was rapidly thickened with settlers, mainly from Great Britain, providing a motley flock for Daniel Muir's circuit preaching. But as the oldest boy, John bore the heaviest share of the farm work and was obliged to stay close to home. Occasionally he traveled to Portage, sixteen miles away, for crop deliveries and supplies. He never ventured to the nearest railroad town, nine miles distant in another direction. His younger siblings went to the district school, but except for a few scattered months John's formal education was suspended. His turning to nature was in part dictated by a lack of other outlets, a pattern to be repeated many times in the early lives of other conservationists.

In Scotland his grandparents and schoolmates had acted as a buffer between the boy and his forbidding father. Without them John was trapped by Daniel's fanatical notions of religion and parenting. The act of burning brush would call forth a sermon on the fires of hell; what a calamity, father warned son, to be thrown into that fire. All the children were admonished, with terrifying sermons, to study and heed the books of Proverbs and Revelation. John in particular was whipped repeatedly, for the slightest act of disobedience or even of simple forgetfulness. "The very deevil's in that boy," Daniel would mutter. John read his Bible and grew pious beyond his years, but he could never please his father. The endless scoldings and beatings made his adolescence a grimly unequal contest of wills with a tyrant blinded by his own righteousness. ("In all the world," Muir said many years later, "I know of nothing more pathetic and deplorable than a brokenhearted child, sobbing itself to sleep after being unjustly punished by a truly pious and conscientious misguided parent.")

Daniel Muir acted like a bully, a very Christian bully. Convinced of his special relation with the Lord, he retreated by degrees into his own world, oblivious alike to the needs of his family and to local curiosity about his peculiar habits. He would retire at seven o'clock in the evening, arise two hours later for a cold tub bath — punishing his flesh even while cleaning it — and then return to bed for the night. He would buy religious books and drive his horse and buggy around the county distributing them; after a time he would return, pick up the books, and leave some more. On Sundays he would deliver sermons in any Christian church that would have him, drawing the line only at Catholics and Unitarians. When his ministries took him from home the family would exhale in relief and begin to enjoy itself. The girls would take out their lace and embroidery, forbidden as productive of vanity. John and the boys would tease the girls, indulging in the general foolishness proscribed by Father. John might break into a jig or a Highland fling, or pantomime the playing of bagpipes by puffing his cheeks and emitting a high, skirling note.

These were rare interludes. Normally every day except the Sabbath, New Year's Day, and the Fourth of July was filled with work — rain or shine, cold or warm. The American settlers in the vicinity maintained smaller fields, stayed indoors during severe weather, rested when tired, and went fishing or hunting when the spirit moved them. Not the Muirs. "Old Man Muir works his children like cattle," the neighbors said. Summertime was the worst, sixteen or seventeen hours a day, with the grinding hand-labor of harvesting and corn hoeing. The hardest work fell to John. He was put to plowing when his head barely reached above the handles. At an early point father and son started splitting fence rails together. "After trying the work with me a day or two," John recalled bitterly, "he gave it up and donated it all to myself. No wonder I was stunted and called the runt of the family." As a matter of pride he would try to surpass the grown hired hands. "Never a word of warning was spoken by father that we were working too hard."

In a few years the land itself was worn out. Frontier agriculture epitomized the boom-or-bust psychology of the day, extending the lure of quick returns even with poor husbandry. The very opulence of the land encouraged an attitude of wasteful extravagance. The burgeoning continent stretched beyond the horizon to infinity. If a man depleted his soil or ran out of trees there was always virgin territory out West or up North. In America, it seemed, old-country frugality might be jettisoned — even by Scotch settlers. Muir and his neighbors in Marquette County put most of their land to wheat and corn, crops that brought good money but wore out the soil. After a few years, a wheat field with an initial yield of twenty-five bushels an acre might produce only five bushels an acre. Thus, after eight years of clearing, grubbing, fencing, and plowing the Fountain Lake farm — with the family at last catching its breath — Daniel Muir bought a half-section of virgin land six miles to the southeast. Despite John's protests, the whole weary process started over again, providing John his first example of the consequences of environmental abuse.

Hickory Hill Farm, as it was called, stood on top of a ridge with no available water. In digging a well, they struck a vein of hard, fine-grained sandstone ten feet down. John was lowered in a bucket with hammer and chisel. For weeks, then months, he chipped his way downward without hitting water. "Father never spent an hour in that well." At eighty feet John was overcome by "choke damp," an excess of carbon dioxide in the air, and was hauled up unconscious. The next day he was back in the well. Ten feet later he struck water. The episode left him with a permanent irritation in his throat, and another grievance against his father. "It shows how they always put the hard work on me," he recalled.

The work was heaviest in summer, but winter brought its own trials. The only heat was provided by a kitchen stove with a small firebox. John and his two brothers slept in a drafty bedroom on the north side of the house, beyond the kitchen's warmth, untouched even by the feeble winter sun. They would awaken with the quilts frozen to their faces. Before the rest of the family they would shiver barefoot down to the kitchen and pull on frozen socks and boots. Father would not allow a fire at that hour, for they would just be going out to do chores. When they took a load of corn to Portage, they would run the sixteen miles behind the wagon to warm themselves. They would lunch on frozen bread and then return to more chores at the farm. (Daniel later gave each of the boys enough land to start a farm. Each one sold the land and took up other work.)

As with his years in Scotland, John probably did not much object to these dreary circumstances at the time. Neighbors knew of Daniel Muir's severity, but none of the children ever complained to them. Years later, when Muir published his autobiography, readers were struck by the contrast between the gentle, cheerful adult and the painful austerity of his childhood. His sister Joanna read the early chapters in tears: "I wished with all my heart it had not been so true," she told Muir.

Even without a switch in his hand the father exuded a formidable presence. His ninety-minute discourses on Sunday about the path of the Lord and the licking, beckoning fires of Hell could only impress his isolated children. Though he would later reject Christianity, at this stage in his life John internalized the message and turned it back on his own acquaintances. His earliest surviving letter, written at eighteen, admonished a friend in the accents of his father: "Where then should you put Jesus. Where *have* you put him? Is he not too often pushed aside among the dear, airy nothings in the most confused corner of your heart? . . . O dear friend let us give our hearts to Christ our Saviour and follow in his footsteps forever."

While accepting the religious message, he bore the other hardships inflicted by his father with the unflinching stoicism he had learned on Scotch playgrounds. Chipping away in bad air at the bottom of a ninety-foot well, outharvesting grown men in the heat of summer, squeezing his chilblained feet into frozen boots, being whipped for imaginary derelictions — the boy grew into a man with the internal resources to make a good mountaineer. He developed within himself a hard, stubborn core beyond the reach of any external situation, a knack for separating his spirit from his physical body. Once he nearly drowned in Fountain Lake. He therefore decided to punish himself "as if my body was one thing and my mind another thing." Rowing out to the middle of the lake, he dove for the first time in his life, headfirst, all the way to the bottom. Back at the surface, he shouted "Take that!" and repeated the process four times, getting even with himself for having lost control.

This granitic self-possession allowed John, in his middle teens, to take his first timid steps outside the world circumscribed by his father. The Gray family, also Campbellites from Scotland, lived a mile to the south of the Fountain Lake farm. They read current books, took good magazines and the New York *Tribune,* and set up a lending library in their home. In this friendly atmosphere John stumbled into a world beyond his ken. "I remember as a great and sudden discovery that the poetry of the Bible, Shakespeare and Milton was a source of inspiring, exhilarating, uplifting pleasure; and I became anxious to know all the poets." A revelation — the Bible as literature, not merely as stern admonition. By selling squirrel and muskrat skins he saved enough money to buy his first books of English poetry, mathematics, and grammar. In stolen moments between the midday meal and returning to the field, or after family worship in the evening, he embarked on an overdue experiment in self-education, his first real intellectual experience since leaving Scotland.

Every night he read until ordered to bed. His father, wearying of the nightly confrontation, finally gave him permission to rise early in the morning instead. That night he went to bed tingling; waking in the darkness, he crept downstairs and looked at the clock: one in the morning. He had five hours all to himself. He fell to his books, devouring history, novels by Scott, theology by the Campbells. For months he slept five hours a night, awakening always at one o'clock to resume his studies.

When winter came his father forbade the use of firewood for such a purpose. Too cold to read but still craving an outlet, he started tinkering with tools to keep himself warm. Always clever with his hands, as a boy in Scotland he had made a wheelbarrow admired by his doting grandfather as "the most notable mechanical wonder of the century." Now, in his basement workshop, he used a few crude tools to make more of his own. From bits of scrap metal he fashioned a fine saw, bradawls, punches, and a pair of compasses. He then set about inventing gadgets, sometimes with the help of books, more typically by using his untapped imagination. His best creations — timepieces and labor-saving devices — implied an unconscious rebellion against circumstances on the farm. He devised a self-setting sawmill (later re-created for James Hutchings), waterwheels, locks and latches, thermometers, hygrometers, pyrometers, barometers, an automatic horse feeder, a lamp lighter, a fire lighter. Carrying bits of wood in his pocket, he would whittle the works for his machines at odd moments during the day. He invented an "early-rising machine" by connecting one of his clocks to a bed balanced on a fulcrum; at the desired hour the occupant would be tipped to his feet.

These creations — whimsical, ungainly, sometimes impractical, but invariably striking — reflected the delayed awakening of a powerful mind, like a glacier starting to move and taking any course available. John nailed his most intricate thermometer high on an outside wall of the house, brandishing it as a trophy. Based on the contraction and expansion of a three-foot iron bar, with the action multiplied thirty-two thousand times by a system of levers, it registered on a dial the body heat of a person approaching within four feet. Neighbors and even strangers came by to study the phenomenon. "It was regarded as a great wonder by all the neighbors," Muir said with pride, "and even by my own father." But generally the father, who by this time devoted himself entirely to his ministries and did no farm work, disapproved of such secular diversions from more essential tasks. John built a large, four-sided clock designed for the top of the barn, where it might advertise its inventor's cleverness for miles around. Daniel scuttled the project, citing the bother of the trampling visitors it would draw, and thus once again stifled his increasingly restive son.

In 1860 John was twenty-two, a year past his majority. With no apparent interest in marriage or in striking out on his own, he was still held to the farm and to the vagaries of his father's will. That summer a neighbor suggested he take his best inventions to the state fair in Madison. Given that exposure, he might be offered a job in a machine shop, and later he might go to college. He thought it over and decided to take the leap. Carrying two clocks and a thermometer in a grain sack, and with fifteen dollars in his pocket, he boarded his first train since arriving in America. Eleven years later, it was his second release — this time alone.

※※

"I am now adrift on this big sinny world," he wrote home, "and I don't know how I feel. Jumping out of the woods I was at once led and pushed and whirld and tossed about by new everythings everywhere. For three or four days my eyes at least were pleased and teased and wearied with pictures and sewing machines and squashes and reapers and quilts and cheeses and apples and flowers and soldiers and firemen and thousands of all kinds of faces, all of them strange." Wide-eyed and wondering, he was living out one of the nineteenth century's favorite literary situations, the drama of initiation as a farm boy comes to town. He looked the part, dressed in rough homespun and with his hair and beard worn long and untrimmed in the farmer style. As the capital and home of the state university, Madison offered a range of traps and enticements. Wanting to trust his fellows, but praying for guidance, the naif determined to make a showing at the fair.

Given space in an exhibition building, he connected one of his clocks to an improvised bed and engaged two small boys for a demonstration. With a whirring and creaking the early-rising machine tipped the boys out, to the laughing applause of onlookers. The next day newspapers hailed the "surprising" creations of the "ingenious whittler." He and his machines became the great hit of the fair. Passed around among his old neighbors in Marquette County, the news brought him characteristic strictures from his father. "Do not let the vanities of this life possess your soul," Daniel warned. "Do not let the praise of men puff you up. Nothing but Christ can keep you from sinking." The advice was redundant: fearing the sin of vanity, John had refused to read his newspaper publicity. But he could not mistake the admiration of the crowds peering at his inventions, or the award from a fair committee with its praise for him as "a genius in the best sense." In its quick, easy success his initiation seemed lifted from a dime novel.

He soon came to earth. Weighing various offers, he accepted the wrong one from an exhibitor showing a steam-powered iceboat, designed to transform a frozen river into a broad thoroughfare for passengers and freight. In exchange for Muir's help with the scheme, this entrepreneur promised lessons in mechanical drawing and foundry work. With the fair over they took the device to Prairie du Chien, on the Mississippi River in the western part of the state. Muir's initial misgivings about his employer — "I hope he is not a Catholic. I noticed a cross on his droll looking boat" — were soon borne out. There seemed little time for the promised lessons. On trial runs the boat failed repeatedly. Toiling in a machine shop, Muir found the work as oppressive in its own way as life on the farm. "It is certainly a dreary thing," he noted, "to file in a great smoky shop among devilish men on two pieces of iron for two or three days to make them fit closely." He could not imagine doing such dull, repetitive work for years on end.

Living in a boardinghouse, he found himself beset by worldly influences. Some of the boarders went so far as to play parlor games involving kissing. Muir rebuked them, quoting from Scripture. He criticized others for their silly conversation and irreverence, and other sins imagined and real. Though he acquired a reputation for Christian sobriety, he still fretted about being led from God. In his rural earnestness he amused the other boarders and found little sympathy among them. With his inventive career stalled, and cut off from co-religionists, he felt thoroughly homesick for the first time. "I am in the world now," he wrote home. "I don't think I know how I like it I guess it has used me better than I could expect but most of its love is very hollow I believe. . . . I don't often think where I am and I don't think I care much. I don't think I can tell you what I am doing or not doing. And I hardly know how I feel I am not unhappy. I generally whistle when I do my chores I guess I am happy."

After three months with the iceboat he went back to Madison. Encouraged by a student who had seen his fair exhibit, he decided to enter the university. Virtually unschooled since the age of eleven, his irregular course of self-education had left him with a precarious grasp of spelling and punctuation, and a mind full of unpredictable gaps. He presented himself to the acting chancellor "with fear and trembling, overladen with ignorance." The school, only a dozen years old, needed students. He was admitted to a preparatory course, then to first-year status in the university. By doing odd jobs, subsisting on a diet of bread and graham mush (and an occasional extravagant potato), and with sometime gifts of ten or twenty dollars from home, he started his college career a few months short of his twenty-third birthday.

The faculty consisted mainly of transplanted New Englanders, like the classics professor James Davie Butler and Ezra Slocum Carr, who taught geology and chemistry. Both men, as disciples of Emerson, spun through one of Boston's outer orbits; both touched the eager, superannuated freshman deeply. Carr in particular opened Muir's mind by showing him the elements of pure science: "the attraction and repulsion of the atoms composing the globe," as he recalled it, "marching and retreating — the harmony, the oneness, of all the world's life." Muir built a small chemical laboratory in his dormitory room, lining the walls with shelves bearing glass tubes and jars and other apparatus, the floor littered with shavings and sawdust from his latest inventions (the proudest of which was a relentless study desk that delivered a book, held it for a time, then replaced it with another). "My room was regarded as a sort of show place by the professors," he said later, "who on Saturdays oftentimes brought visitors to show the wonders."

In tastes and habits he remained the farm boy. The untrimmed beard advertised his origins: another student suggested setting fire to it. He liked to take a book to the campus lake and climb an old basswood tree hanging out over the water. From this perch he might study, or yield to the distraction of watching a hummingbird. To another tree he composed an uncertain ode:

> Fruit of all hues, are on me, and arround
> I bless forever always, and every fruit
> Is on me, to help mankind, and brute.

In the morning, after being tipped out of bed by his early-rising machine, he listened for thrushes. Sometimes they were drowned out by trains and other civilized noises. "Hundreds of common and uncommon sounds make city sounds very phuny," he advised his family.

He was already acquiring a reputation for amiably eccentric social behavior. At a formal college reception he became intrigued by a large square piano. Turning his back to the party, he pried open the top and climbed onto the wires, poking around in the mechanism. Having figured out how it worked, he climbed back down and rejoined the company. The other guests, accustomed to his ways, smiled tolerantly. "Of social life and forms he knew nothing," Ezra Carr's wife Jeanne later declared. "I was anxious to make him at home in my family; and would have felt it a privilege to do so, for the benefit of my children, but no quail ever hid her nest more effectually — or truly enjoyed its privacy."

Though he resisted the social aspects, still the outside world, closed off for so long, began to stretch before his eyes. The clutter in his room offered the choice of science or mechanics, both fascinating to Muir, both marketable to his society. He applied for a patent on his early-rising machine but was turned down. (His brother David submitted a personal objection to the device: "If it was to throw *me* out on the floor I would give it a swift kick and jump in again.") But the man who had chipped through eighty feet of rock was not easily deterred. When he went home to help with the farm work in the summer of 1861, he brought along some of his books and apparatus. At stray moments he showed his brothers a few of the wonders he had learned. Returning to Madison in the fall, he brought David along and enrolled him in the university. The contagion of worldly knowledge was infecting the rest of the family.

A few months into the semester, he was forced by lack of funds to hire out for the winter as a district school teacher in a town ten miles south of Madison. Still callow and awkward, with less than a year of college, he felt terrified when facing his first class. "I did not know where to look," he wrote home, "nor what to say nor what to do and I'm sure looked as bashful as any maid. A mud turtle upside down on a velvet sofa was as much at home." His more recalcitrant scholars required whipping. The act called up the terrors of his youth; every application of the switch made his voice shake for hours afterward. In time the class went more smoothly. He invented various clocks, attaching one to a fire-lighting device that allowed the students the luxury of a schoolhouse already warm on their arrival in the morning. He treated his charges to chemical experiments — placing mice in a jar of hydrogen, firing a cork from a funnel — and to his pet theories of perpetual motion. On Saturday evenings he lectured to the local community on chemistry or natural philosophy. "It does not require much *sapience* to be a district school philosopher," he said, tolerably complacent.

In one year he had gone from the university's preparatory department to learned discourses before an adult audience. He found that he could not only absorb whole new worlds of knowledge, but in turn pass them on — even to an audience of farmers. His letters displayed a surer touch in the sentence structure and spelling. At the same time, his education still had finite limits. According to his college roommate, Charles Vroman, he never read anything but his schoolbooks, the Bible, and the poetry of his fellow Scotsman Robert Burns. Evidently he had no interest in current literature or newspapers and magazines. Nonetheless the speed and facility of his belated intellectual awakening remained impressive, testifying to a supple, versatile mind in emergence.

Back at the university in the spring of 1862, he added a new field of study that in time would crowd out the others. A student named Milton Griswold showed him how to identify a plant specimen by taking it apart and, noting each piece, riffling through the analytical tables of a botany text. The process appealed to Muir as a mechanical operation: treating a plant like a machine of separate parts with known functions, which meshed together in an orderly, purposeful whole. Further, to see apparently unrelated plants in their serried ranks of species, genus, and order reinforced the lesson of Ezra Carr's chemistry course that all the natural world was held together by a single harmonious design. "That is perfectly wonderful," Muir told Griswold. "I am going to get me a Botany at once and then we can ramble the woods together." At home that summer he gathered specimens in the morning, worked all day in the fields, and then toiled over his treasures, sorting and classifying, until midnight. The study of botany combined his boyhood love of nature and life outdoors with his newly aroused fascination for science. Nothing else before the Yosemite glaciers so integrated his life and engaged his mind. "It is the most exciting thing in the form of even amusement much more of study that I ever knew," he declared.

Though as yet unaware of it, he was skirting the nineteenth century's mortal struggle between science and religion. Outwardly his religious life did not change. He held strictly to his regimen of Bible reading and morning and evening prayer. Still imbued with his father's prejudices, he deplored the satanic influence of a Unitarian minister in Madison. Watching a Methodist revivalist in full cry, he thought about pouring a barrel of oysters and ice cream over the preacher's head. He pestered his friends with unsolicited spiritual advice. ("You counsel me not to forget the things of Eternity," one of these victims shot back. "I trust it is not all downhill with me, after all." Another replied: "You are inclined to fear that I shall be tempted to mingle with bad company and the vices of camp. Dear friend, I think I am equal to the task before me.") In his personal life he remained a model of piety, ever worried about losing ground to everyday temptation.

A fine irony: his faith was threatened not by vice or Unitarians, but by the scientific attitude he was so eagerly taking on. Even without the gathering storm over Darwin, science undermined a religious trust in truth perceived by revelation. Instead of simply accepting the word of God as rendered by the King James Bible, science demanded a critical, dismantling approach, the "experimental method." But suppose geology and the word of God disagreed about the age of the earth? Muir, no less pious on a conscious level, was veering toward an ultimate belief in geology. "We obtain all of our knowledge of the laws of nature by experience," he wrote in a college notebook. "Experience is acquired by observation and experiment. . . . Galileo (born in 1564) may be called the father of experimental science. Bacon born in 1561 in his great work Novum Organum shewed this to be the only road to a true acquaintance with nature." The *only* road. This as yet unacknowledged conflict between empiricism and revelation did not at any time undermine his essential reverence. He never doubted the existence of a divine intelligence behind the natural order. But eventually his scientific study of nature would force him out of Christianity and into other religious forms.

For now it led to a bitter break with his father — the completion of a process begun when he had lingered over his books after supper. Daniel Muir saw no need of any book but the Bible. John's inventions then seemed another dangerous tendency. "I wish you may be loving your God much more than inventing machines," said the father. "The world can want machines, but you cannot want salvation so well." His study of botany and geology, with their implication that man might discover some truths for himself, provided the final blasphemy. When John went home from school the two men argued violently — and pointlessly, since they were following different texts with no common ground. It became impossible for John to inhabit the same house with his father; when visiting he generally stayed nearby with one of his married sisters. "Father and I cannot agree at all," he declared. "I could not live at Hickory Hill a single week hardly."

Physically and intellectually, if not emotionally, he was at last freed from Daniel Muir. "I think I love my studies more and more," he noted, "and instead of the time for dismissing them coming nearer, as one term after another passes, it seems to go farther and farther away." He thought about going on to medical school, perhaps at the University of Michigan.

But a new, different kind of restraint was stalking him. The Civil War had begun simultaneously with the start of his college career. It played a mournful threnody in the background as he happily found chemistry, geology, and botany. The fairground — the site of his first triumph, from which so much had followed — was turned into a regimental bivouac, bristling with martial spirit. He worried about moral conditions in the camp and felt no sympathy with its purposes. "I suppose you know by the papers how warlike things are here," he wrote home in the fall of 1861. "Their appearance is very imposing but how can all the great and showy coverings of war hide its real hideousness." A year later: "This war seems farther from a close than ever. How strange that a country with so many schools and churches should be desolated by so unsightly a monster." Enlisting was out of the question, but he worried about the draft calls that started in 1862.

After seeing and feeling so much violence during his grim boyhood, he was instinctively a pacifist. More to the point, he felt no call to join this American Civil War because he did not consider himself an American. In his part of Marquette County, populated mostly by immigrants from Great Britain, the natives were called "Yankees" or "the Americans," with a clear sense of separateness. Muir read his Bobby Burns and proudly retained his Scottish inflections and figures of speech. Occasionally he dreamed about returning to the old country, with its idyllic associations from his earliest years. "My Scottish highlands," he said in 1862, ". . . can have no substitute. *Scotland* alone will ever be Scotland to me. My love for my own Scottish land seems to grow with every pulse so that I cannot see the name or hear it but a thrill goes to every fiber of my body." All his life he felt desperately proud of the homeland — and none too enchanted by the United States. (He did not become an American citizen until he was sixty-five, and only did so then because of passport matters related to a trip around the world.)

Thus John and his two brothers were threatened with conscription by a country for which they held no special allegiance. With the first rumors of a draft his youngest brother Dan fled to Canada to sit out the war. John and David stayed, sweated through the calls in the fall of 1862, and were passed over for the time being. "How glad I am that you are not drafted," one of his sisters wrote John. "I think those that began this war ought to be the only men to fight." After finishing the spring term of 1863, he delivered a triumphant lecture on the properties of heat — "how *smart* I am becoming" — and took off on his first extended botanical trip, tramping hundreds of miles down the Wisconsin River valley into Iowa. Having completed a little over two years of college, he planned to transfer to Ann Arbor for a medical course in the fall.

He was paralyzed by the threat of conscription. With few eligible men still in Marquette County, he might be taken at any time. If he went to Michigan the same could happen there. After all those wasted years on the farm he felt an urgency to get on with his education. Politics still lay outside his ken; he had no strong feelings about the moral aspects of the war. It simply intruded on his life, which had just acquired, at last, an independent purpose. He spent the winter of 1863–1864 living quietly with his sister Sarah and her husband, worrying about his prospects: "I hardly know what to do. War seems to spread everywhere."

In February Lincoln signed an order for a draft of five hundred thousand men to be carried out on March 10. Rather than risk it, Muir decided to join Dan in Canada. "I really do not know where I shall halt," he wrote a friend on March 1, half an hour before catching his train. "I have already bidden all my friends goodbye. I feel lonely again." A few months short of his twenty-sixth birthday, the third release.

❦❦

He headed north. Passing through Upper Michigan, he crossed the border and disappeared into the woods above Lake Huron. For six months he avoided roads and settlements, following an erratic course through the forests and swamps along the eastern shores of Huron and Georgian Bay. Afraid of being pursued, he sent no letters home — or perhaps his family prudently destroyed any evidence of his whereabouts. Generally he behaved like a fugitive, like the British army deserters he occasionally encountered in the swamps. In later years, when recalling this part of his life, he either did not mention his Canadian sojourn or masked it with a quick reference to "botanizing in glorious freedom around the Great Lakes." Embarrassed by the episode, he tried to obscure both the exact location — the future province of Ontario, not the United States — and his reason for going.

Homeless and friendless, he lost himself in collecting botanical samples. The latent tension in his life between human fellowship and the study of nature he felt more acutely than ever before. Temporarily forced from human society, or so he believed, he was drawn to nature all the more. Walking through the woods, he maintained a meticulous herbarium, pressing and labeling the plants and carrying them along wherever he went. In his solitary circumstances the herbarium provided a kind of companionship, with each additional specimen like a newly found friend.

One day in June 1864 he pushed his way through a dense swamp in the late afternoon. As sundown approached he worried about where to spend the night. On the bank of a stream he found the rare orchid *Calypso borealis,* two white flowers against a background of yellow moss. Standing apart from other plants, they reminded him of his own isolation and somehow comforted him. "They were alone," he noted, understanding the condition. "I never before saw a plant so full of life; so perfectly spiritual, it seemed pure enough for the throne of its Creator. I felt as if I were in the presence of superior beings who loved me and beckoned me to come. I sat down beside them and wept for joy." Finally the heavy feeling lifted. He went on through the swamp and found a house for the night.

Years later he ranked this encounter along with meeting Emerson as the two supreme moments in his life. Aside from the emotional release it allowed him, finding *Calypso borealis* in that swamp crystallized an attitude, providing the germ of an idea that would eventually dominate his thinking. Hidden away in a thick tangle of trees and bogs, far from the intentions or even the sight of man, those orchids did nothing "useful." Yet they reassured Muir in his moment of need without performing any practical task, simply by existing for themselves. It set off a train of thought within him: "I cannot understand the nature of the curse, 'Thorns and thistles shall it bring forth to thee.' Is our world indeed the worse for this 'thistly curse'? Are not all plants beautiful? or in some way useful? Would not the world suffer by the banishment of a single weed? The curse must be within ourselves."

Soothed by his plants, he found less sympathy among the humans he encountered. None of these Canadians knew anything about botany; few even knew the meaning of the word. Stolid and hardworking, they treated nature strictly as a commodity, ignoring its beauty. "In vain is the glorious chart of God in Nature spread out for them," he noted. "So many acres chopped is their motto," reminding him of the two farms he had helped clear, "as they grub away amid the smoke of the magnificent forest trees, black as demons and material as the soil they move upon." Again he felt torn between the two poles of his personality. Pushed by humans and pulled by nature, he spent the summer in his solitary excursions.

Moving south along the shore of Lake Ontario, he was joined by Dan at Niagara Falls in September. After taking in "the grandest sight in all the world" they went to the town of Meaford, on the southern end of Georgian Bay, where Dan had been employed in a woodworking factory. The owners, two Scotsmen, hired the brothers to work through the winter. In the spring they learned that their two brothers-in-law had also decided to run from the draft. "I am sorry that John and David have had to leave home," Muir wrote a sister, "but it is better that they go down to sojourn in this American Egypt than to fight American Philistines." A few months later the war ended and Dan went back to the United States. But Muir stayed on, attracted by the unspoiled quiet of the small town and by the chance of giving his mechanical skills full play in the factory. He invented a self-feeding lathe, a machine for making rake teeth, another for boring and driving them, and others that made the bows and handles and bent the handles to the proper arc. The factory's production doubled. Lost in his inventions, with the help of his early-rising machine he worked eighteen-hour days. "Were it not that I have no time to think," he declared, "I would grow homesick and die in a day or two."

At least his employers could grasp and encourage his mechanical work. In his botanizing around Meaford he still found no one to share the esoteric thrill of discovering and naming plants. It remained a solitary passion for him. "It was easy to admire," one of his employers recalled, "but to understand and appreciate him required some knowledge of the subject matter of his studies and his modes of thought." The boss had good cause for being confounded. Muir was undergoing a subtle spiritual conversion. Following up the insight from his encounter with *Calypso borealis,* he no longer defined the world in human terms. All species, no matter how outwardly useless, had their own purposes. In a way that Muir as yet could but dimly comprehend, this new forbearance seemed to pull him away from Christianity toward a direct communion with nature. Somehow the Christian God impeded a proper appreciation of the natural world.

Recruited to teach a Sunday school class, he avoided the usual texts and theological discussions. Instead he took his students outside, instructing them in botany, explaining the use of an herbarium as merely another form of worship. "It may be a bad symptom," he fretted, "but I will confess that I take more intense delight from reading the power and *goodness* of God from 'the things which are made' than from the Bible. ... It is so much easier for us to employ our faculties upon these beautiful tangible forms than to exercise a simple humble loving faith." Recoiling from human manipulations of nature, he urged his friends not to abuse any wild creature, not even insects. He inadvertently choked a cat to death trying to free the bird in its mouth. "Now John is always scolding us about killing spiders and flies," a friend said gleefully, "but when we are away he chokes the cats."

His earnest strictures drew only polite interest — or suppressed laughter — from the people in Meaford. Looking for some kind of support, he wrote his college acquaintances in Madison. A letter to Ezra Carr brought a quick, friendly reply from his wife, Jeanne, herself an amateur botanist. "Your precious letter with its burden of cheer and good wishes has come to our hollow," he wrote back at once. "It came at a time when much needed, for I am subject to lonesomeness at times." Seizing the chance to unburden himself to someone who might understand, he proceeded with an extended review of his recent life and ambitious (if vague) plans. Then he thanked her for proposing "an exchange of thoughts," although "I am altogether incapable of properly conducting a correspondence with one so much above me."

Back came her answer, stilted in the Victorian manner but conveying a dignified warmth and the message he wanted: "Dear Mr. Muir, I was very much gratified by your excellent letter. ... Believe in my cordial and constant interest in all that concerns you, and that I have a pleasant way of associating you with my highest and purest enjoyments." For the next ten years they corresponded voluminously. Most of that time they lived far apart and seldom saw each other in person. But it was a profound friendship, vital to both, based on shared interests and mutual respect. Aside from his family, Jeanne Carr exercised the most significant influence on his early life.

What she brought Muir was his first prolonged contact with a mind of substantial range and ambition. She told him what to read, introduced him to important people, and extended his horizons in a dozen directions. She reinforced his dawning sense that God was best appreciated in nature: "It is only from our Great Mother," she agreed, "that we really learn the lessons of our Father's love for us." Beyond this common ground, she also delved into music, painting, political reforms, feminism, psychic phenomena, landscape gardening, fiction and poetry, and Asian philosophies. All these enthusiasms were pressed on Muir, to greater or lesser effect.

Thirteen years his senior, the descendant of seven generations of New England Puritans, she came from Vermont. Her father was a doctor, and she was brought up in a household of servants and Whig politics. With an extensive family — Carvers and Lees on her mother's side — she was exposed at an early age to a variety of intellectual interests. Inoculated by a noblesse-oblige kind of egalitarianism (she played with black children, and the servants were invited to her wedding), she always felt obliged to do something worthwhile with her life. "Darwin has left us no escape," she said later, "from the necessity of finding our titles to respect in our own characters and not those of our forefathers." After studying at a seminary in her hometown, she married Ezra and accompanied him to the new university in Madison.

Her friendship with Muir supplied deep, partly unacknowledged needs in them both. When he felt isolated by his peculiar ideas she praised him for his unique insight, turning his eccentricity into a badge of pride. "You do not know how we hold you in our memories as one apart from all other students, in your power of insight into Nature, and the simplicity of your love for her," she wrote. "Besides, I like you for your individualized acceptance of religious truth, and feel a deep sympathy in it." Part mother, part sister, part colleague, she measured out her advice and applause with a deftly loving touch. Under her tutelage he bloomed and thrived. Sure of an audience both appreciative and intelligently critical, he deluged her with accounts of botanical trips and unfettered speculations about the cosmos. "I have not before sent these feelings and thoughts to anybody," he said, luxuriating in the floor space she allowed him, "but I know that I am speaking to one who by long and deep communion with Nature understands them, and can tell me what is true, or false and unworthy in my experiences."

For her part, to some degree she lived through her protégé. As a feminist she disliked many of the duties exacted from a housewife in high Victorian America. She hated fashions and housework. Although she taught school and helped Ezra with his work, she felt her life ebbing out in little dribs and drabs. To Muir she described herself as "a woman whose life seems always to be used up in little trifling things, never labelled 'done' and laid away as a man's may be. Then as a woman I have often to consider not the lilies only, in their perfection, but the humble honest wayside grasses and weeds, sturdily filling their places through such repeated discouragements." Ezra was a difficult man who would be fired from his teaching job in Madison and later from his post at the University of California in Berkeley. One of her sons, a railroad brakeman, was killed in a switchyard accident; another committed suicide. Turning from the frustrations and sorrows in her own life, she could always lose herself in long letters to Muir. She envied him his freedom and the great uninterrupted blocks of time he could give to botany and geology. "Write as often as you can," she told him. "Your letters keep up my faith that I shall lead just such a life myself sometime."

Biding his time in Meaford, he explained his prospects to Jeanne Carr. A millwright in the factory was giving him lessons in practical mechanics, and he was allowed a free hand in devising new machines and tinkering with old ones. But he had no wish to spend his whole life among machines. He thought about returning to college to study medicine, but lacked the money. Inspired by the German geographer Alexander von Humboldt, he dreamed of traveling through South America in emulation of the master. "How intensely I desire to be a Humboldt!" Again he was blocked by poverty. For the present he toiled in the factory and saved his money. "It seems as though I should be dragged into machinery whether I would or no," he concluded.

In March 1866 he was dislodged by a fire that destroyed the factory and most of his botanical notebooks and herbarium. Also lost were thirty thousand broom handles and six thousand rakes which Muir had turned out but not been paid for. Offered a partnership to help rebuild the factory, he instead decided to take a note for the two hundred dollars owed him and to leave Meaford. The fire had wiped out his hopes of returning to college. He went back to the United States for the first time in two years. After visiting his brother David in Buffalo, he meandered through New

York, Ohio, Indiana, and Illinois, botanizing at will and looking for work that suited him. In Indianapolis he was offered a job in a large steam-powered factory producing wagon parts. He liked the whirl and clatter of the place (more impressive than the factory in Meaford), and a rich forest of deciduous wood surrounded the city. So he settled for a while, feeling rootless and worried about neglecting his studies. One night he had a tantalizing dream about walking by a deep, pellucid stream that flowed through a hayfield. Ringed by extravagant wildflowers, the hay waved in the wind and shifted colors in the sunlight. "I am myself but a wandering star and move in as crooked an orbit as any star in the sky," he wrote one of his sisters. "I never before felt so *utterly homeless* as now."

His very skill with machinery had locked him into a way of life far from the wilderness. Starting as a sawyer, running a ripsaw at ten dollars a week, he found each promotion binding him closer to the factory. Having become a supervisor at twenty-five dollars a week, he was a victim of his own success, working so hard that he had little time for botany. Against his real instincts, "I suppose that I am doomed to live in some of these noisy commercial centres," he wrote. "Circumstances over which I have had no control almost compel me to abandon the profession of my choice and to take up the business of an inventor, and now that I am among machines I begin to *feel* that I have some talent that way and so I almost think unless things change soon I shall turn my whole mind into that channel." He might, after all, spend his life among machines. Again he applied for patents on his devices. He spent Christmas Day of 1866 in the shop putting up a line shaft. A few weeks later he vowed to take things a little easier, to shirk some of the heavy work. He had begun to resemble a piece of wood being turned on one of his self-feeding lathes.

He fretted over the belt systems that transferred power from central drive shafts to the individual machines. "Gentlemen," he addressed his employers, "the belt system of your shop is in a bad condition and as belting is at once the nerves and sinews of factory life the greatness of the importance of having it kept in good order need scarce be urged." He sketched devices to adjust the belts to variations in temperature and friction. Staying late one night in early March 1867, he was using the sharp point of a file to unlace a belt joining when the tool slipped in his hand. The file flew up and pierced the cornea of his right eye. As he cupped his hand over the socket the aqueous humor flowed out and left the eye sightless. In a few days the left eye also went blind from sympathetic nervous shock.

Now began the great crisis and turning point in his life. "I am shut in darkness," he wrote Jeanne Carr. "My hard, toil-tempered muscles have disappeared, and I am feeble and tremulous as an ever-sick woman." For three days he could neither eat nor drink. The pain spread all through his body. He spent four weeks in bed in a darkened room. Children visited him with flowers, friends read to him, employers offered him an easier job at better pay. But all through those blank, endless days he thought of the natural beauty he might never see again. Tossing in his bed and railing futilely against his fate, he had ample time to think about the course his life had taken. "My days were terrible beyond what I can tell," he wrote home, "and my nights were if possible more terrible. Frightful dreams exhausted and terrified me every night without exception."

The sight returned quickly to his left eye, more slowly to the right. After a month he could see well enough with the right to avoid the furniture in walking through a room; in a full light he might recognize a friend but he could not yet read with it. In a few days he grew stronger, all in a rush, and began to feel like a man risen from the grave. He went for a walk in the woods and invented a clock for his child friends. Jeanne Carr intrigued him by passing along a prophecy rendered the previous summer by a psychic friend of hers: that Muir would eventually come to rest in the Yosemite Valley. A pleasant notion, he replied, "but my faith concerning its complete fulfillment is weak."

Not well enough to work, he went home for the summer, collecting specimens along the way. "I am thankful that this affliction has drawn me to the sweet fields rather than from them," he wrote Carr. "To me all plants are more precious than before." That machinery had all but blinded him seemed an omen, a warning to rethink his priorities. At twenty-nine he still had no family or settled purpose in life. The accident had left him with a chastened sense of his own precarious mortality: life was short; anything could happen. As he visited friends in Madison and tramped over the farmland of his boyhood, thinking it through, he decided to make one last bold gesture. He would take off on a "grand sabbath day three years long." Botanizing through the tropics after the fashion of Humboldt, he would pile up "a stock of wild beauty sufficient to lighten and brighten my after life in the shadows." He might then subside into a civilized existence after a final satisfying fling in the wilderness.

He returned to Indianapolis to arrange his affairs. He would ramble through the South on foot to Florida, then take a boat to South America. Once again he said his goodbyes on the eve of an indefinite journey. "I feel touches of the old depressing melancholy which always comes when I leave friends for strangers," he wrote Dan. "I do not know where I shall go, nor when I shall return." On September 8, 1867, he took a train to Louisville: his final release.

❧❧

A few miles south of Louisville Muir spread his map under a tree and plotted a southeasterly route through Kentucky and Tennessee to Georgia. "I am very ignorant of all things pertaining to this journey," he confided to Jeanne Carr. Carrying a plant press and a bag with three books (Burns, a New Testament, and *Paradise Lost*), he set out on his thousand-mile walk to the Gulf of Mexico. As the days passed he repeated the pattern of his first immersion in the Canadian woods, three years earlier. Once more he felt like an outlaw from society, and especially lonesome at night. Again he found little sympathy for his purposes among the humans he met. Surely, a blacksmith told him, you have something better to do than wandering the country looking at weeds and blossoms. Again he was cheered only by wild nature. Sitting by a stream in Tennessee at the end of a hard day, with the loneliness creeping over him, he was serenaded by a tiny bird. "It had a wonderfully expressive eye," he noted, "and in one moment that cheerful confiding bird preached me the most impressive sermon upon heavenly trust that I ever heard."

A more uplifting sermon than any delivered in a church: during this fall of 1867, in the course of working out his own philosophy Muir made a permanent break from Christianity. Characteristically, he went through the process by himself without discussing it with other people. Nor did he learn or expect much from books. He still read his New Testament — but more for the stately cadences of the prose than for theological ideas. Instead it came down to a private communion between Muir and nature. Under its spell he reached his conclusions by intuitive leaps and flashes. He literally read the face of the land, treating it as a vast book that — given patience and close study — would yield a truer sense of the cosmos.

Departing the faith of Jesus meant reckoning with his father. On one level his religious evolution implied a final rebellion from paternal authority. Daniel preached an especially joyless version of Christianity. "Man naturally is productive of nothing but evil," he had warned his son. Yet when John went to the woods he saw bountiful vegetation that pleased the eye and myriad creatures going about their business, singing, chittering, buzzing, in apparent contentment. This world seemed beautiful to every sense. Where was the evil? Accordingly, he had already rejected those "miserable hymns," heard all through his childhood, that urged such notions as:

This world is all a fleeting show
For man's delusion given.

Several nights spent in a graveyard near Savannah led him to reflect on orthodox attitudes toward death, "the grimest body to be found in the whole catalogue of civilized Christian manufactures." Death was regarded as the ever-threatening enemy of life and as "punishment for the oldest sin." Funeral customs only reinforced the most frightening aspects of the experience. The coffin, church service, black clothing, burial ritual — "the thousand styles and modes of murder to be found in a civilized swarm of Christians so called" — treated death as a uniquely fearful aberration from normal life. But in nature creatures were born, lived, and died with no great upheaval. Dead bodies were not immured in boxes and buried in the ground but simply recycled into the chain of life. Everything fitted together into an ongoing harmony, a "*union* of life and death." Anyone immersed in nature could accept death joyfully: "the grave has no victory for it never fights." (Again the contrast between natural happiness and Christian gloom.)

To this point, his rejection of Christianity included his father's particular interpretation of it, and its less agreeable outward forms. Centering in, Muir next went to the heart of Christian belief. After taking a boat from Savannah to the upper Atlantic coast of Florida, he walked southwest across the state to Cedar Key on the Gulf of Mexico. In this southern latitude he found exotic plants previously unknown to him. Wondering at their remarkable shapes and colors, he began to extend the train of thought initially provoked by his finding *Calypso borealis* in the Canadian woods.

Historically Christianity had dispensed with nature gods, indeed all other gods, in favor of a single deity with a special interest in one creature, man, the only being on earth possessed of an immortal soul. Walking through Florida, marveling at these nonhuman organisms, Muir was struck by the stinginess of the Christian God. "They tell us," he noted, admiring a palm tree, "that plants are not like man immortal, but are perishable — soul-less. I think that this is something that we know exactly nothing about." With that statement he stepped, unequivocally and permanently, outside the Christian tradition. The palm, even though denied the Christian heaven, "preached far grander things than was ever uttered by human priest."

The palm and *Calypso borealis* were attractive and harmless, leading easily to a flirtation with pantheism. His next encounter, with an alligator, pushed his speculations to a disturbing but clarifying linkage. Christian man basked in the certainty of his exclusive claim on heaven. Christian man also sorted out the rest of the natural world according to his own tastes; thus alligators were indicted as ugly and ravenous, and useless to man. Could these two conditions be connected? Did Christian man approach the natural world in a spirit of arrogant manipulation *because* nothing else had a soul, nothing else was so loved by the Christian version of God? "Doubtless these creatures are happy," Muir wrote of alligators, "and fill the place assigned them by the great Creator of us all. Fierce and cruel they appear to us, but beautiful in the eyes of God. . . . How narrow we selfish, conceited creatures are in our sympathies! how blind to the rights of all the rest of creation!"

Thus it seemed that "Lord Man" had committed the ultimate blasphemy by arrogating godlike powers to himself. Instead of God creating man in His own image, as the Bible had it, perhaps the opposite had taken place. Perhaps man had invented a god after *his* own image, a deity with an overweening concern for man. A religion so based would judge all earthly activity by its effect on Christian man. "Let a Christian hunter go to the Lord's woods," Muir wrote in his journal, "and kill his well-kept beasts, or wild Indians, and it is well; but let an enterprising specimen of these proper, predestined victims go to houses and fields and kill the most worthless person of the vertical godlike killers, — oh! that is horribly unorthodox, and on the part of the Indians atrocious murder! Well, I have precious little sympathy for the selfish propriety of civilized man, and if a war of races should occur between the wild beasts and Lord Man, I would be tempted to sympathize with the bears."

At Cedar Key he took a job in a sawmill while waiting for the boat to Galveston. After one day's work he came down sick with a fever which he ignored, having never suffered a serious illness. Two days later he collapsed and was carried home to bed. For two months he lay desperately ill, swimming in and out of deliriums, coming close to death. As he slowly recuperated he took moderate walks and again recorded in his journal his sense of the growing divergence between Christian cosmology and the evidence of nature. "The world we are told was made for man," he noted. "A presumption that is totally unsupported by facts. There is a very numerous class of men who are cast into painful fits of astonishment whenever they find anything, living or dead, in all God's universe, which they cannot eat or render in some way what they call useful to themselves." Claiming dogmatic knowledge of divine intentions, they take sheep as a source of food and clothing, whales as an oil tank, hemp for rope, iron for hammers and plows. Even worse: "Not content with taking all of earth, they also claim the celestial country as the only ones who possess the kind of souls for which that imponderable empire was planned." But possibly animals, plants, and even minerals were endowed with a divine spark of sensation that Christian man in his overweening hubris could not appreciate.

This was the central insight of Muir's life, the philosophical basis of his subsequent career in conservation. The world did not spin at man's whim — despite the teachings of orthodox Christians. Creation belonged not to a manlike Christian God, but to the impartial force of Nature. Christianity rested on a self-serving, man-made artifice. "Nature's object in making animals and plants might possibly be first of all the happiness of each one of them, not the creation of all for the happiness of one. Why ought man to value himself as more than an infinitely small composing unit of the one great unit of creation? . . . The universe would be incomplete without man; but it would also be incomplete without the smallest transmicroscopic creature that dwells beyond our conceitful eyes and knowledge."

When his strength returned he changed plans and went to Cuba, where he admired the tropical plants for resisting the incursions of "their great biped lord." Unable to find passage to South America, and still worn down by his illness, he decided to seek a northern climate while he fully regained his health. He took an orange boat to New York. "I felt completely lost in the vast throngs of people, the noise of the streets, and the immense size of the buildings." So he paid forty dollars for steerage passage to California, by way of the Isthmus of Panama. While waiting for his departure, he saw streetcars bound for "Central Park." The name on the sign intrigued him, but he stuck close to the dock, fearing he would be unable to find his way back. Finally he was on his way to California and the prophesied rendezvous in Yosemite.

3

A Proper Cultivated Plant

As Muir bounced back and forth between the poles of his personality, between the lonely freedom of the wilderness and the social constraint of civilization, he would sometimes declare firm intentions of remaining at one extreme or the other. The intention would then be erased by the next rebound, leaving him once again to despair of exerting any direct control over the course of his life. "We are governed more than we know and are driven as with whips we know not where." Again: "I am bound to my studies, and the laws of my own life. . . . I am swept onward in a general current that bears on irresistibly."

For a few years in Yosemite the prophecy of Jeanne Carr's psychic friend seemed to be holding true. For the first time since leaving Hickory Hill, perhaps even since leaving Scotland, he felt at home. He had the valley and the mountains, botany and geology across a terrain with no apparent limits. Famous people from Emerson down came to see him. He yielded to his wildest tendencies, with only a lingering second thought. "Well," he wrote in his journal in 1872, "perhaps I may yet become a proper cultivated plant, cease my wild wanderings, and form a so-called pillar or something in society, but if so, I must, like a revived Methodist, learn to love what I hate and to hate what I most intensely and devoutly love."

At one pole he always overstated the nature of the opposite extreme. He neither loved the wilderness nor hated civilization as much as he claimed. Within a year of his final confrontation with Elvira Hutchings he had come down from the mountains to settle in San Francisco. He moved his books and papers to the home of John and Mary Swett in the Russian Hill district of the city. Their large, hospitable house on Taylor Street would serve as his base camp for the next four years. There were four children, including young ones, for Muir to regale with stories. John Swett, a local schoolmaster and the former state superintendent of schools, blended friendship with worldly advice ("brother now, papa then," as Muir put it). Relaxing into the bosom of this stable, ready-made family, Muir found the edge taken off his loneliness and was almost reconciled to city life. Civilization planted its first hooks in him. Though he still ran away to the wilderness at regular intervals, he came back sooner, with less grumbling.

Jeanne and Ezra Carr had moved to California in 1869. From their home in Oakland, across the bay, she sent a stream of books, advice, and important visitors to her protégé. In his bashful way he tried to measure up to her promotional work. "Don't believe one-half that Mrs. Carr says," he allowed. She nudged him to write and served as his informal agent, flourishing Emerson's endorsement to gain entry. Essentially because of her untiring efforts, the world began to hear about John Muir. "I owe all my best friends to you," he told her, with no exaggeration.

With one foot in the city, he had to face the problem of how to earn a conventional living. Since quitting the sawmill he had subsisted on savings and the small fees paid for his writing by newspapers and the *Overland Monthly*. That income was erratic at best. How could he turn his Yosemite knowledge into more practical form? "What I have nobody wants," he lamented. "Why should I take the trouble to coin my gold? If I should make an effort to show it, some will say it's fool's gold; no market, and if there was, I feel no inclination to sell. No standard; cannot use it, cannot be given away, much less sold." Even the reliable *Overland*, which had published most of his early work, failed him. It suspended operations in 1876.

Friends suggested that Muir try writing for the major eastern literary monthlies. Done with his glaciers, he could take up the more commercially palatable topics of trees and wildlife, of more universal interest than his icy geological theories. Without much enthusiasm — but prodded by the lack of other options — he rooted around in his old notebooks and began to recast them as articles. He wrote painstakingly, with all the speed of a glacier, littering his pages with revisions and despairing blots. "I have not written enough to compose with much facility," he noted, "and as I am also very careful and have but a limited vocabulary I make slow progress." John Swett told him to let go of his manuscripts sooner, that he need not polish them until an ordinary reader would slip on them. Sometimes he would come downstairs in the Swett home and ask to borrow the baby, explaining that he could write more easily with her creeping around his room. At length he would send his articles to *Harper's* or *Scribner's* in New York. They were always accepted, with the prompt payment of $150 or $200 and a request for more. That he could earn so much money simply with written words seemed peculiar to him.

His developing literary style did benefit from all the fretting. At a time when polite magazines were overflowing with Latinate, polysyllabic, circumlocutory mush, Muir wrote a lean, direct prose, bristling with the energy of hard Anglo-Saxon words and occasional striking neologisms. He re-created the whole sensory feel of life in the wilderness. At its best his writing all but surrounds the reader. Thus an account in *Harper's* of a sudden rainstorm on Mount Shasta: "Presently a vigorous thunder-bolt crashes through the crisp sunny air, ringing like steel on steel, its startling detonation breaking into a spray of echoes among the rocky canyon below. Then down comes a cataract of rain to the wild gardens and groves. The big crystal drops tingle the pine needles, plash and spatter on granite pavements, and pour adown the sides of ridges and domes in a net-work of gray bubbling rills. In a few minutes the firm storm cloud withers to a mesh of dim filaments and disappears, leaving the sky more sunful than before."

Most young writers believe in themselves extravagantly in order to endure early rejections; Muir deprecated himself but was an immediate success, skipping past the initial disappointments of a typical literary career. In transforming his raw bush sugar and mountain meal into magazine cookies and snaps, as he said, he still felt "something not quite honorable in thus dealing with God's wild gold." He retained his muttering suspicions of the vicarious written word. But he obviously had an unstudied gift for it. "You belong to the very rarest class of naturalists and scientists," an admirer wrote from Chicago, "— for you have a literary style incomparable." The articles appealed to his eastern readers on at least three levels: as nature descriptions in the tradition of Audubon and Thoreau, but wilder; as travel accounts of a state unknown to his Europe-facing audience (he helpfully referred to the Sierra Nevada as "the California Alps"); and as adventure stories, since he wrote casually in the first person of his most difficult treks ("It isn't possible that you made all those excursions *alone?*" a man wrote from Boston).

He had gone alone, usually, and thought nothing of it. Transferring that spirit to his articles, he wrote with a light touch that seldom hinted either fear or pride in his lowly human achievements. Literary adventurers in the wilderness typically presented themselves as poised *against* nature, beating back her threats, killing the bear, conquering the mountain. Muir instead stressed the "essential kindliness" of nature, "though making no jot of allowance for ignorance or mistakes." One of his best-received articles recounted a violent windstorm in the valley of the Yuba River of northern California. With trees crashing down around him, he walked through the storm unperturbed, preoccupied with the varying pitch of the wind as it whipped through different species. At the top of the highest ridge in sight, he climbed a hundred-foot Douglas spruce and held on as his perch swung back and forth through a thirty-degree arc. Drinking in all the sights, sounds, and smells, he rode out the storm in unfrightened bliss. From the experience he drew his usual lesson of human forbearance in the presence of nature: "We all travel the milky way together, trees and men; but it never occurred to me until this storm-day, while swinging in the wind, that trees are travelers, in the ordinary sense. They make many journeys, not very extensive ones, it is true; but our own little comes and goes are only little more than tree-wavings — many of them not so much."

Neither above nor apart from nature, he merged so fully with his subject matter as to become indistinguishable from it. In his most popular article of this period, "The Humming-Bird of the California Water-Falls" in *Scribner's,* he unconsciously described himself by sketching the habits of the little water ouzel that flitted happily around the pounding water. "Among all the mountain birds," said Muir, "none has cheered me so much in my lonely wanderings." The ouzel liked to build his nest on a shelf, backed up to a rock, near a waterfall — rather like the hang-nest at the sawmill. The ouzel retraced the route of glaciers in his flights, following the path of streams flowing through channels dug out by glacial action; Muir of course approved this adherence to icy excavation, having traced his share of glaciers. No matter what circumstance, the ouzel always seemed happy and fearless. "The ouzel never sings in chorus with other birds, nor with his kind, but only with the streams." True of bird and Muir both.

Aiming only to make a living, he found himself a minor literary celebrity. A New York publisher suggested making a book of his articles. The novelist Helen Hunt Jackson sent a fan letter — "I know every word you have written" — and said the only time she had wished herself to be a man was after reading about his tree-ride in the valley of the Yuba. The best magazines competed for the right of first refusal. Someone even wrote a poem about him, published in the May 1879 issue of *Scribner's:*

> *His strong heart beat with mighty lyres of pines*
> *On High Sierra; he beheld the light,*
> *Unblenched, where eagles take their daring flight. . . .*

This faithful worshiper at all her shrines
Discerned divinity in every smile
On Nature's face; where'er his footsteps trod,
Alike her strength and beauty did beguile
His heart. . . .

Coaxed and flattered out of his solitude, Muir began to sing more among his own kind. Traces of the old misanthropy still lingered when he measured wilderness and lowland humans against each other. Just before subsiding into life in San Francisco, early in 1875, he had surveyed the results of a flood around Marysville in the Sierra foothills. "True, some goods were destroyed," he said briskly, "and a few rats and people were drowned, and some took cold on the house-tops and died, but the total loss was less than the gain." Rats and people? An odd association, in an odder sequence. During the next few years he met his fellow humans more forgivingly. "Safe in the arms of Daddy Swett," as he put it, he enjoyed a home that offered security with few responsibilities. The palate formerly satiated on oatmeal and crackers learned to appreciate French cooking, fine wines, good tobacco. His domestication had clear limits; any large social gathering still made him restless. (Thanksgiving 1877: "We had what is called a grand time, but these big eating parties never seem to me to pay for the trouble they make.") But now he realized that the isolation of Yosemite had its own problems — in dictating a lack of outlets, in precipitating his final crisis with Elvira Hutchings. Though losing none of his zeal for the wilderness, he no longer wanted to live there. "When you come to the city visit me," he wrote country friends early in 1879, "and see how bravely I endure; so touching a lesson of resignation to metropolitan evils and goods should not be lightly missed."

Newly balanced between mountains and city, Muir undertook his first efforts in behalf of what would later be called conservation. (Over the next century, the American conservation movement would gain most of its troops and money from urbanized people with the same kind of balance: well enough acquainted with the wilderness to appreciate it, but living and working in cities.) Generally he disapproved of reformers. But against his own instincts he became one himself. Stretched across the fault line of his new life, he hoped both to save humans *for* the wilderness and the wilderness *from* humans. When he looked around the city he saw humans working too hard, worrying too much, and living amid a degree of squalor and fetid air that any other animal would have found intolerable. For their own survival, he recommended an annual pilgrimage into the woods and mountains. "Our crude civilization engenders a multitude of wants," he wrote in his journal, "and lawgivers are ever at their wits' end devising. The hall and the theater and the church have been invented, and compulsory education. Why not add compulsory recreation? Our forefathers forged chains of duty and habit, which bind us notwithstanding our boasted freedom, and we ourselves in desperation add link to link, groaning and making medicinal laws for relief. Yet few think of pure rest or the healing power of Nature."

Thus the paradox: if they did come, what would that do to the wilderness? Yet again, humans would benefit at the expense of the natural world. For a long time Muir had been conscious of this delicate tension between human welfare and natural damage. In his sheepherding days he had watched his "hoofed locusts" decimate a mountain meadow. Living in Yosemite, he squirmed while the tourists kept coming and the miserly state legislature provided only a thousand dollars a year for the maintenance and protection of the valley. "The plow is busy among its gardens," he said in 1874, "the axe among its groves, and the whole valley wears a weary, dusty aspect." A year later, camping on the north fork of the San Joaquin River, he observed a cow munching its way through a mountain meadow and wondered whether man would finally spread up and seize everything useful in the mountains: take the meadows for beef and mutton, cut down all the trees for ships and houses. Already new lumber companies were operating in the area, and a flume was being pushed through to connect with the railroad.

The stockmen and lumbermen were only acting out the prevailing philosophy of the age. "To obtain a hearing on behalf of nature from any other stand-point than that of human use is almost impossible," Muir declared. The nineteenth-century industrial revolution enhanced man's notion of his relative supremacy in the natural world, offering further proof of his cleverness and providing new machines with which to subdue greater expanses than ever before. As the American industrial system heated up after the Civil War, a riot of invention and enterprise swept everything before it. Given the implications of his central insight, Muir was not impressed. The dogma "that the world was made especially for the uses of men," he insisted in one article, was the fundamental error of his time. "Every animal, plant, and crystal controverts it in the plainest terms. Yet it is taught from century to century as something ever new and precious, and in the resulting darkness the enormous conceit is allowed to go unchallenged." Such arrogance left every tree and mountain vulnerable to human notions of their value.

Muir could take positions of personal witness. He now felt less inclined to carry off plant specimens when he went into the wilderness, preferring to let them keep growing. He sprinkled his articles with pleas for forest protection. But the times could hardly have been less propitious. Government was withdrawing from any interference in the market economy. Individualism, Darwinian struggle, and laissez-faire dominated the public mind. Writing to a Sacramento newspaper in February 1876, Muir couched his argument for the preservation of mountain conifers in the acceptable vernacular of human use. Without the watershed function of these tree belts on the flanks of the Sierra, he warned, the whole state would become a desert. Yet even the giant sequoias were being lumbered, wastefully, with the choice younger trees taken for lumber and the brittle veterans, the largest trees in the world, burned as worthless. Sheepmen also set fires to burn off old logs and underbrush and so improve pasturage. The situation, Muir concluded, demanded legislative interference: "Whether our loose jointed Government is really able or willing to do anything in the matter remains to be seen. If our law makers were to discover and enforce any method tending to lessen even in a small degree the destruction going on, they would thus cover a multitude of legislative sins in the eyes of every tree lover."

Though nothing was done, the legislators could hardly be blamed. Until trees were understood — how they grew, their interactions with other plants and animals, their real effect on rain and water tables — their salvation would wait. Botanists, preoccupied with naming and classifying species, knew little about such matters. Forestry, the study of trees in their environment, was developing in Europe. The United States had no forestry schools, practically no foresters at all: thus vast ignorance of trees. "Scarce anything definite is known regarding them," Muir pointed out in a paper for the AAAS *Proceedings,* "and the simplest ground-work for available legislation is not yet laid, while every species of destruction is moving on with accelerated speed." A small forestry division was created in the Department of Agriculture in 1876, to start gathering facts and make recommendations. Along with a previously formed committee of the AAAS, it encompassed the approximate extent of American forestry.

In other ways, here and there, American conservation made initial, tentative gestures during the 1870s. The first federal wildlife-conservation bill — a measure to protect buffalo — passed Congress but was vetoed by Grant. Scattered clubs of hunters and fishermen began to ponder the depletion of their quarry. John Wesley Powell of the U.S. Geological Survey published his famous report on the arid lands of the West. A group of professors and mountain lovers in Boston started the Appalachian Mountain Club, the first permanent organization of its kind in the United States. In New York, George Bird Grinnell took over the natural history section of *Forest and Stream* magazine. He would later become the omnipresent pioneer of eastern conservation. And in California, Muir worried about trees and sheep.

ꗇꗇ

A home in the city, a literary career, the beginnings of his conservation work: the mountaineer was starting to resemble that proper cultivated plant. Jeanne Carr added the final element by finding him a wife. Since leaving the farm back in Wisconsin, and especially in Prairie du Chien and Indianapolis, he had carried on friendships hinting elliptically of romance with various women. In 1873 he claimed to have had "many matrimonial possibilities," including a woman with a dowry! (Ever the Scotsman.) But he had always found reasons to avoid a commitment. "If you permit yourself to fall in love," he had advised his brother Dan in 1863, "adieu to study." In the following years he continued to feel a *"slavish fear"* of marriage, associating it with other "calamities" like serious illness or living in a city. Yet after leaving Yosemite he found that a city might be endured, even enjoyed. Further, he craved the company of children and the enveloping warmth a family might offer. All his brothers and all but one of his sisters were married and settled down. In reading their letters, he felt a longing for the same security. "Little did I think," he wrote Sarah in 1877, "when I used to be and am now fonder of home and still domestic life than any one of the boys, that I only should be a bachelor and doomed always to roam far outside the family circle."

By then Jeanne Carr had picked out his wife and Muir was succumbing to his fate, though as yet unaware of it. Through her involvement in the politics of the state Grange she had met the family of John Theophil Strentzel. They lived on a prosperous fruit farm in Martinez, fifteen miles north of Oakland. John Strentzel, educated as a doctor in Poland, had emigrated to the United States to avoid conscription into the Russian army. After marrying a woman in Texas, he had brought her out to California in '49. The family included one surviving child, an unmarried daughter named Louie Wanda. The Strentzel home offered a comfortable oasis of high culture, stocked with fine food and a library of books on science, horticulture, and Polish nationalism. Carr considered the Strentzels her "dearest friends in California." It seemed an obvious match to bring Louie and her protégé together. "I want you to know my John Muir," Carr wrote Louie shortly after his break with Elvira Hutchings, "and I wish I could give him to some noble young woman 'for keeps' and so take him out of the wilderness into the society of his peers."

The lady in question was twenty-six years old in 1873, nine years younger than Muir and verging on spinsterhood by the standards of the day. She shared Jeanne Carr's interests in feminism and botany, maintained an elaborate flower garden, and helped her father run the farm. In walking the hills around Martinez, she felt a measure of her future husband's affinity with the natural world. "Whenever in my wanderings," she wrote Carr, "I look upon rare and perfect trees or flowers, or mayhap the trembling sprays of ferns over dewy banks of emerald moss, and the thought of their loveliness helps and comforts me all the day, I feel quite sure that in some unknown way they understand, and are happier too for the added blessing remaining with them." Her meticulously cultivated flowers seemed "the one relic of Eden's garden brought down to us with no taint or stain of the orthodox Adam's Fall." The garden suggested an esthetic mind, reflected also in her love of the performing arts. She had studied piano at a ladies' seminary in nearby Benicia. (The famous Polish actress Helena Modjeska once stayed with the Strentzels for six months, learning English for her American debut in San Francisco.) In other ways Louie broke from the pattern of Victorian female gentility: she dabbled in astronomy and studiously followed politics and current events.

Reciting her interests may suggest the outer woman, a person of substance and intelligence. To recover a sense of the inner woman, of her personality, is more difficult. In any account of Muir's life she fades into the gray background — always loyal and encouraging, keeping the farm and family together in his absences — but she never steps forward in her own right. Before her marriage she had been isolated by family circumstances and by the lack of social peers in Martinez. She was cut off geographically as well because the railroad had not yet reached her hometown. After finishing school she spent practically all her time with her parents on the farm. "I have seen so very little," she confided to a friend in 1871; "go very seldom even to San Francisco, and then for a day or two only." Round-faced and plain, she disliked facing a camera. The few extant photographs show her to bad advantage, unsmiling and uncomfortable. Even after her marriage she seldom strayed far from home, preferring to drive her horse and buggy around town to perform her good works in her own small world. "She was a clever and noble woman," one of Muir's friends concluded, "but so retiring that she was known to only a few."

It was a long courtship. Muir was equally bashful — and a good deal less anxious to marry. For years he squirmed out of the traps laid for him. Carr arranged an initial meeting in 1874 (the Strentzels happened to drop by when Muir was visiting the Carr home in Oakland); but nothing further came of it. A year later Jeanne Carr showed him one of Louie's letters, written in a fine and graceful hand, with a lyrical description of the natural beauty around Martinez. The subject matter was designed to entice him to the Strentzels, but Muir — perhaps suspecting a plot — commented only on the handwriting. "Louie's letter is a marvelous piece of scribery," he allowed, "almost fairy in fineness and daintiness." Yet he showed no inclination to visit Martinez. "I sent your letter," Carr reported back to her co-conspirator, "hoping it would draw him, but it is even as you see."

In its obviousness the scheme may have offended his closely guarded independence. The two women subsided. On his own Muir let the idea germinate for two more years. In the fall of 1877, after floating down the Merced and San Joaquin rivers to the confluence of the Sacramento River with the San Joaquin, he docked in Martinez and finally showed up at the Strentzel home. In his ragged coat, with his hair hanging down almost to his shoulders, he seemed to be mocking the role of a likely suitor. Nonetheless they took him in, made him rest, and plied him with turkey, chicken, beef, fruits, and jellies. They urged him to stay a month; he lingered for two days and took off for San Francisco. With great enthusiasm he told the Swetts about his scientific discussions with the old doctor. "Did you," Mary Swett inquired, "by any chance observe a young lady about the house?" "Well, yes," he replied, "there was a young lady there."

If he felt any swelling romantic interest it was well concealed. It seems more likely that he was attracted by certain practical aspects. The Strentzels ran an impressive spread, with acres of fields and orchards and well-maintained buildings; Louie was the sole heir. Muir's explorations, now extending up and down the coast and into Utah and Nevada, were growing more expensive. He had recently finished a book on his rambles and discoveries. Never having suffered literary rejection, he had sent it off confidently to a New York publisher. But the manuscript was turned down. Suddenly his income from magazine writing seemed less reliable. For years he had been sending his extra cash to various family members. Now he was forced to turn around and ask them for help. Finally, most of his friends were pressuring him to stop "wasting" his life, to settle down like a normal person. Abstractly, in some moods, he agreed with them. Even if Louie in particular did not spark his passion, the general idea of a home and a secure income appealed to him more as time passed.

He turned forty in the spring of 1878. The season was marked by recurrent visits to Martinez. Still veiling his purposes, he spent much of the time arguing the relative merits of wild and domesticated fruit with the doctor. But he also took solitary walks with Louie through the hills and orchards. Behind the timid exterior he found an acute critic of his writing and a mind that ranged across subjects unknown to him. He spent that summer in Nevada with a U.S. Coast and Geodetic Survey party, keeping in touch through regular letters decorously addressed to all three Strentzels. "I appreciate your motherly care," he told the matriarch, who was worried about rampaging Pah Ute Indians, "but what can a body do? If an explorer of God's fine wilderness should wait until every danger be removed, then he would wait until the sun set." Then a respectful note to the daughter: "Tell Louie that I put a better tail on that Silva fir manuscript. Also rewrote the Will spruce."

When he came back the visits resumed, but during the winter he again lived in San Francisco, fretting over his manuscripts and pondering his future. Though he often celebrated his freedom, he felt paradoxically bound by the very unsettledness of his life, by the distance of his relatives and the lack of a family of his own. "I am pulled with ropes, driven with whips, and ridden with witches or guardian angels, so that I never can forecast my own movements. It is now more than ten years since I saw my mother and sisters."

In this mood he finally took the considerable step of writing his first letter to Louie herself. "Dear Miss Strentzel," he wrote, maintaining his decorous front. "The other day I chanced to find in my pocket that slippery fuzzy mesh which you wear round your neck." (The limits of the written word: evidently the relationship had already reached a certain point.) While he was writing, a messenger arrived with a package of flowers from Louie, breaking down his determined formality. "Boo!!!" he continued. "Aren't they lovely!!! ... An orchard in a bandbox!!! Who wad ha thocht it? A swarm of bees and fifty humming-birds would have made the thing complete." Six days later, contriving an excuse to write again, he reported that the blooms were fading: "We all do fade as a leaf, fade as a bouquet on a bachelor's table." In that offhand reference to his unmarried state, he left himself open to entertaining a change in the condition.

Two months later, in June 1879, he visited Martinez just before leaving on his first trip to Alaska. He would be gone for months; it was time to decide. Late one night John and Louie came to an understanding to marry on his return from the North. "I don't believe," Mrs. Strentzel wrote in her diary the next day, "there were ever four happier people in the world." After seeing him off a few days later, Louie collected his papers and herbarium from his quarters in the city and brought them home, storing them in a trunk outside her bedroom door. Already worried about his safety, she settled in for the long wait. "Dear John," she wrote him, "do not be vexed with me even this time. One can not grow to be brave in an hour or a day, and forgive me that I was so weak and foolish the last day. You would if only you could see and understand how hard I strive to learn patience." Receiving her letter at a stop in British Columbia, he consoled her after his fashion, doling out his affection in jerky little spasms: "Goodbye. Be patient. Heaven bless you."

As he made his initial forays into the last American wilderness, Muir must have sensed that he would never again feel quite so free. His ambivalence about the impending change in his life, along with the unexplored opulence of inlets and bays, mountains and glaciers, stretching before him, left him quivering in a state of giddy intoxication. During the first weeks in Alaska he felt too excited to settle down to systematic work. At Fort Wrangell in the southern end of the Panhandle, a missionary named S. Hall Young took wondering note of his behavior: "From cluster to cluster of flowers he ran, falling on his knees, babbling in unknown tongues, prattling a curious mixture of scientific lingo and baby talk, worshiping his little blue-and-pink goddesses." The coastal mountains offered literally thousands of glaciers to examine; from one vantage point alone he counted two hundred. He could not resist the chance to undertake his first substantial glacial work since leaving Yosemite in 1873. Summer passed into fall and he stayed on. Poking around an obscure inlet east of Cross Sound, he found an unknown bay being steadily enlarged by the retreat of the enormous glacier that would later bear his name.

Meanwhile Louie waited. Writing him in August, she stifled her worries and offered to send him money, explaining it would only be just payment for his botany lessons. He wrote back, briskly, to say he had been thinking of her, but not mentioning any date of return. Two more months passed. "O Friend Beloved," she wrote in a tone of greater urgency, "if ever the dear Lord leads you out from the depths of those blue glacier caves, and will let me once more look upon your face, that I may know you are not become only a white wraith of the northland — there will be no happier woman than I in all the wide world. . . . Fate seems to have willed only punishment for me because I was not patient." "Surely you would not have me away from this work," he wrote the same day, "dawdling in a weak-willed way on your lounge, dozing and drying like a castaway ship on the beach." So much for his notion of conjugal bliss. "O John, John, do not stay too long," she replied. "Surely you can go again next year with the new summer. . . . Ah me! what a blessed Thanksgiving if only you come home."

Through November, still no Muir, not even any new letters. She knew of his whereabouts only through the articles he was sending to the San Francisco *Bulletin.* For his lonely fiancée it was a distressing, even humiliating situation. Lost in his glaciers, he was — even if unintentionally — hurting her grievously. The reaction of his future in-laws may be imagined. Over six years had passed since Jeanne Carr first suggested the match. Calling up some final reserves of love and endurance, Louie wrote once more on December 1: "You must know that my heart is in all your work and that I rejoice over your gains in God's Wilds — but do you think, dear, that I do not understand the costly price you give for it all, in toil and hardship and suffering?" (And in the sufferings of others.) "You yourself are more precious to me than any work. . . . Last night I waited beside the glowing fire till midnight, and then till one, all alone with myself, and your letters. The wind sighed and moaned without ceasing, and I tried to understand but could not, and there was no other voice nor sign. At last in the silence, I know not how, the loving kindness and power of the Heavenly Father seemed to come very near, and clear in my sight, and I believed and was comforted to trust all in His care."

Around the New Year he finally started home. From Portland on January 6 he broke a silence of three months to say he had come ashore to examine the canyon of the Columbia, and then had been detained by requests for lectures; but would soon proceed to California. He offered no expression of love to match those so copiously filling her letters. At the end of the month she learned — from the newspaper — of his recent arrival in San Francisco. She sent a cool note inviting him to Martinez. He showed up in mid-February.

Despite his behavior during the eight months of separation, the reunion went happily. Whatever feelings he had for her were still there. Sensing the significance of his last prolonged immersion in the wilderness, she accepted it. They planned the wedding. After a short time he went back to San Francisco, to stay with the Swetts while he arranged his affairs. "The day I left you seemed intensely light and beautiful," he wrote her, almost but not quite transported by the occasion, "and notwithstanding my dazed, half-aware condition I noticed some telling glacial phenomena as the train glided along the curves of the bay that I had not seen before." By then, presumably, she understood that nothing might take precedence over glaciers.

"You have 'prospects' and he has talent and distinction," Mary Swett congratulated Louie as the day approached. Muir got a haircut, borrowed a coat and a white shirt, and dunned his Canadian employers for a hundred dollars, half of what they still owed him. Worried that the appointed minister might fail to appear, Muir thought about hiring an additional preacher or two for the occasion. Finally John and Louie, forty-two and thirty-three, were married in Martinez on April 14, 1880. "I could not have been more pleased," said Jeanne Carr, "if I had mixed the cup myself" — which of course she had.

Most of his friends and relatives were astonished by the news. Having been given no hint of any romance in Muir's life, they teased him about the sudden change in his economic status. "The Dr. is a millionaire," said a friend in Oakland with some exaggeration, "and the daughter is the only child! Now our dear little Johnny Muir is in clover." The reaction was too cynical, but not by much. He married not for love, mainly, but for stability, children, and a permanent home. When announcing this momentous change in his life to his old comrades, he generally forgot to say anything about Louie. "I was married last April," he wrote Asa Gray two months later, "and now have a fixed camp where I can store burs and grass." Thus the meaning of marriage: a place to keep his specimens. "You have mentioned the name of one party, John Muir," Gray replied, "but you say not a word about the other. Now, who is she?"

※※

After resisting it so long, he made a grudging, unhurried peace with the responsibilities of marriage. For three months he toiled in the orchards and vineyards. At the end of July, with his bride one month pregnant, he departed once again for Alaska. "I shall make haste to you and reach you ere you have time to grieve and worry," he wrote on the boat. "I have been alone, as far as the isolation that distance makes, so much of my lifetime that separation seems more natural than absolute contact, which seems too good and indulgent to be true." Though hardly implying an abandoned passion, he at least wrote in a more loving tone than before the marriage. Three more letters followed in the next two weeks. As the boat took him further from home, his tone cooled to the old forced awkwardness. "Only they who do not love may ever be apart," he offered, kindly, but going through the motions. "There is no true separation for those whose hearts and souls are together. So much for love and philosophy." The letters stopped when he arrived in Alaska. Once more, probably with a measure of relief, he lost himself in his beloved glaciers.

Poor Louie! Her morning sickness lasted all day. It was the hottest part of the summer. She suffered from a draining fever and general debilitation. With her husband away, she wanted him to appreciate her trials; yet she did not want to worry him. So she described her sufferings in loving detail — and then withdrew the complaint. "I have been miserably ill," she wrote. "The whole week after you left, there was almost continuous pain. . . . After the lightest of breakfasts, oatmeal and boiled fruit juice, I rested in bed until nearly sunset when the fever cooled. . . . But all this failed to bring quiet sleep at night until at last my dizzy brain seemed on fire, burning — Oh, my love, do not be troubled because of this. . . . My darling, my darling, I longed so for the touch of your hand, to see you and hear your voice, if only for one moment this side the unfathomable depths of arctic mists." Then, a good Victorian wife, she retreated into self-abnegation. When he came back "I shall know better how to be good to you" (as though she had driven him to Alaska), and together they could wait for the baby, "our own Precious Hope."

Meanwhile Muir, fifteen hundred miles away, had an epochal experience that helped reconcile him to civilized life. After meeting his missionary friend Hall Young at Fort Wrangell, the two men set out to explore glaciers together. Young's dog Stickeen — a mutt of indeterminate heritage, resembling a German shepherd in coloring and markings but about half the size, with an incongruous coat and tail of long, silky hair — insisted on coming along. He looked "small and worthless" to Muir: "This trip is not likely to be good for toy-dogs." But Stickeen, imperturbably self-contained and independent, refused to stay home. After a few days in camp, Muir stopped drawing harsh comparisons between Stickeen and other dogs of his acquaintance. This particular canine would not play games or frisk around for the amusement of humans. He did nothing to ingratiate himself, never obeyed an order. Yet in his detached sobriety he seemed preternaturally wise, anticipating human movements in and out of camp, always aware of what was going to happen next. With no trace of sycophancy he attached himself to Muir. Looking into his eyes, which seemed as old and wild as the hills, Muir felt he was peering into a landscape. "There's more in that wee beastie than I thought," Muir decided.

Early on the morning of August 30 Muir left camp on Cross Sound to explore the Taylor Glacier. Stickeen followed, was ordered back, but as usual had his own way. Man and dog climbed up the glacier's western flank and started to explore northward, leaping a series of latitudinal crevasses up to eight feet wide. Muir kept telling the dog to be careful but "he showed neither caution nor curiosity, wonder nor fear, but bravely trotted on as if glaciers were playgrounds. His stout, muffled body seemed all one skipping muscle." Muir himself grew incautious, turning around too late in the afternoon for an easy trip back. The sky darkened with a slow, thick snowfall. Losing his bearings, Muir tried to navigate by the wind and ice structure as he tacked back and forth through a crevasse field. Facing a wider chasm than any previously leaped, he took a running jump from the higher to the lower side and barely made it. Stickeen followed with his usual aplomb. They found themselves on an ice shelf fifty feet wide facing an unjumpable chasm. A mile to the left, they soon found, was another wide crevasse; a mile to the right the same. They could not go back the same way. With night approaching and the snow piling up, they were marooned.

Only one escape: ten feet below the brink, a sliver of ice stretched diagonally seventy feet across the abyss, hanging slack and motionless like the cable of a suspension bridge, joined to the other side at another ten feet below the edge. "Of the many perils encountered in my years of wandering on mountains and glaciers," he said later, "none seemed so plain and stern and merciless as this." With his ax he cut steps down to the sliver, straddled it, and inched his way across — taking care not to look down. His "other self" clicked in. Again he had the old sensation of moving surely, automatically. "At such times one's whole body is eye, and common skill and fortitude are replaced by power beyond our call or knowledge." Reaching the other side, he cut another set of steps and hauled himself up.

Across the way, Stickeen whined and cried as he desperately ran the length of the ice shelf, seeking some other way out. Then he would hush, examine the sliver critically, and howl some more over the impossibility of it. Muir shouted encouragement and pretended to leave, hoping to bluff him into it. Their eyes met in a riveting moment of trans-species communication. This little dog of such frightening self-possession was exposed in his vulnerability as a comrade, a fellow creature in distress. "So hidden before, he was now transparent, and one could see the workings of his heart and mind like the movements of a clock out of its case. His voice and gestures, hopes and fears, were so perfectly human that none could mistake them; while he seemed to understand every word of mine." At last he lowered himself down to the steps, edged onto the sliver, proceeded across with the slow and regular movements of a clock pendulum; reaching the opposite wall, he studied the steps briefly and rushed up in a whirl. "He flashed and darted hither and thither as if fairly demented, screaming and shouting, swirling round and round in giddy loops and circles like a leaf in a whirlwind, lying down, and rolling over and over, sidewise and heels over head . . . and launched himself at my face, almost knocking me down, all the time screeching and screaming and shouting as if saying, 'Saved! saved! saved!' "

Years later Muir wrote his most popular book, *Stickeen,* about this hairsbreadth escape from the Taylor Glacier. "The most memorable of all my wild days," he declared. Ever since leaving the farm in Wisconsin, he had never opened himself to a domestic animal. He had written tributes to the water ouzel, Douglas squirrel, brown bear, and other wild creatures. But he "knew nothing and cared even less for horses, regarding them as a necessary nuisance," according to a companion of his Yosemite years. Cows and sheep were held in even lower contempt, ruined by humans for their own selfish purposes. Yet on that lowering August afternoon, calling Stickeen across that chasm, Muir felt an unexpected resonance. "He enlarged my life, extended its boundaries," Muir decided. "I saw through him down into the depths of our common nature." Even this domesticated dog, it seemed, might join the wild animals in Muir's pantheistic heaven. "To me Stickeen is immortal." By an ironic twist, this perilous episode in the Alaskan wilderness nudged along Muir's own domestication.

❧❧

With a backdrop of flowers and cherry blossoms, and the songs of larks and linnets, Muir's first child was born on March 25, 1881. After all those years of dandling other people's babies he at last had one of his own. They named the girl Anna Wanda. She at once mingled with glaciers as an object of his deepest affection. "And never since the Glacial Period or Baby Period began on earth were happier people," he exulted to a friend. "How beautiful the world is and how beautiful is the time of the coming of our darling. We are five now, four steadfast old lovers around one little love. She is four days old or four years I scarce remember which."

The happy birth brightened his mood after a difficult fall and winter. During this first prolonged period of domesticity, living in the house of his in-laws, he was afflicted by a vague malaise. Outwardly life went smoothly, with no particular quarrels, as the four awaited the baby. But adjusting to his new situation exacted a psychic cost from Muir, expressed by the deterioration of his normally robust constitution. Nervous indigestion and a persistent bronchial cough took away his strength. Already thin, he grew even skinnier. Old friends looked at his pale face and inquired anxiously after his health. Louie worried about whether she was feeding him properly.

Shortly after Wanda's birth he was asked to accompany an expedition to Alaska. The trip might extend into the following winter. The elder Strentzels objected but Louie gave her consent, yielding to his argument that the trip would improve his health. In May he was gone again. An early letter to Louie after a visit to an Eskimo village hinted at friction in the couple's notions of housekeeping: "I found a little box of child's playthings which might please Anna Wanda, but which I suppose you will not let into the house." Otherwise their letters suggested a subtle shift in their relationship. As he thought about his newborn child, Muir's tone grew more loving; as Louie brandished the child, reminding him of his responsibilities, she felt emboldened to assert her own needs more strongly.

"I will be patient until the wild winter weather," she made clear, "but after that I cannot, I cannot bear it, and our little child will need you." The warning was superfluous: Muir felt a new homeward yearning, perhaps along with a measure of guilt. One morning he awoke suddenly from a dream, imagining the sound of Wanda's cry. Receiving a long-anticipated letter from home in August, he wrote back the same day: "It yet seems as if I had once more been upstairs and held you and Wanda in my arms. Ah, you little know the long icy days, so strangely nightless, that I have longed and longed for one word from you." He came back in October, sooner than expected. The parents spent sunny fall days sitting in the orchard with their baby. "She now loves her papa very much and cries to go to him," Mrs. Strentzel wrote in her diary.

With Wanda as the focus, John and Louie at last settled into married life. For three years he made no more trips into the wilderness. The pendulum of his personality swung further toward civilization than ever before. After Louie's parents built themselves an elaborate new house elsewhere on the property, Muir made the old place his own, adding dormer windows and fireplaces to help ward off his chronic cough. "It is not now so easy a matter to wing hither and thither like a bird," he noted, "for here is a wife and a baby and a home."

All well enough. He felt less satisfaction in returning to the life of a farmer. Taking charge of the family's land, he cut back the old doctor's experiments with many varieties, undertaken in the spirit of a loving amateur, in favor of fewer, more practical species — especially Bartlett pears and Tokay grapes — designed to make money. With some misgivings over the philosophical implications, he changed the operation from a botanical hobby into a burgeoning, profit-making enterprise. To assist the planting he exhumed his old mechanical skills, devising a little machine that helped a man lay down a quick, straight row of seeds. Aside from whatever dour childhood memories his new role may have called up, he now to some extent was forced to regard the natural world in a different light. He loved birds. Now they ate his cherries, their bills running red with the juice, costing him five hundred dollars a year in lost profits.

Tied to his work, he had to slight his scientific and literary pursuits; yet he loved his family more all the time. With these multiple conflicts pulling at him, he sometimes railed at his circumstances with startling vehemence. "I am lost and choked in agricultural needs," he wrote an editor in 1883, turning down her request for an article. "Work is coming upon me from near and far and at present I cannot see how I am to escape its degrading vicious effects. Get someone to write an article on the vice of over-industry, it is greatly needed in these times of horticultural storms." For years he tried to find a satisfactory foreman to relieve him of the supervision of hired hands. Apparently nobody met his exacting standards.

As in his factory days, with a large task before him he worked too hard. Louie and her mother urged him to slow down, but to no effect. Occasionally one of the women would play an irresistible trump by bringing Wanda down to the vineyard where he was toiling away. He would then have to stop, play with the child, perhaps carry her back to the house. Still he looked worn down much of the time. In the summer of 1884 Louie talked him into a Yosemite trip, their first wilderness experience together. "The journey was hard for him," she wrote her parents from the valley, "and he looks thin and pale and tired. He must not leave the mountains until he is well and strong again." Louie herself was no mountaineer. Gamely trying to climb a peak, she faltered on the way up; dropping behind her, Muir pushed a stick into her back to speed the ascent, hurting her and probably not helping her disposition. Eventually a man came along on a horse and gave her a ride. After his years of inexpensive rambles with the barest equipment, Muir was appalled by the cost of transporting his wife's female impedimenta and lodging her in the best available accommodations. The whole trip ran to five hundred dollars, a total that staggered him. Not surprisingly, they never again ventured into the wilderness together.

Aside from a quick stop in Yellowstone on the way to see his parents in 1885, he did not set foot in wild country again until 1888. "I am degenerating into a machine for making money," he told Hall Young. "Condemned to penal servitude," he said, throwing a disgusted glance at his cherries, "with these miserable little bald-heads! Boxing them up; putting them in prison! And for money." All year long he had to superintend from fifteen to forty men on the place. In peak seasons he rose at six o'clock, worked through the day, and after retiring at nine tried to keep up with his reading until midnight. At harvesttime he shipped two thousand boxes of grapes a day, arguing over the price with proper Scotch tenacity. The fruit jobbers in San Francisco knew him as a tough, unyielding businessman. His old friends hardly knew what to make of him at all. "More care-worn," noted Galen Clark of Yosemite, "and not so happy as he used to be when engaged in his excursions and studies."

Certainly Muir often complained of the interruption in what he called his "real work." Cut off from the field studies that provided his research, he wrote little during the 1880s. "I feel that I could still do some good scientific work," he noted in 1885, "if the necessary leisure could be secured." Yet it was not a simple matter of displacement, of the farm crowding out his career as a writer. There was no compelling reason to spend so much time among his despised crops. Louie repeatedly urged him to follow his old instincts, pointing out that a few grapes more or less made no great difference in so profitable an operation. Actually he preferred the farm work to sitting down at his desk and facing a blank sheet of paper. He hated the act of writing even more than those bald-headed cherries. "Writing to me is very hard," he groaned, "for I have no facility in composition and no available vocabulary — only — only invention and imagination." No doubt all writers partake of this mood. By the frequency of his despairing comments, though, and by the testimony of his friends, Muir went through special tortures in coaxing the words out. "It is so difficult," he scribbled in his journal, "to say things that involve thought at once clearly and attractively — to make the meaning stand out through the words like a fire on a hill so that all must see it without looking for it. Yet this is what the times demand in magazine work." He no longer *had* to write to earn a living. Freed of that powerful motive, he seldom wrote. If the grapes and cherries made a hiatus in his literary career necessary, they also made it possible.

Another baby, a girl named Helen, was born in January 1886. Thus he gained a further excuse not to write. When Wanda contracted scarlet fever in 1889, he spent weeks nursing her by himself while Louie and Helen went to live with her parents. The quarantine was imposed because Helen spent her early years in precarious health. (For eighteen months after her birth Muir had scarcely left the farm.) He liked to take the girls on walks around the Martinez hills, pointing out the names of plants and flowers. "For how would you like it," he would ask, "if people didn't call you by your name?" At mealtime the girls prodded Muir into telling stories, some of them quite long, extending over a month or two in daily installments.

Both John and Louie were dutiful parents. Wanda, with her more placid temperament and her love of music, came to resemble her mother. Helen, a mercurial little girl of quick, elfin movements, was her father's special delight. Forever worrying over her health, when away from home he bombarded Louie with instructions on her proper care: "Bathe her frequently and change her clothing in the middle of the day, and again at night. Be specially watchful when after warm days the cold winds set in suddenly from the sea.... Acid fruit with sugar, warm debilitating weather, and nerve-exhausting toothache and irregularity of the bowels, all come together to delicate children and the danger is very great. I charge you, therefore, to be watchful." Louie was thirty-nine at Helen's birth; there were no other children. Given the sex-role conventions of the day, he might have taken a boy child into the mountains at an early age. He did not take his daughters there until they were sixteen and twenty, after which he proudly described them as "good mountaineers."

Having entered the marriage for limited purposes, in those terms he had good reason to feel content. He had home, family, security, a place to keep his specimens. Though he felt tied to the farm, that was largely his own doing. Louie was a good wife and his most trenchant critic (he never sent off a manuscript without first submitting it to her review). Apparently the relationship went that far and no further. In tastes and habits they were quite different people: he tireless on a mountain, she rendered breathless by a horseback ride around the farm; he oblivious to social forms, she respectful of them; he darting and whimsical, she slow and earnest. Louie was a devout, churchgoing Christian, a steadfast member of the local Methodist Episcopal Church. Muir felt it his duty, to keep the house from becoming "most devoutly dull," to tease her and maintain a stream of "sheer blank nonsense and humbug" to lighten the air.

Although bound by their ties of mutual need, they evidently were never quite lost in each other as lovers sometimes are. When Muir described his life or ticked off his reasons for living in Martinez, he still forgot to mention Louie. "This is a good place to be housed in during stormy weather," he told a visitor, "to write in, and to raise children in, but it is not my home. Up there," pointing toward the Sierra Nevada, "is my home."

🐾

Always the faraway look, an effect heightened, when seen head on, by the slight divergence of his right eye — the legacy of his factory accident in Indianapolis. Soon after his marriage an old friend asked him, "Has contact with human nature taken off the natural freshness of your soul and made you more like other people?" Hardly at all. Despite the marked change in his outward circumstances and some signs of aging, like spectacles and a bald spot, his personality and attitudes remained essentially the same. On birthdays he would mark the occasion by noting that he still felt like a boy, no older than when he first left home. Though the farm and family absorbed his time, his spirit might still detach itself and waft away in the direction of the mountains.

Before the marriage he had described himself as "the happiest man I ever saw." Later in life, for all his complaining of home duties, he remained congenitally cheerful. He whistled easily and liked to laugh and provoke laughter in others. In the presence of more morbid souls he might spout a litany of uplifting quotations from favorite authors. From Goethe:

> Keep not standing, fixed and rooted,
> Briskly venture, briskly roam.

Or Thoreau:

> I will not doubt forevermore,
> Nor falter from a steadfast faith,
> For though the system be turned o'er,
> God takes not back the word which once he saith.

Or Emerson:

> Life is too short to waste
> In critic peep or cynic bark,
> Quarrel or reprimand:
> 'Twill soon be dark;
> Up! Mind thine own aim, and
> God speed the mark!

These snatches of invincible good cheer may suggest a mind unacquainted with the moral problem of evil, even a Panglossian naiveté. But they were consistent with the boy who, after nearly drowning, had dived repeatedly to punish his body. All his life Muir was held on course by a hard, unreachable inner self. External conditions at any particular time, however bothersome for the moment, did not much affect him.

His citification, then, had clear limits. Despite Louie's best efforts he kept his beard long and untrimmed, his hair an ungroomed snarl, his clothing careless and random. He determinedly maintained "the outward bearing of an unsophisticated farmer," according to an acquaintance. After decades of making trips into and through San Francisco, he still had no idea of how to find the Cliff House or Golden Gate Park. Chronically late for trains and engagements, he was "not a man for the world to set its watch by." Though he made regular trips to the bank with a laundry bag full of cash from fruit sales, he seemed innocent of the most elementary banking procedures. He made peace with civilization on his own terms: in the city but not of it.

This unruffled detachment from his surroundings was both goaded and expressed by his sense of himself as a Scotsman in America. Clinging to old-country ways, he always felt at one remove from his adopted homeland. "He displayed many Scotch traits," someone recalled. His sentimental affection for Robert Burns; the Scotch cap and gray tweed ulster he wore in cold weather; the flinty suspicion he brought to business matters ("he had the Scotch integrity and knew a rascal when he met one"); ascribing his love of mountains to Highland blood; the uncritical reception he gave anyone from Scotland ("naebody like a Scotchman"); the lingering suspicion of Irishmen. He revealed himself most obviously in his conversation. Especially when he was enjoying himself, his speech would lapse into a broad, playful Scotch. Few Americans, he said, could appreciate the "power and beauty" of the true Scotch vernacular. "It is an upgrowth of pure Saxon," he explained, "enriched with more or less of Danish, Norse and Celtic, thoroughly assimilated, and this has given an affluence, and a delicacy of fibre such as no other branch of the English language has yet attained. These qualities are most fully illustrated in expressing the affections — the life of a pure love-illumined home."

He felt more ambivalent about "that exacting Scotch conscience of mine," a merciless internal monitor he sometimes would have preferred to shake off. As an adult he could recognize the irrational asperities of "the contrary extravagantly self denying doctrine taught in old Scotland that we should never do what we most like to do but only what we like least." His hard childhood memories floated just below the surface: bloody fights in the schoolyard, father and his switches, chipping through eighty feet of rock, being overcome by chokedamp, hobbling out into the winter morning in frozen boots and socks. Whether in Dunbar or America, his early years were scarred by Scotch harshness. "They must practice self denial and subdue their body with its passions; they must keep their bodies subject to the principles that they are taught," he later recalled in anger. If the persistent rumors about his sex life, initially provoked by his friendship with Elvira Hutchings, had any substance, his conduct might be understood as a reaction against the grim Scotch severity of his youth.

Yet a Scotch conscience cut two ways, and he welcomed its advantages. It helped insulate him from discouragement on the one hand and excessive vanity on the other. " 'Never be dowy' as the Scotch say," he declared, "that is downhearted, but struggle on against any fate trusting in Heaven." Resilience, persistence, self-possession — his own best qualities could, as he understood them, be traced directly to his Scotch heritage. More than a sentimental yearning for the homeland, this identification explained salient elements of his personality. "Wherever grit and skill and invincible granite determination and principle are required," he said of Scotsmen, and of himself, "the world cannot do without them."

His best friend was a fellow Scot, the artist William Keith. Jeanne Carr had sent Keith to him in Yosemite in 1872. The two men, born in Scotland in the same year, both of Highland ancestry, had formed an immediate bond cemented by high-spirited, jabbering arguments. "Muir is Scotch, and I'm Scotch, and so we always quarrel," Keith explained. During the 1880s Muir would come down from the farm to San Francisco and, with some difficulty, find his way to Keith's dingy studio on Montgomery Street. After some initial banter, and perhaps lunch at a nearby French restaurant, they might subside into momentary silence "in which they communed in a sort of mystical manner," an onlooker noted. Muir would read, Keith would paint. Then:

"Here, Johnny! What do you think of this?"

"It's ridiculous, Willy. Look at that watershed. Look at those snowfields. And a trickle of water that I could step across. Ridiculous!" More reading and painting.

"Come, Johnny, how's this?"

"What's the hump in the middle of the waterfall?"

"Hump, Johnny! That's a boulder."

"Never could stay there with that force of water behind it."

Another interlude of reading and painting.

"Now, Johnny!"

"That's more reasonable.... You know, Willy, I think if I'd spent as much time messing with paint as you have, I could have been an artist myself."

"Not you! You lack — you lack wildness!"

An amiable form of recreation, in other contexts this hyperbolic chaffing served as a social defense, a way of engaging people while holding them off. Muir's odd social behavior again suggested how little he had changed. Only his real intimates, Keith or John Swett, were granted the privilege of give-and-take. On any other social occasion, even with a small group of fairly close friends, Muir would spew forth an impenetrable wall of language. "I like the feel of words in my mouth better than bread," he declared. Indeed, at table he might rattle on and neglect to eat. Dishes would be placed in front of him, grow cold, be cleared away or emptied by others, and the cascading language never stopped.

Friends put up with it because he spoke so well. The verbal blocks that beset him at his desk cleared away when he opened his mouth. The words tumbled out in crisp sentences and paragraphs, with a complex vocabulary and sentence structure, and a generous allowance for necessary digressions. "Ask him to tell you his famous dog story," someone said, ". . . and you get the whole theory of glaciation thrown in." However rude these discourses might seem, according to his patient listeners they presented Muir at his best, more fluid and charming than even his most polished writing. In the absence of any direct records, the quality of his talk can only be suggested by the recollections of his witnesses. "Scarcely would the guests be seated," one recalled, "when Muir would begin, as if thinking aloud, pouring forth a stream of reminiscence, description, exposition, all relieved with quiet humor, seasoned with pungent satire, starred and rainbowed with poetic fantasy." Another remembered: "I used to keep him talking to me half the night, and if he would begin to get sleepy I would think up some abuse of the Scotch, and off his Jeremiads would start again in full flow. I know one night in this house, we had a steady session of eight hours, in which ninety-five per cent of the time was occupied by his talk, I mixing in merely enough to aggravate or dispute or otherwise stimulate him."

In hogging the floor Muir was not showing off or acting the bully. At a large, formal social occasion or — even worse — when facing a lecture audience, he was normally so terrified he could barely speak. "Sorry can't conquer shyness," he jotted in his journal after being dragooned into giving a talk. If his monologues had been only a form of self-advertisement, he might have blossomed even more in front of a larger group. Rather, they acted as an unconscious defense mechanism against the mystery of two-way social intercourse. Despite the recurring pattern, when someone pointed out his domination of a party, he was always mortified, profuse with apology and resolves to improve his manners. "We have two ears and one mouth that we may hear more and speak less," he noted. "Sometimes it seems as if I had only one ear and a dozen mouths."

As an unconscious tendency, the habit was out of his control. He was a respected naturalist and literary figure — most facile not in writing or lecturing, but in holding forth in someone's living room. With his usual unblinking self-perception he recognized these traits, regretted them, but could not change them. In 1896 Louie sent this explanation to an eastern editor of why Muir could not deliver a certain address: "If a formal speech is required I fear he will bolt like a frightened wild animal. When he meets professors and college presidents in an informal way he takes all the talk to himself and lectures them coolly with an air of superior knowledge, as if they were only boys at the beginning of their studies, but the slightest formality in the way of ceremony frightens him dumb." This unsparing, exasperated description was drafted by Muir himself.

✻✻

Muir's old religious and intellectual habits also remained the same. He continued to admire the Bible as literature ("the best school for English in all the world"). He could still recite whole chapters from memory: a favorite was the description of a good man in Job 29. Otherwise he had no use for Christianity, either as institution or belief system. He expressed no special interest in Jesus and never went to church. Most Christian ministers offended him — "sadly comfortably hidebound" — with their firm and sometimes contradictory ideas about proper conduct. Thus, he noted, they profanely offered themselves as apostles of peace, yet endorsed the hunting of wild animals. They insisted on keeping the Sabbath holy, yet frowned on a reverent Sunday walk through the woods. "We sometimes hear the Lord spoken of as if he were a little, cranky, old-fashioned being," said Muir, "fastened and sealed in by well-established rules, and that the parsons are on confidential terms with Him and know just what He intends."

God was not a person to Muir, especially not an anthropoid person with a narrow interest in human welfare. Christian orthodoxy set man apart from the rest of nature, as a creature of special endowments, and drew further lines between material and spiritual. Muir rejected all such categories as human contrivances. "Earth and heaven are the same," he wrote, "one and inseparable." Life on earth was not merely a preamble to something higher, less gross and physical. Away from human inventions and corruptions, anyone could partake of an immediate eternity, right here and now. Worried about the inexorable passing of time, Christians might wonder about their readiness to enter heaven. But the clock could be stopped by exposing oneself to nature with opened senses. "On a swift flood we are all borne forward," said Muir, "and only when I am in the wilderness is this current invisible, where one day is a thousand years and a thousand years one day."

Muir often spoke in religious accents, leading Christians to suppose him a fellow communicant. But it was religion in his own terms. The "still, small voice" that belonged to God in the Bible became "the still, small voice of Nature." In referring directly to the divine force, he typically called it Beauty or Nature or (compromising) Nature-God rather than God or the Lord, his faith residing in the vast, impersonal power of natural order and harmony rather than in a particular deity preoccupied with human intentions. Once, sitting in a sequoia grove in springtime, he drank in all the sights and sounds of birds and flowers, waterfalls and winds. "Everything busy," he noted, recalling God's edict in Genesis 1:28, "as if hearing the command 'Increase and multiply and replenish the earth.' " He thus turned Genesis on its head, for the original passage ordered *man* to multiply and then to "subdue" the world to his own purposes, to establish "dominion ... over every living thing that moveth upon the earth." In Muir's version, all natural organisms were to reproduce for their own purposes, not to serve man alone.

In his pantheism he felt closer to pagan European and native American religious traditions. A dense grove of oak and mistletoe suggested a fine site for a Druid temple. Again, warming himself at an aromatic fire of rosiny pine logs, he was reminded of the divine force: "No wonder the old nations, with their fresher instincts, had their fireside gods." In his travels he occasionally brushed against Indian and Eskimo cultures, and sensed a corresponding affinity with their religious ideas. Freed of Christianity's human conceits, they prayed to nature gods and allowed nonhuman creatures — like Stickeen — into their heaven. "Indian dogs," he noted with approval, "go to the Happy Hunting Grounds with their master — are not shut out."

Yet Louie was a Christian, and Muir lived in a Christian society and wrote for a Christian readership. Not wishing to offend, he generally kept the precise nature of his religious ideas to himself, confining them to journals, letters, and private discussions. ("You naughty, bad boy!" one of his sisters scolded. "What would the world in general do without churches and Sunday schools?") To the public at large he spoke only in pious generalities. The extent of his disaffection from Christianity remained a secret, both during his lifetime and afterward. In the centennial year of his birth, a Presbyterian minister with unconscious irony claimed him as "one of our Protestant saints." The label would have amused him.

He brought everything to the test of wilderness. As the religion of his youth and then the cataclysmic theory of Yosemite's origins had yielded to his intuitive perceptions of nature, so in maturity Muir preferred a direct immersion in nature to wisdom acquired from books or any disembodied intellectual activity. "Descriptive writing amounts to little more than Hurrah, here's something! Come!" he declared. "Nature's tables are spread and fires burning. You must go warm yourselves and eat." Neither the written word nor an attitude of cool, deductive scientific objectivity persuaded him. All correct knowledge of the natural world, he insisted, began with an impassioned, sensual joy in the environment: "Instead of producing a dissipated condition, the mind is fertilized and stimulated and developed like sun-fed plants."

Judged purely as philosophy, this posture could be defended. As Muir pointed out, the reductive tendency of modern science in breaking knowledge into ever smaller pieces of specialization did obscure the whole picture. He was drawn to unities, not fragments. Botanists spent their lives in minute arguments over how to classify a given species. "While we are disagreeing over the final letter in a name," said Muir, "we are possibly forgetting that the tree is beautiful, and that it is here for us to enjoy." Well and good. But during Muir's lifetime the general naturalist was giving way to the specialist, field studies to the laboratory, direct experience to the microscope. By clinging to his holistic philosophy Muir lost touch with the scientific advance of his day. He seldom did research in books. Once, intrigued by a trip to the petrified forests of Arizona, he actually spent several weeks in a library — complaining all the while. Usually he just relied on his notes gathered from the field. "Had I known what others had written," he explained lamely to a critic, "— just what ground they covered — I might easily have made my glacial article longer. But few will care to read more."

Muir liked to think of himself foremost as a scientist. Yet he spurned the scientific method by reasoning from the general to the particular, from an a priori intuition to preordained conclusions. Attracted to trees, bears, glaciers, and flowers, he studied them all at the cost of finding new information about any of them. Aside from his early glacial work in Yosemite and some of his Alaskan explorations, his scientific career was not distinguished. "To me Muir was a poet rather than a scientific man," his friend Harry Fielding Reid of Johns Hopkins concluded; "he loved Nature and spent his life observing her works; but his observations were the observations of a poet, of a lover, and not the systematic observations of the man of science."

Muir responded characteristically to the nineteenth century's extended debate over evolution. In America the anti-Darwinists were led by Agassiz, Muir's glacial inspiration, while the Darwinians grouped around his mentor in botany, Asa Gray. Initially he veered toward the latter, regarding both Darwin and Gray as "great, progressive, unlimited" men. Darwin was attacked on the same narrow grounds of Christian orthodoxy that

Muir's father had used in criticizing his son's geological studies in Madison. With that stinging memory, and the direct personal influence of Gray, Muir at first declared himself a thoroughgoing evolutionist. "His noble character," said Muir of Darwin, "has suffered from silly, ignorant, and unbelieving men who say much about Darwinism without really knowing anything about it. A more devout and indefatigible seeker after truth than Darwin never lived." As a wide-ranging field naturalist Muir could admire him.

The philosophical implications of Darwinism were less agreeable. Observing the natural world, Muir saw peace and harmony; Darwin saw grim competition, the survival of the fittest. Though Muir accepted the broad process of evolution, he felt bound to reject "Darwin's ungodly word 'struggle.'" *Ungodly:* as the public debate went on, Darwin — or at least the Darwinists — reached even more disturbing conclusions. Like Gray, Muir was an evolutionist who still believed in a divine intelligence. Later in the nineteenth century, evolution as interpreted by Ernst Haeckel and Thomas Henry Huxley was linked with agnosticism. God was dropped from the cosmos in favor of a purely mechanical universe. At that point Muir parted company with the Darwinists. "Every cell," he jotted in his copy of a book by the evolutionist Alfred Russel Wallace, "every particle of matter in the world requires a Captain to steer it into its place." Admiring Darwin as a scientist, Muir rejected him as a philosopher — and thus, on balance, wound up arguing against him. "Evolution! — a wonderful, mouth-filling word, isn't it?" said Muir. "It covers a world of ignorance. . . . Somewhere, before evolution was, was an Intelligence that laid out the plan, and evolution is the process, not the origin, of the harmony." Again he reasoned inductively. If evolutionists even on elaborate scientific grounds argued against his intuitively perceived notion of the cosmos, then they were wrong. What his position lacked in a pure scientist's zeal for the truth, it made up for in consistency.

And in originality. Given Muir's suspicion of books and other people's opinions, and his self-contained detachment from outside influences, any ideas he had were necessarily his own. No written authority ever influenced him as much as his own private speculations in the wilderness. In maturity he embraced Thoreau as his favorite writer. He loved to discourse on the author of *Walden* and frequently urged the book on his friends. As a result, and because of his epochal meeting with Emerson in 1871, Muir has since been described as an intellectual disciple of the Concord transcendentalists. Yet even in these instances, evidently Emerson and Thoreau only corroborated ideas that Muir had already worked out independently.

He first read Thoreau, apparently at the behest of Jeanne Carr, during his Yosemite years. Emerson in his Yosemite visit also spoke with great enthusiasm about his Concord friend. "He said most about Thoreau," Muir noted, "asked me if I knew anyone in Cal this side of the continent any young genius likely to be able to edit his unpublished MS notebooks, etc. — that he must be scholarly acquainted with the Classics — as well as with wild nature etc." Perhaps Emerson hoped Muir would take on the job. In any case, his interest piqued, Muir praised "the pure soul of Thoreau" in one of his early articles. He had finally read *Walden* for the first time in 1872, after a friend in Boston sent her personal copy to him. But this was eight years after discovering *Calypso borealis* in a Canadian swamp, five years after the definitive expression, in Florida, of his central insight ("the world we are told was made for man"). He also was unacquainted with Emerson's poems and most of his essays until the Yosemite period. By then Muir's mature attitudes about wilderness and civilization were already firmly in place.

As it turned out, both Emerson and Thoreau seemed insufficiently wild to him. He littered the margins of his copy of Emerson's essays with dissenting arguments. Emerson and the early Thoreau both appreciated nature from a base in abstract metaphysics. To Muir this seemed to reverse a proper, more reverent approach. Always he began with the natural world and judged everything in its terms: "A little pure wildness is the one great present want." Any philosophical baggage brought to the wilderness merely impeded a true appreciation of nature's handiwork. Ideas must be grounded in an unhumanly humble receptivity to the direct evidence. Accordingly, Muir felt no particular awe toward what he called "the airy wisdom of a Jamaica Plain transcendentalist." He revered Emerson and Thoreau as inspiring personalities who understood part of the truth. Later, when standing at their graves in Concord, he wished that he also might be buried there. But as with everyone else, he thought they needed a strong dose of the Sierra Nevada. "Even open-eyed Thoreau," said Muir, "would perhaps have done well had he extended his walks westward to see what God had to show in the lofty sunset mountains."

Although a person of substantial intellect, Muir was not "an intellectual" in the usual sense because he took so little from books. Essentially a function of his passion for wilderness, this attitude also derived from his spotty early education. After all those lost years on the farm and then his abbreviated studies in Madison, he was conscious of gaps in his learning. (Thus in a revealing moment of intellectual insecurity, he would claim four years at the university — twice his actual stay.) Only after his marriage did time and logistics allow him a broad course of reading. The Strentzels already owned a sizable library. Once settled down Muir added to it steadily; among his first purchases were Humboldt's *Cosmos* in five volumes and the thirty volumes of Carlyle's collected works. His tastes in fiction and poetry remained those of his youth, mainly British novelists and Romantic poets, especially Shelley, Coleridge, and Wordsworth. Hawthorne was the only American novelist he liked. Of contemporary American poets he admired the themes in Whitman — "big ideas, unusual ideas" — but not the jangly, dissonant verse. In nonfiction he favored exploration accounts, Boswell's *Johnson,* and the historical volumes of Francis Parkman.

Muir's reading habits suggest an eclectic Victorian mind: grounded in the creative literature of the past, wary of newfangled literary vogues (none of the younger American realistic novelists), dabbling in history; above all, Anglophile in taste, with an overriding purpose to divert and entertain. Little evidence of this reading crept into his own writing. He wrote only about geology, botany, wilderness — topics he knew at first hand, not through the vicarious mediation of books. In conversation he ranged more widely, expressing firm views on many subjects. As his friend the mammalogist C. Hart Merriam recalled, Muir "had well-digested opinions on a surprisingly large number of topics" — but only when talking. He characteristically offered only fragments of himself in print.

As he spent his evenings during the 1880s filling in random gaps in his knowledge, Muir at last gained a glimmering interest in politics. Previously immune to discussions of social and economic questions, he did take on this one major change in his world view after marriage. Before the 1880s he had no politics as such. "All my inheritance of beliefs, laws and dogmas, rights and wrongs were as yet undeveloped, loose and nebulous on the edges," he recalled in another context. This formless quality applied especially to his political ideas. Once acquired they displaced nothing, but simply filled a void in his thinking.

Instinctively he disliked reformers. Earlier he had urged town dwellers to come rest in the woods — but then disclaimed any grand intentions. "Not that I am seized with a sudden fit of philanthropy," he noted, "for with Thoreau I believe that the profession of doing good is full." Also influenced by the baleful cynicism of "the stern old prophet Carlyle," he doubted that any millennial reform scheme could much affect the snarled dilemmas of modern industrial civilization. Reformers sounded too sure of themselves, he thought, too naive about "the thousand impenetrable mysteries that confront poor, struggling humanity, and in the midst of which the wisest feel compelled to grope."

Apparently his political education was begun by Henry George. In the late 1870s, when George was living in San Francisco, John Swett helped form the first organization to advance George's theories of monopoly and the single tax. Since Muir lived in the Swett home during those years, he could not despite his best efforts avoid hearing about economic problems. Whether Muir attended any George meetings, or ever read *Progress and Poverty,* is not known. But occasionally Georgite ideas and phrases showed up in his writing of this period. Describing a stand of nut pine trees in 1878, he declared: "Fortunately for the Indians and wild animals that gather around Nature's board this crop is not easily harvested in a monopolizing way. If it could be gathered like wheat the whole would be carried away and dissipated in towns, leaving the brave inhabitants of these wilds to starve."

In Martinez, family circumstances immersed him more directly in political questions. All three Strentzels were active Grangers. The old doctor was perennially elected master of the local unit. For obscure reasons Muir at first argued vehemently against the Grange. It functioned in California more as a social and educational institution than as a vehicle for political reform; but it did try to organize farmers to obtain better prices for their crops. In time, perhaps for the sake of family peace, perhaps for economic reasons once he started farming himself, Muir thought better of the Grange and attended local meetings.

Most remarkably of all, Muir actually picked up a few political ideas from books. During the Yosemite period a friend in Oakland had sent him one of John Ruskin's works. All but inevitably, Muir thought Ruskin lacked wildness. "You never can feel that there is the slightest *union* betwixt Nature and him," Muir wrote. "He goes to the Alps and improves and superintends and reports on Nature with the conceit and lofty importance of a factor of a Duke's estate." Years later, though, Muir bought the 1886 edition of Ruskin's collected works and studied the Englishman more closely. He found things to admire: a call to turn away from cities and technology; criticism of a Christian for lamenting the sufferings of Christ instead of his own countrymen's; a proposal to reward landowners for keeping their property in "conditions of natural grace." In particular, in Ruskin's *Time and Tide* Muir read an attack on classical laissez-faire economists for providing an ideological rationale that was allowing the ruin of the English environment. "Legal theft," Muir wrote on the endpaper, as though trying out a new idea, "cold blooded passionless iniquity. The most unpardonable of human crimes so obscure far reaching almost invisible and unpunishable." *Time and Tide* introduced an insurrectionary notion:

that environmental destruction resulted not from the random greed of a few, but from systemic flaws.

Broad social questions still engaged him infrequently. "Muir abhorred politics," according to Hart Merriam. But in these nonsocialist alternatives to the free market — the ideals of George, the Grange, and Ruskin — he found the implicit political basis for his later conservation work. Natural wonders could not be protected within the assumptions of radically individualist capitalism. "The gobble gobble school of economics," as he called it, would need modification.

※※

By 1888 Muir had gone seven years without a real wilderness trip. His old Alaska companion, Hall Young, visited Martinez that spring and found him restive and straining against his traces. "I want to see what is going on," he said. "I'm learning nothing here that will do me any good." In July he took off with Keith for the Cascade Mountains in Washington, with stops along the way at Mount Shasta and other points up the coast. Muir felt the old wild ecstasies returning, mingled with worries about how affairs at home were going. "I hope the ranch is not giving you too much trouble," he wrote Louie. Sensing the lift in his spirits, and conscious of the eclipse of his writing career, she wrote back: "A ranch that needs and takes the sacrifice of a noble life or work, ought to be flung away beyond all reach and power for harm. . . . Dear John, the Alaska book and the Yosemite book must be written, and you need to be your own self, well and strong, to make them worthy of you; there is nothing that has a right to be considered beside this except the welfare of our children."

The trip gave him an even sharper prod to resume writing. At Shasta he found widespread forest destruction and a tawdry lumbermen's town. During his years in civilization, the ax and saw had been chipping away at his beloved trees. If neither money nor science could hold him at his desk, perhaps protecting the wilderness could. Back in Martinez, he talked things over with Louie. They decided to lease or sell major pieces of their land. A few years later Margaret and John Reid, his sister and brother-in-law, came out to take charge of the remaining property. By these gradual steps Muir withdrew from his career as a gentleman farmer — and no longer had any excuse not to write.

During the 1880s he had heard occasionally from an editor in New York, Robert Underwood Johnson of *Century* magazine, successor to the old *Scribner's* magazine that had published some of his best articles of the late 1870s. "We fear you may have abandoned literature altogether,"

Johnson wrote him in 1884, "very much we are sure to the loss of American readers. Has the ink in your fountain entirely dried up?" No reply from Muir, and no further nudges from Johnson. In the spring of 1889 the editor arrived in California to gather material for a series on the state's pioneer settlers. A man of finely tuned eastern sensibilities, he was offended by practically everything in San Francisco: an elevator boy who whistled in the presence of ladies, the "simply horrible" architecture, the "singularly unintellectual" papers given at the Bohemian Club, and the general tone ("low, low, low"). As a believer in civil service reform and clean government, he was especially appalled by the local politics. "In California everybody expects everything in the legislative way to be *bought*. The Southern Pacific has the state by the throat here, and expresses its contempt for the people along its lines in the frankest way." He went about his work, wishing he were back in Manhattan. But the trip seemed worthwhile when he found a local treasure. "My great discovery here," he wrote home, flourishing the news like a gold strike, "is John Muir."

The editor and the silent writer had arranged to meet one night at Johnson's hotel in San Francisco. Acquaintances in the city had warned him to expect a queer man, cranky and reclusive, and the first impression fitted the image. As Johnson dressed for dinner in his room, he heard a plaintive voice down the hall: "Johnson, Johnson! Where are you?" Muir had managed to find his way to the hotel but then had gone astray in the baffling, civilized maze of floors and corridors. Johnson rescued him; they talked for three hours, presumably with Johnson doing most of the listening. In New York he often met striking personalities and famous people at his clubs. Muir still swept him away. He took careful note of his find: "Muir is of my height, slender, thin in the leg, a farmer-looking man, black, curly hair, full long brown beard, graying near the ears where it is more closely kept, a keen gray eye, deep-set, a nose of graceful and delicate profile and with sensitive lines in the high forehead and about the eyes. His temples are rather hollow. He has quite a Scotch air in a fatigue suit of blue with a black slouch hat, and his movements are rather meditative, but show enthusiasm on occasion."

Each man imagined he was stalking the other. Both had ulterior motives — Johnson to revive a stalled literary career, Muir to enlist the prestigious *Century* on behalf of California's threatened wilderness. A few days later Johnson came out to Martinez. Louie impressed him ("a most intelligent woman"), not least as a potential ally ("and deplores the inactivity of Muir's pen"). The two men went for a long drive through valleys filled with birds and flowers, Muir providing a reverent commentary. "He invests every growing thing with human motives," Johnson noted tolerantly. Muir shrugged off the editor's first recruiting effort, explaining that he could not write about Emerson's stay in Yosemite because Emerson had *forced* him to do all the talking. But they did agree, each for his own purposes, to go camping in Yosemite themselves. "How much we will be able to accomplish," Muir confided to Louie, "will depend upon the snow and the legs and resolution of the Century."

The trip brought together a fertile conjunction of magazine, editor, writer, and issue. The *Century* under Johnson's boss, Richard Watson Gilder, was at its height, paying top price to the best writers in America. In fiction it championed the younger American realists; a single issue in 1885 included stories by James, Twain, and Howells. Aiming to be independent of European cultural standards, it was prodding native art and politics toward a greater maturity. With the Civil War still a touchy memory, the magazine's greatest success had been a recent series called "Battles and Leaders of the Civil War," a nonpartisan collection of memoirs by veterans from both sides. Riding that crest, the *Century* had paid $50,000 — an unheard-of fee — for the Lincoln biography by Nicolay and Hay. Johnson's project on California pioneers was planned as an appropriate successor to the Civil War series. In politics the *Century* campaigned for tenement improvement, an international literary copyright, free art, the gold standard, the Australian ballot, and an end to the political spoils system and boss rule. As Muir and Johnson set out for Yosemite, the current issue entered a new list by urging the protection of all forests on federal land and the appointment of a commission to draw up a national forestry plan. Every month a thick copy of the *Century*, with its striking cover designed by Stanford White, went into over two hundred thousand of the most influential American homes. It dominated the field of polite magazines.

Johnson, himself a dominant personality, came along at the right time in Muir's career. During the next decade he would assume the role of Jeanne Carr: introducing Muir to useful people, extending his horizons, pushing him to write, and in general mediating between him and the everyday world. To these varied editorial tasks Johnson brought an irresistible blend of good manners and unrelenting insistence. He passionately observed all the polite amenities of life, refusing to soil himself in the commercial bustle of New York. Arriving at the *Century* office in the morning, he would offer punctilious greeting to every staff member. "Leisurely he would place his hat on top of his desk," another editor recalled, "leisurely seat himself, leisurely take off his glasses and polish them." After sorting his correspondence into neat little piles, he at last would plunge into the day's work. He

Muir at his desk in his upstairs study, about 1912 (Muir Papers, Holt-Atherton Pacific Center for Western Studies)

Jeanne C. Carr, the major intellectual influence on Muir's early life, in 1876 (Muir Papers, Holt-Atherton Pacific Center for Western Studies)

Robert Underwood Johnson, editor of Century *magazine, who served as Muir's mentor and publicist in eastern literary circles (American Academy and Institute of Arts and Letters)*

Charles Sprague Sargent, director of the Arnold Arboretum and Muir's best friend in Boston, photographed in the Arboretum, 1904, by J. Horace McFarland (Permission to reproduce this photograph granted by the Arnold Arboretum. © President and Fellows of Harvard College, 1981)

Gifford Pinchot, creator and first head of the U.S. Forest Service, was Theodore Roosevelt's most trusted advisor on conservation (Yale Alumni Records Office)

John and Louie Muir, with their daughters Wanda (left) and Helen, photographed in 1901 on the front porch of the house in Martinez, four years before Louie's death (Muir Papers, Holt-Atherton Pacific Center for Western Studies)

Muir, the unlikely literary celebrity (extreme left), captioned this August 1910 photograph "Wild mood" (Muir Papers, Holt-Atherton Pacific Center for Western Studies)

After two nights of camping out in May 1903, Muir and Theodore Roosevelt on the Yosemite floor; Half Dome rises in the background (Theodore Roosevelt Collection, Harvard College Library)

Muir holding forth to a Sierra Club outing on the trail to Hetch Hetchy (Muir Papers, Holt-Atherton Pacific Center for Western Studies)

George B. Dorr, Boston Brahmin and spiritualist, who led the movement to establish Acadia National Park (Bar Harbor Historical Society)

George Bird Grinnell, the ubiquitous early leader of eastern conservation, and editor and publisher of Forest and Stream *(Yale Alumni Records Office)*

William Temple Hornaday, director of the Bronx Zoo and a classic example of the repentant hunter (American Museum of Natural History)

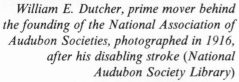

William E. Dutcher, prime mover behind the founding of the National Association of Audubon Societies, photographed in 1916, after his disabling stroke (National Audubon Society Library)

Will H. Dilg, an ardent bass fisherman and the most active founder of the Izaak Walton League (Izaak Walton League)

Willard G. Van Name, maverick conservationist at the American Museum of Natural History (American Museum of Natural History)

Rosalie Edge, exemplar of the amateur conservationist tradition, at the Hawk Mountain Sanctuary, in Pennsylvania, ab 1940 (Courtesy of Peter Edge)

Irving and Hazeldean Brant with their daughter Robin atop Mount Katahdin in Maine in the early 1950s (Courtesy of Robin Brant Lodewick)

was always the last to leave the office. His photographs suggest the hard steel beneath the manners: a handsome, distant man, elegantly dressed and groomed, with an extremely firm jaw. (As late as 1936, he asked Franklin Roosevelt to complete the international copyright law and abolish the spoils system.)

Fifteen years younger than Muir, of Quaker and Scotch Presbyterian background, Johnson grew up in a small town in Indiana. There, according to his autobiography, he "imbibed from its associations a conservatism that it is hard to inculcate in the less stable life of cities." As a junior editor in the 1870s, he left New York for weekend trips into the country. A few years later, in his first act as a conservationist, he helped extend the East River Park some four blocks to Ninetieth Street. A young state representative, Theodore Roosevelt, pushed a bill through the legislature to condemn the land. (When TR ran for mayor in 1886, the *Century* staff turned out en masse.) Nature attracted Johnson essentially on an esthetic level. Unlike Muir, he had no preference between the beauties of nature and human invention. As he summarized the matter in his poem "Divided Honors," written in 1888:

> *Nature rose,*
> *Impressive in her artless pose,*
> *And in a few words fitly chose*
> *(Confined to generalities)*
> *Pleaded the* nature *of the thing —*
> *That singers born to sing* must sing, . . .
> *And hid in trope and allegory*
> *A whole campaign of* a priori. . . .
> *Then Art began to plead* her *cause;*
> *Said Nature's windy words had flaws —*
> *That e'en the larklet soaring high*
> *Must surely once have* learned *to fly*
> *And eke to sing. Moreover, Song*
> *Is something more than baby-prattle;*
> *Or plow-boy's carol to the cattle.*

But in going after articles from Muir, Johnson displayed no such ambivalence.

In June 1889 Muir was ready to be badgered. Having gradually freed himself from the farm, he had more time for trips and writing. The previous summer's travels had pricked his dormant conscience as a defender of the wilderness. For years he had worried intermittently about conditions in and around Yosemite. The original federal grant to the state, which extended only about a mile around the valley perimeter, was slackly administered by a vulnerable commission appointed by the governor. The eight commissioners met only twice a year. Unpaid except for expenses and subject to removal, easily influenced by political pressure, they barely functioned at all as protectors of the valley. Yosemite, one of the most celebrated wilderness spots in the United States, was adorned by butcher shops, vegetable stalls, saloons, lumberyards, wheat- and hayfields, a fragrant pigsty, and ramshackle hostels. One local entrepreneur had even adjusted the flow of Nevada Fall, diverting a side cascade to ensure a more impressive flow for tourists. "Tinkering the Yosemite waterworks would seem about the last branch of industry that even Yankee ingenuity would be likely to undertake," Muir exclaimed. "Perhaps we may yet hear of an appropriation to whitewash the face of El Capitan or correct the curves of the Domes."

As Yosemite had inspired the first stage of his literary career, it now inspired the second. Muir and Johnson arrived on the afternoon of June 3. With all its human improvements, the valley could still bludgeon one's senses. "The first impression is wonder that there should be so much in so small a space," Johnson noted. "The total effect is overwhelming so that you don't take it in at first, but are surprised anew at each new look." Back in his spiritual home, Muir frisked around looking up old friends and sights. Lifting his attention past trampled meadows and tree stumps, he focused on the flowers and sugar pines of the foothills. "All seems so new," he wrote Louie, "I fancy I could take up the study of these mountain glories with fresh enthusiasm, as if I were getting into a sort of second youth or dotage."

After a day in Yosemite they hired mules and a trail cook, and climbed out of the valley into the high country to the north. Once outside the state reservation they found substantial damage from sheep — Muir's beloved hoofed locusts — in the federally owned mountain meadows. Signs of illegal lumbering were also seen. Muir and Johnson spent the first night in a cabin by Lake Tenaya. Next day they pushed on to the meadows and canyon of the Tuolumne River, about a dozen miles north of Yosemite. Here, at a site by Tuolumne Falls, Muir introduced his eastern friend to the High Sierra's outdoor sleeping accommodations: a spruce bed, heavy blankets, and a canopy of what Johnson remembered as "the biggest stars I have ever seen." In the morning the sun rose over the eastern peaks, "a revelation of glory." Johnson was absorbing the intended message.

They spent the day tramping by the river, Muir dancing from rock to rock, Johnson wheezing in pursuit, Muir taking gleeful amusement from the tenderfoot but then rewarding him. "Muir knows of but three other persons who have been down this river," Johnson proudly informed his wife later. That night, lying by the campfire, the two men discussed the situation. Obviously the Tuolumne gorge, in fact all the headwaters feeding into Yosemite, needed better protection. The valley itself, under state aegis, seemed beyond reform. But Johnson proposed the creation of a national preserve on the federal land around the valley proper. It could be modeled on Yellowstone National Park, established by Congress in 1872, the first and as yet the only such protected area in the United States. They struck a bargain: if Muir would write two articles for the magazine, Johnson would add his editorial support and lobby his friends in Washington. The writer, the editor, and the *Century* would launch a campaign for a Yosemite National Park.

❧ II ❧

THE AMERICAN CONSERVATION MOVEMENT

1890-1975

4

Land, Trees, and Water, 1890-1915

THE campaign for Yosemite set a pattern to be repeated many times in future public quarrels over the environment. At stake: a piece of the natural world. On one side: its defenders, spearheaded by amateurs with no economic stake in the outcome, who took time from other jobs to volunteer time and money for the good fight. On the other side: the enemy, usually joining the struggle *because of* their jobs, with a direct economic or professional interest in the matter and (therefore) selfish motives. Politics seldom lends itself to such simple morality plays. But environmental issues have usually come down to a stark alignment of white hats and black hats.

Muir and Johnson, in raising the Yosemite issue, were bearding three entrenched clusters of commercial interest. By pointing out woeful conditions in the valley itself they collided with the local entrepreneurs, notably the Yosemite Stage and Turnpike Company, which brought tourists from distant railroad stations and ran some concessions in the valley. The governing state commission paid close attention to the company's wishes. On a second level, by proposing a federal reserve around the valley Muir and Johnson threatened to displace the cattlemen and sheepherders, and occasional lumbermen, who made free use of the land. Third and most crucially, California politics danced to the tune called by the Southern Pacific Railroad. The SP ran a spur line to Raymond, one of the embarking points for the Yosemite stage, and had a moderate interest in valley conditions. "The valley is going to destruction," Johnson told Gilder at the *Century,* "in the hands of a political Commission owned by the Southern Pacific — as everything and everybody seems to be." The *Century* often inveighed against the corruption of politics by corporate power; Yosemite seemed a case in point. "The valley," said Johnson, "is an instance of monopolies at the public expense." Esthetic matters aside, the issue fitted the magazine's gently reformist political tradition.

The leader of the Yosemite opposition, John P. Irish, was precisely the type of man to curl the patrician whiskers of the *Century*. A Democratic wheelhorse and editor of an Oakland newspaper, Irish also served as secretary and treasurer of the Yosemite board of commissioners. A few years later he acted as agent for a local cattlemen's association. When Muir and Johnson indicted the Yosemite management, they specifically had Irish in mind. Of course Irish took the general criticism personally, as a threat to his own political ambitions (he ran unsuccessfully for Congress in 1890). He dismissed Muir as "a pseudo naturalist." Conversely, Irish reinforced Muir's worst prejudices about politicians feeding at the public trough. As Muir summarized the situation in a letter to Johnson:

> *John P.*
> *Irish he*
> *Says let Yosemite Valley be*
> *Or else you'll catch the Devil*
> *Or me*
> *But who the devil says the people*
> *Is he?*

It came down in Muir's mind to the popular will against interested businessmen and their paid political errand boys.

The approach, then, was to sidestep local politics and appeal to national public opinion through the *Century* for the scheme originally hatched by the two men at a Tuolumne campfire. ("The 'proposed reservation,' " Johnson reminded Muir, "is only proposed by you and me.") During the fall of 1889 Johnson started agitating among his eastern friends and concurrently embarked on a campaign within the campaign: to extract an article from Muir's glacially paced pen. Muir pleaded other work, the farm, the family, the hired hands. Johnson remained implacable. "I began that confounded letter a dozen times," wrote Muir. "You would have written such a letter in half an hour, and no doubt would like to see me hanged for not being able to write it in a month." Again: "I never can tell how anything I begin of a literary kind will end. Sometimes my descriptions are contemptibly mean and lean and scrawny, without any color or atmosphere about them, again they are all fluffily sentimentous drifting about unguided and foundationless as mist, too thin for any terrestrial use." A

Scotch conscience might not hold him to his desk, but it dealt ruthlessly with what he so agonizingly produced. January 1890, still no article for Johnson: "To write to order and measure I am about the worst hand you could find."

By then Johnson had fired his first guns in the magazine with an editorial and supporting statements by other interested Californians. In March a congressman from Los Angeles, William Vandever, introduced a bill for a limited Yosemite reserve of about 288 square miles, excluding both Lake Tenaya and the Tuolumne River watershed. Heading for Washington and a session with the House Committee on Public Lands, Johnson asked Muir for an "emphatic" statement of the need for a larger reserve. Under this duress the obdurate pen moved more quickly, arguing for the inclusion of the Tuolumne meadows and canyon on the north and the Mariposa sequoia grove on the south. The whole park, surrounding the state reservation in the center, was "worthless" for mining or agriculture — "not valuable for any other use," said Muir, "than the use of beauty." The campaign picked up speed. The landscape architect Frederick Law Olmsted, whom Johnson had earlier tried to hire to make a report on the management of the valley, sent an open letter ("a little soft," Muir thought) to the newspapers. The New York *Evening Post* and other eastern papers fell into line. California Senator George Hearst, his influential wife, and his rambunctious son all agreed with the measure. "The Yosemite Century leaven is working finely even thus far throughout California," Muir reported.

Two articles by Muir finally appeared in the August and September 1890 issues of the *Century,* his first appearance in a national publication in eight years. Along with his usual rhapsodic descriptions of the region, he made the case for protection from sheep and certain human species. "Even under the protection of the Government, all that is perishable is vanishing apace," he warned. "The ground is already being gnawed and trampled into a desert condition, and when the region shall be stripped of its forests the ruin will be complete." The proposed park might still be used with due care by humans, but the mindless, unnecessary destruction would be stopped. The Vandever bill should therefore pass in some form.

At this point unlikely help arrived from the dread Southern Pacific. In June 1889, a few weeks after his Yosemite trip with Muir, Johnson had tried to enlist the monarchical hand of Leland Stanford, then head of the railroad. Stanford was noncommittal. The following spring, after a bitter internecine quarrel, Collis Huntington had replaced his old partner as president of the SP. Under Stanford the line had been well hated for its iron control of state politics. In taking over Huntington announced, to general disbelief, a withdrawal from political meddling. "Is it not possible," Olmsted wrote Johnson, "that Huntington's promised reform of the Southern Pacific will have a good influence in this Yosemite matter?" Apparently it did. All but invisibly, so as not to burden the Vandever bill with the SP tarnish, the railroad's lobby moved behind the measure. The park advocates were perplexed. The SP line to Raymond was not heavily traveled, and the railroad had no substantial economic stake in the matter. Perhaps it was just an oblique attempt at improved public relations by the new management. In any case, the Vandever bill, enlarged five times over by Muir's recommended additions, was suddenly enacted in September. "Even the soulless Southern Pacific R.R. Co.," Muir later recalled in wonderment, "never counted on for anything good, helped nobly in pushing the bill for this park through Congress."

Along with outlawing sheep and lumbermen from fifteen hundred square miles of the Sierra, the creation of this second national park had two other effects. It relaunched Muir on a literary career. His readers, it turned out, had not forgotten those vivid pieces about the water ouzel and the Yuba windstorm from the late 1870s. "Everyone has been so delighted to find Mr. Muir again in print," a woman wrote Louie from Washington. "I hope that you will keep him to it." As this new career unfolded, he broadened his range to include public affairs, mainly the protection of the wilderness. He wrote public letters, gave interviews, told his Stickeen story to audiences of politicians, and marveled, he said, "at my temerity in thus plunging into this field." Usually he had the faithful Johnson at his elbow, offering an endless stream of suggestions, introductions, praise, and scolding. "You have taken your hand *off* the plow," said Johnson, "and should not look back."

The park campaign also led to a permanent organization of its friends. In the fall of 1889 Johnson, always popping with ideas, had proposed an "association for preserving California's monuments and natural wonders." At the time Muir was not persuaded: "I would gladly do anything in my power to preserve Nature's sayings and doings here or elsewhere but have no genius for managing societies." The thought of delivering speeches and presiding at meetings rendered him mute, no small feat. Johnson dropped the suggestion, leaving the initiative to Californians.

In the spring of 1892 Henry Senger, a German-born philologist at Berkeley, approached Muir with the idea of starting a local "Alpine club" of mountain lovers. Muir put him in touch with a university colleague, William D. Armes of the English Department. On May 25 the two professors sent out invitations to a meeting at the office of Warren Olney, an attorney in San Francisco, "for the purpose of forming a 'Sierra Club.' Mr. John Muir will preside." (It was necessary, perhaps Muir reasoned, to skirt perils in a good cause.) At the meeting they launched an organization on the model of the Appalachian Mountain Club. Muir was elected president, an office he would hold until the end of his life. He went home jubilant with the news. "I had never seen Mr. Muir so animated and happy before," a supper guest at Martinez recalled. "Hitherto, his back to the wall, he had carried on his fight to save the wilderness. In the Sierra Club he saw the crystallization of the dreams and labor of a lifetime."

Within weeks the club was looking into the cutting of underbrush in Yosemite and fighting off a bill in Congress to reduce the park's boundaries. Muir still chafed in his unaccustomed role ("this formal, legal, unwild work is out of my line"). But with the wilderness at stake he settled grumblingly into the routine of administration, making appointments and calling meetings. With his name and voice as the focus, after a few months the club had 175 members and was launched on its distinguished history. "The battle we have fought," he told the Sierrans in 1895, "and are still fighting, for the forests is a part of the eternal conflict between right and wrong, and we cannot expect to see the end of it." The Yosemite issue would come up again.

❊❊

Conservation began as a hobby and became a profession. The early history of the movement returns again and again to this simple change of such complex implications. The first public alarms about endangered wildlife, trees, rivers, and wilderness were raised by enthusiasts like Muir who might take firmly practical ground in arguing their cases but who acted ultimately from a love of unspoiled nature. Muir might point out the alleged benefits of Sierra forests in regulating rainfall and preventing erosion. But what really piqued him was the wanton blasphemy of cutting down a sequoia grove that predated the Christian era. So it went: Audubon society members would cite the useful role of birds in controlling insects, but they most cared about birdsong and the flash of color on the wing. Within a few years these avocations turned into jobs and conservation was transformed. Forestry became a profession more intent on board feet than esthetics; wildlife protection was lodged in a government bureau responding to political lobbies and gun companies. Embarrassed by its sentimental origins, conservation aimed to be a science.

This evolution took place during the epoch of political and social reforms that historians call the progressive era. As one of these progressive reforms, conservation moved in lockstep with the larger context of the time. The avocational phase in its tone and class aspects duplicated the origins of progressivism: moralistic, evangelical, ethnically nativist if not racist, wealthy, and offended by the corruptions of politics. Antimodern and skeptical of technological progress, it invoked a vision of the pre-industrial community when people lived closer to the land and the natural rhythms of life. This cast of mind was epitomized in the East by the Boone and Crockett Club, the group of gentleman big game hunters organized by Theodore Roosevelt and George Bird Grinnell. Dedicated hunters, the Boone and Crockett men also hoped to preserve big game for its own sake — and as a way of staving off the march of modern progress.

In the early years of the new century this informal, amateur approach yielded to the modernist trends of professionalization and bureaucratization. As a hobby, conservation could enlist only the sporadic attention of its acolytes. "The club gets together once or twice a year and eats a dinner," Grinnell noted in 1904, "and talks about what ought to be done; a few of its members talk from time to time with influential people, trying to push or prevent this or that measure, and that is really all that we do." The times demanded something more. Professional conservationists in government bureaus led the way. Again conservation mirrored broader trends in progressivism: a shift toward expertise, "scientific management," planning, and ideals of economy, efficiency, stability. Instead of looking back to the lost world of nature, the professional conservationists welcomed the urbanized present and future, describing bright prospects in the crisp, desiccated patois of engineering. Nature herself had no rights, no function as a refuge for citified moderns. The world was, after all, made for man. "There are just two things on this material earth," said one professional, "— people and natural resources." User and used, in the spirit of the first chapter of Genesis.

The general acceptance of the term itself, conservation, reflected the triumph of the utilitarian approach. The amateur pioneers typically referred to the "protection" or "preservation" of the environment, often with the goal of absolute exclusion from human use. By contrast, "conservation" as applied to forests as early as 1875 and to rivers by 1890 suggested only a more prudent, more efficient use by humans — not an absolute exclusion. Given these implications, Muir seldom used the term. After 1907 "conservation" was applied to everything that needed environmental protection.

In this broader sense the word passed into everyday language, the original distinction lost.

〰〰

As Muir said, it started as a battle for the forests. Of all living things he liked trees best. They appealed to him as the most formidable, the oldest and biggest, of organisms. In their slow, inexorable life cycles they resembled his beloved glaciers. They lived out their centuries, performing useful tasks without harming anything. In this way, and in their implicit attitude toward the chimeras of progress, they could instruct the humans bustling around their feet with axes. "I never saw a discontented tree," said Muir. "They grip the ground as though they liked it, and though fast rooted they travel about as far as we do." When humans clear-cut an ancient forest, it seemed a metaphor to Muir of where modern civilization had gone wrong. Obviously some timber had to be cut — "for every right use" — but the prevailing wasteful methods and the destruction of old, rare species like the California redwoods were inexcusable even on the most practical economic grounds.

The forestry division of the Agriculture Department, created in 1876, was given neither money nor power by Congress. Real forest protection in America began among dedicated amateurs outside government. Of these the leading figure was the botanist Charles Sprague Sargent, director of the Arnold Arboretum at Harvard. R. U. Johnson considered him nothing less than "the authority on trees." A Brahmin of great personal wealth, born on the edge of Boston Common, Sargent typified early conservationists in his class and ethnic background. His financial independence — and growling irascibility — freed him to join any cause that struck his fancy. Inspired by George Perkins Marsh's pioneering work *Man and Nature,* Sargent in 1880 undertook a survey of American forests for the federal government. The findings convinced him of the need for reform. At his prodding, the American Forestry Association, mainly a group of horticulturists, endorsed his plan for the protection of federally owned timber pending a complete study by a commission of experts. (The *Century* had endorsed Sargent's proposals as Muir and Johnson set out for Yosemite in June 1889.) Asa Gray had introduced Sargent to Muir in 1878, but the relationship had lapsed during Muir's farmer days. In the early 1890s Johnson brought them back together.

A novel idea caught between public indifference and corporate hostility, forest protection was introduced by a combination of subterfuge and executive fiat. In March 1891 an amendment to a general land law passed all but unnoticed through Congress. "Probably no one who read over the bill before it became law understood what the section meant," George Bird Grinnell later recalled. The amendment authorized the President to create "forest reserves" by withdrawing federal land from the public domain. A bench mark in conservation history, this Section 24 was thought up by William Hallett Phillips, a Washington lawyer and society figure. Active in the Boone and Crockett Club, he joined other gentleman sportsmen in their worries over the headlong rush of progress. Every summer he shouldered his gun and escaped to the wilderness. (According to his boon companion Henry Adams, Phillips "loved to play Indian hunter without hunting so much as a field-mouse.") Using the powers granted by Section 24, in two years President Benjamin Harrison, at the behest of Secretary of the Interior John W. Noble, proclaimed fifteen reserves totaling some thirteen million acres — including one of four million acres running along the crest of the Sierra, south of Yosemite, for two hundred miles. "I had no idea," Johnson exclaimed, "that Noble was going to do so much." Under the authority of Section 24, he acted with neither public support nor congressional assent.

Conservation was never more an elitist conspiracy than at its birth. Sargent, Muir, Johnson, and the Boone and Crockett men were leaders without portfolio, often pulling strings without taking their case to the public. When the reaction came, it spoke the rhetoric of bypassed democracy. Section 24 only authorized the establishment of the reserves, leaving undefined the details of administration. In the fall of 1893 Muir and Johnson went to Washington for a talk with Noble's successor at Interior, Hoke Smith, and others involved in forest affairs. Muir no doubt mentioned the error in letting sheep continue to graze the reserves. The following spring, Smith obligingly banned such grazing — to democratic protests from stockmen. Later that year the New York State constitutional convention, under Sargent's influence, declared the vast Adirondack state forest "forever wild." The advocates of absolute protection for forests seemed to be gathering strength. Late in 1894 Johnson gathered a *Century* symposium on Sargent's plan for forestry instruction at West Point and Army patrols to defend the reserves from poachers. "Now, at this darkest time," Muir declared in his contribution, "the light of a better day begins to dawn."

The symposium included a dissenting opinion from an unknown twenty-nine-year-old Yale graduate. Instead of the Army, Gifford Pinchot suggested, supervision of the reserves should belong to "a forest service, a commission of scientifically trained men." As the first American to take up forestry as a profession, Pinchot presumably had himself in mind. Born a Connecticut Yankee, brought up in Paris and Pennsylvania, a man of wealth and family, he shared the genteel love of nature spurring on his associates in conversation. After college he had studied forestry in Europe and returned home with a zeal to transfer the lessons learned in Germany and France: trees could not only be protected but *managed* for sustained yields. Thus in his own person Pinchot embodied the transition from amateur protection to scientific management. Not an originator of ideas, he excelled as a synthesizer, publicist, and self-advertiser. Historians in general have too readily accepted his word that he invented conservation. He is widely regarded as the great pioneer in the movement, while Grinnell, Johnson, and Sargent are barely recognized. Actually, Pinchot appeared on the scene rather late and he borrowed freely from his predecessors.

After meeting Muir in New York in 1893, Pinchot cultivated his friendship, thanking Muir for his "kindness and interest in my work," hoping for a chance to see him again: "I have more than ever to talk over with you, and much advice to ask." In writing one of his forestry teachers in Europe, Pinchot praised Muir's "store of scientific observation" and his "unparalleled acquaintance with the mountains." Separated by twenty-seven years and a social gulf, the two men were never intimates; attracted by motives of forest protection and careerism, Pinchot asked for advice and Muir gave it. Muir told him to strike into the wilderness by himself in order to learn more with fewer distractions. Pinchot tried it for the first time in the spring of 1894. "In a very small way," he told Muir, "I have tried your plan of going alone." He did feel his senses sharpened without companions, although "I am afraid that I shall never be able to do the amount of hard work that you have done, or get along on such slender rations." (A half century later Pinchot recalled this initiation without mentioning Muir as the instigator — a trivial instance of a regrettably too-characteristic trait.)

At first he presented himself to Muir as an acolyte. At the same time he took positions foreshadowing their bitter quarrels of later years. After touring Yosemite he called on John P. Irish, praising the state management of the valley and dismissing the *Century*'s criticisms. At the New York constitutional convention he opposed the "forever wild" clause because it forbade lumbering in the Adirondack forest. He submitted all public questions to a simple formula: "the greatest good of the greatest number in the long run." Unarguably democratic on its face, the formula raised an insoluble question of values. Any effort to compute the greatest good bore an inherent bias toward *material* advantages, to be weighed or counted and factored in. How to quantify a pristine wilderness? What good was it? As a popularizer, Pinchot aimed for the lowest common denominator of public opinion; actually he spent most of his adult life not in forestry but in politics. The amateur pioneers of the movement hated politics and doubted the people could appreciate what they were doing. "We have got to act promptly and secretly in these matters," Sargent once confided to Muir, "or the politicians will overwhelm us." Pinchot ultimately turned out to be a consummate politician.

In December 1894 Pinchot met with Sargent and Johnson in New York to plot strategy toward Sargent's pet project of a government-sponsored forest commission. During the next year they obtained endorsements from business groups — notably the New York Board of Trade and Chamber of Commerce — impressed by their assertions of the effect of trees on water supplies. Stalled in Congress, they again bypassed normal channels by persuading Hoke Smith to ask the National Academy of Sciences to sponsor the commission; then they needed only a congressional appropriation of $25,000 in lieu of a fully detailed bill. With the money the six-man commission set out in the summer of 1896 to make a survey of western forests. For Pinchot, the youngest and least known of the group, the trip meant his big break in national forestry circles. ("It is badly on my conscience," Sargent later recalled, "that I started his career.")

Muir joined the commission in Chicago in an ex-officio capacity. They zigzagged through the West, finding variable food and lodgings, riding "hundreds of miles on animals of mysterious wearisome gait and motion," as Muir noted: "I never before saw men who minded hardship less in urging a way through their appointed work." Only Sargent, it seemed, knew and loved trees as he did. But he also felt himself drawn to Pinchot as they went camping together for the first time. At the Grand Canyon Muir stopped him from killing a tarantula, explaining that "it had as much right there as we did." That night the two men left the others and slept in a cedar grove on the rim of the gorge. Muir — "a storyteller in a million," Pinchot recalled — talked until midnight, recounting his adventure with Stickeen. "In the early morning, we sneaked back like guilty schoolboys." Politics aside, during that cold, cedar-scented night they found common ground in their love of the wilderness.

Differences emerged when the commission tried to agree on a report. The members had seen enough ruined forests to accept some kind of formal protection. "There has been a good deal of volunteer work done in the line of trying to preserve our forests," Muir pointed out. "In fact, about all the work done ... heretofore has been volunteer." Conditions dictated a more professional approach. In the spirit of civil service reform, Muir and H. L. Abbott of the Army Engineers supported Sargent's old scheme to remove forest protection from politics by giving it to the Army. Muir had seen the good results of Army patrols in Yosemite over the last few years. Pinchot, joined by Arnold Hague of the Geological Survey, again urged the creation of a civilian, professional forest service. The Sargent group wanted to keep the reserves inviolate, while Pinchot and Hague favored regulated use. The Sargent view won on most points. The final report favored Army patrols and banned sheep grazing, but did leave the door ajar for lumbering and mineral exploration. Pinchot thought about publishing a minority dissent but finally signed the report, "bad as it is."

In the West a political storm was gathering in reaction to the policy of reserves by executive edict. A congressman from San Diego, William Bowers, warned that soon the whole state would be one large forest reservation. In the Northwest, lumber companies were stirring up their friends in Congress. The storm broke in February 1897, when President Cleveland, in the last days of his administration, approved the Sargent commission's request for thirteen new reserves totalling 21.4 million acres. (Four years earlier, Harrison had also declared most of *his* reserves just before leaving office.) "The western politicians are out for blood," Sargent advised Muir. The Senate amended a sundry civil bill to annul the new reserves; Cleveland threatened to veto the whole bill, and the amendment was withdrawn, leaving the issue to the new administration of William McKinley. Johnson and Sargent went to Washington to lobby the President and Secretary of the Interior Cornelius Bliss, eventually persuading them to keep the reserves.

All that spring of 1897 Congress was sporadically occupied with the issue. According to one observer in Washington, Theodore Roosevelt, less than a dozen senators favored the reserves policy. But did the Senate speak for the people or for a few business interests? Muir addressed the problem in an article for *Harper's Weekly,* his most explicitly political writing to date. "Much is said on questions of this kind about 'the greatest good for the greatest number,' " he wrote, nodding toward Pinchot, "but the greatest number is too often found to be number one. It is never the greatest number in the common meaning of the term that make the greatest noise and stir on questions mixed with money. . . . Complaints are made in the name of poor settlers and miners, while the wealthy corporations are kept carefully hidden in the background." Businessmen, in short, were concealing their simple greed behind democratic sentiment. The public should not be deceived, said Muir; every acre of the remaining federal forest land not suitable for farming needed permanent protection. In the Northwest sheepmen and prospectors were burning off forest cover, regarding trees not even as board feet but as weeds. "Let right, commendable industry be fostered," Muir concluded; "but as to these Goths and Vandals of the wilderness, who are spreading black death in the fairest woods God ever made, let the government up and at 'em."

No use; Congress had lost patience with unilateral action by the White House. In June it passed the Forest Management Act, suspending all but two of Cleveland's reserves for nine months pending further study and — a further blow — reversing Hoke Smith's 1894 ruling by opening the existing reserves to mining and grazing. A few weeks later Secretary Bliss appointed Pinchot his special agent to make the new investigations. Instead of fighting the political reaction, the administration was feeding it by entrusting the reserves to an agent with a known bias toward human use. His old colleagues felt betrayed. "One feeble part of the Forestry Commission," Muir wrote Sargent, "has thus been given the work that had already most ably been done by the whole, without even mentioning what had been done. For a parallel to this in downright darkness and idiotic stupidity the records of civilization may be searched in vain." That summer Bliss, with Pinchot's approval, let sheep into the Oregon and Washington reserves. Pinchot also urged a general policy of regulated lumbering in the reserves. Sargent was humiliated. Having advanced Pinchot's career, he now accused the younger man of selling out the forests for a political appointment. Pinchot, flinching from a thrust rather close to the mark, wanted to reply in kind but was dissuaded. "Keep cool," Arnold Hague advised him. "You owe something to Professor Sargent and much to the Forestry Commission."

Discouraging times for the pioneers of forest protection. "What are we to do about forest matters?" Muir asked Sargent in January 1898. "The sky looks mighty black and blue and I have no plan, system, or trick to save them. I mean simply to go on hammering and thumping as best I can at public opinion." In the spring the Senate tried to abolish all Cleveland's reserves. Muir wrote letters and mobilized the Sierra Club while Sargent and others lobbied Congress, and the measure died in the House. But bad news kept coming. Pinchot was appointed head of the forestry division in Agriculture. Some two hundred thousand sheep were allowed into the Sierra reserve. "Clearly it is time to begin another crusade," Sargent wrote Muir, "but who has the time and strength to do it and what good is coming out of it all?" Sargent's *Garden and Forest* magazine had expired after ten insolvent years. His best proposals were being undone with the approval of a man he had helped. As Pinchot's career took off, Sargent withdrew to his arboretum and retired from the struggle, understandably embittered. "There is no one but you and I," he dolefully wrote Muir in 1902, "who really love the North American trees."

Barely under way, the conservation movement was already split into warring factions of utilitarians and preservationists. "The whole question is a practical one," Pinchot insisted to Muir. This view of nature as a commodity — the world made for man — came to dominate professional circles and government bureaus. Private groups, with no financial or career stake in the matter, and with the time and taste to consider intangibles, took the opposite view. "It is true that trees are for human use," Joseph Le Conte noted in the *Sierra Club Bulletin.* "But there are aesthetic uses as well as commercial uses — uses for the spiritual wealth of all, as well as for the material wealth of some." "While the Club urges with others the economic necessities," said Allen Chamberlain of the Appalachian Mountain Club, ". . . it seems to be its especial province to put forward the aesthetic arguments in the case." The argument boiled down to semantics: Pinchot winced at words like "aesthetic." To Muir such words meant more than board feet and votes in Congress.

In part through Johnson's mediation, Muir and Pinchot stayed in touch with each other. They camped together in the wilderness in 1898 and 1899. But the lines were drawn.

❧❧

All parties to the issue of forest protection agreed on one point. The public domain was running out. The preservers wanted to save the remaining trees, the conservers to use them more wisely, the business adversaries to use them without hindrance. But none could escape the historical context. At the end of its pioneer epoch, American society was being transformed. The census of 1890 had announced the end of the frontier. Over the next thirty years most of the population completed its shift from the country to cities and towns. Oddly, this urbanization occurred when cities could hardly have been less agreeable: dirtier and smellier than ever before or since, marred by grotesque extremes of rich and poor, governed by corrupt boss regimes resistant to the best efforts of wellborn reformers, split into fragmented communities by the "new immigration" from southern and eastern Europe. Still the cities filled up, making all their problems so much the worse. In reaction, what one observer in 1908 called a "widespread turning to nature" grew among the urban, mainly WASP, middle class. Expressed most clearly in the artifacts of popular culture, this nature fad offered fertile ground for the conservation movement.

It started in cities and spread outward in concentric circles.

Cities: the growth of landscaped parks, playgrounds, zoos, and habitat groups in natural history museums; nature study in schools; sociological critiques of urban life; among political reformers, the antiurban blueprints of Henry George and Edward Bellamy; among the avant garde, the vitalist philosophy of Henri Bergson and the neo-Greek paganism of Isadora Duncan and her imitators.

Suburbs: themselves a sign of the trend, implying a geographical separation of home and workplace and a flight to green lawns and trees; bird watching and horticultural magazines; Frank Lloyd Wright and "organic" architecture, building suburban homes designed to harmonize with the natural site; model "garden cities" inspired by the British planners Ebenezer Howard and Patrick Geddes; the founding of country clubs.

Country: back-to-the-land and country life movements, led by Liberty Hyde Bailey of Cornell; agricultural schools; the cowboy novels of Zane Grey and Owen Wister; summer camps for urban children; a second house in the country, used by city folk during summers and weekends.

Wilderness: field sports; Boy Scouts (1910) and Girl Scouts (1912), teaching wild lore to city children; the dominant historical school of the day, spawned by Frederick Jackson Turner, which described the frontier as the source of American democracy and values; natural history authors like John Burroughs, Jack London, Stewart Edward White, James Oliver Curwood, and especially Gene Stratton Porter, author of the four best-selling novels of the time, all on wilderness themes; the publication of Thoreau's collected works in 1906, leading to a revival of his reputation; the vogue of hiking and mountaineering, as national park visitors increased from 69,000 in 1908 to 200,000 in 1910 and 335,000 in 1915. "The tendency nowadays to wander in wilderness is delightful to see," Muir noted. "Thousands of tired, nerve-shaken, over-civilized people are beginning to find out that going to the mountains is going home; that wildness is a necessity; and that mountain parks and reservations are useful not only as fountains of timber and irrigating rivers, but as fountains of life."

All these bits comprised a sprawling, complex whole. At a time of rampant urbanization, the nature craze implied a nostalgic turning back to recover an imagined, idealized past. The trend also provided a safety valve for nativist worries over the new immigrants and their high birthrates. Immersed in the wilderness, the anxious gentry hoped to recover the lost manly virtues — courage, self-reliance, physical strength and dexterity — and so avoid the specter of "race suicide." Yet to cite historical and psychological factors is to miss the larger, simpler, timeless point that humans *belonged* in contact with the rest of nature and by losing contact lost part of themselves. The explosion of interest during the decades around the turn of the century merely exaggerated a persistent thread in American history. As Morton and Lucia White have shown, the best minds of the nineteenth century had nurtured antiurban suspicions and a corresponding preference for the natural world. This attitude has continued down to the present as a ubiquitous counterpoint to modernization. More than anything else, the nature craze drew from basic human instincts.

Muir's own career fed, and fed on, this trend. The *Century* published his first book, *The Mountains of California,* in 1894. The late-blooming author was fifty-six. After selling out its first printing of fifteen hundred copies in a few months, the book went on to total sales of about ten thousand. In 1897 Muir succumbed to Johnson's prodding and wrote down the Stickeen story for the *Century.* But Johnson alarmed him by cutting the piece ("Remember," he told Muir, "that this is my story as well as yours"). The *Century* had previously held another Muir article for three years and had turned down a forestry piece. Accordingly Muir, with Sargent's intervention, allowed himself to be recruited by Houghton Mifflin. "It's like having a child kidnapped," Johnson pleaded, but his discovery had escaped. Muir's series of articles in the *Atlantic* was published by Houghton Mifflin as *Our National Parks* in 1901. In six years the book went through a dozen printings and established Muir as a major voice of the wilderness. "This is the first of your published works I have met," a reader wrote from New York, "and being of stern necessity tied up to an office business, with the hills and streams out of sight and the love of them strong in me, imagining the delight of seeing the Sierras, of breathing the fine clean air, of making acquaintance with those blessed trees of yours . . . ah, it is a treat, a vacation more enjoyed than many."

All his adult life Muir had been warning about cities and preaching the outdoors. No matter how variable his circumstances, he had changed hardly at all. Finally, in his sixties, he found the public more receptive to his message, even forcing him to write. "Though I never intended to write or lecture or seek fame in any way," he told a companion of his Yosemite years, "I now write a great deal and am well known — strange is it not that a tramp and vagabond without wordly ambition should meet such a fate." He did not entirely lack ambition. Conscious of running out of time, he planned a half dozen books to be drawn from his old journals. Still, his belated prominence derived more from the surging nature cults of the day than from any personal zeal to publish and be famous. No one else combined such a direct knowledge of the wilderness with such an agreeable literary style. Thus Muir functioned as a powerful symbol of widespread cultural yearnings. "A man of genius," declared the journalist Ray Stannard Baker: "a complete expression of a deep human instinct which we have often felt, and throttled — the instinct which urges us to throw off our besieging restraints and complexities, to climb the hills and lie down under the trees, to be simple and natural."

Pushed and supported by the spirit of the times, Muir stood out from his fellow nature advocates in two ways. Generally he put his case in religious terms, however elliptically defined so as not to disturb his Christian readers. "In all this rampant nature study," the editor Walter Hines Page wrote him, "since it has become a fad, there is too little said of its bigger aspects." Muir never shied from the bigger aspects: love of nature demanded the rejection of a mechanistic, godless universe. Second, it could not be loved passively or admired vicariously like a painting. Real appreciation required full immersion, engaging the whole body, leading finally to an urgency to protect the wilderness from "progress." Love of nature, in short, implied conservation. "I owe you," Henry Fairfield Osborn of the American Museum of Natural History told Muir, ". . . an altogether new nature-feeling, and a passion to save it from destruction."

Muir's fame as a wilderness defender, by a fine irony, took him away from the wilderness to meet editors and admirers. Cities still bewildered him. When he visited the *Century* staff in New York, an office boy would be dispatched to lead him back to his hotel. (Even when setting forth into his own San Francisco he would plaintively ask friends: "Can't you meet me at the ferry?") Despite himself he yielded to a few civilized advantages. He loved French bread and good coffee, brewed just so from the finest beans. Champagne could tempt him. He wore suits with less grumbling. These small concessions to urban life left him feeling seduced — enjoyably occupied but worried about the moral implications. Staying at Fairfield Osborn's sumptuous home above the Hudson River, he awoke in the morning on a soft bed of embroidered linen. A servant appeared with coffee. "This morning when I was sipping coffee in bed," he wrote his daughter Helen, "a red squirrel looked in the window at me from a branch of a big tulip tree, and seemed to be saying as he watched me 'Oh John Muir! camping tramping tree-climbing scrambler, Churr Churr, why have you left us, Chip Churr, Who would have thought it?' "

Sometimes he heard the siren's song. Then, as in the old days, he would rebound to the wilderness, still the same man who had wept at finding *Calypso borealis.* He could not understand his friend John Burroughs, whom he had met through Johnson in 1896. Burroughs wrote nature books as a detached observer, denied animal intelligence, accepted a godless universe, and — worst — spoke irreverently of glaciers. All these errors, Muir supposed, derived from spending too much time indoors, reading books in a comfortable study. In 1909 he lured Burroughs to Yosemite. "How is that for a piece of masonry, Johnny?" he exclaimed, pointing out El Capitan. Leading the way to Nevada Fall, he bounded down the trail and, reaching the base of the fall, threw up his hands and shouted "HA!" Another member of the party imagined that Muir and the water were saluting each other. Such exultations did not sway Burroughs, who appreciated the valley in his own restrained, bookish way. "It was fine fun," Muir recalled, "to watch John's face so dreamy and philosophic while interviewing El Capitan and Tissiack and the snowy booming falls."

Muir teased and baited the earnest Seer of Slabsides, arguing every point in his playful, relentless way, painting his less glib adversary into conversational corners. "You are a dear anyway," Burroughs wrote him later, "Scotch obstinacy and all, and I love you, though at times I want to punch you or thrash the ground with you." Both loved nature in their separate ways, the one a book naturalist most at ease on paper, the other a field naturalist most at ease in conversation. ("I have more intellect than character," Burroughs noted after Muir died, "while such a man as John Muir had more character than intellect. . . . He has only half expressed himself in his books — the real Muir is only half there. . . . No one could thoroughly know John Muir, or feel his power, or have any idea of the rank, cantankerous, and withal lovable Scot that he was, until he met him.")

Always Muir told people to experience the wilderness, not just read about it. The Sierra Club in its early years almost expired from a lack of wildness. It held meetings, sent letters to Congress, published its *Bulletin,* but it never actually took people into the mountains. Memberships and interest started to dwindle. "The club seems to be losing ground," Muir noted after an aimless directors meeting in 1895. Three years later: "Our Sierra Club seems half dead." To revive the group Muir and the other leaders talked about sponsoring mountain excursions, as the Appalachian Mountain Club and the Mazamas club of Portland were doing. The idea was tossed around for several years until the fall of 1900, when a young mining lawyer, William E. Colby, persuaded the directors to let him plan a

Yosemite outing for July 1901. In announcing the trip in the *Bulletin,* Colby promised that Muir, "our honored President," would accompany the group.

About a hundred Sierrans, including Muir and his daughters, camped in the open for a month. From a Tuolumne base camp they rambled around the park, returning at night to a bonfire and the prodigies of a legendary Chinese camp cook named Charley Tuck. "The Club outing is a great success," Muir wrote Louie. "God's ozone sparkles in every eye. I never before saw so big and merry a camp circle, a huge fire blazing in the center. I had, of course, to make a little speech." The outings were repeated every summer thereafter, making annual converts to the mountains and recruiting new members for the club. No longer a mere paper organization, the club took on social and educational roles. Within three years of the first outing membership had doubled. "The Sierra Club has great and noble purposes, for which we honor it," one outing enthusiast said, "but besides these its name has come to mean an ideal to us. It means comradeship and chivalry, simplicity and joyousness, and the care-free life of the open." Anyone would return home strengthened and purified: "For a little while you have dwelt close to the heart of things."

For club members, the chance of camping with their reclusive president complemented the lure of the mountains themselves. When planning the 1902 outing, Colby told Muir: "They all ask, the first thing, if you are going to be with us." A college student wrote home from another outing, "I had a long talk with Mr. Muir this afternoon — or rather he did all the talking." Never enamored of tourists in the mountains, Muir put up with the lowland ways of the tenderfeet. They walked too fast and missed any sight not pointed out forcibly. " 'Hiking' is a *vile* word," he said. "You should saunter through the Sierra." At the evening campfire, he was sometimes annoyed by riotous jokes and sketches that seemed to profane the Sierra night. On the 1907 outing he gave a characteristically rapt campfire talk about Alaska. But the speech had "but little impression of a durable kind," he wrote in his journal. "Trashy joke stories succeeded in close ranks blurring or obliterating the best mental pictures." Still, after years of telling people to come home to the mountains, Muir on balance was delighted by the outings and by their invigorating effect on the Sierra Club.

His impatience with the moderate half-wildness of Burroughs and the Sierrans again revealed how little the old mountaineer had changed. Spiritually, he never left Yosemite: there lay his power to inspire and provoke people into caring about the wilderness. Perceived as "the nestor of American mountaineers," as one writer described him, for a public figure

Muir left little distance between his image and his reality. He was the genuine article, almost exactly as he described himself, so the public could believe in him. One day in Golden Gate Park he fell into conversation with a young plant lover named Enos Mills. Galvanized by the meeting, Mills went on to a career in forestry and wilderness protection. Calling himself "the John Muir of the Rockies," he led a campaign to establish the Rocky Mountain National Park in Colorado. "I owe everything to Muir," said Mills. "If it hadn't been for him I would have been a mere gypsy."

In his quarrels with utilitarian conservationists, Muir was called sentimental, softheaded, for speaking of intangibles while his adversaries talked in practical terms of material resources and jobs. It was elitist esthetes, Pinchot might say, against democracy and progress. Yet in sheer numbers Muir represented a larger constituency. The utilitarians were better organized and more intent, with money and livelihoods at stake. They had more political power. The preservationists, though more numerous, made up a relatively inchoate, nebulous bloc, lacking the goad of practical self-interest. But Muir, not Pinchot, best articulated the diffuse nature cults of the day. "It is all well enough," declared a New York *Times* review of the revised edition of *Our National Parks* in 1909, "to talk about preserving our natural resources, reforesting our denuded plains and mountainsides, and refilling our empty river basins; but we doubt very much that the masses of our people are vitally concerned in that aspect of conservation, which really seems almost irrelevant to their interests. It is the sentimentalist like Mr. Muir who will rouse the people rather than the materialist." Pinchot spoke for political opinion. Muir spoke for public opinion.

⁂

Somewhere between the two, Theodore Roosevelt all by himself summed up the return to nature. A man of stupefying breadth (if no great depth), among his personalities TR included the birder, the writer of natural history, the gentleman sportsman finding atavistic release in the wilderness, the displaced patrician worried about race suicide, the cowboy riding a hundred miles a day on roundup, the hiker and camper with an esthetic response to the woods, and the historian whose *Winning of the West* anticipated Frederick Jackson Turner's thesis. Last, as a politician he came under Pinchot's influence. In this final role, especially during his second term in the White House, he shifted increasingly to utilitarian conservation. The expansive arc of his interests described in microcosm the sources and conflicts of the young conservation movement.

Like many conservationists, TR first turned to nature for refuge during an isolated childhood. At four years old, as a sickly, asthmatic little boy who never enjoyed more than ten days of uninterrupted good health, he was forced indoors for long periods. In the family library he found a book with pictures of African animals and was hooked for life. When his health improved he ventured outside, sometimes to play with other children, more typically to go off by himself and study birds and other small creatures. In 1865, when he was seven, he began collecting specimens and launched the "Roosevelt Museum of Natural History." Two years later he completed a treatise on insects, his first stab at writing natural history. ("All the insects that I write about in this book inhabbit North America. Now and then a friend has told me something about them but mostly I have gained their habits from ofserv-a-tion.") After lessons in taxidermy from a former associate of Audubon's, the proud acquisition of his first gun, and the addition of eyeglasses to let him see his targets, he began to accumulate what must have been the largest collection of stuffed birds and animals of any American his age. Isolation and his interest in nature fed each other in a circle of cause and effect. Preoccupied with his esoteric pursuits, stained with chemicals and reeking of arsenic, the teenaged Teedie did not invite association. When he entered the room, his sister observed, "you always hear the words 'bird' and 'skin.' It certainly is great fun *for him.*" Markedly less social than other members of the family, he kept himself amused with his books and animals.

At Harvard, TR intended to make a career of his boyhood hobby. His father and, in particular, his uncle Robert B. Roosevelt shared his interests in hunting and natural history, so the family made no objection to his choice. In his college room he maintained an exotic vivarium — salamanders, snakes, a tortoise — and he hunted through the woods around Cambridge. Midway through college, though, he began to lose interest just as he was emerging from his social shell. As though making up for lost time, he plunged into a whirl of dances and parties with Rooseveltian enthusiasm. More attracted to humans, especially to Alice Lee of Chestnut Hill, he drew back from his wild creatures. He quit the Natural History Society and dropped his inveterate habit of taking field notes. Extravagantly in love with Alice, apparently to please her he shifted his course work to politics and planned a new career in law and public affairs. A few years later he gave most of his mounted birds, over two hundred in all, to the Smithsonian.

Yet Alice by no means replaced his first love. He still went birding and hiking. Shortly before his marriage in October 1880, a hunting binge through the Midwest yielded a total bag of 203 assorted victims. As with

Muir, domestication meant a shift in emphasis, an alteration in outward behavior but not an absolute conversion. In the fall of 1883, while stalking his first buffalo, he pushed into the Bad Lands of Dakota Territory. "Here the romance of my life began," he later recalled. And there, the following spring, his life began over. Within a few weeks of the simultaneous deaths of his wife and his mother, he planned a recuperative hunting trip to the Bad Lands. During the first months after the double blow, friends and family had worried about his sanity. That summer, as he rode alone across the desolate landscape and allowed himself the rough company of rough men, he gradually retrieved himself. "I have had good sport, and enough excitement and fatigue to prevent overmuch thought," he wrote home. "I have at last been able to sleep well at night." He learned firsthand the therapeutic potential of the wilderness.

He bought a ranch and spent part of every summer on it, splitting his time between the sport of hunting and the business of raising beef. Still an itchy-fingered sportsman, he also organized a local stockmen's association. Moving between the two perspectives — regarding the land, so to speak, as both an amateur and a professional — he acquired his first conservationist impulses. Years before meeting Pinchot, from his own experience he knew about soil erosion, the need of irrigation in the arid West, and the depletion of prairie game by market gunners. Yet his own roles collided with each other: wild animals were also beset by the guns and fences of stockmen like himself. The bitter winter of 1886–1887 helped resolve the conflict within Roosevelt. After the loss of two-thirds of his stock, his internal balance shifted toward conservation. On a Dakota hunting trip in the fall of 1887 he found no elk or grizzly and few wild sheep. With the beavers removed by trapping, their ponds had burst the neglected dams and dried into hard creek beds. The prairie grass was depleted by overstocking. Riding across this doleful scene, perhaps reflecting on his own responsibility in the causes, TR felt a new urgency to save the remnants. Back in New York, in a few weeks he and Grinnell launched the Boone and Crockett Club.

During the 1890s, in this little group limited to one hundred men who had killed three species of North American big game "in fair chase," Roosevelt continued his evolution from use to protection. At first he favored the Northern Pacific's plans to build a railroad inside Yellowstone. Grinnell, William Hallett Phillips, and other club men talked him around. With the rest of the club he then helped push the National Park Protective Act of 1894 through Congress. A similar shift overtook the three Boone and Crockett anthologies edited in these years by Roosevelt and Grinnell.

Initially preoccupied with the mechanical details of hunting, later the books paid more attention to natural history and game conservation: the focus moved from the human predator to the wild prey. "The older I grow the less I care to shoot anything except 'varmints,' " TR said. "I am still something of a hunter, although a lover of wild nature first." He still maintained his big-game library, which he described as the largest in the United States. In recognition of his scientific work as a mammalogist, a new species of Olympic Mountain elk was named *Cervus Roosevelti* in 1897. Whether writing or shooting, he felt that singular love, incomprehensible to nonhunters, of a gunner for his victims. Even in the act of killing an animal he worried about the depletion of its kind. "When I hear of the destruction of a species," he wrote a leader of the Audubon societies, "I feel just as if all the works of some great writer had perished."

On September 13, 1901, as TR was hiking back down Mount Marcy, the highest mountain in the Adirondacks, he learned that McKinley was dying. President by accident, he suddenly became the first conservationist in the White House. The movement pioneers, discouraged by McKinley's deference to political pressures, perked up with the advent of a friendly administration. "The President is heartily with us in the matter of preserving the forests and keeping out the sheep," Hart Merriam wrote Muir in October. "He wants to know the facts and is particularly anxious to learn them from men like yourself who are not connected with the Government service and at the same time are known and esteemed by the people." A product of conservation's amateur origins, TR instinctively trusted any opinion independent of livelihood and politics. In November he instructed the Secretary of the Interior, Ethan Hitchcock, to ban sheep from the forest reserves. "The forest and water problems," TR declared in his first annual message to Congress, "are perhaps the most vital internal questions of the United States at the present time." During his first year he created thirteen new reserves, increasing the total protected area by one-third.

For a country returning to nature on many levels, TR was the right President at the right time. He knew everyone, read everything, and leaped into nature controversies with the aplomb of a man who had killed a grizzly at close range. On fine spring mornings, right after breakfast, he liked to walk around the White House grounds absorbing the chorus of birdsong, noting with a tuned ear the arrivals and departures of different species. In another mood, he threatened a nearby electrical power plant with criminal action for polluting the presidential air with clouds of dark smoke. Among other ends, in the context of his hyperactive administration his conservationism allowed him a trusty petcock on his overflowing energies. "If I could not — *once in a while* — meet a man like you," he told a wildlife protector at the White House, biting off the words in his usual style, "— and talk about ANIMALS — and forget other matters — I — SHOULD — DIE!!"

In the spring of 1903, on a political swing through the West, he asked Muir to guide him through Yosemite. "I do not want anyone with me but you," TR wrote, "and I want to drop politics absolutely for four days and just be out in the open with you." Although suspicious of politicians, Muir liked what he knew of this one ("an all round strong, bold, good man") and could not miss the chance to lobby for the protection of the Sierra forests north of Yosemite, then under siege from lumbermen and sheep. So he put off a trip around the world with Sargent and took the unprecedented trouble to buy himself a new suit for the excursion, incongruously yellow and short in the sleeve and leg. Embellishing the outfit with a bright new tie, he burst into Keith's studio in San Francisco: "William, what do you think of me?" Keith looked him up and down, struck an astonished pose, and asked, "Johnny, where was the fire?"

"It is only a little trip," Muir told reporters on the eve of departing San Francisco. "You can't see much of the Sierras in four days. . . . After we get to the valley, the President and I will get lost." On the train to Raymond, TR was surrounded by a covey of California politicians, in particular the board of commissioners in charge of the valley reservation. They hoped to monopolize Roosevelt's attention in behalf of continued state control of the valley, while Muir intended to "get lost" with him in the wilder national park surrounding the valley. At Raymond, the party boarded stages for the Mariposa sequoia grove at the park's southern entrance; Muir sat with the President to point out the sights and keep him close at hand. For the first night, Muir planned a private campsite at the grove while the commissioners hoped to lure TR to an elaborate banquet a few miles away at Wawona. After seeing the grove that afternoon, TR asked for his suitcase. By a suspicious accident, it had been sent on to Wawona. The President's jaw snapped shut. *"Get it!"* he said. ("Never did I hear two words spoken so much like bullets," Muir later recalled.) The suitcase was retrieved. On horseback, with a cook and two packers, Muir and Roosevelt set forth by themselves.

Muir made him a bed of crisscrossed evergreen boughs. "It was clear weather, and we lay in the open," Roosevelt noted, "the enormous cinnamon-colored trunks rising about us like the columns of a vaster and more beautiful cathedral than was ever conceived by any human architect." In the evening stillness the old birder heard the song of a western hermit thrush; to TR's surprise, Muir had not noticed the sound and knew nothing about the bird's habits. The nature interests of the two men complemented each other: Muir best knew geology and botany, Roosevelt birds and animals. Since both excelled at talking without listening, they could hold forth on their specialties without treading on the other's expertise. "The hermit thrushes meant nothing to him," TR recalled, "the trees and the flowers and the cliffs everything." "I was surprised," said Muir, "to find he knew so much natural history."

The next day, while the politicians took stages to the valley, Muir and Roosevelt made a hard day's ride cross-country, through forests and snow patches, to the southern rim of the valley. They camped by Glacier Point in a grove of silver fir. Snow began to fall. With the light from the campfire playing against trees and snowflakes, Muir told the story of his telepathic meeting with James Davie Butler in 1869. Next morning they awoke under a literal blanket of four inches of snow. Following an hour on Glacier Point — "everything bright and glorious after the storm," Muir noted — they rode east along the rim to the head of Nevada Fall and finally, late in the afternoon, down into the valley. The commissioners had planned another banquet, along with fireworks and searchlights playing on the granite walls. Again TR ignored them. After briefly paying his respects he continued on down the valley with Muir to a campsite in Bridalveil meadow, with El Capitan looming above them. Here, Muir observed with satisfaction, they rested with the same privacy as when back of Glacier Point. The frustrated commissioners stayed in their hotel.

For two habitual monologists they got on remarkably well. "I never before had so interesting, hearty, and manly a companion," Muir declared. "I fairly fell in love with him." For his part, TR shared Burroughs's impression: "John Muir talked even better than he wrote. His greatest influence was always upon those who were brought into personal contact with him." Indeed, one day after leaving Muir and the valley Roosevelt asked Secretary Hitchcock to extend the Sierra reserve northward all the way to Mount Shasta. In political terms, as well as personal, Muir had succeeded. "We are not building this country of ours for a day," the President said on his way back to civilization. "It is to last through the ages." Surprised to find a trustworthy politician, Muir kept a picture of Roosevelt on the wall of his study. (A few years later TR told him Emerson had made a mistake in not camping out back in 1871. "You would have made him perfectly comfortable," TR wrote, "and he ought to have had the experience.")

The trip again raised the issue of the state's mismanagement of the valley floor. As the two wilderness campers skipped past the lumbering, civilized state commissioners, the problem was all but obscured by the comic-opera aspects of the encounter. But the valley, the natural centerpiece of the park, was still being ruined by frowsy concessions and an endemic lack of supervision. When Muir returned home from the trip he asked William Colby of the Sierra Club to draft another bill for the California legislature to recede the valley to the federal government; TR had promised to help with his end of the procedure. So once again Muir's spiritual home was embroiled in a political fight.

Ever since 1890, R. U. Johnson had been prodding Muir to start a campaign for Yosemite recession. Two bills had already run aground in the legislature, blocked by state pride and commercial interests. The legislature now doled out about $12,000 a year for the valley administration, and it resented any suggestion that the federal government could do better. "A man may not appreciate his wife," Muir remarked, "but let her daddie try to take her back!" And, as in the earlier fight over the national park, the railroads, stagecoach companies, and hotels serving the valley and its access roads had vested interests in maintaining the laissez-faire board of commissioners. So easily manipulated from nearby Sacramento, Yosemite affairs if removed to Washington might respond less readily to local pressures. Muir guessed that nine-tenths of California's citizens, when they thought about it, favored recession. They seldom thought about it. Again, a case of political opinion against public opinion. "Among the other tenth," Muir noted, "are those who are pecuniarily interested, and one man whose pocket is touched to the quick will do more fighting in a case of sentiment and scenery than a thousand who only look at the question in a careless, abstract way, though they look in the right direction."

Once more the Southern Pacific Railroad held the real power. The line had passed into the hands of E. H. Harriman of New York, one of the most influential financiers in the country. Muir had met Harriman in 1899, when he joined a boatload of scientists that Harriman took to Alaska. Wary of this celebrated exponent of the gobble gobble school of economics, Muir had nonetheless been drawn to his personal qualities and to his charming young family. "At first rather repelled," Muir later told Burroughs, "I at last learned to love him." It was surely the strangest friendship in Muir's life. Silent, humorless, distant, forever adding to his private empire of railroads and steamships, Harriman embodied the acquisitive, technological modern syndrome that Muir so hated. No doubt Muir cultivated him in part because of his power, especially in California politics. But essentially the two men, so opposite, found themselves intrigued precisely by the strangeness of the other, each man striking undetected chords in his antithesis. Harriman once apologized for not replying earlier to a

letter from Muir. "The cold everyday facts with which I have been dealing," he wrote, "have held me down so that I did not feel in the spirit of
dealing with your kindly and high-minded expressions as I would like."
Muir meant surcease from his everyday labors. To Muir, by contrast,
Harriman in his unwearied bustling and building seemed a primal force,
"one of the rare souls Heaven sends into the world once in centuries."

In any case, the relationship allowed Muir a direct line to the Southern
Pacific's political lobby. In drafting the new recession bill Colby was as-
sisted by an SP attorney in San Francisco. The railroad kept its role secret;
its prime stooges in the legislature were told to speak out against the bill
during debates and then finally vote for it. The measure also attracted advocates of government economy, such as the state Board of Trade, willing
to let the valley go to save the annual appropriation. Even Muir's old nemesis, John P. Irish, now favored recession for his own reasons. ("Because
the last time that he was there," as Muir explained it to Johnson, "the
saloon-keeper was found so ignorant he did not know how to prepare his
favorite drink.") The opposition was led by the San Francisco *Exam-
iner* — its chief counsel worked for the Yosemite board — and state Senator John Curtin of Sonora, who owned a cattle ranch near the park. Muir
and Colby made nine lobbying trips to Sacramento. The governor's secretary, a Sierra Club member, took them around the capital, introducing
them to key legislators. At the last moment nine votes suddenly shifted behind the bill, and it passed. "Many thanks for your Sacramento Yosemite
work," Muir wrote the SP's chief lobbyist, ". . . covering a multitude of real
or imaginary railroad sins."

Congress still had to add the valley to the surrounding national park.
Boundary disputes held it up for a year. Joe Cannon, the czar of the House,
disliked spending any money — especially for scenery. Muir wrote Harriman, who wrote Cannon, who suddenly suspended House rules and let the
bill through. Roosevelt urged the Senate not to neglect its duty, "either
from indifference or because of paying heed to selfish interests." Finally
the process was completed: inspired by Johnson, powered by Harriman,
signed by Roosevelt. Muir, personal friend to each, was the common element among the sponsors of recession. "The fight you planned," Muir
wrote Johnson, "by that famous Tuolumne campfire seventeen years ago is
at last fairly gloriously won, every enemy down derry down." (Not quite,
as it turned out.)

Aside from approving the completion of Yosemite National Park, TR as
President created fifty-three wildlife reserves, sixteen national monuments,
and five new national parks. His additions to the forest reserves so annoyed

Congress that in 1907 it forbade any further reserves in six western states without its legislative consent. But with the bill on his desk, awaiting his signature, Roosevelt hurriedly declared or enlarged thirty-two reserves totaling seventy-five million acres, thus doubling the forest area under protection. Accused of arrogance and usurpation in the matter, TR explained that he was only defending rightful settlers from "the lumber syndicates."

While such assertions of executive power pleased Muir and the preservationists, Roosevelt's close reliance on Gifford Pinchot did not. Acquainted with Pinchot since the mid-1890s, TR had brought him into the Boone and Crockett Club in 1897. Pinchot then, in a foreshadowing of his effect on Roosevelt's presidency, had changed the club's forest reserve policy from absolute protection to regulated use. Once in the White House, TR made Pinchot a favored member of his inner circle of advisors. With all his formidable panoply of skills, Roosevelt was least astute as a judge of character. "I have one friend," he said of Pinchot, ". . . in whose integrity I believe as I do in my own." Since taking over the forestry division in Agriculture under McKinley, Pinchot had wanted to transfer the reserves from the Interior Department to an enlarged bureau of his own in Agriculture. He urged wider use of the reserves in part to gain congressional support for his plan. Specifically, he assured the Homestake Mining Company of South Dakota that its timber supply would not be threatened under his management. With that guarantee the opposition in Congress disappeared. Moreover, the plan seemed a sensible consolidation of federal forest policy in a single office, and was supported as such by TR, the Sierra Club, and other preservationists. In 1905 it went through and Pinchot became the first head of the U.S. Forest Service, a bureau of the Agriculture Department.

As an administrator and promoter he did brilliant work. Capitalizing on the nature cults of the day, the bureau sent out a blizzard of mailings to magazines and newspapers, describing the importance of trees and the Forest Service. A novel device for a federal agency, the handouts were widely published. The service also maintained a mailing list of private individuals that by 1909 included some eight hundred thousand names. In lobbying Congress for his annual appropriation, Pinchot would invoke his substantial society contacts and background in charming the head of the House Agriculture Committee ("He was one of the Geneseo Wadsworths, some of whom were my friends") and the ranking committee Democrat ("He had lived much abroad, and when he found I could talk French with him he counted it to me for righteousness"). In ten years the Forest Service budget increased over one hundredfold.

The sprawling success of Pinchot and his agency spread his version of conservation over the entire range of federal conservation policy. The term "forest reserves" carried an implication of protecting them from use. Pinchot changed their name to "national forests." His *Use Book,* the manual of the Forest Service, placed no upper limits on timber sales and spoke in positive terms, authorizing certain practices rather than explicitly forbidding others. "The conservation movement," Pinchot declared, "has development for its first principle." In contrast with the ardent pioneers of the 1890s, Pinchot seemed reasonable, practical, reassuringly scientific and accepting of progress, and — above all — political. TR was a preservationist by instinct and avocation but a politician by vocation; hobbies normally gave way to jobs. He explicitly, all but uncritically, put Pinchot in charge of his conservation interests. As Secretary of the Interior, Ethan Hitchcock resisted any commercial use of national parks and opposed livestock permits in the forests and the leasing of federal grazing lands. In 1907 James Garfield, whose attitudes were approved by Pinchot, took Hitchcock's place at Interior.

The great showpiece of Roosevelt's last year as President was the Governors Conference on natural resources. Planned and financed by Pinchot, the meeting brought together forty-four state governors and hundreds of experts — but hardly any preservationists. Muir was not invited. Though Johnson pointed out the conspicuous omission to Pinchot, Muir still was not invited. The Sierra Club sent a statement: "The moral and physical welfare of a nation is not dependent alone upon bread and water. Comprehending these primary necessities is the deeper need for recreation and that which satisfies also the esthetic sense." At the conference, among nearly one hundred speeches and comments only three mentioned non-utilitarian aspects. "P. is ambitious," Muir confided to Johnson afterward, "and never hesitates to sacrifice anything or anybody in his way."

≈≈

Professional conservation was taking over at the national level. It came to dominate conservation affairs in Washington (and, ever since, has commanded the writing of conservation history as well). The older tradition of the zealous amateur still survived, if less visibly, in hinterlands such as Harrisburg, Pennsylvania, and Marin County, California, and Bar Harbor, Maine. The larger story of progressive conservation includes not only familiar figures — Roosevelt and Pinchot — but forgotten individuals like J. Horace McFarland, the man who saved Niagara Falls; William Kent, who gave posterity a stand of virgin coast redwoods and named it Muir

Woods; and George Bucknam Dorr, who put together the first national park in the East. In volunteering their time and money to the cause, these unpaid amateurs carried forward the early work of Muir, Grinnell, Johnson, and Sargent. They nourished an alternative to mainstream conservation that would diminish to a trickle over the next few decades, later to emerge again in a flood of interests after World War II.

Conservation arose when the United States reached a certain point in its industrial development. Until then it had not been imagined, indeed was hardly necessary. By the time that point was reached, most of the East was already developed beyond preservation. The discussion, therefore, mainly involved parks and forests beyond the hundredth meridian, out where urbanization as yet had made a lighter impact.

A stubborn anomaly, Niagara Falls held out as an undeniable natural wonder in a region of headlong progress. After the Civil War it was hemmed in by factories and tourist operations. A preservation campaign led by Frederick Law Olmsted and Charles Eliot Norton of Harvard induced the state, in 1885, to establish a four-hundred-acre park on the American side, extending a mile above the falls. The Canadians a year later followed suit with a park on their side. These reserves soon proved inadequate. Two thousand feet below the American fall, outside the park, the "Bridal Veil" site was taken over by mills and factories. More seriously, the New York legislature granted permits to private power companies to divert water above the falls. First built in the mid-1890s, by 1901 hydroelectric plants were taking 7.3 million gallons a minute, about 6 percent of the total, with options for much more. "Niagara's claim to distinction is now mainly quantitative," H. G. Wells concluded after visiting the falls in 1906; "its spectacular effect, its magnificent and humbling size and splendor, were long since destroyed beyond recovery by the hotels, the factories, the power-houses, the bridges and tramways and hoardings that arose about it." Yet when Wells toured the generating plants — clean, quiet, thrumming with contained force — he accepted the bargain of beauty for progress. "It seems altogether well that all the froth and hurry of Niagara at last, all of it, dying into hungry canals of intake, should rise again in light and power."

The falls found a more persistent champion in J. Horace McFarland, head of the American Civic Association. "We are permitting this one supreme natural glory of America," he said, "to slip into the maws of a few greedy speculators and legislators of America and Canada." For three decades he made Niagara his pet project; though he did not stop the power companies, he at least held them off. McFarland ran a printing company in Harrisburg that specialized in horticulture and the new techniques of color photography. His clients included the Audubon journal *Bird-Lore* and Liberty Hyde Bailey's *Country Life in America* magazine. His interest in public affairs began in the late 1800s, when Harrisburg suffered a typhoid epidemic caused by the polluted water of the Susquehanna River. A crusade for better sewage disposal led to other civic causes — street paving, parks and playgrounds, beautification. Thereafter he was "badly infected with the improvement bacillus," as he put it.

He loved nature in an urbanized way, trimmed and cultivated. Every day in season he spent time in his flower garden, with its eight hundred species of roses. "Nothing else matters while I am doing that sort of thing," he said. The rose garden served as his Yosemite. He wrote books about his favorite flower and started a national society in its honor. Roses summarized his direct interest in nature: an object to be observed and admired esthetically, not to be fully experienced with the whole body. In choosing between the two wings of conservation, though, he aligned himself with Muir. "Pinchot does not see beyond the end of the lumber pile in regard to the forests," he declared. Though apparently he never met Muir, he knew his books and counted himself a disciple. "I trust you may long be spared," he wrote to Muir, "to keep up your great work for the world. You have done more than any other man in the United States to have God's great works left to show forth His handiwork."

Still, he was more repulsed by cities than attracted by nature. Baptized in the field of *civic* improvement, he wanted to save natural beauty not only for its own sake but to help redeem cities and their wretched inhabitants. Almost nothing called progress pleased him — even the favorite new toy of the day, the automobile ("a rampacious grizzly bear on the average highway, snorting and stinking"). A conservative Republican, a Mason and a Sunday school superintendent and Methodist church organist, a nonsmoker and nondrinker who even refused tea, McFarland felt personally threatened by the hordes of Catholics, drinkers, and political radicals he imagined arising from the cities. In political terms, the right sort of conservation meant to him a means of imposing social control over a polity falling apart. "If the country is not roused," he warned Johnson, "the conservation of minerals will still continue to make whole communities hated boarding houses instead of homes, and to furnish to the penitentiary and hospital their largest contingent, and to the ranks of socialism and anarchy growing accessions." The wondrous spread of cities and machinery thus damaged both humans and nature. "Boast we well of civilization and advance, and progress and power," he said. They meant nothing if people could no longer find refuge, a source of refreshment and stability, in natural wonders like Niagara. "For who will care to see a bare cliff and a mass of factories," asked McFarland, "a maze of wires and tunnels and wheels and generators?"

With the New York legislature handing out free diversion permits, McFarland took his case for federal protection to Washington. Roosevelt endorsed the plan ("Turn on Niagara!"), including a formal recommendation in his message to Congress of December 1905. Theodore E. Burton of Ohio, chairman of the House Committee on Rivers and Harbors and the acknowledged congressional expert in the field, agreed to sponsor a bill. It aroused the opposition: Burton was visited by two of the ablest hydraulic engineers in the country, later by a lawyer and more engineers from General Electric, arguing the need for Niagara power. Behind them, directing the power interests, was J. P. Morgan's attorney Francis Lynde Stetson of the Niagara Falls Power Company. "You can little realize," Burton wrote McFarland, "the pressure that will be brought to bear upon the other side."

On his side McFarland tried to mobilize any public opinion retaining sentimental memories or affection for Niagara Falls. His articles in the *Ladies' Home Journal* provoked hundreds of letters, the greatest reader response in the magazine's history to that point, overwhelmingly in favor of protecting the falls. Other preservationists helped out — Enos Mills, the Appalachian Mountain Club, the Sierra Club — as did national journals of moral uplift like the *Outlook* and the *Chautauquan.* "There has been no least doubt," McFarland told Muir, "as to the will of the people in respect to Niagara." The Burton bill, passed in June 1906, took advantage of the international nature of the problem. It removed the permit-granting power from the New York legislature to the War Department, limited for three years the total flow available for diversion, and called for a treaty with Canada to settle the matter permanently. During the next year the Secretary of War received some 6,550 letters from citizens on the granting of further diversions. Of these only a hundred favored more diversions, mostly from the village of Niagara Falls, mostly identical in text but with different signatures.

When aroused, the public spoke emphatically. But the process of negotiating and ratifying the Canadian treaty dragged on for years. The public lost interest and the power companies did not. Elihu Root, first as Roosevelt's Secretary of State and (after 1909) as senator from New York, took the leading role among American negotiators. "Mr. Root now has charge of the matter," TR wrote McFarland at the end of his presidency. "Will you not keep in touch with him?" A formidable adversary, Root operated from a well-established regard for the needs of American business. The Niagara power companies made their own case for more water by generating 300 percent more electricity from 1907 to 1913. Against these capitalized, highly motivated enemies, McFarland had only himself and the twenty-five hundred members of his organization. Slighting his printing business, he spent a third of his time on conservation and piled up a $4,000 debt from the Niagara campaign. "I have a dozen other activities which have nothing to do with making a living," he noted, "and sometimes I get completely flattened out."

Once again a conservation struggle came down to zealous amateurs and practically-minded economic interests. McFarland hoped the treaty would limit diversions to the existing actual usage of 34,000 cubic feet per second. The companies asked for 56,000 cubic feet. The companies won ("a surrender to commercialism," said McFarland). The final treaty seemed an anticlimax after his years of overmatched fighting. "I am a mighty small David," he said, "with an exceedingly diminutive sling, to attempt to reach the forehead of this Goliath who is built of fifty millions in money and with a vast self interest back of him." Yet he could take comfort in wondering how much worse Niagara would have fared in the continued care of the New York legislature. The limit of 56,000 cubic feet was maintained until 1950.

Across the mouth of San Francisco Bay, Marin County was filling up with suburbs and progress. On the slopes and foothills of Mount Tamalpais, the highest point in the county, hundreds of acres of *Sequoia sempervirens,* the coastal relative of the Sierra's Big Trees, were being cut for their prized lumber. In 1900 someone asked Muir to protect these stands of rare coast redwoods. "I would gladly go to Tamalpais," he replied, "and a thousand times farther to stay the ruthless destruction of the forests you refer to. But, alas, all land thereabouts is private property, and what more can I do in the way of protest and efforts to make public opinion for the defense of the trees than I am doing?" All the existing national parks and reservations had been carved from land still owned by the government. The Tamalpais redwoods — in private hands, and expensive to buy — seemed beyond government protection.

In 1907 William Kent left a career of municipal reform in Chicago and moved his family to a large tract on the shoulder of Tamalpais. Descended from old New England stock, he had grown up in Marin County, gone east to school, and then settled into years of political crusading in Chicago. Inheriting a reform tradition from his father, an abolitionist and Lincoln Republican, he had helped launch the urban playground movement, supported Hull House and John Dewey's progressive Laboratory School, fought corruption, urged municipal ownership, and allied himself with the muckrakers of *American Magazine.* Like McFarland, he wanted to reform cities because he disliked them.

A sense of upper-class duty drove him into urban politics; but he felt most alive back in the wilderness, in virgin forests like the redwood groves he had known as a boy. "My life has been largely spent outdoors," he declared. "I have ridden the prairies, the mountains and the desert." He worried, with other nativist conservationists, about the declining vigor of older American ethnic groups softened by too much civilization. They might regain their lost vitality in the snapping challenge of manly field sports. After killing a wild animal, "you are a barbarian, and you're glad of it," said Kent. "You know that if you are a barbarian, you are at any rate a man." (In other ways he defied neat categorization. For all his chest beating, he supported woman suffrage. His wife, Elizabeth Thacher Kent, was a leading feminist.)

His Chicago years had included crusades against the monopolistic practices of private utility companies. The old instincts bristled when, in 1907, a water company in Marin County condemned part of his land for use as a reservoir. The threatened tract, forty-seven acres, included redwoods three hundred feet tall, with diameters of eighteen feet. Kent concluded that the company wanted not so much the site itself as the valuable lumber. So to avoid seizure by eminent domain he gave the land, valued at $45,000, to the federal government as a national monument. At Kent's request, it was named Muir Woods. "I know the dreams we have will come true," he wrote Muir, "and that men will learn to love nature. All I fear is that it may be too late."

In thanking Kent for the gesture, Muir paid the redwoods his ultimate compliment. "Compared with Sequoia," he wrote, "glaciers are young fleeting things, and since the first Sequoia forests lifted their domes and spires to the sky, mountains great and small, thousands of them have been weathered, ground down, washed away and cast into the sea." By preserving these wonders, more venerable even than mountains and glaciers, Kent had performed "in many ways the most notable service to God and man I've heard of since my forest wanderings began," Muir added. "That so

fine divine a thing should have come out of money-mad Chicago! Wha
wad'a' thocht it!"

Down the coast of Maine, just beyond Penobscot Bay, the island of
Mount Desert offered some of the most striking topographical features in
the eastern United States. Scattered through its thirty thousand acres were
springs, rapid little streams, rugged granite outcroppings, thick coniferous
forests on the landward side of hills and in the deeper valleys, and still
lakes, clear and cold. Surmounting the lower granite peaks, Cadillac
Mountain, the highest of them, rose quickly from sea level to fifteen hundred feet. It loomed over the fishing village of Bar Harbor, solitary and incongruous.

During the years after the Civil War this bracing mixture of ocean and
mountain, unique on the East Coast, drew an annual colony of artists,
writers, and rich people to summer homes on the island. The family of
George B. Dorr of Boston built one of the first patrician houses in Bar
Harbor. Among their seasonal neighbors and social peers the Dorrs
counted President Charles W. Eliot of Harvard, a Dana, a Schieffelin, and
various Vanderbilts and Rockefellers. For the embattled gentry at the turn
of the century, Mount Desert offered a literal island of tranquillity, an annual refuge from an urban society cracking open in alarming ways. "The
set at Bar Harbor is exceedingly exclusive," an observer remarked; "it is
inside of the Four Hundred and is made up of the One Hundred tip-
toppers."

In the fall of 1901 Eliot called a meeting of a dozen of the island's wellborn landowners. Progress — in the form of numerous middle-class
owners, who were buying smaller parcels of land and developing them —
was threatening the pristine beauties of Mount Desert. The group
launched a nonprofit landholding trust, the Hancock County Trustees of
Public Reservations, patterned on a Massachusetts group founded earlier
by Eliot's son, a landscape architect. "The time fitted well," George Dorr
recalled, "for it lay between two periods, of the private owner grown suddenly to wealth and that of the multitude set into movement by the new
mechanical age." Mediating between the two, the Hancock County Trustees were chartered by the state legislature to accept private gifts of land
and hold them, tax-free but for public recreational use, in perpetuity. The
land was thus both protected and available to the multitude. After two
small initial gifts, nothing further happened until 1907, when Mrs. Charles
Homans of Boston donated a substantial tract, with a small lake, on New-
port Mountain. Inspired by this addition, Dorr with financial help from

a New York industrialist acquired eighty-five acres on top of Cadillac Mountain, and followed it in 1909 with a large chunk of his family's land. With these additions the initiative passed from Eliot to Dorr. For the rest of his life Dorr made the preservation of Mount Desert his special mission.

"George Dorr is an impulsive, enthusiastic, eager person," noted Eliot, "who works at a high tension, neglects his meals, sits up too late at night, and rushes about from one pressing thing to another; but he is diligent, as well as highly inventive and suggestive." A cousin of Charles Sprague Sargent, he came from the same background of secure privilege. Born near Jamaica Pond, brought up in one of the first homes built on the filled land of the Back Bay, inevitably educated at Harvard, as the last of his family line he symbolized the Indian summer of Brahmin Boston. His father, a banker, served in both houses of the legislature; his maternal grandfather, a Salem sea captain, later made a fortune in business and served as treasurer of Harvard and the Boston Athenaeum. The Dorr home was adorned with oriental ceramics and furniture from the family's years in the China trade. As a boy George knew grace, beauty, and stability: the qualities he later tried to protect on Mount Desert. "My earliest recollections," he said, "are concerned with gardens, our own and my grandmother's before we ever came to Mount Desert." Isolated by a severe stuttering problem, he spent his summers largely by himself, exploring the island, taking special delight in uncovering underground springs. Further distanced from his parents by the Victorian convention of decorously concealed feelings, the three found common ground in their love for the island. "We all three had great reserves, even from each other," he recalled, "and lived our own lives out, not readily opening ourselves out to others." He never married; once, when his mother brought home a likely prospect for him, he climbed a tree until it was safe to come down. After his parents died he lived alone in the house at Bar Harbor, keeping a watchful eye on island affairs, depleting his fortune by adding new parcels of land to the trust.

Around 1909, real estate developers and small landowners started building cottages on Eagle Lake above Bar Harbor, thus endangering the village water supply. Since both Dorr and the local water company wanted to keep Eagle Lake inviolate, the situation threw them together in a peculiar alliance. The company condemned the lake properties and then financed their acquisition by Dorr's group. "I could do what others could not," Dorr noted, "without being open to the charge of acting for some special interest in seeking ... further lands for the protection of the Bar Harbor Water Company." Thus provoked, the local real estate interests in 1913 introduced a bill in the state legislature to annul the charter of the Hancock

County Trustees. Dorr hurried to the capital, talked to the Speaker of the House (a friend from Bar Harbor), and after ten days of lobbying managed to quash the bill.

The narrow escape led Dorr to seek permanent federal protection. Using the precedent of Muir Woods, an earlier gift of privately held land, he offered the tract on Mount Desert to the federal government as a national monument. He and Eliot exploited all their social and political connections in Washington. (Opposition arose from David Houston of Agriculture; but he had taught under Eliot at Harvard, and a letter from his old president converted him.) Through a Boston friend Dorr obtained an interview with Mrs. Woodrow Wilson. In 1916 the President accepted the land as a monument. Two years later it was promoted to park status, and eventually was given the permanent name of Acadia National Park.

Dorr stayed on as self-appointed guardian, living to the age of ninety-one in his echoing old house, ever on the lookout for new donations of land to his park. "Our national parks alone," he said in old age, "can supply the imaginative appeal that is made in older lands by ancient works of art, by ruins and old historic associations." He liked wild nature for the usual reasons of biology, esthetics, and personal freedom. In particular, this witness of the decline of his family, class, and region liked nature for inspiring his historical imagination, implying an unbroken tradition that held him to a fading, chimerical past. American society kept reinventing itself. Nature offered stability.

In varying degrees, efforts to preserve Niagara Falls, Muir Woods, and Acadia were all provoked by water resource problems. Yet the contending parties fell into no pattern. In two cases the preservationist fought against the utility company; in the third, with it. Kent and Dorr were old-money Ivy Leaguers, while McFarland left school at twelve to work in a print-shop. Kent alone defined himself as a socialist; yet McFarland, the most conservative of the three, found himself inveighing against a capitalist monopoly and citing Elihu Root as an argument for the popular election of senators. McFarland was conservative except regarding conservation; Kent was progressive except on the question of progress itself. Dorr claimed the glossiest lineage, yet he wound up admiring Franklin D. Roosevelt, the noted traitor to his class. Dorr and Kent delighted to lose themselves in a real wilderness, while McFarland felt adequately wild at his summer home in the Poconos. The three shared only their concern for nonmaterial conservation and their amateur status in the movement.

Niagara, Muir Woods, and Acadia were all eclipsed at the time by a final showdown over Yosemite. Like these lesser episodes, the last Yosemite struggle derived from a water problem, produced unlikely alliances, and defied analysts who favored symmetrical political explanations. A tangled snarl of interests, with each side claiming to represent the public against private monopolies, the issue four times seemed dead, only to flare up again. For Muir, past seventy during the heaviest fighting, it made an ironic denouement to his lifework. "Ever since the Yosemite National Park was established in 1890 my own real work has been sadly interrupted in trying to assist in its preservation," he noted in 1907. "While a single peak or dome, tree or cascade is left, the poor stub of a park will still call for protection." His career as a pioneer conservationist ended where it started, in a canyon of the High Sierra.

※※

In the northwestern corner of the park the Tuolumne River tumbled down into a long, narrow gorge. It traversed the three and a half miles of the valley floor and passed through the southern end, resuming its course down the mountain range. The valley, called Hetch Hetchy by the Indians in reference to its grassy meadows, first drew Muir's attention in the early 1870s. He described its close resemblance to the more celebrated Yosemite Valley: "formed by the same forces, lying at the same height above sea-level, occupying the same relative position on the flank of the range," and with similar plants and waterfalls. At his urging Hetch Hetchy was included in the national park act of 1890.

Within a few years the city of San Francisco made its first proposal to turn Hetch Hetchy into a water reservoir by plugging the southern end of the valley with a dam. Rebuffed when Muir and the Sierra Club raised a protest, the city tried again in 1901 during the reform administration of Mayor James D. Phelan. For years the privately owned Spring Valley Water Company had been treating the city to high rates and poor service. Phelan, an advocate of municipally run utilities, revived the Hetch Hetchy plan to rescue his city from Spring Valley's acknowledged failings. At his behest a right-of-way bill, allowing water conduits through national parks "for domestic, public, or other beneficial uses," passed Congress in February 1901, zipping through with little discussion. The Sierra Club only learned of it after passage. Under its provisions the city applied to the Interior Department for the rights to Hetch Hetchy. But Ethan Hitchcock rejected the plan in January 1903 and again in February 1905 because of his general policy of keeping utilitarian projects out of the national parks.

After the second ruling, Gifford Pinchot, Hitchcock's persistent adversary in government conservation circles, took up the scheme. A champion of both public utilities and the tapping of park resources, Pinchot declared that Hetch Hetchy might be dammed with no esthetic loss. ("Just the same," Muir wrote Johnson, "as saying that flooding Yosemite would do it no harm.") In November 1906, with his friend James Garfield soon to replace Hitchcock, Pinchot suggested to Marsden Manson, the city engineer of San Francisco, that the application for Hetch Hetchy might fruitfully be renewed. The following summer, with the Sierra Club away on its outing in Yosemite, Secretary Garfield quietly held a hearing in San Francisco. Lawyers and engineers for the city presented their case for the dam. No dam opponents appeared at the hearing. The Sierra Club returned from its outing to find the long process already under way.

At once Muir and Johnson sent protests to their friend the President. Not previously involved in the matter, Roosevelt asked Garfield to investigate alternate water sources. A month later, in early September 1907, Muir recounted for TR the long history of Hetch Hetchy dam promotions. "They all show forth the proud sort of confidence," said Muir, "that comes of a good sound irrefragable ignorance." This latest effort, he added, could only succeed by deceptions and keeping the facts from the public. "As soon as light is cast upon it, nine tenths or more of even the citizens of San Francisco would be opposed to it. And what the public opinion of the world would be may be guessed by the case of the Niagara Falls." Roosevelt sent Muir's letters along to Pinchot and Garfield but remained noncommittal. Abstractly he would like to protect Yosemite, he told Muir, but would have to yield to public opinion: "So far everyone that has appeared has been for it and I have been in the disagreeable position of seeming to interfere with the development of the State for the sake of keeping a valley, which apparently hardly anyone wanted to have kept, under national control." (P.S.: "How I do wish I were again with you camping out under those great sequoias or in the snow under the silver firs!")

Thus challenged by the President, Muir set about rousing public opinion. "This Yosemite fight promises to be the worst ever," he confided to Johnson. With the help of William Colby he put the Sierra Club on record in opposition. They sent recruiting letters to women's clubs and other mountaineering groups. Colby and Johnson talked with private water companies, who for their own purposes provided information against the dam. (As in George Dorr's efforts for Acadia, the preservationists lined up with a private utility.) Reaching back to earlier Yosemite battles, Muir got in touch with former Secretary of the Interior John Noble and William Herrin of the Southern Pacific. His first published broadside appeared in the influential *Outlook* on November 2. Ascribing the plot to "mischief-makers and robbers of every degree from Satan to Senators ... trying to make everything dollarable," he defended the valley's scenic value, deplored the absence of public discussion, and pointed out alternate sources outside the park that would cost more economically but less esthetically. The dam advocates, pricked to respond, attacked Muir in kind. "John Muir loves the Sierras and roams at large, and is hypersensitive on the subject of the invasion of *his* territory," Phelan wrote Garfield. "The 400,000 people of San Francisco are suffering from bad water and ask Mr. Muir to cease his aesthetic quibbling."

Behind the rhetorical sallies, all but obscured by the smoking verbiage, the fight involved more than bad water. To conservationists in the Pinchot camp the concept of "multiple use" implied the highest, most efficient approach to resources. A dam should ideally provide drinking water, regulate floods and erosion, irrigate crops, and — especially — generate electricity. Hydroelectric power could eventually pay the costs of construction; in public hands it also might remove a key utility from monopolistic abuses. Pinchot often warned of "the water-power trust" with its platoons of lawyers and lobbyists. "Whoever dominates power," said Pinchot, "dominates all industry." For their part, the defenders of Hetch Hetchy regarded hydroelectric power as the Trojan horse of the whole fight. Other sites might provide water alone. Hetch Hetchy, as a natural reservoir at a high elevation, was especially suited for both water and power. The dam advocates, though speaking only of San Francisco's need for water, seemed curiously resistant to the consideration of other sites. The preservationists also knew that a generating plant and transmission lines would further disrupt the Yosemite landscape. As the ranks formed overtly over water, the power issue hovered in the background, a source of unspoken mutual suspicion.

In the spring of 1908, as Garfield was deciding whether to grant a permit under the right-of-way law, Muir offered a compromise: take Lake Eleanor, a few miles north of Hetch Hetchy and within the park, in order to save the valley. Using the lake as a reservoir would cause less damage than inundating the valley. "I am trying to see if we can not leave the things on the line that you indicate," TR wrote Muir, "— that is, damming Lake Eleanor and letting San Francisco depend for a generation or so upon that and the Tuolumne tributaries." Roosevelt passed the idea along to Garfield — but only as a suggestion, without his usual snap, leaving the final decision to his cabinet officer. In May, Garfield granted San Francisco a permit, subject to congressional approval, to dam Hetch Hetchy. "I think you must feel, as I do, that a child of ours has been mutilated,"

Johnson wrote Muir. "It was just one of those cases where I was extremely doubtful," TR later told Johnson with un-Rooseveltian hesitancy; "but finally I came to the conclusion that I ought to stand by Garfield and Pinchot's judgment in the matter." The President did ask Garfield to limit the valley's use to supplying water only, with no power development.

Muir's personal influence with TR having failed, as the issue was passed along to Congress the impact of general public opinion increased. Initially Muir ascribed the plot to a few "monopolizing San Francisco capitalists . . . working in darkness like moles in a low-lying meadow." But in November 1908 a city referendum produced a seven-to-one margin favoring the dam — because, Colby supposed, San Franciscans disliked any cause allied with the hated Spring Valley Water Company. For whatever reason, local sentiment resoundingly approved exchanging the valley for better water. The friends of Hetch Hetchy accordingly took their case to the nation at large. "We do not believe that a great national property preserved for the enjoyment of the people of the entire nation," a circular letter of December 1908 declared, "should be thus unnecessarily sacrificed and diverted from its dedicated purposes for the mere pecuniary benefit of a local interest." The national constituency responded: most letters to Congress on the issue came from outside California.

The House Committee on Public Lands held hearings in Washington in February 1909. Preservationist speakers included Johnson, McFarland, and Harriet Monroe, editor of *Poetry* magazine, who had been joining Sierra Club outings since 1905. Among the rebuttals, James Phelan repeated his *ad hominem* attacks on Muir ("I am sure he would sacrifice his own family for the preservation of beauty. He considers human life very cheap, and he considers the works of God superior"). The committee then endorsed the project by so narrow a margin, 8 to 7, that it effectively ruined its chances for further action at that time. After the Senate committee failed to make a report the resolution was withdrawn. A decision on Garfield's permit was delayed for a year, until the next session of Congress.

Meantime a new President, William Howard Taft, and a new Secretary of the Interior, Richard A. Ballinger, had taken office. A strict legal constructionist, Taft listened sympathetically to Johnson's argument that damming Hetch Hetchy would unlawfully nullify the intent of the Yosemite park law of 1890. With congressional action suspended, the park protectors hoped to revoke Garfield's permit. Muir made his best case in October 1909 when he took Taft through Yosemite and guided Ballinger on an inspection of Hetch Hetchy. Taft, a notably less strenuous President than

TR, would not camp out in the valley. He also annoyed Muir with his irreverence: "He refused to regard Yosemite as a place to worship in and
cracked some pretty poor jokes." On the other hand, he listened better
than his predecessor. Filling the presidential ear with one of his monologues, praising the valley and damning the dammers, Muir was impressed
that "he never interrupted me when I was talking." Muir came home from
the trip convinced that Taft and Ballinger would defend Hetch Hetchy.
"All seems coming our way," he told Colby, "and the silly thieves and
robbers seem at the end of their scheme."

Aside from the merits of the case, Taft had political reasons to stop the
dam. Pinchot, his inherited Chief Forester, was criticizing the administration's conservation policies and — in particular — doubting Ballinger's integrity. Since the Hetch Hetchy project was identified with Pinchot, Taft
and Ballinger naturally were inclined to resist it as a way of striking back at
Pinchot. "The Ballinger administration has delayed and obstructed our
work in every possible way," Marsden Manson wrote Pinchot in January
1910, "short of actually forfeiting the City's rights. The Sierra Club has
given us much trouble." A month later Ballinger formally asked San Francisco to show cause why Hetch Hetchy should not be eliminated from the
Garfield permit. At a hearing in May the city asked for more time to gather
facts. Confronted with an unfriendly administration, the dammers adopted
delaying tactics, waiting for a more amenable resident in the White House.
With five extensions the decision was put off two and a half years, until
November 1912.

In the interim both sides had time to launch major national campaigns.
The preservationists included mountaineering groups (the American Alpine Club and Appalachian Mountain Club), wildlife conservationists
(William T. Hornaday, Ernest Thompson Seton, T. Gilbert Pearson, William Brewster), McFarland and the American Civic Association, the Conservation Department of the General Federation of Women's Clubs, and
such prominent individuals as Charles Eliot, Frederick Law Olmsted, Jr.,
Ethan Hitchcock, Enos Mills, the novelist Ellen Glasgow, the journalist
Henry Watterson, and Henry Fairfield Osborn. While Colby and a few
others in the Sierra Club did the trench work of correspondence and
pamphleteering, Muir gave most of the money and, as the most familiar
name among the leaders, served as figurehead and point man. ("JOHN
MUIR," exclaimed an associate of McFarland's in the ACA. "Think of it.
It's grand to be in his presence.") In the summer of 1911, as he prepared
for a trip to South America — playing Humboldt at seventy-three — he

worked fifteen hours a day to finish a book on the Yosemite. It concluded with a ringing chapter on Hetch Hetchy: "These temple destroyers, devotees of ravaging commercialism, seem to have a perfect contempt for Nature, and instead of lifting their eyes to the God of the mountains, lift them to the Almighty Dollar. Dam Hetch Hetchy! As well dam for water-tanks the people's cathedrals and churches, for no holier temple has ever been consecrated by the heart of man."

The most divisive issue yet in the young movement, Hetch Hetchy by no means enlisted general agreement among conservationists. In the Sierra Club one of the founders, Warren Olney, supported the dam. After internal debate the club voted 589 to 161 to oppose the project; for the rest of his life Olney would not allow Hetch Hetchy to be discussed in his home. To ensure their freedom of action Muir and his allies in the club started an *ad hoc* group, the Society for the Preservation of National Parks. In the East, George Bird Grinnell lent his name to the society but, aside from writing a few letters and editorials, gave little help. The Appalachian Mountain Club endorsed Muir's position but offered no money. Muir's friends in Washington, Hart Merriam and Robert B. Marshall of the Forest Service, offered private sympathy but were constrained by their government jobs from taking overt action. "I must tell you," John Burroughs wrote Johnson, "that I can't get up any enthusiasm over Hetch Hetchy. I suppose if there was a lake in that valley and San Francisco wanted to drain it and make meadows in its place, John Muir would howl in the way he does now. . . . Grand scenery is going to waste in the Sierras — let's utilize some of it." William Kent, now representing Marin County in Congress, told a colleague not to take Muir seriously on Hetch Hetchy, "for he is a man entirely without social sense. With him, it is me and God and the rock where God put it, and that is the end of the story."

Granted that sincere conservationists could disagree about the project, the real division was not between utilitarians and preservationists. Rather it was occupational, between those who urged the dam *as part of their jobs* and those who *took time from their jobs* to oppose it. In short, another collision of professionals and amateurs. The dam's prime movers were politicians from the San Francisco area — where public opinion overwhelmingly called for the dam — and engineers and consultants hired by the city. All had a professional stake in pushing through the project. Their opponents by contrast had to steal time from their livelihoods. "We are all persons of small means and we have made considerable sacrifice," Colby noted. "The city has employed experts and skilled attorneys at an expense of thousands of dollars because it has a personal advantage to be gained. The fight has been a most unequal one from this standpoint." "Both Colby and I are hoping that this Hetch Hetchy fight will soon be over," said another of Muir's lieutenants, "or we shall not only be bankrupt but shall have to give up our professions." After donating an estimated five thousand dollars' worth of his time, Johnson finally had to drop the struggle: "The problem of getting three meals a day is too pressing."

Beset on one side by professional politicians and engineers, the friends of Hetch Hetchy found no more support among professional conservationists. By this time only the amateurs brought up esthetic aspects. In 1909 McFarland wrote an article, "Ugly Conservation," on the utilitarian vogue in the movement. A fellow amateur, Allen Chamberlain of Boston, applauded the article but doubted its impact: "Our friends the conservationists, that is the professionals, are exceeding loath to recognize this point of view. Nothing short of a wide public sentiment will ever bring them round, I fear." Actually most articulate public opinion did take the esthetic side in Hetch Hetchy. The *Outlook, Nation, Independent, World's Work, Collier's,* the New York *Times, Tribune,* and *World,* and a hundred or so other newspapers and magazines opposed the project, either for itself or as a precedent for invading the national parks. Again, it came down to public opinion against political opinion.

Rebuffed by Walter Fisher, Ballinger's successor as Secretary of the Interior, at the hearings of November 1912, the dammers waited for the new administration to take office. Woodrow Wilson carried San Francisco in the presidential election. In apparent gratitude, Wilson appointed as his Secretary of the Interior, Franklin K. Lane, an active campaigner who had been city attorney for San Francisco under Mayor Phelan. For the first time in four years, the dammers had a friendly administration in Washington. A bill to take Hetch Hetchy was approved by Lane and then passed Congress as an administration measure late in 1913. In the final Senate vote, eighteen southern Democrats — responsive to the southern Democrat in the White House — provided the margin of victory.

Muir stayed active down to the final votes ("I'll be relieved when it's settled," he told Helen, "for it's killing me"). "Our defeat has weighed heavily on Mr. Muir I think," Colby wrote McFarland a year later. "At least he has been very seriously ill two or three times since the action against us and is now so feeble that he seldom comes to the city." Louie had died in 1905. Muir lived alone in the big house, surrounded by a litter of old journals and manuscripts, working on a book about his Alaskan explorations. Although beaten in his last fight, he could still take some satisfaction in the general spreading of his message. In December 1914 he caught pneumonia and died quickly.

※※

For several years McFarland, Mills, and the Sierra Club had been proposing a national park service, corresponding to the Forest Service, to unify the park responsibilities previously scattered among three cabinet departments. In the wake of Hetch Hetchy, to balance its verdict, Lane and the administration added their support and the new bureau was established in Interior. To head it Lane picked an old friend, Stephen Mather of Chicago, a Sierra Club member and an active enemy of the Hetch Hetchy project. Mather and his disciples would dominate the early history of the National Park Service, often fighting against the utilitarian policies of the Forest Service. Having made a fortune in borax, Mather brought an amateur spirit to government conservation circles; he did not need the job to earn a living. "I got my money out of the soil of the country," he said, "so why should I be praised for putting a little of it back? That's only decent acknowledgment."

The first water from Hetch Hetchy arrived in 1934. The dam cost over $100 million, more than twice the estimate. During the twenty years of planning and construction the city of Oakland, across the bay, tapped a cheaper water source in the Sierra foothills and began to use it. But then the Oakland source provided no hydroelectric power. According to a provision of the 1913 enabling act, any power generated at Hetch Hetchy was to be sold only by public agencies. As it turned out, the transmission lines from the valley stopped at Newark, at the southern tip of San Francisco Bay. George Norris, a leading congressional advocate of the dam in 1913, later recalled: "I underestimated the resourcefulness of the Pacific Gas and Electric Company." To get the power from Newark to San Francisco, it was illegally turned over to the private utility. In the reservoir itself, as the water level rose and fell with the changing seasons the shoreline was marred by slimy mud and decaying vegetation. Nothing could grow at the edge of the artificial lake. Under moonlight, with tree trunks scattered around like so many bodies, it resembled a battlefield one day after the fight: a wasteland bearing stark testimony to man's befuddled ingenuity.

From the perspective of sixty-seven years later, the Hetch Hetchy dam seems a comprehensive mistake. Yet it had a few positive aspects. Never before had such a prolonged fight been waged over an apparent exercise in technological progress. The greatest significance lay in the process, not the outcome. For the conservation movement, Hetch Hetchy left a legacy to future generations: the power of the radical amateur, fueled not by practical or professional motives but by idealism and conviction. Even though eclipsed in the formal movement, the older amateur tradition was not dead.

5
Wildlife Protectors, 1900-1935

HETCH Hetchy brought the early campaigns over land, trees, and water to an ironic climax. Afterward, for the next few decades the conservation movement shifted its focus to the protection of wildlife. Amid the changing issues and personalities, one familiar aspect remained from the early struggles: the clashes between amateurs and professionals, as wildlife protectors indulged in the bloodiest internecine squabbling in the history of the movement.

¥¥

William Temple Hornaday, sixty-six years old in 1920, was the grand old man of wildlife conservation. For two decades he had been the ever vigilant guardian of the endangered wild animals of North America. From his position as director of the Bronx Zoo he poured forth, in books, articles, and news releases, an unquenchable stream of warnings and fretful predictions. "The protection of wild life has become such a burden on my conscience, and so much a part of me," he had confided to a friend in 1912, "that I imagine I never will get free from it." It pricked his conscience because he was a classic instance of the reformed hunter. Once an avid sportsman who exulted at the kill, he then repented and, with all the zeal of the convert, set about atoning for his early sins.

Whether as hunter or protector, all his life he was drawn to wild animals. Growing up in Iowa and Indiana, the youngest child in the family, he spent a lot of time by himself roaming through the nearby woods and marshlands. "As a boy," he recalled, "I was always fascinated by the strange and beautiful things that I discovered day by day in the wild birds and quadrupeds that lived and moved round me." He found his first career in the new craft of taxidermy. During the 1870s he traveled the world, shooting exotic species and sending the mounted remains to American museums. Eventually he moved into zoo keeping and found a permanent mooring when the Bronx Zoo opened in 1896. He was a meticulous, opinionated administrator. Among the zoo's stated purposes was "the preservation of our native animals." He took the clause literally, sometimes to the discomfiture of his board of directors. When frustrated by them he would take his case to the newspapers, who always found him good copy. "The best way is to let Mr. Hornaday speak his mind," one director confided to another, "and then we can meet privately and decide what we are going to do."

Still a hunter, at first he aimed his polemics only at shooters who made excessive kills or otherwise did not behave like gentlemen. Hornaday undertook an initial campaign in support of a picaresque crusader named G. O. Shields who, through his *Recreation* magazine and the short-lived League of American Sportsmen, rained curses on the heads of the hunters he called "game-hogs." In *Recreation* Shields would print lurid pictures of game-hogs and their large kills, with libelous captions ("I pity the dogs that were forced to associate with such miserable swine as these"). Hornaday admired this style of extravagant invective. He became Shields's protector and raised $4,200 for him from 1904 to 1907. But Shields proved too erratic and finally went bankrupt, leaving Hornaday the field.

Thus Hornaday found himself in a delicate situation at the zoo. Its wealthiest patrons included several gentleman hunters. They and many of Hornaday's associates were dismayed by his new course. Madison Grant, his closest ally among the zoo's directors, warned him: "Hornaday, you are losing all your friends." Accordingly, he decided to launch a new organization to separate his protection work from his employment. In 1911 he began raising money for an endowed Permanent Wild Life Protection Fund, to be administered solely by himself. "I decided," he explained, "that inasmuch as I would have to do all the work it would be all right for me to have absolute freedom of action." His initial contributors included Mrs. Russell Sage ($25,000), the photography pioneer George Eastman ($6,000), and Henry Ford and Andrew Carnegie ($5,000 each). In a few years the fund passed its endowment goal of $100,000.

To accompany the fund Hornaday wrote a campaign tract entitled *Our Vanishing Wild Life*. Published in 1913, it was one of the first books wholly devoted to endangered wild animals. It began with a *mea culpa*. "I have been a hunter myself," Hornaday admitted; "but times have changed, and we must change also." Now there were more hunters — some three million — and fewer animals. Some species had been wiped out. The gun companies, moreover, kept improving their products. Instead of the old single- or double-barreled shotgun, hunters now might use automatic weapons that could deliver six shots in as many seconds. Halfway solutions such as bag limits or limited seasons would not suffice. The choice was simple: long closed seasons or a continent with no wild game. Hornaday argued his case with bristling statistics and a relentless urgency that caught the public's attention. A Sierra Club reviewer approvingly remarked of the book, "Its burning and indignant pages remind me of the zeal of the old anti-slavery days when the force of great moral convictions won the day against greed and wrong."

For all his zeal and persistence, Hornaday essentially remained a movement unto himself. By the 1920s he seemed a crotchety, old-fashioned figure, still interested in temperance and phrenology, regarding the Jazz Age with a baleful eye. "The moral standards of the Victorian age are being overthrown and destroyed," he lamented. "The world is going 'modern,' all the way down." He continued his crusade, but he had been sounding his one note for a long time, and he was easily ignored.

His solitary career inevitably raised questions about his motives. Evidently he had no particular affection for animals. A zoo man to the core, he took a manipulative approach to the creatures in his care, expecting them to be docile and tractable. He thought elephants should be dominated for their own good and beaten if necessary. An independent polar bear named Silver King caused him great frustration: "To the last he was savage, dangerous, unreasonable and contrary. Just to spite us, he rarely went into his pool for a swim. . . . In fact, as an exhibition animal Silver King came very near to being a failure." He kept his charges confined to small, barred cages and resisted a trend, pioneered at the St. Louis Zoo and elsewhere, toward letting animals roam in outdoor habitats behind moats.

On the other hand, his interest was not based on a modern scientific curiosity either. An old-fashioned generalist, he resisted the trend toward careful, specialized studies. He once chided an ornithologist for going into a matter too deeply: "I am of a very practical turn of mind, and I like to see practical results accrued or to accrue from the work of an educated man. To be still more frank, I do not see how it is possible to justify devoting any great length of time to the study of parasitism in birds." In the 1920s Aldo Leopold and others were trying to make game management a science by the painstaking investigation of breeding, wintering, and feeding habits. They hoped to preserve game by such methods as controlled breeding and preservation of natural habitats. Hornaday rejected these approaches as diversionary and a waste of time. Instead, he demanded, in writings characterized more by italics and reiteration than by subtlety of argument, a single course: stop the shooting. As an exasperated game expert, William C. Adams of Massachusetts, declared in 1926, "Hornaday belongs to the old school that thought the only way to save game in this country was to put restriction after restriction on the gunner."

In the absence of any compelling sentimental or scientific interest, Hornaday's motives seem to have been largely personal: to expiate his own guilt and to further the cause so identified with his name. He literally kept a list divided into "friends" and "enemies." He inhabited a simple moral universe in which he would smite the opposition merely because it was the opposition. Even his admirers were made uncomfortable by the way he personalized every controversy. "He will take a certain issue at a certain date," one ally remarked, "and the people of that issue and date divide into heroes and villains. . . . [He is] entirely incapable of surveying a field without reference to himself." For Hornaday, protecting animals and defending his own reputation were a single undertaking.

❦❦

A few miles to the south of Hornaday's Bronx Zoo lay the Manhattan offices of the two principal organized defenders of wildlife. The National Association of Audubon Societies, incorporated in 1905, held the various state Audubon groups in a loose union. At least at its inception, the Audubon movement embodied the Muir tradition of the radical amateur in conservation, drawing its strength from dedicated volunteers motivated simply by their love for birds. In contrast, the American Game Protective Association, founded in 1911, implied the Pinchot tradition of professional management for practical returns. The AGPA was, somewhat covertly, a trade group financed by the major gun and ammunition companies. But it included many disinterested sportsmen as well. Thus it represented conservation for mixed motives.

The Audubon movement began with George Bird Grinnell. He had grown up in Audubon Park, a thirty-acre tract in upper Manhattan formerly owned by the great bird painter and protoconservationist. ("All this grand portion of our Union," Audubon had said of Ohio in 1831, "instead of being in a state of nature, is now more or less covered with villages, farms, and towns, where the din of hammers and machinery is constantly heard. . . . Whether these changes are for the better or for the worse, I shall not pretend to say.") As a boy in the 1860s Grinnell hunted muskrats by the Harlem River with Audubon's grandson and attended a school run by the painter's widow. After graduating from Yale he continued to live with his family in Audubon's old home while pursuing a desultory career at his father's Wall Street brokerage office. He spent his summers out West hunting buffalo, riding with the Pawnee, or immersed in paleontological studies. His father's firm almost went under in the Panic of 1873. "The winter was one of great suffering for the family," he recalled, "and in my efforts to divert my mind from the misfortune that had happened, I began to write short hunting stories." When his father retired he dissolved the business and bought control of *Forest and Stream,* the major sportsmen's magazine of the day. As editor Grinnell made it a seminal force in the preservation of natural resources and wild animals.

In 1886 Grinnell proposed an organization for the protection of wild birds and their eggs; naturally he called it the Audubon Society. It attracted distinguished support from John Greenleaf Whittier, Oliver Wendell Holmes, and others. Within two years some fifty thousand members had sent in their dues and pledges to carry out the group's purposes. The staff at *Forest and Stream,* unprepared for such enthusiasm, found itself swamped by administrative tasks. Grinnell then thought better of the scheme and in 1889 quietly let it lapse.

For the time being, bird protection rested with a scientific group, the American Ornithologists' Union. The AOU was founded in 1883 by three New Englanders: Elliott Coues of New Hampshire and J. A. Allen and William Brewster of Massachusetts. Motivated in part by conservationist and esthetic ends, the AOU's main purpose was to help identify and classify bird species. In the absence of modern cameras and optical aids, birders had to kill birds in order to study them. Brewster thus recalled sighting a fine bald eagle: "Its position was very erect, its pose impressively dignified and commanding. 'What a noble creature!' I said to myself" — and then he shot it. Sentiment must yield to science. Yet even so dedicated a collector of specimens as Brewster sometimes had second thoughts. Once, watching a hawk catch a martin, he found himself strangely chilled by the martin's cries. "I was moved by deep pity and fierce wrath to an extent surprising on the part of one who, like myself, has killed thousands of birds without suffering more than an occasional slight qualm." The AOU, perhaps acting on such misgivings, established a committee to protect North American birds and drafted a "model law" to prohibit on a state level the killing of certain endangered species.

The Audubon movement was revived in 1896, when Mrs. Augustus Hemenway of Boston called a meeting to protest the destruction of heron habitats in the South. The protestors formed a Massachusetts Audubon Society and elected William Brewster its president. Later that year a similar group was started in Pennsylvania. By 1898 there were fifteen more, mostly in the Northeast. These state Audubon societies helped pass the first federal legislation for bird protection, the Lacey Act of 1900. Sponsored by Representative John F. Lacey of Iowa, it outlawed the interstate shipment of any birds killed in violation of state laws. It also made the Bureau of Biological Survey in the Agriculture Department responsible for enforcing the law. Although limited to those species already protected by individual state legislation, it at least placed the authority and enforcement powers of the federal government behind the movement for bird protection. Many protected songbirds were being killed and sold across state lines as game birds; other rare species were being hunted for feathers to supply the millinery trade. The Lacey Act, wherever enforced, stopped these practices. Many Audubon members helped out by prowling local markets, on the lookout for illegal merchandise.

In New York the focus of these activities was a middle-aged insurance agent named William E. Dutcher. Long the mainstay of the AOU's protection committee, he took a leading part in organizing the New York Audubon Society. Taking time from his business that he could not well afford, Dutcher spent up to half his working hours on unpaid efforts for birds. In the fall of 1901, along with Frank M. Chapman of the American Museum of Natural History he visited bird shops on Bond Street in New York, looking for violations of the Lacey Act. "In all the places we visited," Dutcher reported with satisfaction, "they got on to the fact that we were looking for illegal birds; Lehmans were angry enough to eat us. They became very abusive and accused me of going around to their trade and inducing their customers to return goods to them."

In states that still lacked bird laws, Dutcher supported lobbying activities by Theodore S. Palmer of the Biological Survey with AOU funds raised by Abbott Thayer, a wildlife painter with access to rich people. Generally, though, the AOU was more interested in scientific work — and shooting specimens — than in protection. Dutcher also felt limited by the straitened finances of the AOU, since its membership consisted mainly of boys and young adults who could barely pay the annual dues of three dollars. "There are very few men who have any means who belong to the Union," he noted, "and those who have are all doing something in one way or another." He therefore decided to revive the idea of a national Audubon group.

In 1901 the state Audubon groups formed a national committee under

Dutcher's leadership. Thinking the new scheme would bring in more money, he expanded his publicity and lobbying efforts. By January 1903, the new committee was seven hundred dollars in debt. Only three state groups — those of Massachusetts, New Hampshire, and Vermont — had sent funds for clerical help. "I am disgusted and tired of the whole matter," Dutcher told Palmer. "It seems to me that if I give at least half my time to the work I should have the necessary clerical aid." A financial angel fortunately appeared in September 1904. Albert Wilcox, a New York bird fancier, paid off all the debts and offered to leave the group over $100,000 in his will — on condition that the organization be broadened to include wild animals as well as birds, and then placed on a more permanent basis through incorporation. Early in 1905 the thirty-six state groups created the National Association of Audubon Societies. "The object of this organization," Dutcher explained, "is to be a barrier between wild birds and animals and a very large unthinking class, and a smaller but more harmful class of selfish people." Wilcox obligingly died in 1906. His total bequests for Audubon work ultimately reached some $320,000.

As president of the new group, Dutcher for the first time had real money at his disposal. He expanded the system of local game wardens hired to enforce the new state laws. (An Audubon warden, Guy Bradley of Florida, was killed by a poacher in 1905.) He hired lecturers and fieldworkers to spread the word. Legislative expenses continued, even in states that had already passed protective laws. Dutcher spent over a thousand dollars in 1907 to keep a lobbyist in Texas simply to prevent the repeal of bird laws passed four years earlier. Ironically, the well-publicized Wilcox bequest made it harder to raise money through normal channels because the association seemed assured of a permanent income. In 1906 Dutcher sent out four thousand appeals for five-dollar memberships. Returns did not even pay the mailing expenses.

Dutcher wore himself out in his multiple roles of insurance agent, fund raiser, drumbeater, and administrator. A man of high principles, utterly dedicated to his mission, he evidently lacked the calculating eye of an efficient manager. He overextended both himself and the association's resources. In the first half of 1907, the association ran up a deficit of over eight thousand dollars. At the end of the year the Audubon board of directors, which had formerly given Dutcher a free hand, sharply questioned his spending practices. After unpleasant exchanges Dutcher resigned as president. The resignation was later withdrawn, but thereafter he functioned with less autonomy. The board of directors was reshuffled to include more people from the New York vicinity, who would thus be able to attend meetings more regularly and maintain tighter control. Dutcher continued as the titular leader but probably chafed under the new regime. In October 1910 he was permanently disabled by a stroke that left him unable to speak or to write anything but his signature. Though he lingered on for ten years his active role was finished.

To succeed Dutcher the directors chose T. Gilbert Pearson, a field-worker since 1904. He would be the dominant figure in Audubon circles for the next quarter century. Cautious where Dutcher was bold, frugal where Dutcher was profligate, he made a sharp contrast to his predecessor. "One of the most pleasant sounds I ever hear," he said, "is the clink of a life membership fee as it drops into the money box." Thirty-seven years old in 1910, he came from an old Pennsylvania Quaker family that had moved to Florida because of his father's health. Like most birders he started young, by making collections of birds' eggs. At thirteen he shot his first specimen — a grackle — and was so proud that he took it to bed. To neighbors these activities seemed odd and worthless. "I lived in a world to myself," he recalled. "Either I was unbalanced or everybody else was stupid." After graduation from the University of North Carolina he became a biology teacher but maintained his bird interests as a hobby. When he published a book of bird stories it brought him to the attention of William Dutcher. In 1902, at Dutcher's urging, Pearson organized a North Carolina Audubon group. Among its 140 charter members were two bank presidents and three college presidents. A year later he pushed a protection bill through the state legislature. In 1904 Dutcher added him to the association's staff.

As Dutcher became more radical, finally opposing even the taking of specimens by naturalists, Pearson acted as a moderating influence. Even before Dutcher's stroke Pearson had assumed some of his duties. After the stroke he was the logical, although not unanimous, choice to succeed Dutcher. Once in power Pearson developed a knack for raising money from wealthy donors, in part by imposing a less extreme image on the association. Toward that end he delivered a "conservative talk" to a group of hunters in Connecticut. "They seemed very glad that I was able to be with them," he reported, "and some of them frankly stated that heretofore they regarded the Audubon Society as a company of long-haired fanatics." Under Pearson no one could make that mistake.

In 1911 the association was offered another financial windfall. Harry Leonard of the Winchester Repeating Arms Company made Pearson an offer: if the Audubon groups would increase their efforts for the protection of game birds, the major gun companies would contribute $25,000 a year for five years. The arrangement would have doubled the Audubon annual income and raised Pearson's salary from $3,000 to $6,000. He submitted the offer to his directors with a recommendation for approval. Two of them, William Brewster and Jonathan Dwight, rejected the proposal. "Just think what a row these subscribers would kick up," Dwight pointed out, "if they did not get what they would expect for their money." The loss of amateur status and (perhaps) of independence had to be weighed against the obvious advantages in money and connections. George Bird Grinnell, one of the most influential directors, at first resisted the offer but then changed his mind. He argued Brewster around as well. The board then voted by a substantial majority to accept the money.

William Hornaday and G. O. Shields, who were not Audubon members, pounced on the news. They accused the association of compromising its principles for blood money. Well circulated by the press, the accusation brought down a torrent of negative publicity. William Dutcher, whose lobbying the gun companies had sometimes opposed, could only look on mutely as his handiwork was corrupted. "If he could speak," his wife wrote Pearson, "he would plainly give you to understand how he does not at all approve of what you have done and so taken advantage of his helplessness. I am greatly disappointed in your friendship for Mr. Dutcher and now look upon you as one of his greatest enemies." Under fire Pearson suddenly changed his mind. Much to Grinnell's disgust, he asked the directors to rescind their action. They did so on June 16, two weeks after the acceptance. "Frank Chapman opened a hole through which the board was able to crawl out of the situation without eating too much humble pie," Grinnell noted. "Of course Hornaday and his friends have won a triumph."

The gun companies under Winchester leadership then launched their own group, the American Game Protective Association. A Grinnell protégé, John B. Burnham, was appointed its president. The new group was endorsed by Theodore Roosevelt, John Burroughs, and other noted sportsmen. Grinnell, transferring his allegiance from the Audubon Association, worked to bring the AGPA into an alliance with his Boone and Crockett Club. He conceded that "the manufacturers are striving to protect the game in order to furnish targets for the persons who purchase their arms." But to Grinnell, "so long as the game is protected and increased, the use to which it is put is of no great importance. These natural things are for the use of man, under reasonable limitations." The AGPA was the first sportsman-supported national organization with a full-time professional staff. As such it represented an important new force — regardless of the motives of the companies paying the bills.

Now the Audubon Association had a competitor, interested in many of the same issues but with a more secure income and more direct ties to the business community. "Our friends in the American Game Protective Association are constantly forging ahead," Theodore Palmer advised Pearson from Washington, "and it seems to me that we must be pretty active to maintain our prestige before the general public in our special field." In 1913 the two groups united behind the most important piece of bird legislation yet passed by Congress. The Lacey Act of 1900, by relying on state laws, had created a patchwork of local regulation and conflicting jurisdictions. For years thereafter conservationists tried to bring migratory birds — which crossed state borders — under the wing of the interstate commerce clause of the Constitution. In 1912 another bill for this purpose was introduced by John W. Weeks of New Hampshire in the House and by George P. McLean of Connecticut in the Senate. (McLean's constituents included Winchester, Remington, and other gun companies.) The Weeks–McLean bill empowered the Biological Survey to regulate hunting seasons and to protect some species entirely. Because it extended federal powers, it was opposed mainly by states' rights congressmen from the South and West.

The bill also attracted the support of a bird lover with great power at his fingertips. "Birds are the best of companions," said Henry Ford. He kept hundreds of birdhouses on his estate in Michigan, including a martin house with no fewer than seventy-six apartments. More enthusiastic than informed, Ford once risked ecological havoc by importing some five hundred alien species from Europe to see if they would like America. When he learned of the Weeks–McLean bill he asked all six hundred Ford dealers to write their congressmen. He also sent one of his top advertising men, Glenn Buck, to Washington with instructions not to return until the bill was passed. Buck and his assistants sent out dozens of publicity releases and thousands of telegrams. The techniques that sold Model T's were applied to bird protection.

Still Congress would not pass the bill. At the end of the session in March 1913, Burnham smoothly played his last card, in a maneuver that recalled the forest reserve act of 1891. The substance of the legislation was attached as a rider to an agricultural appropriation bill. Thus concealed from its enemies, it passed both houses and reached Taft's desk in the last hours of his administration. In the final rush of business he signed the bill without reading it. (Later he said he would have vetoed the bill as unconstitutional had he known its contents.) Ultimately the bill was incorporated in a treaty with Canada and upheld by the Supreme Court. "Wild birds are not in the possession of anyone," Justice Holmes declared, and therefore the states had no claim to them.

With the act's enforcement power resting in the Biological Survey, Secretary of Agriculture David Houston appointed an advisory board of fifteen, including Pearson, Grinnell, Hornaday, and John Lacey. The key position of chairman went to Burnham, the representative of the hunting "industry." The board had no statutory authority and could only make recommendations at its annual meetings. In 1916 it suggested more stringent regulations and was ignored. "*All* our recommendations," Hornaday noted, "were hilariously dumped into the wastebasket by the Biological Survey." But usually the board and the survey agreed on what needed to be done. Spring shooting seasons were abolished. Hunting game to sell at market, previously limited on a piecemeal basis, was totally outlawed. Wood ducks and most shorebirds were protected. The fall hunting season was limited to a maximum of three and one half months, and daily bag limits were set at twenty-five ducks and ten geese per hunter. Under these restrictions the game bird population began a slow recovery that lasted into the 1920s.

After this success the bird protection movement entered a less strenuous period. Alternating rhythms of crusading and administration run through the history of conservation; bursts of energy to pass laws are followed by quieter efforts to execute them. After the passage of the Weeks–McLean bill and other protective measures, Grinnell — who had been in the struggle longer than anyone — saw the risk of complacency. "It seems to me that just now the game protective movement is in some danger of overconfidence," he said late in 1913. "The success of the last year has been so astonishing that some of us may feel that the work has all been done." It appeared that the legislative efforts of two decades had been capped. For the next several years no further laws were proposed.

Wildlife protection by 1920 amounted to a kind of establishment, stretching from Boston to Washington, with minimal links to the South and West. E. W. Nelson, head of the Biological Survey, was on familiar terms with representatives of the gun companies and conservation groups. The principal wildlife protectors belonged to the same clubs and organizations, and they all lived in the East. Hunters elsewhere could plausibly regard bird protection as a plot by the Atlantic seaboard states. The oldest and largest wildlife group, the Audubon Association, had a total of 5,137 members. Of these, 72 percent were residents of New York, New Jersey, Pennsylvania, and New England. "We find it hard to get members in the South," Pearson noted, "and when we do they do not stick." By this time the movement needed new ideas and leaders. But they would come from outside the eastern wildlife establishment.

⚜⚜

On January 14, 1922, a group of fifty-four hunters and fishermen sat down to lunch at the Chicago Athletic Association. They were mostly business and professional people of middle income. Twelve made their living in sales or advertising, the largest single occupational group among them. Aside from two in the sporting goods business, none had a financial interest in the subject at hand. None was connected with the eastern wildlife establishment. They met to swap stories and discuss ways of meeting the latest crisis in wildlife populations. Someone suggested they form a new conservation group; the idea took hold. In March they opened a headquarters in Chicago. In the next five months, as membership dues flowed in from around the Midwest, they twice had to move to larger quarters. The group was named the Izaak Walton League after the "patron saint" of sport fishermen.

The central figure in the league was a fifty-three-year-old advertising man named Will H. Dilg. "Since boyhood," he admitted, "the call of black bass waters has been my chief weakness." In 1921 the *Outlook* had published his enraptured celebration of a recent invention, the cork-bodied black bass fly. ("If you have never taken a fish on a floating bug, you have a series of indescribable sensations ahead of you.") Warmed to his subject, he could be relentlessly persuasive. He had a worn, emaciated face set off by a long jaw and penetrating eyes. He talked fast, unstoppably, in a voice that carried. Well dressed and carrying a cane, he cut a figure of urban sophistication. His favorite idiom was the expansive hyperbole of boosterism.

Just beneath this surface Dilg had a second, more authentic personality: darker-hued, yet sentimental and nostalgic. According to one story, he was driven to found the Izaak Walton League by the death of his young son. In his grief he decided to devote himself to saving the outdoors experience for other young boys. Be that as it may, he did strike many observers as a man possessed by some messianic purpose. "I am weary of civilization's madness," he declared, "and I yearn for the harmonious gladness of the woods and of the streams. I am tired of your piles of buildings and I ache from your iron streets. I feel jailed in your greatest cities and I long for the unharnessed freedom of the big outside." As head of the new league he dropped his advertising work and toiled long hours, doing — he claimed — the work of at least six men. In August 1922 he launched a monthly magazine, at first called the *Izaak Walton League Monthly* and then (after October 1923) *Outdoor America*. Under Dilg's direction it quickly became the most comprehensive journal in the conservation movement.

At the time, the Sierra Club addressed itself to mountaineering and national park matters; Pinchot's National Conservation Association covered forestry and power development; the Audubon Association discussed birds and other wildlife. (In 1921 Pearson confessed that he knew nothing about a certain park issue: "I must not allow this interest to draw me too far from our main line.") The old groups guarded their respective domains and no one asked the large questions. Except Dilg. With a fine impartiality he asked all sorts of questions. Most of the articles in *Outdoor America* reflected his own priorities — water pollution and the indiscriminate drainage of marsh areas (because of their effect on fishing conditions) and the problems of forest fires and reforestation. In addition, Dilg opened his magazine to diverse points of view within the conservation movement, making it a unique forum of conflicting opinion. The magazine also carried regular monthly departments on camping, bird lore, fly casting, firearms, and even (briefly) a women's section.

Outdoor America was thus already unprecedented in its field. But Dilg thought big, and he was not shy. Aiming to make his magazine the first conservation journal with a mass audience, he flattered and badgered writers of large reputation into contributing work for no pay. "I am earnestly hoping that you will send us a story or an article for the magazine," he wrote Hal G. Evarts, a regular contributor to the *Saturday Evening Post*. "It is obvious that each great American who declares himself for us now adds to our national prestige and our convert-drawing ability. You, of course, know what a splendid thing an editorial by you would be for the magazine and the cause it espouses." The writers who succumbed to such blandishments included Zane Grey, Mary Roberts Rinehart, Emerson Hough, Irvin S. Cobb, Albert Bigelow Paine, Gene Stratton Porter, David Starr Jordan, and Henry Van Dyke. John Held, Jr., contributed occasional drawings and cover paintings. In the March 1924 issue, Theodore Dreiser recalled his boyhood in Indiana and his favorite fishing spot on the Tippecanoe River. Later on, said Dreiser, "some local clown or hobbledehoy of the practical variety" had turned his spot into a drainage ditch, arguing for the economic benefits it would bring to the town. "Nonsense. Pish," Dreiser growled. "Can you imagine any sane community anywhere in the world making or permitting any such exchange?"

Dreiser was not simply indulging the nostalgia of middle age for a lost, idyllic youth. He was sounding one of *Outdoor America*'s major themes: a fretful looking back to the old fishing hole and a dawning sense that modern progress was polluting it, filling it in, paving it over. The lament was not merely for lost youth but for a lost America.

The outdoor life, then, seemed a compensation for everyday modern life — a notion that Waltonians sometimes expressed in religious terms. Dilg made frequent reference to an entity he called "the God of Nature." Irvin S. Cobb, a popular humorist and cheerful cynic, let down his guard when confronted by the "wholesome idolatry" of reverence for nature: "There is no religion healthier for a man's spiritual and physical well-being than the pagan worship of the woodsman." The most striking speculations of this sort were made in 1923 by James Oliver Curwood, a popular novelist and later one of the league's national directors. "I fear that I am going to shock many people," he wrote. While growing up on an Ohio farm, he had acquired an early reputation as a hunting prodigy who killed large quantities of game. He was introduced as such to great applause at a country revival meeting. "No one of all those Christians told me that I should stop killing." Instead the message was that man should inherit the earth: "For me, all the universe had been built. For me, the Great Hereafter was solely created. All other life was merely incidental, and made especially for my benefit." Then, in a process that resembled Muir's religious hegira, he became a pantheist not by reading but simply by immersing himself in nature. When engulfed by other organisms, Curwood saw the absurdity in man's thinking that he was "the one toad in the huge puddle of life." That insight led to conservation. Not just wild animals and fishes, but grass, trees and flowers all had their rightful places; "every heart that beats is a spark from the breath of god." Muir would have approved.

Along with these themes of nostalgia and nature worship, Dilg attracted members by creating a clubhouse atmosphere of masculine fellowship. "We are composed of thousands upon thousands of HE MEN," he trumpeted, "and our League will continue to advance in POWER AND INFLUENCE." In camp the Waltonians might tell dirty stories, enjoy them loudly, neglect to shave or wash, and belch and scratch. Unimpressed by Prohibition, they were not ashamed to admit their fondness for drink. In 1925, six years into Prohibition, *Outdoor America* printed the following poem:

If you care to meet a fellow with a drop upon his hip
And can tell a fishing story as you take a little nip,
You're the man that we've been wanting and your fancy we'll intrigue
And we'll treat you like a brother in the Izaak Walton League.

To be treated like a brother: that was the league's most powerful recruiting device. During the 1920s the fraternal service organizations — Lions, Kiwanis, Rotary, and others — were growing fast. Dilg appropriated their methods, addressing members as "brother sportsmen," promising friendship and the warm glow of disinterested public service for common goals. In March 1923 the league hired as executive secretary a man who previously had been office manager at Kiwanis national headquarters. By design, a typical chapter of the league resembled not one of the older conservation groups but rather a Rotary Club that liked to go fishing.

At national headquarters in Chicago, Dilg worked under the nominal direction of a nine-man executive committee. Three of its members were directors of the Continental and Commercial National Bank, one of the largest banks in the country — "and each of these men has practically given us ten thousand dollars," Dilg informed Gifford Pinchot in November 1924. The committee's chairman and most generous member was George E. Scott, the president of a steel foundry. He normally stayed in the background and contented himself with playing silent partner to Dilg. According to one observer, "Dilg was essentially a dreamer, an apostle; Scott is a hard-headed, clear-thinking business man." They complemented each other well and together led the league during its early years of heady expansion.

At a time when the Sierra Club, the AGPA, and the Audubon Association each had a membership of seven thousand or less, the Izaak Walton League had more than one hundred thousand members within three years of its founding. In the month of February 1924, 52 new chapters were formed; in March, another 118; in April, another 124. The local chapters in turn formed state divisions. It was a phenomenon — the first conservation group with a mass membership. Although concentrated in the Midwest, practically every state was represented. The strongest local organizations were in Illinois, Oklahoma, and Iowa. A convention of the Oklahoma division drew a crowd of five thousand; the governor delivered the main address. The Minnesota division helped save the Superior National Forest from inroads by lumber companies. A meeting of the Indiana division was addressed by Judge Kenesaw Mountain Landis, the commissioner of baseball. When Dilg was introduced, Landis jumped to his feet, embraced him, and kissed him on the forehead. The audience cheered.

The league was, apparently, Dilg's personal fief. As salesman, organizer, and editor he had created it. At the first annual convention, held in Chicago in April 1923, he was described in terms recalling the struggles of the early Christian martyrs. "It was as though a second Stephen was preaching a Crusade," one man declared. "And so he has borne the Cross." Another speech compared him to St. Paul, "this prince among men." He was then elected president by acclamation. A year later fourteen hundred delegates retained Dilg in office by a unanimous vote. William Hornaday, who addressed the convention, exclaimed to Dilg: "I have been going to conservation gatherings for more than forty years and I have never seen anything like this convention." The third annual gathering, in 1925, was again a huge success. "In the world of conservation," Dilg said without undue exaggeration, "our League stands forth like a towering mountain set in the center of a vast prairie."

❧❧

As the wildlife conservation movement returned to a period of activism and campaigns for legislation, the Izaak Walton League held the wild cards. It brought new pressures on Congress through its sheer size and because it spoke for a different area of the country. It had Will Dilg as well, with his mercurial personality and headlong enthusiasm. Nobody in the AGPA–Audubon–Biological Survey establishment knew Dilg, and even after meeting him they were not sure what to make of him. ("I had a feeling that he might do or say something unusual at any moment," Pearson recalled.) In the legislative struggles of the 1920s the league acted as a powerful but unpredictable catalyst, stirring up the older forces and precipitating the most bitter internal struggles in the history of conservation.

Although obscured by the smoke and confusion of the squabbling, wildlife was still the point of it all. The first years after World War I brought a crisis in migratory waterfowl populations. Ducks and geese found themselves squeezed between shrinking habitats and more hunters. The marshes and river bottoms that provided feeding and breeding grounds were being drained for human development. At the same time, a cluster of broad social changes — better roads, more automobiles, shorter workweeks, more vacation time, extra cash — sent more hunters into the field than ever before. In 1911, 1.5 million state hunting licenses were issued. That figure increased to 4.5 million in 1922 and 6.5 million in 1928. Thus the debate among conservationists: whether to save habitats or check hunting. The debate became embittered in part because no one truly understood the situation. Wildlife management was not yet a science. The first, tentative waterfowl census was not published until 1930. In the absence of hard facts, people took firm positions depending on what they wanted to believe. But it is important to bear in mind, as one sorts through the tangled history of the next few years, that no one really knew. For the time being it all came down to a matter of opinion.

George Bird Grinnell's opinion commanded respect everywhere except at the Bronx Zoo. (Hornaday had written off Grinnell after the Audubon–gun company issue of 1911, and now referred to him as "the Great Stuffed Prophet.") Relying on reports since he was no longer able to enter the field himself, Grinnell rejected Hornaday's warnings about the dwindling duck population. The ducks *seemed* to be disappearing because their nesting, stopping, and feeding areas were being taken over by man. Pushed out to more remote areas, the ducks continued to breed in numbers beyond human observation and so stretched their shrinking habitats to the limit. Reducing bag limits would therefore only exacerbate this overpopulation. Instead the solution was to increase the federal warden force and save habitats from drainage: in short, to expand the system of federal wildlife refuges. After several decades of game laws, hunters seemed to appreciate the need for more protection and would abide by new restrictions. "Most of us began as ardent hunters," Grinnell said in 1926, "but later our viewpoint changed. To look back on wild life as it was half a century ago is saddening, but the change of sentiment in recent years brings cheer. . . . A new era has begun, and more and more people demand that refuges be set aside where the wild creatures may live and man may not encroach on them."

Beginning in 1920, the eastern wildlife establishment annually tried to push through Congress a game-refuge bill drafted by John Burnham of the AGPA and E. W. Nelson of the Biological Survey. It proposed a system of refuges strung along the migratory paths of ducks, geese, and other waterfowl. Funding would come from a new federal hunting license, which would cost one dollar a year. Most of this money would go toward buying the land for refuges from private owners; the rest would be spent on administration and protection by the Biological Survey. Under the survey's control, the refuges would also be used as public shooting grounds. On the four existing refuges, established under Theodore Roosevelt and Taft, no hunting was allowed. The new bill thus redefined what a federal game refuge should be.

This controversial aspect of the bill suggested the influence of Burnham and his employers. Officially, the AGPA declared itself a conservation group of sportsmen, dedicated to protecting game and preserving the American tradition of free hunting, financed by the contributions of its individual members. "I am an advocate of free shooting from patriotic motives," Burnham told one outsider. Other motives may be inferred from the composition of the board of directors: seven of the twelve were employed by gun and ammunition companies. In 1921, 77 percent of the group's total income of $27,000 was contributed directly by the arms industry, including $5,000 each from Winchester, Remington, and Du Pont. At a directors meeting in May 1921 Burnham neglected to mention his patriotic motives. "We are the insurance for the future of your business," he said. "The American Game Protective Association secured the federal migratory bird laws, which have doubled the number of wildfowl in this country. This increase will not benefit the public unless the public can have places to shoot the birds.... It took $20,000 to put over the first law. It will require as much or more to get the public shooting grounds." That fall the manufacturers gave Burnham an extra $5,000 toward the bill and repeated the favor two years later.

The bill gathered a motley but effective opposition. Hornaday of course objected to the shooting-grounds provision. Since the sponsors would not drop this section, he opposed the entire bill. Will Dilg at first supported it but then changed his mind, outwardly because he objected on principle to a federal hunting license. In Congress, states' rights Democrats from the South and West voted down the bill each year, with some help from Republicans offended by the shooting-grounds provision. "When I was a boy out in Arizona," Hornaday's congressman, Fiorello La Guardia, told the House, "a hunter would shoulder a gun, take to the hills, and hunt game. He had to hunt in the real sense of the word. But can you picture a bird sanctuary fenced in with a stone wall and a line of pikers in close formation advancing into the woods and slaughtering without limit?"

As the annual frustrations in Congress piled up, Burnham detected a cooling of interest among the AGPA's underwriters. In response he described the wildlife situation in ever more desperate terms — and made sure the manufacturers could not miss the bottom line. "I should like to call the attention of the directors of this association," he wrote in July 1924, "to the fact that both the game and free shooting in this country are in a mighty precarious situation, and that your business interests are to that extent at stake." By this time E. R. Galvin, sales director for Du Pont, had decided to seek other opinions about the bill. A questionnaire mailed to a national list of sportsmen and farmers brought a startling response: 90 percent of the replies opposed the bill. Burnham had assured the directors that the bill had no significant opposition. In December 1924 Galvin — evidently without clearing the matter with his bosses — took a public position against the bill. The measure, even if passed, could not succeed without general public support, argued Galvin, and he had been misled about the extent of that support. Recalling that the AGPA had received over $175,000 from the gun companies in recent years, Galvin drew his own bottom line: "A detailed statement showing what benefit has been accomplished by the expenditure of that amount would be interesting, no doubt, to the contributing manufacturers."

Burnham mobilized his allies to meet the defection of Galvin. Two sportsmen's groups in Massachusetts declared a boycott against Du Pont products. Under pressure, Du Pont announced its unbroken support for the bill. In February 1925 Galvin was fired. Burnham rode out the crisis, but his bill remained in legislative stalemate. So long as the gun companies insisted on public shooting grounds and the federal license, the bill could not pass Congress.

Hornaday's solution to the problem — cutting bag limits in half — was blocked by what he called "the Burnham–Nelson–Pearson combine." Hornaday was the sort of man who could find a conspiracy under every rock. In this case, though, his paranoia had a certain validity. Burnham's employers naturally favored their own bill over any scheme that would reduce the sales of guns and ammunition. Nelson's bureau could not enforce Hornaday's suggested cuts with its existing staff of only twenty-four wardens, and moreover stood to gain money, personnel, and power if the AGPA bill were passed. The bureau and the arms companies, then, were acting from a rational self-interest. Pearson's behavior was more perplexing. He presided over the oldest and largest conservation group in the East. Its historic role had been to protect birds, not hunters. Since the gun company issue of 1911 had driven a wedge between hunters and preservers, the state Audubon groups had veered toward the viewpoint of the latter. Pearson persisted in trying to hold the factions together despite criticism from his own members, especially from the active state societies in New Jersey and Massachusetts. Winthrop Packard, a leader of the Massachusetts group, put the question directly to Pearson: "The sportsmen are well organized, backed by great gun and ammunition corporations, represented by powerful magazines, well able to take care of themselves. Do not the Audubon Societies distinctly stand on the other side of the question?" Pearson brushed aside such queries as expressions of "ultra sentiment" by persons not well acquainted with the situation. "Their vision and experience on the whole conservation idea of wild life is not very extensive," he wrote.

Hornaday's Permanent Wild Life Protection Fund yielded an annual income of around thirty-five hundred dollars. With that financial support he took his case to the country, wielding language like a caber, not subtly but effectively. "The sportsmen are led by the men and organizations *in-*

terested in killing," he declared, "— with profits, salaries and emoluments at stake. The *only* money available for our much vaunted 'protection' is the blood money derived from the annual sale of licenses to kill game!!" Hornaday's most receptive constituency lay west of the Alleghenies, where conservationists had no ties with the wildlife establishment and were inclined to view Washington as a foreign capital. The secretary of the New Mexico Game Protective Association, Aldo Leopold, requested two hundred copies of a Hornaday poster and proposed "a thoroughgoing amendment" of the bag-limit law in his state. The Izaak Walton League convention in 1924 endorsed cutting the federal duck bag limit from twenty-five to ten per day. Hornaday also received faithful editorial support from *Outdoor Life,* a monthly published in Denver, and from J. N. Darling, the widely syndicated editorial cartoonist based in Des Moines. A successful barnstorming trip through the Midwest by Hornaday late in 1924 left the eastern establishment fretting about his growing influence. "I am told that he has made a great impression in that western country," Grinnell reported, "and that he has the public with him."

In August 1925 Hornaday published an article in the New York *Times* that not only disagreed with the Biological Survey but accused it of dishonesty and corruption. After sketching the connections from the survey to its advisory board to the AGPA to the gun companies, Hornaday concluded that corporations were dictating game policies for the sake of profits, not in the interest of wildlife. The villain of the piece, Hornaday insisted, was John Burnham. (Two years later Burnham sued Hornaday for libel, claiming that since the *Times* article he had been "shunned and avoided by many of his friends and associates and by persons engaged and interested in the conservation of game.") Clearly Hornaday had drawn blood; his charges, though lacking documentation, were essentially true. But in the East they were granted little credence because Hornaday seemed to be lashing out from frustration, attacking the survey after it would not do his bidding. An editorial in the *Scientific American* rejected the accusations and added a scolding: "The man is reckoned a poor sportsman who, when he is beaten, turns around looking for someone to bite." In effect Hornaday and Burnham had checkmated each other. They could not pass their own bills, but they could block the other side's.

Out in Chicago, meantime, Will Dilg had played his wild card. In the summer of 1923 he learned of a private development plan to drain a three-hundred-mile stretch of river bottoms on the Upper Mississippi, from Lake Pepin in Minnesota to Rock Island, Illinois. This section of the river supported large populations of wildlife and songbirds, and provided spawning grounds for Dilg's beloved black bass. For over two decades he had spent at least sixty days each year fishing the area. Now developers were threatening his favorite fishing spot. Dilg therefore offered an ambitious solution: turn the whole three hundred miles into a federal wildlife refuge financed by a congressional appropriation of $1.5 million. The largest previous sum voted by Congress for a wildlife preserve had been $40,000 for a Montana bison range in 1909.

J. Horace McFarland, who knew his way around Washington, told Dilg his chances were "not quite so thick as tissue paper." A new hand at the business, Dilg did not know enough to be discouraged. With the help of Senator Medill McCormack of Illinois he went to the White House and for forty minutes urged the scheme on President Coolidge. Dilg in full cry was hard to resist; Coolidge promised to sign the bill if Dilg could push it through Congress. It was introduced by McCormack in the Senate and by Harry Hawes of Missouri in the House. Hawes, a fisherman in the Dilg sense of the word, was the bill's main evangelist. ("It is a notable fact," he told the House, "that of the twelve apostles selected by Christ, four were fishermen.") Dilg secured the endorsement of the General Federation of Women's Clubs, with its two million members, and set out for Washington to pursue his campaign on the spot. From a suite at the New Willard Hotel he deployed his forces, wheeling and dealing in a way that astonished the wildlife establishment. "He had a staff of assistants, he had many callers, his messengers constantly came and went," Pearson recalled. "He conducted his campaign on an expensive scale heretofore unknown in conservation circles."

Dilg found a crucial ally in Herbert Hoover, Secretary of Commerce and the rising star of the Republican Party. Amid the earnest pursuits of this dour Quaker's life, fishing stood out as one of his solitary amusements. He belonged to the Izaak Walton League and contributed occasionally to *Outdoor America.* Once, on an inspection tour of Yellowstone National Park, the gregarious park superintendent tried to engage Hoover in conversation during breakfast. Hoover sat there and ate and said not a word. Later, out on the lake, the superintendent rattled on about the park, the lake, the forest. Still no word from Hoover. Then he opened an elaborate tackle box — a gift in recognition of his honorary presidency of the Walton League — and launched a monologue. "He talked about fishing in various countries of the world, Australia through Scandinavia," the superintendent said later. "He talked almost all the way down the lake. Very interesting."

With his bill passed by the House, and needing a vote in the Senate, Dilg went to see his fellow angler. The two men then called on Coolidge, who approved a parliamentary maneuver that cleared the way for a vote. Endorsed by Robert La Follette and other key senators, the bill was passed unanimously. Coolidge signed it on the following day and presented the pen to Dilg. "At last," said Dilg, "the God of Nature and the wild places and wild things WON." The upstarts from Chicago had made their point. "Dilg's name swept the country from coast to coast," Pearson recalled. "Wherever two or more sportsmen met, Dilg and the Izaak Walton League were discussed." It was the height of Will Dilg's career in conservation.

※※

The outward success masked an unhappy fact: Will Dilg was beginning to self-destruct. In a few years he had built the largest organization and most widely circulating magazine in American conservation. The older groups had met nothing but frustration in Congress; he had passed his own considerable bill. Buoyed by these feats, he saw a future in which he and the Walton League would control national conservation policy. Racing toward this large ambition, he ran against his own literal deadline because he was dying of throat cancer. Illness gave his normal sense of urgency an even harder edge. He carried an aura of crisis around with him. After working himself to exhaustion he would disappear on fishing trips for weeks at a time. At some unrecorded point his tightly wound spring snapped, and he crossed the line between zeal and fanaticism, regarding himself not as a prophet but as the messiah.

From the start he had shown little interest in keeping the league within its budget (he and William Dutcher would have understood each other). Busy with the tasks of expansion and publicity, he would let financial matters slide. "In truth," he said early on, "I have not had the time to think of ways and means to raise money." In September 1924, Dilg sent "A Plain Letter" to his members, announcing that thus far the league had spent a grand total of $252,000, nearly twice its income, leaving a deficit of almost $118,000. The league's remarkable achievements had come at no little cost. George Scott, the league's most generous donor, had connections to the East through his membership in the Boone and Crockett Club. The wildlife establishment, embarrassed by the league's success, began to interest itself in Dilg's internal problems. "I feel it is the duty of the conservative conservationists of the country," Pearson declared in private, "to help strengthen in any way they quietly can the arm of the executive committee that is trying to bring order out of chaos." For a time Dilg still controlled matters at the headquarters in Chicago. His opposition was principally organized by two executive committee members from outside Chicago, George H. Selover of Minneapolis and Jack Cunningham of Kansas City. These two men, along with Scott and his eastern friends, formed a growing anti-Dilg nucleus within the league.

With the league in financial trouble, the gun companies sensed an opening. During 1924, at Remington's initiative, they started placing ads in *Outdoor America*. Remington enrolled its traveling salesmen in the league and instructed them to preach the gospel on their rounds. On occasion these salesmen even helped start new chapters of the league. Dilg always insisted that his organization remain independent of commercial interests. But Remington's assistance and advertising revenue, appearing just when the league needed money badly, probably had some moderating effect. Late in 1925, Dilg was removed as editor of *Outdoor America*. He retained only titular authority as president.

In November he was hospitalized for more radium treatments. His conduct grew increasingly erratic, but he had his reasons. A dying man, he now saw the cherished crusade of his last years being corrupted. The scenario played out like a Greek tragedy, with the hero brought down by hubris and the ramifications of his own success. From the hospital he sent out a maudlin "prayer letter" telling members that he was dying, and asking for their prayers and support. Once out of the hospital he took an extended fishing vacation in Mississippi. In his absence Scott and Selover quietly organized a plan to elect a new president, not telling the chapters what they were doing, moving as confidentially as possible. They charged Dilg with wasting money, defying his directors over *Outdoor America* policy, and claiming to work without compensation while actually drawing some $28,000 plus heavy medical expenses from the league over the past two years. The indictment was tightly drawn and probably accurate enough. The matter was effectively settled even before the annual convention met in April 1926.

One observer of the convention called it "the finest piece of machine politics that I have ever witnessed." Dilg tried to claim the chair but was shouted down. On most votes the insurgents had at least a two-thirds majority; Dilg had lost even his popularity among the membership at large. Selover, as chairman of the executive committee and head of the anti-Dilg forces, expected to assume the presidency but stepped aside at the last minute in favor of Charles Folds, the league treasurer and part of the original Chicago leadership. "With his standing," Selover reasoned, "with the Chicago crowd happy as possible, and with peace in the League, we look forward to a wider opportunity for real service." Dilg was voted a pension. The news of the coup raised a flurry of objections among some members. Zane Grey and James Oliver Curwood resigned from the league in protest. But Dilg was too sick to resume the battle, and he died a year later.

A few weeks after the convention, though, Dilg did enjoy a kind of revenge. Hornaday's congressman, Fiorello La Guardia, read into the *Congressional Record* a group of memos and letters that detailed the working relationship between the gun companies and the AGPA. The most incriminating letters were addressed to E. R. Galvin, the Du Pont employee fired for opposing the AGPA bill; Galvin, then, had perhaps sent the documents along to Hornaday. They proved what Dilg and Hornaday had been saying for years: "the unsportsmanlike and selfish purposes urging the passage of this bill," as La Guardia put it. "These lobbyists know," La Guardia went on, "that the sole purpose of this bill is not to conserve birds but to slaughter birds and to create a better market for cartridges, powder, and guns." The revelation of Burnham's frank discussions with his employers shocked the more disinterested supporters of the AGPA bill. "If he wrote these letters," one supporter noted presciently, "he has killed the game refuge bill." It would not be passed in a form the gun companies could approve.

The game kept getting rougher. For years Hornaday's enemies had been trying to control him by exerting leverage through his employer, the New York Zoological Society. In 1925, after he accused Burnham and the Biological Survey of corruption, Grinnell reported a half dozen pointed resignations from the society. In the spring of 1926, as Hornaday continued to press for bag reductions and to oppose the AGPA bill, Burnham obtained a list of the society's directors and began sounding opinion. La Guardia published the Burnham letters, perhaps obtained from Hornaday, on Thursday, April 29; on the following Tuesday Hornaday, under pressure, submitted his resignation from the zoo to take effect on June 1.

Galvin, Dilg, Hornaday: three opponents of the AGPA bill had lost their jobs. The protection of wildlife had never involved such heavy stakes before. It was little wonder that the air was filled with conspiracy theories. But there was no single conspiracy, only a discrete series of smaller plots. Galvin was fired for operating too independently within the Du Pont structure. Dilg's self-immolation was a piece of good fortune for the enemy, which had only to fan the flames. Hornaday's departure merely culminated a tangle of local feuds in New York of many years' standing. Burnham helped out in each case, but the significant power rested in other hands.

Despite these personal coups, the gun companies were losing patience over the uncertain return on their investments. They gave the AGPA $7,000 less in 1926 than the previous year. When La Guardia, and later Senator William King of Utah, spread their confidential documents over the *Congressional Record,* the gun companies were embarrassed into retiring from the struggle entirely. At an AGPA directors meeting in October 1926, the Du Pont man announced that the manufacturers were withdrawing their support "in the belief that it would 'improve the Association's amateur standing' in the eyes of the public." The following summer, Burnham resigned as president of the group.

Thus a final irony: Dilg in losing had ultimately won. Once the AGPA lost its subsidy, and then its influential president, the wildlife stalemate began to loosen up. In the absence of a game-refuge bill, attention was again focused on Hornaday's plan to cut bag limits. The Biological Survey's advisory board approved such a reduction. E. W. Nelson, Burnham's ally, retired as head of the survey in 1927 and was succeeded by Paul Redington, a forester with no fixed opinions on the matter. In 1929 the bags were reduced to fifteen ducks and four geese per day. That same year a revised version of the game-refuge bill was passed. Sponsored by Senator Peter Norbeck, it established a system of waterfowl refuges without the shooting grounds and the federal-license provision that the gun companies had mandated. The bag reductions and Norbeck bill meant a complete, though belated, victory for the forces that had been led by Dilg and Hornaday.

Dilg's creation, the Izaak Walton League, stayed in debt for years. *Outdoor America* was both the league's best recruiting tool and its biggest expense. As of June 1928 the league was still $125,000 in debt, but its largest creditors were league members inclined to be lenient about payment. A wildlife professional, Seth Gordon of Pennsylvania, succeeded Folds as head of the league in 1928. Gordon brought the league into a touchy alliance with the remains of the AGPA and broadened his group's national base. In 1924, 42 percent of the directors came from Chicago; five years later that figure was down to 15 percent, with the difference made up mostly by increased representation from Kansas and Oklahoma. But the league also spread eastward, with a state division in New Hampshire consisting of twenty-three local chapters. Waltonians could still claim, as one official put it, "the one and only nation wide conservation organization." With age and professionalization it lost the early, Dilg-style amateur radicalism. Yet in range and sheer numbers, with three thousand chapters in forty-three states, it remained unique in the field.

※※

Gilbert Pearson was the last survivor from the old wildlife establishment. For almost two decades he had dominated the Audubon Association. As president he was the chief administrator; as virtual head of the board of trustees he oversaw his own presidential activities. His control was complete, almost beyond criticism. He displayed undeniable skill as a speaker, lobbyist, and fund raiser. Most of his accomplishments and enthusiasm, though, had been left behind earlier in the century. "How many people really care," he reflected in 1927, "whether pelicans or herons or ducks live on? After all, why bother about such things? Speeding over miles of paved highways and drinking beer under shady arbors is so much more important anyway." He posed the question rhetorically, but in asking it he betrayed the weariness of a man who had held office too long. Lacking new conservation ideas, he raised money simply to raise money — and to increase his salary, since he received a percentage of Audubon's total annual income. In 1926 that income amounted to $257,000, with an unexpended surplus of $35,000. A year later the income was $390,000 with a surplus of $48,000. He still loved the clink of coins falling into the money box, and tended to hoard them instead of investing in conservation projects.

Pearson's cautious temperament was compounded by Audubon's incestuous relations with other institutions. Theodore S. Palmer, an Audubon founder, still worked for the Biological Survey in Washington and served as first vice-president of the association. In New York the American Museum of Natural History employed several key Audubon figures, notably the treasurer, Robert Cushman Murphy, and Frank M. Chapman, editor of the Audubon journal *Bird-Lore.* For logistical reasons Audubon meetings were generally held at the museum. The boundaries between these three institutions were blurred. If one was attacked, all three would circle their wagons in mutual self-defense. They amounted to one small, exclusive club, conducted in polite discourse by gentlemen and scholars, impervious to the occasional clamor outside.

In 1926 a midwestern journalist named Irving Brant, annoyed by Audubon's support of the AGPA game-refuge bill, wrote an article critical of Pearson and his associates. Brant's viewpoint inevitably led him to Hornaday, who helped him place the article in a New York newspaper. When he tried to publish an enlarged version of the article in a national magazine, he encountered a stone wall. Submitted to the *Nation,* the article was forwarded to Palmer for critical review, who of course dismissed its assertion that Pearson and the Audubon Association were controlled by gun companies. The article, said Palmer, "seeks simply to revive an old contention which interests only a small group of conservationists." Brant took the article to the *Outlook* and other journals with similar results. His argument, as Palmer said, was familiar to wildlife people but not to the general public. There seemed no way of getting the word to outsiders or even to members of the two hundred local Audubon groups, since no hint of the controversy appeared in *Bird-Lore.*

Meanwhile, Willard Van Name, a maverick at the American Museum, tried to reform the Audubon Association from within. A monastic bachelor whose love for wild creatures compensated for his distrust of human beings, he spent most of his income on militant conservation projects initiated — and usually conducted — solely by himself. In the conservation movement he was regarded as a quixotic, truculent curiosity. "The best way to treat Dr. Van Name is to be silent — to him," Grinnell once remarked. "We may try to set right the people that he is trying to put on the wrong track; but let Dr. Van Name severely alone." Isolated by such treatment and by his own radicalism, he fought with practically everyone. Among his colleagues at the museum he solicited support for an effort to depose Pearson. Murphy seemed sympathetic at first but then was brought into line by Chapman. Van Name next wrote and published a pamphlet, *A Crisis in Conservation,* in the summer of 1929. It described an unnamed bird-protection organization, with a large income and a cash surplus, "which owing to entangled alliances performs its work with inertia, incompetency and procrastination." The director of the museum disavowed any connection with the pamphlet. Van Name was told to submit any future writings to an editorial review board at the museum. The wagons were circled.

A copy of the pamphlet was sent to Rosalie Edge, a rich New York society woman. An Audubon life member, like other members she knew nothing of the society's internal affairs. The pamphlet reached her in Paris. She read it, transfixed, pacing up and down her hotel room while her family waited to go to dinner. "For what to me were dinner and the boulevards of Paris," she later recalled, "when my mind was filled with the tragedy of beautiful birds, disappearing through the neglect and indifference of those who had at their disposal wealth beyond avarice with which these creatures might be saved?" Back in New York, she attended the 1929 Audubon annual meeting at the museum. "My entrance made a stir, though no one knew me. That was the trouble; no stranger was expected. This was a family party of directors and office workers, with a few delegates from Audubon societies of other states." She stood up and asked for a response to Van Name's pamphlet. After a hushed silence came rebuttals from Chapman, Pearson, and others. Edge stood up to make further inquiries. Pearson finally said, in effect, that the lady had spoiled the meeting because now there was no time to show the film that was to have been the feature of the gathering, and furthermore lunch was getting cold. Chapman's account of the meeting in *Bird-Lore* did not mention this unseemly debate.

Word got out, though, and brought Edge into contact with the other conspirators. Van Name proposed that she form a committee to publish his pamphlets under her name, thus avoiding censorhip by the museum. "They can prevent my signing them," he said, "but they cannot prevent my writing them." Brant came into the scheme, nominally as treasurer, but actually as a writer and legislative advisor. The Emergency Conservation Committee, founded for the *ad hoc* purpose of reforming the Audubon Association, grew into a permanent crusade. Under Edge's implacable direction, with Brant's assistance, for the next thirty years it represented in its purest form the Muir tradition of the radical amateur in conservation.

Brant had grown up in small towns in Iowa, the son of a newspaperman. When he was thirteen, injuries from a fight with a neighbor boy kept him home from school for a year. To help fill the time he started birding. He subscribed to *Bird-Lore* and, in his first act as a conservationist, protected the songbirds in his yard from hunters. Later he courted his future wife on hikes and canoe trips. A tour of Rocky Mountain National Park left them confirmed mountain lovers. Though making his living in newspaper work, Brant retained a philosophical interest in nature. He read James Oliver Curwood's pantheistic religious speculations with an approving sense of *déjà vu*. "I could not help marvelling," he noted, ". . . that I had come so easily and naturally twenty years ago to the exact religious outlook which Curwood attained by a terrific struggle within himself. . . . The religion of nature came to me as a passive gift." He approached the natural world with a humility that recalled Muir's central insight: "the idea," as Brant put it, "that the world exists in part for its non-human inhabitants."

Rosalie Edge had taken a quite different road to the ECC. Born in a house on Stuyvesant Square, her father a first cousin to Charles Dickens, she grew up in a genteel New York world of finishing school and old culture. She married a British consulting engineer and lived abroad for some years. In 1913 she insisted upon returning to America. On the trip back she met and was fascinated by Lady Rhondda, the militant British suffragist. "It was the first awakening of my mind," she recalled. Settled in New York, she threw herself into suffrage campaigns, learning the rudiments of publicity and organization. "When we suffrage women attacked a political machine," she said later, ". . . we called out its name, and the names of its officers, so that all could hear. We got ourselves inside the recalcitrant organization, if possible, and stood up in meeting. We gave the matter to the press, first doing something about it that should *make news.*" During election campaigns she traveled around the state making speeches and being heckled. Possessed of a quicksilver mind and a deft sense of irony, she relished the thrust and jabbing of stump repartee.

When her family bought a summer home on Long Island Sound in 1915, she developed a second new interest by observing the birds that came into her garden. She was a rare species, a birder by adult conversion rather than by childhood baptism. Once, late for a suffrage meeting, she explained that she had been delayed by a great blue heron in her maple tree. "This did not seem to mend matters," she noted. In the 1920s she went birding in Central Park (she saw a Bewick's wren), on Martha's Vineyard (an Arkansas kingbird), and even on the streets of Manhattan (an occasional peregrine falcon preying on pigeons). Eventually she accumulated a "life list" of 804 species observed, a quite respectable total. Although not a religious person, she explained her love of birds in religious terms: like seeing the divine inspiration in a great work of art, but sensing it more directly. "When we who have a feeling for birds observe a mighty eagle, or the perfection of a tiny warbler," she said, "we see, not the inspiration of God filtered through human agency, but the very handiwork of the Creator Himself."

In 1930 Rosalie Edge was fifty-three years old, bored by social rounds, separated from her husband and with time on her hands. She dabbled in poetry and favored the novels of Jane Austen and cousin Charles. Dressed in conservative style, slightly over medium height, she appraised the world through sharp blue eyes. She spoke in a rich, cultivated voice that reminded people of Eleanor Roosevelt's. Her presence, someone remarked, seemed a blend of Queen Mary and a suspicious pointer. All of this made her easy to caricature as a wealthy dilettante. But she was an utterly serious person with a profound sense of man's fatuous egotism before the natural world. She distilled this sense in her poem "Motor Power," published in *Nature Magazine:*

> *Steel-winged, the humming fan makes slumberous sound*
> *Within my chamber slatted from the sun;*
> *Aeolus' captive, its tempered breezes spun*
> *From vanished forests prisoned underground,*

From long-dead trees and ferns through ages bound
In seams of rock. Such victories man has won.
But, tyrant of the skies, what has he done
To chain the might of living flowers, what found
To rival humming wings of Ruby-throat
Whose motor, smaller than a drop of rain,
Has power beyond what any man can reckon?

Her career with the ECC made her the first woman to have a considerable impact on the conservation movement. As she picked her way through the trousered opposition, she would occasionally express misgivings about her peculiar role to Brant. "It is the policy of the Audubon Association to make it appear that I alone conduct this fight," she wrote, "— a Woman, sentimental, and quite ignorant of conditions; so it is helpful to have you write." Again: "I am all very well in my own way; but as a woman, I do not command the attention that you would get." And again: "People of the West distrust what a lady in New York knows about their problems; many letters come better from a man." But she was still a feminist, accustomed to persuading men in subtle ways. By confessing her qualms to Brant she also appealed to his chivalry, inclining him to offer more help.

Her adversaries were not used to dealing professionally with a woman, and she learned to use her femininity against them. At meetings she would walk up to the men on the other side, smile sweetly, and oblige them to be polite. Then she would sit down among them — to Van Name's horror — and pick up stray bits of information. "Everyone has been kind to me," she reported after testifying before a congressional committee, "and I have chatted and smoked with the worst of them. I have talked to sportsmen, game keepers and all sorts." Opponents who knew only the fulminating language of her pamphlets were startled to encounter a woman of gentle breeding and good manners. Once, after making a speech, she was told: "Mrs. Edge, I never was so surprised as to see that you are a lady." Her allies were delighted to find support from such an unexpected source. Hornaday treated her as a comrade and called her "the only woman in conservation."

In her assault on the Audubon Association, Edge used the methods of her suffragist days, creating news and reforming from within. Leading up to the 1930 annual meeting, she published a pamphlet by Brant, *Compromised Conservation,* which detailed the connections among the association, sportsmen, and commercial sporting interests. She sent the polemic to newspapers and tried to enlist the support of the Bird Club of Long Island

and the Linnaean Society and Camp-Fire Club of New York. Hornaday became an Audubon member in order to be able to speak at the meeting. Roger Baldwin of the American Civil Liberties Union, an Audubon director, promised to help out. The Audubon leadership began to take its opposition seriously. "You probably know Mrs. Edge is on the rampage," Pearson wrote Palmer. "I am sending you a batch of proxies herewith, also a list of our Washington members. Cannot you discreetly get some of these to sign proxies? We do not want to make a general call to members for proxies. I hope that my annual report may be of such a nature that it will not be necessary to go to the mat very strongly with the crowd." As the meeting approached, the plotters gained national publicity in *Time* and received expressions of support from all over the country. "You are fighting the same gang that drove Will Dilg to a premature grave," a man wrote from Iowa.

It was the largest, noisiest Audubon meeting in memory. Hornaday offered a resolution that was quashed after an angry debate. Pearson defended the role of sportsmen in conservation, claiming they were chiefly responsible for protecting game birds and animals. "Perhaps some Utopian-day man will cease killing birds and animals," said Pearson, "but in the meantime we have to take mankind as we find it and struggle along the best we can." To clear the air, a three-man committee under Thomas Barbour of the Harvard Museum of Comparative Zoology was appointed to look into the ECC's charges. At the end of the session Mrs. E. M. Townsend of Oyster Bay, Long Island, moved a vote of confidence in the directors. "I feel that the meeting this morning has not been ideal," she said, "and, in some respects, has been in the direction of destroying the confidence we have always had." The motion was passed overwhelmingly, but some doubts were creeping in around the edges.

A few days after the meeting Edge asked for the mailing list of the association's seven thousand members. Turned down, she hired a lawyer and sued for the list. During the legal proceedings the Audubon attorney referred to her as "a common scold." ("Fancy how I trembled," she remarked.) The odd spectacle of this esteemed organization denying one of its own members its mailing list brought the Audubon leadership a deluge of unfavorable publicity. "Through the daily press all over the United States," Murphy noted, "we have been prodded with the hot end of the poker." Moreover, the ECC "includes more than one man of no inconsiderable cunning." The judge ruled in Edge's favor. Audubon appealed but was enjoined from holding any meetings until the case was decided. With that the association capitulated and gave Edge the list. She sent out requests for proxies for the next annual meeting; Van Name paid the expenses of $1,177.

Under attack, the Audubon leadership was acting defensively. In issuing the report of the Barbour committee it acted dishonorably. The official version of the report endorsed Pearson and dismissed his critics as a self-appointed "zoophile cult." But a confidential appendix, circulated only among the directors and never released to the public, urged the following reforms:

1. That Pearson be paid a fixed wage unrelated to his fund-raising efforts;
2. That Pearson be dropped from the board of trustees, so that he would no longer be passing judgment on his own administrative activities;
3. That Pearson each year prepare in advance an itemized budget to be submitted to the trustees; and
4. That Pearson be relieved of other tasks and hire a new assistant to be director of conservation for the association.

These secret recommendations in effect upheld the ECC's critique of Pearson's hegemony. In withholding this secret appendix the Audubon Association was guilty of a curious breach of faith with its own loyal membership.

Despite the deception the membership was growing more restive. With her proxies in hand Edge prepared for the 1931 annual meeting. "This seems to have become the chief aim of my life," she wrote Brant, "— to spoil the Audubon meetings each year as they come 'round.... It is you and I and Dr. Van Name against a powerful array of rogues." At the meeting she presented her 1,646 proxy votes, a remarkable total given that a year earlier no one in the general membership had even heard of her. But the other side had 2,808 votes, including 400 names not on the mailing list she had been given. The ECC presented two candidates for the board, Roger Baldwin and Mrs. George Seligman, but both were defeated. "Still," Edge noted, "they can't call 1,646 people a 'small, insurgent group.' "

She next asked permission to go through the association's financial records. It was granted after some grumbling. Since 1924 the association had been administering the forty-acre Rainey wildlife sanctuary in Louisiana, supposedly protecting all the wild creatures that lived there. Edge's accountants discovered that from 1929 to 1931 the association had received over $50,000 for the "rental" of the sanctuary. It turned out that hunters had been using the sanctuary to set steel traps, sometimes baited with birds, to catch muskrats for their pelts. The $50,000 was the association's share of the proceeds.

Edge put out a pamphlet on the issue and again solicited proxies for the annual meeting. Again she was beaten. The directors also refused to stop the Rainey trapping. "There is no reforming that organization," she concluded, "because the directors *honestly* believe themselves unimpeachable. They have built up a rich organization and they have the truly American point of view that money is the great end per se." For three years she had been a small but relentless terrier yapping at the heels of the caparisoned Audubon leadership. And after three years, as far as she knew, it had gotten her nowhere.

Behind the scenes at Audubon headquarters, though, Pearson's days were numbered. In January 1933, John H. Baker, a blunt and forceful Wall Street broker, took over as chairman of the board. He was perturbed that since the ECC campaign began, the Aubudon membership had been cut by 60 percent, from eighty-four hundred to thirty-four hundred. He made conciliatory overtures to Edge and Hornaday, and began to limit Pearson's responsibilities. ("Tell me personally," Pearson asked Palmer with unconscious irony, "what is your reaction to turning the Association over in this way to any one man.") Under Baldwin's tactful prodding Chapman and Murphy joined in the palace revolt. In September 1934 Pearson was forced to resign. The presidency was made an honorary position and Baker became the new executive director. As one of his first acts he stopped the trapping in the Rainey sanctuary. "At last a miracle, physiologically impossible, was achieved in the field of morality," Brant later declared with relish: "the National Audubon Society recovered its virginity." Under Baker's direction the association regained some of the spirit of William Dutcher, and Edge directed her attention elsewhere.

In between Audubon meetings the ECC was spontaneously taking on a life of its own. As word got around, strangers would write to Edge "for all the things the Audubon Society ought to be doing for them," as she put it. The letters widened her horizons and made her feel, she said, like a conservation Dorothea Dix. Without much planning it she was pulled into new projects. She published a series of "Teaching Units" on nature subjects aimed at schools and camps. She took on one of Van Name's pet projects, the preservation of a virgin sugar-pine grove south of Yosemite Park. (The grove, one of Muir's favorites, was part of the original cession in 1890 but then was lost to Pinchot's Forest Service during the 1905 reorganization.) The successful five-year campaign for the sugar pines accidentally redefined the ECC. Van Name, an irascible man who rivaled Hornaday as a holder of grudges, regarded Yosemite's superintendent as a sworn enemy. Edge in her ecumenical way befriended the superintendent and even cajoled him into supporting the project. Van Name then withdrew his support of the ECC, thus presenting Edge with a decision. "The whole Committee was started for V.N. and belonged to him," she wrote Brant. "Now that he hates it, and has knifed it, why should I go on?" Brant gave her the desired encouragement. Other projects pushed her along. Edge made the ECC to an even greater degree her own crusade. (Van Name resumed his contributions a few years later. In 1948 he paid Edge a double-edged compliment by calling her "the only honest, unselfish, indomitable hellcat in the history of conservation.")

The ECC, so closely identified with Edge, kept its idiosyncratic nature. It had no membership dues, vested funds, paid officers, or salaried employees. Edge ran the group from an unpretentious one-room office. The annual budget averaged $5,000 and never exceeded four figures. Contributions came at first from disgruntled Audubon members, later from scientists with — according to Edge — large families and small incomes. But the absence of big money and a board of directors left Edge free to act quickly, on her own, at her best. When young people asked her about careers in conservation she always told them to make it a hobby, not a profession. "I have met too many ironed-out, and often bitter, conservationists in professional jobs," she said.

All her campaigns derived ultimately from the central idea in her poem "Motor Power": to break open the tunnel vision imposed by a man-centered view of the universe. She undertook her favorite project on behalf of the migrating hawks that flew by a mountain in eastern Pennsylvania. "Man hates any creature that kills and eats what he wishes to kill and eat," she maintained. "He does not take into account the millions of rodents and insect pests that hawks consume." Instead, hawks were regarded as a threat to poultry and wildfowl, and some gunners thought it sporting to shoot them.

Every fall, with the migrations under way, platoons of gunners drove out to Hawk Mountain in the Pennsylvania Dutch country. Most hawk species were not protected in the state, and the mountain made an ideal shooting grounds. The hawks were shot for sport and left where they fell. The situation came to Edge's attention in the fall of 1932. She urged the Audubon Association to buy the whole mountain, 1,655 acres, for $4,000. Baker and Pearson expressed sympathy but took no action, so the next summer she took an option on the property in the ECC's name. Her signs prohibiting shooting were disregarded as outside interference by the local hunters.

"We must have a warden on the property," she wrote a young ornithologist from Boston named Maurice Broun; "first to post it and then to guard it and get police protection. It is a job that needs some courage." Broun and his wife Irma moved in as resident curators and watchdogs. The shooting finally stopped. In 1938 Edge conveyed the property to the Hawk Mountain Sanctuary Association. "You know," she heard her friends say, "she *likes hawks.*"

꙳꙳

In retrospect, it appeared that wildlife conservation up to 1935 had suffered most from its commercial connections. The gun companies brought alien motives to a movement intrinsically opposed to commercial development. Conservation and business are natural enemies; attempts to reconcile them usually work to the detriment of conservation. In wildlife campaigns this recurrent commercial involvement has been counterbalanced by periodic infusions of the Muir tradition. Radical amateurs — Dutcher, Hornaday, Dilg, Van Name, Edge — in their zealous freedom from practical considerations pushed those with pragmatic tendencies into more principled action. They lost most of the skirmishes but won the wars, and wildlife populations were saved.

The radicals had their own failings. They spent money recklessly and fought over apparently trivial issues. Intent on their crusades, they sacrificed some peripheral vision. Operating on a high level of urgency, they had trouble sustaining that pitch as a way of life. In the larger groups, they eventually had to yield to more moderate managerial professionals like Gilbert Pearson and Seth Gordon.

On a practical level conservation has been sustained by this interplay between professionals and radical amateurs. Professionals keep the movement organized. Amateurs keep it honest. The ghosts of Muir and Pinchot still wrestle for control — in a fractious but symbiotic embrace.

6

Franklin D. Roosevelt and
New Deal Conservation

FRANKLIN Roosevelt became President at the nadir of the gravest national crisis since the Civil War. After three years of hard times one worker in four was jobless. Platoons of unemployed men and women roamed the country. The air was filled with easy talk of revolution. Faced with a run of panicky withdrawals, most banks closed down for an indefinite period. On inauguration day, March 4, 1933, the New York Stock Exchange suspended operations. The new President, as baffled as anyone else, called Congress into special session to meet the banking crisis.

On March 8, the day before Congress was to convene, Roosevelt sent a letter to his forestry advisor in regard to tree planting on the family estate at Hyde Park. "I wish you would make a note of having a careful inspection made of the swamp area planted last year," he wrote. "The permanent tree crop consisted of tulip poplars and black walnuts and these were interspersed with, I think, red cedar and larch. This planting should be filled out to replace trees that have died. During the winter I had all the sprouts cut off from the stumps of the old trees that had been cut." That night Roosevelt outlined his new banking legislation to congressional leaders and then capped his day by calling on Justice Holmes to wish him a happy ninety-second birthday.

During his first week in office, with urgent issues swirling around him, Roosevelt had found time to think about the trees at Hyde Park. The episode was characteristic of his presidency. To a degree unmatched by any other President except his Uncle Ted, FDR took a personal interest in the details of conservation policy. The history of New Deal conservation reflected in large measure Roosevelt's own priorities in preaching what he called "the gospel of conservation." He cared most deeply about land, trees, and water for human use; on a second level he turned his attention to the protection of wildlife; about national parks and wilderness he cared least.

The origins of this order of priorities were buried within the manifold personalities of a deeply enigmatic gentleman. He always presented, as Robert Sherwood put it, a "heavily forested interior." The description fitted him in two senses. The inner man was overgrown, densely shaded, essentially impenetrable; but whatever his nature, it seemed clear that trees were, as he often said, close to his heart. During the 1936 campaign someone suggested that, because of where he had been born and brought up, he naturally reverted to issues of land, trees, and water in approaching any great problem. "I fear that I must plead guilty to that charge," he said.

※※

Scion of an old Dutch family, Roosevelt grew up in Hyde Park in a setting of largely unspoiled natural beauty. The family home stood on a bluff overlooking the east bank of the Hudson, halfway between Albany and New York. To the west, across the river valley, the land stretched for miles, serene and undisturbed — especially in the evening, as the sun set over the river. The Hudson, as yet unpolluted, offered fishing and swimming in summer, skating and iceboating in winter. Surrounding the house was an estate of several hundred acres: lawns, gardens, a greenhouse, a grapery, and finally fields and forests.

Conservationists often trace their interest in nature to a period of isolation during childhood. Few children have been more isolated from normal human contacts than young Franklin Roosevelt. An only child, he was raised by a strong, protective mother who kept him in long hair and dresses until he was five and continued to bathe him into his ninth year. The father, in his late fifties by the time the boy knew him, was kindly but aged and distant. The patrician Roosevelts did not send their boy to the local school, but had him educated at home by a series of tutors until he was fourteen. Thus denied normal relations with siblings, father, and schoolmates, the boy turned to the teeming natural world close at hand and was permanently imprinted by it. He tramped through the woods, hunted rabbits with a bow and arrow, and filled his composition books with descriptions of local trees and other observations. "Tracking is the way to follow a trail," he noted at the age of nine. "You are sure to be fooled as your game will cross other tracks and dodge like a little red devil. I was hunting once and a rabbit led us three times round in a circle!"

Like many boys of his time he took a particular interest in birds, making careful notes on their migrations and habits. The song of blackbirds reminded him of strawberries and cream; if a robin's daily consumption of worms were laid end to end, he noted, it would exceed fourteen feet. On his eleventh birthday he was given a gun for shooting specimens. He promptly went out and bagged a crow. Soon he could regard himself as quite an expert. "Many people do not know what a great variety of birds we have," he wrote, "they can always point out a robin but probably could not tell the difference between a Fox Sparrow and a Song Sparrow and will think that a Nuthatch is a Woodpecker, or a Goldfinch a summer Yellow bird." His specimen collection eventually exceeded three hundred birds and was proudly displayed in glass cases in the front hall. Grandfather Delano made him a life member of the American Museum of Natural History. A highlight of his final year at Groton was a visit to William Brewster's museum in Cambridge — "the *finest private collection of American birds in the world!*" This passion of his boyhood lasted his whole life. Even as President, he would sometimes rise before dawn at Hyde Park and take guests out on birding excursions. As late as 1943 he asked his secretary to complete his file of the journal of the American Ornithologists' Union.

Roosevelt's lifelong interest in forestry also started early. In the summer of 1891 his family went to Germany for a holiday. Riding his bicycle around the countryside near Bad Nauheim, he came to a town with a large forest on its outskirts. The tract, which had been managed to yield an annual timber crop for two hundred years, provided a steady income that paid the town's taxes. "The interesting thing to me, as a boy even," he recalled many years later, "was that the town didn't have to pay taxes. They were supported by their own forest." As an adult he applied the lesson to his own estate. In 1910 he bought twelve hundred acres of adjacent farmland, depleted by generations of poor husbandry, and began a program of annual plantings to reclaim the land and provide a cash crop. When he registered to vote in Hyde Park he described himself as a tree grower.

Most of the land was planted with Norway spruce for the Christmas tree market, but he amused himself by experimenting with many other species. "We have tried all sorts of things," he told a press conference in 1935, "even Douglas fir from the West Coast. That takes a thousand years to grow." ("Is it growing?" a reporter asked. "It is growing up awfully slowly," he replied.) By 1944 he had supervised the planting of over five hundred thousand trees. They appealed to Roosevelt not only for their reclamation and commercial uses. He loved to drive around the estate, admiring his woods and drawing strength from them. He had particular affection for a forty-three-foot yellow poplar he could see from his bedroom window. Occasionally he gave out pointed reports on the annual cash yield of his trees. "Forestry pays from the practical point of view," he said. "I have proved that."

All his life he displayed a wellborn sense of responsibility for the land. It drew on a proud tradition of old, landed wealth, rooted for generations in Dutchess County. It implied both respect for one's forebears and accountability to one's descendants: in sum, an extended view of history. "Growing trees is a long-time proposition," Roosevelt declared. "We are looking at the human race, which we hope won't end in fifty years."

When he began his political career by entering the New York legislature in 1911, it seemed part of the natural order of things that he would take up conservation issues. As chairman of the Forest, Fish and Game Committee he introduced eight bills to regulate fishing and hunting. He also pushed forestry legislation that would have restricted cutting even on privately owned land. To bolster his case he brought Gifford Pinchot to Albany for a lecture before the assembly. Pinchot illustrated his talk with two lantern slides of the same valley in China: one, an old painting, showing a lush sylvan scene in 1500; the other, a photograph taken four centuries later, recording the barren result of land abuse. Roosevelt's bill was not passed but the pictures were seared into his memory. (Thirty years later he still referred to them.)

In 1912 he drew from his conservation experience to formulate a striking statement on the general need of political reform. For the sake of individual liberty, he said, unregulated competition had dominated public affairs in the modern age. But if individual lumber companies were allowed freely to denude the forests, the whole state would suffer the consequences of floods, erosion, and other ills. Thus "competition has been shown to be useful up to a certain point and no further. Co-operation must begin where competition leaves off." Individuals could no longer be allowed free rein with their private property because "there are to-day men of the State who for the sake of lining their pockets during their own life-time are willing to cause the same thing that happened in China." To avoid such a future the liberty of the individual must yield to "the liberty of the community." The same principle of state regulation for the common good should be applied to economic monopolies, educational reform, unfair rebating, the control of common carriers, and new experiments in political administration. Starting from a base in conservation, Roosevelt thus extended the liberty of the community to the whole cluster of reform movements that made up the progressive era.

During the "New Era" after World War I, with Muir and TR dead and Pinchot diverted by a political career, conservation lost its connection with political liberalism and became an adjunct to the business-minded Republican Party of the 1920s. Changes within the American Forestry Association illustrated the trend. Formerly a professional group of foresters and conservationists, after 1923 it was led by Ovid M. Butler and George Dupont Pratt, conservative Republicans friendly to the lumber industry. The major forestry legislation of the period, the Clarke–McNary Act of 1924, codified the new alliance of conservation and business by offering cooperation and incentives, not penalties and force, for the improvement of privately owned timber. Approved by the new AFA, the act was opposed by Pinchot and other advocates of stricter regulation. Older conservationists like Robert Underwood Johnson resigned from the AFA in protest. Pinchot remained in the group but had little influence on its policies. Most graduates of forestry schools were entering private industry, not government service. In 1928 even the head of the Forest Service, William B. Greeley, quit to become general manager of the West Coast Lumbermen's Association. In a development that paralleled the dominant role of gun companies in wildlife conservation, lumber industry trade groups supplied most of the funding for the AFA.

The marriage of business and conservation fitted perfectly the New Era's ideals of professional management and efficiency. It avoided wasteful political battles by conferring the power of decision on practical men in private conference. But the marriage was an unequal partnership on terms too controlled by business. "Today the conservation movement is led by sober business men and is based on the cold calculations of the engineers," an observer noted in 1933. "Conservation, no longer viewed as a political issue, has become a business proposition." The Muir tradition of the radical amateur was in temporary eclipse.

When Franklin Roosevelt became President, the organized conservation movement was controlled by members of the opposition party. John Baker and Kermit Roosevelt of the Audubon Association, Joseph Knapp of More Game Birds, Wallace Atwood and William P. Wharton of the National Parks Association, Fairfield Osborn, Jr., of the American Museum of Natural History, Horace Albright of the American Planning and Civic Association, and Arthur Newton Pack of the American Nature Association were all Republicans. Even FDR's own forestry advisor for Hyde Park, Nelson Brown of the New York State College of Forestry, belonged to the GOP. In his first conservation appointments Roosevelt stayed within the accepted political framework. To head the two cabinet departments most closely involved with conservation, Interior and Agriculture, he named two apostate Republicans, Harold Ickes of Chicago and Henry A. Wallace of Iowa. Yet the appointments suggested a new direction for conservation: Ickes was a progressive, an old Bull Mooser, and Wallace had renounced his ancestral Republicanism in 1928. Both men had supported the Democrats in 1932.

When the top jobs in the Park Service and Forest Service became vacant in late 1933, Roosevelt appointed the first Democrats to hold either office. The new boss at the Park Service was Arno B. Cammerer, a career service employee since 1919. A stolid functionary who exasperated Ickes in meetings by chewing gum, vigorously, with his mouth open, Cammerer served without distinction. Perhaps instructed by this example, FDR brought in an outsider, Ferdinand B. Silcox, to direct the Forest Service. A graduate of the Yale Forest School, he had spent a dozen years in the Forest Service before a career in labor relations in New York during the 1920s. Regarded as an alien by service veterans, Silcox with great skill and imagination pushed his bureau back into an adversary relation with the lumber industry. "He loved to thrust and parry with the lumbermen," William Greeley recalled, "to show up weak spots in their position and to needle them into action. He carried it off with a personal charm and aplomb that blunted the edge." Pinchot took satisfaction in the rejuvenation of his old agency. In June 1934, he declared that the Forest Service was again becoming "the aggressive agent and advocate of the public good, and not the humble little brother of the lumbermen."

Of course not all of Roosevelt's conservation appointments were made in such a disinterested spirit. The *effect* of appointing Democrats was to sever the union of business and conservation, since the GOP was preeminently the party of business. But the effect was sometimes unintended, and some appointments seemed sheer politics with no particular conservation motive behind them. In 1935, for example, Senator Joseph Guffey of Pennsylvania objected when two Republicans were given important Forest Service jobs. Roosevelt agreed that the positions should instead be filled by Democrats. "If it is true that these gentlemen were politically active," he told Wallace, "I do not see why they should be retained. The Forestry Service cannot afford it." Though covering himself with a high-minded concern for the service, FDR actually interfered in the interest of party unity and patronage.

Yet there was no mistaking his real concern — within the limits of his Pinchot-style understanding of conservation. The projects directly initiated by him predictably involved trees and land reclamation: Hyde Park writ large. Campaigning in Montana in 1932, FDR conceived one of the most ridiculed New Deal projects, a scheme to plant a "shelterbelt" of trees one hundred miles wide along the 100th meridian from Canada to Texas. Considerably scaled down and financed only by relief funds, the project ended as a moderate success.

More celebrated was his favorite New Deal agency, the Civilian Conservation Corps. Within a few weeks of taking office he sent Congress a proposal to deploy an army of unemployed men into the country to do "simple work, not interfering with normal employment, and confining itself to forestry, the prevention of soil erosion, flood control, and similar projects." He insisted on supervising the details of CCC organization himself, treating it as his personal agency and creating a bottleneck by forcing every decision through his office. But the job was done and by July over three hundred thousand young men were at work planting trees, digging reservoirs, building dams and fire towers. In their zeal to improve the land they sometimes offended conservationists of the Muir persuasion. The CCC director, Robert Fechner of the machinists' union, once proposed to dam the headwaters of Upper Yosemite Fall so the water could be turned on and off like a faucet to coincide with the presence of tourists. That bizarre proposal was stillborn, and in general the CCC had a salutary effect on both the land and its 2.5 million workers.

The Tennessee Valley Authority embodied the Pinchot tradition at its finest: the harnessing of an unruly river system for human purposes and the production of fertilizer and electrical power by a public agency. For Roosevelt, and for the dirt-poor farmers of the region, the TVA meant a clear application of the liberty of the community against private interests. "Power is really a secondary matter," Roosevelt told a press conference. "What we are doing there is taking a watershed with about three and a half million people in it, almost all of them rural, and we are trying to make a different type of citizen out of them. . . . TVA is primarily intended to change and improve the standards of living of the people of that Valley." Like the CCC, the TVA refashioned the natural landscape for human uses. But it was done so skillfully and with such tangible advantage to the impoverished region that the TVA at first received little criticism from conservationists.

In short order the Republican conservation movement began to embrace the Democratic President. "Thank God that I — although always heretofore a Republican — voted for you," Fairfield Osborn, Jr., wrote the White House. "You are outstripping the highest hopes of your friends." In 1935 the Society of American Foresters gave Roosevelt its most prestigious medal. In accepting the award he pointedly urged the foresters to regard trees as more than just so many thousand board feet of lumber to be harvested. A forest, he said, "is an integral part of our natural land covering, and the most potent factor in maintaining nature's delicate balance. . . . The preservation of the forests must be lifted above mere dollars and cents considerations." By striking this ecological, noncommercial note Roosevelt aligned himself with the most liberal thinking among conservationists. In action, though, the New Deal usually favored the more practical style of the Pinchot tradition. Yet even the liberal economist Stuart Chase, concluding an alarmed book in 1936 about the depletion of natural resources, had only praise for Roosevelt. The President "really cared about the continent," said Chase. "One cannot fail to appreciate his devotion to land and water."

For Franklin Roosevelt, conservation meant not only a family responsibility or a political maneuver or a mechanism to relieve unemployment. At bottom it was an avocation. He seemed to turn to conservation matters with a sense of relief, giving them unprecedented blocks of presidential time because they offered surcease from the everyday burdens of his office. One day in 1937, he entertained himself by drawing a chart of Niagara Falls, sketching in a construction project to regulate the tidal flow and prevent erosion. "These are 2 Power Houses," he noted, "not Honey Mooners." Then he signed it with a flourish: "FDR Civil Engineer." ("Not so civil," added his secretary Missy LeHand.)

☙❧

In wildlife protection the New Deal again reflected the President's own priorities. FDR was not unaware of the needs of wild animals, but he seemed to care more about the humans above them and the "lower" forms below them.

After Roosevelt lost the use of his legs, his personal involvement with hunting game was reduced to that of a spectator. He prohibited hunting on the Hyde Park estate, hoping that wood ducks would use Valkill Creek as a refuge. From a seated position he still enjoyed deep-sea fishing. In the spring of 1935, cruising through the Bahamas on a fishing holiday, he noticed a scarcity of brown pelicans and asked the Audubon Association to look into the matter. (John Baker reported that the pelicans were protected and had a stable population of sixty-five hundred.) At other times he seemed obtuse to dangers to waterfowl. He brushed off protests over the destruction of breeding marshes by the Santee–Cooper project in South Carolina. "He seems to think that the migratory water fowls will adjust themselves to changed conditions," Harold Ickes confided to his diary. FDR regarded the issue as another episode in the long feud between landed gentry and field laborers, with the gentry in this instance being rich, anti–New Deal absentee landlords from the North who liked to shoot ducks. The project, he said with finality, "will develop power, it will prevent floods, and will, first and last, give a tremendous amount of work. The complaint that it will kill all the ducks from Florida to Maine is silly. As an old-time professional ornithologist, I vouch for this!" Again he favored land and humans over wild animals.

Given these priorities, wildlife protection by the New Deal normally originated not by White House initiative but in response to outside pressure. The heaviest pressure came from Jay Norwood "Ding" Darling of the Des Moines *Register*. In 1934 a poll of newspaper editors named him the outstanding editorial cartoonist of the past half century. Syndicated in three hundred newspapers, his work punctuated the breakfasts of millions of Americans and made him a kind of visual Will Rogers. Born in 1876, the son of a Congregational minister, he had grown up in Iowa. His first cartoon, after he was hired by the *Register* in 1906, dealt with air pollution caused by the burning of soft coal. Irving Brant worked on the *Register* for a few years and joined Darling in the warm sessions of a debating club. "Darling was an extreme extrovert," Brant said later, "awed by nobody, overflowing with self-confidence." Darling listed his hobbies as Roquefort cheese, dairy farming, rock gardening, black bass fishing, ornithology, and duck shooting.

Especially duck shooting. Darling was a conservationist in the tradition of George Bird Grinnell, who loved to hunt but hated game hogs and sloppy shooting. On his fortieth birthday in 1916 he drew a cartoon on this theme that brought him to the attention of the New York *Herald-Tribune* syndicate and launched his national career. During the bitter controversies of the 1920s Darling was one of William Hornaday's trusted midwestern allies. His cartoons helped create the public support that led to the protection victories at the end of the decade.

Those measures were soon rendered inadequate by another crisis in the ealy 1930s. The usual problems of encroaching progress and more hunters were compounded by a prolonged drought in the plains states that dried up breeding and feeding areas. By one estimate the duck population sank from 100 million in 1930 to 20 million four years later. Once again conservationists urged the Biological Survey to cut back on the hunting season and bag limits. But conservationists were mostly Republicans, and now the survey was controlled by Democrats for the first time since the war. Darling had served on the resolutions committee at the 1932 GOP convention, and he generally disapproved of the New Deal. But Henry Wallace, whose department included the survey, was another old friend from Iowa. For a time Darling muted his criticism so as to keep Wallace's confidence. He urged the survey to suspend its predator control and patrol activities in favor of more restoration and fieldwork — in effect to function more as a biologist than a policeman — but he refrained from any major attacks.

His discretion was rewarded toward the end of 1933, when he was appointed to the President's Committee on Wild Life Restoration along with Aldo Leopold, recently named the first professor of wildlife management at the University of Wisconsin, and Thomas Beck, president of the Crowell–Collier Publishing Company of New York. Avid duck hunters concerned about the depletion of their quarry, the three were charged with devising a program to rescue it.

The committee's report, issued in January 1934, proposed an ambitious program of spending $50–$75 million to buy some seventeen million acres of submarginal farmland for use as refuges. The report produced little response from the White House. After two months Wallace reminded Roosevelt of the political risks. "Mr. Beck determines policies for the Collier's Publishing Company," he wrote, "and on that score I think his feeling in the matter would be well worth considering; in addition, he is highly public-spirited in his service on this committee." The suggested program was admittedly too expensive, he continued, but its general drift seemed wise. Furthermore: "I have been amazed to find how universal has been the praise of the report . . . representing unification in groups ranging from the rabid conservationists to the game slaughterers." Still no action from the White House. Frustrated by the experience, Darling began to draw cartoons more critical of the administration's wildlife policies.

Over the years Darling had nurtured an outsider's suspicion of conservation bureaucrats. At one point he estimated that in a quarter century some $100 million had been wasted by stupid management. "If there was a deserving party worker who needed a job," he said, "but was too dumb to do anything else, he was made game warden." In the tradition of the radical amateur, Darling relished his role as a freewheeling critic of those in power. He therefore resisted when, in the spring of 1934, Wallace offered to make him head of the Biological Survey. Darling hated making speeches, had never been an administrator, and enjoyed an income several times that of a government employee. But Wallace talked him into taking the job for six months, long enough to preside over a reorganization of the bureau. Suddenly the erstwhile critic found himself inside the house of the enemy, exchanging total freedom but no direct power for some power but less freedom.

As an independent cartoonist he had been allied with the most radical of amateurs, Rosalie Edge. He served on the ECC board of directors. Since 1931, though, Edge had been scourging the Biological Survey for its whole-sale slaughter of predators like the coyote and for its poisoning of small mammals disliked by western livestock interests. A classic instance of human self-importance, this interplay of predator control and poisoning set off an unforeseen, uncontrollable cycle of extermination. As Brant pointed out when Darling took over the survey, killing predators meant a population explosion among the rodents on which they fed. "Rodents mul-tiply and must be poisoned. Birds are poisoned by the rodent poison and insects multiply and must be poisoned. We will just get deeper into the mire if this practice is continued." Now Darling's new job put him in po-tential conflict with his friends from the ECC. Edge hoped for the best and reminded Darling, "We are, I believe, the one group that cannot be inti-midated by the Big Stick. I might say of myself 'He who is low need fear no fall.' " Darling in reply hoped she would bear with him: "I almost find myself ducking instinctively when I hear the swish of your sword and your stalwart battle cry."

Darling soon experienced the frustrations of being on the inside. His main concern was to save the ducks. Other aspects of the job held less in-terest for him. In a speech to the Wool Growers Association he endorsed the poisoning program, thereby incurring Edge's wrath. Brant as the friend of both arranged a peace conference in July 1934. The two spent an ami-able evening jousting back and forth. "I had to keep a cool head," Edge later told Brant, "and judge when he was trying to bluff me and when he was really giving me his confidence. It was hard not to yield to the tempta-tion to drop business and have a delightful evening talking of every-thing — his art, Manchuria, and lots of other things. What a thoroughly delightful and likeable man he is." Darling scolded her for dumping a lot of mail on his desk and urged her to attack someone else, such as the Rec-lamation Service. But he also found the occasion pleasant if not altogether instructive. "She really seemed to enjoy being kidded and I did my best to amuse her," he reported to Brant. "She is not, I find, a very good listener, and when we parted she still maintained that the Bureau of Biological Survey ought to be completely eradicated." As usual Edge smiled politely while inserting her knife.

Caught between the ECC on one side and zealous hunters on the other, Darling issued a compromise set of regulations for the 1934 hunting season that pleased neither group. Edge decided that he had capitulated to the sportsmen and was no longer fit for his position ("He knows nothing but ducks, if indeed he knows them"). For his part Darling was tired of pointlessly courting her favor. "I've dined with her, squandered evenings and given her access to my innermost convictions," he complained to Brant. "She just loves to see the heads fall into the basket when her ax falls. She knows very little about any angle of her work except the techniques of poisoned dart making." Obviously stung by the darts, Darling like Edge took refuge in a general accusation of ignorance. But the real difference between them was less a matter of knowledge than the implications of their different roles. Edge could say anything she pleased; Darling had to balance constituencies. Brant tried to convince him that the ECC was being helpful: "You are in a more comfortable position to have us fanatics criticizing you than if we were all whooping it up for this year's regulations, as it takes the other side off your back." But it didn't. The more conservative sportsmen continued their attacks while poor Darling felt betrayed by a lack of support from his friends on the other side. As he later told Hornaday, "Your criticism during my first year in the Biological Survey hurt me deeply. I was struggling alone against the tremendous tide and I thought I deserved your sympathetic support rather than your quite violent criticism." After six months the prospect of returning to Iowa doubtless appealed to him.

He stayed on past his intended six months because of his success in creating new wildlife refuges. As part of the survey's reorganization, Darling formed a Migratory Waterfowl Division within the bureau. The Duck Stamp Act of 1934, mandating a one-dollar federal hunting license, provided additional money for waterfowl. Darling also displayed great skill in prying money from Congress and from various relief agencies, especially the FERA and WPA. After one year he had acquired nineteen major and thirteen secondary refuges, a total of 840,000 acres, concentrated in duck breeding grounds in the upper Midwest. During that first year he came up with a total of $8.5 million for wildlife, an unprecedented amount. His feat created an undercurrent of jealousy at the White House, a sentiment not helped by Darling's tendency to lecture Roosevelt about wildlife issues. As Missy LeHand insisted, "the President knows just as much about 'wild life' as Ding does!"

In July 1935 Darling obtained another $6 million from Congress. Not satisfied, he asked FDR for $4 million more: "We can make better use of retired agricultural land than anybody. Others grow grass and trees on it. We grow grass, trees, marshes, lakes, ducks, geese, fur-bearers, impounded water and recreation.... We did a good job last year. Why cut us off now?" The request caught Roosevelt in a testy mood. In recent months the Supreme Court had wiped out a central New Deal measure, the NRA, while lower federal judges handed down a flurry of injunctions to stop other welfare programs. At the same time the courts approved Darling's reclamation plans. So Roosevelt was not kindly disposed toward the Biological Survey's request for more millions for ducks. He accused Darling of being the first man in history to hold up the U.S. Treasury and get away with it. "You hold an all-time record," he wrote Darling in a spirit of begrudged admiration. "In addition to the six million dollars ($6,000,000) you got, the Federal Courts say that the United States Government has a perfect right to condemn millions of acres for the welfare, health and happiness of ducks, geese, sandpipers, owls and wrens, but has no constitutional right to condemn a few old tenements in the slums for the health and happiness of the little boys and girls who will be our citizens of the next generation! Nevertheless, more power to your arm!" No further funds were delivered. Relations between the survey and the White House were deteriorating.

Soon Darling parted company in public with the administration's wildlife policies. He could resume his cartooning career at any time, and had nothing to lose. The gun companies brought him a proposal to raise a $10 million endowment fund for wildlife protection by pledging 10 percent of their annual sales — on condition that the government drop its existing 10 percent excise tax on guns and ammunition. (The gun companies were nothing if not persistent. The proposal raised echoes of the Audubon controversy of 1911 and AGPA activities in the 1920s.) But the administration was not agreeable, overtly because of the disapproval of Henry Morgenthau, Secretary of the Treasury. Darling found the rejection "more than my placid disposition can accept," he said: "Continuity is essential. I know of no other way to accomplish the necessary reversal from down hill slide to upward climb for wildlife resources." He was also angry over quarrels with the Reclamation Service and in regard to the Hart Mountain antelope range in Oregon. Neither Darling nor Roosevelt was in a mood to smooth over differences. Finally, in September 1935 Darling decided to resign. "It now seems the strategic moment," he wrote Wallace, "to demand my resignation for insubordination, murder, incest and the good of the service."

Darling left in November with two strong and related impressions from his twenty months of government service: first, that Roosevelt was personally more friendly to wildlife conservation than political pressures allowed

him to express, because the exploiters of natural resources were better organized and politically more astute than conservationists; and second, that
the scattered wildlife forces somehow had to cooperate under a single powerful leadership. "I have come to realize that most of our wildlife conservation troubles are due to lack of organization," he said. "Wildlife interests
remind me of an unorganized army, beaten in every battle, zealous and
brave, but unable to combat the trained legions who are organized to get
what they want."

The gun companies and their money were still at hand. During the three
months that the administration spent mulling over their endowment fund
proposal, Darling arranged a quiet dinner with their representatives in
New York. Together they decided to create a new umbrella organization,
the American Wildlife Institute, ecumenical in nature and financed by
business interests. Seth Gordon, of the American Game Association (the
old AGPA), merged his association with the new group and became its secretary; Carl Shoemaker of the Senate Wildlife Committee became field
secretary; Thomas Beck was the president. Formally organized in August
1935, the AWI was the lineal descendant of the AGPA but avoided its
mistake of masquerading as a disinterested conservation group. Instead it
aimed to speak frankly for all industries with a financial stake in hunting,
not only gun and ammunition companies but automobile, oil, and railroad
corporations as well. As the group declared, "The Institute is amply financed by officers who, fortunately, have selfish interests." The board of
trustees, chaired by Walter P. Chrysler, included the presidents of
Remington, the Burlington Railroad, U.S. Rubber, Standard Oil of California, Packard, and the Chicago North Western Railroad, and other top
executives of Remington, Du Pont, Hercules Powder, Socony-Vacuum, and
General Motors. The AWI announced itself in favor of restoration, not
restriction, and pledged $30,000 a year for five years for game management
research at ten land-grant colleges. The new group was obviously powerful but somewhat limited. Its impressive board included no zoologists,
botanists, or biologists. And its devotion to conservation was questioned
when Walter Chrysler was convicted of various hunting violations in 1936.

It may not have been exactly the organization Darling had in mind, but
it was the best available vehicle. "The bricklayers have been smarter than
all the conservation groups together," he told an Audubon meeting, "because they've got an organization and when they want a thing they get it."
The AWI at least had the kind of money and connections that politicians
would notice. With help from Roosevelt's staff it staged a huge wildlife
conference in Washington in February 1936. Silcox of the Forest Service

headed a committee that sent out one hundred thousand invitations to conservationists of varied persuasions. Some forty thousand posters were distributed by the Post Office and by railroads and sporting goods dealers. The North American Wild Life Conference drew an attendance of twelve hundred. Tightly run, it was declared a great success. According to the *Sierra Club Bulletin,* "Probably nothing has happened in recent years to stimulate the conservation movement more than the Wild Life Conference." The meeting was endorsed by representatives of thirty-six thousand wildlife groups. They combined to form yet another new group, the General Wild Life Federation, and elected Darling its president. He had taken no public role in planning the occasion but clearly was the popular choice for leadership.

The outward unanimity was hard to believe. The AWI's business connections also bothered some conservationists. "The Wild Life Institute is still in command," Edward Preble of the Biological Survey noted afterward. "All the enemies were coached long in advance to amalgamate their forces." The federation held its second meeting in St. Louis a year later, funded by the AWI and with less government cooperation. The group was organized on a permanent basis and Darling was again elected president. But its focus was narrower, restricted — as *Nature Magazine* put it — to those "selfishly" interested in wildlife conservation. Later in 1937 the federation helped pass the Pittman–Robertson bill, which in effect established the gun companies' endowment fund plan rejected by Roosevelt in 1936. In 1938 the group changed its name to the National Wildlife Federation and dropped any pretense of being a general clearinghouse for conservation. At that point Darling lost interest in the group because it functioned too often as a lobby for the gun industry. But as such it usually advanced conservationist purposes. Carl Shoemaker, editor of the federation's *Conservation News,* was regarded by Irving Brant as "a good conservationist in spite of gun and ammunition affiliations." With a large membership, the NWF exerted great influence in behalf of wildlife.

As an alternative Darling was attracted to the reformed Audubon Association. Under John Baker's emphatic direction it represented the best combination of principle and widespread influence. In the fall of 1936 Darling joined the Audubon board of directors. Baker hired talented new personnel — like the artist Roger Tory Peterson — and expanded research programs and teaching centers. *Bird-Lore,* as edited by Frank Chapman for over three decades, had been narrowly focused on dry ornithological reports. With a new editor, William Vogt, and a fresher layout, it ranged more agreeably over a spectrum of conservation issues. The 1936 annual meeting included a report by Kenneth Reid of the Izaak Walton League on water pollution, and another by Harold Bryant of the National Park Service on the beneficial functions of predators. These papers implied a broader, more ecological approach: "the importance," as one Audubon staff member said, "of consideration of the effect of all elements in the environment of any threatened wild-life species."

Yet the degree of Audubon reform should not be exaggerated. Rosalie Edge left the group alone mainly because she had developed other causes, not because it met her standards. Baker ran the office like a tyrant, leading by fear as much as by example. Local societies were still not consulted on policy matters. In 1938 Vogt rounded up other conspirators on the staff and tried to lead an office coup, but Baker was supported by his trustees and Vogt departed. "Though Baker is no less firmly entrenched than Pearson," Edge said afterward, with typical restraint, "everyone hates him, outsiders and office workers alike." On occasion the association still seemed oddly timid about offending major commercial interests. In the late 1930s, the Agriculture Department launched a program of killing deer on the Seminole Indian reservation in Florida, on the theory that the deer harbored cattle ticks dangerous to local livestock. An Audubon field study denying the theory was informally passed on to the government, but the association would not formally publish the report because of pressure by the agriculture lobby. In the end Roosevelt intervened personally to stop the killing. "The point is that no one knows whether these unfortunate animals are hosts to cattle ticks or not," he instructed Agriculture. "You might also tell the Bureau of Animal Industry that they have never proved that human beings are not hosts to cattle ticks. I think some human beings I know are. But I do not shoot them on suspicion — though I would sorely like to do so!"

The episode suggested one of Roosevelt's best qualities: he was educable. Darling, the Izaak Walton League, the Audubon Association, and others gradually made him see the need of taking concerted action for wildlife. After the first term his wildlife record improved. He recommended closing all government lands to duck hunting; refused to extend hunting seasons despite unusual weather conditions; stopped operations on an artillery range in Utah because they endangered a colony of trumpeter swans. The duck population gradually recovered, from a total of 40 million in 1937 to 70 million four years later. Darling's successor at the Biological Survey, Ira N. Gabrielson, continued the program of acquiring new refuges. By 1940 the New Deal had created 159 new refuges, a total of 7,549,-823 acres, more than doubling the federal holdings as of 1934. Roosevelt in

1940 took the Bureau of Fisheries from the Commerce Department and the Biological Survey from Agriculture and combined them into a new agency, the Fish and Wildlife Service in the Interior Department. Under Gabrielson's direction it imparted a new coherence and continuity to federal wildlife policy.

꽃꽃

As a Hudson River patrician Roosevelt had traveled more widely in western Europe than in the western United States. Before 1933 he had seen little of the national park system. The only national park in his region of the country, Acadia, struck him as rather small, properly a national monument rather than a park. When as President he began to visit the national parks of the West, they also sometimes left him unimpressed. "It looks dead," he said of the Grand Canyon. "I like my green trees at Hyde Park better. They are alive and growing." But other parks — especially those with fine stands of timber — reminded him of home. In the summer of 1934 a tour brought him to Glacier National Park for the first time. Straddling the continental divide in the mountains of western Montana, hard by the Canadian border, the park moved Roosevelt to give nationalistic expression to his old idea of conservation as the liberty of the community. "There is nothing so American as our national parks," he declared. "The scenery and wildlife are native and the fundamental idea behind the parks is native. It is, in brief, that the country belongs to the people."

With other conservationists, FDR regarded the parks as a vital source of spiritual rejuvenation for the frazzled residents of modern cities. As the Depression lifted, tourist travel to the national parks and monuments shot upward, from 6.3 million in 1934 to 16.2 million in 1938. Roosevelt applauded the trend and hoped to make the parks more accessible — especially for the congested, urbanized East. At the dedication of Shenandoah National Park in Virginia in 1936, he lovingly invoked a vision of how vacationers would come to the park to find an open fire, the smell of the woods, the wind in the trees. "They will forget the rush and the strain of all the other long weeks of the year, and for a short time at least, the days will be good for their bodies and good for their souls. Once more they will lay hold of the perspective that comes to men and women who every morning and every night can lift up their eyes to Mother Nature." Then he closed by recalling a favorite figure in Greek mythology, the giant Antaeus, invincible on the ground but crushed by Hercules when he lost contact with earth. "There is merit for all of us in the ancient tale," he said.

At Hyde Park FDR liked to play Antaeus in a snappy 1936 Ford

Phaeton convertible, dark blue with whitewall tires. The car was specially equipped to compensate for his disability. To the driver's right was a conventional long-handled floor shift. To his left was another lever resembling a floor shift; pushed halfway forward, it disengaged the clutch; pushed further it applied the brakes. On the right of the steering column was a ratcheted throttle; on the left was a gadget that dispensed lighted cigarettes for the presidential holder. Installed behind the wheel, he enjoyed a degree of mobility otherwise impossible to him. Treating himself to his beloved trees and scenic views of the Hudson, he put thousands of miles on that car as he drove around the old roads he had known since boyhood. He liked to take risks on the road, showing his skill with the special controls, perhaps to make the point that a crippled man could still drive. Churchill recalled such an occasion in 1942: "The President drove me all over the estate, showing me its splendid views. In this drive I had some thoughtful moments. . . . I confess that when on several occasions the car poised and backed on the grass verges of the precipices over the Hudson I hoped the mechanical devices and brakes would show no defects. All the time we talked business, and though I was careful not to take his attention off the driving we made more progress than we might have done in formal conference."

Roosevelt's personality was essentially tactile and intuitive. Usually he absorbed new information not by reading but by experience or conversation or through his pores. As a conservationist he thus *knew* about — or at least could remember — trees, land reclamation, hunting, wildlife, and the restorative power of life outdoors. But a true wilderness experience of hiking or mountaineering far from civilization was beyond him. In dedicating the Whiteface Mountain Memorial Highway in 1935, he made one of his infrequent references to his disability: "I wish very much that it were possible for me to walk up the few remaining feet to the actual top of the mountain." Again, when Irving Brant urged him to keep roads out of the Bogachiel Valley of the proposed Olympic National Park, Roosevelt reduced the discussion to a simple issue: "How would I get in?" Since he could not *experience* the wilderness, it remained his one major blind spot as a conservationist.

Wilderness enthusiasts found a more amenable friend in Harold Ickes, whose purview at Interior included the National Park Service. "I do not happen to favor the scarring of a wonderful mountainside," he said after two years in office, "just so that we can say we have a skyline drive. It sounds poetical, but it may be an atrocity." The statement measured how much Ickes had learned in two years. He had joined the cabinet after a long career as an urban reformer in Chicago. His slight interest in conservation derived from an association with Gifford Pinchot, a political ally since the Bull Moose campaign of 1912. "I learned the principles of conservation at your feet," he told Pinchot during the Hundred Days. Now he found himself at the head not of Pinchot's Forest Service, with its utilitarian tradition of conservation for human use, but of the rival Park Service, with its corollary tradition of esthetic conservation. A quick study, Ickes soon was exchanging insults with his old mentor Pinchot.

Ickes took firm charge of a cabinet department historically notorious for corruption. Interior administered the public lands and thus received loving attention from private interests. Prior secretaries, notably Albert Fall under Harding, had succumbed to temptation. At the same time, since 1916 Interior had claimed the Park Service with its relative incorruptibility. Inheriting this collection of cutthroats surrounding one vestal virgin, Ickes bent them all to his will. He roamed the halls looking for slackers and even tapped the telephones of some subordinates. He was said to breakfast on nails and brickbats. One disappointed congressman accused him of having "the soul of a meat ax and the mind of a commissar." In guarding the public interest Ickes used any weapon at hand, resorting at the last extremity to a spluttering rage. (In private FDR used to call him Donald Duck.) With his ferocious integrity and self-righteous posturings, and with his special privileges as one of the New Deal's inner circle, he made Interior over as an effective agency of conservation.

Official tours brought Ickes to the national parks for the first time. A new world opened before him. After seeing Yosemite in 1934 he declared, in the tones of a man stumbling on a strange new idea, "One should get away once in a while as far as possible from human contacts. To contemplate nature, magnificently garbed as it is in this country, is to restore peace to the mind." At Acadia in 1937 he found George Dorr, still keen at the age of eighty-four despite serious eye trouble. "I must say that he is gallant about it all," Ickes noted. "He is a man of real culture and I note no impairment of his intellectual vigor." A year later an inspection tour took him to Glacier Bay in Alaska. As he passed through the Muir Channel, by the Muir Inlet, to the Muir Glacier, Ickes envisioned a new national park. (He was there because FDR, in the Pinchot spirit, wanted to open the region to mining. "It seems to me a refinement of conservation to prevent mining on a glacier," said Roosevelt. "Let us cut red tape and get the thing started." The mining studies went forward, at some risk to the geological record that was being revealed as the Muir Glacier retreated.)

Ickes feuded interminably with Henry Wallace of Agriculture for the federal control of conservation. By the Taylor Grazing Act of 1934 Ickes acquired — over Agriculture's objections — jurisdiction of ninety million acres of public rangeland. But a year later Ickes lost his Soil Erosion agency to Wallace. So it went, with Roosevelt playing the two men against each other and extracting the best efforts from both. The Forest Service (in Agriculture) had a formidable lobby, originally built by Pinchot and carefully maintained since. It came in layers: professional foresters in and outside the service; major conservation groups (Izaak Walton League, American Forestry Association, Appalachian Mountain Club, National Parks Association); farm groups (National Grange, American Farm Bureau); lumber interests (National Lumber Manufacturers Association, West Coast Lumbermen's Association); grazing interests (National Livestock Association). The lobby drew from both conservation and commercial interests. The Appalachian Mountain Club approved the Forest Service for its management of the White Mountain National Forest in New Hampshire, the favorite source of recreation for most AMC members. But national forests also were used for commercial purposes, unlike the national parks. When Ickes looked for supporters he found few allies among businessmen because no major commercial groups benefited from the park system.

Yet he did not fare much better among conservationists. "Most conservation organizations swallow hook, line, and sinker anything that they are told by the Forest Service," he lamented. "Even such an organization as the Izaak Walton League sneezes whenever the Forest Service takes snuff." He was fighting not only an expert lobby but several decades of tradition: the Forest Service as the clean, efficient spearhead of natural resource protection; the Interior Department as the despoiler of public lands.

The Emergency Conservation Committee, new enough to the field to disregard such traditions, was led by two ardent New Dealers, Rosalie Edge and Irving Brant. The ECC provided Ickes his most reliable support among conservationists, and Ickes in turn gave the group favored treatment. Early in 1937 Brant asked Ickes for help with the ECC's campaign to save a grove of Yosemite sugar pines. "I like the majesty, the symmetry and the denseness that one finds in a grove of sugar pines," Ickes noted. They brought the case to Roosevelt. He reviewed the matter and wrote a longhand memo that implied a veering toward the Park Service's viewpoint. "Forest Service not so good on report — no protection in right place," the President wrote. "Have we the money? $1,000,000 wd do most of it." Ultimately Ickes came up with $2 million in PWA funds to buy the trees.

For Edge and Brant, being on the inside left them in the same vaguely disquieting position as Darling's: closer to power, but less freewheeling. Edge was delighted by the new crop of idealists in the wildlife division of the Park Service. For his part Ickes came to view the ECC as his allies. Occasionally he would ask Brant to have Edge publish a pamphlet on a particular topic; once Ickes even wrote one himself. It was a mutually helpful arrangement, but still bothersome. "I feel that we have perhaps moved too far from our old policy of arousing public interest *first,* and then enlisting the support of the government," Edge confided to Brant in 1941. "It was wonderful when Mr. Ickes worked with us . . . but should we fail to bring before the notice of the public other matters merely because Mr. Ickes is not personally interested?" A strange question for Rosalie Edge to ask. She perhaps was relieved when, in 1942, the birder Florence Page Jaques could still describe her as "the most belligerent of all the conservationists."

With due credit to New Deal achievements, the most striking new direction in conservation at this time took place outside the New Deal, in the development of Muir's ideal of wilderness preservation — not by the Park Service or its supporters but by noncommercial elements within the Forest Service lobby.

During the 1920s, the central figure in wilderness work had been Robert Sterling Yard, a Park Service founder and later its unrelenting critic. He operated from the tradition of the eastern literary lover of wilderness, as defined by Muir's associate Robert Underwood Johnson. (The lineage could be traced directly: Yard briefly succeeded Johnson as editor of the *Century* in 1913.) A Princeton graduate in 1883, Yard had embarked on a career in New York journalism. At the *Sun* he met Steve Mather and served as best man at his wedding. When Mather took charge of the national parks in 1914 he brought Yard to Washington to handle publicity, paying his salary himself. "I became his interpreter and mouthpiece," Yard said later, "because he was naturally incoherent." His articles helped create legislative support for the National Park Service, established in 1916. Shortly thereafter a new law prohibited the salary arrangement between Mather and Yard. The two men in 1919 launched the National Parks Association, with an initial $5,000 from Mather. Friction between the NPA and NPS developed at once, and Mather eventually disassociated himself from the group.

The quarrel between the two old friends embraced many issues. Mather, little interested in wildlife, accepted the Biological Survey's efforts to exterminate predators; Yard criticized the program as early as 1924. But essentially the argument came down to Mather's administration of the parks. He had a weakness for plush accommodations and city comforts. To obtain them he turned over park concessions to private operators, who often were more concerned with profits than with scenery. The results offended Yard's cultured sensibilities. Visiting Yosemite in 1926, he found crowds, automobiles, and a honky-tonk atmosphere. An evening's entertainment at Camp Curry drew an audience of two thousand. "The specialties of a jazz band were followed by vocal solos, quartettes, and amusing stunts. One of the latter was so flagrantly vulgar that I wished myself out of hearing, but the crowd apparently adored it." Later the crowd drove two miles down the valley to witness the Bear Show: "The bears are fed from platforms on a clearing brilliantly lighted by electric lamps in trees. . . . They scrap delightfully. Believe me, with eight to a dozen bears gorging what the announcer calls 'swell swill,' dumped on the platforms from a truck, it is some spectacle." The evening ended with dancing at the outdoor camps. "Once when I waked at midnight in my redwood cabin an eighth of a mile away, the air still palpitated with jazz. If only the Yosemite Night could be transferred to an environ of New York City it would make its promoter a millionaire." Above the valley, Muir's mountains were out of reach and still intact. But "so far as my sympathies are concerned, the Valley's lost."

In short order Yard became unwelcome at the Park Service. Mather's assistant and successor, Horace Albright, perceived Yard as a zealot, remained courteous to him, but kept him out of substantive discussions. Mather gave no money to the NPA after his first donation. Yard accordingly looked elsewhere. "Thousands of business and professional men of degree are very personally interested in the work," he wrote Franklin Roosevelt in 1923. "There ought to be tens of thousands." Roosevelt begged off, and in fact the NPA membership under Yard never exceeded a thousand.

William Greeley's Forest Service, at the urging of Arthur Carhart and Aldo Leopold, began in 1924 a program of setting aside "primitive areas" in the national forests. Aside from protecting wilderness, this program allowed the service to claim — when competing with the Park Service for control of public territory — that it preserved land as well as opened it to human use. The Forest Service never permitted bear shows or jazz bands. Further, the Park Service on occasion tried to create new parks out of land that Yard deemed insufficiently grand to meet his park standards. In such cases Yard preferred the land to go to the Forest Service, where Greeley happily received it. So for these reasons, esthetic rather than commercial, Yard and the NPA drifted into the Forest Service lobby. He later praised

Greeley as "the best advocate of national park standards I ever knew in official life." Yard's NPA worked so closely with the American Forestry Association that William Wharton and George Bird Grinnell of the AFA suggested the two groups be merged.

This alliance with forestry interests damaged the NPA's reputation. Yard, a pure idealist without financial ambitions, found himself rejected by fellow idealists like Willard Van Name, who regarded the NPA as merely a stalking horse for the Forest Service. At the same time, Yard's forestry friends gave more generously of advice than money, and they in turn were bothered by his intensity. "I do not wholly trust his balance," said Grinnell. "With the best intentions he sometimes swings off too far in one direction or another." The NPA's income averaged only $14,700 a year, with one third of the total up to 1930 coming from two major donors, Wharton and John D. Rockefeller, Jr. Yard split his time between crusading and fund raising. Trying to do both, he believed he did neither well. As an old journalist his most cherished hope was to publish a fine magazine for the NPA; he could never afford it. Cut off from his natural allies in the national parks, manipulated but not supported by the Forest Service lobby, Yard often felt isolated and unappreciated. "Waking in the low-tide hours of the night," he wrote in 1926, "I wonder whether I'm justified in forcing this work upon people who seem to care so little about it. . . . Having sacrificed everything personal, myself, if, after seven years, the cause has won neither financial nor personal support, is it really a cause? Am I not merely an impracticable dreamer?"

In the late 1920s his forestry advisors persuaded Yard to accept a reorganization of the group. George Dupont Pratt of the AFA suggested John Burnham as the new president: "What if he isn't identified with the Association's educational program?" Yard fought that off, but some of his tactical maneuvers with Congress had left him open to criticism by his top officers. They forced him in 1930 to accept Pratt's man, Lorne Barclay, as director in charge of fund raising. Yard stayed on in a subordinate role but the group no longer belonged to him. On a smaller scale his experience recalled the work of William Dutcher and Will Dilg: the founding of a conservation group by a radical amateur, full of zeal, whose problems with money ultimately brought a takeover by a more conservative group of officers.

With all his sincerity and dedication, Yard's crucial limitation was that his love of wilderness remained an abstract philosophical attitude, lacking the substance of direct experience. As a rule he did not hike or climb mountains or camp outdoors or study geological formations and plant life.

The only park he knew well, he joked, was Central Park. "I am a tenderfoot. I have no right to stand up here talking to mountaineers," he said on one occasion. "Nevertheless I have got the stuff inside of me. When I am in the woods I feel closer to God than anywhere else." But he spent little time in the woods. He had a writer's personality, most comfortable indoors and on paper. Acolytes of the wilderness experience, like those in the Sierra Club, admired his writing but sensed a distance. "The mountaineer feels a sense of kinship with the stern high country, is at home there," Muir's disciple Marion Randall Parsons noted, "while the dweller in cities is awed but chilled by it. Nature to him is best described in terms of art as a masterpiece, a composition. . . . Mr. Yard proclaims himself to western mountaineers as with us but not yet of us."

A fuller embodiment of the Sierra Club tradition appeared during the New Deal years in the person of Robert Marshall, the first mountaineer in the conservation movement since Muir to approach his combination of firsthand experience, scientific interests, and writing skill. Under his leadership the wilderness concept took on more permanent standing within government and an influential new organization outside government; these were accomplished before his death at thirty-eight. (At that age Muir had yet to write his first book.)

Marshall grew up in New York, son of the wealthy constitutional lawyer and civil libertarian Louis Marshall. Like Irving Brant's, his interest in the natural world was prodded by a period of enforced idleness during childhood. Sick in bed with pneumonia when he was eleven, he read a story about the Lewis and Clark expedition. The book so held his imagination that he reread it annually for the next ten years. His family spent summers in the Saranac Lake region of upstate New York. The boy took long walks into the wilderness in the spirit of Lewis and Clark. "We admired the fine trees, beautiful flowers, lights and shades among the trees," he wrote at fifteen, "and the hundreds of other things which make the woods so superior to the city." That year he climbed his first mountain; eventually he claimed all forty-six of the four-thousand-foot peaks in the Adirondacks. By his junior year in high school he had decided on a career in forestry. "I love the woods and solitude," he said. "I like the various forms of scientific work a forester must do. I should hate to spend the greater part of my lifetime in a stuffy office or in a crowded city."

His formal education included forestry degrees from Harvard and the New York State College of Forestry, and a Ph.D. in plant physiology from Johns Hopkins. In some ways, though, the most educational episode in his life was the fifteen months he spent in the Koyukuk region of north central

Alaska in 1929–1931. He recounted the experience in a best-selling book of 1933, *Arctic Village*. In a remote settlement of 127 whites, Eskimos, and Indians, two hundred miles from Fairbanks, he found the happiest civilization he had known. Living in the village and befriending the residents — he was called Oomik Polluk, "big whiskers" — he concluded they were happy because their lives so little resembled those of modern urbanites. They were surrounded by a beautiful landscape. They routinely encountered hazards and adventures, testing their skills and courage. They did interesting and varied work that brought direct benefits, not simply wages. They all felt independent ("I'm my own boss") and were not pushed around by distant, impersonal economic forces. "Most important of all," he concluded, "happiness in the Koyukuk is stimulated by the prevalent philosophy of enjoying life as it passes along. The absence of constant worry about the future and remorse about the past destroys much that tends to make men miserable." He returned to modern life with his distaste for cities confirmed.

As a conservationist Marshall made his initial mark in forestry. During the 1920s, in the New Era of harmony between the Forest Service and lumber companies, he was one of the profession's Young Turks calling for stricter regulation. "The period for voluntary private forestry is over," he declared in 1929. "The government must step in and compel the private timber owner to leave the forest which he exploits in a productive condition." Soon he moved from mere regulation to public ownership as the solution. Early in 1933 President-elect Roosevelt asked Gifford Pinchot to recommend a forestry policy. Pinchot, out of touch with his old calling, picked Marshall to draft a statement. He brought the draft to Pinchot's home in Pennsylvania, where he was introduced to Pinchot's wife and beautiful niece. With surprising ease he persuaded Pinchot of the need for public ownership. "Then they had the decency to retire at 9:30," Marshall reported to a friend, "leaving the evening to the beautiful Rosalyn and myself. So, I am all for Pinchot now, and shall certainly support him on the basis of his Forestry and his niece." Marshall developed the case for public ownership in a second book published in 1933, *The People's Forests*. Arguing that the history of utility regulation in the United States had largely resulted in private interests regulating regulation, and that private ownership in its focus on immediate profits could not provide the continuity essential to forest management, he concluded that every acre of woodland in the country should belong to the people.

Within this socialist vision, Marshall intruded an unabashed elitism, producing a curious tension in his thought. He proposed that fifty-five million acres of the national forests be set aside for recreation, including thirty million acres in primeval and wilderness conditions. But what of the objection that only a small minority of hikers and campers would benefit from these thirty million acres? "There are certain things that cannot be enjoyed by everybody," he replied. "If everybody tries to enjoy them, nobody gets any pleasure out of them." The greatest threat to the wilderness, according to Marshall, was the misapplication of the utilitarian doctrine — so often invoked by Pinchot — of the greatest good for the greatest number. For most people trees implied lumber. For Marshall and his minority they implied higher intangibles: beauty, adventure, release from the psychological repressions of modern life. For some individuals they even inspired intellectual activity. "Many of our greatest American thinkers," he said, "men of the caliber of Thomas Jefferson, Henry Thoreau, Mark Twain, William James, and John Muir, have found the forests an effective stimulus to original thought." By including Muir in his American pantheon Marshall parted company with most professional foresters. The Pinchot forestry tradition cut down trees so humans might use them in improving on nature. The Muir tradition protected trees for their own sake, as an instructive counterpoint to what Marshall called "the puniness of man."

Marshall, again in the Muir spirit, found his deepest sense of human insignificance in climbing mountains. At the summit he felt the peculiar blend of achievement and humility known only to mountaineers. "The sense of adventure which one gets in the wilderness reaches its perfection, for many people of good equilibrium, in the romance of mountaineering," he wrote. "There is nothing comparable in its demands for physical competence and deftness and stamina and courage." It was the most rarefied, elitist aspect of the already elitist wilderness experience. Scaling a difficult peak, he could be sure of encountering no other humans beyond an occasional climbing partner. In that impregnable solitude he could inhale the view and ponder his private thoughts with no distractions. "A person might die spiritually," he said, "if he could not sometimes forsake all contact with his gregarious fellowmen, and the machines which they had created, and retire to an environment where there was no remote trace of humanity."

Yet when he came back to civilization he led a vigorous social and political life, with many friends in New York and Washington. His interests were neatly compartmented into socialism, civil liberties, and conservation. He liked to stage parties for a disparate group of his friends, plying them with dubious drinks and provoking arguments. A homely man with prominent ears and protruding eyes, his appearance was redeemed by a supercharged vitality and an overpowering, enthusiastic manner. His acquaintances, without sharing all his enthusiasms, could hardly avoid being pulled in by his energy and charm. "I'm glad you have had so glorious a time," Justice Benjamin Cardozo wrote after receiving a letter from Alaska. "How I'd hate it all, much as I love to read of it! . . . Don't stay away too long, but give me a glimpse of your radiant presence and a sample of your racy speech."

Ultimately Bob Marshall's strenuous life was held together by an attitude, born perhaps of his awareness that a congenital heart lesion might kill him at any time. Even when he went out dancing he would curse impatiently during the floor show, anxious to be in motion once again. "Four walls seemed to cramp him," a friend recalled, "and all small confining situations. Only on wilderness trails did his wild free spirit find release and satisfaction." On more than two hundred occasions he hiked over thirty miles in a single day. Once in 1936 he hiked *seventy* miles through the Fort Apache reservation in Arizona — and then, after going sleepless for thirty-four hours, he went off to a meeting and nearly fell asleep.

Few conservationists could match Marshall's intellectual range and physical energy. Early in the New Deal he was offered jobs by various government agencies. In his orderly way he compared the Forest and Park Services as protectors of wilderness. The Park Service had built unnecessary roads and was unduly controlled by its concessionaires; but it defended primeval areas by prohibiting logging. "On the whole," he decided, "it has been a pretty even break." So he split his allegiance between the feuding cabinet departments. From 1933 to 1937 he was director of forestry for the Bureau of Indian Affairs in Interior. As such he created sixteen wilderness areas on Indian reservations. Then, over the objections of Ickes, he transferred to the Forest Service in Agriculture. Silcox opened a new job for him as head of the Division of Recreation and Lands. In two years he pushed through restrictions on roads and developments covering fourteen million acres of national forest land. Spending half his time in Washington and half in the field, he put up with the usual constraints on an amateur radical caught up in administration. Occasionally he would criticize his agency, but only in private. "Obviously, my name should be kept completely out of this," he would say; or, "this is only a personal opinion and not official Forest Service policy. Therefore, please do not quote me."

A fervent New Dealer, Marshall was appalled by one of the major thrusts of New Deal conservation. As he explained the dilemma to Ickes, work relief projects threatened primitive areas precisely because roads and forest improvements functioned so well as unemployment measures: labor-intensive and relatively undemanding of skills, they put large numbers to work quickly. Projects were undertaken more to dispense wages than to make needed improvements. "The bulldozers are already rumbling up into the mountains," Marshall wrote Silcox in 1935. "Unless you act very soon on the seven primitive area projects I presented to you a month ago, eager CCC boys will have demolished the greatest wildernesses which remain in the United States." But Roosevelt for his own reasons would not keep parkways and the CCC out of the wilderness.

In the East, a primeval Appalachian Trail proposed by the forester Benton MacKaye in 1921 was gradually being stitched together over the two thousand miles from Maine to Georgia. Now it was threatened by proposed skyline drives and other developments. While working for the TVA in Knoxville, MacKaye began to discuss protective measures with a local hiking enthusiast named Harvey Broome. They in turn exchanged ideas with an associate in Washington, Harold Anderson, founder of the Potomac Appalachian Trail Club. In August 1934 Anderson planted the seed for a new organization. "You and Bob Marshall have been preaching that those who love the primitive should get together and give a united expression to their views," he wrote MacKaye. "That is what I would like to get started."

When Marshall visited Knoxville on government business — ironically, a survey for a proposed parkway — MacKaye and Broome enlisted his support for a group to protect the Appalachian Trail. Broome was especially concerned about inroads on the Smoky Mountains. "It was that wilderness," he told Marshall, "which a half decade ago we were so eagerly seeking to bring under the *protection* of the Park Service, and which now some of us are just as eagerly seeking to protect *from* the Park Service." Marshall picked up the idea and expanded it to embrace wilderness issues on a national scale. He brought in Ernest Oberholtzer, the prime mover behind the Quetico-Superior wilderness area in Minnesota, and Aldo Leopold. Marshall had long admired Leopold's writings on primitive areas, and though bothered by his former connection with gun company money, respected him because "he has done some of the most effective work yet done to save various areas from mechanical invasion." In Washington, Marshall added a final key member to the group, Robert Sterling Yard. For Yard it meant a new lease on life, and his favorite cause, at the age of seventy-four. With a baptismal donation of a thousand dollars from Marshall, the group was officially launched in January 1935.

That September Yard put out the first issue of a new magazine, the *Living Wilderness.* "The Wilderness Society is born of an emergency in conservation which admits of no delay," he declared. "The craze is to build all the highways possible everywhere while billions may yet be borrowed from the unlucky future. The fashion is to barber and manicure wild America as smartly as the modern girl. Our duty is clear." The society's platform sought to move wilderness discussion beyond esthetics, to connect it with practical resources like coal and timber. Defining wilderness as "the environment of solitude," and as "a human need rather than a luxury or plaything," it proposed that primitive areas be regarded as a public utility needing protection from commercialization. Such areas should be sharply distinguished from nonprimitive forests, with the line between them drawn by roads and automobiles. "Motorway and solitude together constitute a contradiction," the founders insisted. Stepping back from these immediate issues, Leopold capped the magazine's first number by locating the new group in a philosophical context, a variation on Muir's denial that the world was made especially for man. The Wilderness Society, said Leopold, implied "a disclaimer of the biotic arrogance of *homo americanus.* It is one of the focal points of a new attitude — an intelligent humility toward man's place in nature."

According to initial plans, Marshall would assume the presidency. But Ickes, anticipating criticism of his Park Service, would not hear of it. Marshall then suggested Leopold, who in turn demurred in favor of someone on the scene in Washington. So Yard took the position. All parties agreed that the membership should remain small and sympathetic to the group's ideals. "We want no straddlers," said Marshall. MacKaye ("a grand fellow but very eccentric," according to Marshall) was even more suspicious of new allies. "I have in mind a long list of people who should NOT be admitted," he said. "We want those who *already* think as we do; not those who have to be shown." The founders set up a virtual oligarchy to run the group and defend its principles. With that protection, prominent outsiders such as John Collier of the Bureau of Indian Affairs and Arthur Morgan of the TVA were allowed to join. "If we keep the proper executive committee," Marshall pointed out, "I do not think there is any danger that these big shots will run the Society in the ground as they have done in the National Parks Association."

That prospect was unlikely in Marshall's lifetime because he essentially controlled Wilderness Society policy. The group belonged to him even more tightly than the early Izaak Walton League belonged to Will Dilg — because, unlike Dilg, as a man of independent wealth he was his own

financial angel. Presiding at the annual meetings, he would introduce a resolution. After long and contentious discussion, he would bring the matter
to a vote. "Everybody would shout aye," Yard recalled later. "Then Bob
would introduce another subject. Then another. Then another. And so
we'd put in a whole morning and afternoon, and it would all be Bob."
They could hardly resist his personality — or the fact that he contributed
$2,500 or $3,000 a year while income from other sources averaged only
$700. Yard depended entirely on Marshall's generosity for his living. Prob-
ably both men disliked the situation. "My contribution to the Wilderness
Society has been out of proportion to what one contributor should do,"
Marshall noted in 1938. But the group's radicalism and exclusiveness cut
off other sources of income.

In its size, principles, and independence from commercial interests, the
Wilderness Society most resembled the ECC. Yet by an accident of politics
one belonged to the Forest Service lobby, the other to the Park Service
lobby, so cooperation between the two groups was limited. Marshall and
Rosalie Edge, alike in many ways, circled each other warily and kept their
respective allegiances. Marshall resented her attacks on his boss Silcox;
Edge could not forgive Yard's connection with the forestry-dominated
NPA. Nonetheless, Marshall gave the ECC a hundred dollars a year: "On
the whole," he told Edge, "I approve of your general attitude." She shot
back: "We are just about to put out valuable publications, which I venture
to hope that you, *even you,* will approve." On another occasion, after Brant
persuaded Silcox to withdraw his objections to the proposed Olympic park,
she tried flattering Marshall ("Mr. Brant is such another as yourself —
entirely sincere"). The two half-seriously talked about taking a pack trip
together in the summer of 1938. "I believe the trip should be educational to
both of us," said Marshall. But it never took place. On some park issues
they opposed each other bitterly. It was a relationship of mutually respectful skepticism. "I never trusted Bob Marshall," she said after his death,
"— though I liked him, and liked his money."

꙲꙲

A hundred miles southeast of Yosemite, the Kings River cascades down
from some of the highest peaks in the Sierra Nevada, splits into three forks,
and then resumes its course southward. The south fork, called the Kings
Canyon, is longer and deeper than Yosemite. Ten miles long and a half
mile wide with walls of purplish gray granite, the canyon floor is more than
a mile below the general surface of the surrounding mountains. Muir ex-
plored the three forks during one of his mountaineering excursions in

1875 — "when it was wild," he said later, "and when the divine balanced beauty of the trees and flowers seemed to be reflected and doubled by all the onlooking rocks and streams as though they were mirrors." Even then, though, he found an ominous sign tacked to a tree: "We, the undersigned, claim this valley for the purpose of raising stock." Thereafter he periodically returned to the region to check on conditions. On his fourth visit in the spring of 1891 he found giant sequoias, fifteen feet in diameter, being cut for lumber. In the valleys, even the groves under government protection had been hacked and scarred by campers and sheepherders. Fresh from his successful campaign for the Yosemite National Park, he urged that park status be conferred on the Kings River area. "This region contains no mines of consequence," he pointed out in the *Century*, "it is too high and rocky for agriculture, and even the lumber industry need suffer no unreasonable restriction. Let our law-givers then make haste before it is too late ... and the world will rise up and call them blessed."

Muir and the Sierra Club pursued the matter but were resisted by lumbermen and stockmen, and later by water power interests in Los Angeles. Instead of a park, the region became a national forest under Forest Service jurisdiction. After Muir's death Steve Mather tried to transfer the area to his Park Service. He reread Muir's writings on the Kings Canyon and, according to Yard, "was more enthusiastic about it even than about his beloved Yosemite," making the transfer his pet project. Muir's disciple William Colby rounded up support in the Sierra Club. "I wish John Muir were alive now to help," he said in 1925, "... but his prophetic voice still carries the gospel abroad and helps to carry on the good work." Bills to make the region a national park were introduced in Congress a half dozen times but were defeated by the Forest Service lobby. Meantime the service allowed hunting, grazing, mining, and logging in the area. But these were conducted on a limited scale because the region was inaccessible to the outside world.

In 1935, as part of the New Deal public works program, construction began on a major highway into Kings Canyon, bringing the prospect of real commercial development. Senator Hiram Johnson of California introduced another park bill but it was stalled in committee. The new road gave park advocates a stronger case, though, and for the first time they began to make headway. Bob Marshall asked Ickes to take up the cause. Perhaps at his urging, Ickes decided to push for a new kind of national park — one that would avoid the excessive roads and hotels that defaced Yosemite. Ickes proposed to treat Kings Canyon as "a primitive wilderness, limiting roads to the absolute minimum, maintaining foot and horse trails, excluding elaborate hotels, admitting all responsible packers, promoting good fishing," and restoring wildlife.

A bill incorporating this new definition was introduced by Representative B. W. Gearhart, whose district included most of the proposed park. Ickes hoped the bill with its wilderness provisions would meet the exacting standards of the NPA's wealthy president William Wharton. But Wharton naively took his conservation policies from the American Forestry Association's Ovid Butler ("the slickest, slipperiest weasel that ever paraded as a ground squirrel," according to Brant). Butler, a leader in the Forest Service lobby, advised Wharton to oppose the Gearhart bill unless it absolutely excluded future water-power development from the region. Butler presumably had other reasons to fight the bill, but behind that pretext he lined up opposition from the Izaak Walton League, American Nature Association, American Wildlife Institute, and National Wildlife Federation.

The conservation group closest to the situation, the Sierra Club, at first took no part in the controversy. Since Muir's time it had become a quiet, largely social organization, and had even lost its traditional connection with mountaineering. "It is not necessary to be a mountaineer in the physical or athletic sense, to be eligible for Club membership," a new policy statement declared in 1935. "To explore the mountains is the joyous privilege of all who can; but to assist in the preservation of their glories is both a privilege and a duty of conscientious citizens." Individual members like Colby still did their duty, but as an organization it seldom bestirred itself in active conservation fights. In the 1930s most of the three thousand members were middle-aged Republicans. To attract a new generation, annual dues were halved for those under the age of twenty-one. Younger Sierrans like Ansel Adams and David Brower still saw few of their contemporaries at meetings in San Francisco. The meetings of the southern California chapter in Los Angeles were better attended — because they were more fun. On weekends there were dance parties at the Muir Lodge in the Santa Anita canyon, and monthly parties in Los Angeles. It was very agreeable and very far from Muir's spirit. "I don't want people to join the Sierra Club just to fight for conservation," a leader of the Southern California chapter said later. "I want them to join the Sierra Club because they enjoy it."

Historically the club had aligned itself with the Park Service. Steve Mather and Horace Albright, both Californians, were club members. During the New Deal, with the Park Service in the hands of a nonentity and with the Forest Service being reformed by the expert leadership of Silcox, the club gradually shifted its allegiance and became an occasional ally of the Forest Service lobby. One club leader, Duncan McDuffie, served as West Coast representative on the NPA council. When the Wilderness Society was founded it was allowed to use the Sierra Club's mailing list to recruit new members. In the summer of 1937 Bob Marshall strengthened the tie by taking some club members on a Forest Service inspection trip of the High Sierra and soliciting their recommendations. Greatly impressed, the club president, Joel Hildebrand, praised Marshall as "a man of courage and high ideals."

As the congressional fight over the Kings Canyon park approached a showdown, Brant and the ECC tried to pull the Sierra Club's influence behind the Gearhart bill. But the Forest Service regional office in San Francisco was lobbying actively against the measure, despite Silcox's orders otherwise, and most club members seemed aligned with the regional office. The ECC's man on the West Coast, William Schulz, decided the group was hopeless. "As a club it is snobbish and smug," he told Brant, "and feels that all matters regarding the Sierra and the California outdoors are its own special province."

Precisely: without Sierra Club support the Kings Canyon bill was dead. In August 1938, Brant as Ickes's envoy went out to look over the territory of the proposed park. With Hildebrand and other Sierrans he took a six-day pack trip into the region. Afterward he was told the club still could not support the bill because it lacked safeguards against commercial inroads. Next Ickes, with Brant as mediator, made the overtures. He asked to meet with leaders of the Sierra Club during a trip to San Francisco in October. They sat down together at the Bohemian Club on the evening of October 21. "We gave him a very nice dinner," Hildebrand recalled. "He was in an expansive mood, talked freely. He told us about his troubles with Henry Wallace." Ickes held forth for an hour, charming his audience with inside details, in an atmosphere of fraternal cooperation. According to Hildebrand, the Sierrans stressed the need to avoid "another Yosemite with an Ahwanee Hotel. We wanted a wilderness park." Ickes agreed and invited their advice in refining the bill's wilderness provisions. By the end of the evening the Sierra Club leaders had promised to help pass the measure.

That fall a librarian from the San Francisco area named Linnie Marsh Wolfe launched an effort to attach Muir's name to the proposed Kings park. (In 1945 Wolfe would publish a Pulitzer Prize–winning biography of Muir.) She argued that Muir should be so honored as an early explorer of the canyon and as one of the first advocates of according park status to the area. Moreover — as Brant pointed out to Ickes — including Muir's name in the Gearhart bill would help assure the Sierra Club's support. In January 1939 Ickes and Brant broached the matter to Roosevelt, who readily endorsed the change. A month later Ickes in full cry delivered a rousing sermon at the Commonwealth Club in San Francisco. "John Muir engaged in a ceaseless campaign, a never-ending struggle, to arouse the American people to the need of preserving the wonder spots of nature," he declared. "It is no empty gesture, no undeserved capitalization of fame, that causes the name of John Muir to be attached to the proposed national park in the country he loved so well." The Gearhart bill began to gather momentum in California. The governor and the mayor of San Francisco sent endorsements to Roosevelt. The Sierra Club, drifting from the Forest Service toward the Park Service, dropped its affiliation with the NPA and urged the Wilderness Society to join the cause. "The bill must pass," David Brower wrote in the *Sierra Club Bulletin.* "Wilderness destruction proceeds on a one-way road. From mile to mile the course of destruction may seem justifiable enough. But when the road's end is reached, there is no turning back. The wilderness is gone, and with it the values of the primeval places to civilization — values that cannot be stated in dollars." (For the twenty-six-year-old Brower, the effort was his baptism in national conservation struggles.)

Back East, Rosalie Edge added a slogan to her ECC letterhead: "The John Muir National Park in 1939." As the bill made its way through the House Committee on Public Lands, unknown parties in California revived the old stories about Muir and Elvira Hutchings and sent them to Washington, intending to prove that Muir was unworthy of having a park named for him. In committee his name was dropped from the bill, officially because "it has not been customary to name national parks after individuals." In any case, the bill even without Muir's name was virtually assured of passage when the opposition made a clumsy attempt to entrap Gearhart in a payoff scheme. Engineered by Charles Dunwoody, lobbyist for the California Chamber of Commerce, the ruse was ludicrously transparent. When Gearhart revealed the plot's details in Congress on May 2, 1939, he securely lodged his bill on the side of the angels. It passed the House that summer and the Senate in the following February. The new Kings Canyon National Park embraced 438,000 acres, all three forks of the river, and peaks as high as fourteen thousand feet. Its wilderness provisions were essentially intact. For William Colby, the park ended thirty-five years of intermittent campaigning, undertaken originally at Muir's request. "I feel now that I can 'die in peace,' " he wrote Ickes. "At least you have added the greatest possible joy to my remaining years."

☙☙

From the CCC to Kings Canyon, the Roosevelt administration after two terms had made a fine record in conservation. Beyond the individual achievements, in a larger sense the New Deal brought about a political realignment of the conservation movement, linking it for the first time with both political liberalism and the Democratic Party. Robert Marshall, as the first prominent socialist in conservation, epitomized in an extreme form the new alliance. Because Democrats held the White House for twenty years after 1932, federal conservation agencies came to be well stocked with Democrats. Especially in the lower echelons, these agencies were run by younger political liberals, as were the newer conservation groups like the ECC and the Wilderness Society.

In the older groups this change toward liberal politics took place more slowly. As Rosalie Edge pointed out, with a nod to the Audubon Association and the American Museum of Natural History, "all the *anti* forest-preservation agencies are also anti New Deal. All so-called conservation is anti New Deal." But among conservationists — as she defined the term — Republicans were becoming hard to find. During the 1940 presidential campaign Edge was asked to recommend a Republican to advise presidential candidate Wendell Willkie on conservation issues. No one who met her standards came to mind. "Has the Republican Party any conservationists?" she asked Brant. He mulled it over and wrote back, "I don't know anybody in that damn party to which I once belonged who would do it." The exchange revealed the most important New Deal contribution to the movement. After Franklin Roosevelt, most conservationists were Democrats.

7

Six Free-Lancers

By the 1940s the conservation movement could claim a respectable maturity. The major groups — Audubon, Sierra Club, Izaak Walton League, Wilderness Society, and National Wildlife Federation — were established and reasonably stable. Yet the leaders of these groups toiled away in public anonymity, unknown to anyone except fellow conservationists.

Outside the movement proper, certain individuals revived the amateur tradition and promoted conservation through their own individual prominence. Celebrated in other fields, they helped bring the word to audiences that otherwise would have had no exposure to conservation. A detailed look at the careers of a half dozen of these free-lancers can suggest, in microcosm, salient qualities of their less familiar counterparts in the movement itself.

❧❧

Conservation is often accused of being a plaything of the rich, an indulgence of wealthy people with nothing else on their minds. According to this view, affluent conservationists have cared more for birds and trees than for their less fortunate fellow human beings. A moot point; yet conservation leadership, especially in the modern period, has included very few individuals of great wealth. Rich people have often given money, but little else. Decision making, lobbying, and the grubby everyday work of public education have generally been carried out by people of moderate income. Wealthy conservationists have paid many bills but have not exerted much direct influence on the course of the movement.

With one notable exception: John D. Rockefeller, Jr., was the most generous philanthropist in the history of conservation. By the sheer extent of his gifts — amounting to tens of millions of dollars over four decades — he wielded an implicit power, even though he seldom wrote or spoke on behalf of conservation and though his interest was essentially restricted to the protection of trees and land from commercial development. His preservationist instincts were further encased by a personality accustomed to urban luxuries and plush accommodations. Not a hiker or climber, he liked to enjoy the wilderness from the comfort of good roads and hotels. Such tastes made him a controversial friend of the national parks. But his bottomless checkbook had a way of smoothing out difficult issues.

"I think perhaps I have always had an eye for nature," Rockefeller said toward the end of his life. "I remember as a boy loving sunsets." As the only son of the most celebrated of all the nineteenth-century robber barons, he grew up in wealthy isolation somewhat after the fashion of Franklin D. Roosevelt. Surrounded by sisters and a very attentive mother, his father a revered but distant figure, Junior was a detached, self-contained little boy who seldom played with other boys. Instead, again after the fashion of FDR, he turned to nature — but without getting his clothes dirty. He watched those sunsets from his bedroom window in the family home on West Fifty-fourth Street in New York. At the family estate outside Cleveland he developed a love for the woods, well-manicured woods. "I remember what the sycamore trees looked like and the maple trees," he recalled. "Every time I ride through the woods today, the smell of the trees — particularly when a branch has just been cut and the sap is running — takes me back to my early impressions in the woods." As a young man he did a little hunting in Nova Scotia but never cared for it, and the habit did not persist. His interest in nature remained passive and esthetic, an experience to be absorbed rather than a directed activity.

At the turn of the century, fresh from college, young Rockefeller entered his father's employ and promptly lost a million dollars in a bad investment. Perhaps chastened by this baptism, he never matched the old man's entrepreneurial passion. In a few years he began resigning his inherited directorships and withdrew from the business world. Instead, he devoted himself to philanthropy and, incidentally, to salvaging his father's reputation from the attacks of muckrakers. To serve both ends he constructed an empire for giving away money. "I did not seek nor choose to be the recipient of great wealth," he said in a rare moment of self-revelation. "It has not meant the greatest happiness." He fancied himself a master builder, whether of Rockefeller Center or the restoration of Colonial Williamsburg or one of his park roads. He would lose himself in the details of blueprints and engineering technicalities; wherever he went he carried a folding rule in his pocket, always ready to take a measurement. All his building and giving, as he explained it, were intended to burnish his father's image. "I have ever been proud to lay the credit for things accomplished at his feet, where alone it belonged," he wrote. "I have gloried in the greatness of his unparalleled achievements in industry and his world wide services to humanity. I have never sought anything for myself." He gave away nearly half a billion dollars. Of this total about 5 percent went to conservation projects.

Rockefeller's interest in the national parks had begun shortly after his early retirement from the family business. In 1910 he bought a summer place at Seal Harbor on Mount Desert Island and thus came to the attention of George Dorr, then in the initial stages of putting his park together. At a crucial juncture in 1915 Dorr, through Charles Eliot, appealed to Rockefeller for $15,000. Rockefeller gave $17,500, his first big money for conservation, and followed it a year later with a gift of twenty-seven hundred acres worth a quarter million dollars. The land was given on one condition: that Rockefeller be allowed to build roads on it to his own specifications. He liked to enjoy nature behind a team of fine horses; he hated the idea of automobiles on the island. So the roads he built were carefully integrated into the natural landscape, with stone overpasses to avoid intersections, and constructed with careful grading and a lavish use of hand labor — but without a hard surface, and too narrow for two-way automobile traffic. To critics they intruded on the park and the private lands they crossed, yet were unsuitable for the cars driven by most tourists.

Rockefeller's fetish for carriage roads presented Dorr with a dilemma. "One of the main difficulties I have had to overcome at Washington," he told Rockefeller, "is the impression that ... the Island is a place for wealthy people only, and I am exceedingly anxious to show uses of the park that lie within the reach of everyone." That implied automobiles, finally granted entrance in the 1920s over Rockefeller's objections. Not persuaded of their benefits, he continued to honeycomb the park with his own roads. Ultimately it was a system of sixty miles of roads and bridges, with a cost to Rockefeller of two million dollars. Dorr disliked the system but was caught between Rockefeller's money and the criticism of park purists such as Robert Sterling Yard. "Who is willing to tell rich men truths which may discourage their giving?" Yard asked. Dorr was not. In the interest of future Rockefeller contributions he publicly supported the road building.

Rockefeller retained the self-contained personality of his boyhood. As Dorr delicately put it, he "does not welcome suggestions for which he does not ask." When Dorr had something to propose he would plant it with one of Rockefeller's people instead of taking it directly to the rich man himself. Even with his own employees and friends Rockefeller was formal and withdrawn, never addressing anyone by first name. Essentially he remained a Victorian gentleman beset by the twentieth century. Harold Ickes tried to warm up to him but finally concluded that he was "somewhat dull," with little interest in world affairs or anything except his own projects. He invariably said grace before every meal — "the only man of his generation and class who does this," Ickes thought. But regardless of his unbending ways he was still an immensely wealthy man who liked to underwrite conservation projects. Yard criticized him in private but happily accepted his two thousand a year to the National Parks Association. Dorr's unflagging tolerance was rewarded in 1935 when Rockefeller made a final gift of 3,835 acres to Acadia (on condition that he be allowed to build three more road projects). Ickes accepted with thanks.

The pattern established at Acadia was repeated in Rockefeller's most controversial undertaking in conservation: the creation of a new park at Jackson Hole in the Grand Teton Mountains of Wyoming. The project began in the summer of 1924 when Rockefeller, on a western tour with his three oldest boys, arrived in Yellowstone and met the park superintendent, Horace Albright. In riding around the park he noticed that the roadsides were cluttered with brush and fallen logs. Disliking such untidiness, he sent Albright the money for clearing away the debris. Two years later Rockefeller returned, and Albright, sensing a high roller, took him on a trip to the Tetons. He was bowled over by the view above Jackson Lake — "quite the grandest and most spectacular mountains I have ever seen," he exclaimed — but was dismayed by the human improvements along the road below: billboards, gas stations, telephone lines, dance halls, and bootlegger establishments. He asked Albright to draw up plans for buying the privately held land and restoring it to a natural state.

Albright had cleverly planted the idea without seeming to do so: the honky-tonks made their own argument. He brought Rockefeller a proposal to spend $250,000 on buying up the eyesores. Rockefeller rejected the scheme with the comment that only an "ideal" project would interest him. Albright came back with a plan to spend a million dollars to buy ten thousand acres. Rockefeller gave his approval this time. The Snake River Land Company was organized to mask his involvement and keep the prices down. However prudent, this subterfuge proved to be a political mistake as the project went forward. "There were rumors," a resident of the valley later recalled, "about many ranches up-country being bought by some mysterious somebody for some mysterious something." By 1933 Rockefeller's agent had gained control of some thirty-five thousand acres at a cost of $1.4 million.

When Congress was urged to combine this land with one hundred thousand acres of the Teton National Forest and other public lands to create a new national park, the Forest Service and local cattlemen rose up in high dudgeon. Regardless of their real motives, their strongest argument was that Rockefeller had acquired his land dishonestly, keeping his identity secret and without divulging his intentions. The Forest Service of course did not want to lose its land, and if the national forest became a park the cattlemen would no longer be allowed to graze their stock on it. For these varied reasons the Forest Service lobby and its allies among western politicians blocked the efforts of Rockefeller and Albright to get a park bill through Congress. For ten years Rockefeller bided his time, paying taxes on the property and waiting for congressional action.

Finally in 1943, acting on the advice of his assistant Kenneth Chorley and of Albright, Rockefeller tried another ploy: either the government would find some way of accepting the land or he would return it to private ownership. "He is now almost seventy years old," Ickes explained to the White House, "and, with the heavy additional taxes that he will be called upon to pay, he wants to get his affairs in order." Ickes urged the President to circumvent Congress and declare the land a national monument by executive order. Roosevelt did so in March 1943, thereby detonating another explosion in Wyoming: the order took in Rockefeller's gift, 140,000 acres of federal land, and 18,000 acres of land still in private hands. "We GAVE them the Tetons!" said one citizen of Jackson Hole. "What *more* do they want?" Far from dead, the controversy was only heating up.

Western congressmen pushed through a bill to abolish the Jackson Hole National Monument. It reached Roosevelt's desk in December 1944. Most conservationists — including Rosalie Edge, the Izaak Walton League, the Sierra Club, the National Parks Association, and the American Planning and Civic Association — urged a veto. Roosevelt did veto it, but Senator Joseph O'Mahoney of Wyoming attached a rider to Interior's annual appropriation bill that prohibited any funds for the maintenance of a national monument in Jackson Hole. At last, a few years later, a compromise was arranged. Congress would guarantee the protection of grazing rights on the private land and would compensate the county for its loss of tax revenue. Rockefeller presented his land to the government in 1949, capping a struggle that had lasted over twenty years.

In all that time his love of the region had never wavered. He returned every summer to look at the mountains and check on conditions. When the land was finally safe he built a six-million-dollar hotel on Jackson Lake. Questioned about the wisdom of constructing such an elaborate hotel to be open only three months a year, he declared: "I am not making an investment. I am making this hotel a gift to the American people." (It also provided him suitable accommodations for his own stays at Jackson Lake.)

The Acadia and Jackson Hole episodes displayed Rockefeller's tenacity and his particularly civilized tastes in admiring the wilderness. In their controversial aspects they were not typical of his conservation efforts. Other projects — $5 million for the Great Smoky National Park, $2 million for California coast redwoods, $1.65 million for Yosemite sugar pines — went through in relative serenity and spared him the pain of having his generosity spurned or his motives questioned.

The precise nature of his motives can only be surmised. He gave away money because he was a Christian gentleman and because he wanted to save his father's reputation. He underwrote conservation projects because he loved natural beauty and, with other conservationists, found in it evidence for a religious argument from design. "I never had any doubt about the existence of a divine being," he said. "To see a tree coming out in the spring was enough to impress me with the fact that God existed."

One other motive for his gifts to conservation suggests itself, probably on a level of which he was not consciously aware. In the same way that Steve Mather, the borax king, decided to put something back in the ground, perhaps Rockefeller took the proceeds of a fortune built on oil and returned it to the earth. "His actions are curiously symbolic," Fairfield Osborn, Jr., pointed out, "for much of the wealth that has made possible his munificent contributions for the purposes of conservation has been derived from the depths of the earth. . . . He is part of a self-created epic that expresses the completion of a cycle."

※※

Bernard DeVoto, a writer from Cambridge, Massachusetts, packed up his family and headed west in the summer of 1946. He traced the route of Lewis and Clark to the mouth of the Columbia and followed a zigzag course through a dozen national parks and forests. In three months of rambles he was offended by the lack of good food and drink, and he quickly saw his fill of mountains. Nonetheless the trip was a conversion experience — "by far the best thing I ever did in my life," he said. He slept on the ground, on the floors of ranger stations, on air mattresses, on the slope of a mountain. Despite himself he was bowled over by Glacier National Park and by crossing the Nevada desert at night. As he immersed himself in these unfamiliar habitats, studying local geography, talking with park rangers and forest lookouts, conservation gained its most effective spokesman between Franklin Roosevelt and Rachel Carson. "It is imperative to maintain portions of the wilderness untouched," DeVoto concluded at the end of his tour, "so that a tree will rot where it falls, a waterfall will pour its curve without generating electricity, a trumpeter swan may float on uncontaminated water — and moderns may at least see what their ancestors knew in their nerves and blood."

On a personal level the trip meant an ironic homecoming for DeVoto at the age of forty-nine. He had grown up in Ogden, Utah, the son of a Catholic father and a Mormon mother. Stifled by the lack of intellectual outlets in Ogden, as soon as he could he went east to Harvard. Eventually, settling down to a life of free-lance scholarship within walking distance of Harvard Yard, he liked to call himself an apprentice New Englander. As such he looked out at the rest of the country with the amused tolerance of his neighbors in Cambridge. Having outgrown his youthful impatience with the West, in the summer of 1946 he could see the region more clearly. Twelve miles east of Ogden, he stumbled into an unappreciated valley. "One of the beauty spots of the world," he reflected. "I guess I was too mad to realize it before now." But he was not quite reconciled. He was still disgusted by cowboy songs, loud extroverts, and the regional inferiority complex. On the whole trip he met only three people that came up to his civilized standards. "My God," he said, "how good it was to get back to the coiled and interknit neuroses and psychoses of Cambridge." His subsequent writings about the West retained the alien tidiness of a city slicker at a dude ranch. (A few years later he declared with finality that horses were the dumbest of animals, thereby revealing his lack of acquaintance with cows and sheep.)

As a conservationist DeVoto had an advantage over anyone else in the field: a large reputation as a writer and, therefore, a measure of national influence. His monthly column in *Harper's* provided a regular pulpit, and he also enjoyed access to such important magazines as *Fortune* and the *Saturday Evening Post*. On his western trip, in the course of doing other research, he accidentally learned of a development that had been neglected by other writers. "One of the biggest land grabs in American history," he called it. At the end of 1946 he broke the story in two characteristic broadsides in *Harper's,* and thus began his active career in conservation.

During World War II, various western business interests — stockmen, lumbermen, mining companies and oil companies — had brought legislation to Congress to open up the federal lands of the West. Though resisted by conservation groups, under emergency conditions some inroads had been made. Grazing in the national parks, for example, was increased as a war measure. In the postwar reaction, with a Republican Congress, western businessmen hoped to build on those precedents. "Federal ownership or control of land," declared a spokesman for a stockgrowers association, "is a form of communism." As reported by DeVoto, these threats were focused on national forests and Taylor Act grazing lands in the five-state region of Idaho, Utah, Nevada, Arizona, and New Mexico. The stockmen hoped to use the grazing land with fewer restrictions, and ultimately to have the government sell the Taylor lands back to the states and then to private individuals. Lumber interests aimed to transfer some twenty-seven million acres of national forests back to the states. These designs were clothed in the attractive rhetoric of home rule, economic individualism, and the mystique of the noble cowboy. Recalling past examples of ruggedly individualistic land abuse by western mining, lumbering, and overgrazing, DeVoto predicted ecological disaster if this assault on the West's public resources was not stopped. "In a single generation," he concluded, such an assault "could destroy the West and return it to the processes of geology."

For DeVoto this new campaign represented a striking break from his previous career. He had always scorned reformers and idealistic political movements. With some pride he described himself as the only member of his literary generation who had never cast a vote for Eugene Debs. Suddenly, in middle age, he was bemused to find that he had taken up a cause about which he cared deeply. "This is the only time I ever served as a midwife to a revolt," he told a friend, "and needless to say I am getting a hell of a kick out of it."

Moreover, in his historical work he had made a firm distinction between what he called "regressive" historical forces and "those that are dynamic, of the future." In two books on the westward movement, *The Year of Decision* and *Across the Wide Missouri,* both written before his conservation phase, he had taken a cheerleading approach as the dynamic Americans subdued the land and the Indians. Manifest Destiny was inexorable and salutary; the mountain men and Indian traders were heroic and wise; critics like Thoreau ("Henry") were misguided and faintly ridiculous.

Apparently DeVoto saw no parallel between 1846 and 1946. But the land-grabbers of 1946 were simply the ideological descendants of the brave mountain men. They wanted to reduce the land to human purposes, and brooked no interference from the government or anyone else. Although DeVoto would have bristled at the accusation, he now served as spokesman for what he otherwise would have called regressive forces.

Conservationists quickly brought the new recruit into camp. "If I have ever read a better article on conservation," William Vogt told him, ". . . I cannot recollect it." The Sierra Club reprinted parts of the land-grab articles and made him an honorary life member. (The editor of the *Sierra Club Bulletin* suggested that *Harper's* was exercising editorial leadership in the tradition of Johnson's *Century*.) *Audubon Magazine* also reprinted some of DeVoto's work, and the society joined the cause. "The grazing interests of the western states are on the warpath," John Baker declared. "It is perhaps the biggest conservation battle since the Ballinger controversy." Even Rosalie Edge thought about turning DeVoto's work into an ECC pamphlet.

Without planning it, he found himself serving as a free-lance clearinghouse for conservation, bringing the movement into contact with more general sources of public opinion. He helped the forester Arthur Carhart place an article in the *Atlantic,* and he berated friends in the media, such as Elmer Davis, Marquis Childs, and his old student Joseph Alsop. He searched — without success — for some bright young man in Congress to take up the cause and make a career of it. He extolled the policies of his favorite conservation group, the Izaak Walton League, and its executive secretary, Kenneth Reid, whom he considered "the best-informed man, over the whole field, in the country." He also respected Edge ("the one-woman army"). But he faulted conservationists for their internal squabbling and for being less intent than their adversaries on the cause. "The trouble with our side," he reflected, "is that we quit at five o'clock and go home to relax over a good drink without ever helping one another out, whereas the boys on the other side are well drilled in teamwork and neither relax nor sleep."

His side did stop the land-grab, though. Following his lead, the conservation movement launched a full campaign and found unexpected support in some parts of the West. Small stockowners, fearing unregulated competition from larger operators, urged their congressmen to support federal control. Thus the terms were changed: instead of noble cowboys against Washington, the issue became big business against the little guy. The Idaho legislature passed a resolution to that effect in the spring of 1947. The Forest Service and the Agriculture Department deployed their lobbies against the land-grabbers. As a veteran of literary controversies, DeVoto was not averse to unlimbering his considerable polemical skills when the fight became personal. "The active land-grabbers are only a small minority of Western stockgrowers, a still smaller minority of Western citizens, and an infinitesimal fraction of the American electorate," he thundered in *Harper's.* "These babies can be stopped." In response, a Wyoming stockman wrote to *Harper's:* "There is only one thing worse than a dude ranch historian, and that is a dude ranch conservationist." Conservationists had existing laws and institutional inertia on their side; the enemy's bills remained in committee. In the 1948 elections the big stockmen lost one of their key allies in Congress. The issue died, to flare up again in the early 1950s. When it did, DeVoto remounted the barricades.

"A man has to do these things when called on," he explained. His "damn crusade," as he termed it, stole time from his other work, delayed books already under contract, and exasperated his editors. Frederick Lewis Allen of *Harper's,* although a loyal Audubon member, periodically urged DeVoto to turn his attention to something else. A stubborn man, outspoken in his enthusiasms, DeVoto would not relinquish "the most important issue in the world today." But he did come to appreciate the recurrent dilemma of the radical amateur in conservation: that the cause closest to one's heart paid no bills. (Which helped explain why the enemy seemed more intent. Those on the other side made a living at it; conservationists usually took up the fight expecting to pay, not to be paid.) "I cannot afford the time that all this is going to take," DeVoto would say; or, to Kenneth Reid, "I only hope I get a chance occasionally to practice the profession that is supposed to support my family." "I have spent so much time on pious works, meaning conservation," he complained to Horace Albright in March 1949, "that I am practically broke." He resolved to limit his activities and to push forward on the overdue books.

Within a year he was pulled into another damn crusade. He had undertaken his land-grab battle on *behalf* of government bureaus — the Forest Service and the Park Service — against private interests. Now he turned his guns *against* other government agencies — the Army Corps of Engineers and the Interior Department's Bureau of Reclamation — which themselves threatened the national parks and forests. Again his interest was sparked by a trip through the West. In the summer of 1950 he and two other writers, William Lederer and A. B. Guthrie, started in Three Forks, Montana, and traversed the length of the Missouri River, with facilities provided by the Army Engineers. He praised his hosts for the skill and spirit with which they undertook their large construction projects. "It shows the human intelligence mastering the environment," he said, "and the human will dominating the contrary and hostile will of nature." But he was appalled by the Engineers' lack of attention to conservation values and the national interest. They just liked to build dams and irrigation systems. Larger questions were met with blank looks. "Don't you think," a member of the Corps replied to DeVoto, "that is a hell of a philosophical question to ask a poor engineer?" Yet the public had no way to subject the arcane designs of the engineers to expert criticism, and therefore no chance to express its will. DeVoto wrote an article for the *Saturday Evening Post,* describing Reclamation's designs on the Dinosaur National Monument in Colorado and thereby touched off the major conservation struggle of the 1950s.

As a historian, DeVoto placed his conservation work squarely in the tradition articulated by Gifford Pinchot. The Bureau of Reclamation and the Army Engineers also worked in the Pinchot tradition — "the human will dominating the contrary and hostile will of nature" — but in their obtuseness to anything except slide rules and bulldozers they carried the engineering mentality further than DeVoto was willing to go. He deplored their blindness, yet endorsed their general attitude toward the natural world. He publicized Pinchot's autobiography in a *Harper's* column in 1948 and considered him, with the two Roosevelts, as one of the three greatest leaders in conservation history. "We need a mid-twentieth century Pinchot," he said in 1954.

Conversely, DeVoto was not impressed by Muir or his ideas. In *The Year of Decision* he accused Muir of plagiarizing the work of C. E. Dutton on the Grand Canyon. When DeVoto's friend Ansel Adams published a book of Yosemite photographs, with descriptive passages culled from Muir, DeVoto told him: "In the face of your pictures, Muir is just some unnecessary rhetoric. . . . Muir is empty and a little fatuous in the same book with them." On his visits to the national parks he was irritated by the "religious breathlessness" of some Park Service naturalists. "I shrink from the uplift," he wrote the head of the Park Service. "I think that the man who just likes to look at geysers has as much right to do so as the one who likes to look at a geyser and see God."

DeVoto was a sentimental man who hated sentimentality in any form. He disapproved of birds, had no interest in studying their habits, but paid his dues to the Audubon Society. He disliked fishing, hunting, camping, hiking, horseback riding, and canoeing. But he thought life intolerable if he could not visit the woods and mountains at short intervals. Shortly before his death in 1955, he summed up his attitude in words that verged closer to Muir than to Pinchot. "I have got to have the sight of clean water and the sound of running water. I have got to get to places where the sky-shine of cities does not dim the stars, where you can smell land and foliage, grasses and marshes, forest duff and aromatic plants and hot underbrush turning cool. Most of all, I have to learn again what quiet is. I believe that our culture is more likely to perish from noise than from radioactive fall-out." Then he finished with a characteristic disclaimer: "Nothing in this is sentimental or poetic. It is necessity."

❧❧

Joseph Wood Krutch, a contemporary of DeVoto's, underwent a similar conversion in the latter part of his life. For three decades he worked in New York as a drama critic and an English professor, spending most of his time on literary matters. Then, in 1952, he moved to Arizona and took up a second career as a conservationist and amateur naturalist. Probably he never matched DeVoto's influence in the movement because his work reached a smaller audience. Where DeVoto wrote a column for *Harper's*, Krutch wrote one for the *American Scholar*. His conservation phase remains of interest, particularly because of the *process* that brought him from New York to Arizona, from a book on Samuel Johnson to a book on the Grand Canyon. The shifts within Krutch's mind by their stark contrasts illuminate the historic tension between conservation and modern culture.

In his background as in his writing career Krutch was self-defined, independent, hard to categorize: a disembodied mind floating freely across the intellectual landscape. He grew up in Tennessee, the son of a mother from Brooklyn and a father descended from German immigrants. He stayed in his hometown of Knoxville to attend the state university. (Though his later work showed an affinity with the antiprogressive posture of the Vanderbilt literary agrarians gathering down the road in Nashville, he apparently never associated himself with that group, or any group.) After travel in Europe, where he admired the "sense of stability" in Paris, Krutch married a French Basque woman in New York and took his doctorate at Columbia. During the 1930s he was on the anti-Marxist left, radically alienated from the existing political order but unwilling to abide the conventions of novels about noble proletarians.

Krutch's most popular and enduring book, *The Modern Temper*, summarized his generation's disillusionment with the cheery prewar faith in inevitable progress. Published in 1929, it argued that science, the proudest achievement of Western man, had accidentally undermined Western man's understanding of his place in the universe and left him stranded in a bleak nothingness: more powerful, but less wise and less happy. Traditional religion had been rendered untenable by Darwin and scientific skepticism. With his overdeveloped intellect, man was thrown back on believing in his own powers, for did not his intellect set him apart from the rest of creation? But modern biology and psychology described man as a creature of glands and primitive impulse, not of judgment and understanding. He acted not from choice or will but from conditioned biological urges. Men were animals, and animals were machines, and machines lacked both soul and purpose. Modern literature, the field Krutch knew best, reflected these diminished victims of science: the creative writing of the day was strewn with little people in trivial situations, without vision or heroism, bumping into each other in a trackless void.

In light of his later career, the most striking parts of *The Modern Temper* were Krutch's baleful descriptions of nature. The natural world was presented as cold, threatening, and indifferent to humans. If nature had any purpose of her own, it probably did not include man and surely could not be perceived by him. "Nature, in her blind thirst for life, has filled every possible cranny of the rotting earth with some sort of fantastic creature, and among them man is one — perhaps the most miserable of all." Because of man's intellectual arrogance he could not even emulate an animal's unreflective, straight-ahead approach to living; he must ask big questions about the point of it all. In short, Krutch still operated from the Judeo-Christian certainty that man was the most important creature on earth — but without the Judeo-Christian faith that man was uniquely blessed among the earth's creatures. "Ours is a lost cause," he dolefully concluded, "and there is no place for us in the natural universe, but we are not, for all that, sorry to be human. We should rather die as men than live as animals."

Despite this grim coda, Krutch himself was a happy man, not immune to the mundane pleasures of life. When he gave lectures about *The Modern Temper* he sometimes surprised audiences because he did not habitually wear a pained, existential expression. The book described a condition of modern life, one of the incidental drawbacks of modern science, but the author maintained a certain distance from his own argument. Again his characteristic independence asserted itself. Though his name was associated with alienation and despair, when a different perspective came his way he could be persuaded to it.

In 1930 Krutch read *Walden* for the first time. Thoreau also distrusted modern science, yet for him this attitude finally led to a strengthened religious belief, not an anguished loss of faith. At once the Concord recluse became one of Krutch's favorite authors. He started spending weekends in a small town fifty miles from New York; away from pavements and sky-scrapers, he began to notice plants and animals. Eventually he spent only three days a week in Manhattan. By slow degrees, in a process that en-gaged his other senses as well as his intellect, he moved away from an urban cast of mind.

His study of Thoreau culminated in a biography published in 1948. In describing his subject's intellectual journey Krutch described, perhaps un-wittingly, his own as well. The early Thoreau as a good transcendentalist postulated a spiritual truth intuitively, and looked for examples in the nat-ural world to substantiate it. The mature Thoreau *began* with his observa-tions of nature, and by piling them up deduced from them a scientific pan-theism. Instead of arguing from God to nature, he argued from Nature to gods. Krutch evidently approved this turnabout. Almost twenty years after *The Modern Temper,* the natural world seemed more friendly to him: "Now a feeling of fellowship with the animals, with the vegetables even, can remain a warm thing. With the first we are linked by the common pos-session of consciousness and emotion, with the second at least by the fact that all protoplasm is the same and that hence we must possess in common certain characteristics." But he drew the line when Thoreau saw divinity in rivers and stars. To suggest that man be happy like the Concord River im-plied an extreme kind of pantheism that would break the final link with humanity.

Nonetheless, Krutch himself was headed in that direction. In a Thoreauvian spirit he read extensively in the classics of English nature writing, the work of Gilbert White and W. H. Hudson, and also dipped into Muir and Burroughs. One day in the late 1940s, Krutch sat down and wrote his first nature essay. It was a paean to the spring peeper, the familiar harbinger of the end of the New England winter. "On that day," the start of spring, "something older than any Christian God has risen. The earth is alive again." As plants and animals reappeared they seemed not indiffer-ent to him, but happy to see him, and he in turn greeted them as friends. He finished this first essay with an expression of what he later called "a kind of pantheism." To the peeper he whispered an admonition that also expressed a newly discovered faith: "Don't forget, we are all in this to-gether." With that assertion of solidarity he stepped outside the Judeo-Christian tradition.

Krutch had not changed his diagnosis of the modern syndrome, but he had found a crack in it that left him enough room to create a small, com-fortable niche for himself. His contemporaries in literature, psychology, and sociology still described man as a creature without will or judgment, stumbling around in a lonely, amoral environment. Krutch read their explanations of the human condition and rejected them. Instead, he traveled backward in history, past the Industrial Revolution, the Renaissance, finally past the dawn of the Christian era, until as a neopagan he engaged the natural world on his own terms. In studying plants and animals he felt consoled by them. They assured him that, modern progress notwithstanding, he was part of something larger than himself or his society.

He decided to live in Arizona, overtly because of his health. The move also extended the process that had begun with *Walden*. In the bright, dry air he felt happier and healthier; and the unfamiliar flora and fauna further stimulated his study of nature. Freed of his teaching and reviewing chores, he changed his hobby into a full-time occupation by turning out professionally respected studies of desert life. When questioned about the anomaly of his two incongruous careers, he explained: "I probably know more about plants than any other drama critic and more about the theater than any botanist." His reputation among intellectuals brought his nature studies to the attention of a rarefied audience that ordinarily disdained such books. He became the thinking man's conservationist. "His peculiar strength," noted the ecologist Paul Sears of Yale, "lies in the fact that, with his literary craftmanship and great respect for scientific accuracy, he has been able to exert a wide influence over the country."

Krutch was not reconciled to modern life. He never went to movies and thought humans would be better off without airplanes. He disliked the functionalism of modern architecture. He argued for high cultural standards, strict English, the importance of the beleaguered humanities, and the teaching of classical literature in its undiluted form. He must have been the last essayist in English letters to sprinkle his work with obscure, unidentified quotations of poetry. "Neither our society, our civilization, nor our technology has paid off as we believed it would," he said in 1957. "And we neither know why nor what we can do about it. We can only go on seeking more wealth, more security, more comfort and more power."

As a conservationist he was closer to Muir than to Pinchot. Like Muir, he was essentially a field man who resorted to books for information but took his attitudes from an intimate, visceral relation with nature herself. Immersed in the natural world, it seemed evident that man was not the only creature with a soul. He therefore concluded, with Muir, that the world was not created solely for man. Accordingly he disapproved of the utilitarian notions that still dominated conservation in the 1950s. "What is commonly called 'conservation' will not work in the long run," he declared in 1955, "because it is not really conservation at all but rather, disguised by its elaborate scheming, only a more knowledgeable variation of the old idea of a world for man's use only. That idea is unrealizable."

Later, as the environmental crisis worsened, the conservation movement veered back toward Muir because the utilitarian approach seemed both ethically and practically impossible. Late in life, Krutch for the first time could bring himself to embrace a social movement as his own. Accustomed to being a minority unto himself, he saw increasing signs that nature was perceived not merely as a prelude to man (*pace* Darwin) or a kindly, beneficent spirit (*pace* the Romantic poets) but as the ultimate creative force, a kind of religion: "a modern version of ancient pantheism." Modern man seemed to be losing his arrogance and turning back to the start of a cycle.

❧❧

Something was happening at the end of the Second World War: DeVoto suddenly turning his historical forces upside down; Krutch emerging from a study of Thoreau by heeding his injunction to simplify; both rebounding from the aftermath of the war, in a complex internal process of rethinking played against whatever the deadliest war in history might have meant. It seemed at the time that Western civilization was poised on a fulcrum, teetering in precarious balance after the war. DeVoto and Krutch were shifting their weight, one as a historian, the other as a thinker and naturalist. Neither had ever fully embraced the technological mentality, recently capped by Hiroshima, from which they now drew back. On this point they were less disillusioned, having never bought the illusion, than the man usually perceived as the embodiment of technological progress.

The image of Charles Lindbergh that survives him still seems accurate: a lone man flying by instinct, trusting his own senses, not so much above public opinion as impervious to it. "I'm a stubborn Swede," he would explain. Nothing knocked his internal gyroscope askew. At twenty-five, his flight to Paris made him one of the most powerful symbols of modern progress. "The Icarus of the twentieth century," the New York *Times* declared, "a son of that omnipotent Daedalus whose ingenuity has created the modern world." Indeed, Lindbergh spent most of his working life in the service of aviation, tinkering with airplane design and preaching the benefits of the air age.

But always, within his own personality, the "flying fool" coexisted with the farm boy who craved simplicity and natural surroundings. In 1928, harried by crowds and reporters, he landed his plane on the Great Salt Desert in Utah. In the unaccustomed solitude he felt himself become part of the desert. For a moment he savored the heightened awareness, the sense of soaring beyond power and possessions. Then he got back in his plane and flew off to the next appointment. Eventually Lindbergh emerged from this interplay between his two selves and became a conservationist. "If I had to choose," the great aviator finally decided, "I would rather have birds than airplanes."

With that statement he returned to his boyhood. While growing up on a Minnesota farm, he fished and hunted by the river and listened to his father's stories about the plentiful game that had been largely wiped out in a generation by settlers. The boy, who was given a gun on his sixth birthday, absorbed this initial lesson in wildlife conservation. His countervailing interest in technology also appeared early, when he replaced the farm's horses with a tractor. He liked to play with engines, bought himself a motorcycle, and caught the flying bug. He still loved farming, but "I loved still more to fly," he recalled. Yielding to the greater love, he took up an anonymous life of barnstorming and flying the mail. Then, an overnight hero whose fame would not diminish, he committed himself to the future of aviation. He hoped it would break down prejudices among nations, linking them together through air travel. The boy hero and the fledgling industry matured together. "It's fascinating," he told his wife, "to grow up with a new development like that, watch its growth." At such heady moments the engineer in him overcame the misgivings of the simple farm boy.

In 1930 an interest in medical research brought Lindbergh into contact with the major intellectual influence of his life, the Nobel Prize–winning biologist Alexis Carrel. Coming from a background of religious skepticism, and at the height of his infatuation with the airplane, Lindbergh was startled by Carrel's forays into mystical and occult phenomena. But he had the unfettered mind of the autodidact, and with Carrel's help he began to read books of a more speculative and philosophical kind. At this point he saw no conflict between science and religion. In fact, science by revealing the positive design behind nature seemed to bear out theological notions of immortality. "The more I go into science," he said in 1932, "the more I feel that one cannot say that everything ends with the death of the body." He posited a theory of scientific reincarnation: since all life consists of atomic particles, the life spark attached to those particles is simply redistributed when a body dies. He sought out mediums and conceded the existence of thought transference. In 1937 he flew to India for a religious conference in Calcutta. Such activities left his aviation associates a little worried: "You'd better drop this religion stuff, you know!" said one.

He had only met the mystics halfway. He acknowledged the truth of their intuitions, but relied finally on science to *prove* them. He still grounded himself in rational deduction and the experimental method. Confronted with the unhealthy aspects of modern cities, he distinguished between science (the disinterested effort to understand the universe) and technology (the physical result of that effort). Retaining his faith in the one, he became more skeptical of the other. He thus could doubt the excesses of progress without inquiring too deeply into their origins.

By 1939, he was urging his contemporaries to reject a synthetic environment and the "modern Idol of mechanical efficiency" when they crowded out every trace of a natural life. "How long can men thrive between walls of brick," he asked, "walking on asphalt pavements, breathing the fumes of coal and of oil, growing, working, dying, with hardly a thought of wind, and sky, and fields of grain, seeing only machine-made beauty, the the mineral-like quality of life?" The farm boy spoke through the twentieth-century Icarus: "This is our modern danger — one of the waxen wings of flight."

The wings melted away in the crucible of World War II. Before the war he had admired and feared Germany's military and technological strength. Flying by instinct, he had joined with other isolationists in trying to keep out of a war with Germany; for his efforts he was called an anti-Semitic Nazi and, after Pearl Harbor, was not allowed to enlist. For a time he worked in a civilian job at the Ford River Rouge plant — "the home of Faustian man in his highest state of development," he thought. Eventually he drew assignments in the South Pacific and flew unofficial combat missions. When he visited the occupied islands, his conservation instincts were stirred as he noted the absence of trees and wildlife. "War is like a flame," he wrote in his journal. "Where it sweeps, life disappears, the birds and the trees with the Japanese."

A few weeks after V-E Day he made an inspection tour of Germany. As he sifted through the rubble, he must have confronted his own previous admiration for the feats of German technology. At Nuremberg he felt surrounded by death; only the sky, which man had not yet defiled, seemed to hold any hope. The illusion of technology as progress was destroyed with macabre emphasis by the V-2 rocket site at Nordhausen. Adjacent to the sophisticated rocket installations were gas ovens that had killed twenty-five thousand people in eighteen months. "The height of human accomplishment," he recalled decades later, "and the depth of human degradation were there at the underground tunnels of Nordhausen; the two had somehow joined together to show the catabolic tendency of our civilization's science."

The war tipped the balance within Lindbergh's personality. Afterward, regardless of his external activities, the aviator gave way to the farm boy. His distinction between science and technology no longer made sense in the practical world. Science had been overwhelmed by its own technologists, he believed, perverted to the material uses of industry and war. Perhaps a pure scientist had never intended his work to produce Hiroshima; but an atomic bomb could hardly be construed as anything but an instrument of massive destruction.

In 1948 Lindbergh published a short book, *Of Flight and Life,* which seemed a *mea culpa* for his early life. "I grew up as a disciple of science," he wrote. "I know its fascination. I have felt the godlike power man derives from his machines." But now he drew an unsparing indictment of science: it sacrificed cities full of children, twisted medicine into biological warfare, turned workers into factory robots, undermined religious faith, and unbalanced the human temperament by emphasizing mind to the neglect of body and spirit. To restore sanity to this metallic, intellectual existence, he proposed a remedy outside man and his works. "We must surround our people with the physical security, bodily vigor, and spiritual peace that come from close contact with earth and sky."

Krutch and DeVoto had come to a similar point, largely by drawing on years of scholarship and thinking. In contrast Lindbergh was again flying by instinct, responding within himself to whatever he saw and felt. From a quarter century of flying over the country, he had witnessed with unique clarity the extension of civilization across land formerly wild. "Somehow I feel every road and oil well is an imposition, an intruder on the solitude which once was mine as I flew over it," he noted in his journal. "Looking down on them from the air, those marks seem like a disease — a rash spreading slowly over the earth's surface." Back on the ground, he was no less offended by human conceits seen at closer hand. He went to zoos to find a touch of wildness, but was depressed by the deadened eyes of the animals. Walking along a befouled beach on Long Island Sound, he longed for "real wilderness with its cleanness and solitude, away from the crowded litter of cities." At night he stood by the ocean looking at the stars, wondering why humans preferred their own baubles to such gifts from God. "I must teach my children to know and to love the earth itself," he vowed. "I must teach them how to keep this civilization we are building from deadening their senses."

In light of these sentiments, it seems odd that Lindbergh still had little contact with American conservationists. Despite a marked agreement with their ideas, he remained the lone flyer. Instead, in the mid-1950s, he began to visit "primitive" tribal groups in Asia and Africa, approaching conservation through wild humans rather than wild animals. On these trips he attempted to merge completely with the people and their cultures. In the Philippines he joined the Agta tribe in eating wild boar and fruits, and drinking fresh coconut milk. He slept in the open with a shoe for a pillow and a light nylon raincoat for a blanket. Talking through an interpreter with the Agta, he was eager and inquisitive, seeking wisdom instead of expecting to impart it. "The major difference between an Agta hunter and myself," he decided, "lies in the invisible mass of knowledge my culture has crammed into my head." Otherwise he felt at home. He was reminded of the values of simplicity and balance in contrast with the luxury and excess of civilization.

Among the Masai of East Africa, Lindbergh felt his rational mind yielding without effort to his intuitive faculties. His mind and body merged along with his senses and intellect. A civilized notion of measured time gave way to a timeless vision of life fusing with death in a miraculous scheme of immortality. In a culture outside progress, time lost its meaning because there was nowhere to go: only the moment right at hand. He no longer demanded that religious insights be proved by science. On the contrary, "in instinct rather than in intellect is manifest the cosmic plan of life." Primitive peoples still knew this; civilization had forgotten it and had become deranged. "The primitive teaches that life itself, unforced life, is progress."

Finally, in the early 1960s, he carried through the logical implication of his thinking since the war by becoming an active conservationist. Though congruent with his previous ideas, this last phase of his life also represented a departure from habits of long standing. Ever since his flight to Paris, and especially since the kidnap murder of his first child in 1932, he had shunned reporters and publicity. Now he courted them, knowing their value to his conservation campaign. He took them along on his trips to the wilderness, posed for pictures, granted exclusive interviews. The most private of men, Lindbergh even showed up at cocktail parties for conservation, signing autographs and cheerfully making the small talk he detested.

In addition, he had always been a political conservative suspicious of big government and protective of individual liberties. (At the New York World's Fair in 1940, he had been offended by the Perisphere's "extremely subtle Communistic propaganda.") After the war he continued to associate with conservative institutions like the U.S. Air Force, and to write for conservative magazines like *Reader's Digest* and the *Saturday Evening Post*. But his mentor in conservation was Ira Gabrielson, the old New Dealer still on the job for a private group in Washington in the 1960s. Lindbergh had disapproved of the New Deal. Under Gabrielson's influence, however, he was forced to rethink the role of government. "Few people value individual freedom more than I," he concluded, "but with respect to the use of our resources I have to say, reluctantly, that government must step in and . . . monitor and guide how we use our environment. Individual volunteer action is grand — it should be encouraged — but it is not sufficient to meet national needs."

He spoke out most often in behalf of wilderness and especially of wildlife, working mainly through such international groups as the World Wildlife Fund and the Nature Conservancy. "On every continent, and in almost every country, the crisis for wildlife is acute," he said in 1964. "This is why I have been devoting attention to the wildlife I flew over with too little thought in decades past. There is no time to lose." In Alaska four years later, he broke a public silence of ten years by addressing the legislature: "There is nothing we can do anywhere in the world that is more important than protecting our natural environment." Later that same year he turned up in Taiwan: "We're on the edge of time. Time is literally running out."

Wherever he went, Lindbergh used his fame to open doors that an ordinary private citizen would have found shut. Forty years after his flight, his name still brought a gasp of recognition and immediate deference. In Brazil he could discuss wildlife problems along the Amazon with high government officials. In the Philippines, his close relationship with the president shook loose a directive protecting the tamarau, a small water buffalo. On a trip to Peru to investigate whaling operations directed against the endangered blue whales and humpback whales, he learned that the company was run by a firm back in Minneapolis. "The chairman of the board turned out to be a fellow Scandinavian," he noted, "and I wrote him a letter." Eventually the firm agreed to restrict its kill.

Lindbergh now declared that civilization's highest achievement lay in conservation, not aviation; airplanes had made their greatest impact in war, in killing rather than creating. If he were to start over in 1967, he said, he would pick a career that kept him in touch with nature instead of a scientific job. During the national debate over the supersonic transport plane in the early 1970s, he for the first time opposed a new aviation product. "Many developmentalists believe that the progress of mankind depends on ceaseless technological improvement, measured by such elements as speed," he wrote. But there were other criteria: the SST wasted fuel and disrupted the environment with its sonic boom and the effect of its exhausts on the upper atmosphere. No technological need demanded the plane, Lindbergh insisted. Rather, certain political and commercial interests had contrived the project for their own ends. Did these interests make it impossible for modern man to protect his own environment? "Is the quality of life or the advance of technology to guide us?"

Having spent most of his career on the latter, he devoted his twilight years to values that could not be weighed or counted. The quality of modern life could only be appraised by comparing it subjectively to life in the wilderness. "Man must feel the earth to know himself and recognize his values," he said in one of his last articles. He liked to feel the earth by camping out. With the odor of roasting meat in his nostrils, the warmth of the fire in his face, surrounded by the stars, he felt the spirit of his primitive ancestors. He wondered whether perhaps his genes still carried an unconscious memory of those times, triggered by any renewed contact with the wilderness. "God made life simple," he thought. "It is man who complicates it."

※※

For thirty years after the death of Franklin Roosevelt, Justice William O. Douglas of the Supreme Court was the most prominent conservationist in public life. As an especially visible and controversial member of the Court, he could attract publicity for conservation simply by casting a fly or going for a hike. He looked more at home in jeans and an old shirt than in the robes of his august office. As DeVoto did for the readers of *Harper's,* and Krutch for the intellectuals, and Lindbergh for the technologists, Douglas brought conservation issues to a constituency that otherwise might have ignored them. Because he stayed on the case so long, his career epitomized two essential aspects of the conservation movement in the decades after World War II: its connection with political liberalism, and its ideological shift from Pinchot to Muir.

In the course of an awesomely vigorous life, Douglas tramped, climbed, and canoed across an ample portion of the world. But, like Muir, he always belonged spiritually to the mountains of the western United States. "All the roots I had in life," he said, "were in the Yakima Valley." Growing up in this unspoiled section of south-central Washington State, he was drawn outdoors at an early age. To the west of the valley, the Cascade Mountains sent down cold, clear streams. Their peaks and foothills dominated the horizon and kindled the boy's imagination. After recovering from a mild case of polio, he started going on long hikes and climbs to strengthen his legs. He felt a sense of mastery over the disease when he was able to hike all day and through the night, a total of forty miles with a pack. In the mountains he developed an interest in botany, geology, and trout fishing. He continued his trips to the mountains even after the last traces of polio disappeared. One spring night, a warm chinook wind sparked an eerie resonance within him. "It became for me that night a measure of the kindliness of the universe to man, a token of the hospitality that awaits man when he puts foot on this earth," he later recalled. "I felt that I was a part of the universe, a companion to the friendly chinook that brought the promise of life and adventure."

In his teens, Douglas's mountain rambles produced the first stirrings of the conservationist in him. The public lands of the Cascades were being besieged by stockmen and lumbering. Cattle were set loose to leave their droppings at campsites and to turn pristine lakes into muddy wallows. A dam on the Tieton River destroyed one of his favorite high meadows. Recoiling from such "improvements," the boy's earliest ambition was to follow in the footsteps of the most famous forester of the time. "Maybe some day I could take Gifford Pinchot's place," he thought. "I could carry on his fight for conservation. He loved the mountains; so did I." Pinchot remained the most enduring influence on his youth and middle years. Though he chose law over forestry as a career, in his leisure time he was still an outdoorsman of the Pinchot persuasion. He regarded nature with a certain man-centeredness and gloried in the human conquest of "angry" rivers and "unproductive wastelands." Implicitly he operated from the Judeo-Christian tradition of the world for man's use.

During the summer of 1951 Douglas set out alone on a 250-mile hike through the Himalayas. At the end of the trip he stayed at a Buddhist monastery for three days and was exposed for the first time to a non-Christian philosophy. He presented a fishing rod to the spiritual leader, but the gift was rejected: "It might tempt him to catch fish." Buddhists, who regarded all forms of life as sacred, could not eat flesh. To this animistic viewpoint, each man and animal and flower posessed a "being" to be valued equally with all other "beings." "That idea," he said later, "became an article of faith that greatly altered my relationship to the outdoors." He studied other religions — Hinduism, Zoroastrianism, American Indian faiths — and found in each one a reverence for all life and a sense that wilderness, instead of being an obdurate foe to be subdued, expressed the unity and harmony of the universe. Man now seemed a ruthless, dangerous, strutting fool.

Accordingly, Douglas transferred his allegiance from Pinchot to Muir.

As a boy he had read Muir's accounts of tramping around the Sierra Nevada, and while reveling in them had not quite accepted their spirit. "I was with him when the great winds blew," Douglas recalled, "and the pine and fir forests played their symphonies. I shared his winter exploits and alpine feats. Best of all, I knew from him the glories of the sculptured domes of Yosemite, the music of its waterfalls, and the brightness of its meadows." The religious passion behind these descriptions escaped Douglas until his own spiritual awakening in the Himalayas. Once he saw man not as the lord of creation but as the spiritual brother of chipmunks and mountain goats, he returned to Muir with sharpened insight. He published a biography of Muir for children, calling him the most influential conservationist in American history. In his later conservation books he quoted Muir, not Pinchot. The frontispiece of *My Wilderness: The Pacific West* (1960) offered one passage from Thoreau and two from Muir. In their spirit he stopped hunting and fishing. He still honored Pinchot as his first boyhood hero. "But he left behind a group of 'experts' who specialize in conquering nature," Douglas ultimately concluded.

Douglas emerged as a reborn preservationist by leading the fight to save the Chesapeake and Ohio Canal in 1954. The canal with its adjacent territory made up a ribbon of relatively wild land, two hundred feet wide and stretching 189 circuitous miles from Washington into the Maryland hinterland. Abandoned for commercial purposes in the 1920s, it had been acquired by the federal government at FDR's behest. Under federal ownership it had been left intact, an artificial waterway that with age had taken on a patina of naturalness. In the early 1950s someone proposed to turn the canal into a highway, and the Washington *Post* added its powerful editorial support. Douglas offered a dissent in a letter to the *Post* in January 1954. "Hundreds of us still use this sanctuary for hiking, and camping," he wrote. "It is a refuge, a place of retreat, a long stretch of quiet and peace at the Capitol's back door." He proposed that if the *Post*'s editorial writer would only accompany him in hiking the canal from one end to the other, he would have to join in urging its preservation. "One who walked the canal its full length could plead that cause with the eloquence of a John Muir," Douglas suggested.

The man at the *Post,* Merlo Pusey, was game. So on a rainy day in March, Douglas, Pusey, and two dozen others set out from Cumberland, Maryland. The party was filled out with members of the Wilderness and Audubon societies and other conservationists. With Douglas setting a brisk pace, the marchers — not all of whom were in the best shape — averaged twenty-three miles a day. "We are torn between a feeling of appreciation to Justice Douglas for luring us into this venture," said Pusey, "and irritation over the increasingly pathetic condition of our feet. But blisters heal and memories linger." Pusey dropped out after sixteen miles on the first day and later rejoined the group at intervals. The stalwarts maintained their spirits by inventing new verses to the old "C&O Canal Song":

> *From Cumberland to Washington*
> *Is one-eight-nine they say;*
> *That doesn't faze this dauntless band,*
> *It's downhill all the way.*

> *The duffers climbed aboard the trucks*
> *With many a groan and sigh,*
> *But something faster passed them up*
> *The Judge was whizzing by.*

With logistics organized by the Wilderness Society, the marchers were sheltered at sportsmen's clubs along the way. One night Douglas regaled the group with an account of how to lasso a mountain lion in Arizona. Bemused by such anecdotes, the national media gave the march wide coverage.

Nursing his blisters, Pusey changed his mind about the proposed highway. "Experience on the trail is an excellent leavening influence to which even editors occasionally should be subjected," he declared. The *Post* joined an *ad hoc* committee to protect the canal. A bill to accord it park status passed the Senate but not the House. In 1960, just before leaving office, Eisenhower made it a national monument. Finally in 1971 it became a national historic park. Throughout that period, Douglas hiked the canal in an annual pilgrimage. At the age of seventy-one, with his heart regulated by a pacemaker, he had only slowed down to a pace of three miles an hour.

The C&O battle offered an instructive lesson in conservation politics. The National Park Service at first had supported the highway scheme: the federal agency that should have protected the canal was not on the job. Douglas, as a liberal and civil libertarian in a time of political conservatism and anti-Communist hysteria, for years had been looking down from the bench with suspicion on what the executive and legislative branches were up to. With that background, and nudged by the C&O episode, he had little faith in the federal conservation agencies. Instead he operated from the Muir tradition of the radical amateur in conservation. "I concluded that the so-called experts had come close to ruining our environment," he recalled, "that a return to common-sense judgments of laymen was essential." He found his friends not in Washington offices but in the burgeoning conservation movement. He joined the Sierra Club and was quickly made a director. He resigned that position in 1962 to avoid a possible conflict of interest over the Glen Canyon suit brought by the club, but he remained "our own hot line to the judiciary," as a club leader put it.

Immersed in the movement and an independent figure as well, Douglas became increasingly militant with age. His protean energies seemed to diminish not at all. (In his early sixties he walked all twenty-one hundred miles of the Appalachian Trail.) "I took part in almost innumerable crusades across the country to save a river here, a lake there, a bit of woods somewhere else," he recalled. The culprit, he found, was usually a federal agency. Even the pet projects of the New Deal had aged badly: the TVA was "an ensconced bureaucracy" and, said Douglas, the worst strip miner in the nation; the Soil Conservation Service, once the farmer's friend, had turned to flood-control projects that made rivers into flumes and killed all the life on the river bottoms. The Park Service, dominated by concessionaires, was preoccupied with developing facilities and increasing its mass recreation statistics — in order to make money, not to protect the wilderness. The Forest Service, in league with the lumber industry, justified any intrusion by the concept of "multiple use," which Douglas traced back to Pinchot and dismissed as a disguise for mercenary intentions. Most dangerous of all were the Army Corps of Engineers and the Bureau of Public Roads, both well organized, efficient, articulate in the patois of engineers, and politically powerful in Washington. "These Twin Gods," he warned, "can bulldoze, pave, and dam the country until most of our sacred precincts are gone."

None of this endeared him to certain Washington circles. His outspoken views no doubt helped spawn the periodic attempts by political conservatives like Gerald Ford to impeach him. But he was safe on the Court, more or less, and served longer than any justice in history. From this base he made his periodic forays into the wilderness, recovering there the sense of adventure and self-reliance he had first found in the Cascade foothills. Gradually he would again feel the unity with nature that he had discovered in the Himalayas. Far from Park Service improvements, he could avoid the dread Washington bureaucrats. "In this wildness the body cells are once more in rhythm," he wrote. "The sound of wind in birches, the conversation of swamp crickets, the gentle swish of trout feeding on the surface make the music man needs to survive the mad rush of the machine age."

᛭᛭

Aside from Muir, the conservation writer most respected by Douglas after his Himalayan conversion was Aldo Leopold. In the course of perhaps the most distinguished career in twentieth-century conservation, Leopold went through an intellectual evolution broadly resembling that of Douglas: from a Pinchot-like attitude of manipulating and exploiting the natural environment to a Muir-like stance of human forbearance and humility. The shift overcame Leopold in slow increments during three decades of fieldwork and reading. In that time he made significant contributions as a technical forester, pioneered the wilderness concept in national forests, laid the groundwork for turning wildlife management into a legitimate science, served prominently in a half dozen organizations and helped found the Wilderness Society. Yet today he is best known as the author of a posthumously published book, *A Sand County Almanac*. Since it appeared in 1949 it has become easily the most admired, most quoted, most influential book in modern conservation. *Sand County* "taught me man's responsibility to the earth," Douglas said. "Leopold articulated the need for a land ethic — a challenge that consumed much of my energies in the latter part of my life."

Leopold was born in Burlington, Iowa, in 1887, the son of a prosperous furniture maker, and grew up in a mansion on top of a hill. He was the third generation in his family with a deep interest in the outdoors. The Mississippi River, close at hand, offered duck marshes on its eastern side and upland woods with quail and partridge to the west. "My earliest impressions of wildlife and its pursuit," Leopold recalled, "retain a vivid sharpness of form, color, and atmosphere that half a century of professional wildlife experience has failed to obliterate or to improve upon." At an early age he was given a single-barreled shotgun — with the admonition that he could shoot partridges only when they were in flight. The boy's dog was adept at treeing partridges; to give up an easy shot in the tree for a hard shot on the wing became Leopold's first exercise in ethical restraint. After a boyhood dominated by camping, hunting, and bird studies, he went east to preparatory school and then to Yale. With a degree from the forestry school endowed by Pinchot's family, he took a job with Pinchot's Forest Service. All but inevitably he absorbed the master's utilitarian notions of conservation.

But not to the exclusion of those vivid boyhood memories. Leopold's attitude toward nature always mingled a purely esthetic appreciation with the more practical aspects of his education and professional employment. His later veering toward Muir reflected a subtle shading of his viewpoint, not a marked and sudden conversion in the fashion of Douglas. Thus, even as a young man, fresh out of the Yale Forest School, he was offended by the sightseeing facilities in Yosemite Valley. "I can't say whether it was more pleasure to see Yosemite than pain to see the way most people see it," he wrote home. "The tourists all gape at Yosemite but what none of them see is the fifty miles of foothills on the way in. They are almost a relief after the highly frosted wedding-cake (and the wedding-guests) on the other end." In the 1920s, when he started agitating for the reservation of wilderness areas within national forests, he specifically wanted to avoid the kind of "improvements" being carried out by Steve Mather's National Park Service.

As initially conceived, these areas would not exclude all the works of man. The first such area, a tract of 574,000 acres in the Gila National Forest of New Mexico, was established with the vigorous support of local stockmen, who used it for grazing their cattle and did not want the range invaded by tourists. No hotels or permanent roads could be built, but the cows were still allowed to roam freely and the stockmen to draw their profits. At this point Leopold had not yet moved beyond the Pinchot tradition. In that spirit he protected deer, a species valued by man, and urged the eradication of its predators, especially wolves and coyotes.

According to his later recollection, this attitude was first dislodged by an encounter in the Arizona wilderness with a mortally wounded wolf. From a high rimrock he saw a mother wolf and her grown pups playing by the river below. Believing that fewer wolves meant more deer, he squeezed off a flurry of shots ("I was young then, and full of trigger-itch"). He ran down to the river and met the old wolf's eyes, dying with a fierce, unvanquished green fire. "I realized then, and have known ever since, that there was something new to me in those eyes." He sensed — in a sudden, inexplicable insight — that the wolf had as much right to that land as he did; that to sort out species into good and bad categories and then to eradicate the bad was an act of arrogant supererogation.

A Forest Service assignment took Leopold to Madison, Wisconsin, in 1924. He joined the local chapter of the Izaak Walton League and turned his mind to the problems of wildlife management. The old technique of closed seasons no longer sufficed, he explained to the readers of *Outdoor America*. The game's habitat must be considered, along with the delicate relations between hunters and local landowners. Federal regulations would have to be adjusted to regional conditions. Leopold was groping toward an approach stressing the interrelationships of *all* the organisms in a piece of land, instead of imposing an artificial control on only one or two. At the time, exact knowledge of the life cycles of wild animals was rudimentary at best. As he told the Walton League convention in 1928, the key question in game conservation had shifted from *whether* to preserve game to *how* to do it. "This will require a different mental attitude," he warned, "— perhaps less courage but more patience, less oratory but more thought, less legislation but more education, less opinion and more research. Agriculture and forestry began to apply science to their crops decades ago. Game management must now do so, or fail."

(Leopold could cite a precise example of his own previous shortsightedness. Before his encounter with the wolf's dying green eyes, he had helped wipe out the wolf population in the Gila wilderness. In short order, with the predators removed, there were too many deer. "Here my sin against the wolves caught up with me," he said later. A road was built to allow hunters access to the burgeoning deer, so as to trim them back. Because of no wolves, Leopold's wilderness was split in two. "I was hoist of my own petard.")

In 1928 he left the Forest Service to make a game survey for the Sporting Arms and Ammunition Manufacturers' Institute. Despite this commercial connection, his reputation for flinty integrity kept him in the good graces of even William Hornaday. Leopold's textbook, *Game Management,* is still considered a classic. A teaching position was created for him at the University of Wisconsin in 1933, and he stayed there the rest of his life. He bought an abandoned farm in the sand counties of central Wisconsin, thirty miles west of where Muir grew up. (Because Muir in 1865 had tried to establish a wildflower sanctuary on the Fountain Lake property, Leopold considered that year the beginning of "mercy for things natural, wild, and free" in Wisconsin.) He spent weekends at the farm with his family in a decrepit structure called the shack. Every spring a week was devoted to a ritual of pine-tree planting, as many as six thousand a year, to reclaim the cropped-out land. A working laboratory in land health, the farm provided the setting for the opening sections of *Sand County Almanac.*

Among the conservationists of his day Leopold was a universal man. At a time when the movement was fragmented into specialized groups — wildlife, natural resources, wilderness, national parks — he touched all bases and was exasperated by the stubborn demarcations maintained by such leaders as John Baker of the Audubon Society. "I sense a deep difference in viewpoint between John and the rest of us," he confided to a fellow member of the Wilderness Society. "He seems to think that wildlife is the only justification for wilderness areas!" Leopold pointedly urged Audubon members to acknowledge such conflicts, to grapple with them instead of avoiding the problem. Yet his own Wilderness Society had its peculiar myopia; he was regarded as its liaison to sportsmen, who in general could not seem to grasp the wilderness idea. The conservation movement, in Leopold's view, lacked a ruthless critical judgment and a capacity for self-examination: two prominent aspects of his own evolution. "We face a future marked by a growing public zeal for conservation," he told a National Wildlife Federation meeting in 1937, "but a zeal so uncritical — so devoid of discrimination — that any nostrum is likely to be gulped up with a shout."

Once an advocate of easy nostrums himself, Leopold knew better. If a proposal seemed widely popular, he dug in his heels and asked disagreeable questions. Essentially, though he belonged to more conservation boards of directors than he could attend to, he remained an outsider, universally respected but a little cantankerous. When Bob Marshall rounded up Wilderness Society support for a plan to take groups of boys into the wilderness, Leopold couldn't bring himself to go along with it. "I know I am 'out of step with the company' but I can't help it," he told Marshall. "The only real reason for predigested trips is that thousands are to take them, and if thousands are to take them what's left of the wilderness? This business is only one degree removed from roads. It takes all the individuality out of wilderness recreation. I can't see it."

In small groups of friends Leopold was affable in a laconic way. But probably he was more comfortable at his desk, adding to the bibliography that eventually exceeded three hundred articles. A man of scholarly mien with grave, even severe features, he did not look like an outdoorsman. His students referred to him generically as "the professor," a label that pleased him. "He was the embodiment of mind," noted Harvey Broome of the Wilderness Society, "— almost always serious, or thinking of serious problems." "The man was a living question mark," another associate recalled. From a lifetime of work he could draw on an expansive range of field experience and reading; yet his questions seemed only to lead to further questions.

A sense of knowledge without certainty is the pervading hallmark of *Sand County Almanac.* A reader clearly feels himself in the presence of considerable erudition. Leopold wrote of birds as an ornithologist, of soil as an agronomist, of trees as a forester, of ducks and geese as a hunter, of philosophical issues as an ecologist. But the tone is modest, self-effacing, with a ready admission of past mistakes and current ignorance. The author refers to himself as "me, a mere professor." He evokes the inscrutable mystery of nature's processes and suggests that man should never understand them all — that he already has too high an opinion of himself.

Much of the book's lasting appeal derives from the quality of the writing itself. In contrast with the overblown earnestness of most nature prose, Leopold had a light, witty touch, neither frivolous nor sententious. (He was able to read the books of Donald Culross Peattie only in small doses. "The man is devoid of humor," Leopold thought, "and there is no salt in his dishes.") He imparted the esthetic wonders of nature without using words like "glorious" or "beautiful" or "sublime"; he just stood back and recorded his amazement at the show.

The sounds of an early morning in a Wisconsin marshland: "A single silence hangs from horizon to horizon. Out of some far recess of the sky a tinkling of little bells falls soft upon the listening land. Then again silence. Now comes a baying of some sweet-throated hound, soon the clamor of a responding pack. Then a far clear blast of hunting horns, out of the sky into the fog. High horns, low horns, silence, and finally a pandemonium of trumpets, rattles, croaks, and cries that almost shakes the bog with its nearness, but without yet disclosing whence it comes. At last a glint of sun reveals the approach of a great echelon of birds."

An epitaph to the passenger pigeon: "He was the lightning that played between two opposing potentials of intolerable intensity: the fat of the land and the oxygen of the air. Yearly the feathered tempest roared up, down, and across the continent, sucking up the laden fruits of forest and prairie, burning them in a traveling blast of life. Like any other chain reaction, the pigeon could survive no diminution of his own furious intensity. When the pigeoners subtracted from his numbers, and the pioneers chopped gaps in the continuity of his fuel, his flame guttered out with hardly a sputter or even a wisp of smoke."

Nature writing of a high order. Large claims have also been made for the ethical discussions that conclude the book. Yet *Sand County* ultimately seems grounded in history, not philosophy. The book is studded with some two dozen references to history or historians. "A sense of history should be the most precious gift of science and of the arts," Leopold wrote. His final appeal derives not from abstract notions of right and wrong but from the empirical record of what man has done to the earth. That record, stripped of metaphysical flights, was telling man that the world was not made especially for his purposes. Nature implied a community of which he was just another member, not a commodity for his private manipulation. Or so Leopold read history. "We should, in the century since Darwin, have come to know that man, while now captain of the adventuring ship, is hardly the sole object of its quest, and that his prior assumptions to this effect arose from the simple necessity of whistling in the dark."

♫♫

Douglas and Leopold were typical of most conservationists after World War II. An interest in nature that began in childhood and was never interrupted ultimately found expression within the framework of the organized conservation movement. In response to external conditions, the philosophies of both men shifted from a domination of nature, in the Pinchot tradition, to a more cooperative harmony with nature in the Muir tradition. By their prominent names Douglas and Leopold stood out in sharp relief from the general movement. But their experience was not so different from that of thousands of anonymous associates.

As for DeVoto, Krutch, and Lindbergh, one is struck most by how untypical their conservation activities were. That these three strong personalities should have veered off in middle age, into work that in some sense denied their previous careers, is something to ponder. The new phase often ran counter to their temperaments. It offered no financial inducements, in fact usually cost time and money that could have been invested elsewhere. It was not reinforced by friends and peers, but instead was met with incredulity and faintly repressed laughter. But all three men were exceptionally independent and self-sufficient. They knew their own minds. In some inchoate fashion they were responding to changes in American society in the aftermath of the war. Their newly acquired tastes anticipated the expansion of the conservation movement in the 1950s.

8

Muir Redux, 1945-1965

 Son of the Wilderness, Linnie Marsh Wolfe's biography of John Muir, won the Pulitzer Prize in 1945 and thereby augured a revival of the Muir tradition in American conservation. In 1948 Ansel Adams published his collection of Sierra photographs, interspersed with the Muir quotations that left DeVoto so unimpressed. Conservationists after the war turned to Muir's books with a deepening regard for his ideas about wildness and the natural rights of the natural world. In 1954 Edwin Way Teale, the most widely read naturalist of the day, edited an anthology that made Muir's best work readily available for the first time in decades.

Meantime Muir was largely ignored by the academy. His papers were locked up by his family after Wolfe finished with them. Denied access to the raw materials, historians not surprisingly tended to slight Muir in favor of Pinchot. But the conservation movement, immersed in current issues, came back to Muir.

❧❧

In broad outlines the history of the conservation movement in the 1950s repeated the pattern of the 1920s. An "establishment" based in Washington and New York, with its strength drawn mainly from wildlife groups, controlled most of the available money and personnel. Within this establishment the key individuals knew each other well and met for social and business purposes at the Cosmos Club in Washington. Sometimes they congenially changed jobs from one group to another inside the establishment. This inbreeding of leadership facilitated cooperation but, inevitably, exacted a price in isolation from the hinterlands. Though less complacent than the wildlife establishment of the 1920s, the leaders of the 1950s again needed the stimulation of an outside catalyst. Once again the catalyst blew in from west of the Alleghenies.

At the center of the establishment stood the substantial figure of Ira Gabrielson, the lineal successor to John Burnham. The American Game Protective Association, Burnham's vehicle during the wildlife wars of the 1920s, had evolved with the support of the arms industry into the American Wildlife Institute and finally, in 1946, into the Wildlife Management Institute. In this final incarnation the WMI acquired instant legitimacy when Gabrielson, having retired as head of the federal Fish and Wildlife Service, became its first president. The presence of gun company money still bothered some conservationists, especially those with long memories. The WMI sponsored an annual wildlife seminar, the North American Wildlife Conference, which brought together an assortment of conservationists for speeches and discussions. Though well respected as a source of education and cross-fertilization, these conferences sometimes left unsettling hints of the industry funding behind them — for example, the sudden presentation of a resolution that federal wildlife refuges and sanctuaries be opened to public shooting.

In general, though, the WMI was more highly regarded than the AGPA had been. Gabrielson was a large, affable man with an encyclopedic knowledge of conservation and a reputation for independence and integrity. Despite his employment by the gun companies he remained his own man. In the tradition of Grinnell and Leopold he personally bridged the gap between hunters and bird lovers. A lifelong Audubon member, he had accumulated one of the longest life lists among North American birders. During the 1950s and 1960s he was a ubiquitous figure, the grand old man of conservation, "the glue in the conservation movement," according to David Brower. "Some fourteen years ago," Gabrielson told an Audubon meeting in 1959, "I retired to go fishing and to lie in the sun and do whatever else struck my fancy. Except for a few short weeks, I have done less of either than before my alleged retirement." When Charles Lindbergh became interested in conservation he, being Charles Lindbergh, could talk to the best man in the field. He naturally turned to Gabrielson.

The Izaak Walton League, the obstreperous western catalyst of the 1920s, had long since settled its quarrel with the wildlife establishment. Geographically it remained apart, with headquarters still in Chicago and most of the membership drawn from the Midwest. But tactically and financially it was more conservative than during the freewheeling years under Will Dilg. His casual ways with budgets and finances had left the league with a persistent indebtedness that by 1933 amounted to over $380,000. Under that chastening burden the league operated with an un-Dilg-like caution. In addition, the league seemed less the unbridled mustang because of changes in the wildlife establishment. The gun companies never recovered the power they had enjoyed in the halcyon days of Burnham's AGPA. Under Ding Darling and Gabrielson, federal wildlife policy had paid more attention to beleaguered species than to the arms industry's profits. Nelson Brown, FDR's forestry advisor, was a vice-president of the league; as such he brought its viewpoint directly to the President's attention. Finally, the league no longer stood out as the only group taking an ecological approach to the entire range of conservation issues. Starting in the 1930s, the older groups had abandoned their parochial viewpoints for one that recognized all conservation questions as aspects of a single problem.

The league reached its peak in influence and prestige during Kenneth Reid's tenure as general manager from 1938 to 1949. The old debts were retired and the league, effectively represented by Reid at national meetings, regained a measure of its former prominence. The fishermen in the league and the bird lovers in the Audubon Association still had their occasional arguments, as on the issue of using wild-bird plumage for fish flies. John Baker regarded this usage as a commercialization of wildlife, but Reid insisted that the feathers of common domestic birds were less enticing to fish. ("These fly-tyers are a peculiar lot," Reid explained. "They are artists.") In general, however, Reid worked persistently for more cooperation among the major conservation groups. Toward that end, in 1946 he was instrumental in starting the Natural Resources Council, a coordinating body founded by two dozen disparate organizations. Rosalie Edge, whose standards were undiminished by time, regarded him as "one of the finest figures in conservation." Once, at a hearing in Washington, she watched with relish as he acquainted two federal bureaucrats with their mistakes, speaking to them "as though he were Dr. Arnold lecturing two naughty boys. He did it superbly, with a gentle kindliness that was very stinging."

In 1945 Reid first applied the word "land-grab" to the public lands controversy that launched Bernard DeVoto's career in conservation. For some years the IWL branch in Wyoming had been urging the national leadership to take up the general issue of the abuse of federal grazing lands. When western congressmen introduced bills to return these holdings to the states, the league was the first national group to raise a protest. With a budget of $60,000 and about forty thousand members, it was still the largest conservation organization. But the membership figure was deceptively large because the western-lands fight was geographically and emotionally distant from the fishing and hunting grounds of most Waltonians. "We relied largely on volunteers," a league official later recalled, "and ruefully recognized that about 95 percent of all members were more interested in enlarging and extending outdoor recreational pursuits than attending to basic resource realities." Federal lands in Wyoming had no apparent relevance to the local fishing stream in Illinois.

Nonetheless Reid and others in the league hierarchy, notably Arthur Carhart and William Voigt, Jr., plunged in and fed ammunition to DeVoto for his *Harper's* polemics. DeVoto called Reid "my stay and comfort" and praised the league as "the best single organization" in the field. In three years the league distributed a half million pieces of literature on the issue. The successful campaign, the most notable victory for the league since Dilg's crusade for the Upper Mississippi wildlife refuge, was also a kind of swan song for Reid and the organization. A second major stroke left him incapacitated in 1949. Under subsequent leadership the league gradually lost influence. Membership figures declined for a time. They recovered later, but no leader of the league after 1949 was able to match Reid's reputation and influence within the movement.

As the league receded, the National Wildlife Federation took its place as the largest group with a particular interest in fishing and hunting. Organized like a pyramid, the federation represented thousands of local sportsmen's groups. These local clubs elected state representatives, who in turn elected regional directors, who in turn chose the national leadership. This democratic process gave hundreds of thousands of sportsmen a hand in setting national policy; by the same token it diffused authority and gave the federation a certain formless quality. In addition, the local groups paid no dues to the national office. Ever since its founding in 1936 the federation had been beset by financial problems. Ding Darling's plan to raise money by selling wildlife stamps had been botched by the leadership, and for that and other reasons Darling had parted company with the group by 1940. "Although the leaders in the federation were sincere conservationists," an NWF official said later, "some of them were anything but good administrators. The federation had quite a struggle in those years."

In this early period the American Wildlife Institute, which had sponsored the NWF's founding convention, came to the rescue with loans that eventually were written off. In 1945, for example, notes worth some $30,000 were forgiven by the institute, and this capped previous instances of gun company gifts — through the institute — to the federation. For some conservationists this arrangement raised the question of undue influence by gunning interests on federation policies. "In several states," Edward

Robert Sterling Yard, R. U.
Johnson's successor as editor of
the Century *and as the voice of*
eastern literary conservation
(The Living Wilderness)

Robert Marshall, forester and
wilderness explorer, was one of
the founders of the Wilderness
Society and its financial angel
(*Mable Abercrombie Mansfield*
and The Living Wilderness)

FDR tells a fish story off Port Aransas, Texas, May 1937 (UPI/Acme)

Jay Norwood "Ding" Darling, the popular editorial cartoonist, was instrumental in the founding of the National Wildlife Federation (J. N. "Ding" Darling Foundation, Inc.)

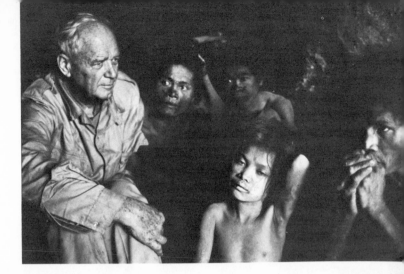

Charles Lindbergh listening to a Tasaday bird call in the Tasaday Caves, Mindanao, Philippines, April 1972 (© John Nance — Magnum Photos)

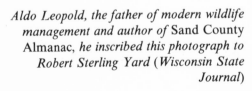

Supreme Court Justice William O. Douglas leads a party of hikers protesting plans to build a highway through Olympic National Park, 1964 (Wide World Photos)

Aldo Leopold, the father of modern wildlife management and author of Sand County Almanac, *he inscribed this photograph to Robert Sterling Yard (Wisconsin State Journal)*

John D. Rockefeller, Jr., philanthropist and controversial friend of the wilderness (Wide World, Inc.)

Bernard DeVoto, the Harper's conservationist, on one of his western trips in the early 1950s (U.S. Forest Service, courtesy of Avis DeVoto)

Joseph Wood Krutch, drama critic and Thoreau biographer, found in his second career as a naturalist his own antidote to "the modern temper" (Bill Sears — Black Star)

William E. Colby (second from left), organizer of Sierra Club outings in the High Sierra and a club leader for sixty years, on an outing in the 1930s with Dick Leonard and David Brower (to his left), and Oliver Kehrlein (Courtesy of the Sierra Club)

Ansel Adams, wilderness photographer, Muir's successor as the artistic voice of the Sierra, and a Sierra Club leader since 1919 (Courtesy of the Sierra Club)

Howard Zahniser, editor of the Living Wilderness, *one of the least known and most influential conservationists since World War II* (The Living Wilderness)

Olaus J. Murie, wilderness biologist, photographed with his wife Margaret at the 1953 meeting of the Wilderness Society, of which he was then president (James Marshall, courtesy of the Wilderness Society)

Rachel Carson, writer and marine biologist, at Rosalie Edge's Hawk Mountain Sanctuary, 1945 (Shirley A. Briggs, courtesy of the Rachel Carson Council, Inc.)

Richard Leonard, attorney and mountaineer, a prime mover in transforming the Sierra Club after 1945, and a link between the club and the Wilderness Society (Courtesy of the Sierra Club)

David Brower, Muir reincarnate, the most prominent conservationist of the postwar period and founder of Friends of the Earth in 1969 (Tom Turner, Courtesy of Friends of the Earth)

Preble reported in *Nature Magazine,* "only delegates representing organized gunning groups have been welcomed, or even tolerated at their meetings. Under such conditions, it is difficult to see how any reforms beneficial to wildlife can result." The group's financial arrangement with the arms industry apparently ended when Gabrielson took over the Wildlife Management Institute in 1946. The wildlife stamp program was revived and, better managed, it became the main source of the federation's income.

But the NWF retained its reputation as essentially a group of and for hunters. It opposed strict gun-control legislation, insisting on the constitutional right to bear arms. On occasion it resisted the creation of new national parks from national forest land — because hunting was prohibited in the parks but not the forests. On more general conservation issues the federation typically took moderate, prudent stands. "We must be realists — as well as idealists," declared a NWF spokesman. "If we continually ask for the moon we might wind up with nothing at all." The federation's journals frequently presented both sides of a given issue and refrained from taking any firm positions.

The NWF was, as claimed, the "largest private conservation group in the world." Yet on issues outside hunting it lacked a firm edge. "I think extremism is indulged in by minority groups who need to make a lot of noise to be heard at all," executive director Thomas Kimball later explained. "But the federation, as the world's largest conservation organization, represents too many people to do that." Instead, as an educational outlet it dispensed information, helped coordinate the activities of its members, and sold various items related to wildlife. Though it seldom took the lead in legislative campaigns, once they were begun by others it might swing the latent power of its vast organization into a supportive role. In general, the example of the NWF suggested that size was no index of effectiveness.

☙❧

At Audubon House in New York, the oldest wildlife group continued to evolve into a general conservation organization. The name was changed in 1940 from the National Association of Audubon Societies to the National Audubon Society, a streamlining that also reflected John Baker's tight management of the national office and his feud with certain state societies, especially Massachusetts Audubon, for control of the Audubon name. The newly reorganized society launched a branch plan whereby members of local affiliates, by paying a single annual fee, gained membership in both the local group and the national; previously the dues had been separate. The effect was to build a network of local branches with a loyalty to the national society, thereby isolating those local groups, such as Massachusetts Audubon, that remained aloof. The St. Louis Bird Club was the first to join, followed by affiliates in Detroit, Milwaukee, South Bend, and Topeka. By 1949 the society had thirty-six such branches. They attended to local matters while the national office concentrated on federal issues.

Staff members had begun to broaden the group's range of concerns in the mid-1930s. The name of the bimonthly magazine was changed from *Bird-Lore* to *Audubon Magazine* in 1941 because, as Baker explained, the organization had come to embrace "the whole field of conservation of wildlife resources." Two years later he flung his net wider to include soil, water, and plants. "The preservation of birds and other wildlife will remain the primary objective of your Society," he told the membership, "but with due regard for the interplay of other natural resources and with recognition of the need for active cooperation with those primarily concerned with the preservation of those other resources." In 1947 the leadership decided to stop publishing detailed ornithological reports in the magazine since its readership included so many nonbirders. Such reports were thereafter issued in a separate publication, *Audubon Field Notes,* that went only to those members with a traditional Audubon interest in technical birding.

These changes took place simultaneously with the development of ecology as a new branch of biological science. Previously, species had been studied in isolation, cast in a Darwinian mode of a solitary struggle for survival. By contrast, as Leopold pointed out in one of his most striking images, ecology implied the act of thinking in a plane perpendicular to Darwin. Slicing across the biotic community revealed not a solitary organism fighting all comers, but many species in a mysterious symbiotic interdependence. That perception demanded a reversal of specialization: an all-seeing eye instead of the narrowly aimed binoculars of a bird watcher. The Audubon leaders, along with everyone else in conservation, read their *Sand County Almanac.* During the 1950s ecological notions appeared with increasing frequency in Audubon publications. "We should set before our large membership," Guy Emerson, the treasurer, urged in 1952, "the idea that ecology for us means not merely birds and the earth, and growing things upon the earth, but includes the vast oceans around us," and even the sky and the stars. At the fiftieth annual convention in 1954, Baker declared that the society had moved from the idea of simple protection of birds to an emphasis on habitats and interrelationships. The "era of protection," he said, had given way to the "era of conservation."

The lesson was driven home by innovations that encouraged members to participate and experience instead of simply being aroused by words.

These included educational summer camps (begun in 1935), wildlife tours (1940), and film lectures called screen tours (1942). Roger Tory Peterson, hired by Baker early on, rewrote the Audubon school leaflets on a more accessible level. The Junior Audubon Clubs, aimed at schoolchildren, reached a peak of some four hundred thousand affiliates. Later the leaflets were rewritten again, dropping the old focus on individual species in favor of an interrelated ecological approach.

Membership figures, decimated by Rosalie Edge's campaign against Gilbert Pearson, slowly climbed upward. The total regained the pre-Edge high point of eighty-four hundred in 1947; it stood at twelve thousand in 1951 and then nearly doubled in the next three years. The national office moved into larger quarters and opened two regional offices outside New York. In 1954 the society had an endowment of some $3 million and an annual budget of $750,000. Both sums were unrivaled by any other conservation group. (But, as Baker pointed out, even the Audubon Society's resources seemed puny measured against those of other educational enterprises. "The few organizations in the conservation field that are sometimes inaccurately described as 'wealthy,' " he said, wincing at the familiar word, "have tiny endowments when compared with even small-sized colleges or museums.")

With all these advances, the society had two large problems. According to a poll taken in 1963, more than three-fourths of the members were over forty years of age. This left a demographic gap between the Junior Audubon schoolchildren and the general membership; the society seemed to have trouble attracting young adults. The older members did not always hear the ecological warnings of the leadership. Ludlow Griscom of the Harvard Museum of Comparative Zoology, the most widely respected ornithologist of his day, stated the matter bluntly at the 1953 Audubon convention: "What is vitally necessary is that the members of the National Audubon Society should become realistic. They must snap out of the historic thinking current in the Protective Era, and become more conservation-minded about current biological problems." The society's reputation as the gray lady of American conservation derived in part from all the gray hairs on its members.

The second problem was Baker himself. Like Pearson before him, he held sway for a quarter century — probably too long. Although an improvement on his predecessor, he shared some of Pearson's secretiveness and lack of imagination. He refused to publish budget reports in the magazine and was often strangely vague about membership figures. The annual convention, with one exception, was held in New York every year. He resisted Peterson's campaign to add more scientists to the Audubon board, arguing that "we could easily get some that would be primarily a headache." Most seriously of all, he refused to let the society flex any of its considerable muscle in support of conservation legislation. "Laws not adequately supported by public opinion are seldom enforced," he maintained. "We therefore stress education." He feared that even a small legislative effort would jeopardize the society's tax-exempt status and diminish the growth of the endowment. Perhaps he listened too intently for an echo from Pearson's clinking money box.

The dread scourge of the Audubon leadership was still on the job, though she had long since written off the society as hopeless and unworthy of her time. On occasion Rosalie Edge still attended the annual meetings and amused herself by inserting her disagreeable questions. But it was only sniping, not a wholesale assault. "Baker strongly resembles a crook," she advised Irving Brant in 1942. "No man is so disliked by his own executives without some good cause. Emerson is a pleasant gentleman, well tailored, but without much intelligence or force. I believe he and others are hoodwinked." After the 1946 meeting she reported that capital funds were the major subject of discussion, and that "bird" was not uttered once.

Edge spent most of her energy on her own projects through the Emergency Conservation Committee and her favorite undertaking, the Hawk Mountain Sanctuary Association. The ECC was still tiny, with a membership in 1947 of nine hundred and a budget under $3,000. She wondered why even rich people never seemed to give her more than five dollars at a time. But, with a new generation of ecological conservationists, her efforts received a measure of belated recognition. In 1948 the *New Yorker* ran an amused but respectful profile by Robert Lewis Taylor ("I think I could have been just as funny described accurately," she retorted). Her opinions — about the vulgarity in national parks, or about plans by Robert Moses for turning a marshland into a golf course — did not mellow with time. Nor was she reconciled to the limits of old age. "I don't know how to get to political leaders," she lamented in 1955 at the age of seventy-eight. "To them I am just an old woman." Three years later: "The ECC does little these days except to answer questions, and direct correspondents to sources." Then the old spirit flickered once again: "On the other hand, Hawk Mountain grows in wisdom and stature, etc."

She also presumably brightened at the news of Baker's retirement in 1959. The new boss was Carl W. Buchheister, vice-president under Baker since 1944. Outwardly it seemed an orderly dynastic succession. But though he was Baker's protégé, once in power Buchheister proved to be his own man. He changed many policies of long standing, usually to the society's benefit. A native of Baltimore, he had spent his early career as a Latin teacher in preparatory schools; in the summer he ran boys' camps. The latter work brought him the job of running the first Audubon adult camps for teachers in the 1930s. Then, after a stint as executive director of Massachusetts Audubon, Buchheister joined the national staff — a symbolic gesture of reconciliation, given the durable animosity between the two groups. At Audubon House he took charge of relations with branches and affiliates. When Baker finally retired and handed down the mantle, Buchheister was fifty-eight years old.

Within a few years Buchheister, taking his cue from more activist groups, had rejuvenated the society. He hired a lobbyist, Charles Callison, who wrote a report from Washington in each issue of *Audubon Magazine.* The national membership was implicitly recognized by moving the annual meetings outside New York, to Atlantic City, Corpus Christi, Miami, Tucson, and elsewhere. A detailed financial report was published each year. The society became more political, more open, and more controversial. It took particular umbrage at the use of chemical and biological controls by wildlife agencies. "The world must be on guard," said Buchheister, "against the myopic technologist who, assuming the aura of 'science,' arrogantly thinks he can play God." The rising militancy helped attract a tide of new members. In the single year of 1961–1962 the membership rose 24 percent, to forty-one thousand.

In the final years of her life Rosalie Edge at last saw the fruition of the crusade that had launched her conservation career more than thirty years earlier. In Buchheister she finally had an Audubon leader she could like. "His administration has brought new life and new spirit into the society," she declared, "his executives working in a happy atmosphere of high endeavor and progress. I feel myself personally blessed to have lived to see my hopes fulfilled." At the 1962 annual meeting Buchheister introduced her to a standing ovation. She died three weeks later.

※※

The Wilderness Society, with five thousand members in 1952, was the smallest of the major conservation groups. Its power derived not from numbers but from the reputations and personal qualities of an extraordinarily capable staff and council. Like the National Wildlife Federation, the Wilderness Society suggested that size might be inverse to influence in conservation circles. Though Bob Marshall and Aldo Leopold were dead, the society continued to attract the most respected names in conservation.

The new leaders still embodied the militancy and (to some extent) the exclusiveness of the founders. In the spirit of Marshall and Leopold they took leading parts in the noisiest conservation fights of the 1950s. "I think we shall always be a very small minority," Harold Anderson remarked, "but there is no good reason why our influence should not be out of all proportion to our numbers."

The society had been started mainly by easterners, and in the early years most members lived along the Atlantic seaboard. Yet most of the wilderness areas the society aimed to protect lay in the Rocky Mountain and Pacific West. As early as 1948 only 44 percent of the members lived in the East, and California was home to more society loyalists than New York. But headquarters remained in Washington. The two top leaders epitomized this continental identity. Olaus J. Murie, the director, lived in a wilderness cabin in Moose, Wyoming. Howard Zahniser, the executive secretary, prowled the halls of Congress and the Cosmos Club in Washington.

Both men had come to the society after not altogether contented careers with the Biological Survey. Murie, sixty-three years old in 1952, was an old-fashioned field naturalist who had never been reconciled to the laboratory and microscope. His particular interest was in large mammals, and he had recently published a definitive book on the elk of North America. His fieldwork served as a plausible excuse for spending his life outdoors. Like Muir, he was intoxicated by a lifelong, unaffected, childlike passion for the simple joy of life in the wilderness. Of Norwegian descent, he had grown up along the flatlands of the Red River in Minnesota. "There were woods, birds, mammals," he recalled. "It was living close to the earth — you know what that does to you. Gee, it was wonderful!" After college he joined the Biological Survey and was sent to Alaska, where he met his wife. In 1927 he was transferred to Jackson Hole, Wyoming, to find out why the elk of the region were dying off. (The problem, it turned out, was not starvation but unnatural forage. Chewing on sharp fibers caused lesions in the mouth that brought on lethal infections.)

By 1929 Murie was disagreeing with the survey's predator policy that so annoyed Rosalie Edge and, later, the Audubon Society. Taking its cue from farming and ranching interests, the survey regarded wolves, coyotes, and even some rodents as harmful species to be eradicated by mass poisoning and bounty campaigns. Murie's dissent from this policy was tolerated by the survey but not heeded. Again after the fashion of Muir, he cherished every living creature, even garter snakes, and did not sort them out according to their human uses. "I think we should go beyond proving the rights of animals to live in utilitarian terms," he said. "Why don't we just admit we like having them around? Isn't that answer enough?" In 1945 the survey's successor, the Fish and Wildlife Service, refused to publish his study of coyotes because it criticized the eradication policy. When Robert Sterling Yard died that same year, Murie was prevailed on to quit the service and take a half-time appointment as director of the Wilderness Society — with the provision that he could stay in Wyoming. The Murie family settled into a former dude ranch, fourteen miles north of the town of Jackson. During the first winter they were snowed in for five months; Murie would ski out for supplies every two weeks.

This new phase of Murie's career required a different set of skills. Previously he had written technical studies as a mammalogist. Now he had to write more general articles, give lectures, travel to hearings, keep abreast of conservation journals, and maintain a large correspondence. "We had become immersed in the conservation battle," his wife Margaret said later, ". . . and we both knew that life was blooming, expanding, growing because of the new work Olaus had undertaken. It demanded a great deal of us both." Though lacking the intellectual range and verbal deftness of a Leopold, Murie resembled Leopold in the universal respect he commanded. He had a presence often called Lincolnesque, suggestive of homely simplicity and strength masked by gentleness. Something about his manner forced an audience to trust and believe him. As a symbol and spokesman he was invaluable to the wilderness cause. In awarding him its highest medal the Audubon Society called him the "personification of the spirit of wilderness." The Sierra Club gave him its second John Muir Award "in gratitude for his carrying forth in spirit and in deed the historic work of John Muir." These awards by rival organizations themselves bespoke the ecological mood of cooperation and interrelatedness that Murie, somewhat quixotically, had tried to impress on government agencies.

Life in Wyoming reinforced his distaste for most of the modern world. Sounds heard in a city seemed just noise; at his cabin the bugling of an elk or the call of a coyote seemed beautiful. He regarded conventional ideas of progress as literally pathological, a sickness. "We are in a fever," he said, "of almost hysterical emphasis on science as a material weapon; on increasing economic wealth, ability, invention, as a weapon. . . . Our civilization needs to adopt the mountaineer pace, somewhat slower, but steady and upward." He differed from Marshall, who never stopped rushing, and agreed with Muir that one should "saunter" in the wild, at a deliberate, observant tempo. A mountaineer pace allowed all the senses to function. In 1954 Murie traveled from Moose to join Justice Douglas on his C&O hike. "He was a good hiker," Douglas recalled, "but always brought up the rear because he went in an unhurried way so as not to miss a flower, or the track of an animal, or the flight of a bird." Muir would have approved. Murie, as someone pointed out, was quite Muir-ie himself. His life bore everyday witness to the ideals of the city-bound Wilderness Society membership.

In Washington, Howard Zahniser handled the society's administrative chores and edited *Living Wilderness.* Seventeen years younger than Murie, he looked like a misplaced librarian, bald, bespectacled, and bookish. His favorite recreation in any city was to inventory a secondhand bookstore; he especially favored the works of Dante, Blake, and Thoreau. His enormous personal collection of nature books was eventually donated to the Conservation Center of the Denver Public Library, the main repository of historical materials on conservation. The books reflected the man: Zahniser had one of the sharpest, best-stocked minds in conservation. Previously, *Living Wilderness* had appeared at erratic intervals. Under Zahniser, and later Michael Nadel, it turned into a brightly edited quarterly that extended generous coverage to other groups in the movement. Aside from his editing and office chores, Zahniser also became a conservation ombudsman on Capitol Hill, keeping track of bills, plotting strategies, and buttonholing Congressmen. With his left hand he conducted a monthly books column in *Nature Magazine.* All of this left him intolerably busy. In 1952 he suffered a serious coronary spasm "brought on," he admitted, "by the unrelieved tension of too much writing and editing, without enough — oh shame! — of the outdoors preached by that writing and editing." Though unknown to the outside world, he was one of the most effective conservationists of the postwar period.

Zahniser grew up in a small town in Pennsylvania, the son of a Free Methodist minister. His interest in nature began in the fifth grade, when he joined a Junior Audubon Club. (Murie harked back to the old field naturalists; Zahniser represented the newer generation of city-bred nature lovers.) Joining the Biological Survey in 1931, he worked for Edward Preble, who like Murie was one of the agency's tolerated mavericks; Zahniser later named a son after Preble. During the war he transferred to another bureau within the Agriculture Department. A thoughtful man, Zahniser was evidently affected by the war in somewhat the same way as Charles Lindbergh: a dawning sense that modern man had made a Faustian bargain he could not win. Hiroshima presented the possibility of total destruction. "As we constantly become more and more nearly lords of creation," he said afterward, trying to sort it out, "there is nothing so much to be feared as ourselves, yet we know so little about fearsome us." The wisest course seemed a united effort "to understand the cosmos we now perceive before we shatter its whole into disintegrating atoms."

His own contribution toward that end was to quit a secure civil service job for a none too certain future in conservation. In 1946 the Wilderness Society's total income was only $19,867, of which all but $3,367 was provided by Marshall's bequest. Zahniser had a young family to support; he switched jobs, at half his former salary, with some misgivings. As he later explained it, he supposed it was the evangelistic spirit of his father that pushed him toward the society. "We deeply need the humility to know ourselves as the dependent members of a great community of life," Zahniser wrote, "and this can indeed be one of the spiritual benefits of a wilderness experience." In civilization man was surrounded and impressed by his own achievements. Removed from them, it was possible "to recognize one's littleness, to sense dependence and interdependence, indebtedness, and responsibility."

The viewpoint recalled Muir's central insight into man's proper place in the world. Zahniser in fact had a particular regard for Muir, whom he called "our prophet of the wilderness." In 1938, in recognition of the centennial of Muir's birth, Zahniser had reread all his books, the highest tribute an inveterate reader could pay. "It will be a sorry time," Zahniser said on that occasion, "if the pressure of current writings ever forces John Muir from the attention of American readers." In Muir himself he found an antidote for the modern condition. One day in 1946, while reading Wolfe's biography of Muir on a Washington streetcar, Zahniser noticed a woman perusing a sober volume entitled *The Neurotic Personality of Our Time*. It required "decorous restraint" on his part, he recalled, to keep from pressing the Muir biography on her with an air of look — read this — it has the answer. As a student of conservation history he respected both Pinchot and Muir but clearly preferred the latter. "Gifford Pinchot made conservation practical," he pointed out. "It is, of course, John Muir's leadership to which we are more directly committed in our preservation efforts."

That balanced judgment suggested one of Zahniser's finest qualities. He had firm opinions of his own, but in dealing with other conservationists he was courteous, good-humored, diplomatic, ecumenical, an earnest advocate who also listened well. During the fractious campaigns of the 1950s, he was the common denominator, holding the center together and in touch with everyone, implacable but imperturbable. "As a follower of Muir," he said at the 1963 Audubon convention, ". . . and as one who also knew and respected Pinchot, I am inspired to gain from each of them and to draw a circle that takes us all in, encompassing all of conservation." The Audubon Society under Buchheister was ready to hear the message.

The most hopeful sign of the postwar movement was that conservationists seemed willing to converge around the ecological imperative. Murie, Zahniser, and other Wilderness Society leaders had all been friends of Leopold's; for them *Sand County Almanac* hit home with a special impact. "The Wilderness Society should push Aldo's book to the limit," Benton MacKaye urged Zahniser. Excerpts were printed in *Living Wilderness*. Society spokesmen invoked Leopold's name and put his ideas into practice on two levels. Philosophically the ecological cast of mind implied treating all conservation issues as aspects of a single problem; practically it meant cooperating with other groups. The society's overt purpose, Zahniser noted, was still to preserve wilderness areas. "Yet we find that to accomplish this we need to cooperate in every sound conservation enterprise and to support as actively as we can the whole conservation movement." For example, mass demands threatened wilderness parks because more accessible parks had been ruined by pollution. Accordingly the society helped the Izaak Walton League in its ongoing crusade to clean up waterways. "I feel I am here among friends," Ernest Griffith, the treasurer, said at the 1950 Walton convention.

A more natural alliance was forged with the Sierra Club. Despite an obvious affinity as defenders of wilderness, the two groups had previously disagreed on occasion — as in advocating the Kings Canyon park — and historically the club was associated with the Park Service lobby, the society with the Forest Service lobby. But the deaths of Marshall and Yard had removed the society's two strongest ties to the Forest Service. After the war the two main wilderness groups started working in concert. Leopold's seat on the society council was taken by Richard Leonard of the Sierra Club. George Marshall, Bob's brother, was also a prominent figure in both organizations. For a Muir acolyte like Zahniser the new alliance was a heady experience. "When I remember my boyhood and later respect for the Sierra Club," he confided to Murie, "I almost have to pinch myself to realize that here we are working as a part of that Club."

As an outsider Leonard brought a vital new perspective to meetings of the Wilderness Society council. The council functioned as the society's board of directors, setting policy and giving directions to Murie and Zahniser. The council chose its own members, who seldom quit, were never fired, and even took their time about dying. The general membership had no input whatsoever. This oligarchy, as Bob Marshall had called it, had been set up to ensure that the society would be run by a small coterie of true believers. But the self-perpetuating nature of the council carried at least a potential source of abuse. Most of the founders were still on hand in the 1950s. Council meetings sometimes resembled a final encampment of the Grand Army of the Republic, with grizzled veterans on every side. A few of the old-timers resisted Zahniser's more activist impulses in editing the magazine.

For the most part, this situation remained a problem only in theory. The men on the council were highly principled, like-minded, and meticulous about attending meetings and keeping abreast of events. They operated by consensus, not by majority vote; if everyone could not agree on an issue the matter was tabled or deferred. Thus in 1947 everyone but Leopold had approved a resolution in favor of federal regulation of private lumbering. (Leopold was never shy about acting as a minority of one.) Since he could not be budged, the society took no public action. The effect of this consensus approach protected minority opinions and imparted a certain deliberate gravity to council proceedings. Any precipitate actions were constitutionally unlikely.

On most issues Murie and Zahniser were left a free hand. For practical purposes they *were* the Wilderness Society. The Wildlife Federation and the Audubon Society, for all their larger budgets and memberships, had no leaders of the stature of these two. They functioned as the legitimate heirs of Bob Marshall and Aldo Leopold.

※※

The most startling surprise of this period was the emphatic reemergence of the Sierra Club on the national scene. It swooped in from the west, much as the Izaak Walton League had done in the 1920s, and showed a similar disregard for given arrangements. A quiet regional group of mountaineers in 1945, two decades later the Sierra Club had become the focal point of modern American conservation under the leadership of a man who seemed to be Muir reincarnate. At a time when Muir's ideas and reputation were undergoing a general revival, with an uncanny historical synchronicity his group also sat up and stretched itself for the first time since 1914.

This rebirth was made possible by a generational succession within the club. Younger members who had joined in the 1920s and 1930s worked their way upward in the club hierarchy and then took over in the years after the war. The people they replaced — men like Joel Hildebrand, Duncan McDuffie, and Francis Farquhar — were all good conservationists within the parameters they set for the club. They regarded the organization as a bastion of uncorrupted amateurism, without paid employees beyond a small clerical staff. They made their livings outside conservation: Hildebrand was a chemistry professor, McDuffie a real estate developer, Farquhar an accountant. For them the club was essentially a hobby, not a vehicle for political activism. "When I was first in conservation," one of these proud amateurs later recalled, "if we wanted to go somewhere we supplied the gas, and we took our lunches, and if we had to sleep overnight we arranged to sleep in somebody's house."

On an individual level the tradition of the amateur in conservation could still allow for effective work, as Rosalie Edge showed repeatedly. On an organizational level, though, it was outmoded. Other conservation groups had long since hired professional staffs. The Sierra Club's resistance to professionalization both reflected and reinforced a certain provincial quality in the leaders. They directed an organization of lovers of the Sierra Nevada, period. On national conservation issues they might exert an informal power through personal ties to decision makers. "We did not have any paid lobbyist," Hildebrand said later. "We had members of the board of directors who were men of influence, and they would alert all their friends in the East to apply pressure." Sometimes, as in Kings Canyon, this informal approach proved adequate. But in general it was too haphazard for a modern conservation group, lacking continuity and dependent on the particular identity of the friends back East and the positions they happened to hold at the time. It operated on a specific, personal basis instead of the more general, politically derived influence of the larger groups.

The club was still best known for its outings into the Sierra, now augmented by ski trips in the winter. Muir's faithful lieutenant William Colby, hale at sixty-nine in 1945, had led the summer trips for twenty-eight years with a ruthless eye for overweight dunnage bags and an undisturbed confidence in the face of adversity. His invariably optimistic estimates of the distance to the next campsite had contributed the legend of the "Colby mile" to club folklore. "I, like a modern Moses," he said, "literally have led the disciples of John Muir into the wilderness." Though retired from active leadership in the outings, Colby persisted in the original faith that anyone set down in the Sierra became a mountaineer, and that anyone so converted would protect the mountains from human abuse. But for most members the outings answered social and recreational needs, little else. Marjory Bridge Farquhar recalled her impression of the outings: "That was where you got a man." And in fact that was where she met Francis. The outings remained as a device for recruiting both spouses and new club members; the conservationist passion of these new members could be questioned. In reviewing *Sand County Almanac,* Harold Bradley, the son of a club founder, predicted that the book would please those imbued with the traditions of the Muir era — but would not interest newer members "more preoccupied with the varied physical opportunities provided by the club."

Still: although most members escaped a true conversion on the outings, these excursions had a powerful impact on a few key individuals. All the Young Turks who refounded the club after the war could trace their interest to experiences in the Sierra Nevada. Richard Leonard first visited Yosemite in 1926 at the age of eighteen. A few years later, in a park in Berkeley, he tried out the new techniques of rock climbing with rope and piton. Having learned the rudiments, he moved on to unscaled faces around Yosemite; and with that he was hooked. In 1932 he formed a Rock Climbing Section within the Sierra Club over the objections of some club fathers. ("They felt that it was more a sport than it was an outlook toward conservation," according to Marjory Farquhar.) The arcane lore of rock climbing did on occasion seem far removed from conservation. Leonard once published a thirty-three-page article in the *Bulletin* titled "Belaying the Leader," including data on the tensile strength of various ropes. But for Leonard, at least, rock climbing led to conservation work and ultimately to a militant conservationist philosophy. In 1947, after the Wilderness Society had helped out on a club project in California, Leonard in turn joined the society's campaign for the Quetico-Superior wilderness — "although," he wrote Murie, "it is quite a long way from the high mountains of California." He was added to the Wilderness Society council in the following year.

The most widely known of the club's Young Turks was the photographer Ansel Adams. As a publicist for the Sierra Nevada he ranked with Muir. A Sierra Club member since 1919 and a director since 1936, he constantly pushed the club to be more aggressive, to take risks. His prominence in the art world made him the most effective friend of the Sierra since Muir — with whose tradition Adams explicitly aligned himself. "John Muir was one of those exceptional men whose writing touches us deeply, revealing the world which is potentially available to us all," Adams declared. "The quality of Muir's vision has undeniably colored my own moods of response and clarified the statements of my camera."

Adams was born in San Francisco in 1902. As a little boy, he spent a lot of time by himself, walking on the beach and exploring the dunes near his home at the western edge of the city. "In grammar school, as a kid," he recalled, "I was considered 'unusual' — not in my right mind, so to speak."

Obviously gifted, and a prodigy on the piano, he was indulged by a sympathetic father. In the spring of 1916 the father announced a first trip to Yosemite; the boy prepared himself by reading the Yosemite guidebook by Muir's old rival James Hutchings. Primed with great expectations, Adams arrived in the valley and was not disappointed. Thereafter he returned every year, Brownie camera in hand. He spent four summers as custodian of the Le Conte Lodge, Sierra Club headquarters in the valley. He met his future wife at her father's Yosemite art studio. When her father died, in 1937, they took over the studio and became year-round residents. Over the next two decades Adams published a half dozen books on the Sierra Nevada. In its major phases his career paralleled Muir's: a shock of recognition on first seeing the valley, followed by a period of residence and then a reputation as the artistic voice of the Range of Light.

On a trail high in the central Sierra in the summer of 1933, Adams was fiddling with his camera when a tall young man ambled by. "Ansel Adams was complaining about the clouds when I first met him," David Brower said later. Brower was then twenty-one years old, a dropout from the University of California without firm prospects but with a rising interest in the mountains. He also had some of Adams's skill with camera and piano, and the two became friends at once. That fall Adams sponsored Brower for Sierra Club membership. Francis Farquhar invited the young man to his Berkeley home for a tour of his mountaineering library and a discussion of routes through the Sierra. Brower, something of a social misfit, relaxed in the warm embrace of a Sierra Club family. The mountains yielded their own pleasures and other benefits as well. "The Farquhars and their growing family," Brower recalled, "helped me through various prewar nadirs, giving me the run not only of the library but also of the beautifully equipped Farquhar darkroom." As editor of the *Bulletin* Farquhar appointed Brower to the club's editorial board in 1935. Brower later became associate editor and then took over the magazine in 1946.

Like Adams and many other conservationists, Brower had a solitary childhood that turned him toward nature. An accident in infancy had knocked out his front teeth, and the second set came in crooked when he was twelve. Schoolmates referred to him as "the toothless boob." He grew up shy, afraid to smile, wary of human contacts. He roamed the Berkeley hills collecting butterflies and discovered a species that was subsequently named after him. His mother was blind; guiding her on hikes through the hills and describing the scenery sharpened his own eye. The family went camping on the fringes of Yosemite Park, where the boy heard stories about the battle over Hetch Hetchy. When he was twelve he read Muir's

My First Summer in the Sierra and began to think about venturing into the high mountains. After leaving college he marked time by clerking in a candy factory. Meeting Adams and joining the club gave him a direction that eventually transformed his life. Marjory Farquhar remembered him as "very sensitive" and "very shy and quiet" when he first entered their family circle.

Like Muir, he had one personality in town, another in the wilderness. On a mountain Brower was bold, unfettered, and imaginative. At the summit he found his true self. "Who, once having enjoyed it," he wrote in the *Bulletin* in 1935, "does not long for the deep satisfactions of beholding a panorama from a vantage-point, access to which has cost something in effort and training ... of being awed by the great, but remaining proud of the success of the organized effort of the small?" He made thirty-three first ascents in the Sierra, many in the company of Richard Leonard. Once he climbed three 14,000-foot peaks in twelve hours. On another occasion, at the end of ten weeks in the mountains, he wondered if he had hit a saturation point; another peak was possible but instead he returned to camp and thence to civilization. "By the time I reached Berkeley," he said, "the answer was certain: This person was not coming home — he had just left it!"

He carried this insight to its logical conclusion by moving to Yosemite in 1935. For three years he made a spare living as part of the park staff and spent his time skiing, hiking, and climbing mountains. His ardor as a skier briefly overcame his nascent preservation instincts: he proposed a tramway from the valley floor to the top of Mount Hoffmann. A Sierra Club member forcibly persuaded him otherwise. In 1941 Brower went back to Berkeley and got a job with the University of California Press, where he met the woman he married two years later. (A small historical irony here: Anne Hus Brower was the granddaughter of John P. Irish. Muir reincarnate was married to the granddaughter of Muir's old political nemesis.)

When the war came Brower enlisted as a private. Assigned to the Tenth Mountain Division, he instructed troops in climbing techniques and served as a battalion intelligence officer during operations in Italy, from the Apennines to the Alps. Along with three battle stars and a Bronze Star, he picked up an increased urgency about saving wilderness. "The Alps confirmed my belief in wildness," he recalled. "All those mountains in Switzerland punched so full of holes that they have to be held together with cables. They strengthened my desire to protect the places in the Sierra Nevada."

Brower returned with a new glint in his eye. He had a magical quality that reminded people of Muir, some indefinable extra element that made him more than the sum of his attributes: the charisma of a born leader, perhaps, or the late-maturing compensations of the boy afraid to open his mouth in public. Whatever it was, he had *it*. Club members were sometimes awed by Brower's mountaineering exploits. One veteran spoke of him as "the friction climber, the advocate of dynamic balance who seemed somehow to be able to move on slight discolorations of the rock." Another member glowingly described him on the 1948 outing: "The tall young leader stood forward in the firelight.... If newcomers wondered that a man so youthful in appearance could speak with such quiet authority, it was because they did not know his background: already more years of mountain experience and leadership — summer and winter, in peace and in combat — than might be crowded into a score of ordinary lifetimes." (Even after Adams and Leonard quarreled bitterly with him, they still acknowledged his special gifts. "He is a genius," said Adams. "He is an evangelist with great persuasive powers," said Leonard. "He is reminiscent of Muir.")

In the years after the war these three insurgents took control of the Sierra Club. A new militancy was at once apparent when they tried to abolish the Southern California chapter for being too social and snobbish, and too oblivious to conservation. The dominant northern contingent in the club had long been dismayed by the southern cousins, whose executive committee was colloquially known as the Booze Brothers. "Most of those that joined," a southern leader later admitted, ". . . were more interested in meeting people and the social end of it . . . than they were in the objectives of conservation." At a club directors meeting a motion by Adams to abolish the chapter failed of a second, but the insurgents went on to stack the board at the next election of directors. Well canvassed by the insurgents, the membership returned only one representative of the southern chapter to the board instead of electing its usual complement of five of the fifteen members.

It was power politics, to a degree not seen in the club since Hetch Hetchy. The new leaders again showed a willingness to drop a gentlemanly decorum over the issue of road construction in the upper region of Kings Canyon. The matter went to the heart of the Sierra Club's purpose. In 1892, the founders had bound themselves "to render accessible" the mountains of the Pacific Coast — at a time when most of those mountains were beyond easy reach. As the years passed, and more roads and facilities were built, "to render accessible" meant increasingly to improve and despoil. As early as 1930, Muir's friend Marion Randall Parsons warned that spreading campgrounds and parking areas had rendered the old policy obsolete. "Our problem is no longer how to make the mountains better traveled and better known," she wrote. "Rather, it would seem, how from the standpoint of the mountain-lover 'to render accessible' may be made more truly compatible with 'to enjoy.'" Yet most club leaders adhered to the original policy, arguing that roads meant people who would support the parks. William Colby, citing Muir's support for railroad spurs to Yosemite, was especially adamant.

The lines were drawn after the war, when the Park Service announced plans for a major new road in Kings. Brower and Leonard rounded up enough directors to oppose the scheme, and they worked out a compromise with the Park Service. Colby bore the defeat like a good soldier. "We have a new crop of very zealous conservationists growing up who have taken over," he told another veteran, Horace McFarland, "and all I do nowadays as far as the club is concerned is to make a suggestion from the standpoint of an 'old timer,' which the Board sometimes follows and sometimes ignores, which is as it should be." Shortly thereafter the new leadership deleted the "render accessible" clause from the club's articles of incorporation. With that Colby decided he could no longer serve on the board of directors after a half century of indefatigable service. "And so dear Colby resigned," Leonard recalled. "All of us loved him deeply and elected him honorary president of the Sierra Club until his death in 1964."

In effect, the club was redefining its conception of the wilderness experience to make it wilder and less harmful to the land. Among the casualties of this policy was that humble symbol of a Sierra Club High Trip, the mule. At the founding meeting in 1892, Warren Olney had declared: "We shall learn much from mules." In pre-backpacking days they carried everything on outings, including a cast-iron stove; at night they grazed in mountain meadows; on dangerous trails they were sensible and sure of foot. At the fiftieth anniversary dinner in 1942, Willis Linn Jepson paid the beast a heartfelt tribute. "Of wisdom and intelligence, of patience and fortitude, of caution and self-reliance," he said, "this club has learned more from His Honor, The Mule, than from any other one element in the Sierra Nevada." But His Honor's fondness for succulent mountain grass exacted a toll. A study in 1947 by Richard Leonard and Lowell Sumner, a Park Service biologist, found too many meadows depleted of vegetation, with packed soil alternately dust and quagmire. A year later Brower proposed the question: "Are Mules Necessary?" The answer was apparently no. Along the same lines, the old practices of cutting blazes in trees, taking saplings for beds and lean-tos, and building a large bonfire came under scrutiny. The postwar tendency was to rely solely on human locomotion and to tread lightly. "It is still fun to play Indian," said Brower, "and it is still a challenge to emulate the freely translated Indian motto, 'Where I go I leave no sign.' "

All these changes left bruises on the club's old guard. For some veterans a wilderness experience was not possible without mules. If more kind to the mountains, the new policy was less kind to some people who had sustained the club for years. Under Brower's direction the *Bulletin* gave more space to park and wilderness battles, less to the familiar accounts of outings and climbing trips. "Just about everything that could be written about a Sierra High Trip has been written," he maintained. Instead he envisioned a general magazine, a *National Geographic* of the wilderness, less intimate and personalized than the old *Bulletin* but with a correspondingly wider range. Such changes were not welcomed by Brower's old mentor and protector, Francis Farquhar. He described himself as "very much disappointed" by the new format of the journal he had edited so long — but supposed it a necessary aspect of expansion.

Club membership, stable at around 3,000 for decades, climbed to 4,000 just after the war, then 6,000 in 1948, and 7,000 two years later. In 1949 the club held the first of its biennial wilderness conferences, which on the model of the North American Wildlife meetings brought together experts in the field from all over the country. In 1950 the first chapter outside California, the Atlantic chapter, was started by members who had moved to the East. The Sierra Club was gaining a wider, more national base. Professionalization logically followed. In 1952 Leonard as president appointed Brower to be the first executive director; Brower quit his publishing job and assumed the tasks formerly done by several volunteers. Over the next few years he expanded both his responsibilities and the size of his staff. The Sierra Club moved irrevocably into the big time.

In seven years under Brower's aegis the membership doubled again, and the conservation budget alone went from $5,000 to $30,000. He always pushed forward, intent on transforming the club from "the small, compact, face-to-face group that used to enjoy reading about each other's summer trips and climbs." (During the 1930s, Farquhar recalled, "we all knew each other very well.") A directors meeting in October 1953 debated the question of expansion, and agreed not to set any geographic limits on the formation of new chapters. Many new members joined not to go on outings but to support the club's conservation efforts. "We need more money," said Brower. "The National Wildlife Federation and the National Geographic Society testify eloquently that bold ideas can work. We could do enormously more with wilderness outings, publications, and films than we have done, and almost all the rest of the program could be carried as a result."

An established mountaineering group with a fifty-year history had, in slightly over a decade, been transformed into something quite different. To the old guard the new Sierra Club sometimes seemed unfriendly and ill-mannered. Brower seldom approved of the Park Service and the Forest Service, and he was inclined to embroider his criticisms by impugning their motives. The old club did not operate that way, according to Joel Hildebrand: "We were often consulted by the chiefs and superintendents, and we treated each other as gentlemen." But when the Forest Service violated wilderness protections in the Cascade Mountains or allowed logging on the Kern plateau south of Mineral King, or when the Park Service built an unneeded road to Tenaya Lake in Yosemite, the new club might neglect its manners.

The old guard could be circumvented. The club played for higher stakes when it bearded the Internal Revenue Service. In 1954 the Supreme Court in *United States* v. *Harris* outlined strict if vaguely worded rules against lobbying activities by tax-exempt organizations sustained by deductible contributions. For activist conservation groups with small budgets, like the Wilderness Society and the Sierra Club, the ruling set up two unpalatable choices: risk even greater poverty or become politically innocuous. Brower's impulse was to damn the torpedoes, but even his fellow insurgents in the Sierra Club had doubts. "I often get a guilty feeling," Leonard told Howard Zahniser, "that you and Dave feel at times a frustration that 'we blankety blank attorneys' are holding up conservation." By Leonard's estimate, loss of the favored IRS status would mean estate taxes of 30 to 50 percent on bequests to the Sierra Club, which averaged $25,000 a year at that time. To avoid such a possibility he set up the Sierra Club Foundation, a nonactivist shelter that could safely receive large contributions regardless of the club's fortunes with the IRS. Brower could then proceed as before, not without trepidation. "The Sierra Club is deductible," he said, "but willing to explore at some risk into the never-never land of undefined undeductibility so as to do in the public interest what John Muir founded it to do."

It was Brower, preeminently Brower, who transformed the Sierra Club into (as the New York *Times* said) "the gangbusters of the conservation movement." To a rare degree he had the quality which he valued most highly in Muir: the "ability to transcend his powers as an observer and to become in addition a keen advocate." He stood with Muir and Marshall in the line of great mountaineer-conservationists.

※※

The Sierra Club and Wilderness Society prospered during the 1950s because they had the best leaders — and because the two major conservation issues of the decade involved wilderness, the central concern of both groups. Brower and Zahniser led the fight to prevent another Hetch Hetchy. Then, instructed by the experience, they spearheaded a legislative campaign to give national wilderness areas permanent statutory protection. Hanging over both episodes were the ghosts of Muir and Pinchot.

The battleground that raised the specter of a second Hetch Hetchy was the Dinosaur National Monument, on the Utah border in the northwest corner of Colorado. Originally established to protect a deposit of dinosaur skeletons, it had been enlarged in 1938 to include a hundred miles of wild, isolated canyons of the Green and Yampa rivers. Hidden away in forbidding country, beyond the reach of good roads, it was practically unknown to anyone except paleontologists. "No one had ever heard of Dinosaur National Monument," Leonard said later. In the late 1940s the Bureau of Reclamation of the Interior Department drew up ambitious plans for a billion-dollar Colorado River storage project that included an Echo Park dam within the monument. Newton B. Drury, director of the Park Service, protested this utilitarian intrusion on his domain. But Secretary of the Interior Oscar Chapman, faced with an intramural quarrel between two of his agencies, leaned toward Reclamation, which had a much larger staff and budget than the Park Service.

Before making a final decision, Chapman in April 1950 held a hearing in his office on the Echo Park dam issue. Conservationists submitted their objections on a general level, citing the proposed dam as a dangerous precedent. In a letter to Chapman, Irving Brant described the proposal as "one more move in the incessant drive to break down the national park system by subordinating all values not measurable by dollars." As an alternative site, outside the parks and monuments, conservationists suggested Glen Canyon in Arizona as an equivalent source of irrigation and electrical power. Reclamation and the Army Engineers were building up strong, commercially backed lobbies. Having no expectations of stopping them, conservationists hoped to divert them.

The matter reached the public when Bernard DeVoto heard about it. With information secretly provided by Herbert Evison of the Park Service, he wrote an angry article for the *Saturday Evening Post,* an oracle of mainstream public opinion. The article was accepted early in June 1950, but before it could be published Chapman gave his approval to the Echo Park dam. "It goes without saying that we share your feeling of disappointment," Drury told DeVoto; "also that, as a bureau of the Department of Interior, we cannot encourage individuals or organizations to oppose the dams further." Thus the formal position. But when the article was published in July, Drury added a less formal note: "Fine medium! Fine position! Fine writer!" Chapman's decision only cleared the administrative channels; the project still needed money from Congress. With DeVoto's *Post* article, later reprinted in *Reader's Digest,* the battle was on.

The Wilderness Society council met in Jackson Hole that summer. Afterward, Murie, Leonard, and others drove down to take a look at Echo Park. Though accustomed to wilderness with trees, they found the arid scenery surprisingly attractive. They also discovered ancient Indian pictographs that would be submerged by the dam. The case against the dam became more specific: not only a mischievous precedent in invading the park system, it also would have ruined an unexplored but substantial scenic resource.

The issue came along at the right time in the history of the conservation movement. Under the ecological imperative, and with *Sand County Almanac* as the text, all the major groups had started thinking at right angles to Darwin. Philosophically they were ready to cooperate, given a major issue like Echo Park. Ira Gabrielson of the Wildlife Management Institute, *Nature Magazine,* and the Audubon Society — all technically preoccupied with wildlife — joined in the fray. Seventeen groups banded together under an emergency committee of Brower, Zahniser, Gabrielson, and William Voigt, Jr., of the Walton League. Allied with private power interests opposed to federal projects, they held up congressional authorization of the Colorado River plan as long as it included Echo Park. "For the first time in the history of conservation," Irving Brant noted, ". . . practically all organizations devoted to it have been stirred up to a joint campaign." The movement had matured since the wildlife wars of the 1920s and the ECC's assault on the Audubon Society.

As a burgeoning political issue, Echo Park was passed on to the White House. Brant sent President Truman a three-page statement and suggested he take a raft trip down the river. "It has always been my opinion," Truman wrote back, "that food for coming generations is much more important than bones of the Mesozoic period but I'll be glad to talk to you about it sometime." (Actually the dinosaur deposits, in another part of the monument, were not threatened by the dam.) Toward the end of 1951 Chapman in addressing the Audubon convention hinted that Echo Park might be saved. But the Democratic senator from Utah, Elbert Thomas, who was running for reelection in 1952, told Truman his chances depended on passage of the entire Colorado project. Consequently Truman ordered Chapman to continue to press for the whole package. Nonetheless its enemies held it off through the election year. Thomas lost his seat and the Democrats lost the White House, thereby presenting the conservationists with a fresh set of adversaries.

Dwight D. Eisenhower ran on a platform that called for "restoration of the traditional Republican lands policy," meaning free enterprise without federal meddling. (As DeVoto pointed out, the Republican tradition included the work of Pinchot and Theodore Roosevelt, but the platform committee's memory evidently did not reach back that far.) Once in office, the Eisenhower administration in its first term compiled a conservation record so execrable that it reinforced the recently forged alliance between conservation and the Democrats. Top positions in conservation bureaus were taken off civil service and given to dubious political hacks. The technical staff of the Soil Conservation Service in Agriculture was emasculated. The Federal Power Act was hamstrung by administrative interference. A new, more subtle edition of the land-grab against the national forests was encouraged by the White House. "A business administration means business, doesn't it?" asked DeVoto. During the Truman years, natural resources had been assaulted by members of Congress and defended by federal agencies. After two years under Eisenhower, as John Baker — a Republican — pointed out, those roles had been reversed: "The administration is the aggressor, and the Congress the defender. This is not a political opinion, it is a fact."

Conservationists were especially appalled by the Secretary of the Interior, Douglas McKay, an automobile dealer from Oregon. For his friendliness to private interests he was called Giveaway McKay. He opened practically all the national wildlife refuges to gas and oil leasing. He decimated the Fish and Wildlife Service, downgrading career employees to negligible positions. Clumsy to the point of comedy, when confronted with difficult issues McKay would say, "Well you know, I'm just a Chevrolet salesman." Yet in most cases McKay was only the scapegoat. Decisions at Interior were usually made by his under secretary, an engineer named Ralph Tudor, or by Sherman Adams, Eisenhower's chief of staff. Tudor was particularly intent on purging the department of those he called "screwballs," "rabid New Dealers," and "persons who did careless things for which they might be intimidated or blackmailed by communists." McKay absorbed the criticism for actions undertaken by others. Understandably, he bristled all the more when attacked. After his department endorsed a new Colorado bill including Echo Park, and was duly lambasted, he referred to his critics as "punks" — an interesting variation on such traditional labels as bird watchers and posy pickers.

Officially the Park Service was constrained to support the full project. Unofficially it gathered friends for Echo Park by enlarging the program of raft trips down the Green and Yampa rivers. Dinosaur had less than thirteen thousand visitors in 1950, and over seventy thousand four years later. In the summer of 1953, two hundred Sierra Club members floated through the monument; Brower went along with two of his sons. "I have seen a lot of outstanding scenery in the last thirty-five years," he said afterward. *"I have never had a scenic experience to equal that one —* and as a native Californian I fully expect to be hanged from a yardarm in San Francisco Bay for saying so." At congressional hearings in 1954 he recounted this trip, vividly re-creating the sights and warning about the effect of a dam and reservoir on them. To drive the point home he revived the Hetch Hetchy case; once again, forty years later, a Sierra Club leader brandished photographs of what the valley had looked like in its natural state. Then he showed recent photos of the monotonous Hetch Hetchy reservoir with its ugly, stumpy shoreline, covered with mud instead of lush vegetation. "If we heed the lesson learned from the tragedy of the misplaced dam in Hetch Hetchy," said Brower, "we can prevent a far more disastrous stumble in Dinosaur National Monument."

But esthetic arguments might soar beyond the engineering mentality. Brower took care to come down to its level. The Sierra Club might include some "strange people," he allowed, but it also claimed an assistant U.S. attorney general, presidents of a railroad, a mining firm, and a drug company, a past president of the American Society of Civil Engineers, a current president of the American Society of Radio Engineers, and the incoming president of the American Chemical Society. Reclamation still insisted that the Echo Park site would lose significantly less water by evaporation than any alternate site. In his most telling presentation, Brower showed that Reclamation had made a serious miscalculation and that other sites were actually preferable in terms of water loss. With that the case for the Echo Park dam began to evaporate too. Greatly embarrassed, Secretary McKay reprimanded the head of Reclamation for his "inexcusable negligence." Stalemated in 1954, both sides resumed the struggle on the floor of Congress in the following year.

By then Echo Park had grown into the biggest conservation issue in decades, probably the biggest since Hetch Hetchy itself. With Echo Park as the goad, the movement was booming as never before. "I am amazed," said Rosalie Edge, "at the aroused spirit of conservationists and their greatly increased numbers. Something should be done to unify the thousands who constitute a seething mass opposed to the Echo Park dam." During the House debates in 1954, constituent mail ran 80 to 1 against the dam. Faced with that deluge, and discomfited by Brower's display of Reclamation's erroneous figures, supporters of the dam began to panic. A prominent eastern friend of Echo Park, Richard Pough of the conservation department of the American Museum of Natural History, was fired in the spring of 1955, apparently because of his opposition to the dam. "Certain members of the board had interests that were to benefit from the dam at Echo Park," as Pough later recounted it, "and they were incensed that an organization of which they were trustees would be credited with playing a key role in its being defeated." (Pough went on to start the American branch of the Nature Conservancy.)

Other dam opponents were not so vulnerable. Alfred Knopf, head of the distinguished publishing house, answered to nobody. After publishing Wolfe's biography of Muir in 1945, he had developed a connoisseur's interest in the parks. DeVoto helped arrange a western tour for him in 1948; Knopf came back blazing, much as DeVoto had done two years earlier. "I never saw a man get religion as fast," DeVoto marveled. In 1950, at DeVoto's suggestion, Knopf was appointed to the Interior Department's advisory board on national parks. Thereafter he made annual pilgrimages to the parks, where he was known for his electric-blue shirts and the case of vintage wine in the trunk of his car. He spent three days in Dinosaur in 1954, floating down the Green River in a raft. After following the machinations of the dam's advocates for five years, Knopf remarked acidly that he had never seen an issue with such a tendency to "turn otherwise honorable men into such God damn liars."

Knopf contributed to the cause by publishing a book, *This Is Dinosaur,* at breakneck speed. Edited by Wallace Stegner, with chapters by Knopf, Brower, and others, the volume took only three months from completion of the manuscript to publication date. Its text and pictures vividly conveyed a sense of the threatened river canyons. A copy was sent to every member of Congress, along with a folder containing an artist's idealized conception, drawn in 1913, of what the Hetch Hetchy reservoir would look like — and a photo of the actual result. Noting the "bleak expanse of dead water," Hubert Humphrey declared in the Senate: "You have only to look at the picture of Hetch Hetchy today to see how wrong were the prophets of 1913." A Senate amendment to delete Echo Park from the Colorado bill was introduced by Richard Neuberger and supported by Humphrey and their fellow Democrats Clinton Anderson, Paul Douglas, and Wayne Morse. But most western senators opposed the amendment in a bloc, and the whole bill went on to the House.

As Brant pointed out, the states with no direct interest in the Colorado project had a vastly greater proportionate membership in the House. The five-year campaign finally paid off in 1955, when Echo Park was removed from the bill. The final compromise, worked out by Zahniser, stipulated that the project as passed would not violate any national park or monument. With that change, some 120 votes in the House shifted in favor of the project — an unprecedented display of the conservation movement's political power.

In a *realpolitik* sense the movement came of age during Echo Park, and Brower was its Bismarck. The issue and the man fed off each other, a happy conjunction that threw the Sierra Club back onto the national stage. The conservationists, perhaps to their own surprise, beat down powerful federal bureaus and private commercial interests. They even influenced the cabinet politics of an unfriendly administration: when McKay resigned in the spring of 1956, he was replaced by Fred Seaton, who proved more amenable to conservation viewpoints. Usually, when the Echo Park combatants were disentangled, the trail led back to Brower. "The Sierra Club is certainly making an all-out effort on Dinosaur," Sigurd Olson of the Wilderness Society had remarked in 1954. "Thank God for Dave Brower and his boundless energy."

彩彩

In its conception the Echo Park dam served as a warning that Hetchy Hetchy might be repeated. In its defeat the dam inspired conservationists to convert their unprecedented public support into a new law that would permanently outlaw any such schemes in the future. Instead of merely reacting defensively to attacks on wilderness, after Echo Park the movement took the offensive. The shift from protective response to aggressive initiation was symptomatic of a movement suddenly stronger and more popular than ever before.

The wilderness problem came down to this: wild areas in national parks and forests were maintained by administrative whim. The Park Service in most of its jurisdiction could destroy a wilderness with roads, trails, and cabins if the people in charge at any particular time were partial to them.

In the forests, the roadless areas established at the urging of Leopold and Marshall could be wiped out by the stroke of a pen in Washington. Given the conservation style of the Eisenhower administration, that seemed a real danger. To prevent it, a bill was introduced in Congress — two months after the saving of Echo Park — to establish a national wilderness system, shielded by law from administrative caprice.

The idea had a long history. As early as 1940 Harvey Broome of the Wilderness Society, worried about the vulnerability of Marshall's wilderness areas in national forests and Indian reservations, had looked into legislative means to make them permanent. That same year Irving Brant persuaded Ickes to support a wilderness bill. Thrown into the legislative hopper, it "progressed like a glacier moving backward with the bill underneath," according to Brant's later recollection. After the war, with a growing divergence between the conservation movement and federal conservation agencies, the idea took on greater urgency. No such law seemed necessary when the conservationists and bureaucrats were cooperating, treating each other (as Joel Hildebrand said) like gentlemen. When the two sides squared off, they needed a statutory buffer more substantial than a gentleman's agreement. "I am getting slightly nauseated at the official attitude of calmness and no hurry with our wilderness slipping away under our noses," Sigurd Olson exclaimed in 1946. "When will they wake up, and get fighting mad and do something tangible to bring their declared official policies into fruition?" At an early meeting of the Natural Resources Council in 1949, a committee under Kenneth Reid presented a program calling for a legislated wilderness system. But the council declined to endorse the idea.

As Echo Park marked the arrival of David Brower, the wilderness bill precipitated Howard Zahniser into the front rank of conservationists. He started talking about such a proposal at the Sierra Club's wilderness conferences in 1949 and 1951. In Washington he broached the matter informally among the assorted conservationists who gathered for lunch at the Cosmos Club. Those club members associated with forestry interests did not greet the suggestion warmly. "What's the matter," Ovid Butler of the American Forestry Association riposted, "aren't the wilderness areas there anymore? Why save them twice?" Zahniser as an advocate was unfailingly polite and well tempered — but relentless. As he pressed his case, his forestry colleagues at the club began to perceive him differently. "Up to that time," James Craig, editor of *American Forests,* later recalled, "Howard had been known as an entertaining individual with a nice wit and a flair for amusing light verse that sometimes found its way into the club's house organ. Everyone knew he had a lively mind; not everyone realized he had depth." Zahniser drafted the wilderness bill, persuaded Hubert Humphrey and Representative John Saylor to introduce it, wrote speeches for congressional advocates, filled *Living Wilderness* with hortatory articles, saw the bill through sixty-six rewritings, traveled around the country attending nine series of hearings over eight years — and wore himself out.

As originally submitted, the bill's two most controversial provisions called for a ban on mining in national forest wildernesses (an "essential reform," according to Zahniser) and for the establishment of a supervisory council divided between private citizens and federal administrators. The first was of course strenuously resisted by the mining industry. "Certainly the Soviet Union, the enemy of the free world," said a man from Kennecott Copper, "would be delighted with the passage of such legislation." The proposed council was condemned by professional foresters and administrators as an intrusion on their domain by amateurs. One forestry spokesman called it "an attack on the integrity of the forestry profession." On these grounds both the Park Service and the Forest Service rejected the bill at first. When the council provision was removed, the Forest Service gave lukewarm support, but the Park Service, still offended by the notion that it could not protect its own wilderness areas, remained in opposition.

To meet these adversaries Zahniser plugged into the campaigning apparatus built for Echo Park. That victorious campaign had left the movement uncommonly united and flushed with success; Zahniser found support for the wilderness bill almost everywhere he turned. At an early point he went to New York for a meeting with John Baker at Audubon House. Baker agreed that an educational campaign of several years would be necessary, and with Zahniser in his office he called in the editor of *Audubon Magazine* to plan an article. Then Zahniser went to lunch with John Oakes of the New York *Times* editorial staff, who brought up the wilderness bill himself and promised his support. The Izaak Walton League endorsed the measure at its 1959 convention. Zahniser also went outside the movement proper, gathering a varied group of allies that included the national Jaycees, Karl Menninger, the General Federation of Women's Clubs, Eleanor Roosevelt, and Adlai Stevenson. Members of Congress received more mail on this issue than any other in 1962.

Most of the bill's advocates in Congress were Democrats, and the Democratic administration of John Kennedy brought the measure its first support from the executive branch. But its most obdurate foe was a Democratic congressman from Colorado, Wayne Aspinall, who used his position as chairman of the House Committee on Interior and Insular Affairs to delay the measure for years. Zahniser's efforts had built up overwhelming favorable majorities in both houses of Congress; but as the price of passage Aspinall inserted a clause guaranteeing all established mining claims and permitting new claims until 1984. With that concession the bill in the summer of 1964 sailed through the Senate, 73 to 12, and the House, 373 to 1. The ample margins meant another high watermark for the political power of the conservation movement.

The Sierra Club had doubled its membership during the struggle over Echo Park. The Wilderness Society did even better in pushing the wilderness bill, growing from seventy-six hundred members in 1956 to twenty-seven thousand in 1964. Most of the credit belonged to Zahniser, who regrettably died three months before the final vote on his cherished legislation.

۞

Seen in the light of history, Echo Park and the Wilderness Act of 1964 reversed the verdict of Hetch Hetchy. The utilitarian notion of nature for man's use gave way to a preservationist forbearance. The world, we were told, was not made for man. The rest of creation had its own purposes.

Gifford Pinchot, the utilitarian champion, continued to fare well at the hands of historians. Such writers as J. Leonard Bates, David Cushman Coyle, and Samuel Hays, in treating the origins of American conservation, still placed him at center stage and reduced Muir to a walk-on part. New scholarly biographies of Pinchot continued to appear and treat him respectfully. But his *popular* reputation ebbed steadily away. His own Forest Service was taken over, especially in the lower echelons, by foresters who took their cues from Leopold or Marshall, not the old Chief. "Nobody has a higher regard for Gifford Pinchot than I," said a director of the American Forestry Association in 1965, "but I think it is time we realized that something was deficient in his view."

By contrast Muir was still relatively ignored by historians. But he rose steadily in popular esteem as the movement returned to his viewpoint. Muir became the subject of a dozen juvenile biographies and picture books, a treatment not accorded Pinchot. Stewart Udall's bellwether book of 1963, *The Quiet Crisis,* called for "modern Muirs" to step forward and carry on his fight. To mark the fiftieth anniversary of his death in 1964, his home in Martinez was made a national historic site; a commemorative stamp was issued; and a half-million-acre tract in the High Sierra was renamed the John Muir Wilderness Area. In 1965 Muir became the second member, after TR, of the National Wildlife Federation's Conservation Hall of Fame. (Pinchot was named eighth, after Leopold, Darling, Audubon, Thoreau, and Hugh Bennett of the Soil Conservation Service.) Among conservationists and the general public, Muir had finally won his quarrel with Pinchot. "The real father of conservation," *Time* magazine explained in 1965, "is considered to be John Muir, a California naturalist."

9

The Last Endangered Species

As a nineteenth-century naturalist Muir recognized no categories in nature. He took it all in, through all his senses, and pronounced it a single pulsating harmony, held together by physical laws reflecting a cosmic design so vast that it made human intentions seem puny. In his own day scientists were chopping up their work into specialties, to learn more about ever smaller swatches of the natural world. Muir — at the cost of making new discoveries — shrugged off the tendency. He was drawn to biotic communities, not individual species. Long before the growth of ecology as a branch of biology, he was an intuitive ecologist. "When we try to pick out anything by itself," he wrote during his first summer in the Sierra, "we find that it is bound fast by a thousand invisible cords that cannot be broken to everything in the universe. I fancy I can hear a heart beating in every crystal, in every grain of sand and see a wise plan in the making and shaping and placing of every one of them. All seems to be dancing in time to divine music."

A century later the conservation movement, even without quite hearing the divine music, was ready to acknowledge that everything is indeed connected. For most of its history conservation had focused on nonhuman parts of the natural world: wildlife, natural resources, and wilderness. When humans themselves were added to the list, the circle was closed and the movement underwent a fundamental transformation. Modern man believed himself the lord of creation. Now it seemed he was only another victim of his own cleverness, merely the last endangered species. "Our new concern centers upon people," declared a speaker at the North American Wildlife Conference of 1965. "There is a new battle to be waged," *Audu-*

bon Magazine agreed two years later, "— to keep man's technology in check while promoting the welfare of man himself."

This last phase followed logically from the ecological tendencies that had been overtaking the movement for decades. In the late 1960s the ecological drift found expression in a new, all-inclusive label: "environmentalism." The term embodied the ecological imperative to study every problem in its context. Under this banner millions of people suddenly declared themselves environmentalists. The movement exploded. Conservationists had always thought of themselves as a tolerated minority — when the survival of a bird species or a river canyon was at stake. But everything changed when *human* survival became the issue. On that score, at least, humans cared deeply.

ⅩⅩ

Early in 1962 a writer named Murray Bookchin, under the pseudonym of Lewis Herber, published a book bearing the contentious title *Our Synthetic Environment.* It set forth the full range of modern technology's incidental effects: polluted air, food with pesticide residues, milk contaminated by strontium 90, intolerable living conditions in cities, water not fit to drink, diets of chemical additives, and so on. The book, although polemical in tone, offered a comprehensive, well-argued case against a technology run amok. Behind it were a noted editor, Angus Cameron, and a prestigious publisher, Alfred Knopf. But after gathering a few reviews it disappeared from sight, a failure. Bookchin later blamed a conspiracy among the political and commercial interests indicted by the book. Actually the book was probably undone by its very comprehensiveness. In casting his net so widely Bookchin took the edge off his case and gave the reading public more bad news than it cared to absorb.

Six months after the appearance of *Our Synthetic Environment,* Rachel Carson brought out her *Silent Spring.* Although she also nurtured a comprehensive suspicion of modern technology, she concentrated on a single aspect of the problem, the misuse of synthetic pesticides and insecticides — DDT in particular. The book sold a half million copies in hard cover, stayed on the New York *Times* best-seller list for thirty-one weeks, and provoked a ferocious controversy, with implications far beyond the specific matter of DDT. From this controversy the burgeoning of man-centered conservation may be dated. *Silent Spring* became one of the seminal volumes in conservation history: the *Uncle Tom's Cabin* of modern environmentalism.

Rachel Carson herself illustrated the shift from traditional conservation to a focus on human welfare. Like Olaus Murie, Howard Zahniser, and Ira Gabrielson, she came from a working career in the Fish and Wildlife Service. Her early books, squarely in the literary naturalist mode of Muir and Burroughs, were designed to reacquaint citified moderns with the outdoor world they were losing. "Most of us walk unseeing through the world," she said, "unaware alike of its beauties, its wonders, and the strange and sometimes terrible intensity of the lives that are being lived about us." Active in Audubon circles in Washington, she was a serious birder who kept a life list. At her summer home in Maine she helped organize a local chapter of the Nature Conservancy. Her initial alarm over pesticides was aroused within this framework of traditional conservation: a friend told her about songbirds killed by an aerial spraying of DDT. As she dug into the issue she found more subtle dangers to humans, and the book took on larger implications.

She had grown up in a small town outside Pittsburgh. Isolated by family circumstances (two siblings much older than she, and a protective mother), she had a conservationist's childhood. "I was rather a solitary child," she recalled, "and spent a great deal of time in woods and beside streams, learning the birds and the insects and flowers." Her mother taught her their names, and admonished her to release insects outdoors rather than kill them in the house. Rachel stayed home from school frequently, because of illnesses real or anticipated, and was tutored by her mother. After college in Pittsburgh she entered graduate school in marine zoology at Johns Hopkins. At the end of the first semester, her parents moved the two hundred miles to Baltimore to live with her. They remained with her for the rest of their lives.

As a child she had acquired her tastes in nature and literature from her mother. "Her love of life and of all living things was her outstanding quality," Carson later declared. "More than anyone else I know, she embodied Albert Schweitzer's 'reverence for life.'" As an adult, after her father's death, Carson became the breadwinner while her mother did housekeeping and typing chores, along with the incidental ego-bolstering required by any neophyte writer. This family circle was enlarged and made even more binding by the addition of nieces and a grandnephew. Because the two women lived together they seldom corresponded, and so left little record of their relationship. But the few surviving letters suggest the depth of the emotional tie. "O, darling, that is my last reading these nights," the mother wrote of one of Carson's books. "I sit in the big chair and read and read it, and think how *wonderful* that you could ever write such a book, and how beautiful it is. O, you are so wonderful and so dear, honey." By the same token, these family loves and responsibilities exacted a price in isolation from the outside world. Carson would have liked to marry, she confided to a friend, but apparently was inhibited by the familial cocoon. In dress and manner she was neat, quiet, and old-fashioned. "There was something about her of the nineteenth century," an acquaintance noted, "of the times when there really had been young ladies." She paid no attention to popular amusements, had no interest in radio or television programs.

The great passion of her life was the ocean. In childhood — before her first trip to the Atlantic — she dreamed about it and read all the sea literature she could find. As a marine zoologist she was one of the first two women to hold a professional civil service position at the Fish and Wildlife Service. Practically any piece of wild land reminded her of the ocean. At the Hawk Mountain Sanctuary she thought of the streams running down the hills, eventually into the Atlantic; in the Everglades she felt "a curious sense of the sea." Her first three books all dealt with the ocean and its environs.

These books were written at odd hours snatched from her expanding responsibilities as an editor and writer for Fish and Wildlife. She was proud of her anomalous role among her male co-workers, but she disliked certain policies of the bureau — notably in regard to predators — and chafed at the restrictions imposed on government prose. In the mid-1940s she tried to find other work (with *Reader's Digest,* the New York Zoological Society, National Audubon), but nothing turned up. In 1947, with her fortieth birthday approaching, she felt trapped by her job and frustrated in her literary career. "I write nothing," she dolefully told a friend, "and am fast coming to feel that I have lost what it takes to produce a companion to that first and solitary book. No, my life isn't at all well ordered and I don't know where I'm going!" The mood passed. Associates at work noticed her distinctive tread coming down the hall: direct, forceful, no hesitation. In a few years the enormous popularity of *The Sea Around Us,* published in 1951, let her quit her job and become at last a full-time writer.

Running through that book's plangent sea prose was a subtle line of tension. The first chapter ended with a rebuke to the technological presumption of modern man: "He cannot control or change the ocean as, in his brief tenancy of earth, he has subdued and plundered the continents. In the artificial world of his cities and towns, he often forgets the true nature of his planet and the long vistas of its history." The ocean appealed to her precisely because it seemed beyond man's tampering. Like Howard Zahniser, she had been shaken by the doomsday implications of the Atomic Age. Recoiling from the grim possibilities, believing that humans should address the universe with more humility, she began to think in increasingly ecological terms. In the course of writing *The Edge of the Sea* in the early 1950s, she recast the book from a series of individual life histories of various species to a study of three different kinds of living communities. She set forth the delicate interdependencies in each, and the looming danger of human interference.

As a conservationist in the 1950s Carson was furious over Douglas McKay's depredations on her Fish and Wildlife Service: "a politically minded administration returns us to the dark ages of unrestrained exploitation and destruction." She worked for the Democrats in the 1956 campaign, though politics did not appeal to her, and in subsequent years supported the wilderness bill and antipollution legislation. The focus of her work shifted from nature's wonders to man's offenses. Even the impregnable ocean was endangered by the dumping of radioactive wastes — "the most dangerous materials," she said, "that have ever existed in all the earth's history."

In this mood she turned to the question of pesticides. These synthetic agents — principally chlorinated hydrocarbons and organic phosphates — had first been widely applied during World War II. After DDT was credited with preventing a typhus epidemic in Italy, one enthusiast called it, with unconscious irony, "the atomic bomb of the insect world." Its toxicity and persistence caused immediate misgivings among entomologists and conservationists. Edwin Way Teale published an early warning in *Nature Magazine* in March 1945. The Audubon Society launched a full campaign, with thirty articles and editorials on the issue in *Audubon Magazine* between 1945 and 1962. "The damaging possibilities of the broadcasting of DDT outdoors call for restraint and utmost caution in its use," John Baker declared. "Let us not open another Pandora's box." Carl Buchheister likened the widespread use of pesticides to "handing a loaded .45 automatic to a child and telling him to run out and play."

Such statements, however prescient in retrospect, had no discernible effect. From 1947 to 1960 the manufacture of DDT and its even more toxic relatives increased by 500 percent. Until 1954 they could be marketed without prior testing of their toxic power. Even when tests were done, they were carried out in laboratories, not in biotic communities; generally they dealt only with immediate toxicity and involved no wild species, no birds or fishes. Test results were passed along by the manufacturer to the Agriculture Department, with its bias in favor of human use. The Fish and Wildlife Service had no part in the process, and the accumulating examples of unintended damage to wildlife were sloughed off. Despite these warnings the Agriculture Department went ahead with two pesticide fiascos in the late 1950s, directed against gypsy moths in the Northeast and the fire ant in the South. Both programs bludgeoned innocent plants and wildlife while having no important effect on the targeted species. The whole pesticide problem derived not from a lack of scientific knowledge but from a chronic failure of the federal regulatory process.

Carson had been worried about DDT for a long time; as early as 1945, she proposed a warning article to *Reader's Digest*. By 1958 she saw the matter as only one aspect of the larger issue of environmental pollution from domestic sewage, nuclear fallout, and chemical and radioactive wastes. She decided to attack the entire deluge of pollutants by way of the single, dramatic issue of pesticides. She postponed her other writing commitments and began the research for a book quite unlike anything she had previously written. She corresponded with experts at the Audubon Society and with her old mentor Clarence Cottam, formerly of the Fish and Wildlife Service. Conscious of the reception awaiting her, she kept the project secret as long as possible so as to avoid what she elliptically called "the extremely powerful pressures that can be applied."

The working title was "Man Against the Earth." Gradually she sensed the extent to which man's war against the environment ricocheted against himself; the title could as well have been "Man Against Man." Her main contribution to the ongoing discussion of pesticides was to point out the *human* dangers. With that significant addition, conservation started to evolve into environmentalism. Aside from their toxicity, it appeared that pesticides had genetic and carcinogenic implications as well. "At one point I thought the evidence rather shaky," she told a colleague in December 1959; "now I find it is extremely strong. . . . Now that I have tabulated all the pesticidal chemicals that disturb cytochrome oxidase, a great light is breaking in my mind." She decided to devote a chapter to the cancer hazards. A few months later, by a cruel coincidence, a lump in her breast was diagnosed as malignant. The operation was not fully successful.

She was two years into the book. In the interim her mother had died, leaving to her the care of the young grandnephew. Aside from her cancer therapy, Carson was afflicted with a malevolent range of medical problems that included sinus infections, an underactive thyroid gland, occasional diverticulitis, and a duodenal ulcer. But she got on with the book. "Somehow I have no wish to read of my ailments in literary gossip columns," she joked to a friend. "Too much comfort to the chemical companies!" Early in 1962 she sent the completed manuscript to William Shawn of the *New Yorker* for the preparation of prepublication excerpts that were to appear in the magazine. The most respected of editors, he responded enthusiastically. "I knew from his reaction that my message would get across," she noted. After putting her ward to bed she sat down and listened to the Beethoven violin concerto. "And suddenly the tension of four years was broken and I let the tears come. . . . The thoughts of all the birds and other creatures and all the loveliness that is in nature came to me with such a surge of deep happiness, that now I had done what I could — I had been able to complete it."

The book, retitled *Silent Spring,* was organized around recurrent themes: a parallel between nuclear radiation and chemical pollutants, pesticides as a symptom of several modern fallacies, and the need to replace clumsy chemical controls with selective biological and natural alternatives. Pesticides could still be used under certain conditions, given proper testing and safeguards, she conceded — but only with due regard for the ecological principle of biotic diversity. The engineering mentality sacrificed diversity, wiping out any nearby species in the interest of the task at hand. Carson, following the work of the ecologist Charles Elton, argued that diversity was the key to biological health. It was imperiled by the human conceit that sorted out wild species according to their human uses and eliminated the "bad" ones. At the end of the book she summarized her case in terms that recalled Muir's central insight: "The 'control of nature' is a phrase conceived in arrogance, born of the Neanderthal age of biology and philosophy, when it was supposed that nature exists for the convenience of man."

Carson also placed the issue in a political context by describing the apparent collusion between universities and chemical companies. (The point suggested a conservationist's variation on the "military-industrial complex" that Eisenhower had warned of in his farewell address in 1960.) Pure science, Carson argued, had been corrupted into a counterfeit version intent only on corporate profits. The chemical industry gave money to colleges and professional groups for research on chemical pesticides; no comparable funds were available for biological control studies. Thus the puzzling advocacy of pesticides by outstanding entomologists who should have known better. "Inquiry into the background of some of these men," she noted, "reveals that their entire research program is supported by the chemical industry. Their professional prestige, sometimes their very jobs depend on the perpetuation of chemical methods. Can we then expect them to bite the hand that literally feeds them?" Ultimately, therefore, the pesticide fallacy was no accident. Derived initially from the modern notion of conquering nature, it was then reinforced by a cozy arrangement between business and academia.

She bearded the lion in its den, and the beast growled. A chemical trade group spent $250,000 to demonstrate that Carson was "a hysterical fool." Her publisher, Houghton Mifflin, was warned that sinister influences were attacking the chemical industry in order to bring American food production down to parity with that of the Communists. An attorney for the Velsicol Chemical Corporation threatened *Audubon Magazine* with court action if it printed excerpts from the book. "I thought she was a spinster," a federal pest controller remarked. "What's she so worried about genetics for?" CBS News prepared a TV documentary on the controversy; three sponsors withdrew at the last minute, but the show went on.

Even among conservationists, *Silent Spring* started many arguments. The journal of the National Wildlife Federation ran a negative review (Carson blamed the commercial sporting interests behind the federation). In the Sierra Club, members with a chemical background generally disliked the book. Joel Hildebrand, a chemistry professor, did not read *Silent Spring* but dismissed it as "not a scientific book." Thomas Jukes, a life member and the founder of the New York chapter, eventually quit the club over the issue because, as a chemist, he equated the rejection of pesticides with the rejection of his profession. David Brower both read the book and agreed with it. After he printed an alarmed article by Clarence Cottam in the *Bulletin,* a club member employed in the agricultural chemical industry replied, "I cannot help viewing this type article with some alarm" — it was "at the best negative and at the worst possibly socialistic."

But conservationists without a professional ax to grind generally embraced *Silent Spring.* In the fall of 1963, on a trip to San Francisco, Carson met Brower and others in the Sierra Club. Brower took her on a tour of Muir Woods. That same year, the National Wildlife Federation, belying her suspicions, presented her with its first Conservationist of the Year Award. She was also the first woman to receive the Audubon Society's highest medal. "A prophet is not always honored in his own country," she said at the ceremony, "but the National Audubon Society *is* my country — I belong to it — and from its own strength and devotion to the cause of conservation I have drawn strength and inspiration."

The public debate over pesticides raged on for years. Eventually all twelve of the most toxic agents described in *Silent Spring* were banned or restricted. The Toxic Substances Act of 1976 tightened federal controls, correcting many of the abuses that Carson had described. She did for pesticides what DeVoto had done for the land-grab: by using the leverage of her fame, she brought the issue to a general audience, not just a small band of conservationists. More broadly, she opened up the whole subject of environmental pollution — including its philosophical and political aspects. *"Silent Spring* was really the beginning," an environmentalist declared in 1973. "It showed for the first time, and on a grand scale, that a meticulously researched and lucidly written account of a faulty technology could arouse the public to demand a more rational approach to problems of the environment."

Silent Spring was her last book. "I keep thinking," she told a friend, "— if only I could have reached this point ten years ago! Now, when there is the opportunity to do so much, my body falters, and I know there is little time left." She died at the age of fifty-six in the spring of 1964. She left her estate to her family, the Sierra Club, and the Nature Conservancy.

※※

Carson's great insight was to move from the particular to the general by revealing chemical blunderbusses as only a symptom of the modern syndrome. Far from an incidental mistake, they vividly revealed structural flaws in American politics and technology. Carson was by no means the first conservationist to address the pollution issue. Previously, aspects of the problem had been attacked in piecemeal fashion. But Carson pulled the threads together and brought them to public attention.

Water pollution had a long history as a conservation issue. The nation's waterways had been befouled ever since the late 1800s, when they had begun to receive the by-products of industrialization and indoor plumbing. Protests were first raised by sportsmen who noticed a change in the fishing. "We are a water drinking people," said George Bird Grinnell in 1900, "and we are allowing every brook to be defiled." A few years later a sportsmen's group in Maryland, concerned about fewer bass in the Potomac, traced the matter to wood-pulp shavings from mills at Harpers Ferry. Birders were also concerned about waterfowl killed by oil slicks from wrecks at sea.

The Izaak Walton League was the first conservation group to campaign against water pollution with some persistence. "The old swimming hole," Will Dilg declared at the outset, "of those of us with a touch of gray in our hair is now, ten to one, polluted and the boy of today is apt to be stricken with typhoid who swims in it. Pollution is the big thing that this mighty national crusade has got to battle." In 1926 the league's twenty-seven hundred chapters were asked by President Coolidge, a fisherman, to take samples of local streams and have them analyzed. The results were chastening: even at that early point, 85 percent of the inland waters were found to be polluted. In many parts of the country Waltonians encouraged the construction of modern sewage plants. Occasionally they also prevailed on offending industries to mend their ways.

On a national level the problem was to enforce existing statutes. The Rivers and Harbors Act of 1899 prohibited the dumping of any nonliquid refuse matter into navigable waterways. But as administered by the Army Engineers the law was a dead letter. When Senator Augustine Lonergan of Connecticut made inquiries in 1933, the Army reported back: "This department is not advised that sewage laden with quantities of solid matter has been and is being discharged into the navigable waters of New York and Connecticut. . . . The preservation of the purity of the water . . . more properly belongs to the States for regulation under their police powers." In other words, pass the buck. Lonergan sponsored a conference of some forty conservationists on the issue in Washington in December 1934. From this meeting eventually came a House resolution asking the Army to report on how many federal installations were discharging raw sewage into waterways. The chief of the Engineers came up with the extraordinary finding that of 2,486 federal facilities, only 103 needed corrective measures; therefore no further legislation was called for. Lonergan had previously suggested using the NRA codes, as urged by the Walton League, to enforce proper disposal of industrial wastes. But the White House was not agreeable.

So Lonergan, with support from the Waltonians and the American Nature Association, filed a new bill with real enforcement provisions. Kenneth Reid of the Walton League took his case to the Audubon annual meeting in 1936. Describing water pollution as the "result of Man's utterly selfish and short-sighted business economy," he asked for help with the Lonergan bill. John Baker did write some letters but, given his wariness of jeopardizing Audubon's tax status by too much lobbying, left most of the work to the Waltonians.

The bill in different versions almost passed three times between 1936 and 1940. "Water has been the orphan stepchild of the entire conservation picture," Reid told FDR, "and our polluted streams have been a national disgrace for many years." Since water flowed downhill with a fine disregard for human political boundaries, it seemed self-evident to Reid that the only solution was federal control of the watershed. In his advocacy he impressed Roosevelt, as he later impressed DeVoto and Edge. FDR offered him a job as head of the Bureau of Fisheries (which incidentally would have made him Rachel Carson's boss). But he was not interested, and Roosevelt gave little help to the Lonergan bill. When pressured, the White House passed the matter along to the PWA or its National Resources Committee. Harold Ickes later got behind the bill but it was still stalled when World War II came.

Aside from its philosophical effect on the minds of many conservationists, the war acted as a conservation watershed by fomenting new industrial processes that speeded up environmental deterioration. Under wartime pressures, unapplied discoveries in physics and chemistry were precipitately converted into usable technologies with no time for testing their incidental effects. DDT was the classic example among many others. In addition, war shortages forced the concoction of new synthetic materials and wider use of available synthetics: high-phosphate detergents instead of soap, synthetic fibers for cotton and wool, aluminum and plastic for steel and lumber, inorganic fertilizers for organic varieties. All these materials took more energy — especially oil — to produce, and they left behind wastes of great durability. In the decades after the war, the production of all these unprecedentedly dirty innovations increased exponentially. With the economy itself in a postwar boom, the American industrial system embarked on an orgy of pollution.

The Walton League resumed its crusade for federal enforcement of clean water. An experimental law, passed in 1948, again was not enforced. A stronger law in 1956 encouraged state programs by offering limited funds for construction and research; it was pushed through by Representative John Blatnik of Minnesota, a state with many Waltonians. Another bill in 1960 would have doubled these federal grants. Eisenhower vetoed it: "Water pollution is a uniquely local blight," he said. The federal involvement in this local blight was administered from a tiny office within HEW. The delayed effect of the efficient pollutants arising from the war would belatedly come to public attention in the environmental crisis of the late 1960s.

Air pollution, for example, crept slowly into public awareness. It had long been more or less tolerated as a by-product of the Industrial Revolution. Occasional incidents — like the temperature inversion that combined with factory smoke to kill fourteen people in Donora, Pennsylvania, in 1950 — provoked momentary concern that then blew away with the smoke. But the new synthetic processes spewed forth more dangerous debris into the air. Even more ominously, automobiles — running on leaded fuels at higher compression, on vast new highways and interstate networks — replaced factories as the main source of air pollution. A new phenomenon, smog, was first noticed in Los Angeles in 1943 and by 1957 had been authoritatively traced to car exhausts. Smog was not restricted to factory towns; it accompanied the ubiquitous automobile. After the war,

David Brower had built a home in the sylvan hills behind Berkeley. "We built here for the view of San Francisco Bay and its amazing setting," he wrote in 1956, his eyes smarting. "But today there is no beautiful view; there is hideous smog, a sea of it around us. 'It can't happen here,' we were saying just three years ago. Well here it is." Three years later the Surgeon General's office drew a connection between air pollution and lung cancer. In the year of *Silent Spring*'s publication, the U.S. Public Health Service called a national conference on the problem.

By the late 1960s, even among traditional conservationists these new issues were rivaling the old concerns. A poll commissioned by the National Wildlife Federation in 1969 found the public most worried about air pollution, water pollution, and pesticides; open spaces and wildlife came last. "Today," Joseph Wood Krutch noted, "concern over such amenities seems to some almost frivolous since we realize, as only a decade ago we did not, that there are more desperate threats and problems." A Sierra Club spokesman agreed: "The state of the environment has so deteriorated that all the natural resources won't be worth a tinker's dam if we all suffocate in our own wastes." Postwar technology had replaced open windows with air conditioning, returnable bottles with disposables, streetcars with buses, trains with cars and planes: all at some cost to the environment. Now the debts were coming due.

The most perceptive analyst of this mess was Barry Commoner, a biology professor at Washington University in St. Louis. Building on Carson's insights, he argued that the environmental crisis — insofar as it involved pollution — derived not from growth or affluence or overpopulation, but essentially from a flawed technology. Where Carson traced this technology to an obsolete philosophy of conquering nature, Commoner blamed the reductionist tendency of modern science and (in particular) the American economic system that valued private profits over social benefits. In taking these positions Commoner stirred up sharp debates among environmentalists. But even his adversaries in these quarrels had to acknowledge his gift for lucid, accessible exposition of esoteric scientific matters. Though often called an ecologist, he functioned more as a superb popularizer, shuttling back and forth between the arcane world of professional science and his general reading public. To the world at large he was the pollution man.

Commoner's background rebutted those polluters who took refuge in calling environmentalism an upper-class diversion. The son of Russian immigrants, he grew up poor in Brooklyn; his father worked as a tailor. With education as his outlet, he made his way to the Upper West Side of

Manhattan. "In the 1930s," he recalled, "it was not simple for a Jewish boy from Brooklyn to get into Columbia." From there he went on to Harvard for graduate work and received his doctorate at the age of twenty-three. Two episodes during his wartime naval duty foreshadowed his future career. Involved with DDT experiments against insect-borne diseases, he was startled by their unexpected effects on fish and reptile populations. Just after the war, he was assigned to congressional duty for the Navy, and helped defeat a bill that would have given the control of nuclear development to the Pentagon.

As it turned out, the resulting civilian control under the Atomic Energy Commission had its own limitations. The AEC carried out dual and contradictory roles: regulating nuclear energy and setting safety standards, but also promoting its development by private enterprise. Usually the AEC tilted toward promotion, not regulation, as hazards were consistently underestimated. In 1953 Troy, New York, was showered with radioactive fallout from atomic bomb tests in Nevada. The incident, explained as the capricious result of unanticipated currents in the stratosphere, spurred Commoner to look into the problem further. "I was shocked to learn that nuclear radiation is never harmless, to the ecosystem or to man," he said later. "It was the AEC that turned me into an ecologist." With others in St. Louis he founded the Committee for Nuclear Information in 1958.

Concurrently, he was disturbed by developments in his professional field of cellular biology. The most advanced research, borrowing concepts from physics and chemistry, was breaking the cell into its component parts, isolating each for the study of its particular function. The Watson–Crick model of DNA carried the trend to the point of describing the origins of life in chemical terms. Intuitively, indeed esthetically, Commoner disliked this trend and preferred the classical approach of standing back far enough to see the whole living unit. Almost alone among legitimate biologists, Commoner refused to accept the DNA model. To him it was symptomatic of the same cast of mind that could carry on bomb tests without considering their effect on the whole biological community. Pulled by his deepening environmental concern and pushed by isolation from his own colleagues in biology, he shifted his focus 180 degrees: from the smallest units of life to the largest. "We were learning more and more about smaller and smaller parts of the cell," he said, "while terribly important things were happening out there in nature about which we were totally ignorant."

It was too easy to remain ignorant: that was the great danger. As Commoner pointed out, earlier environmental offenses at least had the advantage of high visibility. No one could miss a denuded forest or the Dust

Bowl. But contemporary perils were more insidious. Carcinogens in the air, strontium 90 in milk, and synthetic by-products in water could easily be overlooked. Undetected by the normal senses, their effects might not surface for decades. Since knowledge of these effects was peculiar to scientists, it became their responsibility to spread the news. "A new conservation movement is needed to preserve life itself," Commoner declared in 1966. His group in St. Louis, prompted originally by the AEC's derelictions, evolved into an environmental organization. The changing name of its journal reflected this evolution: *Nuclear Information,* then *Scientist and Citizen* (1964), and finally *Environment* (1969).

Commoner's strength lay in diagnosis. Prognosis and remedial action fell to others. Historically, conservation had relied on the traditional techniques of American pressure groups: education, publicity, letter writing, and lobbying, all with the goals of converting the heathen and redeeming past sins. With souls *and* bodies at stake, a new and less genteel slogan was heard: *Sue the Bastards.* Environmental lawsuits arose as an aspect of public interest litigation, dependent on the rejection of the old doctrine of sovereign immunity. The breakthrough came in 1965, when the Sierra Club joined in a suit to protect Storm King Mountain in New York State from a power project; the court broke precedent by recognizing the club's non-economic interest in the case. A year later an attorney on Long Island, Victor Yannacone, filed a class action suit to prevent an aerial spraying of DDT. The suit brought Yannacone together with Charles Wurster and other scientists at the State University campus in Stony Brook. This union of legal and scientific minds, organized formally as the Environmental Defense Fund in 1967, raised environmental litigation to an art form. In a few years the EDF was joined by the Natural Resources Defense Council and the Sierra Club Legal Defense Fund.

More direct than education, often quicker than legislation, lawsuits offered conservationists a new tool. "A court of equity is the *only* place to take effective action against polluters," said Yannacone, who was not given to understatement. "Only in a courtroom can a scientist present his evidence, free from harassment by politicians. And only in a courtroom can bureaucratic hogwash be tested in the crucible of cross-examination." Yannacone came from a background in civil rights and the labor movement. Citing examples from these fields of lawsuits leading to overdue legislation, he urged the same course on environmentalists; he dismissed polite letters to the editor as worthless. Instead, he insisted that "the right to a salubrious environment" was one of the unenumerated rights guaranteed by the Ninth Amendment and protected by the due process and equal protection clauses of the Fifth and Fourteenth amendments. In other words, pollution was unconstitutional.

Judges might argue the point, but the new field of environmental law became a growth industry, fueled by platoons of idealistic young law school graduates. By 1976 the two largest environmental law firms in the country had a combined budget of $3.5 million. With the National Environmental Policy Act of 1970 as the Magna Carta, hundreds of suits were brought to compel industries to submit environmental-impact statements — and then to stick by them. By suing the bastards, private citizens gained a mechanism that let them operate on a parity with government agencies. Injunctions could override administrative decisions and sometimes achieve greater permanence. But they had their own limits. "No lawsuit will, *ultimately,* win any conservation issue," James Moorman of the Sierra Club Legal Defense Fund pointed out. "We must never forget that Congress or the state legislatures can always overrule hard-won court victories." Injunctions might buy time and ventilate the issues, but in the long run public opinion still had the final say.

The most effective single influence in mobilizing public opinion against pollution was Ralph Nader, a movement unto himself. He struck a third major theme in analyzing the roots of the problem. Carson had grounded her critique in science, Commoner in economics. To Nader it was essentially a political issue: the free enterprise system was sound, merely corrupted by big corporations against the best interests of a supine public. If the people rose up and smote the corporations, said Nader, they would gain the environment they deserved. "The question is not whether we can build a car that won't pollute the air," Nader said in 1967; "the question is whether we can overcome the resistance of the auto industry and the oil industry to get it built." Toward that end — and for his proliferating other causes, most of which involved the protection of humans from one environmental ill or another — he set up public-interest firms to seek legislation and bring the corporations to rein.

Nader resembled Commoner in his immigrant origins and in the brush with DDT that provided his environmental baptism. (As a junior at Princeton in 1955, Nader wrote a letter to the campus newspaper protesting the killing of songbirds by the DDT aimed at Dutch elm disease.) But ideologically the two men could not have differed more. To Commoner pollution was the natural expression of the free economy. To Nader pollution was its denial. Most Americans, when they thought about it, agreed with Nader. With his legendary asceticism — which put him beyond the corruptions of ordinary mortals — and with his hollow-eyed charisma, he was perhaps the most influential American in private life. He set about his announced task of the qualitative reform of the Industrial Revolution. "This country is on fire," he warned in *National Wildlife* in 1971. "It just isn't the visible form. This is the first society in history that has the capability to destroy itself domestically, inadvertently."

What united all these new crusaders against pollution, despite their varied diagnoses of the problems, was a certain distaste for the traditional conservation movement. It was hard to imagine Nader even stepping outdoors; he once lamented that more people were drawn to bird watching than to Congress watching. Commoner likewise had little interest in the outdoor pastimes of most conservationists. Disapproving of "a passive admiration of nature," he made his priorities clear: "I happen to think that people are more important than whooping cranes." Charles Wurster of the Environmental Defense Fund, although a birder himself, indicted conservationists for "talking to themselves in a closed eco-system. They are legally weak, scientifically naive and politically impotent. They lack an offense." Which, arguments aside, could never be said of the EDF.

The conservation movement, after dealing with pollution for years in its own way, no doubt had mixed feelings about these upstarts. The allies were welcome; but they seemed to lack a proper deference to their elders in the struggle. "I think," said Brower, "there needs to be more consultation with some people who are older and stuffier." "Wildlife people," countered an EDF man, "have some very impractical ideas." In general these two wings of the fight against pollution held to their respective biases and spoke to different constituencies, and stayed out of each other's way.

⚶⚶

An even graver problem, the related issues of population growth and resource depletion, eventually displaced pollution as the heart of man-centered environmentalism. No matter how its origins were traced, pollution at least held out the possibility of a technological fix. No one doubted that, given the proper nudges, modern industry *could* clean up the air and water and dispose of wastes more tidily. But the population/resource nexus seemed less manageable. Technology in the form of medical care, hygiene, and better diet had vastly lowered the death rate; thus more people. At the same time, indeed as part of the same process, technology had sucked up ever greater quantities of the world's nonrenewable resources, both in total amounts and on a per capita basis, to provide for all those people; thus resource depletion. "Contemporary conservation thinking as distinguished from that of a generation ago," DeVoto observed in 1948, "tends to focus on the implications of these diverging curves."

This contradiction bore only a superficial resemblance to the worries that had animated resource conservationists of the Pinchot era. They had been preoccupied with half the nexus, resources — in particular trees, water, and soil, all of which as renewables could respond and thrive given better management and federal regulation. For instance, the larger private lumber companies (which could afford to think in the long term) turned from mining trees to planting them. As concern over renewables diminished, the new industrial processes spawned by World War II put spiraling demands on nonrenewables. In the decades after the war, Americans used 5.4 percent more oil each year, pouring it into every major industry, in many instances replacing renewable products with oil-derived synthetics.

For a few years after the war conservationists were clairvoyantly agitated over these tendencies. Two widely read books, both published in 1948, summarized the mood. *Our Plundered Planet,* by Fairfield Osborn, Jr., focused in a Pinchot spirit on renewables but added overpopulation to the equation. The book acquired its sense of urgency from the wartime shortages of wood and food, with their residual effect on postwar attitudes toward prudent management. In the land-grab spirit, peacetime industry apparently intended to extend the emergency precedents for superheated consumption. Thus the nation's forests, grasslands, and water sources were endangered. "The tide of the earth's population is rising, the reservoir of the earth's living resources is falling," said Osborn. "There is only one solution: Man must recognize the necessity of cooperating with nature." But with this reorientation, man might save himself; soil depletion and erosion could be corrected. Osborn remained hopeful despite himself.

The second book, William Vogt's *Road to Survival,* sounded a much darker theme: "The Day of Judgment is at hand." Strident in tone and laced with black humor, the book represented a kind of revenge for its author. After leading his abortive revolt against John Baker at Audubon headquarters in 1939, he had remained outside the inner circles of conservation leadership. During the war, he had taken a job with the conservation section of the Pan American Union. As he monitored wartime conditions in Latin America, the implacable mixture of hopeless poverty, large families, and the Catholic Church's resistance to birth control turned him into a neo-Malthusian. He launched a solitary crusade to persuade ecologists to include human populations in their thinking. In 1946, while making a survey of Mexican wildlife, Vogt convinced one of Aldo Leopold's sons of the urgency of the problem. But when Starker Leopold entered graduate school at Berkeley, he encountered massive skepticism: "I was the only one on this campus who would stand up and defend Bill Vogt and his ideas."

Such resistance made the success of *Road to Survival* all the more remarkable. It became the best-selling conservation book before *Silent Spring*. With the postwar baby boom emitting its first squalls, Vogt declared the United States overpopulated at 147 million inhabitants. With the nation emerging from two decades of emergency austerities, Vogt indicted the American ethos as luxurious, self-indulgent, and doomed to extinction. With the relaxation of economic controls imposed by the war, Vogt deplored the effects of free competition and the profit motive on the health of the land. Few books have ever sold so well while decrying the major currents of their time. To ram home his generalizations, Vogt imperturbably picked on the bellwether of American industry, the automobile. Engines were too big and wasteful, he said, and cars were driven at speeds dangerously, pointlessly high. "Our tensions find outlet in racing motors," said Vogt. "We drive them hundreds of millions of miles a year in pursuit of futility." The approaching petroleum famine, inevitable but unacknowledged, merely symbolized the mindless loss of purpose that defined the modern syndrome. "We need a revolution," Vogt concluded, "in Kropotkin's sense of a profound change of fundamental ideas."

Bernard DeVoto was so impressed by the book that he appointed himself its literary publicist. "I am more steamed up about it than I can remember having been about any book for years," he exclaimed. In a conversation with Walter Lippmann, DeVoto plugged the book nonstop for half an hour. For months he made himself a pest about it and helped ensure its success. The publicity sold the book; and, incidentally, put Vogt's job at the Pan American Union in jeopardy. "Whether or not the R.C. Church will swing into action," Vogt confided to DeVoto, "and whether or not the Union would be able to withstand pressure from that quarter, we shall have to wait and see." In 1949 Vogt resigned when he was told to stop writing magazine articles. He then went on to a new career as the national director of Planned Parenthood.

The Malthusian specters raised by *Road to Survival* were stamped with the imprimatur of a government commission in 1952. A panel chaired by William Paley of CBS agreed with Vogt that the United States was running out of resources and that no adequate replacements were in sight. Even *Time* magazine, which had rejected *Road to Survival,* acquiesced in the Paley report: "The fat years of the U.S. have ended." With that pronouncement the Vogt school of thought reached its apogee. Over the next few years, new books in the Vogt spirit by Samuel Ordway and Harrison Brown were reviewed and excerpted in conservation journals, but stirred little response from the general public. Most conservationists themselves turned to more pressing issues, such as Echo Park or pesticides. In 1956, only eight years after *Road to Survival* and four years after the Paley report, David Brower practically apologized for doubting the wisdom of economic expansion: "There is not yet much embarassment about the daily homage to the great god Growth, so secure in his chrome-plated niche. This very statement, if it were to be widely read, would probably cause widespread resentment."

What had happened? Partly a change in the political milieu, to the Rotarian sensibility of the Eisenhower administration. Partly an expansion in the overseas operations of American capitalism; as early as 1955, the United States was consuming half of the world's nonrenewable resources. Partly just dumb luck, as a cycle of warm weather yielded a string of bumper crops. In any case, Vogt's gloomiest forecasts seemed premature. Except for an occasional recession, the country enjoyed general prosperity in the 1950s. A disciple of Vogt like Brower had to contend with the general human tendency of preferring good news to bad — and the specifically modern tendency to be cut off from history, either past or future. "When I personally get to speculating about this problem of conservation," Eisenhower said at a resources conference in 1954, "and let my mind run on into the future, I get into such an intricate problem that I am forced back, willy-nilly, to the immediate problem of the day, and that is: What do we do now in order that we may get to the next step?"

The varied history of the organization Resources for the Future suggested the resilience of the cornucopia tradition. The group — which operated in the twilight world ringed and influenced by business, government, labor, and the foundations — was launched in a surge of concern following the Paley report. Conceived in meetings among Osborn, Horace Albright, and other New York conservationists, RFF started up with an initial grant of $100,000 from the Ford Foundation, which charged that the group devise a rational plan for resource consumption. But almost at once, Eisenhower's aide Sherman Adams objected to the presence of idealists and New Dealers; new leaders were installed. The group's conservation edge was further dulled by the addition of a broadly based Council of Sponsors, which included chambers of commerce and trade associations. This catholic approach shook loose more Ford money — $3.4 million for the first five years — but required a degree of blandness sufficient to please all constituents. RFF became a richly endowed clearinghouse, officially constrained from recommending policy but actually veering toward positions pleasing to the business community. In 1963 RFF came out with a massive report, five years in the making, that in effect refuted the Paley commission by citing new discoveries of oil and iron, new methods for extracting oil from shale and tar sands, improved nuclear technologies, and a more favorable reappraisal of the timber supply. "There is little danger," said the president of RFF in 1965, "of any general running out of resources before the end of this century, and probably for some time thereafter."

Confronted by such "expert" testimony, conservationists could still bring up the population half of the population/resource nexus. As social movements, population control and conservation shared parallel histories, intersecting at many points over the years. Earlier in the century, both had embraced the pseudoscience of eugenics, with its zeal for protecting native populations — human and otherwise — from the assaults of other ethnic groups. After World War II the birth control movement retained an unlovely hint of WASPy condescension. Vogt had approved H. L. Mencken's suggestion of sterilization bonuses: "Since such a bonus would appeal primarily to the world's shiftless, it would probably have a favorable selective influence." From the 1950s on, though, conservationists with an interest in population control typically shifted their rationale from eugenics to wilderness protection. Instead of defending urban areas against selected "inferior" races, they hoped to protect wild areas from *all* groups of marauding humans. Accordingly, within the conservation movement population issues were raised most persistently by those groups with a special interest in wilderness. "Our movement becomes all the more critical with the growth of the population," said Harvey Broome of the Wilderness Society in 1957. "The clash between the way man lives and the basic environment of the wilderness grows sharper. . . . We must not become so engrossed in fights that we lose sight of this major responsibility."

No less than Eisenhower, conservationists were inclined to let immediate issues displace the perplexities of long-range thinking. The Sierra Club under Brower managed to juggle the two perspectives more successfully than other groups. At its Wilderness Conference of 1959, a zoologist from UCLA, Raymond Cowles, read a controversial paper arguing the need for population control on ecological grounds. Later that year Starker Leopold declared in the *Sierra Club Bulletin* that the population problem transcended all other conservation questions; in the same issue his brother Luna agreed: "the population issue is the basic problem in conservation." At the Wilderness Conference of 1965, one speaker called for an enforced limit of two children per family. The club that year adopted a policy statement indicting overpopulation for threatening wilderness and wildlife while damaging the general quality of life. "We feel that you don't have a conservation policy unless you have a population policy," Brower explained in 1966. "There's no point in ignoring the root of our troubles."

Meanwhile conservation was turning into environmentalism, spurred on mainly by the pollution issue. To Paul Ehrlich, a biology professor at Stanford, this focus on pollution seemed to be missing the point. As an entomologist he appreciated the dangers of misused chemicals; in his first act of environmental concern he had protested the Agriculture Department's fire ant program in 1957. But his interest in population went back even further. During his college days in the early 1950s, *Road to Survival* had exerted "a major influence" on his thinking. Ten years later he started giving informal talks before student groups about various social problems of the day. A population speech at the Commonwealth Club in San Francisco in 1967 launched him on a new career. "David Brower of the Sierra Club heard me," Ehrlich recalled, "and asked me to write a short book for them. And my life was destroyed from then on." *The Population Bomb,* issued in paperback by Ballantine and the Sierra Club, sold three million copies over the next decade. It was the best-selling conservation book ever. Population and its corollary of resource depletion were routinely injected into environmental discussions. Ehrlich became the movement's most familiar media star.

"The battle to feed all of humanity is over," his book announced. "At this late date nothing can prevent a substantial increase in the world death rate." The only palliative — since no solution existed — was rigid birth control, "hopefully through a system of incentives and penalties, but by compulsion if voluntary methods fail." The reference to compulsion provoked uncomfortable memories of the eugenicists, as did Ehrlich's critique of Catholic politicians. But he went on to lay greater blame on America's mindless enthusiasm for economic growthmanship. And while he traced environmental ills in the short run to too many people, he concluded by reversing the causal relationship: "In the long view the progressive deterioration of our environment may cause more death and misery than any conceivable food-population gap." Thus the book was curiously double-edged, presenting overpopulation as both catalyst and symptom of larger environmental crises. However muddled the book's message, no one could mistake its apocalyptic tone. In his endless round of lectures, interviews, and TV appearances, Ehrlich — with his thundercloud visage and deeply resonant voice — seemed the very personification of the Voice of Doom.

"If we don't get action by the 1972 election," he said in 1970, "it'll be too late; and if we *do* get it then, I won't be needed anymore, so I can go back to doing what I like."

As it happened, neither alternative took place. Instead, environmentalists were treated to a none too edifying quarrel between their two most prominent spokesmen. Barry Commoner pounced on Ehrlich's offhand reference to compulsion, calling it "immoral, misleading, and politically retrogressive." Indeed, the whole population issue to Commoner was merely a camouflage for political repression. Instead of cutting the birthrate as a means to the just society, said Commoner, the process should be turned on its head. "Powerful, sustained social action to remove the economic and political barriers that keep people and whole nations in poverty" would lead eventually to a "demographic transition." As societies became wealthier and more industrialized, population growth would taper off naturally through voluntary limitation.

"I agree with Commoner when he worries about the political implications of what I'm saying," Ehrlich conceded. "I worry about them myself." But Commoner, in his "preoccupation with pollution," implied that the whole problem had only begun in the 1940s. Ehrlich properly noted that environmental abuse had a longer history than that. He also criticized Commoner's manipulation of statistics (a favor Commoner returned), and pointed out affluent, industrialized societies that still had a high rate of population growth. So it went, until the two principals wearied of the quarrel. In time Ehrlich softened his position to include the emphases of Commoner. "Population growth," he wrote in 1974, "is just one of the three key factors that, multiplied together, threaten the quality of life for all of us" — along with growing affluence and faulty technologies.

Commoner by contrast hardened his own position. In an earlier book, published in 1966, he had included population as one of the sources of pollution; but once he started arguing with Ehrlich, he never mentioned population except to dismiss it. In general the quarrel did Commoner less credit. He was not above smearing Ehrlich with the less inhibited strictures of his population colleague Garrett Hardin. The logic of Commoner's position drove him to intellectual contortions in order to deny any crisis in resource depletion. (Because the United States had enough oil reserves to last *fifty to sixty years,* "there is no need to act as though we are now running out of oil, for we are not.") Moreover, in Commoner's sweaty earnestness lurked more than a hint of professional ego. If he had not provoked the debate with the populationists, he said, "I might have escaped their critical wrath. But this act would have violated my duty to science and to the public."

Since the Sierra Club had published the book that started it all, most of its members not surprisingly sided with Ehrlich. A new group, Zero Population Growth, was launched under the leadership of club members. Brower, with his long interest in population limitation, doubted the feasibility of Commoner's demographic transition: "The resources aren't there to bring the other peoples up to this standard. It is cruel to let them think that they are. And that's where I believe Commoner's big error is." Aside from the Sierra Club, most other conservationists seemed to line up with Ehrlich. The National Wildlife Federation adopted a resolution in 1970 calling for restricting the U.S. population to its current level. The Ehrlich position also received implicit outside support with the development, after 1972, of a "limits to growth" school of economists — a viewpoint quickly embraced by most environmentalists.

In any case, the rhetoric of battle obscured the vital common ground among the combatants. Pollution, overpopulation, and resource depletion all could be traced to a runaway technology, to the unintended side effects of the dazzling discoveries of modern physics and chemistry. Ehrlich and Commoner — and Rachel Carson and Charles Wurster — were all biologists, appalled by what the chemists and physicists were up to. In *Silent Spring*, "chemical" was virtually a dirty word: chemical control, chemical war, chemical assault, chemical destruction. Commoner resisted DNA because it applied models from physics and chemistry to living cells, thereby wiping out the vital distinction between animate and inanimate matter. Without that distinction, modern technology was free to manipulate inanimate nature with a blithe inattention to any implications for living creatures. Ehrlich predictably objected to the tendency of Presidents to appoint physicists as their science advisors. What the situation needed, said Ehrlich, was a good biologist in the job.

❧❧

These disgruntled biologists symbolized the absorption of environmentalism into American society through the medium of professional expertise. Historically, the conservation movement since Muir had been catalyzed by its amateur radicals — Dilg, Edge, Darling, Krutch, Brower, Douglas — whose unflinching zeal had compensated for their lack of formal training in the field. When biologists, lawyers, and economists turned their professional knowledge to environmental problems, the movement reached a new maturity and legitimacy. Yet matters were by no means relinquished entirely to outside professionals. The traditional conservation groups continued to prosper. Between 1965 and 1975 all the major organizations except the Izaak Walton League marked steady increases in memberships and (therefore) in budgets and activities (see the accompanying table).

The National Wildlife Federation remained the largest, richest, and most conservative group. Its budget, just under $11 million in 1971, had, by 1975, grown to $17.3 million. The federation was the last stronghold of Pinchot-style conservation for use. "We believe," said the executive director, Thomas Kimball, in 1971, "that conservation means wise use as determined by the professional people who are trained in this Nation's best educational institutions in wildlife management." Proponents of a complete ban on hunting, he added, were "acting from emotion rather than from knowledge." Hounded by such groups as Cleveland Amory's Fund for Animals, hunters were themselves starting to feel like an endangered species. Even in the NWF, most of the new members seemed to join in order to receive *National Wildlife* rather than to enjoy the company of sportsmen. In the 1970s only 30 percent of the members were hunters; fully 20 percent, in this group traditionally regarded as the sportsman's voice, were *opposed* to all hunting. The environmental revolution could apparently sweep through even so substantially entrenched a group as the federation. "At a time of growing anti-hunter sentiment," said a Winchester employee at a meeting in 1976, "hunters must become a wheelhorse in the trend to broaden wildlife concerns from game animals to include nongame species, as well."

The National Audubon Society, which had been responding to the ecological imperative since the 1930s, dealt more effectively with the expansive new circumstances. "Conservation is no longer for the birds," *Audubon* declared in 1971. "It is for people, simply because there are now so many of us, armed with such powerful technologies and making such exorbitant demands on the environment." The society parlayed the wave of new concern into a staggering growth in membership: an eightfold increase from 1965 to 1975. This jump was prodded by a direct-mail campaign and the advice of an outside consulting firm — and by the quality of the nature photographs published in the magazine. The society expanded so quickly that, when Buchheister stepped down in 1969, he was succeeded by a professional administrator with no previous conservation experience. The job at that point seemed to call for a manager, not a traditional bird lover. Though the national headquarters in New York retained a degree of its old muscle-bound quality, the system of affiliates launched under Buchheister

ANNUAL MEMBERSHIP GROWTH IN FIVE MAJOR CONSERVATION GROUPS
1966–1975

YEAR	IZAAK WALTON LEAGUE	NATIONAL AUDUBON SOCIETY	NATIONAL WILDLIFE FEDERATION	SIERRA CLUB	WILDERNESS SOCIETY	TOTAL	ANNUAL GROWTH	ANNUAL GROWTH RATE (PERCENT)
1966	52,600	45,000	271,800	35,000	35,000	439,400	—	—
1967	52,700	52,000	324,100	45,000	35,000	508,800	69,400	13.6
1968	56,000	62,000	364,600	58,000	39,000	579,600	70,800	12.2
1969	51,800	70,000	465,200	70,000	50,000	707,000	127,400	18.0
1970	53,600	81,500	540,000	113,000	54,000	842,100	135,100	16.0
1971	54,200	148,000	505,100	135,000	70,000	912,300	70,200	7.7
1972	56,100	193,000	524,700	137,000	67,000	977,800	65,500	6.7
1973	56,400	221,500	555,600	140,000	68,000	1,041,500	63,700	6.1
1974	51,200	275,500	594,000	141,000	76,000	1,137,700	96,200	8.5
1975	50,000	321,500	612,100	147,000	87,000	1,217,600	79,900	6.6

Total Growth, 1966–1975: 778,200 (177 percent)

in the late 1940s injected new ideas and personalities into the Audubon bloodstream. "Today the chapters *are* the National Audubon Society," a staff member noted in 1973. "The society isn't just a group of professionals working in New York City — the pros are working for and with the people who make up the chapters." The amateur tradition in American conservation still thrived in the hinterlands.

The Sierra Club by the mid-1960s was regarded as the most influential group in the traditional movement. It offered the best combination of considerable size and innovative leadership. Overtly that leadership was provided by Brower and his professional staff. But actually decisions emerged from a delicate minuet between Brower and his amateur, unpaid board of directors. As the last major group to become professionalized, the Sierra Club stubbornly held on to vestiges of the old amateur tradition through the powers retained by its board. The occasional differences between Brower and his board — between the pros and the amateurs — could be subtle to the point of mystification, matters of style and tone rather than of substantive policy. All hands agreed on the club's well-established role of vanguard militancy; all hands evoked the shade of the founder in support of that role. "We were born fighting," said Brower, with a nod to Muir. At the seventy-fifth anniversary dinner in 1967, the amateur president drew the obvious historical parallel: "Muir epitomized the Sierra Club of his day — and even the club of our day. . . . From his own consuming enthusiasm, he would kindle the fire in others. . . . And our labors are the greatest tribute we can pay him."

The only major group with headquarters on the Pacific Coast, the Sierra Club operated a legislative office in Washington and maintained branches and crusades all over the country. Aside from the Storm King case in New York that had opened up the field of environmental law, the club also intervened in behalf of the Great Swamp in New Jersey, the Red River gorge in Kentucky, the Allagash wilderness in Maine, the North Cascades National Park in Washington, the central Great Smokies in Tennessee, national seashores on Cape Cod and Point Reyes, and the Canyonlands National Park in Utah. Amid almost any gathering of stockmen, lumbermen, or real estate developers, "Sierra Club" was the grossest of epithets.

Whether reviled or admired, the club was *recognized.* People who had never heard of the Wilderness Society or the Izaak Walton League knew about the Sierra Club. The most effective single device in broadcasting its name was a bold publishing program, Brower's favorite project, especially its opulent series of Exhibit Format photography books. Before 1960 the club had issued occasional guidebooks and other Sierra materials, with total annual sales of around $10,000. Brower, from a background in publishing, cajoled the board into expanding the program. "You have heard it often," he declared, "and may have even said it yourself: 'The trouble with conservationists is that they are always talking to themselves.' " The first Sierra Club book aimed at a general audience, *This Is the American Earth,* appeared in 1960. A collection of Ansel Adams photographs, with format and layout designed by Brower, the book became a moderate success. The program really took off two years later with *In Wildness Is the Preservation of the World.* The book included quotations from Thoreau and an introduction by Joseph Wood Krutch. But what caught the public's attention were the color photographs by Eliot Porter, so vividly clear and textured they seemed three-dimensional. A browser in a bookstore, leafing through the lacquered pages, usually found his sales resistance dwindling despite the book's $25 price. "A kind of revolution was under way," one such victim later recalled. "For with the publication of this supremely well-crafted book, conservation ceased to be a boring chapter on agriculture in fifth grade textbooks, or the province of such as bird watchers."

The club's Exhibit Format books offered an ironic variation on Muir's old scheme of creating conservationists by depositing them in the Sierra. Instead of bringing people to the wilderness, Brower's publishing program brought the wilderness to people — with much the same conversion effect — through books that were hard to put down. Over the first four years, fifty thousand were sold, 80 percent through bookstores and mainly to nonmembers of the Sierra Club. The number of buyers was further increased by a distribution arrangement with Ballantine Books of New York. A cheaper edition of *Wildness* was the best-selling trade paperback of 1967. Two Exhibit Format books were published each year (one in 1964 reprinted excerpts from Muir's *My First Summer in the Sierra*). By 1969 total sales amounted to $10 million.

Brower picked the topics, selected the authors, argued about the contracts, designed the layouts, set the prices, oversaw the distribution — did everything but sew the bindings. He carried a moderate administrative load at headquarters, overseeing the steady expansion of his professional staff. He flew around the country to testify at hearings and deliver the standard speech he called The Sermon. All this activity made him the only leader in the traditional conservation movement with an outside reputation. Kimball of the NWF and Buchheister of the Audubon Society presided over larger budgets and memberships, but to the public at large they were unknown. Brower was called "the club's slow-burning but incandescent firebrand" by *Newsweek* and "his country's No. 1 working conservationist" by *Life*. "Even his enemies," added the *Nation*, ". . . regard him with a respect tinged with awe." At a time when other groups were led by anonymous bureaucrats in gray suits, Brower retained that faraway look in his eye. Sometimes, when engulfed by too many overdue projects, he would slip off to the mountains for a few days, schedules be damned. Well, he might say, if Muir were here . . .

It was both his greatest gift and fatal flaw. Like Muir, Brower felt most at home among mountains and wild creatures; like Muir, he arrived at his positions by an internal, self-contained process of leaps and insights — not by measured, external solicitation of diverse opinions, rationally appraised; like Muir, he pursued his ends with little attention to social amenities and given procedures. For his board of directors, he resembled Muir rather too closely. His work habits were frenetically disorderly. Although often out of town — in New York or London — he would not delegate authority. "He was always trying to accomplish too much," Richard Leonard said later. "Thus many important matters were never completed on time." Even his prominence in the movement had its negative aspects. "Dave Brower got to the point," another former club president recalled, "where he was out to tell the world what was wrong about the wilderness." Joel Hildebrand put it more strongly: "He became a sort of fair-haired boy or knight in shining armor and got carried away with his own self-importance."

The publishing program, for all its success as an educational device, diverted enormous chunks of time and money from the club's traditional activities. As early as 1962, some members complained that the *Bulletin* was coming out late because Brower was preoccupied with his books. Two years later came rumors that club dues were underwriting the heavy production costs of Exhibit Format books. "Through these books," said Brower, denying the charges, "we frequently induce the heathens to pay for their own conversion. . . . Has any other activity of the club gained it wider recognition or garnered it more praise?" Obviously no. But what were Brower's priorities? He gravitated between dual roles as the leader of the Sierra Club and the most visible conservationist of his time. As the former he was bound to advance the interests of the club and keep its balance sheet in black ink; as the latter he aimed above all to reach the heathens and convert them. When the roles clashed, which should he favor?

Brower's directors, at least, felt an overriding commitment to the club's health. The conspicuous success of *Wildness* concealed the more typical commercial failure of other books in the series. Brower, believing the books a triumph in conservation, if not financial, terms, disregarded the warnings of his directors and plowed more money into the program. Once he asked the Publications Committee, which included his old mentor Francis Farquhar, for permission to go ahead with an Exhibit Format book. Turned down, he imperturbably replied: "But I've already spent $10,000 on it." Such collisions delayed the execution of contracts and the payment of royalties, poisoning relations between Brower and some of his most prominent authors, including Porter, Krutch, and Loren Eiseley. "We have not been able yet to solve the problems that arise when there must be a mixture of volunteer and professional management of an operation," he told Krutch. "You are quite correct that the explanation should have come sooner. So should almost everything else I do." From 1964 on, the books program lost an average of $60,000 a year. Until that point Brower had handled finances well, building up the club's net worth and staying more or less within his budgets. But in 1965, with a cash-flow bottleneck created by book inventories and unpaid accounts, the club's expenses ran $268,000 over budget.

The developing scenario had parallels in conservation history: Dutcher and the Audubon Association, Dilg and the Walton League, Yard and the National Parks Association. In each case, a gifted but headstrong leader strained against the traces held by a more cautious board of directors. The leader had created the group by making financial sacrifices and working long, unappreciated hours. He thus had a proprietary interest: it was *his* group. The board, drawn from practical men of affairs, guarded its own prerogatives and disapproved of budget deficits. The leader found his board lacking in zeal for the larger struggle. The board found its leader uncontrollable and financially irresponsible. Conservation is at stake, said the leader. Money is at stake, said the board. (Dutcher, Dilg, and Yard had all lost their quarrels.)

The Sierra Club's major crusade of the 1960s involved the Bureau of Reclamation's incredible plan to build a pair of billion-dollar dams in the Grand Canyon. Reclamation fell within the purview of Stewart Udall, the most conservation-minded Secretary of the Interior since Ickes. "The one overriding principle of the conservation movement," Udall had said in 1960, "is that no work of man (save the bare minimum of roads, trails, and necessary public facilities in access areas) should intrude into the wonder places of the National Park System." In his cabinet post, Udall generally remained true to this declaration. But in the case of the Grand Canyon, he yielded to pressures from the White House and from his congressman brother Morris and accepted the dam proposals. "He has to live the political life every day," Brower noted, "and I think he's been too mindful of that."

The club as a tax-exempt organization was constrained from "substantial" political lobbying. In 1960 the board had authorized Brower to push the definition of "substantial" to its limit. The club, in a conscious assumption of risk, decided to engage in lobbying as vigorously as possible within the law. The Grand Canyon issue turned out to be the test case. In June 1966 Brower spent $15,000 on full-page ads in the New York *Times* and the Washington *Post*: "This time it's the Grand Canyon they want to flood. *The Grand Canyon.*" The advocates of the dams were at once deluged with calls and telegrams. The very next day, the club received a hand-delivered directive from the Internal Revenue Service: pending a full investigation into the club's political activities, its exempt status was suspended, and contributions to it were no longer deductible. The swift action seemed explicitly punitive. As a political gambit it proved counterproductive by bringing a wave of sympathy to both the club and its campaign against the dams. Brower blamed the action on Udall and Wayne Aspinall, the old nemesis of conservation, still ensconced as chairman of the House Interior and Insular Affairs Committee. But Udall was probably innocent. He claimed as much in a private, handwritten note to Krutch — and added his impression that the episode had actually bolstered the club's membership and morale. "I hope this is the case," said Udall, "as the Sierra Club is the one indispensable national conservation organization."

The IRS action did attract thousands of new members. But, given the club's cash-flow problems, it came at precisely the wrong time. Large contributions fell off sharply. "The IRS keeps saying their investigation is routine," said Brower. "The hell it is. They've never done this before. Our ads for the Redwoods Park in California were far more extensive and we never heard a word from them." As the investigation went on, Brower continued to spend money on ads and other lobbying efforts against the dams. The dams were stopped, and the club finally lost its tax status. Some $50,000 was spent on fruitless appeals. Despite the deepening financial problems, neither Brower nor his directors behaved less militantly. "That didn't turn us around," one club leader later recalled. "After we lost our status there was no turning back." When confronting its adversaries, the club could still generally close ranks behind a common policy.

Within the club, the issue between Brower and his nonprofessional officers was essentially money — with an implicit argument over the extent to which his independence had caused the heavy annual deficits. The club lost over $100,000 in 1967, again in 1968, and $200,000 in 1969. Early in 1967 an open letter signed by seven former club presidents censured Brower's leadership; but the board rejected the criticisms and affirmed its support. "I feel that the basic difficulty from then on was not Dave," Leonard recalled, "but his overzealous supporters. They were the ones who harmed Dave." In preparing for the 1968 election of directors, the candidates split into factions for and against Brower. The Brower forces won a majority. But bitter feelings remained, and were not improved by the behavior of the victors.

The final crisis began in the fall of 1968. Leonard and Adams — Brower's two best friends in the club, who had helped him transform it after the war from a regional group of mountaineers into the organized second coming of John Muir — formally charged him with insubordination and financial recklessness and called for his removal. Probably all three men, in that moment when the gauntlet was thrown down, felt torn by currents of loss and betrayal, of personal memories and affections forcibly disregarded in the perceived greater interest of the Sierra Club. The board entertained the charges and rejected them. Brower's majority still held. Then, in a self-immolation that recalled Will Dilg's last throes, Brower lost his majority by a series of defiant initiatives undertaken without the board's consent. His culminating offense was a $10,000 ad in the New York *Times* for — inevitably — Sierra Club books. By a vote of 7 to 6, the board removed his spending power. "Do I have authority to do what I am authorized by this board to do without requiring consultation?" Brower demanded. "What I cannot see continue to happen is constant review, review, and re-review." "Brower's ideas leave no place for the amateur," said director William Siri, who two years earlier had proposed the motion of support that rejected the former presidents' letter. "They want to run this place like a bank," Brower replied.

He took a leave of office and campaigned around the country for his own slate of prospective directors. The annual election normally drew a quarter of the membership. In April 1969 it drew 60 percent. Anti-Brower candidates won all five of the open seats, and Brower departed gracefully. "There will be no retreat and no further pause," said the new president. "There must be dynamic movement ahead — without compromise of principle." The new leadership, in attempting to prove itself as militant as Brower, lost $200,000 a year in the next two years. Four years after the denouement, Brower's strongest supporter on the board was elected president.

Brower lost no time in starting his own groups, the nondeductible Friends of the Earth and the deductible John Muir Institute for Environmental Studies. "We cannot be dilettante and lily-white in our work," he said, not at all subdued. "Nice Nellie will never make it. . . . We cannot go on fiddling while the earth's wild places burn in the fires of our undisciplined technology." The bitter feelings roused by the final showdown hung in the air briefly. Anne Brower refused for a time to talk to Leonard or Adams. But in a few years Brower was made an honorary vice-president of the Sierra Club, and a few years after that the club gave him its highest honor, the John Muir Award.

An ironic footnote: in 1976 Congress passed tax reforms that allowed substantial lobbying by tax-exempt organizations.

⚥⚥

The environmental revolution of the 1970s drew equally from the surging traditional conservation groups and from the newer man-centered leaders like Commoner, Ehrlich, Nader, and the Environmental Defense Fund. Despite this powerful if prickly convergence of forces, the real explosion of the movement into public awareness awaited one final development. As late as May 1968, a prestigious conference of three hundred environmental experts at Rockefeller University in New York attracted little press attention, even from the omnivorous *Times*. In the presidential election that fall, environmental issues made a late, inconsequential impact. Environmentalism finally attained maturity when it intersected with the heterogeneous social movements of the day. Reaching its crest at the end of a decade of social activism, the environmental revolution borrowed from all the major movements and, at last and none too soon, took off on its own.

The most obvious affinities were with the fuzziest of the movements, the hippie counterculture. Conservationists had always urged an ethic of naturalness, primitivism, antiurbanism, antimaterialism, and technophobia. All these themes reverberated among hippies. In their neighborhoods, ecological notions mingled inseparably with incense, marijuana, and the I Ching. "The earth, seen wholly, is holy ground," said an acolyte of the San Francisco scene. "There is no waste, only matter-energy, all transformable into life and life support." In Arizona, a hippie poet named Stephen Levine, who described himself as a spiritual ecologist, sat with the dying Joseph Wood Krutch, "our conversation about animal communications a glowing directive from a man of considerable knowledge and sensitivity, though his illness could be felt across the room." When Krutch died, Levine — in the argot of his peers — eulogized him as "a planet steward who gave himself to his vision of man's more complete return to the Planet Family." Howard Zahniser's son Ed (the child named after Edward Preble) contributed verse and reviews in the hippie manner to *Living Wilderness*. Even Brower was apparently influenced by the ecological impulses of his college-age children. Most traditional conservationists were offended by the hippie style. But beneath the hair and clutter the more perceptive observers found a striking congruence of ideas. "I think it would be well," suggested Ehrlich, who was surrounded by hippies at Stanford, "if those of us who are totally ensnared in the non-hip part of our culture paid a great deal of attention to the movement, rather than condemn it out of hand.... At the very least they are asking the proper questions."

Ideological similarities could also be discerned with some feminists. The most visible leaders in the women's movement, those pushing for political and economic advancement, were committed to a rationale for absolute equality. As such they dismissed apparent differences in male and female behavior as the product of external conditioning. By contrast, feminist artists and poets typically spoke of a separate feminine sensibility, biologically based. This sensibility upon examination turned out to be quite similar to traditional stereotypes, with the substitution of positive terms for the corresponding negatives: mystical for irrational, nonaggressive for passive, natural for nonmechanical. When applied to the environment, this feminine identity treated man as the violent manipulator and woman as the gentle, embracing friend. Thus, Diane Wakoski, in "A Poet Recognizing the Echo of the Voice":

> *We are the earth*
> *We wake up*
> *finding ourselves*
> *glinting in the dark*
> *after thousands of years*
> *of pressing....*
>
> *A man says, "it is mine,"*
> *but he hacks,*
> *chops apart the mine*
> *to discover,*
> *to plunder,*

what's in it/Plunder,
that is the word.
Plunder.

To the extent that feminists took their cues from such poetic definitions, the women's movement articulated a viewpoint — of forbearance, harmony, cooperation — that had many points of contact with environmentalism.

With the two most vociferous movements of the 1960s, civil rights and antiwar, environmentalism had practically nothing in common, despite labored efforts to discover common elements among them. Blacks scorned conservation as an elitist diversion from the more pressing tasks at hand. A black minister in Washington called Nader "the biggest damn racist in the United States" because of his efforts against pollution. The two causes spoke different languages to separate constituencies. One spoke of jobs, schools, discrimination, and other such breadbasket issues; the other spoke of wilderness, clean air and water, endangered species, and spiritual intangibles. "You can't be saving national parks and improving minority housing at the same time," said one environmentalist. "We have to make our political force as specific as possible." "There is not enough in the pie," said another, "once you let the powerful have what they've got, for both the blacks and the environmentalists." When the Sierra Club membership was polled on the question of increased involvement with urban poor and minorities, the proposal was rejected three to one. Asked if the club had any black members, Richard Leonard could not think of any. "We feel a little embarrassed," he said.

Relations between environmentalists and war protesters were not much friendlier. On college campuses the former typically wore long hair, read *Sand County Almanac,* radiated good vibes, and liked to climb mountains and go camping. The latter typically wore short hair, read Mao and Marx, furrowed their brows, and liked to leaflet a factory. One liked the Grateful Dead, the other the Rolling Stones in their proletarian stage. One talked about cultural revolution and *The Greening of America,* the other talked earnestly about the prospect of political revolution in America. Away from the colleges, the two persuasions were less distinguishable by their external habits. But a clear division remained. "The ecology movement was remote, separate and cut off from the revolutionary surge sweeping through American society," declared the radical journalist James Ridgeway. "It had no bearing on the war, political repression, blacks, the poor, or any other factor which created the currents of stress in the society."

The real bond between environmentalism and the civil rights and anti-war movements was *chronological.* By 1970 the two great crusades of the 1960s were losing momentum; activists who wanted to keep fighting turned to the environment as the best available cause. When civil rights changed from its integrationist, southern, legalistic phase to its nationalistic, northern, economic phase, white liberals were squeezed out. Groups like CORE and SNCC, increasingly dominated by blacks, refused to hire whites on general principles. One of Nader's Raiders, a veteran of struggles in Mississippi and North Carolina, described his shift to environmentalism: "I didn't succeed in getting a job in any civil rights organization I was interested in, so I ended up working for Ralph." Concurrently the antiwar movement was retiring in frustration, having had no more effect on Richard Nixon than on Lyndon Johnson. After years of marches and demonstrations, thousands of activists were left with alienated politics and a comprehensive distrust of corporate America — and no medium for their expression. "Now a lot of us are turning to the environment," said a Columbia graduate student. "It's right here. It's something we can do something about. And — for a change — we just might win this one."

Whether from hippie, feminist, civil rights, or proto-Marxist backgrounds, young people flooded into the conservation movement as never before, providing most of the foot soldiers as it assumed the character of a mass crusade. Of the twenty-eight contributors to the Sierra Club's manual *Ecotactics,* published in 1970, over half were under thirty and only two were over forty. Conservation could claim, if nothing else, a decorous, well-mannered history. Now, in the prop wash of 1960s activism, came a rash of irregular guerrilla actions. A legendary figure in Chicago known as The Fox retained his anonymity while carrying on several years' worth of escapades, such as staining a rug at the U.S. Steel home office with a bottle of the effluent dispensed into Lake Michigan by one of the company's factories. In Miami, a group of commandos added yellow dye to the sewage flowing into treatment plants suspected of failing at their job; the next day half of the Dade County canals turned bright yellow. In the vicinity of Ann Arbor, a group of students set to cutting down billboards at night. Eventually a youth-oriented group in Washington, Environmental Action, established a Golden Fox trophy for the best "ecotage" ploy.

The youthful cast of the swelling movement was revealed in startling proportions by the largest environmental demonstration in history, Earth Day, on April 22, 1970. The idea originated with Gaylord Nelson of Wisconsin, the most conservationally inclined member of the Senate. With a federal grant of $125,000, three Harvard graduate students set up an office in Washington to coordinate the occasion. "The small conservation organizations have done their best," they announced, "but the time has come to involve the whole society." At a cabinet meeting in March, Spiro Agnew urged the Nixon administration to have nothing to do with Earth Day. But Walter Hickel, the maverick Secretary of the Interior, went ahead and told his staff to take part — thus persuading political radicals that the whole affair was set up by Nixon to divert attention from the war. On the appointed day, rallies were held at some fifteen hundred colleges and ten thousand schools. In Boston, thirteen demonstrators were arrested for protesting an airport expansion; hippies at Indiana University plugged offensive sewage pipes with concrete; in Atlanta, piles of Coke cans were dumped on the lawn in front of Coca-Cola headquarters. Dow Chemical sent out speakers equipped with kits providing suggested answers and cautioning the speakers to pause five seconds before replying, so as not to seem too primed.

Earth Day was a symptom of how far the movement had spread. "Now, suddenly, everybody is a conservationist," *Audubon* remarked. All the diverse conservation forces generated during the 1960s were pushing, if not together, then at least along parallel lines. Shortly before Earth Day, the venerable *New Republic* had dismissed "the ecology craze" as an irrelevant sideshow, supported by "the biggest assortment of ill-matched allies since the Crusades." Six months after Earth Day, the *New Republic* devoted an entire issue to the environment. Earth Day, said the editors, had been "not just a channel for frustrated antiwar energies, as we thought. It signaled an awakening to the dangers in a dictatorship of technology." Congress began to construct a whole new apparatus of environmental legislation and — more important — enforcement agencies. Will Dilg would have been pleased by the $25 billion water-pollution bill passed in 1972; Congress overrode Nixon's veto by votes of 52 to 12 and 247 to 23. In the congressional elections that year, environmental lobbies made Wayne Aspinall their special target and had the pleasure of retiring him to private life. Over the next few years environmentalists increasingly found themselves on the inside of government. The Environmental Protection Agency became the largest regulatory body in the country.

ℳℳ

As revolutions will do, this one kept raising the ante. When an environmental activist took a government job and moved to the other side of the desk, he found his old colleagues holding him to even higher standards. The situation never stabilized. One victory led only to the next struggle. An apparent solution to a problem later became just another problem.

At one time nuclear energy seemed the magical remedy for both air pollution and resource depletion. "The supreme conservation achievement of this century," said Udall in *The Quiet Crisis:* "The atomic physicists who uncovered the edge of an infinite dynamo brought fire, like the gods of Greek mythology, from seemingly inert elements, and allayed our fears of fuel shortage once and for all." On a western tour in the fall of 1963, John Kennedy predicted a giant nuclear reactor in the West by the end of the decade; conservationists seized the suggestion as an argument for opposing hydroelectric dams. At the Sierra Club Wilderness Conference of 1965, Senator Clinton Anderson of New Mexico urged the alliance of conservation and the atom: "It would avoid ugly slag heaps, high stacks, and barge traffic. It would not pollute the atmosphere." Another speaker at the conference proposed that radioactive wastes be simply poured into empty oil wells in Texas.

Eventually the matter of waste disposal would become the heart of the nuclear controversy. Luna Leopold had already raised the question at an earlier Wilderness Conference, in 1960. But for the most part, during these years no one gave the problem much thought. This inattention to materials that stayed deadly for hundreds of years was the perfect expression of the truncated present-mindedness of the modern age. "Nobody was telling us we were going to have trouble with radioactive waste," Brower said later. Conservationists started arguing about nuclear energy by way of other considerations.

In the late 1950s a utility company announced plans for a reactor at Bodega Bay, fifty miles north of San Francisco. Local citizens raised a protest, thus precipitating one of the first controversies over nuclear plant siting. The Sierra Club joined the fray, initially on grounds unrelated to nuclear energy itself. "The proposed reactor will take a priceless scenic resource for its site," the club said in an *amicus* brief, "but will produce nothing but common kilowatts." Other opponents brought up the issues of waste disposal, low-level radiation, and thermal pollution from hot water dispensed into the ocean. The opposition was largely frustrated until 1963, when new earthquake faults were discovered within a half mile of the site. The AEC, vacillating as usual between its contrary roles of regulation and promotion, issued conflicting reports. A month later, in November 1964, the utility withdrew its application. The Bodega project was a landmark because it was rejected by criteria peculiar to nuclear power. A conventional plant disrupted by an earthquake meant no special threat; a nuclear plant in such circumstances might wreak inconceivable damage.

Still, Brower and the Sierra Club had no general objection to nuclear power under normal conditions. When another plant was proposed for the Nipomo Dunes south of San Francisco, the club arranged a deal with the utility company: no plant at the dunes, but instead at an alternate site nearby in Diablo Canyon. Only one board member, Frederick Eissler, opposed the exchange. In 1966 he urged the club to consider not only the site but the larger questions of nuclear contamination and waste disposal. Submitted as a referendum to the club, the Diablo site was approved by 69 percent of the members. But Eissler did convert Brower to a general position against nuclear power. They and others like-minded campaigned hard for the 1968 club elections. Four new directors, all opposed to the Diablo plant, were elected. The new board then reversed its earlier approval of Diablo.

It was the only substantive policy issue between Brower and his adversaries in the club. Ansel Adams, previously a Brower man, turned against him because he believed the reversal put the club's integrity and credibility at stake. Once again the matter was submitted to the general membership. Adams and William Siri urged a rejection of the latest board decision, arguing that the club had already exhausted its rights of appeal. The plant's opponents countered with the ultimate argument: "John Muir would have voted YES." Diablo Canyon became entangled with the larger quarrel over Brower's leadership. In the same election that sealed his fate as executive director, the site was approved by a three-to-one margin. (Construction went ahead. In 1975, after six years and nearly a billion dollars, a major new earthquake fault was found in the vicinity.)

Diablo Canyon marked the end of the honeymoon between conservationists and nuclear power. In September 1969, in Vermont, the AEC for the first time was pressured into making its case for a plant in public. Previously the agency had concealed many dubious practices behind a facade of security considerations. That same year, three respected scientists criticized the AEC's standards for safe radiation. In 1970 the Sierra Club joined two suits to require more stringent safeguards for plants on Lake Michigan and Chesapeake Bay. Such interventions, by the club and other groups, forced utility companies to meet tighter limits on thermal pollution and waste disposal than those imposed by the AEC. "Back in the old days before intervenors," a pronuclear congressman said in May 1971, "we had a press conference to give the natives a look. The natives usually didn't show up. Then the people from Mills Tower — the Sierra Club — they began to show up. Why do we have to have hearings? Why don't we make it discretionary?"

Nuclear power gradually became the most controversial issue for the present and future among environmentalists. Paul Ehrlich and Barry Commoner agreed on at least this one point. Brower's Friends of the Earth from its creation opposed all new nuclear construction. The Sierra Club and Wilderness Society adopted similar policies in 1974, and soon even the National Wildlife Federation was leaning in the same direction. Ralph Nader also urged a general moratorium on new plants. Under these pressures the nuclear industry fell on hard times. Orders for new reactors reached a peak in 1972–1973 and then tapered off, perhaps never to revive. The existing plants and their wastes remained — like "a brontosaurus that has had its spinal cord cut," as Amory Lovins of Friends of the Earth put it, "but is so big and has so many ganglia near the tail that it can keep thrashing around for years not knowing it's dead."

Delivering a mortal blow to such an enormous beast was one measure of the movement's power in the 1970s. At mid-decade the heady expansion that followed Earth Day tapered off somewhat, prompting a spate of hopeful articles in business magazines about an "environmental backlash." But it never really took place. By the end of the decade the movement was still marking gains in membership, income, and influence. With the combined power of some three thousand groups, conservation seemed a permanent force in American political and social life.

Such status came as a revelation for a movement accustomed to regarding itself as a tolerated minority. Some of the high points in conservation history — the forest reserve act of 1891, TR's last-minute creation of sixteen million acres of national forest in 1907, the migratory-bird act of 1913 — had been accomplished, in the absence of widespread public support, by subterfuges of one sort or another. "The conservation conscience can be dominant in American life from time to time and place to place, without once representing a conviction on the part of a majority of the people," said a speaker at the North American Wildlife Conference in 1959. "This is inevitably the best for which we can hope." Twenty years later, conservationists hoped for more.

⚜ III ⚜

CONSERVATION IN
AMERICAN HISTORY

10

The Amateur Tradition:
People and Politics

From 1890 to 1975 — from the legislative campaign for Yosemite National Park to obstructions at nuclear plant sites — amid the changing issues and personalities, the role of the radical amateur was the driving force in conservation history. The movement depended on professional conservationists and government agencies for expertise, staying power, organization, and money. The amateurs by contrast provided high standards, independence, integrity. Unhampered by bureaucratic inertia or a political need to balance constituencies and defend old policies, they served as the movement's conscience. Neither group could have done its work as well without the other. Each was necessary. But judged by such criteria as flexibility, vision, innovation, honesty, and zeal, the amateurs played their parts more admirably: in the tradition of John Muir.

Excelling as adversaries, the amateurs bearded their enemies in three distinct confrontations. In society at large conservationists typically found themselves opposed by business interests. Accused of resisting progress and the American way of life, they usually preferred to describe their foe as the simple human greed of a few interested parties instead of the larger aspirations of a technological society. After all, random greed was easier to fight than the entire modern syndrome. In any case, as the least commercial of all conservationists, the amateur radicals led the fight against progress/business. "I am pleading as one amateur to another," Ernest Griffith of the Wilderness Society told the Izaak Walton League convention of 1950. "You and I have no commercial interest in this. We can make no money by the wilderness. But I believe that if we stand fast on the belief that there is something we are fighting for which is very precious, the generations yet to come will rise up and thank us for it."

Caught between the movement and the political muscle of economic interests, government conservation agencies presented another target to the zealous amateurs. Usually the interests, with their lobbies and campaign budgets, could muster political opinion on their side. The amateurs countered with votes, not money, by appealing to public opinion at large. Driven by more practical motives, the interests often outlasted the amateurs. The massive latent public sympathy for the natural world might be aroused, but it suffered from a short attention span. After a flurry of editorials and letters to Congress, public opinion might drift away while paid lobbyists bided their time in Washington anterooms. Still the inchoate popular will offered the amateurs their heaviest club over the heads of government bureaucrats. "If the voice of reform comes," Justice Douglas said in 1972, "it will come from the people, not the agencies. Only an active, enlightened citizenry can keep the bureaucracy energized and on the straight and narrow path."

Finally, within the conservation movement itself the amateurs prodded, criticized, and (if necessary) bypassed their professional colleagues. Some groups — such as the National Wildlife Federation, especially in its early years — depended on commercial interests for financial support. Even in groups without such ties, the best conservationists might suffer from a hardening of leadership arteries or organizational inertia. "The members will want to educate everybody else," Aldo Leopold complained of all organizations, "but many will be unwilling to study themselves." The amateurs, working alone or in groups too small to become inert, did not worry about the effect of a campaign on their jobs and careers. Since they did not depend on conservation for a living, they could act on the merits of the case, with speed and total freedom from organization charts. "There is *no one at all* who has done anything for conservation," Rosalie Edge declared in 1938, "who has not had independent means (or a livelihood apart from conservation)." Twenty-six years later the Yale ecologist Paul Sears made the same point in more measured language: "As a general comment, I would say that much the most effective work in conservation is done by people who have it as an avocation with other means of support."

Whether confronting business interests, bureaucrats, or professional conservationists, the radical amateurs comprised the heart and soul of American conservation. Who were these obscure heirs of the Muir tradition? Why did they plunge into struggles that offered no material inducements, that indeed might steal from their incomes and careers?

❧❧

To generalize about the motives of so disparate a group as the amateur conservationists only invites arguments. Outwardly altruistic, concerned for posterity and the rights of the natural world instead of material gain, the amateurs still had selfish purposes. Rosalie Edge, the most vivid of the breed, needed an outlet for her ample energies and indignation after the end of her suffrage work, marriage, and child-raising years. By assaulting the hapless Pearson she gained a purpose, even a measure of fame and prestige, not otherwise available to her. "There is nothing in the world I love like my conservation work," she said. The statement could have been echoed by William Dutcher, Will Dilg, Robert Sterling Yard, Howard Zahniser, and many others rescued by conservation work from more mundane lives.

Still, in dealing with such a group it seems wisest to take them literally, as they described themselves, and not to invent complexities where simple motives apparently dominated. They were amateurs in the literal sense. At an early point, usually in childhood, often during a period of relative isolation from human contacts, they began to love some aspect of the natural world. Nurtured into maturity, that love was then expressed in conservation work. "Most plant lovers can remember their special interest and susceptibility from childhood," Joseph Wood Krutch noted of his particular fascination, "and often can connect it with a specific incident or moment." A vivid flash of revelation — Muir finding *Calypso,* Justice Douglas feeling the chinook, David Brower leading his mother around the Berkeley hills — stamped the individual with a lifelong attitude. Generally conservationists were neither born nor made but reborn in a riveting instant of immediate conversion. The early flash was then called up by later exposures, and the insight was renewed. "We little suspect that the youth of all the world is in us," Muir wrote in his journal in 1873. "In the most solitary and secluded valleys gazing for the first time upon lakes and meadows never neared by human foot, we recognize them as familiar in some measure as if we must have seen them before, answering to the images forming the warp and woof of our lives."

Amateur conservation thus began in some form of outdoor activity. In the East, although the Appalachian Mountain Club was the first permanent group, the early impetus came mainly from hunters and fishermen. Their leading figure, George Bird Grinnell, insisted that a gun merely provided a good excuse for being outdoors. The immersion in nature meant more than the quarry itself. With an independent income, Grinnell pioneered in conservation work in the same spirit: for the visceral love of it. "I have never made any money at it," he said of his conservation career, "but I have had barrels of fun; in fact, I suspect that there is no one living who ever had so good a time during his life." In over forty years of campaigning he never lost the amateur spirit. Conservation remained his hobby.

The familiar syndrome of the repentant hunter suggested that a love of nature did indeed draw sportsmen outdoors more strongly than a love of killing. William Temple Hornaday carried penance to an extreme by leading a national crusade for game preservation. Many other former hunters — including James Oliver Curwood, Irving Brant, Justice Douglas, Sigurd Olson, Edward Abbey, and Arthur Carhart — later testified to their loss of enthusiasm for the chase and kill; yet all remained strong conservationists, in fact, stopped killing as part of their mature conservationism. "The hunter knows the excitement of stalking and the excitement of the kill," said Douglas. "Yet in time he often comes to realize that satisfaction of his atavistic desire serves an ignoble end and that preservation of wildlife ranks higher." Even Aldo Leopold, whose unalloyed enthusiasm for hunting mars *Sand County Almanac* for some contemporary readers, eventually met the repenters halfway by giving up his rifle in favor of bow and arrow. As an archer Leopold killed little game; with Grinnell, he claimed that killing was not the point. "I think all of us start out as pretty bloodthirsty young hunters who want something in the bag," one of Leopold's sons said to an audience of sportsmen in 1972. "We later come to appreciate that the enjoyment of hunting is something quite apart from the killing."

For hunters unwilling to give up the chase entirely, fishing offered a compromise. Most sportsmen at first engaged in both activities; with time they typically put down the gun and took up the rod. As a "lower" order, submerged from sight, fish drew less sympathy than a graceful deer or a soaring game bird. The act of fishing itself, more passive and sedentary than most hunting, allowed the sportsman time to appreciate his surroundings. "The contemplation of the eternal flow of streams," noted Herbert Hoover, a serious angler, "the fine stretch of mountains and forest, is a fine reducing agent for the egotism which we get out of our narrow occupations in these lives of strenuous culture." Gifford Pinchot hunted bear in his youth but later found his greatest thrill in life in catching a substantial pickerel with a streamer fly on a three-ounce rod. Muir disapproved of hunting, indeed of any life-taking; as an adult he seldom ate meat. But he tolerated fishing because it took its disciples into the wilderness and opened their senses. "Catching trout with a bit of bent wire is a rather trivial business," he said, "but fortunately people fish better than they know. In most cases it is the man who is caught."

Like hunters, birders went through an analogous process from intrusion to forbearance. As children they were drawn to birds by the challenge of identifying species, the mysteries of flight or migration, the music of birdsong — often triggering a memory of a specific time and place — or the quiet observation of feeding and nesting habits. "I have never met a dedicated ornithologist," Frank Chapman recalled, "who did not pursue his interest in birds so early in life that he cannot remember exactly when it started." (A poll of the fellows of the American Ornithologists' Union once revealed that 90 percent had started birding by the age of ten.) As with Theodore Roosevelt, this early obsession with birds often reinforced the social shyness that had helped provoke the obsession itself. Gilbert Pearson and Roger Tory Peterson, both solitary children, found refuge in their early birding. At the turn of the century, in the absence of adequate cameras and field glasses, birders were perforce hunters. Only a bird in the hand could be definitely identified and studied. As equipment improved, the birders did less shooting. The gun money episode of 1911 split the birders and hunters into separate camps, which were led thereafter, respectively, by the National Audubon Society and the American Game Protective Association (and its lineal descendants down to the National Wildlife Federation).

The record of the National Audubon Society has been one of the singular mysteries of conservation history. After incorporation in 1905 it was usually the richest, most stable, potentially most useful of all conservation groups. Perhaps *too* stable: under Pearson and John Baker it raised money and maintained existing programs but seemed frozen in memories of the old battles. Acutely in need of fresh leadership, it still resisted the more activist impulses of the state societies, especially Massachusetts Audubon. A young birder from Boston, Maurice Broun, recalled the stories he began to hear about Rosalie Edge in the early 1930s: "Here was this woman in New York City who was *doing* things in conservation — very militant, very strident, very abrasive, but she was *doing* things. Getting things done" — in contrast with National Audubon. Not until the 1950s, and particularly with the advent of Carl Buchheister as president, did the group really start to bestir itself. True to the pattern, Buchheister had converted a boyhood fascination into a career. He energized the society in part by never forgetting the origins of both the group and his job. "How little could I know," he said on assuming the presidency, "when as a boy roaming the countryside of my native state, Maryland, looking for birds' nests, that that romantic childhood interest would lead to this!" A career professional, he held on to his amateur zeal.

However deficient their main organization, birders did excel as writers and thinkers. Perhaps the most literate and best read of all conservationists, birders included among their ranks Theodore Roosevelt, John Burroughs, T. S. Palmer, Rosalie Edge, John Kieran, Brooks Atkinson, Hal Borland, Louis Halle, Ira Gabrielson, Edwin Way Teale, William Vogt, and Rachel Carson: a disproportionate share of the best minds in conservation. No other outdoor activity was analyzed at such length with such penetration.

Birders could occupy themselves in a backyard or a city park. Sportsmen might find their quarry in farming country. Wilderness lovers had the farthest to travel — and by the same token found the sharpest goad to conservation. In general, the degree of conservationist zeal varied directly with the difficulty and wildness of the catalyzing activity. No one else suffered as willingly as hikers and mountaineers, or so mystified outsiders. As Bernard DeVoto imagined the calling: "A hiker staggering along a cluttered trail, his face bloated by mosquito bites, his stomach queasy from the charred eggs he cooked over a smudge, his shoulders galled by the straps of a pack that is filled with beloved but idiotic equipment for the outdoor life, his muscles agonized by unfamiliar strain — such a man has no truck with so paltry a thing as pleasure." DeVoto seldom strayed from the amenities of Cambridge. Yet his grim prejudices about life in the wilderness were sometimes echoed even by the enthusiasts: at odd moments of hunger, thirst, cold, or exhaustion, they wondered what the hell they were doing there. "Imagine someone at home telling me: 'Tomorrow you will get up at 5:15,' " a mystified enthusiast reflected after a Sierra Club outing in 1951. " 'You will spend the day carrying seventeen pounds up 2,600 feet and down 2,600 feet — net gain 0. You will tread on rocks that are flinty, on rocks that roll underfoot. You will find a bed site on a granite mountain and bathe in snow water. Tomorrow you will wash your dust- and sweat-soaked clothes. For this toil *you* will pay *me* five dollars a day.' I was crazy."

More than uncomfortable, mountaineering and wilderness hiking were the most dangerous of outdoor pursuits. Usually done without weapons, far from ambulances and hospitals, at high altitudes, the simplest hike could be threatened by wild animals or capricious weather or rockslides — or a stumble on the trail. At moments of extreme peril, an "other self" like Muir's might click in, imparting an uncanny clarity of mind and sureness of touch. The crisis past, wilderness conventions called for dismissing the occasion with some form of throwaway humor. In 1928, on a Sierra Club outing in the Canadian Rockies, a snow bridge gave way under a woman. The rope saved her from falling into a crevasse; the man who hauled her up later explained that "he had spent three hours cobbling her shoes on the previous day and he saw all of his handiwork disappearing." Robert Marshall, when climbing a ridge in the Brooks Range in 1930, heard a loud crack and looked up to see a six-foot boulder crashing toward him. He started to run but slipped and fell in its path. "I lay just as flat as I could, knowing that chunks like this, as they go bounding down the mountainside, hit the ground only now and then. Fortunately the spot where I was lying was neither now nor then."

Even when accidents did happen, mountaineers accepted them with an almost cold-blooded aplomb. "Hard on him," a Sierra Club member noted of a fall in 1892 that broke three ribs, "but will make a good paper for some future meeting of the club." On the 1907 outing, Muir offhandedly noted the events of the day in his journal. July 13: "All who spent the night at Moro Lake returned to main camp by trail except 2 one of whom a daring girl fell about 200 feet and was instantly killed near camp in throat of grand arroyo body rolled into torrent." Matter of fact, no great excitement, the death almost an afterthought. July 14: "All except 12 start for Whitney. A few also for Williamson. I meant to go also but my horse was required by party who conveyed body to Mineral King." Another death occurred on the 1934 outing. "Everyone appreciated the dignity with which this tragic event passed into club history," ran the account in the *Bulletin*, "and soberly the camp resumed its accustomed ways."

Why this humor over narrow escapes and stoicism in the face of death? In part they functioned as necessary psychological defenses. Wilderness lovers voluntarily subjected themselves to unpleasant, dangerous situations. Knowing the risks, free to avoid them but drawn on by other considerations, mountaineers in particular had to adopt attitudes that would cushion the impact of accidents that — if examined too closely — might wreak greater psychic damage. Perhaps more to the point, the wilderness experience taught humans not to value themselves too highly. Man shared the wilderness on equal terms with other forms of life; the other forms died quietly, without bother; a human death meant nothing special. Normally a wilderness trip was the least social of outdoor activities. "Climb a fine mountain all alone," said William Hornaday. "In that way one sees things and feels things that are veiled by the presence of any other human being." Benton MacKaye of the Wilderness Society divided people into "the gregarious and the solitary" — with wilderness lovers emphatically belonging to the latter category. "A large number of people in a band can not have the individual freedom to get the message of wilderness," Olaus Murie insisted. "The highest form of communion with nature can be had individually, to be alone with nature." A private bond between nature and a single human imposed its own set of blinders, obscuring even the impact of a human death.

Misanthropic in this sense, the wilderness lover paid a social price for corresponding rewards. Muir spent his life rebounding between the human comforts of the city and the sanctuary of the mountains. Poised between the two, he and his ideological descendants in conservation appraised the terms and made a clear choice. "In spite of sore feet and weariness," Muir wrote in his journal after a climb near Kings Canyon in 1891, "and the spiky bush leveled against you like bayonets and the rough rocks in battle array, you climb in a kind of natural ecstasy as if lifted by the very spirit of the mountains . . . and when the glorious summits are gained, all the weariness vanishes in a moment as the vast landscapes of white mountains are beheld reposing in the sky. . . . This is the true transportation." The hardship and danger yielded a sharpened appreciation, more reward for more effort. When mountaineers gropingly listed the reasons for climbing — including courage, independence, freedom, a slower pace, natural beauty, an antidote to anthropocentrism and materialism — the litany amounted to an indictment of the civilization that routinely denied such qualities.

In the wilderness, especially in the mountains, the antipathy between conservation and modern culture seemed as clear as the air. Muir believed that anyone brought to the Sierra peaks would then help protect them. The history of the Sierra Club, and of the conservation movement generally, eventually bore him out. "The appeal of mountaineering," David Brower said in 1952, "has brought to the club many men who have stayed to fight *for* mountains long after they were willing or able to fight *with* them. Of the fifteen present directors of the club, for example, at least thirteen have mountaineering-conservation case histories to which this concept would apply — except that none would admit he was no longer able to climb or ski-mountaineer if he wanted to." In the conservation movement at large, each of the great mountaineer-conservationists — Muir, Marshall, Brower — was the most effective militant of his time.

The wildlife groups dominated conservation affairs from 1920 into the 1950s. Thereafter the wilderness groups, although the Wildlife Federation and Audubon Society had larger memberships and budgets, provided the most creative, uncompromising leadership. Muir regarded hunting as a childish indulgence to be outgrown; in a sense conservation outgrew hunting. From 1970 to 1976, while other outdoor activities were exploding, the ranks of hunters actually decreased by one-fourth. Even in the Wildlife Federation, only 30 percent of the members hunted while 20 percent opposed hunting in any form. Among the major groups, the Sierra Club and Wilderness Society represented the present and future of American conservation.

❧❧

Of the leading figures in the amateur tradition only two, Rosalie Edge and Rachel Carson, were women. Surrounded by male colleagues, they stood out prominently — yet were not quite so anomalous as they seemed. To approach any reform movement only through its top leadership will obscure the full story. Women in particular, usually working as supporters and helpmeets in the background, are invisible to history. For these two reasons most accounts of American conservation, including this one, have understated the participation of women in the movement. "Few people realize," Gifford Pinchot said as early as 1910, "what women have already done for conservation."

However muffled and cosseted, women took part from the beginning. The Appalachian Mountain Club admitted women to membership at its second regular meeting in 1876. "There are few climbs or mountain expeditions from which a vigorous woman need shrink," the ladies were told. In a day of hobbling female fashions, women had to devise a trail costume both modest and liberating. A woman AMC member suggested "the emancipation waist," a good flannel bathing suit over loose Turkish pants, and shoes selected without undue attention to appearance. "Our dress has done all the mischief," she said. "For years it has kept us away from the glory of the woods and the grandeur of the mountain heights. It is time we should reform." Properly equipped, they set out to hike with the men. In 1879 another AMC woman, in a report titled "Camp Life for Ladies," gave the verdict: "They may, if they will, do almost the same mountain work as men."

So much for the gentle peaks of the White Mountains. But what of the Sierra Nevada? In 1897 an experienced male mountaineer took four women on a hike through the rough country along the Tuolumne River. "I found them considerably slower than athletic young men," he reported in the *Sierra Club Bulletin,* "but fully as able otherwise to cope with all the physical difficulties; and their capacity of endurance of cold water, loss of sleep, snow, and certain forms of muscular fatigue, somewhat greater, perhaps, than that of the average young mountaineer of the other sex." The first Sierra Club outing in 1901 included women students from Stanford and Berkeley. "Their vigor and endurance were a revelation to all of us," a man concluded. The note of surprise in these male testimonials reflected current assumptions about the delicacy of women. At a time when men worried about the debilitating effect of too much education on the female constitution, these trips into the Sierra amounted to feminist gestures.

Whether from feminist or conservation motives, women always took a prominent part in the Sierra Club. Marion Randall Parsons met her husband on a High Trip and worked closely with Muir in his last years, going out to Martinez after Louie's death to feed him and serve as his secretary. On the club outings, women sometimes outnumbered men and did their share of the work. "One of my earliest impressions," a Sierran recalled of the 1920s, "was that men and women were equal on the trips." Aurelia Harwood served as the first woman president of the club, from 1927 to 1929. Marjory Bridge Farquhar, who also met *her* husband on an outing, was one of the foremost woman climbers of her day, with several first ascents in the Sierra. "I never thought of it as a men's club," she said later. "There are mostly men on the board, and there always were; but there were an awful lot of women that did other things. . . . Maybe some of the harder work was done by the women."

Women were even more influential in local Audubon circles. Bird watching attracted more women to conservation than any other nature activity; Edge and Carson were both birders. At the turn of the century, women authors — including Olive Thorne Miller, Florence A. Merriam, and Mabel Osgood Wright — wrote popular books about birds and their habits. The first state Audubon group was founded in 1896 by a group of women in Boston. Two years later Wright launched the Connecticut Audubon Society with the help of other women. In fact, women dominated most of the early state groups. After the local societies formed the national association in 1905, men took over the leadership. When Edge began her assault on the male leadership in 1929, she felt like a quail menaced by peregrine falcons. But on the local, less visible level, women never relinquished their leadership in bird protection.

On the national level women pressed for conservation measures through their own groups, especially the General Federation of Women's Clubs. At its 1902 convention the GFWC created the Committee on Forestry and Irrigation on a motion by Mary Eno Mumford, a relative of Pinchot's. Most of the two million members of the GFWC approached conservation by way of tree planting, nature study, national park campaigns, and bird protection. As with the general population, the utilitarian aspects held less appeal. "Appreciation of the aesthetic value of trees and forests," said Mary Gage Peterson of Chicago, chairman of the Forestry Committee in 1907, "is much more common than a definite grasp of the economic meaning and importance of forestry." Her successor, Mary Belle Sherman, head of the committee from 1914 to 1920, started conservation work after coming under the influence of Enos Mills during an extended vacation at Longs Peak, Colorado. From Muir to Mills to Sherman, the mountains pulled in another convert. In 1916 Sherman sent out seven hundred personal letters urging the establishment of the National Park Service. Known as the "National Park Lady" for her persistence, she returned to the Rockies in the same way that Muir went back to Yosemite. "It is a great relief to be here in my log cabin in the mountains once more," she wrote Horace McFarland, "where things and people seem saner than at the convention in New York."

The GFWC drew most of its members from middle-class married women. Lacking independent incomes, they gave not money but time to conservation. Of 6,450 protesting letters sent to the War Department in 1906–1907 over the diversion of Niagara Falls, about one-third were written by women. "The organized women are not at all great about raising money for wild life conservation," Hornaday noted. "They can, however, do no end of circular work and publicity of all kinds." Women made up over half of the National Parks Association's membership. "It is they who get the men started," wrote Robert Sterling Yard. "Their federated clubs are invaluable as local propagandists and ground breakers. If once women see the light, the militant kind will fight forever against any odds." After 1930 the GFWC fell on hard times. In 1937 its Conservation Committee had a budget of only eighty dollars. But for specific campaigns it could still call forth an avalanche of mail and letters to the editor. In 1948, according to DeVoto, the GFWC provided "the strongest single opposition" to threatened commercial inroads on the Olympic National Park.

Partial to trees, parks, and birds, women generally disliked hunting and fishing — because of the killing, apparently, and not because of a general aversion to roughing it, as every Sierra Club outing proved. The Boone and Crockett Club and the American Game Protective Association were stag affairs. Will Dilg tried to attract women to the Izaak Walton League. "No Chapter can become a great Chapter that does not allow the women of their community to membership," he said at the 1925 convention. "And while it is true that most of our women do not fish or hunt, it is certainly true that all of them love a beautiful land." On two occasions in the 1920s the Walton journal *Outdoor America* tried a woman's department. Both times it quickly expired, evidently from a lack of interest. Most women simply did not care for the sporting life. During the three decades that wildlife interests dominated the conservation movement, women had notably less impact than in the periods before and after.

During this hiatus Rosalie Edge embarked on her solitary crusades. Time and again she found herself opposed by commercial interests. Since most women did not directly work for a living, and thus were relatively independent of such interests, it seemed to Edge that they made natural conservationists. "I wish that more women would work for conservation," she said. "Most of the conservation measures are so closely related to business that it is sometimes difficult for men to take a strong stand on the side of the public interest. But women can do it, and they should." She also believed that women put loyalty to measures above loyalty to friends. A male politician once told Edge that he defended the Audubon Society because of his friendship with Frank Chapman. "To a woman," she said, in the spirit of her suffragist days, "loyalty to the cause is of first importance, and the obligations of friendship must, if necessary, be sacrificed. To a man, the friendship comes first, and causes must be adjusted." Nothing deflected Edge from her causes. Yet despite her ironic strictures on male sentimentality, most of her allies were men: Hornaday, Willard Van Name, Irving Brant.

After World War II, with the revival of the amateur tradition and a building concern over the environment, women took more prominent roles. In the Sierra Club, Charlotte Mauk and Doris Leonard organized the biennial wilderness conferences that helped bring the club back into the mainstream of the movement. Eleanor Anthony King edited *Audubon Magazine,* broadening its editorial scope and recruiting such noted naturalists as Olaus and Adolph Murie, until her premature death in 1949. Celia Hunter joined the council of the Wilderness Society and later became its first woman president. In local communities, unnumbered anonymous women took up specific causes. A housewife named Claire Dedrick, trying to stop a road in San Mateo County, California, in 1966, was told by an exasperated engineer: "Get back in your kitchen, lady, and let me build my road!" The remark launched a career in conservation. Joining the local Sierra Club chapter, Dedrick went on to the club's board of directors and, in 1975, became California's Secretary for Resources.

All these fragmentary references can only suggest the importance of women in conservation. Given the limits of historical evidence, the full record is buried. Women exerted influence in their homes, on their husbands and families, in subtle ways not recorded for posterity or made public at the time. Thus in 1921, when the California legislature voted $300,000 for the Save the Redwoods League, the governor seemed unwilling to sign the bill. But his wife, a GFWC member, talked him into it. When male field biologists went off on their trips, the wives often came along as the first assistants. "Most of us are obliged to acknowledge in all fairness," one such biologist said in 1946, "that our wives have contributed at least half to our success on the good jobs for which we have taken the credit." From incomplete evidence it appears that Hazeldean Brant, Marcelline Krutch, Margaret Murie, Avis DeVoto, and Anne Morrow Lindbergh all crucially reinforced their husbands' conservation work.

Whether these women were acting specifically as women is a moot point. Stereotypical female behavior and values — including nurture, prudence, the protection of life, a love of beauty — do lend themselves to conservation. "With true mother instinct," said Mrs. Francis E. Whitley, chairman of the GFWC Conservation Committee in 1925, "women want to keep for the children of the future all the best that the past has known." "Man has always been the thoughtless destroyer," said a woman Waltonian, whereas women stand for "the saving of the good things which beneficent nature has granted." To the extent that stereotypes are only generalizations run amok, perhaps women in conservation were in fact acting out their womanly tendencies. In any case, they deserve a large chapter in conservation history.

❧❧

By its nature the amateur tradition drew support from people with a little extra time and money. Amateur conservation work paid no bills, actually submitted its own bills in expenses and volunteered hours. Accordingly, it typically appealed to a certain economic class. Most of the early pioneers — Muir, Grinnell, Johnson, Sargent, the Sierra and Appalachian Mountain clubs, the women behind the state Audubon groups, TR and the Boone and Crockett men, Hornaday, Burnham and the American Game Protective Association — held positions in society of relative privilege, if not of great wealth in most cases. "The impression still seems to exist," an AMC member noted as early as 1908, "that we are an aggregation of millionaires." "I was not born in a log cabin," said Hornaday with perverse pride, "I never swept any office but my own, and glory be! I did not have to work my way through college." In the early 1900s, a privileged status usually implied an Anglo-Saxon Protestant background and limited enthusiasm for the aspirations of other, poorer, economic groups. Thus from the beginning conservation was accused of elitism and racism, often by business interests that themselves displayed little sympathy for the poor. But the charges had, and continued to have, enough substance to complicate the politics of conservation down to the present day.

Historians realize the unfairness of judging a previous generation by standards accepted now but not then. Racism, as the term is now understood, was all but universal in Muir's day. He used the word "nigger" in everyday conversation, apparently with no particular hostility toward blacks. In the same way, he disapproved of a Jewish merchant in Martinez ("the wolf-Jew"), yet bought all his food at a Jewish grocery in San Francisco. Any charge of racism, however obvious by current standards, would have baffled him. Furthermore, to some degree pride in one's own group implies, even demands, hostility toward other groups. The two attitudes are often indistinguishable, each reinforcing the other. Muir proudly identified himself as Scotch, then British, then Anglo-Saxon: the successive labels by themselves required no invidious comparisons with other groups, simply an affirmation of Muir's own stock. "Anglo Saxon folk have inherited love for oaks and heathers," he said. Again: "Anglo Saxons seldom take any retrograde steps. Therefore the movements toward forest salvation however wavering and slow we may well believe will be onward." He meant no offense by such remarks. But non-Anglo-Saxons might justifiably take them as implicit criticisms, or worse.

For conservationists, a bland sense of differentness slid over into nativism and racism when a given category of foreigners went so far as to resist conservation. In the early 1900s, the "new immigrants" from southern and eastern Europe sometimes disregarded American protective laws by continuing old-country hunting customs, especially the shooting of songbirds. In Massachusetts the federated women's clubs tried to stop this slaughter "by Italians and other foreign residents," a leader wrote in the GFWC journal, "through educating them to an understanding of our laws and a respect and love for bird life." Others adopted harsher measures. John M. Phillips of Pittsburgh, a member of the AGPA and the Boone and Crockett, pushed through a state law in 1910 prohibiting unnaturalized aliens from owning a shotgun or a rifle. When the law was challenged he paid the expenses for the Supreme Court test case that upheld it. Some nativists used the alien/hunting issue as a pretext for larger attacks. David Starr Jordan, president of Stanford and an honorary officer of the Sierra Club, declared that American agriculture was threatened by immigration because aliens killed the birds that ate the insects that destroyed crops. "The fruit grower pays a high price," said Jordan in 1926, "for the ignorance and carelessness of the 'oppressed of every nation,' 'the beaten men of beaten races,' whose very presence here contributes to our own oppression."

Obviously Jordan had something more in mind than endangered fruit. The old WASP gentry, the same class that invented conservation, felt besieged by the new groups. By recalling America as it was, or as it was imagined, and by calling forth the sturdy pioneer values now seemingly passing on to the aliens, conservation offered psychic release from the new tensions. Conservation seemed clean, efficient, invoking a vision of rushing streams and fragrant forests and cultural homogeneity, all in sharp contrast to the redolent immigrant districts of most cities. Daniel Carter Beard, founder of the Boy Scouts, drew cartoons depicting alien game-hogs "with plenty of black curly hair, cigarettes and ear-rings," as he pointed out. Good "American" hunters smoked proper pipes and put no rings in their ears. Just west of his Bronx Zoo, Hornaday found aliens plinking away at birds in Little Italy. In his landmark book of 1913, *Our Vanishing Wild Life,* he devoted a chapter to the problem. "All members of the lower classes of southern Europe," he said with a grand sweep, "are a dangerous menace to our wild life." Warming to the subject, Hornaday then digressed from animals long enough to warn about Italians in American life: "They are strong, prolific, persistent and of tireless energy. . . . Wherever they settle, their tendency is to root out the native American and take his place and his income. . . . The Italians are spreading, spreading, spreading." This in a book about wildlife!

Conservation and nativism met at the highest level in a Park Avenue aristocrat named Madison Grant. A founder of the Bronx Zoo, a trustee of the American Museum of Natural History, a leading member of the Boone and Crockett Club and the Save the Redwoods League, Grant was also — according to a student of the subject — "intellectually the most important nativist in recent American history." His two hobbies fed into each other. As an amateur naturalist he argued in the Muir spirit that nature had rights of its own, independent of human intentions. This sympathy for animals informed his nativist tome, *The Passing of the Great Race,* published in 1916. The Judeo-Christian tradition had gone astray in its central concept "that man is something fundamentally distinct from other living creatures." Actually humans and other animals differed not in kind but only in degree of development, said Grant, and were controlled alike by heredity rather than environment. People from northern Europe — "Nordics" — thrived on heavy farm work but withered in factories and crowded cities, where the dark Mediterranean races bred and prospered. The Nordics were doomed. The future belonged to Jews, with their "dwarf stature, peculiar mentality, and ruthless concentration on self interest." Grant's racial ideas were shared, to some degree, by many other conservationists of the time, including George Bird Grinnell, Abbott Thayer, George Dorr, Theodore S. Palmer, Henry Fairfield Osborn, Emerson Hough, and Will Dilg.

Racist by modern standards, their attitudes cannot be separated from historical factors specific to the period: the new immigration, the tensions of modernization and rampant progress, cancerous urbanization complemented by the end of the frontier, and the bunker mentality among the old, displaced patricians. Progressive-era conservationists expressed nativist ideas more as prisoners of their time than as conservationists. The amateur tradition inherently drew from a privileged class; at the time that class belonged to WASPs; therefore the amateur pioneers in the movement were WASPs. Later, as the middle class opened to more diverse groups, so did conservation. Two of the Wilderness Society founders, Robert Marshall and Bernard Frank, were Jews. As editor of the *Century* Robert Sterling Yard had deplored the diminishing flow of "the desirable blood of northern Europe" in American life. In his last years, as president of the Wilderness Society, Yard by a lovely irony depended on the largesse of a descendant of Russian Jews.

The New Deal revolution in conservation politics further encouraged ethnic and class diversity in the movement. Again the demographics of conservation reflected larger currents of the day. Liberal Democrats infiltrated the old conservation leadership of conservative Republicans, especially through federal agencies, the Wilderness Society, and the Emergency Conservation Committee. Marshall, Frank, Benton MacKaye, Irving Brant, and others shuttled back and forth between the amateur movement and jobs in the federal government. To some degree conservation was democratized. "One of the arguments most frequently raised against wilderness areas," *Living Wilderness* noted in 1939, "is that the average person can't afford to visit them." True enough, the writer conceded, in the old days when heavy equipment and mule caravans forced expenses of ten dollars per day per person. But with modern equipment and backpacking, costs were substantially reduced. After the war, as the Sierra Club phased out mules, its outings also became cheaper and at least potentially attractive to blue-collar hikers.

The matter went beyond economics, however. The major groups, especially at the level of local chapters and branches, were also *social* units. Even with an acceptable income, potential members from ethnic minorities might find a discouraging lack of their peers at conservation meetings. A

WASP hegemony still controlled the movement. "Many of our first- and second-generation immigrants, drawn from Europe's marginal populations," said Roger Tory Peterson in 1957, "are enjoying prosperity for the first time and perhaps have not had time to develop judgment." The second coming of Madison Grant! In the Sierra Club, an applicant needed the sponsorship of two members to gain entrance. The Southern California chapter thereby screened out minorities, even Jews, from its meetings and parties. The more liberal members from the San Francisco area deplored the policy; in 1959 Brower, declaring the club open to people of "the four recognized colors," pointedly approved the admission of a black woman to the southern chapter. The woman did join, but was not active and soon dropped her membership. Later the board considered a resolution against the exclusion of minorities. "Now wait a minute," said director Bestor Robinson, "— this is not an integration club; this is a conservation club." The resolution did not pass.

Despite the changes in postwar American society, the conservation movement for long retained its ethnic homogeneity. During the twenty years after 1945, every major conservationist without exception could trace his background to Christian immigrants from northern Europe. In that time not even the Wilderness Society's precedent of introducing Jews to national leadership circles was repeated. If the WASP hegemony of progressive conservation was reinforced by its era, the continued hegemony ran *against* profound currents of the two decades after the war, suggesting that conservation amounted to a nativist ethnic movement.

Yet, in a seeming paradox, it often cited "primitive" peoples as examples of sound ecological conduct. Charles Lindbergh, in his prewar isolationist campaigns, made statements widely perceived as racist. "It is time to turn from our quarrels and to build our White ramparts again," he said in urging a union of European countries against the hordes of Russia and Asia. After the war he saw previously unnoticed qualities in non-European races: natural instincts, reverence for nature, a sensible aversion to technological progress. As a conservationist he found himself oddly at home among the Agta and Tasaday of the Philippines and the Masai of Africa. No longer the repository of civilization in its highest forms, the European countries could actually learn from colored races. "It seems to me," he concluded, "that the average intellectual superiority of the white race, for instance, is countered by the sensate superiority of the black race. Even though I was born and live in the framework of the white race, I believe it is quite possible that the black race will achieve a better balance of life eventually. . . . I become more and more doubtful that the superiority in science and technology of European man is leading him to a better life than that achieved by other peoples."

As always Lindbergh spoke only for himself. But he was tapping a deep vein in conservation history. Ever since Muir, conservationists had been praising native American peoples as wise stewards of the land. Muir admired their pantheism, supposing that — as in his own case — it demanded a respectful forbearance toward all natural phenomena. "To the Indian mind all nature was instinct with deity," he noted approvingly. "A spirit was embodied in every mountain, stream, and waterfall." As a young man George Bird Grinnell rode with the Pawnee and was inducted into the tribe. After retiring from *Forest and Stream* in 1911 he spent the rest of his life turning out substantial ethnological studies of the Plains Indians, especially the Cheyenne. He agreed with Muir that conservationists might learn from Indian practices. "He protected the beasts on which he depended," Grinnell said of the Indian hunter, "and practiced methods of economy in hunting that American sportsmen may well take to heart." Other statements in the same mode may be quoted all but interminably:

Caption on a cover painting of *Outdoor America,* 1928, depicting an Indian spearing a fish: "He had unpolluted waters to fish in and he never took more than he needed."

Robert Marshall, 1933: "They had for the most part an attitude of preservation, a realization that their life came from a nature which it would be catastrophic to destroy."

Gifford Pinchot, 1947, noting the practice of family hunting grounds among the Algonquin: "Centuries before the Conservation policy was born, here was Conservation practice at its best."

Stewart Udall, 1963: "Today the conservation movement finds itself turning back to ancient Indian land ideas, to the Indian understanding that we are not outside of nature, but part of it."

William Douglas, 1974: "Although the Indians took their living from the wilderness, they left that wilderness virtually intact. . . . Indeed, their judicious use of fire was a technique that ecologists were to adopt years later."

Sigurd Olson, 1976: "Indians believe the land is God's and no one has the right to manipulate it, that it is to be used not only by man but equally by all living creatures."

In one sense this pervasive theme in conservation literature balances the movement's outward appearance as an aggregation of WASPs. When comparing aboriginal attitudes and practices with those of modern, progressive whites, conservationists typically found their own people deficient — stupid at best, perhaps willfully selfish and shortsighted, in any case less wise than the native populations they displaced. "Whatever the virtues of our race may be," said Pinchot in 1906, "and they are very many, it is a fact that wherever the white man, and especially the Anglo-Saxon, sets his foot, the first thing he does is take the cream off the country."

In another sense, conservationists' interest in Indians was curiously manipulative and vicarious. Few conservationists dealt with actual living Indians, or listened to their problems in a white man's world, or helped them maintain the old ways of which conservationists spoke so reverently. Grinnell did campaign for Indian rights, but even he hoped the reservations would be broken up and the Indians dispersed into white society. "There is nothing more important for the Indian child than association with white people," he said, ". . . for only by such association can he learn to use his naturally intelligent mind as the white man uses his, and be taught to reason as a white man reasons." In the 1930s Marshall, without consulting the affected tribes, established roadless areas on sixteen reservations. Twenty years later, when the tribes regained a measure of self-determination, they voted to abolish all but two of those areas. Perhaps Marshall, in regarding Indians as an idealized abstraction, assumed they would favor the protection of wilderness.

Until the mid-1960s, then, with the conspicuous exceptions of Marshall, Frank, and a few others, conservation was ethnically a WASP preserve. No other American reform movement of a general nature was so exclusively the province of one ethnic group. At least the movement could exploit the advantages of elitism. What it lost in range and democracy it gained back in stability and cohesiveness. The ethnic narrowness surely discouraged some potential allies of different backgrounds. But it also eased the way into corporate boardrooms and congressional offices. Conservationists wielded influence beyond their numbers because they knew the right people, or at least had gone to their schools.

❧❧

As yet, historians have no idea of where to locate amateur conservation in the context of American reform history. In fact the question has hardly been addressed. Of the existing historical overviews of conservation, one (by J. Leonard Bates) treats it as a democratic protest against selfish economic interests; another (by Samuel P. Hays), as an exercise in scientific management and modernization; a third (by Michael Lacey), as a reaction against Herbert Spencer in favor of an evolutionary positivism that urged human intervention in the natural world. But all three deal only with professional or utilitarian conservation. All three accept the usual notions of modern progress, with modifications, and all three make man the measure of all things. "The world we are told was made for man." The Muir tradition of the radical amateur in conservation has barely been acknowledged, much less interpreted.

Philosophically, this tradition belongs to the antimodernist thread in American thought. Drawn from an incongruous range of intellectual and political backgrounds, antimodernist thinkers converge on a single point: modern progress — implying cities, technology, and human arrogance — as ambiguous at best, probably nothing more than a harmful illusion that exchanged sanity and wholeness for less important physical improvements. Although overcome by the general course of events, antimodernist thinkers comprise an impressive roster of the most powerful and original minds in American history: Jefferson, Emerson, Thoreau, Henry George, Frederick Law Olmsted, Thorstein Veblen, Henry Adams, Mark Twain, Frank Lloyd Wright, T. S. Eliot, Robert Frost, Lewis Mumford, Edmund Wilson.

As a social and political movement, amateur conservation shared affinities with other, more ephemeral eruptions of antimodernism. Henry George, especially in the early years of the movement, exercised the strongest single political influence on conservation. *Progress and Poverty,* in stressing the treatment of land and natural resources, fed naturally into conservation. All people hold equal rights to the land, said George, in the same way they share equal rights to breathe the air. Private property grants no monopolistic privileges. Only a temporary tenant, a landowner could not benefit from the undeserved appreciation — the "unearned increment" — of his property's value. Any such unmerited appreciation should be confiscated by a "single tax."

Many early conservationists — including Muir, Pinchot, William Kent, and Daniel Carter Beard — could trace their political awakening to George, if not to the single panacea of the single tax, then to his general treatment of monopoly and resources. George's ideas saturated the politics of the progressive era, showing up in the minds of even conservative conservationists like Horace McFarland. "I am outraged personally," McFarland told a single-taxer, "at values added to land by no work, thought, help, or even decent interest on the part of the man who gets the benefit of the value." Pinchot never identified himself as a George disciple, but Georgite ideas and language appeared in his writing and in Forest Service policies. "My own money," he once declared in explaining his political career, "comes from unearned increment on land in New York held by my grandfather.... Having got my wages in advance in that way, I am now trying to work them out."

The George influence persisted among some conservationists for decades after the progressive era. Irving Brant, converted to "left-of-center" democracy by a reading of George in 1913, as late as 1935 made a Georgish speech about land values inflated by speculative buying. Benton MacKaye, a friend of the single-tax publicist Louis Post, brought the viewpoint to the Wilderness Society. In 1937 John Collier wrote a *Living Wilderness* article about "unearned increment from the land." Even Franklin Roosevelt praised George as "one of the really great thinkers produced by our country. I do not go all the way with him, but I wish that his writings were better known and more clearly understood, for certainly they contain much that would be helpful today." Newton B. Drury, director of the National Park Service in the 1940s and a leader of the Save the Redwoods League, came from an ardently Georgite family. "I was always a very mild devotee of the single tax theory," Drury said, "but I still think it's sound." The old faith was kept alive most persistently by Judson and Bertha King. Through their National Popular Government League, for almost half a century they campaigned for public utilities and rational resource policies, as defined by Henry George.

At scattered points in the twentieth century, individual antimodernists — sometimes inspired by George — put their ideas into practice by going "back to the land." In 1906 George H. Maxwell, a lawyer from California, started his Homecrofter movement to return urbanites from the "wrong environment" of cities to a healthier farming life. Appalled by the absorption of public lands into speculative private ownership, without settlement or any beneficial use, Maxwell urged that any male willing to farm be given a free acre of land. "We must approach the ideals of Socialism," he said, "by a slow process of education and evolution." But not socialism as commonly understood. The Marxist form, like capitalism, removed humans "from the environment in which God Almighty intended they should live." Instead, drawing on Ruskin, Kropotkin, and George, Maxwell proposed a libertarian socialism of self-sufficient communities that recalled the utopian socialists of the 1840s. Indeed, Maxwell liked to quote Emerson on the virtues of owning and using your own land — and no more.

In the 1920s Ralph Borsodi, an economist and single-taxer from New York, took up the theme of decentralized homesteads. Modern America, he declared from his farm in Rockland County, was unnatural and ugly: "a civilization of noise, smoke, smells, and crowds." Only a few miles from Manhattan, his family produced its own food and clothing and enjoyed, he said, "the inner discipline that comes from communion with the land."

After an unsatisfactory experiment with a New Deal subsistence home-stead in Ohio, Borsodi opened his School for Living in Suffern, New York. For ten years his *Free America* magazine served as a forum for the diverse antimodernisms of the Vanderbilt agrarians (Allen Tate, John Crowe Ransom, and others), Herbert Agar and his Distributists movement, con-sumer cooperatives, the Catholic Rural Life Conference, and unreformed single-taxers.

The most familiar recent exponents of back-to-the-land were Scott and Helen Nearing. In 1932, after spending years at a single-tax colony in Arden, Delaware, they decided to seek "an alternative to Western civiliza-tion and its outmoded culture pattern" by moving to a farm in rural Ver-mont. "We hoped to replace worry, fear and hate with serenity, purpose and at-one-ness." In Vermont, and at a later farm in Maine, they thrived on a regimen of the most ascetic simplicity: no alcohol, tea, coffee, tobacco, candy, pastries, meat; no telephone, radio, TV. They still called themselves socialists, but in a pre-Marxian, native American sense of the term. Their testament of 1954, *Living the Good Life,* quoted Thoreau nine times, Marx not once. "Marxism has laid great emphasis on economic development," said Scott Nearing. "It confines its attention chiefly to society. It by-passes the individual and the cosmos." Like the agrarian hippies that took up the cause in the 1960s, the Nearings ultimately described their work in reli-gious terms.

Together these disparate groups — amateur conservationists, Georgites, agrarians, homesteaders, hippies — made up a unique form of native American radicalism. The dominant radical tradition in this country, as defined by the popularizers of Marx and as diluted and installed by the progressive–New Deal lineage in government, was characteristically

- oriented toward cities,
- skeptical about religion,
- materialist in values,
- lower and middle class in sympathy,
- attuned to ethnic minorities, and
- partial to a liberal view of history as progress.

By contrast the antimodernist tradition was

- oriented toward rural and wilderness areas,
- strongly if quirkily religious,
- esthetic and spiritual in values,

- middle and upper class in sympathy,
- attuned to WASPs, and
- informed by a radically conservative view of history
  as decline and regression.

The antimodernist tradition seemed less coherent because it never found its Marx. To Marxists, Marx served as prophet, historian, and philosopher. To antimodernists, Thoreau served as prophet, Henry Adams as historian, Lewis Mumford as philosopher. The conservation movement, the most successful exercise in antimodernism, corresponded to the Russian Revolution. Muir was its Lenin. Pinchot was its Stalin.

※※

After 1965, conservation underwent a fundamental transformation in evolving into environmentalism. With man, the newly endangered species, as the overriding focus, the movement drew recruits who lacked a traditional conservationist's interest in hiking, birding, fishing, or hunting. Paradoxically, by narrowing its focus to man the movement attracted a broader range of people. The old WASP hegemony ended. The major leaders of environmentalism included Barry Commoner and Paul Ehrlich (Jews), Ralph Nader (Lebanese), and Victor Yannacone (Italian). And to some degree, the lines between mainstream political radicalism and political antimodernism were blurred.

The quarrel between Commoner and Ehrlich reiterated the issues between these two reform traditions. Commoner spoke from a Marxist perspective — the first major conservationist since Robert Marshall to do so. A holistic philosophy, said Commoner, closely resembled the process of dialectical materialism: "The whole idea is to find the decisive relationship in a complex situation, the red thread." Ehrlich by contrast spoke in the tones of Malthus, one of Marx's favorite whipping boys, and the population issue had a long history among traditional conservationists. Ehrlich also accepted the ecological imperative. "These attitudes are the antithesis of those of the Old Left," he said, "of Socialism and Communism, which resemble Judeo-Christian attitudes in encouraging the exploitation of nature." Predictably enough, as a Marxist Commoner resisted the population issue. ("I didn't understand it and I had the left-winger's natural uneasiness about it.") At the outset, Commoner and Ehrlich argued from sharply opposed political traditions. Yet the most striking feature of their quarrel, once it was under way, lay in how quickly it evaporated. On a practical level most environmentalists cared about both pollution and population, and worked at both problems with no sense of conflict. Sharply contested in theory, the confrontation lost its impact in the context of actual politics.

The folksinger Pete Seeger, for example, came to environmentalism from three decades of Old Left causes. At his home in Beacon, New York, near the Hudson, he knew firsthand about water pollution. ("I would not drink water in Poughkeepsie," Franklin Roosevelt had said in 1938.) In the late 1960s Seeger led a drive that built a sailing sloop, the *Clearwater,* to sail the dirty river and, as he said, "to reach a Main Street audience" with the environmental word. Blending his Old Left background and his newly found ecological sense, Seeger simply split the difference between Commoner and Ehrlich. "Commoner has convinced me," he wrote, "that technology and our private profit politics and society must be radically changed and quickly. But I'm still working hard for Zero Population Growth. . . . Achieving ZPG will be good education for everyone. Everyone can and must cooperate."

The traditional conservation groups still appealed mainly to an elite constituency. In the Sierra Club, 52 percent of the members held professional jobs, 19 percent were students, and only 7 percent worked in clerical and blue-collar occupations. Audubon Society members in 1976 claimed an average income of $35,700; 85 percent had gone to college, 43 percent to graduate school. Thus Norman Podhoretz suggested that environmentalism was nothing more than "the issue on which the WASP patriciate . . . hopes to reassert its primacy." But the situation had changed in two crucial ways since the early 1900s. A position of privilege no longer implied a WASP identity. In 1970 the Audubon Society added two blacks of impeccable credentials to its board of directors; Marshall Kuhn, a Jew, was an active Sierra Club leader in San Francisco. Second and more important, the traditional groups no longer dominated amateur conservation. The newer man-centered groups appealed to younger, more diverse memberships.

Finally, by the mid-1970s almost every sector of American society had some appreciation of the environmental crisis. Historically the province of a particular class and ethnic group, conservation at last belonged to everyone. In 1969, according to one poll, only 33 percent of American blacks urged greater attention to the environment. Seven years later that figure had risen to 58 percent. Increasingly, not without some rough edges, conservation and ethnic minorities accepted each other. "We are concerned with the quality of life," said the president of the Sierra Club. "To us, that means adequate housing and transportation, clean air and water, good schools and inner-city parks." A spokesman for the National Wildlife Federation pointed out, "It takes a while to get over the mistrust, theirs of environmentalists and ours of the urban-poverty coalition. But once past the rhetoric, we have a lot in common." At rallies against nuclear power, feuding Marxist sects and aging hippies together invoked the specter of another Three Mile Island. The friends of the proletariat and the enemies of modernism found themselves in unlikely agreement. The amateur tradition in conservation, catalyzed by a campaign to stop a hydroelectric project in Hetch Hetchy, was reinvigorated by a crusade against a more baleful form of electricity generation.

1 1

Lord Man:
The Religion of Conservation

ALONG with such achievements as air pollution, industrial carcinogens, acid rain, and nuclear wastes, modern progress left its characteristic
mark on the influence of religion in American life. Just as progress did not
intend to foul the air, so it undermined religion in an offhand, incidental
way. As science and technology prospered, they dominated the public
mind and displaced religion as the highest expression of human uniqueness and genius. Science encouraged not faith and awe, but a dismantling
cast of mind: take it apart, figure it out, make it better. Religion demanded
reverence before the unknowable; science promised that, given enough
R and D, nothing was unknowable. Religion did not surrender easily. Periodically, every few decades, would come a wave of revivalism and com-
mentaries on the renewal of faith in a secular age. But the long-term trend
seemed inexorable. Religion mattered less in 1900 than in 1820 and less
still in 1980. Every generation appeared less pious than its predecessor.
Progress waxed and religion waned.

Conservation, the most durable expression of antimodernism, was often
described as a religious movement — by friends and enemies alike. The
label fitted well enough. Conservation resisted every aspect of the modern
syndrome, not least the loss of faith. In a particular way, however. Conservation religiosity hardly resembled the churched version under assault
by progress. "All devotees of nature and the outdoors are prophets and
promulgators of a kind of gospel," declared the naturalist Alan Devoe
in *Audubon Magazine* in 1945. "Expressly or implicitly, as a defined
doctrine or as only a pervasive and informing under-conscious mood,
a quality of *credo* and *hosanna* runs through their thoughts and writings. They are communicants of a common faith." As his prime ex-

ample, Devoe cited the missionary zeal of John Muir. What made him special, said Devoe, was not his scientific work or travels or writing. Rather, Muir distinguished himself by the passion of his nature mysticism and evangelism. "Of all the prophets of the nature-faith," Devoe suggested, "Muir was the most religiously exalted and sustained."

Here lay the ultimate meaning of Muir's life, indeed of conservation itself. Traced back to its ideological roots, conservation amounted to a religious protest against modernity.

※※

Contemporary discussion of this issue usually begins with a paper read by the medieval historian Lynn White, Jr., to a meeting of the American Association for the Advancement of Science in December 1966. Writing just as the environmental revolution started to break from the confines of traditional conservation, White aimed to explain the ecological crisis in historical terms and thus (by inference) to show a way out of the mess. He traced the culprits, Western science and technology, back to their origins in medieval Europe — a culture saturated with Christian thinking. He then followed Christianity to its earliest stirrings and placed the final blame on Judeo-Christian anthropocentrism: one God with a special interest in man, the only earthly creature with a soul, gifted with special powers and privileges, instructed by the first chapter of Genesis to subdue the earth and establish dominion over all her creatures. The world, as Muir said, made for man. "The victory of Christianity over paganism was the greatest psychic revolution in the history of our culture," wrote White. "By destroying pagan animism, Christianity made it possible to exploit nature in a mood of indifference to the feelings of natural objects." Asian and Greco-Roman religions posited ideals of stasis and harmony, with a concept of time as cyclical and repetitive. The Judeo-Christian story of creation introduced the notion of linear time, progress, with its corollary injunctions of human endeavor and improvement. Fueled by these twin notions of human uniqueness and progress, Christianity begat science and technology which begat environmental abuse. As the way out, White proposed nothing less than a rethinking of the Christian tradition, with Francis of Assisi as the patron saint of ecologists.

Later published in *Science* and the *Sierra Club Bulletin* and then widely anthologized (and restated by Arnold Toynbee in 1973), the White thesis provoked a flurry of discussion among both conservationists and theologians. Critics pointed out non-Christian cultures with sorry records of land abuse, and other Christian cultures with better records than the industrial West. Textual interpreters claimed that the key passage, Genesis 1:28, enjoined a wise stewardship rather than mindless exploitation. One rebutter blamed the ascetic dualism of the early Church, which led to a separation of matter and spirit; others inverted this sequence, praising the early Church but damning the Protestant Reformation.

The most detailed response, by the Australian philosopher John Passmore, conceded that the Hebrew tradition, in sharply distinguishing between God and nature, had led to a desacralization of the natural world. But he cited Old Testament passages showing God's concern for all of nature: instructing Noah to save every beast; causing rain to fall on all the earth for all creatures, not only man; praising the righteous man for valuing the life of his beast. According to Passmore, Christianity only became dangerous to nature when it was grafted to the Greek Stoic tradition, freed by Aristotle from the historical Greek fear of human hubris. Centuries later, this bristling hybrid was refined by Bacon and Descartes into a specifically *Western* viewpoint inaccurately ascribed to Christianity. Thus, Passmore concluded, the environmental crisis required "not so much a 'new ethic' as a more general adherence to a perfectly familiar ethic" with available Christian sources.

On the other hand, many conservationists — and Christian thinkers with an interest in conservation — agreed with White. "I really don't feel very sympathetic," said Margaret Murie, "with the old Judeo-Christian ethic that man is the master of the universe and should have dominion over it, because I think we have abused that dominion." "The Judeo-Christian idea of man dominating nature," Paul Ehrlich proposed, "must be replaced by the goal of living in harmony with nature." In response to White, some Christian theologians tried to discover a full ecological tradition within Christianity. But even such writers — including H. Paul Santmire, Frederick Elder, Francis A. Schaeffer, Conrad Bonifazi, John B. Cobb, Jr., Ian Barbour, and Roger L. Shinn — had to concede that most of historical Christianity denied their efforts. Francis of Assisi, though one of the most beloved saints, had few disciples in his ministry to the birds. To grant absolute value to every human individual *necessarily* devalued the rest of the natural world. Modern Christian theology, especially the Protestant forms, still borrowed most heavily from mechanistic German writers influenced by Kant and Newton. "Today," Frederick Elder suggested, "the most adequate 'theologian' is not Karl Barth but someone like the naturalist John Muir." (Perhaps Elder did not realize the extent of Muir's apostasy from the faith of Jesus.)

Such discussions could be spun out indefinitely. The Bible of course offered grist for anyone's mill. The priestly account of creation in the first chapter of Genesis recorded the successive appearance of vegetation, animals, and man, with each seen as good and told to multiply, and the focus on God rather than man. The Yahwistic account in the second chapter of Genesis introduced man first, followed by vegetation, animals, and finally woman, with man given clear priority in the new scheme. Similarly, a passage in Deuteronomy apparently warned against forest destruction: "When thou shalt besiege a city a long time, in making war against it to take it, thou shalt not destroy the trees thereof by forcing an axe against them." Fine; but wait: "For thou mayest eat of them, and thou shalt not cut them down. . . . Only the trees which thou knowest that they be not trees for meat, thou shalt destroy and cut them down." In the same anthropocentric mode, Paul cited the law of Moses that prohibited the muzzling of oxen engaged in grain threshing. "Doth God take care for oxen?" Paul asked. Of course not: "Or saith he it altogether for our sakes? For our sakes, no doubt, this is written: that he that ploweth should plow in hope."

Citations may pile up, leading nowhere. Biblical exegesis on this point was essentially irrelevant. "The historical impact of Christianity upon ecology," White said in replying to his critics, "has depended not on what we, individually, at present, may think that Christianity should have been, but rather upon what the vast 'orthodox' majority of people who called themselves Christians have in fact thought it was." And conversely, on what conservationists have had to say about religion in general and Christianity in particular.

☙☙

As Muir said, the question always returned to the relative eminence Lord Man assigned himself in the cosmos. In civilization man was surrounded by his works and therefore impressed by his own cleverness. If returned to the natural world, though, this singularly assertive biped seemed less special: hairless and none too agile, possessed of a large brain but dim of sight, faint of smell, barely able to take care of himself. When Muir made his early forays into the Canadian woods, and then walked his thousand miles to the Gulf of Mexico, he intuitively grasped the error in the Judeo-Christian conceit. Operating from experience, he derived a theological conclusion without the intercession of the theological process. After him, many other conservationists independently reached the same insight by a similar direct immersion. "A tree, a rock, has perfect poise and content," noted Cedric Wright of the Sierra Club. "In its life, a life enclosing whole solar systems within the atom, there surely is a consciousness utterly beyond our comprehension. . . . In the contemplation of this, one begins to doubt whether man is, after all, the highest form of life." "I defy anyone to live intimately with spring, to be witness at the rebirth of the green world, and still think that man owns the earth," said Hal Borland. "Out here we know who didn't make the hills, even if we aren't altogether positive who did."

Carried to its logical implications, this human humility before the natural world set up an obvious tension in conservationist ideology. Given the WASP hegemony in the movement, most conservationists were brought up as Christians, and as adults continued to regard themselves as followers of Jesus. But as friends of nonhuman nature they had to dislodge Christian man from his comfortable niche as the favored child of the Creator. "It is the way of Christian man," William Hornaday admitted in 1913, "to destroy all wild life that comes within the sphere of influence of his iron heel." The historical record seemed clear enough. How to reconcile a Christian faith with a love of nature? In 1950 Ernest Griffith of the Wilderness Society suggested a way out of the dilemma: God had actually inspired *two* Bibles, one the familiar written record of humans struggling toward salvation, the other the natural expression of his handiwork in wild places unimproved by man. Both Bibles embodied the Creator's highest intentions and were equally valid.

But could a Bible of nature remain within Christian orthodoxy? In 1954 the naturalist Alexander Skutch, writing in *Nature Magazine*, noted the absence among Western philosophers of any discussion of the ethics of killing wildlife. Asian religions did speak to the issue. "I find it more difficult to imagine," Skutch noted, "how Jesus would have treated the problem." Citing Paul's assurance that God had no concern for oxen, Skutch blamed the Western mistreatment of wild animals on this narrow Pauline concept. Indeed, no major religion in the modern West taught the sanctity of nonhuman life. "Hence in this part of the world it is among those who love the woods and fields and all their varied creatures, rather than among the staunchest adherents of the established creeds, that we find the deepest respect for living things as such."

Conservationists, in doubting the national myths of technology and progress, already had enough problems on their hands. To question the implications of *Christianity,* in an overtly Christian society, only complicated their efforts. The available record of such questioning probably understates its true extent among conservationists. "These voyagers and discoverers in the realm of spirit are often reticent about their sentiments in this matter," Skutch noted, "which as outgrowths of individual experience lack the weight of prestige and authority that invests them when taught by a venerable religion, as in the East." Nonetheless, in the early 1960s a growing number of conservationists declared their reservations about the Judeo-Christian tradition. Joseph Wood Krutch, converted to pantheism by his encounter with the spring peeper, pointed out the Hebraic desacralization of nature and its triumph over the nature gods of ancient Greece. Roland Clement of the Audubon Society declared that the deepening environmental crisis needed "an almost religious humility" on man's part — "but none of our churches have yet helped man to acquire it." Christians, said C. Edward Graves of the Wilderness Society, "should be more concerned as Christians with understanding the spiritual nature of wilderness experiences." Paul Brooks, a Sierra Club director and Rachel Carson's editor at Houghton Mifflin, criticized the Christian tradition for placing both God and man above nature by "the doctrine that this world was only a sort of Ellis Island on the threshold of the Heavenly Kingdom."

Other writers — including Aldous Huxley, Albert Burke, Peter Farb, Kenneth Boulding, and Ian McHarg — spoke in the same mode at this time. When Lynn White wrote his article in 1966, he was merely summarizing ideas with a long history among conservationists. Previously these ideas had appeared in obscure publications, often buried in articles on other topics. White's contribution was to bring the viewpoint to a larger audience, with the authority and literary panache of a skilled historian. He did for conservation religiosity what DeVoto had done for the land-grab and Carson for pesticides — that is, he popularized an issue already familiar to conservationists.

All but invisibly, often apologetically, ever since Thoreau naturalists and conservationists had embraced a variety of non-Christian religions. Sometimes the faith had no specific name but merely embodied (as Ansel Adams described his attitude) "a vast impersonal pantheism — transcending the confused myths and prescriptions that are presumed to clarify ethical and moral conduct." However deeply felt, a pantheist faith was typically expressed at some risk within the constraints of a Christian society. In 1858, in an article for the *Atlantic*, Thoreau declared his faith in the immortality of a pine tree and its prospects for ascending to heaven. The *Atlantic* ran the piece without the offending sentence, thereby eliciting a furious letter from the author. Later nature pantheists might actually see their heresies in print but they still cringed over the anticipated impact. James Oliver Curwood hoped his ideas would not shock the readers of *Outdoor America*. In the same way, the English naturalist W. H. Hudson broached his concept of "pantheistic Christianity" with a delicate touch. "It is not my wish to create the impression that I am a peculiar person in this matter," he apologized. "I differ from others only in looking steadily at it and taking it for what it is." Others might cover their intuitions with a jest. "Come for a Sunday," Benton MacKaye wrote Bob Marshall in 1935, "so that we can get in a good all-day expedition in Pantheism."

The early pioneers in conservation often gave their nature-faith a classical patina. Educated in the languages and traditions of ancient Greece and Rome, the pioneers found kindred spirits among the old pantheons of naturalist deities. At an early meeting of the Appalachian Mountain Club, Thomas Wentworth Higginson was reminded of "some weird council of old Greek wood-gods, displaced and belated, not yet quite convinced that Pan was dead, and planning together to save the last remnants of the forests they loved." In his book of 1915, *The Holy Earth*, Liberty Hyde Bailey borrowed from the ancient faith: "We should find vast joy in the fellowship, something like the joy of Pan." For some the ancient myths represented more than an offhand allusion, penetrating even the unconscious mind. In 1918 William Brewster of Massachusetts Audubon was bereaved by the death of his cherished Irish terrier. A few nights afterward, Brewster dreamed that Charon was ferrying him across the river Styx. Approaching the opposite shore, Brewster saw his dog, "there to greet me with wagging tail and smiling loving eyes, and when I landed he whirled around and around. . . . All this seemed very real." (The Christian heaven, of course, included no dogs or other "lower" forms of life.)

For other conservationists, the characteristic interest in aboriginal peoples included a respect for their religious ideas. On one of his Alaskan trips, Muir admired the Tlingit belief that animals also had souls, that it was unlucky even to speak disrespectfully of the creatures that supplied food for the tribe. The killing of such animals, a writer noted in *Bird-Lore* in 1938, amounted to a religious sacrament, carried out with reverence and a proper respect for ecological balance. Ernest Oberholtzer of the Wilderness Society immersed himself in Indian cultures, adopting their standards of beauty and tape-recording Ojibway religious myths. Such conduct, no less than a toying with pantheism, might expose a conservationist to popular ridicule. "Lo the poor Indian," one of Muir's friends twitted him, "— whose untutored mind sees God in storms and hears Him in the wind. Shall I class you with the Indian?" Actually Muir had more in common with Indians than with most civilized Christians. In the same fashion, years later Charles Lindbergh found agreeable theologies among the Masai of

Africa. "We believe God is in everything," a Masai told him. "We sing songs to the mountains and the trees because God is in them."

Asian religions in particular attracted conservationists as a sound basis for the nature-faith. Hindu, Zen Buddhist, and Taoist ideas were more contemporary than ancient Grecian myths, more substantial and less exotic than fugitive aboriginal religions, and they had long recorded histories and hundreds of millions of adherents. When conservationists spoke in philosophical terms, they invoked these Asian traditions more often than they mentioned Christianity. The Asian point of view generally treated man as just another animal, no more significant, in some cases actually less privileged, than other animals. Further, Asians retained a cyclical concept of time and typically greeted Western notions of progress with a tempered skepticism.

Most conservationists encountered Asian texts fairly late in life. The texts then corroborated ideas of long standing instead of acting as a primary influence on their formation. In Muir's case, he was first exposed during his Yosemite years when Jeanne Carr sent him a Hindu book, which he read "with much interest." More prolonged contact waited until years later, during his trip around the world in 1903. After traveling through Europe, Russia, Manchuria, and China, he left the company of Charles Sargent and went on alone to India. "This so far is the most interesting part of my trip," he wrote home. In Bombay he approvingly noted the tameness of the wild monkeys: "The Hindoos however poor always try to help their tailed neighbors in getting a living." He copied Hindu texts and aphorisms into his journal. His contemporary William Hornaday also liked to cite Hindu practices as a good example for benighted Americans, as did such later conservationists as Cedric Wright and Guy Emerson of the Audubon Society.

For William Douglas, his stay at a Buddhist monastery in the Himalayas in 1951 actually sparked a revolution in his conservation attitudes, changing him from a Pinchot utilitarian to a Muir acolyte. "I realized that Eastern thought had somewhat more compassion for all living things," he recalled: "man was a form of life that in another reincarnation might possibly be a horsefly or a bird of paradise or a deer. So a man of such a faith, looking at animals, might be looking at old friends or ancestors. In the East the wilderness has no evil connotation; it is thought of as an expression of the unity and harmony of the universe."

For David Brower, more typically, Buddhism later took the place of the Judeo-Christian ethic he had rejected earlier. "We cannot forever continue to multiply and subdue the earth," he said in 1956. During the 1960s the hippie counterculture, the fullest expression of antimodernism at the time, embraced Zen Buddhism and ecological ideas in equal measure. Perhaps from this milieu, perhaps from his own college-age children, Brower picked up an awareness of Zen. "We are in a kind of religion, an ethic with regard to terrain, and this religion is closest to the Buddhist, I suppose," he said in 1970. "We can take some cues from other religions. There is something else to do than bang your way forward."

China offered a choice between the Yang of Confucius (strong, aggressive, masculine) and the Yin of Lao-tse and Taoism (receptive, intuitive, mystical). Conservationists naturally preferred the Yin:

> As for those who would take the whole world
> To tinker it as they see fit,
> I observe that they never succeed:
> For the world is a sacred vessel
> Not made to be altered by man.
> The tinker will spoil it;
> Usurpers will lose it.

Apparently Charles Lindbergh was the first American conservationist to make significant use of Lao-tse. He first read the Taoist's work in 1940 on the recommendation of his wife. "He was greatly influenced by it and quoted it all his life," Anne Morrow Lindbergh recalled. Entering his ken just as he was turning toward conservation, Lao-tse confirmed and extended the new direction in his thinking. In his *Autobiography of Values* Lindbergh quoted the Taoist more than any other author ("The wise are not learned; the learned are not wise. Let your learned mind take leaven from the wisdom of your heart").

After World War II, Lao-tse showed up in conservation writing with increasing frequency. "The love of Tao is the love of nature," Alan Devoe declared in 1946. "There is an endless strength when (in the words of John Muir, that Tao-minded westerner) we 'lie back upon nature' and hush our hearts." Sigurd Olson liked to read Lao-tse's poems during long airplane trips; he gained a sense of poise and serenity as he dreamed the old Chinese dreams and the sound of airplane engines drifted away. Later the Taoist way was occasionally cited as a model of good conduct in ethical discussions provoked by Lynn White's article. "Western man has been at heart Promethean," wrote Huston Smith of MIT; "therein lies both his greatness and his absurdity. Taoism does not try to beat or cajole the universe or the gods; it tries to join them."

Asian ideas entered the minds of two of the most prominent postwar conservationists, Aldo Leopold and Rachel Carson, at one remove — through the mediation of a non-Asian writer. A man of flinty independence, Leopold seldom credited any external influences on his thinking. Except one: the Russian mystic Peter Ouspensky, best known in the West for his *Tertium Organum* and biography of Gurdjieff. First exposed to Ouspensky in the 1920s, when the gaze of a wolf's dying eyes sparked his rethinking of man's part in the ecological balance, Leopold was impressed by the Russian's melding of Western science and Eastern mysticism. Every particle in the universe, Ouspensky taught, in pulsing with consciousness denied both Newtonian mechanics and the Western separation of man from nature and matter from spirit. Everything, as Muir said, is bound fast to everything else. In Ouspensky's formulation, Asian mysticism fitted perfectly with the conservation Muir advocated, and reinforced Leopold's dawning sense of "the indivisibility of the earth." Accordingly, Leopold moved away from the Judeo-Christian tradition. "Industrialism, imperialism, and that whole array of population behaviors associated with the 'bigger and better' ideology," said Leopold, "are direct ramifications of the Mosaic injunction for the species to go the limit of its potential, i.e., to go and replenish the earth." In *Sand County Almanac* he used Ouspensky's concept of the "numenon," the imponderable essence of material things — although he characteristically referred to Ouspensky only as "a philosopher."

Carson accepted an Asian viewpoint by way of Albert Schweitzer, whom she admired as "the one truly great individual our modern times have produced." Schweitzer's "reverence for life" philosophy was essentially pantheist. Christian theologians have placed it outside the orthodox Christian tradition, as a new teaching without any Christian analogues. Schweitzer had arrived at the concept in the same way that Muir reached his central insight, by a direct immersion in the wilderness. In September 1915, recoiling from the World War and the dazzling effectiveness of modern war technology, Schweitzer embarked on a slow boat ride up the Ogowe River in Africa. As he floated past the teeming flora and fauna of the jungle, he pondered man's place in the cosmos. At sunset on the third day, the key phrase flashed in his mind: the German *Ehrfucht* conveying more than the English "reverence," suggesting a harder-edged awe and fear before a great force. Like many American conservationists, he felt a sudden sense of human puniness and forbearance toward the natural world. According to Schweitzer's biographer James Brabazon, this new perspective was implicitly Buddhist. Later Schweitzer read Buddhist texts and admired the concept of the unity of all life, an idea which he found nowhere in Western philosophy. For Carson, Schweitzer represented the purest expression of the respect for all living things she had originally learned from her mother. She dedicated *Silent Spring* to him with a grim quotation from his own writing: "Man has lost the capacity to foresee and to forestall. He will end by destroying the earth." The book brought her a handwritten note and an inscribed photograph from Schweitzer. "I can't think of anything that has pleased me more," she said.

From these varied sources — pantheism, classical Greece, American Indians, Asian religions, and Western interpreters of Asian viewpoints — conservationists took the philosophical affirmations that seemed absent from the more familiar Judeo-Christian tradition. They may have still called themselves Christians. But their ideas came from elsewhere.

❧❧

Some of them came from the middle kingdom of psychic phenomena. These inexplicable oddities — called spiritualism in the nineteenth century, studied as parapsychology more recently — occupy a special category of conservation religiosity. Not exactly religious, yet far removed from everyday reality, psychic experiences run through the personal histories of many conservationists. They defy much analysis but seem to mean *something*.

A properly skeptical Scotsman, Muir had no use for popular fads that smacked of humbuggery. As a boy in Wisconsin, he observed that only those neighbors with no fixed moral or religious principles succumbed to the vogue for spirit rappings and table-levitating parties. Later, in San Francisco, he gleefully disrupted a reverent séance held by his friends. Still ... Back in Wisconsin, Jeanne Carr's psychic friend had predicted that Muir would find his way to Yosemite and settle there, and that had come to pass. During his first summer in the Sierra he had his telepathic meeting with James Davie Butler. Emerson, perhaps responding to the Butler story, told Muir in 1871 about Swedenborg's experiences with talkative angels and voices from the dead. Muir was sufficiently intrigued to remind Emerson, the following spring, of the Swedenborg book he had promised to send.

One day in 1885, sitting in his study in Martinez, Muir suddenly put down his pen and felt an eerie inner compulsion. "I am going east," he told

Louie. "Somehow I feel that if I don't go now I won't see father again." He summoned his siblings to their father's home. "I just kind of feel it, that's all — I have no reason." When they reached Daniel Muir, he seemed well enough. But he started to fail and died two weeks later. The pattern repeated itself in 1896. At work in his study, he felt a sudden impulse to go home to Portage. "Why, John," his sister said when he arrived, "God must have sent you because mother is very sick." She died shortly thereafter. "For all I know," Muir later concluded, "these cases may be only good guesses, but not so the Butler incident."

Willie Keith was a Swedenborgian, and other friends of Muir's — J. E. Calkins, Charles Keeler, the novelist Mary Austin — were intrigued by psychic phenomena. Calkins found Muir "remarkably receptive of telepathic influences," and Austin recalled, "I know something of what went on in Muir. For him, quite simply, the spirits of the wild were angels, who bore him on their wings through perilous places." In his last years Muir collected articles by spiritualist authorities. When he finished dictating his autobiography in 1908, he added a final section, "Mysterious Things," almost as an afterthought that could not be denied. Recounting the Butler episode and the deaths of his parents, he expressed a belief in phenomena "now called supernatural, that are as natural as any other forces with which we are acquainted." The field admittedly was littered with frauds and exploiters. "There is yet at the bottom of all such humbugs a basis of truth, founded on natural laws, which perhaps some day we may discover."

Among the eastern pioneers of conservation, George Dorr of Acadia was the most persistent student of psychic fields. His parents had earlier been swept up in the wave of spiritualist activity during the decades before the Civil War. After the death of George's brother in the 1870s, they communicated with his spirit, so they believed, by automatic writing. A few years later, when George was debilitated by a mysterious illness, his mother engaged a faith healer. "I had an open mind," he recalled, "but was not superstitious or ready to take up on faith doctrines I could not understand or give rational credit to." After two weeks of treatment he felt a surge of energy which leveled off, then built up again to a complete cure.

Dorr joined William James and other Boston Brahmins in the affairs of the American Society for Psychical Research. James and the society's secretary, Richard Hodgson, were frequent guests of the Dorrs at Bar Harbor. To Dorr, Hodgson seemed too credulous, too uncritical of the often bizarre reports that came his way. Dorr's interest in psychic phenomena was waning when, in 1905, Hodgson suddenly dropped dead on a handball court. Shortly thereafter Dorr fell into conversations through a medium with Hodgson's departed spirit, discussing Bar Harbor episodes that the medium could not possibly have known. The experience left Dorr "with a suspended judgment," he said later. "Were it but possible to arrive at definite evidence of survival, no subject in the world could touch it in importance, altering our whole outlook upon life." He had no doubt of the reality of extrasensory perception, which he regarded as an "intermediate intelligence" below the conscious level.

Stewart Edward White, whose widely selling wilderness novels impressed the young Aldo Leopold, wrote some forty books on outdoor topics before turning to psychic subjects. When camping in remote areas, he was sometimes intrigued by the mysterious ability of Indians to transmit news telepathically across wide distances. But "such things did not especially concern me" until 1919, when a frivolous experiment with a Ouija board led his wife Betty to try automatic writing. After some initial static, the process yielded a coherent narrative. Betty then went on to speaking directly, in voices and personalities not known to her or to White. For the next twenty years she articulated daily contact with "the Invisibles." "I'm having such a good time!" a spirit said on one occasion. "I'm just skipping and tripping along the top of the Sierra Nevada. The sky is deep blue — and it's such a nice touchable sky! I can swirl the glistening snow around, and feel the sting of its warmth." ("Anyone who lives close to the mountains," Muir had said, "is sensitive to these things.") After Betty's death in 1939, White maintained regular contact with her spirit and wrote his last books about these adventures into the unknown. "Reason is not the end of the line," he declared. "Beyond it lies perception."

Other conservationists could report similar forays. Gifford Pinchot, who knew Dorr and Hodgson, for several years in the 1890s communed with the spirit of his fiancée after her traumatizing death. "A happy day," he wrote in his diary in 1896. "My Dearest and I were on a mountain top together. I am learning from Swedenborg." Again: "Tonight my Dearest and I twice went by Uncle Frank's house together." In the 1930s Charles Lindbergh delved into clairvoyance, believed in telepathy, sought out a medium in London, and flew to India to study yogis. Sigurd Olson, like White, noticed clairvoyant powers among aboriginal peoples. On a canoe trip in wild country, Olson once lost track of a young boy. After miles of fruitless searching he sat down to ponder the problem. "Somehow in the process I must have aligned myself with forces, thoughts, and feelings beyond understanding, dipping once again into that great unplumbed pool of darkness involved with the spiritual background of all mankind. . . . I rose and started off through the woods, following a route as unerringly as though it were blazed." Three miles away he found the boy, "and when I saw him, I was not surprised."

Historically these phenomena were associated with occult religions that denied the Christian concept of a personal God, accepted reincarnation, and rejected the Christian separation of the natural and supernatural. Nineteenth-century spiritualism was fought most strenuously by Christian churches in America. They accused spiritualists, often for good reason, of pantheistic heresies. "God is not a person, but a principle, permeating all things," said a spiritualist journal. "Nothing is outside of God," another spiritualist agreed, "and God is not outside of anything. Every particle that exists, every human soul, possesses within itself that which is absolutely and essentially divine." If God did not stand apart from nature, and every particle claimed divinity on equal terms with humans, perhaps the world was not made especially for man. For conservationists, then, psychic phenomena offered another alternative to Christian orthodoxy.

❦❦

So much for conservationists and Christianity. Turning the issue around, the record of Christians and conservation is equally revealing.

Christian ministers, in the past, have helped lead most American reform movements. Over the years, conservation leaders have included a few members of the Christian clergy. Muir's first biographer, William F. Badè, edited the *Sierra Club Bulletin* for a time. Preston Bradley, a Unitarian minister in Chicago, helped found the Izaak Walton League and admired Muir's writings. A Presbyterian minister from Virginia, James J. Murray, served as secretary of the Audubon Society during the 1940s. Robert M. Hatch, an Episcopal bishop in New England, wrote articles for *Living Wilderness* and *Audubon Magazine* in the 1950s. But none of these, indeed no Christian minister, was ever counted among the real movers and shakers of conservation. To a unique degree among American reform movements, conservation was preached without much help from Christian clergy. No Christian minister in conservation ever exercised the sustained national influence of (for example) Anna Howard Shaw in feminism, Norman Thomas in socialism, A. J. Muste in the peace movement, or Martin Luther King in civil rights.

Conversely, Christian doctrine was sometimes cited as a rationale for environmental abuse. Seventeenth-century New England Puritans, on their errand into the wilderness, supposed it their divine mission to subdue

the new land and establish dominion over her creatures. "The early settlers," Muir noted, "claiming Heaven as their guide, regarded God's trees
as only a larger kind of pernicious weeds." On the Wisconsin frontier, an
old pioneer explained to Muir that passenger pigeons were made to be
killed and eaten even as the Lord had sent quails to the starving Israelites
in the desert.

The pioneer attitude survived into the conservation era. In the late
1890s, a man shooting terns for the millinery market explained his trade to
Gilbert Pearson: "The good Lord put us here and the Good Book says,
'Man shall have dominion over all creatures.' They're ourn to use." Eighty
years later, a Michigan game official defended hunting to another Audubon member: "Now the Bible tells us that man should have dominion over
the fowls of the air and the cattle that roam the hills and the game and the
wild animals. And I believe that, because man is superior." Stephen
Levine, the spiritual ecologist in Arizona, encountered the same justification from a game warden in his state.

Yet Christians might bristle when conservationists dared object to the
first chapter of Genesis. Joseph Wood Krutch, on a Tucson radio program,
once denied that man should wield exclusive dominion over the beasts. An
agitated fundamentalist called in to denounce him as blasphemous: "Only
man, she said, was valuable in God's sight, whereas I had put myself on the
devil's side when I had confessed that I should not like to see even such
'noxious' creatures as the tarantula and the scorpion totally exterminated."
In 1957 Albert Burke, writing an NBC television script for a series on resources, cited Genesis 1:26 as the reason for land abuse in the West. After
some debate the network censor cut the offending passage. "It was too
touchy a topic," Burke was told. "It would be better not to air the concept."

Later, with the start of the environmental revolution and especially the
publication of Lynn White's article, the implications of Genesis could be
discussed more openly. Some of the sharpest criticism of environmentalism, logically enough, came from Christian spokesmen. "What a remarkably hopeless future for man," said Richard Neuhaus, a Lutheran minister,
"when the *locus* of God's presence is to be found in the wilderness and not
in human industry." Neuhaus's book of 1971, *In Defense of People,* was
perhaps the most virulent anticonservation screed ever written by anyone
outside the business community. Citing Biblical warnings against the idolatry of worshipping nature, Neuhaus listed ancient Canaanites, Thoreau,
Muir, and Hitler as typical idolators. Conservation was only "an upper-
class anxiety," a way of avoiding more serious social problems — in Christian terms, simply an unnecessary diversion. "The idea that nature," Neu-

haus said in another context, "— the presumed imperatives of nature — has a role in determining public policy is classically fascist."

At lesser length but no less vehemently, other Christians denounced the environmental movement. "We too want to clean up pollution in nature," said an editorial in *Christianity Today,* "but not by polluting men's souls with a revived paganism." A Jesuit writing in the Catholic journal *America* described ecology as "an American heresy" that challenged those faiths concerned primarily with man: "For Christians, nature cannot be fully nature except through man." R. V. Young, Jr., declared in *National Review:* "There is no 'democracy' of all creatures; a single human soul is worth more than the entire material creation. Just as man is here to serve God, so nature is here to serve man." Another writer warned in the *Christian Century* about "a sort of mindless ecological imperative . . . ultimately reactionary and antihuman, as well as anti-Christian." The theologian Thomas Sieger Derr noted an "open antihumanism" among some environmentalists, "an expressed preference for the preservation of nonhuman nature against human needs wherever it is necessary to choose."

It amounted to a genuine quarrel drawn from genuine differences. Many conservationists *did* articulate Christian heresies. Leaders of the Sierra Club and Wilderness Society *did* worry more about wild land than helping the urban poor. And conservationists could justifiably point to a lack of ecological concern in Christian circles. These recent exchanges simply reiterated the historical tension between the Judeo-Christian ethic and ecological forbearance.

As Robert Nisbet has shown, the Western idea of progress cannot be separated from a Judeo-Christian cosmology, indeed would not have existed without the philosophical basis provided by the dominant religion of Western history. Thus, to the recurrent question of whether conservationists are against progress, the answer would seem to be yes — *at least to progress as it has normally been defined in the West.* Standing as they do outside the Judeo-Christian tradition, conservationists naturally see progress in their own way. In this dual sense, in the striking connection between its religiosity and its skepticism toward the onward march of secular events, conservation implies a vision radically different from the American norm. For all their conservative aspects, conservationists ultimately are more radical than any Marxists. Dissenting from both the capitalists and the communists, they declare that history is not a line but a circle; that meaning resides less in matter than in spirit, less in striving than in stasis, less in humans than in Nature, less indoors than outdoors.

※※

In early October Muir climbed out of Yosemite Valley and headed east, toward the peaks of the upper Merced basin. On the first day he followed a trail of glacial mud to a living glacier, his first discovery of an actual remnant of the forces that had carved out the valley. To celebrate, he climbed Mount Clark, 11,522 feet, a difficult ascent up the east side. During the climb he noticed a hawk and some of his favorite plants. At the summit he watched a fine sunset. "It had been cloudy all day until towards evening," he wrote in his journal; "then the sun broke through the cloud gloom, irradiating the edges with a purple-and-golden flood of light, which fell on the mountain, making it glow in richest creamy yellow — intensely fine and spiritual in tone."

In the darkness he ran down the mountain to his camp by Lake Washburn, four miles to the northeast. By touch he recognized the soft sedge and shore mosses and the carpet bushes. Looking up, he watched the stars and mountain shadows. A solitary bird sang somewhere in the darkness. Just before dawn, he saw the earliest beamless morning light creeping over the landscape, trees and mountains merging together in the background, gaining definition as the day brightened.

Sauntering around the lake, he happened on a dead bear. It provoked a line of thought as he recorded the day in his journal: "Toiling in the treadmills of life we hide from the lessons of Nature. We gaze morbidly through civilized fog upon our beautiful world clad with seamless beauty, and see ferocious beasts and wastes and deserts. . . . We deprecate bears." But bears seemed to belong in the Sierra, magnificent creatures worthy of their magnificent home — not companions of men, but tenderly loved children of God. They roamed at will, feared no one, ate practically anything, and seemed not to mind rain or snow. "There are no square-edged inflexible lines in nature. We seek to establish a narrow lane between ourselves and the feathery zeros we dare to call angels, but ask a partition barrier of infinite width to show the rest of creation its proper place. . . . Bears are made of the same dust as we, and breathe the same winds and drink of the same waters. A bear's days are warmed by the same sun, his dwellings are overdomed by the same blue sky, and his life turns and ebbs with heart-pulsings like ours, and was poured from the same First Fountain. And whether he at last goes to our stingy heaven or no, he has terrestrial immortality."

After three days by the lake he fashioned a pair of bark snowshoes and skimmed over a new snowfall back down to the valley.

ACKNOWLEDGMENTS

BOOKS BY JOHN MUIR

MANUSCRIPT
COLLECTIONS

ABBREVIATIONS
OF SOURCES

CHAPTER NOTES

INDEX

Acknowledgments

I am grateful to the following people for reading and criticizing the manuscript in whole or part: Shirley Briggs, Paul Brooks, Avis DeVoto, Peter Edge, John Allen Gable, Robert Emmett Ginna, Richard Leonard, Robin Brant Lodewick, George Marshall, Margaret Murie, Michael Nadel, Christina Ward, and Jean Whitnack.

For other kinds of assistance I owe thanks to C. Francis Belcher, Milan Bull, Wallace Finley Dailey, James G. Deane, Maitland De Sormo, Sherry R. Fisher, John Ripley Forbes, Stanley Freeman, Jack Lorenz, Stephanie Moore, John Nance, Gladys O'Neil, Richard Pough, the Eleanor Roosevelt Institute, Deborah Seymour, William Voigt, Jr., and Douglas West.

Ronald H. Limbaugh and the staff of the Holt-Atherton Pacific Center for Western Studies at the University of the Pacific guided me through the John Muir Papers.

Eleanor Pihl Fox again helped me compile the index.

Finally, Chloe and Theo Goodfellow kept my sights aligned on the question of whether the world is, indeed, made for man.

Books by John Muir

Picturesque California (co-author) (New York and San Francisco: J. Dewing, 1888)

The Mountains of California (New York: Century, 1894)

Our National Parks (Boston: Houghton Mifflin, 1901). Cited as *Parks*

Stickeen (Boston: Houghton Mifflin, 1909)

My First Summer in the Sierra (Boston: Houghton Mifflin, 1911). Cited as *First Summer*

The Yosemite (New York: Century, 1912)

Edward Henry Harriman (New York: Doubleday, 1912)

The Story of My Boyhood and Youth (Boston: Houghton Mifflin, 1913). Cited as *Boyhood*

Travels in Alaska (Boston: Houghton Mifflin, 1915)

Letters to a Friend (Boston: Houghton Mifflin, 1915). Cited as *Letters*

A Thousand-Mile Walk to the Gulf (Boston: Houghton Mifflin, 1916)

Steep Trails (Boston: Houghton Mifflin, 1918)

John of the Mountains: The Unpublished Journals of John Muir, ed. Linnie Marsh Wolfe (Boston: Houghton Mifflin, 1938). Cited as *Journals*

Studies in the Sierra (San Francisco: Sierra Club, 1949)

The fullest Muir bibliographies to date are *John Muir: A Reading Bibliography,* edited by William F. Kimes and Maymie B. Kimes (Palo Alto, 1977), and a compilation by Ann T. Lynch in *Bulletin of Bibliography,* Apr.–June 1979.

Manuscript Collections

I would like to thank the staffs of the libraries listed below for all the courtesies they extended to me.

Acadia Historical Papers, Acadia National Park, Me.
American Academy Papers, The Archives of the American Academy and Institute of Arts and Letters, New York City
Audubon Papers (National Association of Audubon Societies), New York Public Library Annex, New York City. Cited as AuP
Daniel Carter Beard Papers, Manuscript Division, Library of Congress
Bidwell Family Papers, Bancroft Library, University of California, Berkeley
Boone and Crockett Club Papers, Theodore Roosevelt Birthplace, New York City
Irving Brant Papers, Manuscript Division, Library of Congress. Cited as BrP
Jeanne C. Carr Papers, Huntington Library, San Marino, Calif.
Rachel Carson Papers, Yale Collection of American Literature, Beinecke Rare Book and Manuscript Library, Yale University
Century Collection, New York Public Library, New York City
William E. Colby Papers, Bancroft Library, University of California, Berkeley
Morris L. Cooke Papers, Franklin D. Roosevelt Library, Hyde Park, N.Y.
Ina B. Coolbrith Papers, Bancroft Library, University of California, Berkeley
George Davidson Papers, Bancroft Library, University of California, Berkeley
Bernard DeVoto Papers, Manuscripts Division, Department of Special Collections, Stanford University Libraries. Cited as DeVP
George B. Dorr Papers, Bar Harbor (Me.) Historical Society
Charles W. Eliot Papers, Harvard University Archives
Ralph Waldo Emerson Papers, Houghton Library, Harvard University. Cited as EP
Hal G. Evarts Papers, Special Collections, University of Oregon
George Bird Grinnell Papers, Connecticut Audubon Society, Fairfield, Conn. Cited as GBGP
Katherine P. Hooker Papers, Bancroft Library, University of California, Berkeley
William T. Hornaday Papers, Manuscript Division, Library of Congress
Harold L. Ickes Papers, Manuscript Division, Library of Congress
Gardner Jackson Papers, Franklin D. Roosevelt Library, Hyde Park, N.Y.
Robert Underwood Johnson Papers, Bancroft Library, University of California, Berkeley. Cited as JPB

Robert Underwood Johnson Papers, Rare Book and Manuscript Library, Columbia University. Cited as JPC

David Starr Jordan Papers, University Archives, Stanford University

Charles A. Keeler Papers, Huntington Library, San Marino, Calif.

William Kent Papers, Yale University Library, Yale University

Joseph Wood Krutch Papers, Manuscript Division, Library of Congress

Le Conte Family Papers, Bancroft Library, University of California, Berkeley

Theodore P. Lukens Papers, Huntington Library, San Marino, Calif.

J. Horace McFarland Papers, Division of Archives and Manuscripts, Pennsylvania Historical and Museum Commission, Harrisburg, Pa. Cited as McFP

Robert Marshall Papers, Wilderness Society, Washington, D.C. Cited as RMP

Robert Marshall Papers, Franklin D. Roosevelt Library, Hyde Park, N.Y. Cited as RMPR

John C. Merriam Papers, Manuscript Division, Library of Congress

John Muir Papers, Holt-Atherton Pacific Center for Western Studies, University of the Pacific, Stockton, Calif. Cited as MP

John Muir Papers, Bancroft Library, University of California, Berkeley. Cited as MPB

John Muir Papers, Yosemite National Park, Calif. Cited as MPY

Muir Family Papers, Huntington Library, San Marino, Calif. Cited as MFP

"National Parks: Kings Canyon," National Park Service: Central Classified File 1933–1949, RG 79, National Archives, Washington, D.C.

Overland Monthly Papers, Bancroft Library, University of California, Berkeley

Theodore S. Palmer Papers, Manuscript Division, Library of Congress. Cited as PP

Parsons Family Papers, Bancroft Library, University of California, Berkeley

James D. Phelan Papers, Bancroft Library, University of California, Berkeley

Gifford Pinchot Papers, Manuscript Division, Library of Congress. Cited as GPP

Franklin D. Roosevelt Papers, Franklin D. Roosevelt Library, Hyde Park, N.Y.

Theodore Roosevelt Papers, Manuscript Division, Library of Congress

Paul Bigelow Sears Papers, Yale University Library, Yale University

Sierra Club Papers, Bancroft Library, University of California, Berkeley

Strentzel Family Papers, Bancroft Library, University of California, Berkeley

Henry A. Wallace Papers (microfilm), Manuscript Division, Library of Congress

"Water Supply for San Francisco," National Park Service: Central Files 1907–1939, RG 79, National Archives, Washington, D.C. Cited as WS

Wilderness Society Papers, Wilderness Society, Washington, D.C. Cited as WSP

Abbreviations of Sources

A	*Audubon*
AF	*American Forests*
AM	*Audubon Magazine*
AuP	Audubon Papers
Badè	W. F. Badè, *The Life and Letters of John Muir* (1924)
Boyhood	John Muir, *The Story of My Boyhood and Youth*
BrP	Irving Brant Papers
DeVP	Bernard DeVoto Papers
EP	Ralph Waldo Emerson Papers
FDR	Franklin Delano Roosevelt
First Summer	John Muir, *My First Summer in the Sierra*
GBGP	George Bird Grinnell Papers
GPP	Gifford Pinchot Papers
JM	John Muir
Journals	*John of the Mountains: The Unpublished Journals of John Muir*, ed. L. M. Wolfe (1938)
JPB	R. U. Johnson Papers, Bancroft Library, University of California
JPC	R. U. Johnson Papers, Rare Book and Manuscript Library, Columbia University
Letters	John Muir, *Letters to a Friend*
LW	*Living Wilderness*
McFP	J. Horace McFarland Papers
MFP	Muir Family Papers
MP	John Muir Papers, University of the Pacific
MPB	John Muir Papers, Bancroft Library, University of California, Berkeley
MPY	John Muir Papers, Yosemite National Park
Nixon	Edgar B. Nixon, ed., *Franklin D. Roosevelt and Conservation* (1957)
NW	*National Wildlife*

OA	*Outdoor America*
OM	*Overland Monthly*
Parks	John Muir, *Our National Parks*
PP	Theodore S. Palmer Papers
RMP	Robert Marshall Papers, Wilderness Society, Washington, D.C.
RMPR	Robert Marshall Papers, Franklin D. Roosevelt Library
SCB	*Sierra Club Bulletin*
TR	Theodore Roosevelt
Wolfe	L. M. Wolfe, *Son of the Wilderness: The Life of John Muir* (1945)
"WS"	"Water Supply for San Francisco"
WSP	Wilderness Society Papers

Chapter Notes

In the notes below, a bylined article in a periodical is cited in the following form: "Theodore Roosevelt in *Outlook,* Jan. 6, 1915."

1. THE YOSEMITE PROPHET

Page

4 "You have to go": Thérèse Yelverton, *Teresina in America* (1875), 2:59.

4 "This valley": James B. Thayer, *A Western Journey with Mr. Emerson* (1884), 76.

5 "Do not thus": JM to R. W. Emerson, May 8, 1871, EP.

5 "His party": JM, *Parks,* 132.

5 "I wanted to": JM to J. B. McChesney, June 9, 1871, MP.

6 "Would you were here": JM to R. W. Emerson, Jan. 10, 1872, EP.

6 "I have everywhere": Badè, 1:259–260.

6 "The squirrel hoards": R. W. Emerson, *Prose Works* (1870 ed.), 1:183. (JM's copy of v. 1, annotated with his marginal comments, is now in the Beinecke Library, Yale.) Subsequent citations here are to pp. 184, 329, 368, 509, 511, 516.

7 "transparent eyeball": JM to Sarah Galloway, Dec. 19, 1872, MP; and see JM in *Scribner's,* Feb. 1879.

7 "The most serene": JM, *Journals,* 436.

7 Emerson's list: R. W. Emerson, *Journals* (1914), 10:357.

7 "I am lost": JM to Daniel Muir, Jr., Apr. 17, 1868, MFP.

8 "I never was": JM to John and Maggie Reid, Jan. 13, 1869, MP.

8 "If I want": Ibid.

8 "Now we are": JM, Journal, June 6, 1869, MP.

8 "Perhaps no such": Ibid., June 16, 1869.

8 "hoofed locusts": JM, *First Summer,* 113.

9 "When such places": Ibid., 155–156.

9 "I therefore concluded": Ibid., 158.

Page

9   "I suddenly stopped": Autobiography, 455, in folder 31.3, MP.

10   "This is the most": Ibid., 462.

10   "Hawthorne, I fancy": JM, *First Summer,* 257.

10   "I am told": JM to Jeanne Carr, Nov. 15, 1869, MP.

10   "I have run wild": JM to Daniel Muir, Jr., Mar. 24, 1870, MFP.

11   JM's climbing clothes: Typescript, n.d., in folder 37.26, MP.

11   "the sole forms": Ibid.

11   "dancing rhythm": Ibid.

11   "The crackers": Memoir, ca. 1875, in folder 37.17, MP.

11   "A very strong": Ibid.

11–12   "then all tied": Ibid.

12   "I would start up": JM in *SCB,* 1924 annual issue.

12   "The higher the peak": Memoir, ca. 1875, in folder 37.17, MP.

12   "Who wouldn't": JM, *First Summer,* 206.

12   "I feel like": JM to W. H. Trout and Charles Jay, Nov. 28, 1871, MPB.

13   "Then my trembling": JM in *Scribner's,* July 1880.

13   "There is no mystery": JM, *Journals,* 107–108.

13   "a beautiful animal": MS fragment, n.d., in folder 38.12, MP.

13   "I can't understand": JM, *First Summer,* 57–58.

13   "The gross heathenism": JM to J. B. McChesney, Sept. 19, 1871, MP.

14   "I ran back": JM, Autobiography, 167, in folder 33.2, MP.

14   "more to show": JM, Journal, July 12, 1869, MP.

14   "All sorts of ": JM, *Letters,* 80–81.

14   "hoping thereby to": JM in San Francisco *Bulletin,* Sept. 21, 1875.

14–15   "Oh, then": JM, *Parks,* 320.

15   "Idle sentimental": JM, Journal, Jan. 6, 1873, MP.

15   "What on earth": Thérèse Yelverton, *Zanita: A Tale of the Yo-Semite* (1872), 4. Subsequent citations are to pp. 5, 6, 7, 8, 231.

16   "desperately bashful": JM, *First Summer,* 242.

16   "I am always": JM to Annie Muir, Aug. 15, 1868, MPY.

16   "I have not made": JM, *Letters,* 49.

16   "I am lonely": Ibid., 77.

17   " a slight semi-girlish": Yelverton, *Zanita,* 19.

17   "ill mated": Henry Randall to JM, Mar. 9, 1902, MP.

17   The Hutchingses' marital problems: Summary of a letter from Gertrude Hutchings Mills, Mar. 29, 1932, in folder 71.10, MP.

17   "I boarded": Autobiograph, 294–295, in folder 31.1, MP.

17   "all vigor": Yelverton, *Zanita,* 21–22.

17   "I have a great deal": JM to J. Carr, Apr. 5, 1870, MP.

17   "My father had": G. H. Mills to W. F. Badè, Jan. 23, 1923, in folder 66.23, MP.

18   "apparently accepted mission": J. M. Hutchings, *In the Heart of the Sierras,* (1886), 159.

18   "Hers is the only": Yelverton, *Zanita,* 81–82.

18   "Kenmuir wept": Ibid., 96.

18   "J. M. Hutchings wasn't": H. Randall to JM, Dec. 15, 1901, MP.

Page

18   "Were it not": JM to J. Carr, Dec. 22, 1870, MP.

18   "I am more lonely": JM to David Muir, Dec. 1, 1871, MP.

19   "Mrs. Hutchings is": JM to J. Carr, July 27, 1872, MP.

19   "I have a low": JM, *Journals,* 94–95.

19   "There is no": JM's note in his copy of John Tyndall's *Hours of Exercise in the Alps* (1871), MP.

19   "It is astonishing": JM to R. W. Emerson, Mar. 18, 1872, EP.

20   "intelligent face": Joseph Le Conte in *SCB,* Jan. 1900.

20   "If you could be": JM to J. Le Conte, Dec. 17, 1871, Le Conte Family Papers.

20   "you know how gladly": JM to J. Le Conte, Apr. 27, 1872, Le Conte Family Papers.

20   "This entire region": JM, *First Summer,* 266.

21   "landscapes fresh": JM, Journal, July 14, 1869, MP.

21   "most devoutly": JM, *Letters,* 76.

21   "You might have heard": JM to R. W. Emerson, July 6, 1871, EP.

22   "My friends regarded": JM in *OM,* Dec. 1872.

22   "I have no": JM to C. L. Merriam, Aug. 20, 1871, MP.

22   "the grandest marvel": Horace Greeley, *Recollections of a Busy Life* (1868), 381.

22   "I have been drifting": JM in New York *Tribune,* Dec. 5, 1871.

23   "He soon said": JM to R. W. Emerson, Mar. 18, 1872, EP.

23   "My life work": JM to Ann G. Muir, Sept. 27, 1872, MFP.

23   Issues containing JM's articles: *American Journal of Science,* Jan. 1873, May 1874; AAAS *Proc.,* Aug. 1874.

23   "This was my": JM in *OM,* Aug. 1873.

23   "a slight reconnaissance": JM in *Harper's,* Nov. 1875.

24   "that shepherd": Thurman Wilkins, *Clarence King* (1958), 189–190.

24   "It is to be hoped": Francis P. Farquhar, *History of the Sierra Nevada* (1965), 163.

24   Later geological conclusions: see, e.g., William R. Jones in *A,* Jan.–Feb. 1967.

24   "What a splendid": Asa Gray to JM, Jan. 4, 1872, MP.

24   "They told": JM to Annie Bidwell, Apr. 19, 1890, Bidwell Family Papers.

24   "so you can set": A. Gray to JM, Sept. 21, 1872, MP.

24   "and to all": JM to A. Gray, Oct. 10, 1872, Gray Herbarium, Harvard.

24–25   "The last days": JM in *OM,* Aug. 1873.

25   "In all God's": JM, *Journals,* 89.

25   "To live without": Ibid., 138.

25   "Dear friend": This letter is taken from an undated, unidentified typescript copy in the Muir Papers. In 1923 Muir's authorized biographer, William F. Badè, sent Gertrude ("Cosie") Hutchings Mills a copy of a letter which her mother had sent to Muir upon leaving James Hutchings. Badè dated this letter "about 1872" and described it as "an intimate document . . . noble in its spirit," and doing "great credit both to her and to John Muir" (Badè to Mills, Apr. 11, 1923, in folder 66.24, MP). The unidentified typescript fits this description and appears from internal evidence to be a statement by a person in turmoil, leaving one situation for another, and confiding in a close friend. Further, the typescript appears to have been copied on the type-

Page

writer Badè used to make his copies of other Muir correspondence. This letter does not appear in either the Badè or Wolfe biographies.

The date of September 1873 is assigned because of Muir's surprising movements during the following year, because of his explicitly not wanting to see Elvira Hutchings on his return to Yosemite in September 1874, and because in September 1873 Muir inexplicably returned a letter to his confidante Jeanne Carr which she had forwarded to him. "I sealed it without reading it," he wrote Carr, "thinking that it would be better for you to read it first knowing that you could easily bring it to Tahoe if you wished me to see it" (JM to Carr, Sept. 13, 1873, MP). Carr was a close friend to both Muir and Hutchings; the document in question may have been the letter Hutchings sent Muir on leaving her husband.

Muir's letters to Carr are the major source of information on the Muir–Hutchings relationship. Later in life Muir tried to recover these letters from Carr. But she, growing somewhat erratic with age, gave the letters to George Wharton James, an outdoors writer described acidly by Muir as "an unscrupulous ex-minister who tried to get hold of anything in any way to make money." Muir and his friends devised various strategies to get the letters from James. Ultimately, in April 1909, Muir was shown copies. He requested that seven letters be destroyed entirely, ten others in part. Apparently his wishes were carried out. James had already published some of the letters in *Impressions Quarterly* (Dec. 1904) and in *Craftsman* (Mar. 1905). Badè as Muir's literary executor published most of the letters after Muir's death in *Letters to a Friend* (1915). Muir's prolonged efforts to recover the letters, and then to censor them, raise questions about what they might have revealed of his friendship with Elvira Hutchings. See Muir to Theodore P. Lukens, June 10, 1897, Jan. 16, Nov. 13, 1901, Lukens Papers; Muir to R. U. Johnson, Dec. 15, 1906, and undated letter, American Academy Papers; G. W. James to Muir, July 16, 1908, MP; A. H. Sellers to Muir, Jan. 11, 1909, MP; notes by Muir on the letters, Apr. 1909, in folder 39.8, MP.

26   "Tell me what": JM, *Journals,* 191.

26   "I have not seen": JM to J. Carr, Sept. 1874, MP.

2.   BEFORE YOSEMITE: NATURE AND THE BIPED LORD

27   "We never know": JM, *First Summer,* 331.

28   "a comet": JM to Sarah and David Galloway, Apr. 25, 1872, MP.

28   "A representative Scotch woman": Badè, 1:16.

28   "and nature does": Autobiography, 74, in folder 33.1, MP.

28   JM's memories of Scotland: See JM, *Journals,* 84; JM, *Letters,* 72; JM, *Journals,* 115; JM, Journal, Feb. 2, 1873, MP.

29   "Damn it!": Autobiography, 47, in folder 33.1, MP.

29   "But, mark you!": Ibid., 41.

29   "The Scotch simply": Ibid., 32–33.

29   "Public opinion": Ibid., 34.

30   "by heart": JM, *Boyhood,* 31.

30   "With all that": Autobiography, 66, in folder 33.1, MP.

30–31   "I was set down": Ibid., 235, in folder 31.7, MP.

31   "We cannot": Ibid., 149, in folder 33.11, MP.

Page

31 "The very deevil's": Ibid., 176–177, in folder 33.2, MP.

31 "In all the world": JM to James Whitehead, Feb. 13, 1913, MP.

32 "Old Man Muir": Wolfe, 45.

32 "After trying": Autobiography, 180–181, in folder 33.2, MP.

32 "Never a word": Ibid., 181.

33 "Father never": JM, *Boyhood,* 234.

33 "It shows": Autobiography, 187, in folder 33.2, MP.

33 "I wished": Joanna M. Brown to JM, Oct. 7, 1913, MP.

34 "Where then": JM to Bradley, 1856, in folder 27.1, MP.

34 "as if my body": Autobiography, 158, in folder 33.1, MP.

34 "I remember": JM, *Boyhood,* 244–245.

35 "the most notable": Autobiography, 196, in folder 33.1, MP.

35 "It was regarded": Ibid., 328, in folder 31.7, MP.

36 "I am now": JM to S. Galloway, Oct. 1860, MP.

36 "surprising": Wolfe, 59.

36 "Do not let": Daniel Muir to JM, Oct. 14, 1860, MP.

36 "a genius": Wolfe, 61.

37 "I hope": JM to S. Galloway, Oct. 1860, MP.

37 "It is certainly": JM to Daniel Muir, Jr., Nov. 19, 1860, MFP.

37 "I am in the world": JM to S. Galloway, Nov. 1860, MP.

37 "with fear": Wolfe, 64.

38 "the attraction": Autobiography, 238, in folder 33.2, MP.

38 "My room": Ibid., 241, in folder 33.2, MP.

38 "Fruit of all hues": JM to Mrs. Pelton, 1862, MP.

38 "Hundreds of common": JM to Mary Muir, May 1861, MP.

38 "Of social life": MS note, n.d., Carr Papers.

39 "If it was": David Muir to JM, 1861, MPB.

39 "I did not know": JM to Sarah and David Galloway, Feb. 9, 1862, MP.

39 "It does not": Ibid.

39 JM's reading: Charles E. Vroman in *Wisconsin Alumni Magazine,* June 1915.

40 "That is perfectly wonderful": M. S. Griswold to W. F. Badè, Mar. 30, 1917, in folder 66.10, MP.

40 "It is the most": JM to S. and D. Galloway, June 1, 1863, MP.

40 "You counsel me": J. L. High to JM, Nov. 14, 1863, MP.

40 "You are inclined": Alfred R. Brown to JM, Nov. 26, 1862, MP.

40–41 "We obtain": College notebook, "Principles of Physics or Moral Philosophy," 1861, in folder 39.29, MP.

41 "I wish": Daniel Muir to JM, Apr. 17, 1861, MP.

41 "Father and I": JM to Daniel Muir, Jr., Dec. 20, 1863, MFP.

Page

41   "I think I love": JM to S. and D. Galloway, fall 1862, MP.

41   "I suppose": Ibid., fall 1861, MP.

41   "This war seems": Ibid., fall 1862, MP.

42   "My Scottish highlands": JM to Mrs. Pelton, Sept. 28, 1862, MP.

42   "How glad I am": Mary Muir to JM, Nov. 15, 1862, MP.

42   "how *smart* I am": JM to S. and D. Galloway, June 12, 1863, MP.

42   "I hardly know": JM to Daniel Muir, Jr., Dec. 20, 1863, MFP.

42   Lincoln order: *The Collected Works of Abraham Lincoln,* ed. by Roy P. Basler (1953), 7:164.

42–43   "I really do not": JM to Emily Pelton, Mar. 1, 1864, MP.

43   "botanizing in glorious freedom": Badè, 1:120.

43   "They were alone": *Boston Recorder,* Dec. 21, 1866.

44   "I cannot understand": Ibid.

44   "In vain": JM, *Letters,* 11–12.

44   "the grandest sight": JM to Annie Muir, Oct. 23, 1864, MP.

44   "I am sorry": JM to Mary Muir, Mar. 5, 1865, MP.

44   "Were it not": Ibid., Dec. 24, 1865, MP.

45   "It was easy": W. H. Trout, "The Coming of the Muirs," in folder 65.15, MP.

45   "It may be": JM to Jeanne Carr, Jan. 21, 1866, MP.

45   "Now John is": JM to Mary Muir, Dec. 24, 1865, MP.

45   "Your precious letter": JM, *Letters,* 8 (letter misdated 1866).

45–46   "Dear Mr. Muir": J. Carr to JM, Sept. 24, 1865, MP.

46   "It is only": Ibid., July 30, 1869, MP.

46   "Darwin has left": J. Carr, "My Own Story," MS in Carr Papers.

46   "You do not know": J. Carr to JM, Oct. 12, 1866, MP.

46–47   "I have not": JM to J. Carr, Oct. 1866, MP.

47   Carr as feminist: Reminiscence by Mrs. McChesney, Sept. 22, 1916, in folder 68.5, MP.

47   "a woman whose life": J. Carr to JM, Sept. 24, 1865, MP.

47   "Write as often": Ibid., May 28, 1870, MP.

47   "How intensely": JM, *Letters,* 9.

47   "It seems": JM to E. Pelton, Nov. 12, 1865, MP.

48   JM's dream: JM to Henry Butler, Apr. 22, 1866, MPB.

48   "I am myself": JM to S. Galloway, May 1866, MP.

48   "Circumstances over which": Ibid.

48   "Gentlemen": MS fragment, ca. 1866–1867, MPB.

48–49   "I am shut": JM, *Letters,* 15.

49   "My days were": JM to S. and D. Galloway, Apr. 12, 1867, MP.

49   "but my faith": JM, *Letters,* 22.

49   "I am thankful": Ibid., 24, 30.

49   "grand sabbath day": Memoir, ca. 1875, in folder 37.17, MP.

49–50   "I feel touches": JM to Daniel Muir, Jr., Sept. 7, 1867, MFP.

50   "I am very ignorant": JM, *Letters,* 35.

50   "It had a wonderfully": JM to Rachel Trout Beach, Sept. 13, 1870, MPB.

50   "Man naturally": Daniel Muir to JM, Feb. 24, 1866, MP.

50   "miserable hymns": JM to E. Pelton, 1865, MP.

51   "grimest body": JM, Journal (fall 1867), 50, MPY.

51   "the thousand styles": Ibid., 51.

51   "*union* of life": Ibid., 51–52.

51   "They tell us": Ibid., 90.

52   "Doubtless these creatures": JM, *A Thousand-Mile Walk to the Gulf* (1916), 98.

52   "Let a Christian": Ibid., 122.

Page

52   "The world we are told": JM, Journal (fall 1867), 150–156, MPY. Muir later revised the first two sentences to read: "The world, we are told, was made especially for man — a presumption not supported by all the facts." The passage was published in this revised form in the posthumous *Thousand-Mile Walk*. But the original, more pointed version more accurately represents Muir's thinking as of 1867. See *Thousand-Mile Walk,* 136.

53   "their great biped lord": JM, Journal (fall 1867), 180, MPY.

53   "I felt completely": JM, *Thousand-Mile Walk,* 186.

3.   A PROPER CULTIVATED PLANT

54   "We are governed": JM to Sarah Galloway, Jan. 12, 1877, MP.

54   "I am bound": Ibid., Jan. 16, 1875, MP.

54   "Well, perhaps I may": JM, *Journals,* 90.

55   "brother now": JM to Jeanne Carr, July 31, 1875, MP.

55   "Don't believe": JM to C. W. Stoddard, Feb. 2, 1872, MPB.

55   "I owe all": JM to J. Carr, spring 1872, MP.

55   "What I have": Memoir, ca. 1875, in folder 37.17, MP.

55   "I have not written": JM to S. Galloway, Jan. 12, 1877, MP.

56   "Presently a vigorous": JM in *Harper's,* Sept. 1877.

56   "something not quite": JM to the Strentzels, Jan. 23, 1879, MP.

56   "You belong": John McLandburgh to JM, June 13, 1879, MP.

56   "the California Alps": JM in *Harper's,* July 1877.

56   "It isn't possible": George W. Pierce to JM, Oct. 18, 1875, MP.

56–57 "essential kindliness": JM in *Harper's,* Sept. 1877.

57   "We all travel": JM in *Scribner's,* Nov. 1878.

57   "Among all": JM in *Scribner's,* Feb. 1878.

57   "I know": Helen Hunt Jackson to JM, June 8, 1885, MP.

57–58 "His strong heart": Marie Mason in *Scribner's,* May 1879.

58   "True, some goods": JM in *OM,* June 1875.

58   "Safe in the arms": JM to J. Carr, May 4, 1875, MP.

58   "We had what": JM to S. Galloway, Nov. 29, 1877, MP.

58   "When you come": JM to the Strentzels, Jan. 28, 1879, MP.

59   "Our crude civilization": JM, *Journals,* 234.

59   "The plow is busy": JM in *OM,* Sept. 1874.

59   The cow: JM, *Journals,* 215.

59   "To obtain": JM in *OM,* Apr. 1875.

59   "that the world": Ibid.

60   Pleas for forest protection: JM in San Francisco *Bulletin,* Aug. 13, Nov. 17, 1875; JM in *Scribner's,* Jan. and Mar. 1879; JM in *Century,* Aug. 1882.

60   "Whether our loose": JM to Sacramento *Record-Union,* Feb. 9, 1876.

60   "Scarce anything": JM in AAAS *Proceedings,* Aug. 1876.

61   "many matrimonial possibilities": JM to Maggie Lander, Mar. 1, 1873, MP.

61   "If you permit": JM to Daniel Muir, Jr., Dec. 20, 1863, MFP.

61   *"slavish fear":* Ibid., May 7, 1866.

Page

61 "calamities": JM to David Galloway, May 1870, MP.

61 "Little did I": JM to S. Galloway, Jan. 12, 1877, MP.

61 "dearest friends": J. Carr to the Strentzels, May 20, 1876, in folder 65.13, MP.

61-62 "I want you": J. Carr to Louie Strentzel, Oct. 29, 1873, in folder 65.13, MP.

62 "Whenever in": L. Strentzel to J. Carr, Mar. 21, 1875, in folder 65.18, MP.

62 "I have seen": L. Strentzel to Nellie, Nov. 28, 1871, in folder 65.14, MP.

62 "She was a clever": C. H. Merriam in *SCB,* Jan. 1917.

63 "Louie's letter": JM to J. Carr, Apr. 8, 1875, MP.

63 "I sent": J. Carr to L. Strentzel, Apr. 19, 1875, MP.

63 "Did you by": Wolfe, 196.

63 JM's book: MS fragments in folders 27.26-28, 28.1-10; JM to S. Galloway, Apr. 23, 1877, MP.

63 JM's request for help: David Muir to JM, Apr. 2, 1878, MP.

63 JM's "wasting" his life: Annie K. Bidwell to JM, Sept. 4, 1878, MP.

64 "I appreciate": JM to Mrs. Strentzel, June 20, 1878, MP.

64 "I am pulled": JM to A. K. Bidwell, Feb. 17, 1879, Bidwell Family Papers.

64 "Dear Miss Strentzel": JM to L. Strentzel, Apr. 18, 1879, MP.

64 "We all do": Ibid., Apr. 24, 1879, MP.

64 "I don't believe": Wolfe, 204.

65 "Dear John": L. Strentzel to JM, June 27, 1879, MP.

65 "Goodbye": JM to L. Strentzel, July 10, 1879, MP.

65 "From cluster": S. Hall Young, *Alaska Days with John Muir* (1915), 19-20.

65 "O Friend": L. Strentzel to JM, Oct. 9, 1879, MP.

65 "Surely you": JM to L. Strentzel, Oct. 9, 1879, MP.

65-66 "O John": L. Strentzel to JM, Oct. 24, 1879, MP.

66 "You must know": L. Strentzel to JM, Dec. 1, 1879, MP.

66 JM breaks silence: JM to L. Strentzel, Jan. 6, 1880, MP.

66 Louie's cool note: L. Strentzel to JM, Jan. 27, 1880, MP.

66 "The day I left": JM to L. Strentzel, Feb. 1880, MP.

66 "You have 'prospects' ": Mary Swett to L. Strentzel, Apr. 8, 1880, MP.

67 "I could not": J. Carr to JM, June 3, 1880, MP.

67 "The Dr. is": J. G. Lemmon to JM, June 4, 1880, MP.

67 "I was married": JM to Asa Gray, June 19, 1880, Gray Herbarium, Harvard.

67 "You have mentioned": A. Gray to JM, June 28, 1880, MP.

67 "I shall make": JM to Louie Strentzel Muir, Aug. 2, 1880, MP.

67 "Only they who": JM to L. S. Muir, Aug. 10, 1880, MP.

68 "I have been": L. S. Muir to JM, Aug. 23, 1880, MP.

68 "small and worthless": JM, *Stickeen* (1909), 4.

68 "There's more": Young, *Alaska Days,* 136.

68-69 "he showed neither": JM, *Stickeen,* 35. The next four quotations are from ibid., 51, 54, 61, 66-67.

Page

70 "knew nothing": Merrill Moores in *SCB,* Apr. 1938.

70 "He enlarged": JM, *Journals,* 277.

70 "To me Stickeen": JM, *Stickeen,* 74.

70 "And never since": JM to A. K. Bidwell, Mar. 29, 1881, MP.

71 "I found": JM to L. S. Muir, July 4, 1881, MP.

71 "I will be patient": L. S. Muir to JM, June 7, 1881, MP.

71 JM's dream: JM to L. S. Muir, May 17, 1881, MP.

71 "It yet seems": Wolfe, 226.

71 "She now loves": Diary of Louisiana E. Strentzel, Oct. 21, 1881, Strentzel Family Papers.

71 "It is not now": JM to the Bidwells, Jan. 1, 1881, Bidwell Family Papers.

72 "I am lost": JM to Millicent Shinn, Apr. 18, 1883, *OM* Papers.

72 "The journey": L. S. Muir to the Strentzels, July 6, 1884, MP.

72 Louie's climbing: JM to Wanda Muir, July 16, 1884, MP.

72 Cost of the trip: French Strother in *World's Work,* Apr. 1907.

72 "I am degenerating": Young, *Alaska Days,* 204, 206.

73 JM as businessman: Arno Dosch in *Sunset,* Feb. 1916.

73 "More care-worn": Galen Clark to J. Carr, Dec. 3, 1894, in folder 65.19, MP.

73 "I feel": JM to L. S. Muir, Sept. 10, 1885, MP.

73 "Writing to me": JM to Janet Moores, July 2, 1891, MP.

73 "It is so difficult": JM, Journal, Feb. 12, 1895, MP.

73 "For how would": Wolfe, 231.

74 "Bathe her": JM to L. S. Muir, June 16, 1893, MP.

74 "good mountaineers": JM to Emily Hawley, Mar. 1903, MP.

74 "most devoutly dull": JM to David Muir, Aug. 8, 1893, MP.

74 "This is a good": R. S. Baker in *Outlook,* June 6, 1903.

74 "Has contact": Anne W. Cheney to JM, Feb. 13, 1881, MP.

74-75 JM's birthday notes: see, e.g., JM, Journal, Apr. 21, 1895, Apr. 21, 1896, MP.

75 "the happiest man": JM to Katherine Graydon, Apr. 12, 1880, MP.

75 "Keep not standing": H. F. Osborn to JM, Oct. 5, 1904, MP, and JM in *Atlantic,* Jan. 1898.

75 "I will not doubt": JM to Katherine P. Hooker, Sept. 15, 1910, Hooker Papers.

75 "Life is too short": JM to Mrs. H. F. Osborn, Dec. 1913, MP.

75 "the outward bearing": Charles Keeler in *SCB,* Jan. 1916.

76 "not a man": Bailey Millard in *Bookman,* Feb. 1908.

76 "He displayed": R. U. Johnson, *Remembered Yesterdays* (1923), 284.

76 "he had the Scotch": Ibid., 284.

76 "naebody like": JM, *Journals,* 338.

76 JM's suspicion of Irishmen: JM, Journal, Nov. 8, 1897, MP.

76 "It is an upgrowth": JM in San Francisco *Bulletin,* Apr. 20, 1878.

76 "that exacting": JM to William E. Colby, Feb. 10, 1908, MPB.

76 "the contrary extravagantly": JM to Katherine P. Hooker [1913?], Hooker Papers.

76 "They must practice": Autobiography, 160-161, in folder 33.1, MP.

Page

77 "Never be 'dowy' ": JM to Ina B. Coolbrith, Dec. 13, 1907, Coolbrith Papers.

77 "Wherever grit": JM to Mr. Murdoch, Mar. 22, 1902, MP.

77 "Muir is Scotch": Wolfe, 261.

77 "in which they": Augustin S. MacDonald in *California Historical Society Quarterly,* Mar. 1938.

77 "Here, Johnny": M. R. Parsons in *SCB,* June 1939.

77 "I like the feel": Clara Barrus in *Century,* Aug. 1910.

78 "Ask him to tell": C. Barrus, *Life and Letters of John Burroughs* (1925), 1:360.

78 "Scarcely would": Melville B. Anderson in *American Museum Journal,* Mar. 1915.

78 "I used to keep": Charles F. Lummis to William F. Badè, July 3, 1919, in folder 66.17, MP.

78 "Sorry can't": JM, Journal, May 25, 1905, MP.

78 "We have two ears": MS fragment, n.d., in folder 39.16, MP.

79 "If a formal": L. S. Muir to R. U. Johnson, 1896, in folder 37.21, MP.

79 "the best school": Millard in *Bookman,* Feb. 1908.

79 "sadly comfortably": JM, Journal, Nov. 5, 1897, MP.

79 "We sometimes hear": Baker in *Outlook,* June 6, 1903.

79 "Earth and heaven": MS fragment, n.d., in folder 37.20, MP.

79 "On a swift": JM to Janet Moores, July 2, 1891, MP.

79–80 "the still, small voice": JM, *Journals,* 312.

80 "Everything busy": JM, Journal, n.d., in folder 39.37, MP.

80 "No wonder": JM in San Francisco *Bulletin,* Apr. 3, 1878.

80 "Indian dogs": JM, *Journals,* 277.

80 Privacy of JM's religious views: L. M. Wolfe to Wilson Follett, Mar. 14, 1944, in folder 70.10, MP.

80 "You naughty": Joanna M. Brown to JM, Feb. 12, 1880, MP.

80 "one of our": G. C. Hunter in *Religion in Life,* spring 1938.

80–81 "Descriptive writing": JM to Mrs. Richard Swain, Oct. 21, 1900, MP.

81 "Instead of producing": JM in *Scribner's,* Feb. 1879.

81 JM on modern science: JM, *Journals,* 434.

81 "While we are": Baker in *Outlook,* June 6, 1903.

81 JM in a library: JM to Helen Muir, June 3, 1906, MPB.

81 "Had I known": JM to C. H. Merriam, July 8, 1900, MP.

81 "To me Muir was": H. F. Reid to W. F. Badè, July 16, 1919, in folder 66.17, MP; see also T. D. A. Cockerell in *Dial,* Jan. 6, 1916.

81 "great, progressive": JM, *Letters,* 125–126.

82 "His noble character": JM to A. K. Bidwell, Feb. 1, 1878, Bidwell Family Papers.

82 "Darwin's ungodly word": JM, *Journals,* 118.

82 "Every cell": JM's note in his copy of A. R. Wallace's *The World of Life* (1911), MP.

82 "Evolution!": French Strother in *World's Work,* Mar. 1909.

82 Muir as transcendentalist: Hans Huth, *Nature and the American* (1957), 105; Roderick Nash, *Wilderness and the American Mind* (rev. ed., 1973), 125–127; Joseph M. Petulla, *American Environmental History* (1977), 230–231.

Page

83 JM's first reading of Thoreau: JM, *Letters,* 84.

83 "He said most": MS fragment, n.d., in folder 38.2, MP.

83 "the pure soul": JM in Boston *Evening Transcript,* Mar. 21, 1873.

83 JM's first reading of *Walden:* Abba G. Woolson, a Boston reformer and the wife of a scientific colleague of JM's, sent her copy of *Walden* to JM in March 1872. "It will give you infinite delight," she wrote JM, citing another reader to whom she had loaned the book: "and he learned to love Thoreau from it, too." The implication is that JM had not previously read the book. He kept Mrs. Woolson's copy of *Walden* in his personal library for the rest of his life. See Abba G. Woolson to JM, Feb. 4, Mar. 21, 1872, MP; Edith Jane Hadley, "John Muir's Views of Nature and Their Consequences" (Ph.D., thesis, University of Wisconsin, 1956), 215.

83 JM and Emerson's writings: JM to R. W. Emerson, July 6, 1871, EP.

83 "A little pure": JM in *OM,* Apr. 1875.

83 "the airy wisdom": JM to C. S. Sargent, Mar. 25, 1900, MP.

83 JM at Concord graves: JM to L. S. Muir, June 13, 1893, MP.

83 "Even open-eyed": MS fragment, n.d., in folder 40.1, MP.

83 Length of JM's stay at the university: JM to C. L. Merriam, Aug. 20, 1871, MP; Autobiography, 228, in folder 33.2, MP.

84 "big ideas": Strother in *World's Work,* Apr. 1907.

84 "had well-digested": Merriam in *SCB,* Jan. 1917.

84 "All my inheritance": Memoir, ca. 1875, in folder 37.17, MP.

84 "Not that I am": JM, Journal, July 9, 1876, MP.

84 "the stern old prophet": JM in San Francisco *Bulletin,* Aug. 21, 1880.

85 JM and H. George: C. A. Barker, *Henry George* (1955), 244; Wolfe, 181-183.

85 "Fortunately for": JM in San Francisco *Bulletin,* Oct. 22, 1878.

85 JM and the Grange: Strentzel Diary, Jan. 22, 1882, Strentzel Family Papers; JM to L. S. Muir, Apr. 20, 1892, MP.

85 "You never can": JM to J. B. McChesney, Jan. 10, 1873, MP.

85 "Legal theft": JM's note in his copy of John Ruskin's *Time and Tide* (1886 ed.), MP.

86 "Muir abhorred": Merriam in *SCB,* Jan. 1917.

86 "The gobble gobble school": Wolfe, 102.

86 "I want to see": Young, *Alaska Days,* 207.

86 "I hope the ranch": JM to L. S. Muir, July 23, 1888, MPY.

86 "A ranch that needs": L. S. Muir to JM, Aug. 9, 1888, MP.

86 Shasta conditions: JM, Journal, July 12, 1888, MP.

86-87 "We fear": R. U. Johnson to JM, Oct. 28, 1884, MP.

87 Johnson's visit to San Francisco: R. U. Johnson to Katherine Johnson, June 13, 1889, and to R. W. Gilder, May 18, 1889 (two), June 11, 1889, JPC.

87 "In California": R. U. Johnson to R. W. Gilder, May 18, 1889, JPC.

87 "My great discovery": R. U. Johnson to K. Johnson, May 27, 1889, JPC.

87 "Johnson, Johnson!": Johnson, *Remembered Yesterdays,* 279.

87 "Muir is": R. U. Johnson to K. Johnson, May 27, 1889, JPC.

87 "a most intelligent": Ibid.

87-88 "He invests": Ibid.

88 "How much": JM to L. S. Muir, June 3, 1889, MPY.

Page

88 The *Century's* circulation: Johnson, *Remembered Yesterdays,* 97.

88 "Leisurely he would": L. Frank Tooker, *The Joys and Tribulations of an Editor* (1923), 62.

97 Johnson and FDR: R. U. Johnson to FDR, Nov. 4, 1936, PPF 1742, FDR Library.

97 "imbibed from": Johnson, *Remembered Yesterdays,* 17.

97 "Nature rose": R. U. Johnson, *Poems* (1908), 78–79.

98 "Tinkering": JM, *Journals,* 283.

98 "The first impression": R. U. Johnson to K. Johnson, June 3, 1889, JPC.

98 "All seems so": JM to L. S. Muir, June 3, 1889, MPY.

98–99 "the biggest stars": Johnson, *Remembered Yesterdays,* 283.

99 "Muir knows of": R. U. Johnson to K. Johnson, June 8, 1889, JPC.

4.   LAND, TREES, AND WATER, 1890–1915

103 "The valley is going": R. U. Johnson to R. W. Gilder, June 11, 1889, JPC.

104 "a pseudo naturalist": J. P. Irish to George F. Parker, Jan. 9, 1893, in *Iowa Journal of History and Politics,* July 1933.

104 "John P./Irish he": JM to R. U. Johnson, May 13, 1891, JPB.

104 "The 'proposed reservation' ": R. U. Johnson to JM, July 22, 1891, MP.

104 "I began that": JM to R. U. Johnson, Oct. 29, 1889, JPB.

104 "I never can tell": JM to R. U. Johnson, Dec. 6, 1889, American Academy Papers.

105 "To write to order": JM to R. U. Johnson, Jan. 13, 1890, American Academy Papers.

105 "emphatic": R. U. Johnson to JM, Apr. 29, 1890, MP.

105 "not valuable for": JM to R. U. Johnson, May 8, 1890, MP.

105 "a little soft": JM to R. U. Johnson, Apr. 19, 1890, MPB.

105 "The Yosemite Century leaven": Ibid.

105 "Even under": JM in *Century,* Aug., Sept. 1890.

106 "Is it not possible": F. L. Olmsted to R. U. Johnson, Apr. 15, 1890, *Century* Collection.

106 SP lobby: Holway R. Jones, *John Muir and the Sierra Club* (1965), 46–47.

106 "Even the soulless": JM in *SCB,* Jan. 1896; and on railroads and national parks generally, see Alfred Runte in *National Parks and Conservation Magazine,* Apr. 1974.

106 "Everyone has been": Eliza R. Scidmore to Louie S. Muir, Dec. 31, 1890, MP.

106 "at my temerity": JM to R. U. Johnson, May 27, 1890, American Academy Papers.

106 "You have taken": R. U. Johnson to JM, Sept. 20, 1890, MP.

106 "association for preserving": R. U. Johnson to JM, Nov. 21, 1889, MP.

106 "I would gladly": JM to R. U. Johnson, Dec. 6, 1889, American Academy Papers.

106 Senger and Armes put in touch: JM to Henry Senger, May 10, 1892, MPB.

Page

107 "for the purpose": H. Senger and W. D. Armes to JM, May 25, 1892, MP; and see E. O. Easton in *SCB,* Dec. 1969.

107 "I had never seen": Samuel Merrill in *SCB,* Feb. 1928.

107 "this formal, legal": JM in *SCB,* Jan. 1896.

107 "The battle we have": Ibid.

108 Boone and Crockett activities: John F. Reiger, *American Sportsmen and the Origins of Conservation* (1975), 27–30.

108 "The club gets": G. B. Grinnell to Madison Grant, June 1, 1904, Boone and Crockett Club Papers.

108 "There are just": Gifford Pinchot, *Breaking New Ground* (1947), 325.

108 "conservation" as concept: M. Nelson McGeary, *Gifford Pinchot* (1960), 86; Samuel P. Hays, *Conservation and the Gospel of Efficiency* (Atheneum ed., 1969), 5n.

109 "I never saw": JM, *Journals,* 313.

109 "for every right use": Ibid., 351.

109 "the authority": R. U. Johnson to JM, Mar. 20, 1893, MP.

109 Sargent inspired by Marsh: C. S. Sargent to R. U. Johnson, Nov. 25, 1908, JPB.

110 "Probably no one": G. B. Grinnell to John W. Noble, Feb. 28, 1910, GBGP.

110 Role of Phillips: Ibid.; J. W. Noble to G. B. Grinnell, Mar. 11, 1910, Boone and Crockett Club Papers. On Phillips, see L. O. Howard, *Fighting the Insects* (1933), 237–238; *The Letters of Theodore Roosevelt,* ed. Elting E. Morison (1951–1954), 1:306; Reiger, *American Sportsmen,* 258–259.

110 "loved to play": *The Education of Henry Adams* (1918), 350.

110 "I had no idea": R. U. Johnson to JM, Feb. 21, 1893, MP.

110 "Now, at this": JM in *Century,* Feb. 1895.

110 "a forest service": G. Pinchot in *Century,* Feb. 1895.

111 Pinchot as latecomer: see, e.g., Reiger, *American Sportsmen,* 50, 150.

111 "kindness and interest": G. Pinchot to JM, Apr. 8, 1894, MP.

111 "store of scientific": G. Pinchot to W. Schlich, June 19, 1893, MP.

111 "In a very small": G. Pinchot to JM, May 23, 1894, MP.

111 Pinchot's later recollection: Pinchot, *Breaking,* 63.

111 Pinchot and Irish: J. P. Irish to G. F. Parker, Jan. 9, 1893, in *Iowa Journal of History and Politics,* July 1933.

111 "the greatest good": Harold K. Steen, *The U.S. Forest Service* (1976), 75.

112 "We have got": C. S. Sargent to JM, Jan. 13, 1897, MP.

112 "It is badly": C. S. Sargent to R. U. Johnson, June 4, 1923, JPB.

112 "hundreds of miles; JM in *Harper's Weekly,* June 5, 1897.

112 JM drawn to Pinchot: JM, Journal, July 16, 17, 1896, MP.

112 "it had as much": Pinchot, *Breaking,* 103.

112 "a storyteller": Ibid.

112 "There has been": Portland *Morning Oregonian,* July 23, 1896.

113 Sargent group: C. S. Sargent to JM, Apr. 6, May 3, 1897, MP.

113 "bad as it is": G. Pinchot to H. L. Stimson, May 5, 1897, GPP.

113 "The western politicians": C. S. Sargent to JM, May 5, 1897, MP.

113 TR as observer: *Letters of TR,* ed. E. E. Morison, 1:657.

113 "Much is said": JM in *Harper's Weekly,* June 5, 1897.

Page

114 "One feeble part": JM to C. S. Sargent, Oct. 28, 1897, MP.

114 "Keep cool": Arnold Hague to G. Pinchot, Feb. 11, 1898, GPP.

114 "What are we": JM to C. S. Sargent, Jan. 3, 1898, MP.

114 JM's letter writing: JM to Theodore P. Lukens, Apr. 25, 1898, Lukens Papers; JM to D. S. Jordan, Apr. 26, 1898, Jordan Papers.

114 "Clearly it is": C. S. Sargent to JM, Jan. 26, 1899, MP.

115 "There is no one": C. S. Sargent to JM, Dec. 26, 1902, MP.

115 "The whole question": G. Pinchot to JM, Dec. 30, 1897, MP.

115 "It is true": Joseph Le Conte in *SCB,* June 1902.

115 "While the Club": Allen Chamberlain in *Appalachia,* June 1908.

115 JM and Pinchot, 1898 and 1899: Pinchot Diary, Mar. 5-6, 1898, GPP; Pinchot to JM, Aug. 20, 1899, MP.

115-116 "widespread turning": Peter J. Schmitt, *Back to Nature* (1969), 19; see this book for a full discussion of progressive-era nature fads.

116 "The tendency": JM in *Atlantic,* Jan. 1898.

116-117 Antiurbanism in the 1800s: Morton and Lucia White, *The Intellectual Versus the City* (1962).

117 "Remember that this": R. U. Johnson to JM, July 9, 1897, and JM to Johnson, July 27, 1897, MP.

117 JM recruited by Houghton Mifflin: W. H. Page to JM, Sept. 1, 29, Oct. 7, 29, 1897, MP.

117 "It's like having": R. U. Johnson to JM, Dec. 14, 1897, MP; and see JM to Johnson, Mar. 3, 1911, *Century* Collection.

117 "This is the first": Anonymous, New York, to JM, Aug. 10, 1903, MP.

117 "Though I never": JM to Henry Randall, Dec. 20, 1901, MP.

118 "A man of genius": R. S. Baker in *Outlook,* June 6, 1903.

118 "In all this": W. H. Page to JM, Oct. 3, 1904, MP.

118 "I owe you": H. F. Osborn to JM, May 7, 1912, MP.

118 "Can't you meet": MS fragment, n.d., Hooker Papers.

118 "This morning": JM to Helen Muir, Nov. 4, 1898, MP.

119 "How is that": Clara Barrus in *Century,* Aug. 1910.

119 "It was fine fun": JM to Katherine P. Hooker, May 12, 1909, Hooker Papers.

119 "You are a dear": John Burroughs to JM, Dec. 28, 1909, MP.

119 "I have more": C. Barrus, *The Life and Letters of John Burroughs* (1925), 2:320.

119 "The club seems": JM, Journal, June 24, 1895, MP.

119 "Our Sierra Club": JM to T. P. Lukens, Dec. 28, 1898, Lukens Papers.

120 "our honored President": W. E. Colby in *SCB,* Feb. 1901.

120 "The Club outing": JM to L. S. Muir, July 20, 1901, MP.

120 "The Sierra Club has": Marion Randall in *SCB,* Jan. 1905.

120 "They all ask": W. E. Colby to JM, May 21, 1902, MP.

120 "I had a long talk": letter of July 18, 1908, inserted in C. Nelson Hackett memoir (Sierra Club History Committee).

120 " 'Hiking' is a *vile*": Ibid., 2.

120 "but little impression": JM, Journal, July 19, 1907, MP.

120 "the nestor": John Ritchie, Jr., in Boston *Evening Transcript,* May 24, 1911.

Page

121 Mills and Muir: Enos Mills to JM, Jan. 13, 29, 1903, May 1, 1906, July 30, 1907, Jan. 31, 1913, Nov. 24, 1914, MP.

121 "I owe everything": *Literary Digest,* July 14, 1917.

121 "It is all well": New York *Times,* Dec. 5, 1909.

122 "All the insects": Edmund Morris, *The Rise of Theodore Roosevelt* (1979), 47.

122 "you always hear": Ibid., 65.

122 TR's solitariness: Carleton Putnam, *Theodore Roosevelt* (1958), 100.

123 "Here the romance": Morris, *Rise of TR,* 214.

123 "I have had good": Ibid., 285.

123 TR in Dakota Terr., fall 1887: Ibid., 382-383.

123 TR and the Yellowstone railroad: Paul Schullery in *Montana,* summer 1978.

123 Boone and Crockett books: Paul Russell Cutright, *Theodore Roosevelt the Naturalist* (1956), 78.

124 "The older I grow": Frank Graham, Jr., *Man's Dominion* (1971), 116.

124 "When I hear": *Letters of TR,* ed. E. E. Morison, 2:948.

124 "The President is": C. H. Merriam to JM, Oct. 28, 1901, MP.

124 "The forest and water": Wolfe, 288.

124-125 "If I could not": W. T. Hornaday, "Eighty Fascinating Years," Hornaday Papers.

125 "I do not want": TR to JM, Mar. 14, 1903, MP.

125 "an all round": JM to Benjamin Wheeler, Mar. 23, 1903, MP.

125 "William, what": Augustin S. MacDonald in *California Historical Society Quarterly,* Mar. 1938.

125 "It is only": Stockton *Evening Mail,* May 15, 1903.

125 "Never did I hear": MS fragment, n.d., Hooker Papers.

125 "It was clear": TR in *Outlook,* Jan. 6, 1915.

126 "The hermit thrushes": TR, *An Autobiography* (1921), 322.

126 "I was surprised": JM to C. H. Merriam, June 4, 1904, MP.

126 "everything bright": JM to L. S. Muir, May 19, 1903, MP.

126 "I never before": JM to L. S. Muir, May 19, 1903, and to the Merriams and the Baileys, Jan. 1, 1904, MP.

126 "John Muir talked": TR in *Outlook,* Jan. 6, 1915.

126 "We are not": Cutright, *TR the Naturalist,* 171.

126 "You would have": TR to JM, Jan. 27, 1908, MP.

127 JM's request to Colby: W. E. Colby in *SCB,* Dec. 1962.

127 "A man may not": JM to R. U. Johnson, Mar. 4, 1890, MPB.

127 "Among the other": JM to R. U. Johnson, Jan. 13, 1893, MP.

127 "At first rather": JM to John Burroughs, Sept. 23, 1909, MP.

128 "The cold everyday": E. H. Harriman to JM, July 31, 1908, MP.

128 "one of the rare": JM, *E. H. Harriman* (1912), 39.

128 JM and the SP lobby: JM to E. H. Harriman, Jan. 5, 25, 1905, MP; Jones, *JM and the Sierra Club,* 67.

128 SP stooges: W. E. Colby in *SCB,* Dec. 1962.

128 "Because the last": JM to R. U. Johnson, Mar. 6, 1905, MP.

Page

128   "Many thanks": JM to W. F. Herrin, Feb. 26, 1905, MP.

128   Harriman and Cannon: E. H. Harriman to JM, Apr. 16, 1906, Alex Miller to JM, May 10, 1906, MP.

128   "either from indifference": *Letters of TR,* ed. E. E. Morison, 5:293–294.

128   "The fight you planned": JM to R. U. Johnson, July 16, 1906, JPB.

129   "the lumber syndicates": *Letters of TR,* ed. E. E. Morison, 5:604.

129   "I have one": McGeary, *Pinchot,* 55.

129   Pinchot and wider use of reserves: Hays, *Conservation,* 39–40; Steen, *Forest Service,* 74.

129   "He was" and "He had": Pinchot, *Breaking,* 154–155.

130   *Use Book:* Steen, *Forest Service,* 79–80.

130   "The conservation movement": G. Pinchot, *The Fight for Conservation* (1910), 44.

130   Hitchcock as Secretary of the Interior: Hays, *Conservation,* 72–73.

130   Omission of JM: G. Pinchot to R. U. Johnson, Apr. 13, 1908, Johnson Papers.

130   "The moral": *SCB,* June 1908.

130   "P. is ambitious": JM to R. U. Johnson, June 2, 1908, American Academy Papers.

131   Olmsted–Norton campaign: A. Runte in *New-York Historical Society Quarterly,* Jan. 1973.

131   "Niagara's claim": H. G. Wells in *Harper's Weekly,* July 21, 1906.

131   "We are permitting": J. H. McFarland in *Ladies' Home Journal,* Sept. 1905.

132   "badly infected": J. H. McFarland to Stephen Mather, Dec. 6, 1912, McFP.

132   "Nothing else matters": J. H. McFarland to R. B. Watrous, Dec. 14, 1912, McFP.

132   "Pinchot does not": J. H. McFarland to C. R. Woodruff, Apr. 13, 1908, McFP.

132   "I trust you": J. H. McFarland to JM, Jan. 10, 1914, McFP.

132   "a rampacious": J. H. McFarland to E. Mills, Apr. 20, 1912, McFP.

132   "If the country": J. H. McFarland to R. U. Johnson, Feb. 4, 1909, JPB.

133   "Boast we well": McFarland in *Ladies' Home Journal,* Sept. 1905.

133   "Turn on Niagara!": J. H. McFarland to Ernest McFarland, Apr. 9, 1943, McFP.

133   "You can little": T. E. Burton to J. H. McFarland, Apr. 10, 1906, McFP.

133   Response to McFarland's articles: Edward Bok to J. H. McFarland, Apr. 19, 1906, McFP.

133   "There has been": J. H. McFarland to JM, June 19, 1911, McFP.

133   The 6,550 letters: *Chautauquan,* Aug. 1907.

134   "Mr. Root now": TR to J. H. McFarland, Oct. 24, 1908, McFP.

134   "I have a dozen": J. H. McFarland to T. E. Burton, May 1, 1912, McFP.

134   "a surrender": J. H. McFarland to T. E. Burton, Jan. 27, 1914, McFP.

134   "I am a mighty": J. H. McFarland to J. S. Pray, Mar. 4, 1914, McFP.

134   "I would gladly": JM to Mrs. Howard, Sept. 1900, MP.

135   "My life": Roderick Nash, *Wilderness and the American Mind* (rev. ed., 1973), 172.

135   "you are a barbarian": Ibid., 153.

Page

135   The water company's condemnation: Jonathan E. Webb in *California Out-of-Doors,* Oct. 1919, copy in box 112, William Kent Papers.

135   "I know": William Kent to JM, Jan. 17, 1908, MP.

135–136   "Compared with Sequoia": JM to W. Kent, Feb. 6, 1908, Kent Papers.

136   "The set at Bar Harbor": William E. Dutcher to T. G. Pearson, July 9, 1907, AuP.

136   "The time fitted": MS fragment, n.d., Dorr Papers.

137   "George Dorr": C. W. Eliot to Ellen Bullard, Sept. 1, 1915, Dorr Papers.

137   "My earliest": MS fragment, Jan. 26, 1940, Dorr Papers.

137   "We all three": MS fragment, Dec. 22, 1938, Dorr Papers.

137   Cottage building: Bar Harbor *Times,* Oct. 31, 1963.

137   "I could do": MS fragment, Oct. 15, 1941, Dorr Papers.

138   Muir Woods precedent: G. B. Dorr, *Acadia National Park* (1942), 28.

138   "Our national parks": "What Do National Parks Stand For?", MS in Dorr Papers; and on this historical/cultural rationale for national parks, see A. Runte in *Journal of Forest History,* Apr. 1977.

138   Dorr and FDR: G. B. Dorr to FDR, June 25, 1940, PPF, FDR Library.

139   "Ever since": JM to J. R. Garfield, Sept. 6, 1907, "WS."

139   "formed by": JM in San Francisco *Bulletin,* Aug. 13, 1875.

139   "for domestic": Jones, *JM and the Sierra Club,* 90.

140   "Just the same": JM to R. U. Johnson, Mar. 23, 1905, MP.

140   Pinchot's suggestion: G. Pinchot to Marsden Manson, Nov. 15, 1906, in *Transactions of the Commonwealth Club of California,* June 1907.

140   "They all show": JM to TR, Sept. 9, 1907, "WS."

140   "So far everyone": TR to JM, Sept. 16, 1907, MP.

140   "This Yosemite fight": JM to R. U. Johnson, Sept. 2, 1907, JPB.

141   "mischief-makers": JM in *Outlook,* Nov. 2, 1907.

141   "John Muir loves": James Phelan to J. R. Garfield, Nov. 21, 1907, "WS."

141   "the water-power trust": Pinchot, *Fight,* 27–28.

141   JM's compromise: JM to TR, Apr. 21, 1908, in folder 65.31, MP.

141   "I am trying": TR to JM, Apr. 27, 1908, Roosevelt Papers.

141   TR's action: TR to J. R. Garfield, Apr. 27, 1908, "WS."

141   "I think you must": R. U. Johnson to JM, May 23, 1908, MP.

142   "It was just": TR to R. U. Johnson, Dec. 17, 1908, JPB.

142   TR's request to Garfield: William Loeb, Jr., to J. R. Garfield, Dec. 17, 1908, "WS."

142   "monopolizing San Francisco": JM in *SCB,* Jan. 1908.

142   Colby's supposition: W. E. Colby to R. U. Johnson, Nov. 19, 1908, McFP.

142   "We do not": JM et al., "To All Lovers of Nature and Scenery," Dec. 21, 1908, in box 7, PP.

142   "I am sure": Wolfe, 316.

142   Taft and Johnson's argument: R. U. Johnson to JM, Sept. 7, 1909, MP.

143   "He refused": *Bookman,* Feb. 1915.

143   "he never": Frank Swett memoir, p. 13, in "Recollections of John Muir" (1965), Bancroft Library.

143   "All seems coming": JM to W. E. Colby, Oct. 21, 1909, MPB; and see R. A. Ballinger to JM, Dec. 27, 1909, MP.

Page

143 "The Ballinger administration": Marsden Manson to G. Pinchot, Jan. 9, 1910, GPP.

143 "JOHN MUIR": R. B. Watrous to J. H. McFarland, Oct. 14, 1912, McFP.

144 "These temple destroyers": JM, *The Yosemite* (1912), 261–262.

144 Olney would not allow: E. O. Easton in *SCB,* Dec. 1969.

144 JM's friends in Washington: C. H. Merriam to JM, Jan. 21, 1909, and R. B. Marshall to JM, Jan. 21, 1910, Jan. 19, 1913, MP.

144 "I must tell you": John Burroughs to R. U. Johnson, Oct. 20, 1913, American Academy Papers.

144 "for he is a man": William Kent to Sidney Anderson, July 2, 1913, Kent Papers.

144–145 "We are all": Jones, *JM and the Sierra Club,* 132.

145 "Both Colby and I": W. F. Badè to J. H. McFarland, Feb. 17, 1909, McFP.

145 "The problem": R. U. Johnson to J. H. McFarland, Dec. 29, 1913, McFP.

145 "Ugly Conservation": J. H. McFarland in *Outlook,* Mar. 13, 1909.

145 "Our friends": A. Chamberlain to J. H. McFarland, Mar. 13, 1909, McFP; see, e.g., W. H. Badè in *Independent,* Oct. 13, 1910.

145 Wilson's apparent gratitude: see, e.g., Franklin K. Lane to James D. Phelan, July 19, 1912, Phelan Papers.

145 "I'll be relieved": JM to Helen Muir, Nov. 15, 1913, MPB.

145 "Our defeat": W. E. Colby to J. H. McFarland, Nov. 27, 1914, McFP.

146 "I got my money": R. S. Yard to John C. Merriam, July 1, 1929, Merriam Papers.

146 "I underestimated": George Norris, *Fighting Liberal* (1945), 165.

5. WILDLIFE PROTECTORS, 1900–1935

148 "The protection": W. T. Hornaday to D. C. Beard, Apr. 10, 1912, Beard Papers.

148 "As a boy": *Mentor,* May 1929.

149 "The best way": William Bridges, *Gathering of Animals* (1974), 300.

149 "I pity the dogs": Frank Graham, Jr., *Man's Dominion* (1971), 113.

149 The $4,200 for Shields: W. T. Hornaday to T. S. Palmer, Apr. 27, 1907, PP.

149 "Hornaday, you are": W. T. Hornaday to Mrs. Irving Brant, Feb. 3, 1930, BrP.

149 "I decided": W. T. Hornaday, *Thirty Years War for Wild Life* (1931), 183.

149 "I have been": W. T. Hornaday, *Our Vanishing Wild Life* (1913), x.

150 "Its burning": W. F. Badè in *SCB,* June 1913.

150 "The moral standards": W. T. Hornaday, "Eighty Fascinating Years," Hornaday Papers.

150 Hornaday's approach to animals: Bridges, *Gathering,* 117–118, 253–254, 412.

150 "To the last": Hornaday, "Eighty Fascinating Years."

150 "I am of a very": Bridges, *Gathering,* 407.

151 "Hornaday belongs": W. C. Adams to F. A. Dallett, Mar. 31, 1926, AuP.

Page
151   "He will take": I. Brant to Rosalie Edge, Feb. 3, 1931, BrP.

151   "All this grand": Wayne Hanley, *Natural History in America* (1977), 78-79.

152   "The winter was": John F. Reiger, *The Passing of the Great West* (1972), 79.

152   "Its position was": William Brewster, *October Farm* (1937), 116.

152   "I was moved": W. Brewster, *Concord River* (1937), 60.

153   "In all the places": W. E. Dutcher to T. S. Palmer, Oct. 17, 1901, AuP.

153   "There are very": W. E. Dutcher to L. A. Fuertes, Dec. 13, 1901, AuP.

154   "I am disgusted": W. E. Dutcher to T. S. Palmer, Jan. 8, 1903, PP.

154   "The object": Graham, *Man's Dominion,* 51-52.

154   Wilcox bequest: T. G. Pearson, *Adventures in Bird Protection* (1937), 143.

154   Dutcher's appeals: W. E. Dutcher to T. S. Palmer, July 9, 1906, PP.

154   The $8,000 deficit: W. E. Dutcher to T. G. Pearson, May 23, 1907, AuP.

154   Dutcher questioned: W. E. Dutcher to T. S. Palmer, Dec. 8, 1907, PP; Palmer to Dutcher, Dec. 10, 1907, AuP.

155   "One of the most": T. G. Pearson to T. S. Palmer, Mar. 12, 1913, AuP.

155   "I lived": Pearson, *Adventures,* 19.

155   "They seemed": T. G. Pearson to T. S. Palmer, Mar. 11, 1913, AuP.

156   "Just think": Jonathan Dwight, Jr., to T. S. Palmer, May 31, 1911, AuP.

156   Grinnell and the gun companies' offer: G. B. Grinnell to H. F. Osborn, May 23, 1911, GBGP; Grinnell to W. W. Grant, May 29, 1911, AuP.

156   "If he could speak": *Congressional Record,* 69 Cong., 1 Sess., 9907.

156   "Frank Chapman opened": G. B. Grinnell to W. Brewster, June 19, 1911, GBGP.

156   "the manufacturers": G. B. Grinnell to Madison Grant, Feb. 7, 1912, GBGP.

157   "Our friends": T. S. Palmer to T. G. Pearson, Apr. 6, 1912, AuP.

157   "Birds are": Henry Ford, *My Life and Work* (1922), 236-237.

157   Buck's activities: Hornaday, *Thirty Years War,* 164.

157   Burnham's maneuver: G. B. Grinnell to Witmer Stone, Mar. 12, 1913, GBGP.

157-158   "Wild birds": Harry B. Hawes, *Fish and Game: Now or Never* (1935), 106-107.

158   "*All* our recommendations": W. T. Hornaday to T. S. Palmer, Aug. 214, 1916, PP.

158   "It seems to me": G. B. Grinnell to T. G. Pearson, Oct. 10, 1913, GBGP.

158   Audubon membership figures: T. G. Pearson to T. S. Palmer, Jan. 20, 1920, PP.

158   "We find it hard": T. G. Pearson to T. S. Palmer, Jan. 31, 1920, PP.

159   The fifty-four founders: *OA,* Apr. 1928.

159   "Since boyhood": W. H. Dilg in *OA,* Feb. 1925.

159   "If you have": W. H. Dilg in *Outlook,* May 25, 1921.

159   Description of Dilg: Harry B. Hawes, *My Friend, the Black Bass* (1930), 275-276.

159   Death of Dilg's son: *Congressional Record,* 69 Cong., 1 Sess., 9896.

159   "I am weary": W. H. Dilg in *OA,* Oct. 1927.

Page

160   "I must not": T. G. Pearson to J. H. McFarland, Apr. 12, 1921, McFP.

160   "I am earnestly": W. H. Dilg to H. G. Evarts, Mar. 19, 1923, Evarts Papers.

160   "some local clown": Theodore Dreiser in *OA*, Mar. 1924.

161   "wholesome idolatry": I. S. Cobb in *Izaak Walton League Monthly*, Feb. 1923.

161   "I fear": J. O. Curwood in *Izaak Walton League Monthly*, Jan.–Mar., June, 1923.

161   "We are composed": W. H. Dilg in *OA*, Nov. 1925.

161–162   "If you care": *OA*, Nov. 1925.

162   "and each of these": W. H. Dilg to G. Pinchot, Nov. 25, 1924, GPP.

162   "Dilg was essentially": Hawes, *My Friend*, 276.

162–163   "It was as though": *Izaak Walton League Monthly*, May 1923.

163   "I have been": W. H. Dilg to H. G. Evarts, Oct. 14, 1924, Evarts Papers.

163   "In the world": *OA*, May 1925.

163   "I had a feeling": Pearson, *Adventures*, 361.

164   "the Great Stuffed": W. T. Hornaday to I. Brant, Sept. 26, 1930, BrP.

164   Grinnell re duck crisis: G. B. Grinnell to John Burnham, Dec. 1, 1923, May 12, 1925, GBGP.

164   "Most of us": G. B. Grinnell to J. Burnham et al., Feb. 4, 1926, GBGP.

164   "I am an advocate": J. Burnham to I. Brant, Jan. 28, 1928, BrP.

165   AGPA income: *Congressional Record*, 69 Cong., 1 Sess., 8477.

165   "We are the insurance": Ibid., 9908.

165   "When I was": Ibid., 8478.

165   "I should like": Ibid., 9913.

166   "A detailed statement": Ibid., 9910.

166   "the . . . combine": W. T. Hornaday to I. Brant, Apr. 8, 1927, BrP.

166   "The sportsmen are well": Winthrop Packard to T. G. Pearson, Nov. 16, 1923, PP.

166   "ultra sentiment": T. G. Pearson to W. P. Wharton, Nov. 17, 1923, PP.

166–167   "The sportsmen are led": W. T. Hornaday to I. Brant, Nov. 17, 1926, BrP.

167   "a thoroughgoing": Aldo Leopold to W. T. Hornaday, Oct. 8, 1923, PP.

167   "I am told": G. B. Grinnell to J. C. Phillips, Dec. 17, 1924, GBGP.

167   Hornaday article: New York *Times*, Aug. 12, 1925.

167   Burnham suit: New York *Times*, July 17, 1927.

167   "The man is": *Scientific American*, Oct. 1925.

168   "not quite so": J. H. McFarland to W. H. Dilg, Jan. 7, 1924, McFP.

168   "It is a notable": *OA*, Mar. 1924.

168   "He had a staff": Pearson, *Adventures*, 360.

168   "He talked about ": "The Reminiscences of Horace M. Albright" (Columbia Oral History Collection, 1962), 424.

169   "At last": *OA*, July 1924.

169   "Dilg's name": Pearson, *Adventures*, 360.

169   "In truth": W. H. Dilg in *Izaak Walton League Monthly*, May 1922.

169   "A Plain Letter": W. H. Dilg, "A Plain Letter," Sept. 20, 1924, in box 111, Merriam Papers.

169   "I feel it is": T. G. Pearson to Lee Miles, Mar. 24, 1926, AuP.

Page

170 Remington's activities: Remington statement in *OA,* Nov. 1924.

170 Charges against Dilg: Statement by G. H. Selover, 1926, in box 183, AuP.

170 "the finest piece": David Madsen to T. G. Pearson, Apr. 13, 1926, AuP.

170 "With his standing": G. H. Selover to T. G. Pearson, Apr. 16, 1926, AuP.

171 Grey and Curwood: New York *Times,* June 13, 1926.

171 "the unsportsmanlike": *Congressional Record,* 69 Cong., 1 Sess., 8476.

171 "If he wrote": E. H. Forbush to T. G. Pearson, Oct. 19, 1926, AuP.

171 Hornaday's enemies: G. B. Grinnell to Charles Sheldon, July 23, 1924, GBGP.

171 The resignations: G. B. Grinnell to T. G. Pearson, Oct. 13, 1924, AuP.

171 Burnham and the list: J. S. Barnes to T. G. Pearson, Apr. 7, 1926, and W. C. Adams to Pearson, Apr. 21, 1926, AuP.

171 Hornaday's resignation: Bridges, *Gathering,* 409. According to Bridges, Hornaday had been expected to retire in the spring of 1926. Yet, although Hornaday wrote a letter of resignation on May 4, no public announcement of the resignation was made until May 20, and the news was then received with surprise. "I don't feel so badly about it now," Hornaday told the press, "but wait until a week after I leave; then it will hit me hard." His statement, and the fact that only twelve days would elapse until his formal departure, suggest the decision was made hastily. See New York *Times,* May 21, 1926. Hornaday later maintained that he had resigned of his own volition (interview with John Ripley Forbes, July 1980).

172 "in the belief": Minutes of AGPA meeting, Oct. 20, 1926, GBGP.

172 "the one and only": *OA,* Nov. 1928.

173 "How many people": Pearson, *Adventures,* 245.

173 Audubon income: *Bird-Lore,* Nov.–Dec. 1926 and Nov.–Dec. 1927.

173 Brant and Hornaday: I. Brant, "Adventures in Conservation," 10–12, BrP.

174 "seeks simply": T. S. Palmer to W. P. Mangold, Jan. 20, 1928, PP.

174 "The best way": G. B. Grinnell to R. S. Yard, Apr. 21, 1922, GBGP.

174 Van Name solicited support: W. G. Van Name to I. Brant, Dec. 28, 1931, BrP.

174 "which owing to": *Forest and Stream,* Nov. 1929.

174 "For what to me": Rosalie Edge, "Good Companions in Conservation: Annals of an Implacable Widow" (MS in custody of Peter Edge, Chicago), 6.

174 "My entrance": Ibid., 15.

175 "They can prevent": Ibid., 26.

175 "I could not help": I. Brant to Enos Mills, Aug. 5, 1921, BrP.

175 "the idea": Brant, "Adventures," 151.

175 "It was the first": R. L. Taylor in *New Yorker,* Apr. 17, 1948.

176 "When we suffrage": Edge, "Good Companions," 7.

176 "This did not": Ibid., 9.

176 "When we who": Ibid., 9A.

176 Edge's presence: Taylor in *New Yorker,* Apr. 17, 1948.

176 "Motor Power": R. Edge in *Nature Magazine,* Dec. 1940.

177 "It is the policy": R. Edge to I. Brant, Dec. 17, 1931, Apr. 16, 1947, and Nov. 3, 1931, BrP.

177 "Everyone has been": R. Edge to I. Brant, Apr. 6, 1932, BrP.

Page

177 "Mrs. Edge, I never": Edge, "Good Companions," 57.

177 "the only woman": Ibid., 27.

178 "You probably know": T. G. Pearson to T. S. Palmer, Oct. 15, 1930, PP.

178 *Time* publicity: *Time,* Nov. 3, 1930.

178 "You are fighting": B. Shimek to I. Brant, Oct. 20, 1930, BrP.

178 "Perhaps some": *Bird-Lore,* Nov.–Dec. 1930.

178 "I feel that": Ibid.

178 "Fancy how I": Edge, "Good Companions," 43.

178 "Through the daily": R. C. Murphy to T. S. Palmer, Aug. 6, 1931, PP.

179 "zoophile cult": Audubon news release, Sept. 3, 1931, BrP.

179 The confidential appendix: T. G. Pearson to T. S. Palmer, Aug. 20, 1931, PP.

179 "This seems": R. Edge to I. Brant, June 5, 1931, BrP.

179 "Still, they can't": Ibid., Oct. 27, 1931, BrP.

179 The $50,000 rental: Edge, "Good Companions" 69–70.

180 "There is no": R. Edge to I. Brant, Nov. 5, 1932, BrP.

180 "Tell me": T. G. Pearson to T. S. Palmer, Sept. 14, 1934, PP.

180 Pearson's resignation: R. C. Murphy to T. S. Palmer, Sept. 24, 1934, PP.

180 "At last a miracle": Brant, "Adventures," 89.

180 "for all the": R. Edge to I. Brant, Nov. 9, 1931, BrP.

181 "The whole Committee": Ibid., Oct. 20, 1937, BrP.

181 "the only honest": Taylor in *New Yorker,* Apr. 17, 1948.

181 Contributions to the ECC: R. Edge to Robert Marshall, Apr. 2, 1938, RMP.

181 "I have met": Edge, "Good Companions," 230.

181 "Man hates": Ibid., 144.

182 "We must have": Maurice Broun, *Hawks Aloft* (1949), 13.

182 "You know": Edge, "Good Companions," 218.

6. FRANKLIN D. ROOSEVELT
AND NEW DEAL CONSERVATION

183 "I wish you": Nixon, 1:131.

184 "the gospel": Ibid., 1:433.

184 "heavily forested": Arthur M. Schlesinger, Jr., *The Coming of the New Deal* (1959), 576.

184 "I fear that": Nixon, 1:572.

184 "Tracking is": Composition book, Sept. 1891, FDR Library.

185 Song of blackbirds: Composition book, June 1896, FDR Library.

185 "Many people": Composition book, Nov. 1893, FDR Library.

185 "the *finest*": Frank Freidel, *Franklin D. Roosevelt: The Apprenticeship* (1952), 27.

185 FDR as birder: see, e.g., L. S. Ashton in *AM,* May–June 1955.

185 AOU file: Grace G. Tully to Rudyard Boulton, Jan. 7, 1943, PPF 5547, FDR Library.

185 "The interesting": Nixon, 2:603.

Page

185 "We have tried": Ibid., 1:356.

186 "Forestry pays": Ibid., 1:605.

186 "Growing trees": Ibid., 2:633.

186 "competition has": A. M. Schlesinger, Jr., *The Crisis of the Old Order* (1957), 337, and Freidel, *Apprenticeship,* 133.

187 Johnson resignation: Ovid M. Butler to R. U. Johnson, June 5, 1924, JPB.

187 AFA Funding: Note by Irving Brant, Sept. 30, 1965, in box 17, BrP.

187 "Today the conservation": Arthur A. Ekirch, Jr., *Man and Nature in America* (1963), 120.

187 GOP conservationists: *Who's Who in America,* 1930–1935.

188 "He loved to": William B. Greeley, *Forests and Men* (1951), 212.

188 "the aggressive agent": M. Nelson McGeary, *Gifford Pinchot* (1960), 406.

188 "If it is true": FDR to the Secretary of Agriculture, Apr. 22, 1935, OF 1-C, FDR Library.

189 "simple work": F. Freidel, *Franklin D. Roosevelt: Launching the New Deal* (1973), 260.

189 Fechner plan: Horace M. Albright and Newton B. Drury, "Comments on Conservation, 1900 to 1960" (Bancroft Library, 1962), 45.

189 "Power is really": Nixon, 1:333.

189 "Thank God": Fairfield Osborn, Jr., to FDR, Oct. 2, 1933, PPF 872, FDR Library.

190 "is an integral": Nixon, 1:346.

190 "really cared": Stuart Chase, *Rich Land, Poor Land* (1936), 302.

190 "These are 2": MS chart, 1937, OF 1193, FDR Library.

190 Baker's report: John H. Baker to FDR, May 27, 1935, PPF 2543, FDR Library.

190–191 "He seems to": Harold L. Ickes, *Secret Diary* (1954), 1:488.

191 "will develop": Nixon, 2:329.

191 "Darling was": I. Brant, "Adventures in Conservation," 100, BrP.

191 Darling's hobbies: *Literary Digest,* Nov. 18, 1933.

191 Estimate of the duck population: Brant, "Adventures," 18.

192 Darling and the survey: J. N. Darling to I. Brant, July 13, 1933, BrP.

192 "Mr. Beck determines": Nixon, 1:266.

192 "If there was": *Business Week,* Jan. 6, 1935.

193 "Rodents multiply": I. Brant to H. A. Mason, May 17, 1934, BrP.

193 "We are, I believe": R. Edge to J. N. Darling, May 12, 1934, BrP.

193 "I almost find": J. N. Darling to R. Edge, May 17, 1934, BrP.

193 "I had to keep": R. Edge to I. Brant, July 31, 1934, BrP.

193 "She really seemed": J. N. Darling to I. Brant, Aug. 2, 1934, BrP.

194 "He knows nothing": R. Edge to I. Brant, Aug. 27, 1934, BrP.

194 "I've dined": J. N. Darling to I. Brant, Oct. 1, 1934, BrP.

194 "You are in": I. Brant to J. N. Darling, Sept. 28, 1934, BrP.

194 "Your criticism": J. N. Darling to W. T. Hornaday, Jan. 21, 1936, Hornaday Papers.

194 "the President knows": M. A. LeHand to Marvin McIntyre, Jan. 25, 1935, OF 378, FDR Library.

194–195 "We can make": Nixon, 1:404.

195 "You hold an": Ibid., 1:405–406.

Page

195   "more than my": Nixon, 1:418.

195   "It now seems": J. N. Darling to H. A. Wallace, Sept. 19, 1935, Wallace Papers.

195   FDR more friendly: J. N. Darling to I. Brant, Jan. 6, 1936, BrP.

196   "I have come": J. N. Darling in *Current Biography* (1942), 177.

196   The dinner in New York: J. N. Darling to Seth Gordon, Apr. 13, 1960, Boone and Crockett Club Papers.

196   "The Institute": *Bird-Lore,* Sept.–Oct. 1935.

196   Chrysler convicted: *Nature Magazine,* Jan. 1937.

196   "The bricklayers": New York *Herald-Tribune,* Oct. 30, 1935.

197   "Probably nothing": *SCB,* May 1936.

197   "The Wild Life Institute": E. A. Preble to W. T. Hornaday, Feb. 14, 1936, Hornaday Papers.

197   The "selfishly" interested: *Nature Magazine,* May 1937.

197   Darling's loss of interest: J. N. Darling to S. Gordon, Apr. 13, 1960, Boone and Crockett Club Papers.

197   "a good conservationist": Brant, "Adventures," 596.

198   "the importance": *Bird-Lore,* Nov.–Dec. 1936.

198   "Though Baker": R. Edge to I. Brant, Mar. 26, 1939, BrP.

198   "The point is": John Collier, *From Every Zenith* (1936), 292.

199   "It looks dead": Schlesinger, *Coming,* 588.

199   "There is nothing": Nixon, 1:322.

199   "They will forget": Ibid., 1:538–539.

199–200   FDR's car: The car is on exhibit at the FDR Library.

200   "The President drove": Winston S. Churchill, *The Hinge of Fate* (Bantam ed., 1962), 327–328.

200   "I wish very": Nixon, 2:137.

200   "How would I": Brant, "Adventures," 235.

200   "I do not": *LW,* Sept. 1935.

201   "I learned": Donald C. Swain, *Wilderness Defender* (1970), 220.

201   "the soul of a meat ax": Ibid., 218.

201   "One should get": Ickes, *Diary,* 1:176.

201   "I must say": Ibid., 2:203.

201   "It seems": Nixon, 1:518.

202   Forest Service lobby: Richard Polenberg, *Reorganizing Roosevelt's Government* (1966), 105.

202   "Most conservation": H. L. Ickes to C. E. Merriam, Mar. 1, 1940, in "National Parks: Kings Canyon."

202   "I like the": Ickes, *Diary,* 2:38.

202   "Forest Service not": FDR memo, Feb. 19, 1937, OF 6-P, FDR Library.

203   "I feel that": R. Edge to I. Brant, Feb. 19, 1941, BrP.

    "the most belligerent": F. P. Jaques, *Birds Across the Sky* (1942), 182.

203   "I became his": R. S. Yard to J. C. Merriam, Jan. 12, 1925, Merriam Papers.

204   "The specialties": R. S. Yard to G. B. Grinnell, Sept. 18, 1926, Merriam Papers.

204   Albright and Mather: R. S. Yard to W. P. Wharton, Oct. 29, 1931, Merriam Papers.

Page

204 "Thousands of": R. S. Yard to FDR, June 25, 1923, Group 14, FDR Library.

205 "the best advocate": R. S. Yard to Olaus Murie, Aug. 13, 1935, WSP.

205 "I do not wholly": G. B. Grinnell to W. R. Cross, Oct. 10, 1928, GBGP.

205 NPA income: R. S. Yard to Duncan McDuffie, Apr. 14, 1930, Merriam Papers.

205 "Waking in the": R. S. Yard to J. C. Merriam, ca. Nov. 26, 1926, Merriam Papers.

205 "What if he": G. D. Pratt to R. S. Yard, Apr. 8, 1929, Merriam Papers.

206 "I am a tenderfoot": *LW,* Dec. 1945.

206 "The mountaineer": M. R. Parsons in *SCB,* Jan. 1920.

206 "We admired": George Marshall in *LW,* autumn 1951.

206 "I love the": Ibid.

207 "Most important": Robert Marshall, *Arctic Village* (1933), 378–379.

207 "The period for": R. Marshall in *Nation,* Aug. 28, 1929.

207 "Then they had": R. Marshall to Raphael Zon, Jan. 23, 1933, RMPR.

208 "There are certain": R. Marshall in *LW,* summer 1954.

208 "Many of our": R. Marshall, *The People's Forests* (1933), 69–70.

208 "the puniness": R. Marshall to Irving Clark, Oct. 26, 1935, RMP.

208 "The sense": R. Marshall in *LW,* summer 1954.

208 "A person": R. Marshall in *LW,* autumn 1951.

209 "I'm glad you": R. Marshall, *Alaska Wilderness* (2d ed., 1970), xxix.

209 Marshall's awareness of lesion: John Collier, *From Every Zenith* (1963), 276.

209 "Four walls": Sigurd Olson in *LW,* spring 1948.

209 "On the whole": R. Marshall to I. Clark, Mar. 19, 1935, RMP.

209 "Obviously, my name": R. Marshall to Ernest Oberholtzer, Apr. 12, 1939, RMP.

209 "this is only": R. Marshall to Kenneth Reid, Feb. 17, 1939, RMP.

209–210 Threat of work projects: R. Marshall, memo to H. L. Ickes, Apr. 25, 1935, RMP.

210 "The bulldozers": R. Marshall to Ferdinand Silcox, June 24, 1935, RMP.

210 "You and Bob": Harold Anderson to Benton MacKaye, Aug. 12, 1934, WSP.

210 "It was that": Harvey Broome to R. Marshall, Aug. 21, 1934, RMP.

210 "he has done": R. Marshall to Alvin G. Whitney, May 1, 1935, RMP.

211 "The Wilderness Society": R. S. Yard in *LW,* Sept. 1935.

211 "a disclaimer": Aldo Leopold in *LW,* Sept. 1935.

211 "We want no": R. Marshall to Harold Anderson, Oct. 24, 1934, WSP.

211 "a grand fellow": R. Marshall to R. S. Yard, Oct. 26, 1935, WSP.

211 "I have in mind": B. MacKaye to R. S. Yard, June 25, 1935, WSP.

211 "If we keep": R. Marshall to Bernard Frank, May 13, 1935, RMP.

212 "Everybody would": R. S. Yard to S. Olson, July 10, 1942, WSP.

212 "My contribution": R. Marshall to R. S. Yard, Feb. 3, 1938, WSP.

212 "On the whole": R. Marshall to R. Edge, Mar. 11, 1936, RMP.

212 "We are just": R. Edge to R. Marshall, Apr. 23, 1935, RMP.

212 "Mr. Brant is": R. Edge to R. Marshall, Apr. 2, 1938, RMP.

Page

212 "I believe": R. Marshall to R. Edge, Dec. 15, 1937, RMP.

212 "I never": R. Edge to I. Brant, Mar. 5, 1940, BrP.

213 "when it was wild": JM in *Century,* Nov. 1891.

213 "This region": Ibid.

213 "was more enthusiastic": R. S. Yard in *LW,* Dec. 1942.

213 "I wish": W. E. Colby to J. H. McFarland, Nov. 17, 1925, McFP.

213 "a primitive": *Nature Magazine,* May 1940.

214 "the slickest": I. Brant to Mike Frome, May 4, 1972, BrP.

214 "It is not necessary": *SCB,* Feb. 1935.

214 "I don't want": Marion Jones memoir (Sierra Club History Committee), 15.

215 "a man of": Joel Hildebrand to I. Brant, Dec. 24, 1938, BrP.

215 "As a club": W. G. Schulz to I. Brant, Oct. 13, 1938, BrP.

215 "We gave him": J. Hildebrand memoir (Sierra Club History Committee), 17–18.

216 Brant pointed out: I. Brant to H. L. Ickes, Oct. 8, 1938, BrP.

216 "John Muir engaged": *Congressional Record,* 76 Cong., 1 Sess., Appendix, 1086.

216 "The bill must": David Brower in *SCB,* Apr. 1939.

216 ECC slogan: R. Edge to I. Brant, Apr. 24, 1939, BrP.

216 Elvira Hutchings stories: L. M. Wolfe to Mrs. Atkinson, May 16, 1940, in folder 70.9, MP.

216 "it has not been": *Congressional Record,* 76 Cong., 1 Sess., Rpt. No. 718.

216 Dunwoody's scheme: I. Brant to FDR, May 5, 1939, BrP.

216 Gearhart revealed: *Congressional Record,* 76 Cong., 1 Sess., 5033–3040.

216–217 "I feel now": W. E. Colby to H. L. Ickes, Feb. 20, 1940, in "National Parks: Kings Canyon."

217 "all the *anti*": R. Edge to I. Brant, Mar. 15, 1940, BrP.

217 "Has the Republican": R. Edge to I. Brant, Oct. 7, 1940, BrP.

217 "I don't know": I. Brant to R. Edge, Oct. 17, 1940, BrP.

7. SIX FREE-LANCERS

219 "I think perhaps": Raymond B. Fosdick, *John D. Rockefeller, Jr.* (1956), 302.

219 "I remember": Ibid., 302.

219 "I did not": Peter Collier and David Horowitz, *The Rockefellers* (1976), 138.

220 "I have ever": Ibid., 138.

220 "One of the ": George B. Dorr to J. D. Rockefeller, Jr., Jan. 2, 1920, Eliot Papers.

220 "Who is willing": R. S. Yard to W. P. Wharton, Sept. 21, 1927, Merriam Papers.

220 Dorr supports road building: MS fragment, Apr. 14, Dorr Papers.

221 "does not welcome": G. B. Dorr to Herbert L. Satterlee, May 14, 1935, Acadia Historical Papers.

221 "somewhat dull": Harold L. Ickes, *Secret Diary* (1954), 2:502.

221 "the only man": Ibid., 2:503.

Page

221 "quite the grandest": Fosdick, *Rockefeller,* 316.

221 Plans for purchase: "The Reminiscences of Horace M. Albright" (Columbia Oral History Collection, 1962), 225–227.

222 "There were rumors": Margaret and Olaus Murie, *Wapiti Wilderness* (1966), 110.

222 "He is now": Nixon, 2:570.

222 "We GAVE them": Murie and Murie, *Wapiti,* 123.

223 "I am not making": William Manchester, *A Rockefeller Family Portrait* (1959), 119.

223 "I never had": Fosdick, *Rockefeller,* 129.

223 "His actions are": Ibid., 325–326.

224 "by far the best": Bernard DeVoto to Robeson Bailey, Aug. 11, 1946, DeVP.

224 "It is imperative": B. DeVoto in *Fortune,* June 1947.

224 "One of the beauty": B. DeVoto to R. Bailey, Aug. 11, 1946, DeVP.

224 "My God": B. DeVoto to Madeline, Jan. 18, 1947, DeVP.

224 DeVoto on horses: B. DeVoto in *Harper's,* Nov. 1948, Sept. 1951.

224 "One of the biggest": B. DeVoto in *Harper's,* Jan. 1947.

225 "Federal ownership": B. DeVoto in *Harper's,* July 1948.

225 "In a single": B. DeVoto in *Harper's,* Dec. 1946.

225 "This is the only": B. DeVoto to Robert van Gelder, Aug. 4, 1947, DeVP.

225 Historical forces: B. DeVoto in *Harper's,* Mar. 1946.

226 "If I have ever": William Vogt to B. DeVoto, Jan. 21, 1947, DeVP.

226 "The grazing interests": John H. Baker in *AM,* Mar.–Apr. 1947.

226 "the best-informed": B. DeVoto to Mr. Perry, June 21, 1948, DeVP.

226 "the one-woman": B. DeVoto to Eric Larrabee, July 13, 1948, DeVP.

226 "The trouble": B. DeVoto to Mrs. Gifford Pinchot, May 25, 1948, DeVP.

227 "The active land-grabbers": B. DeVoto in *Harper's,* Jan. 1948.

227 "There is only": J. Elmer Brock in *Harper's,* Sept. 1948.

227 "A man has to": B. DeVoto to J. P. Baxter, Jan. 28, 1949, DeVP.

227 "the most important": B. DeVoto to Mr. Henry, May 13, 1948, DeVP.

227 "I cannot afford": B. DeVoto to Walter Dutton, Feb. 13, 1948; to Kenneth Reid, Mar. 2, 1948; to H. M. Albright, Mar. 16, 1949, DeVP.

227–228 "It shows": B. DeVoto in *Harper's,* Aug. 1950.

228 "Don't you think": Ibid.

228 *Post* article: B. DeVoto in *Saturday Evening Post,* July 22, 1950.

228 "We need": *The Letters of Bernard DeVoto,* ed. by Wallace Stegner (1975), 374.

228 JM accused: B. DeVoto, *The Year of Decision* (1943), 360.

228 "In the face": B. DeVoto to Ansel Adams, Dec. 24, 1948, DeVP.

228 "I shrink": B. DeVoto to Newton Drury, Feb. 3, 1949, DeVP.

229 "I have got": B. DeVoto in *Harper's,* Sept. 1955.

229 "sense of stability": J. W. Krutch, *More Lives Than One* (1962), 105.

230 "Nature, in her": J. W. Krutch, *The Modern Temper* (Harvest ed. 1956), 7.

230 "Ours is a lost": Ibid., 169

231 "Now a feeling": J. W. Krutch, *Henry David Thoreau* (1948), 212.

231 "On that day": J. W. Krutch, *The Twelve Seasons* (1949), 7.

Page

231 "a kind of pantheism": Krutch, *More Lives,* 294–295.

232 "I probably know": Ibid., 329.

232 "His peculiar strength": Paul Sears to Guy Emerson, Apr. 12, 1961, Sears Papers.

232 "Neither our society": J. W. Krutch, *And Even if You Do* (1967), 34.

232–233 "What is commonly": J. W. Krutch, *The Voice of the Desert* (1955), 199.

233 "a modern version": J. W. Krutch, *A Krutch Omnibus* (1970), 339.

233 "The Icarus": J. W. Ward, *Red, White, and Blue* (1969), 33.

234 "If I had to": Charles A. Lindbergh in *Reader's Digest,* July 1964.

234 "I loved still more": C. A. Lindbergh, *Boyhood on the Upper Mississippi* (1972), 46.

234 "It's fascinating": Anne Morrow Lindbergh, *Bring Me a Unicorn* (1972), 223.

234 "The more I go": A. M. Lindbergh, *Hour of Gold, Hour of Lead* (1973), 304.

234 "You'd better": A. M. Lindbergh, *The Flower and the Nettle* (1976), 151.

235 "How long can": C. A. Lindbergh in *Reader's Digest,* Nov. 1939.

235 "the home of": C. A. Lindbergh, *Wartime Journals* (1970), 747.

235 "War is like": Ibid., 919.

235 "The height of": C. A. Lindbergh, *Autobiography of Values* (1978), 349.

236 "I grew up": C. A. Lindbergh, *Of Flight and Life* (1948), 49.

236 "We must surround": Ibid., 47.

236 "Somehow I feel": Lindbergh, *Journals,* 199–200.

236 "real wilderness": Ibid., 359.

236 "I must teach": Ibid., 10.

237 "The major difference": Lindbergh in *Reader's Digest,* Nov. 1972.

237 "in instinct": Lindbergh in *Life,* July 4, 1969.

237 "The primitive": Lindbergh, *Autobiography,* 273.

237 "extremely subtle": Lindbergh, *Journals,* 398.

238 "Few people": Alden Whitman in *New York Times Magazine,* May 23, 1971.

238 "On every continent": Lindbergh in *Reader's Digest,* July 1964.

238 "There is nothing": New York *Times,* Mar. 20, 1968.

238 "We're on the edge": New York *Times,* Oct. 31, 1968.

238 "The chairman": New York *Times,* June 23, 1969.

238 Lindbergh's choice of career: Lindbergh in *Life,* Dec. 22, 1967.

238 "Many developmentalists": New York *Times,* July 27, 1972.

239 "Man must feel": Lindbergh in *Reader's Digest,* July 1972.

239 "All the roots": William O. Douglas, *Of Men and Mountains* (1950), 15.

240 "It became for me": Ibid., 31.

240 "Maybe some day": Ibid., 129.

240 "angry" rivers: Ibid., 327.

240 "It might tempt": W. O. Douglas, *Beyond the High Himalayas* (1952), 157.

240 "That idea": W. O. Douglas, *Go East, Young Man* (1974), 203.

241 "I was with him": W. O. Douglas, *My Wilderness: The Pacific West* (1960), 170.

241 Douglas's book on Muir: *Muir of the Mountains* (1961), 179.

Page

241   "But he left": Douglas, *Go East*, 205.

241   "Hundreds of us": Douglas in Washington *Post*, Jan. 19, 1954.

241–242 "We are torn": Washington *Post*, Mar. 22, 1954.

242   "From Cumberland": *LW*, spring 1954.

242   "Experience on the": Washington *Post*, Mar. 22, 1954.

243   "I concluded": Douglas, *Go East*, 216.

243   "our own hot line": Fred Grunsky in *SCB*, Oct. 1963.

243   "I took part": Douglas, *Go East*, 211.

243   "an ensconced": Ibid., 212.

243   "These Twin Gods": W. O. Douglas, *A Wilderness Bill of Rights* (1965), 169.

243–244 "In this wildness": W. O. Douglas, *My Wilderness: East to Katahdin* (1961), 289.

244   "taught me man's": Douglas, *Go East*, 204.

244   "My earliest": Aldo Leopold, *A Sand County Almanac* (Ballantine ed., 1970), 128.

245   "I can't say": Charles Steinhacker with Susan Flader, *The Sand Country of Aldo Leopold* (1973), 9.

245   Stockman support: A. Leopold to R. S. Yard, Feb. 13, 1942, WSP.

245   "I was young": Leopold, *Sand County*, 138.

245–246 Leopold on old technique: A. Leopold in *OA*, Nov. 1924.

246   "This will require": A. Leopold in *OA*, June 1928.

246   "Here my sin": S. L. Flader, *Thinking Like a Mountain* (1974), 102.

246   Leopold and Hornaday: W. T. Hornaday, *Thirty Years War for Wild Life* (1931), 262.

246   "mercy for things": Leopold, *Sand County*, 17. The actual year was 1871; see JM to David Galloway, Sept. 8, 1871, Apr. 25, 1872, MP; and JM in *SCB*, Jan. 1896.

246–247 "I sense a deep": A. Leopold to O. Murie, Nov. 1, 1946, WSP.

247   Leopold's urging: A. Leopold in *Bird-Lore*, Jan.–Feb. 1937.

247   "We face a future": *Nature Magazine*, May 1937.

247   "I know I am": A. Leopold to Robert Marshall, Nov. 21, 1938, RMP.

247   "He was the": Harvey Broome Journal, Apr. 27, 1948, WSP.

247   "The man was": Roberts Mann in *AF*. Aug. 1954.

248   "me, a mere": Leopold, *Sand County*, 77.

248   "The man is devoid": Aldo Leopold to O. Murie, Apr. 16, 1942, WSP.

248   "A single silence": Leopold, *Sand County*, 101.

248   "He was the lightning": Ibid., 118

248   "A sense of history": Ibid., 171.

249   "We should": Ibid., 117.

8. MUIR REDUX, 1945–1965

251   "the glue in": David Brower in *Not Man Apart*, Apr. 1975.

251   "Some fourteen years": Ira Gabrielson in *AM*, Jan.–Feb. 1960.

252   Walton League debt: H. G. Rossell to James Roosevelt, Apr. 13, 1933, PPF 383, FDR Library.

252   "These fly-tyers": *AM*, Nov.–Dec. 1941.

Page

252 "one of the finest": Rosalie Edge to Irving Brant, Dec. 3, 1947, BrP.

252 Reid and "land-grab": William Voigt, Jr., *Public Grazing Lands* (1976), 100.

253 "We relied largely": Ibid., 102.

253 "my stay and comfort": Bernard DeVoto to Kenneth Reid, Mar. 2, 1948; to Mrs. Blake, Jan. 12, 1948, DeVP.

253 "Although the leaders": C. R. Gutermuth in *Forest History*, Jan. 1974.

253 AWI loans: Ibid.

253 "In several states": Edward Preble in *Nature Magazine*, Aug.–Sept. 1941.

262 "We must be": Russ Neugebauer in *SCB*, Apr. 1966.

262 "largest private": *NW*, Oct.–Nov. 1963.

262 "I think extremism": Thomas Kimball in *NW*, Oct.–Nov. 1968.

263 "the whole field": John H. Baker in *AM*, Jan.–Feb. 1941.

263 "The preservation": J. H. Baker in *AM*, May–June 1943.

263 Leopold's image: Aldo Leopold, *A Sand County Almanac* (Ballantine ed., 1970), 189.

263 "We should set": Guy Emerson in *AM*, May–June 1952.

263 "era of protection": J. H. Baker in *AM*, Jan.–Feb. 1955.

264 "The few organizations": J. H. Baker in *Annals*, May 1952.

264 1963 poll: *AM*, Mar.–Apr. 1964.

264 "What is vitally": *AM*, Mar.–Apr. 1954.

265 "we could easily": J. H. Baker to Paul Sears, July 21, 1960, Sears Papers.

265 "Laws not adequately": J. H. Baker in *National Geographic*, Nov. 1954.

265 "Baker strongly": R. Edge to I. Brant, Jan. 21, 1942, BrP.

265 Profile of Edge: R. L. Taylor in *New Yorker*, Apr. 17, 1948.

265 "I think I": R. Edge to I. Brant, June 6, 1948, BrP.

265 "I don't know": R. Edge to I. Brant, Oct. 10, 1955, Jan. 14, 1958, BrP.

266 "The world must": Carl Buchheister in *AM*, May–June 1961.

266 "His administration": R. Edge, "Good Companions in Conservation: Annals of an Implacable Widow" (MS in custody of Peter Edge, Chicago), 83.

266 1962 annual meeting: New York *Times*, Dec. 1, 1962.

267 "I think we": Harold Anderson to Olaus Murie, Oct. 18, 1948, WSP.

267 "There were woods": P. S. Curry in *AM*, Nov.–Dec. 1963.

267–268 "I think we should": Ibid.

268 "We had become": Margaret and Olaus Murie, *Wapiti Wilderness* (1966), 275.

268 "personification of": *AM*, Jan.–Feb. 1960.

268 "in gratitude": *LW*, spring 1963.

268 "We are in a fever": MS, Mar. 21, 1958, WSP.

268–269 "He was a good": William O. Douglas, *Go East, Young Man* (1974), 220.

269 "brought on": Howard Zahniser in *Nature Magazine*, Apr. 1952.

269 "As we constantly": H. Zahniser in *Nature Magazine*, Oct. 1945.

270 WS income, 1946: H. Zahniser to C. E. Graves, Apr. 26, 1956, WSP.

270 "We deeply need": H. Zahniser in *LW*, spring 1952.

270 "our prophet": H. Zahniser in *Nature Magazine*, Feb. 1955.

270 "It will be a sorry": H. Zahniser in *Nature Magazine*, Apr. 1938.

Page

270 "decorous restraint": H. Zahniser in *Nature Magazine*, Aug.–Sept. 1946.

270 "Gifford Pinchot": *AM*, Jan.–Feb. 1964.

270–271 "As a follower": Ibid.

271 "The Wilderness Society": Benton MacKaye to H. Zahniser, Jan. 29, 1950, WSP.

271 "Yet we find": H. Zahniser in *LW*, Mar. 1946.

271 "I feel I am here": *LW*, spring 1950.

271 "When I remember": H. Zahniser to O. Murie, Nov. 18, 1952, WSP.

272 The old-timers' resistance: H. Broome to O. Murie, Jan. 2, 1956; H. Anderson to Murie, Nov. 14, 1956, WSP.

272 Leopold and regulation: H. Zahniser to B. MacKaye, Jan. 14, 1947, WSP.

273 "When I was first": Nathan Clark memoir (Sierra Club History Committee), 76.

273 "We did not have": Joel Hildebrand memoir (Sierra Club History Committee), 24–25.

273 "I, like a": W. E. Colby in *SCB*, Feb. 1931.

273 "That was where": Marjory B. Farquhar memoir (Sierra Club History Committee), 2.

274 "more preoccupied": Harold Bradley in *SCB*, May 1951.

274 "They felt that": M. B. Farquhar memoir, 16.

274 "Belaying the Leader": Richard Leonard and Arnold Wexler in *SCB*, Dec. 1946.

274 "although it is": R. Leonard to O. Murie, Mar. 28, 1947, WSP.

274 "John Muir was": Ansel Adams, *Yosemite and the Sierra Nevada* (1948), xv.

274 "In grammar school": Nancy Newhall, *Ansel Adams* (1963), 27.

275 "Ansel Adams was": Ibid., 114.

275 "The Farquhars": D. Brower in *Not Man Apart*, Dec. 1974.

275 "the toothless boob": John McPhee, *Encounters With the Archdruid* (1971), 28.

276 "very sensitive": M. B. Farquhar memoir, 44.

276 "Who, once having": D. Brower in *SCB*, Feb. 1935.

276 "By the time": Ibid.

276 "The Alps": Harold Peterson in *Sports Illustrated*, Apr. 14, 1969.

277 "the friction climber": Bestor Robinson in *SCB*, Feb. 1940.

277 "The tall young": Charlotte Mauk in *SCB*, June 1949.

277 "He is a genius": Peterson in *Sports Illustrated*, Apr. 14, 1969.

277 "He is an evangelist": Richard Leonard memoir (Sierra Club History Committee), 337.

277 "Most of those": Philip Bernays memoir (Sierra Club History Committee), 23, 28.

278 "Our problem": M. R. Parsons in *SCB*, Feb. 1930.

278 "We have a new": W. E. Colby to J. H. McFarland, Mar. 10, 1948, McFP.

278 "And so dear": Leonard memoir, 20.

278 "Of wisdom": W. L. Jepson in *SCB*, May 1947.

278 1947 study: Lowell Sumner and R. Leonard in *SCB*, May 1947.

278 "Are Mules": D. Brower in *SCB*, May 1948.

279 "It is still fun": D. Brower in *SCB*, Feb. 1962.

Page

279   "Just about everything": D. Brower in *SCB*, Nov. 1959.

279   "very much disappointed": F. P. Farquhar memoir (Sierra Club History Committee), 66.

279   "the small, compact": D. Brower in *SCB*, May 1959.

279   "We all knew": F. P. Farquhar memoir, 71.

279–280   "We need more": D. Brower in *SCB*, May 1959.

280   "We were often": J. Hildebrand memoir, 17.

280   "I often get a": R. Leonard to H. Zahniser, Nov. 21, 1956, WSP.

280   "The Sierra Club is": D. Brower in *SCB*, Jan. 1963.

280   "the gangbusters": New York *Times*, Dec. 11, 1967.

280–281   "ability to transcend": D. Brower in *NW*, Dec. 1964–Jan. 1965.

281   "No one had ever": Leonard memoir, 112.

281   "one more move": I. Brant to Oscar Chapman, Apr. 3, 1950, BrP.

282   *Post* article: B. DeVoto to Herbert Evison, May 22, 1950, DeVP; DeVoto in *Saturday Evening Post*, July 22, 1950.

282   "It goes without": Newton Drury to B. DeVoto, July 19, 1950 (two), DeVP.

282   "For the first": I. Brant to Harry Truman, Feb. 16, 1951, BrP.

282   "It has always": H. Truman to I. Brant, Feb. 20, 1951, BrP.

283   Thomas–Truman role: Note by I. Brant, Mar. 16, 1957, in box 21, BrP.

283   Republican tradition: B. DeVoto in *Harper's*, Oct. 1952.

283   *"A business": B. DeVoto in Harper's*, May 1953.

283   "The administration is": J. H. Baker in *AM*, Sept.-Oct. 1954.

283   "Well you know": Elmo Richardson, *Dams, Parks & Politics* (1973), 89.

283–284   "screwballs": Ibid., 94.

284   "punks": B. DeVoto in *Harper's*, Aug. 1954.

284   "I have seen": D. Brower in *SCB*, June 1954.

284   "If we heed": Ibid.

284   "strange people": Ibid.

284   "inexcusable negligence": Richardson, *Dams*, 144.

285   "I am amazed": R. Edge to I. Brant, June 13, 1955, BrP.

285   "Certain members": Richard Pough to author, Apr. 20, 1979; see, e.g., New York *Times*, May 3, 1955.

285   "I never saw": B. DeVoto to H. Evison, Oct. 6, 1948, DeVP.

285   "turn otherwise": Richardson, *Dams*, 147.

285–286   "bleak expanse": H. Zahniser in *Nature Magazine*, June–July 1955.

286   Brant's observation: I. Brant to R. Edge, July 23, 1955, BrP.

286   Shift of 120 votes: Leonard memoir, 116.

286   "The Sierra Club": Sigurd Olson to C. E. Graves, May 5, 1954, WSP.

287   Broome, 1940: Harvey Broome to R. S. Yard, May 4, 1940, WSP.

287   "progressed like": I. Brant to R. Edge, Dec. 5, 1956, BrP.

287   "I am getting": S. Olson to O. Murie, Aug. 4, 1946, WSP.

287   Reid's committee, 1949: Henry Clepper in *AF*, Oct. 1967.

287   "What's the matter": James B. Craig in *AF*, June 1964.

287–288   "Up to that time": Ibid.

288   "essential reform": D. Brower in *SCB*, Sept. 1964.

288   "Certainly the": Frank Graham, Jr., *Man's Dominion* (1971), 302.

Page

288   "an attack on": *AF*, Apr. 1957.

289   "Nobody has": Maurice Goddard in *AF*, Apr. 1965.

289   "modern Muirs": Stewart Udall, *The Quiet Crisis* (1963), 179.

290   NWF Hall of Fame: *NW*, Dec. 1964–Jan. 1965.

290   "The real father": *Time*, Sept. 17, 1965.

9.   THE LAST ENDANGERED SPECIES

291   "When we try": JM, Journal, July 27, 1869, MP. Muir later revised the first sentence to read: "When we try to pick out anything by itself, we find it hitched to everything else in the universe" (*First Summer*, 211).

291   "Our new concern": *AF*, Apr. 1965.

291–292   "There is a new": *AM*, Mar.–Apr. 1967.

292   Bookchin's accusation: Murray Bookchin, *Our Synthetic Environment* (rev. ed., 1974), xiii.

293   "Most of us walk": Rachel Carson, *Silent Spring* (Fawcett Crest ed., 1970), 220.

293   "I was rather": Paul Brooks, *The House of Life* (1972), 16.

293   "Her love of life": R. Carson to Marjorie Spock, Dec. 4, 1958, Carson Papers.

293   "O, darling": Maria Carson to R. Carson, Tuesday night, n.d., Carson Papers.

294   Carson's desire to marry: Philip Sterling, *Sea and Earth* (1970), 143; Brooks, *House*, 242.

294   "There was something": Brooks, *House*, 97.

294   "a curious sense": Ibid., 82.

294   "I write nothing": R. Carson to Ada Govan, Feb. 15, 1947, Carson Papers.

295   "a politically minded": Brooks, *House*, 155.

295   "the most dangerous": Sterling, *Sea*, 155.

295   "the atomic bomb": James Whorton, *Before Silent Spring* (1974), 249.

295   "The damaging": John Baker in *AM*, Mar.–Apr. 1946.

295   "handing a loaded": Carl Buchheister in *AM*, July–Aug. 1961.

296   "the extremely powerful": R. Carson to Clarence Cottam, Jan. 19, 1959, Carson Papers.

296   "At one point": R. Carson to Morton Biskind, Dec. 3, 1959, Carson Papers.

296   "Somehow I have": R. Carson to M. Spock, Apr. 12, 1960, Carson Papers.

297   "I knew from": Brooks, *House*, 271–272.

297   "The 'control of nature' ": Carson, *Silent Spring*, 261.

297   "Inquiry into the background": Ibid., 229.

298   "a hysterical fool": Paul Brooks, *The Pursuit of Wilderness* (1971), 206.

298   "I thought she": Frank Graham, Jr., *Since Silent Spring* (1970), 50.

298   NWF review: *NW*, Feb.–Mar. 1963.

298   Carson's blame: R. Carson to Ruth Scott, Feb. 8, 1963, Carson Papers.

298   "not a scientific": Joel Hildebrand memoir (Sierra Club History Committee), 32.

Page

298   Jukes's resignation: T. H. Jukes to P. Brooks, Mar. 6, 1963, Carson Papers.

298   "I cannot help": Adrian Hale in *SCB*, Apr.-May 1963.

298   "A prophet is": *A*, Mar.-Apr. 1964.

299   *"Silent Spring* was": Kevin P. Shea in *Environment*, Jan.-Feb. 1973.

299   "I keep thinking": R. Carson to Lois Crisler, Mar. 19, 1963, Carson Papers.

299   "We are a water": *OA*, Feb. 1925.

299   Group in Maryland: O. M. Dennis to T. S. Palmer, May 24, 1904, PP.

299   "The old swimming": Will H. Dilg in *Izaak Walton League Monthly*, Sept. 1922.

299   Walton League report, 1926: Frank Graham, Jr., *Disaster by Default* (1966), 47.

300   "This department": George H. Dern to A. Lonergan, Nov. 8, 1933, OF 114-A, FDR Library.

300   Engineers' report: FDR to Speaker of House, May 13, 1936, OF 114-A, FDR Library.

300   "result of Man's": Kenneth Reid in *Bird-Lore*, Nov.-Dec. 1936.

300   "Water has been": Nixon, 2:209.

301   "Water pollution is": William O. Douglas, *Go East, Young Man* (1974), 309.

302   "We built here": David Brower in *SCB*, Dec. 1956.

302   NWF poll, 1969: *NW*, Apr.-May 1969.

302   "Today, concern over": J. W. Krutch in *American Scholar*, winter 1970.

302   "The state of": *Business Week*, May 23, 1970.

302   Commoner blames reductionism: Barry Commoner, *The Closing Circle* (1971), 189, 270.

303   "In the 1930s": Alan Anderson, Jr., in *New York Times Magazine*, Nov. 7, 1976.

303   "I was shocked": *The American Environment*, ed. by Roderick Nash (2d ed., 1976), 241.

303   "We were learning": Anne Chisholm, *Philosophers of the Earth* (1972), 128.

304   "A new conservation": B. Commoner, *Science and Survival* (1966), 127.

304   "A court of ": F. Graham, Jr., in *New Republic*, Jan. 13, 1968.

304   "the right to": Victor Yannacone in *AF*, Apr. 1970.

305   "No lawsuit will": James Moorman in *SCB*, Jan. 1972.

305   Nader's solution: Ralph Nader in *NW*, June-July 1971.

305   "The question is not": Patrick Anderson in *New York Times Magazine*, Oct. 29, 1967.

306   "This country is": Nader in *NW*, June-July 1971.

306   Nader and bird watching: Hays Gorey, *Nader and the Power of Everyman* (1975), 261.

306   "a passive admiration": Chisholm, *Philosophers,* 138: Alan Anderson in *New York Times Magazine*, Nov. 7, 1976.

306   "talking to themselves": Gilbert Rogin in *Sports Illustrated*, Feb. 3, 1969.

306   "I think there needs": Luther J. Carter in *Science*, Dec. 22, 1967.

306   "Wildlife people": Bil Gilbert in *Sports Illustrated*, Dec. 20-27, 1976.

306-307   "Contemporary conservation": B. DeVoto to Stuart Rose, Oct. 6, 1948, DeVP.

Page

307 "The tide": Fairfield Osborn, *Our Plundered Planet* (1948), 201.

307 "The Day of Judgment": William Vogt, *Road to Survival* (1948), 78.

308 "I was the only": Chisholm, *Philosophers*, 64–65.

308 "Our tensions find": Vogt, *Road*, 68.

308 "We need": Ibid., 143.

308 "I am more steamed up": B. DeVoto to Harry Scherman, Apr. 12, 1948. DeVP.

308 "Whether or not": W. Vogt to B. DeVoto, Aug. 8, 1948, DeVP.

308 Vogt resigns: Howard Zahniser to Benton MacKaye, Oct. 26, 1949, WSP.

308 "The fat years": *Time*, June 30, 1952.

309 "There is not yet": D. Brower in *SCB*, Dec. 1956.

309 "When I personally": Samuel H. Ordway, Jr., *Prosperity Beyond Tomorrow* (1955), 131.

310 "There is little": *Future Environments of North America*, ed. by F. Fraser Darling and John P. Milton (1966), 272.

310 "Since such a": Vogt, *Road*, 282.

310 "Our movement": Harvey Broome to Olaus Murie, Feb. 17, 1957, WSP.

310 The Leopolds in *SCB*: A. S. and L. B. Leopold in *SCB*, Sept. 1959.

311 "We feel that": *Newsweek*, Oct. 3, 1966.

311 "a major influence": Chisholm, *Philosophers*, 145.

311 "David Brower of": Ibid., 146.

311 "The battle to feed": Paul Ehrlich, *The Population Bomb* (Sierra Club ed., 1969), 5.

311 "hopefully through": Ibid., 6.

311 "In the long view": Ibid., 39.

312 "If we don't": P. Ehrlich in *Playboy*, Aug. 1970.

312 "immoral": Commoner, *Closing Circle*, 235.

312 "Powerful, sustained": Commoner in *Environment*, Apr. 1972.

312 "I agree": Chisholm, *Philosophers*, 148.

312 "preoccupation with pollution": P. Ehrlich and John P. Holdren in *Environment*, Apr. 1972.

312 Statistics criticized: P. Ehrlich and B. Commoner in *New York Times Book Review*, Feb. 6, 1972.

312 "Population growth": Paul R. and Anne H. Ehrlich, *The End of Affluence* (1974), 5.

312 Commoner, 1966: Commoner, *Science*, 24.

312 Use of Hardin: Commoner in *Ramparts*, Aug. 1975.

312 "there is no need": Commoner, *The Poverty of Power* (1976), 57.

312–313 "I might have": Commoner in *Environment*, Apr. 1972.

313 "The resources aren't": *American Environment*, ed. by Nash, 347.

313 Commoner and DNA: Commoner, *Science*, 25.

313 Ehrlich re science advisors: David M. Rorvik in *Look*, Apr. 21, 1970.

314 "We believe": Thomas Kimball in *Environmental Action*, Oct. 30, 1971.

314 NWF hunting members: *NW*, Oct.–Nov. 1973, Oct.–Nov. 1977.

314 "At a time": John Madson in *NW*, June–July 1976.

314 "Conservation is": *A*, Nov. 1971.

316 "Today the chapters": C. W. Buchheister and F. Graham, Jr., in *A*, Jan. 1973.

Page

316 "We were born": *Newsweek*, Dec. 25, 1967.

316 "Muir epitomized": *SCB*, Nov. 1967.

317 "You have heard": D. Brower in *SCB*, Sept. 1960.

317 "A kind of ": *Smithsonian*, Oct. 1974.

317–318 "the club's slow-burning": *Newsweek*, Oct. 3, 1966; *Life*, May 27, 1966.

318 "Even his enemies": Scott Thurber in *Nation*, Feb. 27, 1967.

318 "He was always": Richard Leonard memoir (Sierra Club History Committee), 366.

318 "Dave Brower got": Harold Crowe memoir (Sierra Club History Committee), 10.

318 "He became": J. Hildebrand memoir, 30.

318 "Through these books": D. Brower in *SCB*, Feb. 1965.

319 "But I've already": Francis P. Farquhar memoir (Sierra Club History Committee), 72.

319 poisoning relations: Eliot Porter to J. W. Krutch, Apr. 20, July 5, 1968, Krutch Papers.

319 "We have not": D. Brower to J. W. Krutch, Dec. 5, 1967, Krutch Papers.

319 "The one overriding": *Current Biography* (1961), 465.

320 "He has to live": *Life*, May 27, 1966.

320 "This time it's": Roderick Nash, *Wilderness and the American Mind* (rev. ed., 1973), 229.

320 "I hope this": Stewart Udall to J. W. Krutch, Aug. 12, 1966, Krutch Papers.

320 "The IRS keeps": *Newsweek*, Oct. 3, 1966.

320 "That didn't turn": Richard Searle memoir (Sierra Club History Committee), 28.

321 "I feel that": Leonard memoir, 346.

321 "Do I have authority": D. Brower in *SCB*, Mar. 1969.

321 "Brower's ideas leave": Robert A. Jones in *Nation*, May 5, 1969.

321 "They want to run": Ibid.

321 "There will be": *SCB*, May 1969.

322 "We cannot be": New York *Times*, May 4, 1969.

322 "The earth, seen": Rasa Gustaitis, *Wholly Round* (1973), 5.

322 "our conversation": Stephen Levine, *Planet Steward* (1974), 226.

323 Ed Zahniser: E. Zahniser in *LW*, spring 1974, autumn 1974.

323 "I think it": Ehrlich, *Population Bomb*, 153.

323–324 "We are the earth": *Psyche*, ed. by Barbara Segnitz and Carol Rainey (1973), 211–212.

324 "the biggest damn": Robert F. Buckhorn, *Nader* (1972), 47.

324 "You can't be": *Environmental Quality and Social Justice*, ed. by J. N. Smith (1974), 45–46.

324 "There is not": Ibid., 47.

324 Sierra Club poll: *SCB*, Jan. 1973.

324 "We feel": Leonard memoir, 34.

324 "The ecology movement": James Ridgeway, *The Politics of Ecology* (1970), 204.

325 "I didn't succeed": Charles McCarry, *Citizen Nader* (1972), 219.

Page

325   "Now a lot": *Ecotactics*, ed. by John G. Mitchell and Constance L. Stallings (1970), 53.

326   "The small conservation": *LW*, spring 1970.

326   The cabinet meeting: Walter J. Hickel, *Who Owns America?* (1971), 239–240.

326   "Now, suddenly": *A*, May 1970.

326   "the ecology craze": *New Republic*, Mar. 7, Oct. 31, 1970.

327   "The supreme conservation": S. Udall, *The Quiet Crisis* (1963), 174.

327   "It would avoid": *Wilderness in a Changing World* (1966), 151.

327   "Nobody was telling": *U.S. News and World Report*, July 5, 1971.

327   "The proposed reactor": *The Silent Bomb*, ed. by Peter Faulkner (1977), 226.

328   Eissler's opposition: Frederick Eissler in *SCB*, July–Aug. 1966.

328   Adams against Brower: Ansel Adams and William Siri in *SCB*, Feb. 1969.

328   "John Muir would": Martin Litton and Frederick Eissler in *SCB*, Feb. 1969.

328   AEC in Vermont: F. Graham, Jr., in *A*, Mar. 1970.

328   "Back in the old": Richard S. Lewis, *The Nuclear-Power Rebellion* (1972), 263.

329   Antinuclear policies: *SCB*, Feb. 1974; *LW*, autumn 1974; *NW*, Apr.–May 1975.

329   "a brontosaurus": Boston *Globe*, Oct. 8, 1978.

329   Three thousand groups: *The Unfinished Agenda*, ed. by Gerald O. Barney (1977), 161.

329   "the conservation conscience": Monroe Bush in *AM*, July–Aug. 1959.

10.   THE AMATEUR TRADITION: PEOPLE AND POLITICS

333   "I am pleading": Ernest Griffith in *LW*, spring 1950.

334   "If the voice": William O. Douglas, *The Three Hundred Year War* (1972), 188.

334   "The members will": Aldo Leopold to Morris L. Cooke, May 28, 1940, Cooke Papers.

334   "There is *no one*": Rosalie Edge to Irving Brant, Sept. 11, 1938, BrP.

334   "As a general": Paul Sears to T. A. Brindley, Nov. 30, 1964, Sears Papers.

335   "There is nothing": R. Edge to I. Brant, Sept. 11, 1931, BrP.

335   "Most plant lovers": J. W. Krutch, *And Even if You Do* (1967), 305.

335   "We little suspect": JM, Journal [1873], MP.

336   "I have never": G. B. Grinnell to E. G. Judson, May 26, 1925, GBGP.

336   "The hunter knows": W. O. Douglas, *A Wilderness Bill of Rights* (1965), 36.

336   "I think all": A. S. Leopold in *NW*, Oct.–Nov. 1972.

336   "The contemplation": Herbert Hoover in *OA*, Mar. 1926.

336–337   "Catching trout": JM in *Atlantic*, Nov. 1898.

337   "I have never": *Frank M. Chapman in Florida*, ed. by Elizabeth S. Austin (1967), 4.

Page

337 AOU poll: John C. Devlin and Grace Naismith, *The World of Roger Tory Peterson* (1977), 162.

337 "Here was this": Michael Harwood, *The View From Hawk Mountain* (1973), 69.

337–338 "How little": Carl Buchheister to Paul Sears, Oct. 29, 1959, Sears Papers.

338 "A hiker": Bernard DeVoto in *Harper's*, Sept. 1951.

338 "Imagine someone": Paul H. Pfeiffer in *SCB*, May 1951.

339 "he had spent": Walter L. Huber in *SCB*, Feb. 1929.

339 "I lay just": Robert Marshall, *Alaska Wilderness* (2d ed., 1970), 45.

339 "Hard on him": William D. Armes to JM, Sept. 25, 1892, MP.

339 "All who spent": JM, Journal, July 13–14, 1907, MP.

339 "Everyone appreciated": Ruth R. Currier in *SCB*, Feb. 1935.

339 "Climb a fine": W. T. Hornaday, *Camp-Fires in the Canadian Rockies* (1906), 145.

339 "the gregarious": Benton MacKaye in *LW*, Mar. 1939.

340 "A large number": Olaus Murie to Ida J. Sherriffs, Nov. 30, 1960, WSP.

340 "In spite of": JM, Journal, June 7, 1891, MP.

340 "The appeal": David Brower in *SCB*, Sept. 1952.

341 Decrease in hunters: *Statistical Abstract*, 1971–1978.

341 "Few people realize": Gifford Pinchot, *The Fight for Conservation* (1910), 105.

341 "There are few": *Appalachia*, June 1877.

341 "Our dress has": Mrs. W. G. Nowell in *Appalachia*, June 1877.

341 "They may": M. F. Whitman in *Appalachia*, June 1879.

341–342 "I found them": T. S. Solomons in *SCB*, Jan. 1897.

342 "Their vigor": E. T. Parsons in *SCB*, Jan. 1902.

342 "One of my earliest": Nathan Clark memoir (Sierra Club History Committee), 18.

342 "I never thought": Marjory B. Farquhar memoir (Sierra Club History Committee), 51.

342 Women in state groups: R. H. Welker, *Birds and Men* (1955), 206.

343 "Appreciation of": *Federation Bulletin* (GFWC), Mar. 1907.

343 Sherman's letters: Peter J. Schmitt, *Back to Nature* (1969), 159.

343 "It is a great": M. B. Sherman to J. H. McFarland, June 28, 1916, McFP.

343 Protest letters: *Chautauquan*, Aug. 1907.

343 "The organized women": W. T. Hornaday to T. S. Palmer, Feb. 14, 1923, PP.

343 Women in NPA: R. S. Yard to R. L. Wilbur, Jan. 31, 1929, Merriam Papers.

343 "It is they": R. S. Yard to John C. Merriam, July 1, 1926, Merriam Papers.

343 "the strongest": B. DeVoto to Mr. Perry, June 21, 1948, DeVP.

343 "No Chapter can": Will H. Dilg in *OA*, May 1925.

344 "I wish that": Edwin J. Becker in *Independent Woman*, Apr. 1946.

344 "To a woman": R. Edge, "Good Companions in Conservation: Annals of an Implacable Widow" (MS in custody of Peter Edge, Chicago), 54.

344 "Get back": *Ladies' Home Journal*, Apr. 1976.

Page

345   The wife of the governor: Newton B. Drury, "Parks and Redwoods, 1919–1971" (Bancroft Library, 1972), 137.

345   "Most of us": Becker in *Independent Woman,* Apr. 1946.

345   "With true mother": Mrs. Francis E. Whitley in *OA*, Feb. 1925.

345   "Man has always": *OA*, Mar. 1927.

345   "The impression": Harland A. Perkins in *Appalachia*, June 1908.

345   "I was not born": W. T. Hornaday, "Eighty Fascinating Years," Hornaday Papers.

346   JM's use of "nigger": JM to Wanda and Helen Muir, Oct. 8, 1898, MP; Autobiography, 396, 399, 400, 402–403, in folder 31.3, MP.

346   "the wolf-Jew": JM, Journal, May 7, 9, 1895, MP.

346   "Anglo Saxon folk": JM to Asa K. McIlhaney, Jan. 10, 1913, MP.

346   "Anglo-Saxons seldom": MS fragment, no date, in folder 38.2, MP.

346   "by Italians": Mary L. Tucker in *Federation Bulletin*, July 1911.

346   Phillips's action: J. M. Phillips to W. T. Hornaday, Sept. 6, 1910, Hornaday Papers.

346–347   "The fruit grower": D. S. Jordan in *OA*, Apr. 1926.

347   "with plenty of ": D. C. Beard to W. T. Hornaday, Sept. 25, 1912, Beard Papers.

347   "They are strong": W. T. Hornaday, *Our Vanishing Wild Life* (1913), 100–102.

347   "intellectually the most": John Higham, *Strangers in the Land* (Atheneum ed., 1970), 155.

347   "that man is": Madison Grant, *The Passing of the Great Race* (1916), 4.

347–348   "dwarf stature": Ibid., 14.

348   "the desirable blood": *Century*, Dec. 1913.

348   "One of the arguments": *LW*, Mar. 1939.

349   "Many of our": R. T. Peterson in *AM*, Mar.–Apr. 1957.

349   Southern Calif. chapter screened: Glen Dawson memoir (Sierra Club History Committee), 14–19; Richard Leonard memoir (Sierra Club History Committee), 34.

349   "the four recognized": Thomas Amneus memoir (Sierra Club History Committee), 15–16, 33.

349   "Now wait": Clark memoir, 83.

349   "It is time": Charles A. Lindbergh in *Reader's Digest*, Nov. 1939.

349   "It seems to me": Wayne S. Cole, *Charles A. Lindbergh and the Battle Against American Intervention in World War II* (1974), 81–82.

350   "To the Indian": JM, *Journals*, 315.

350   "He protected": George B. Grinnell in *Forest and Stream*, Mar. 1916.

350   "He had unpolluted": *OA*, June 1928.

350   "They had for": R. Marshall, *The People's Forests* (1933), 15.

350   "Centuries before": G. Pinchot, *Breaking New Ground* (1947), 25.

350   "Today the conservation": S. Udall, *The Quiet Crisis* (1963), 12.

350   "Although the Indians": W. O. Douglas, *Go East, Young Man* (1974), 70–71.

350   "Indians believe": Sigurd Olson, *Reflections from the North Country* (1976), 103.

351   "Whatever the virtues": G. Pinchot in *Appalachia*, May 1906.

Page

351 "There is nothing": G. B. Grinnell, *The Indian of To-Day* (1900), 155.

351 Roadless areas abolished: John Collier, *From Every Zenith* (1963), 270–273.

351 The existing overviews: J. Leonard Bates in *Mississippi Valley Historical Review,* June 1957; Samuel P. Hays, *Conservation and the Gospel of Efficiency* (Atheneum ed., 1969); Michael J. Lacey, "The Mysteries of Earth-Making Dissolve: A Study of Washington's Intellectual Community and the Origins of American Environmentalism in the Late Nineteenth Century" (Ph.D. thesis, George Washington University, 1979).

352 "I am outraged": J. H. McFarland to C. H. Ingersoll, Feb. 5, 1914, McFP.

352 Pinchot and George: Frank E. Smith, *The Politics of Conservation* (1966), 88; Harold T. Pinkett, *Gifford Pinchot* (1970), 62; and see Bates in *Mississippi Valley Historical Review,* June 1957.

352 "My own money": M. Nelson McGeary, *Gifford Pinchot* (1960), 3.

353 Brant and George: I. Brant, "Adventures in Conservation," 6, 134, BrP.

353 MacKaye and George: Frederick Gutheim in *LW,* Jan.–Mar. 1976.

353 "unearned increment": J. Collier in *LW,* Dec. 1937.

353 "one of the really great": F. C. Leubuscher to FDR (quoting FDR), Aug. 2, 1939, PPF 6152, FDR Library.

353 "I was always": Drury, "Parks and Redwoods," 17.

353 "wrong environment": G. H. Maxwell in *Maxwell's Talisman,* July 1906.

353 "We must approach": Ibid., Sept. 1905.

353 Re Borsodi: William H. Issel in *Agricultural History,* Apr. 1967.

353 "a civilization of ": Ralph Borsodi, *This Ugly Civilization* (1929), 1.

353 "the inner discipline": R. Borsodi in *New Republic,* July 31, 1929.

354 "an alternative": Helen and Scott Nearing, *Living the Good Life* (1970 ed.), 5.

354 "We hoped to": Ibid., xviii.

354 "Marxism has laid": S. Nearing, *The Making of a Radical* (1972), 272.

355 "The whole idea": Anne Chisholm, *Philosophers of the Earth* (1972), 129.

355 "These attitudes": David M. Rorvik in *Look,* Apr. 21, 1970.

355 "I didn't understand": Chisholm, *Philosophers,* 135.

356 "I would not drink": Nixon, 2:257.

356 "to reach a Main Street": Pete Seeger in *Environment,* May 1969.

356 "Commoner has convinced": P. Seeger in *Environment,* June 1972.

356 Sierra Club members: *SCB,* July–Aug. 1972.

356 Audubon members: *A,* Jan. 1977.

356 "the issue on": Norman Podhoretz in *Commentary,* June 1970; and see Barry Weisberg, *Beyond Repair* (1971), 31, and James Ridgeway, *The Politics of Ecology* (1970), 13.

356 Blacks and the environment: *SCB,* Nov.–Dec. 1977; and see August Piper, Jr., in *Black Scholar,* May 1975.

356 "We are concerned": *Newsweek,* Oct. 8, 1979.

357 "It takes a while": Ibid.

11. LORD MAN: THE RELIGION OF CONSERVATION

Page

358 Conservation as a religious movement: See, e.g., Charles E. Fay in *Appalachia*, June 1879; Frank M. Chapman, *Autobiography of a Bird-Lover* (1933), 82; E. C. Kemper in *OA*, July 1925; Harry B. Hawes, *My Friend, the Black Bass* (1930), 24; Charlotte E. Mauk in *SCB*, May 1947; Rosalie Edge, "Good Companions in Conservation: Annals of an Implacable Widow" (MS in custody of Peter Edge, Chicago), 168; Maurice Broun, *Hawks Aloft* (1949), 139; William O. Douglas, *The Three Hundred Year War* (1972), 198; John McPhee, *Encounters with the Archdruid* (1971), 159; William Tucker in *Harper's*, Aug. 1978.

358 "All devotees": Alan Devoe in *AM*, May–June 1945.

359 "The victory of ": Lynn White, Jr., in *Science*, Mar. 10, 1967.

359 Restatement by Toynbee: Arnold Toynbee in *Horizon*, Aug. 1973, and in New York *Times*, Sept. 16, 1973.

359–360 Critics of White's thesis: Anne Chisholm, *Philosophers of the Earth* (1973), 34; Rene Dubos in *A*, Sept. 1972; T. S. Derr in *Worldview*, Jan. 1975.

360 Interpretation of Genesis: Francis A. Schaeffer, *Pollution and the Death of Man* (1970), 69–70.

360 Rebuttals: *Earth Might Be Fair*, ed. by Ian G. Barbour (1972), 150; Michael W. Foley in *CoEvolution Quarterly*, fall 1977; Richard A. Baer, Jr., in *Christian Century*, Jan. 8, 1969.

360 Passmore's views: John Passmore, *Man's Responsibility for Nature* (1974), 8.

360 "not so much": Ibid., 185.

360 "I really don't": Margaret Murie in *Sierra*, July–Aug. 1979.

360 "The Judeo-Christian": Paul Ehrlich in *A*, May 1970.

360 The Christian theologians: H. Paul Santmire, *Brother Earth* (1970), 6–7; Frederick Elder, *Crisis in Eden* (1970), 82; Schaeffer, *Pollution*, 85; *This Little Planet*, ed. by Michael Hamilton (1970), 203, 223; John B. Cobb, Jr., *Is It Too Late?* (1972), 32–35; *Earth Might Be Fair*, ed. by Barbour, 156, 142–143.

360 "Today the most adequate": Elder, *Crisis*, 141n.

361 Creation in Genesis: Ibid., 84–86.

361 "When thou shalt": Deut. 20:19–20.

361 "Doth God take": 1 Cor. 9:9–10.

361 "The historical impact": L. White, Jr., in *Science*, May 12, 1967.

361–362 "A tree, a rock": Cedric Wright in *SCB*, Feb. 1935.

362 "I defy anyone": *A Documentary History of Conservation in America*, ed. by Robert McHenry and Charles Van Doren (1972), 84.

362 "It is the way": William T. Hornaday, *Our Vanishing Wild Life* (1913), 82.

362 Griffith's suggestion: Ernest Griffith in *LW*, spring 1950.

362 "I find it more": Alexander Skutch in *Nature Magazine*, Apr. 1954; and see Frank Graham, Jr., in *A*, Mar. 1979.

362 "Hence in this": A. Skutch in *Nature Magazine*, May 1954.

362–363 "These voyagers": Ibid.

363 Krutch's observation: J. W. Krutch, *If You Don't Mind My Saying So* (1964), 336–338.

363 "an almost religious": Roland Clement in *AM*, July–Aug. 1962.

Page

363 "should be more": C. E. Graves in *LW*, winter–spring 1963.

363 "the doctrine": Paul Brooks, *Roadless Area* (1964), 233.

363 The other writers: *Documentary History*, ed. by McHenry and Van Doren, 349; *Wilderness in a Changing World* (1966), 81; Peter Farb, *Ecology* (1963), 164; *Future Environments of North America*, ed. by F. Fraser Darling and John P. Milton (1966), 230, 302, 396.

363 "a vast impersonal": Ansel Adams, *My Camera in the National Parks* (1950), n.p.

363 Thoreau and the pine tree: J. W. Krutch, *Henry David Thoreau* (1948), 226.

364 "It is not my": W. H. Hudson, *Far Away and Long Ago* (1946 ed.), 233.

364 "Come for a Sunday": Benton McKaye to Robert Marshall, Dec. 12, 1935, WSP.

364 "some weird council": T. W. Higginson in *Appalachia*, Apr. 1884.

364 "We should find": L. H. Bailey, *The Holy Earth* (1915), 10.

364 "there to greet": William Brewster, *October Farm* (1937), 285.

364 JM and Tlingit belief: JM, *Travels in Alaska* (1915), 235–236.

364 Writer in *Bird-Lore*: Frank G. Speck in *Bird-Lore*, July–Aug. 1938.

364 "Lo the poor": Julia M. Moores to JM, Mar. 10, 1880, MP.

365 "We believe God": Charles A. Lindbergh, *Autobiography of Values* (1978), 276.

365 "with much interest": Badè, 1:320.

365 "This so far": JM to family, Oct. 3, 1903, MP.

365 "The Hindoos": JM to family, Oct. 23, 1903, MP.

365 Cited Hindu practices: W. T. Hornaday, *Camp-Fires in the Canadian Rockies* (1906), 153; Hornaday, *Vanishing*, 82; Cedric Wright in *SCB*, June 1957; Guy Emerson in *AM*, May–June 1946.

365 "I realized": W. O. Douglas, *Go East, Young Man* (1974), 203.

365–366 "We cannot forever": David Brower in *SCB*, Dec. 1956.

366 "We are in": McPhee, *Encounters*, 84; on Zen and conservation, see Hwa Yol Jung in *Christian Century*, Nov. 15, 1972.

366 "As for those": Lao Tzu, *The Way of Life* (Mentor ed., 1955), 81.

366 Lindbergh and Lao-tse: C. A. Lindbergh, *Wartime Journals* (1970), 327.

366 "He was greatly": Anne Morrow Lindbergh to author, Feb. 12, 1979.

366 Lao-tse and Lindbergh's thought: Lindbergh, *Of Flight and Life* (1941), vii, 38, 50.

366 Lao-tse quoted by Lindbergh: Lindbergh, *Autobiography*, 152, 214, 265, 268, 286–287.

366 "The love of Tao": Alan Devoe in *AM*, Nov.–Dec. 1946; and see Paul Sears in *SCB*, Oct. 1959.

366 Olson and Lao-tse: Sigurd Olson, *Reflections from the North Country* (1976), 150; Olson to Charles Woodbury, Oct. 20, 1955, WSP.

366–367 "Western man has": *Earth Might Be Fair*, ed. by Barbour, 80–81; and see *Ecology*, ed. by Richard E. Sherrell (1971), 70–72, and Cobb, *Too Late*, 43.

367 "the indivisibility": Susan L. Flader, *Thinking Like a Mountain* (1974), 18.

367 "Industrialism": Aldo Leopold, *Game Management* (1933), 49.

367 "numenon": A. Leopold, *A Sand County Almanac* (Ballantine ed., 1970), 146.

Page

367 "the one truly": Paul Brooks, *The House of Life* (1972), 315.

367 Christian theologians and reverence for life: Schaeffer, *Pollution*, 25; Cobb, *Too Late*, 48; John W. Laws in *Intellect*, Mar. 1975.

368 According to Brabazon: James Brabazon, *Albert Schweitzer* (1975), 242.

368 "I can't think": Rachel Carson to Christine Stevens, Mar. 28, 1963, Carson Papers.

368 JM's meeting with Butler: W. F. Prince, *Noted Witnesses for Psychic Occurrences* (1928), 37.

368 JM intrigued: JM to R. W. Emerson, Apr. 3, 1872, EP.

368–369 "I am going": Autobiography, 467–468, in folder 31.3, MP.

369 "I just kind": Ibid., 470.

369 "Why, John": Ibid., 473.

369 "For all I know": Ibid., 312, in folder 31.7, MP.

369 "remarkably receptive": J. E. Calkins statement, 1942, in folder 71.4, MP.

369 "I know something": Mary Austin, *Earth Horizon* (1932), 188.

369 "now called": Autobiography, 444–445, in folder 31.3, MP.

369 "I had an open": MS fragment, n.d., Dorr Papers.

370 Dorr's séances: *William James on Psychical Research*, ed. by Gardner Murphy and Robert O. Ballou (1960), 150–158.

370 "with a suspended": MS fragment, n.d., Dorr Papers.

370 "such things did": S. E. White, *The Betty Book* (1937), 16.

370 "I'm having such": S. E. White, *Across the Unknown* (1939), 203.

370 "Anyone who lives": Wolfe, 257.

370 "Reason is not": White, *Betty Book*, 127.

370 "A happy day": G. Pinchot Diary, Mar. 22, May 7, 1896, GPP.

370–371 "Somehow in the": S. Olson, *Open Horizons* (1969), 11–12; and see Elmo Robinson in *SCB*, Apr. 1938.

371 "God is not": R. Laurence Moore, *In Search of White Crows* (1977), 52.

372 "The early settlers": JM in *Atlantic*, Aug. 1897.

372 The old pioneer: JM, *Boyhood*, 161.

372 "The good Lord": T. G. Pearson, *Adventures in Bird Protection* (1937), 51.

372 "Now the Bible": John G. Mitchell in *A*, May 1979.

372 Levine and the warden: Stephen Levine, *Planet Steward* (1974), 213; and see Devereux Butcher in *NW*, Aug.–Sept. 1963, and Paul Brooks, *Speaking for Nature* (1980), 274.

372 "Only man": J. W. Krutch, *Grand Canyon* (1958), 226.

372 "It was too touchy": *Wilderness in a Changing World*, 80.

372 "What a remarkably": Richard Neuhaus, *In Defense of People* (1971), 139.

372 Neuhaus's listing: Ibid., 147, 160, 136, 35, 124.

372–373 "The idea that nature": *Environmental Quality and Social Justice in Urban America*, ed. by J. N. Smith (1974), 65.

373 "We too want": *Christianity Today*, Apr. 10, 1970.

373 "an American heresy": James V. Schall in *America*, Mar. 27, 1971.

373 "There is no": R. V. Young, Jr., in *National Review*, Dec. 20, 1974.

373 "a sort of mindless": J. Patrick Dobel in *Christian Century*, Oct. 12, 1977.

373 "open antihumanism": T. S. Derr, *Ecology and Human Need* (1975), 83, 85.

Page

373 Nisbet's view: Robert Nisbet, *History of the Idea of Progress* (1979), 47–76, 352.

374 "It had been": JM, *Journals*, 80.

374 "Toiling in the": Ibid., 82–83.

Index